DRUGS

POLICY, SOCIAL COSTS, CRIME, AND JUSTICE

Lisa Anne Zilney
Montclair State University

Prentice Hall
Boston Columbus Indianapolis New York San Francisco Upper Saddle River
Amsterdam Cape Town Dubai London Madrid Milan Munich Paris Montreal Toronto
Delhi Mexico City Sao Paulo Sydney Hong Kong Seoul Singapore Taipei Tokyo

Editor in Chief: Vernon Anthony
Acquisitions Editor: Eric Krassow
Editorial Assistant: Lynda Cramer
Director of Marketing: David Gesell
Marketing Manager: Adam Kloza
Marketing Assistant: Les Roberts
Senior Marketing Coordinator: Alicia Wozniak
Senior Managing Editor: JoEllen Gohr
Production Manager: Meghan DeMaio
Creative Director: Jayne Conte
Cover Designer: Suzanne Duda
Cover Art: Getty Images
Full-Service Project Management/Composition: Aparna Yellai, GGS Higher Education Resources, PMG

Text Font: 10/12 Minion

Credits and acknowledgments for materials borrowed from other sources and reproduced, with permission, in this textbook appear on the appropriate page within text.

Library of Congress Cataloging-in-Publication Data

Zilney, Lisa Anne.
Drugs : policy, social costs, crime, and justice / Lisa Anne Zilney. — 1st ed.
p. cm.
Includes bibliographical references and index.
ISBN-13: 978-0-13-227535-4
ISBN-10: 0-13-227535-X
1. Drug control. 2. Drugs—Government policy. 3. Drug abuse and crime. I. Title.
HV5801.Z55 2011
362.29—dc22

2010008345

Prentice Hall
is an imprint of

PEARSON

www.pearsonhighered.com

ISBN 10: 0-13-227535-X
ISBN 13: 978-0-13-227535-4

Dedication

To my canine companions:

Huxley—my precious snowball, who stayed with me through every moment of writing this book, nudging me with his nose for a cuddle break at all the right times,

and

Parker—my lovebug, whose zest for life reminds me that today is the moment that matters,

and

Anna – my sweet pea, whose joy is inspiring and whose energy is never-ending!

BRIEF TABLE OF CONTENTS

CONTENTS

PREFACE

Drugs: Policy, Social Costs, Crime, and Justice is designed to serve as a comprehensive text for courses dealing with drugs and society from both a national and international perspective, in a variety of social science disciplines. By incorporating observations from sociology, criminology, and public policy, this text provides for a fuller understanding of the issues surrounding drugs. The primary purpose of this work is to teach students about the dynamics of drugs (both legal and illegal) in American society informed by historical law creation and current law enforcement. Some of the topics that are new and major additions to this text from existing texts are: the history of drugs in the United States and the integral role of race in the creation of drug laws, the elaboration of the global trade in drugs, as well as U.S. drug control policies and the impact of the U.S. drug war on international relations.

Depending on the issue, the treatment of the material in this text is succinct and expansive, and conceptual and practical, as a combination of these approaches is necessary to teach the material effectively. The intended audiences are students who have basic knowledge of their discipline and are ready to apply that knowledge to the social problem of drugs. Students will benefit from the consistent conceptualization and organization of material in this work, a "real life" examination at the start of each chapter, important terms highlighted at the end of each chapter and a glossary at the end of the text, research topics to provide suggestions for assignments, as well as critical thinking questions to allow for greater insight into the issues analyzed. In addition, graphics in the form of charts, graphs, or maps are used to elaborate the varied nature of drug use; drug trends over time; and other relevant issues essential to increase student comprehension.

The book is organized by first framing the issue of drugs and the use of drugs in society, providing an overview of the creation of the drug program, theoretical explanations for drug use and an examination of studies regarding who uses drugs. It then proceeds to analyze legal, medical, and illegal drugs, explores the history and effects of drug use, and details how drug use is controlled. This is accomplished in fourteen chapters.

Chapter One is designed to contextualize the issue of drugs and the use of drugs in society. Students learn various definitions of drugs and that these definitions are relative and fluid. As well, three frames of reference for understanding and defining drugs are explained, as are objective classification systems used to organize types of drugs. A distinction is made between appropriate and inappropriate drug use and between drug use, harmful use, hazardous use, misuse, and drug abuse. Finally, students learn the differences between physiological and psychological dependence, tolerance, and withdrawal. Chapter Two discusses how media sensationalism influences attitudes toward drugs and drug users. This chapter applies the tenets of a moral panic to the social problem of drugs and does so using various examples of how different types of drugs have been construed as a moral panic at various points in history. Students will understand how the moral panic surrounding illicit substances impacts and drives criminal justice policy. Chapter Three compares and contrasts the general premises of biological, psychological, and sociological theories. This chapter uses six sociological theories to explain drug use: social reaction theory, social learning theory, social control theory, strain theory, cultural deviance theory, and conflict theory. Chapter Four elaborates the methods by which drug use statistics are reported and teaches students the three critical questions to ask when confronted with statistical data. This chapter also evaluates the strengths and weaknesses of the surveys conducted to determine drug-use trends, leading to an understanding of the extent of drug use and how drug use varies by age, gender, race/ethnicity, and geographical location. This chapter ends with an exploration of drug use through qualitative research and how this type of research can lend itself to varied perceptions of the issue. Chapter Five begins with a discussion of the role of the Food and Drug Administration in drug regulation. It then proceeds to examine the basic pharmacology, use trends, benefits and consequences, and current issues associated with the use of the legal drugs, such as caffeine, tobacco, alcohol, inhalants, herbal supplements, and diet drugs. Chapter Six starts with an exploration of the growth of the pharmaceutical industry. This chapter then proceeds to examine the basic pharmacology, use trends, benefits and consequences, and current issues associated with the use of medical drugs, including ADD/ADHD drugs, substances used for female and male sexuality, HIV drugs, and drugs used in sports. Chapter Seven examines the basic pharmacology, use trends, benefits and consequences, and current issues regarding the use of illegal drugs such as marijuana, opiates, hallucinogens/psychedelics, methamphetamine, and cocaine. Chapter Eight unearths the historical development of drug control policy in the United States and helps students in understanding the purpose of drug control legislation. This chapter discusses the types of controls created by the major pieces of drug legislation and conveys the policies of recent presidential administrations on drug control. This chapter is integral in explicating the role of race in the formation of drug control legislation. Chapter Nine elaborates the relationships between drugs and various types of crime and provides the theoretical explanations for a drugs-crime link. This chapter helps students understand the structure of the illicit drug trade and explores current trends in domestic and global drug trafficking using the examples of domestic trafficking of methamphetamine and the global trafficking of cocaine. This chapter also discusses the role of women in the drug economy. Chapter Ten is guest authored by Lauren M. Caravaglia, who has an MSW and focuses on understanding the effects drug and alcohol abuse have on an individual's personal social functioning, health, and well-being. This chapter explains how substance abuse affects the family system, including the effects alcohol and drug use have on an individual's ability to parent effectively, the consequences of alcohol consumption during pregnancy, and the effects parental substance abuse have on children. This chapter ends with a discussion of the impact of drugs on community life. Chapter Eleven contextualizes the U.S. war on drugs, elaborating incarceration trends for drug offenses, specifically the varied impacts of drug laws by race and gender. This chapter also focuses on drug war strategies such as asset forfeiture, interdiction policies, eradication policies, certification policies, and varied types of street-level enforcement in the drug war. Chapter Twelve details prevention strategies, including drug education, public service announcements, drug testing, and zero tolerance policies. The types and effectiveness of these programs as well as the controversies surrounding these programs are explored. Chapter Thirteen explores treatment for drug use and abuse, including the use of drug courts in the United States as a diversion from traditional criminal justice. This chapter elaborates the varied aspects of treatment methods such as pharmacological treatment, residential treatment, outpatient treatment, anonymous self-help treatment programs, and prison-based and compulsory treatment programs. Finally, Chapter Fourteen ends the text with a discussion of how other nations address the issue of drugs and what the United States could learn from these alternate approaches.. Advantages and disadvantages of legalization and decriminalization are elaborated, as is the harm reduction approach. As well, this chapter discusses the effects of U.S. drug control policy on other nations.

ACKNOWLEDGMENTS

I did have some assistance in the research of this project, and for that I am enormously grateful. Randall Greenman, a student at Montclair State University provided assistance in researching for a couple of chapters, which was very beneficial. A significant contribution in terms of research was made by Lauren Caravaglia, who also co-authored a chapter in the manuscript. Lauren was a former student of mine at Montclair State University whose ability I cannot praise enough. She is extremely intelligent and so her willingness to assist me in researching for this project was greatly appreciated. Her chapter on "Drugs and Collateral Damage" is a wonderful addition to the book, and she was an ideal candidate to write this section, due to her educational background and work experience. My heartfelt thanks goes to Lauren for all of her contributions to this project! Despite all the input on this project, the errors and interpretation remain my own.

There were wonderful people at Montclair State University who asked regularly (but not too often) about the progress of this book: Norma Connolly, Jessica Henry, Venezia Michalsen, Gale Morganti, Susan O'Neil, Vicki Toffler and Francine Raguso. Your thoughtfulness and your friendship are so very much appreciated! As with all of my life endeavors, a special acknowledgement and thanks goes to my parents, Mary and Nicholas Zilney, who always stand beside me and assure me that this is just one more obstacle that I without doubt can overcome and will, in the end, make me stronger! For their tireless confidence, I am overwhelmingly grateful! For each step of this long journey, my love and partner Steve has also been there encouraging me and giving me the strength to continue when this project seemed more frustrating than worthwhile . . . thank you for pushing me when I needed to be pushed!

I also wish to thank the following reviewers: Tammy Garland, University of Tennessee-Chattanooga; Gary Potter, Eastern Kentucky University; Carleen Vincent, Florida International University; Courtney Waid, North Dakota State University.

ABOUT THE AUTHOR

Lisa Anne Zilney is an associate professor in the Department of Justice Studies at Montclair State University, Montclair, NJ. She holds a Ph.D. in sociology with specializations in criminology and environmental sociology from the University of Tennessee. She has an M.S. in criminal justice from Eastern Kentucky University, and a B.A. in psychology from the University of Windsor in Canada.

1

Framing Drugs and Their Use

"When I use a word," Humpty Dumpty said in a rather scornful tone, "it means just what I choose it to mean—neither more nor less."

—THROUGH THE LOOKING GLASS ~ LEWIS CARROLL

OBJECTIVES:

When you have finished this chapter, you should be able to:

- Recognize that the definitions of drugs and their use are relative
- Explain the three frames of reference for understanding and defining drugs
- Describe objective classification systems used to organize types of drugs
- Discuss the difficulty in distinguishing appropriate and inappropriate drug use
- Differentiate drug use, harmful use, hazardous use, misuse, and drug abuse
- Understand the difference between physiological and psychological dependence, tolerance, and withdrawal

REAL LIFE

The prevalence of opium users is very high in Rajasthan (India) with particular concentrations in the Western desert districts of the state. The use of opium is not distinguished by caste, creed, religion, or financial status and it has now established itself as a staple intoxicant . . . The cultural practices surrounding opium use make it an object central to the life of the people of Rajasthan. The users are mostly considered to be decent people, well accepted within their society. The neonate is nurtured with a dosage of opium and thereafter males graduate to infancy and adolescence by taking the substance in family gatherings and, at times, with peers, on occasions of joy, celebration and conviviality. It is a social lubricant, has a symbolic place in birth, marriage and other ceremonies, and a great deal of its usage has been recognized as medicinal for generations in rural and urban Rajasthan. The multifarious uses to which opium is put only add to its social acceptance . . . Opium consumption in various forms, at small social or political gatherings and at larger, more public, village gatherings, has an evident symbolic and functional importance deriving from earlier times and now integrated into the contemporary setting. Such interdependency between opium and the people is a characteristic image of typical Rajasthan. Rather than opium being understood as a destructive force as it is in the West, the social fabric is understood to be strengthened by its presence and use in a number of ways: its use is instrumental in social gatherings, enhancing the interactions of individuals on a one-to-one level but also—depending on the form and objective of the gathering—local traditions, group inter-relationships this type of use may have helped to maintain a dynamic equilibrium between the negative and positive effects of opium use and consequently to have provided an important niche for the substance in this society (Ganguly, 2004, pp. 97–98).

DEFINING DRUGS

The definition of drugs is relative rather than absolute. That is, it carries with it many meanings, all dependent upon the context in which it is being understood. The segment above depicting the social place of opium in Rajasthan contradicts the view in the United States of opium as a harmful and illegal substance. It illustrates that the definition of drugs is relative rather than absolute. The meaning of what constitutes a drug and whether the use of the drug is socially acceptable varies by historical time period, culture, location, person, and situation.

Historical Context

The definition of drugs may be situated in historical or temporal context and thus change over time. In early America, most drugs were dried plant parts used to treat ailments; legal standards were not attached to their therapeutic uses. In the United States, federal laws and regulations to legally define the medical use of drugs did not exist prior to the passing of the Pure Food and Drug Act in 1905 and the subsequent establishment of the Food and Drug Administration (FDA). Today in the United States, the FDA is solely responsible for approving what products can legally be prescribed or sold as medicine in the United States and for regulating their safety. The FDA may approve a drug and then recall it later thus labeling it legal and appropriate for medical use at one point in time and then illegal and not appropriate for medical use at a later time. This certainly differs from a century ago when there were no fixed legal or formal definitions of drugs.

Geographic Context

The meaning of drugs can also change geographically. **Dry counties** or jurisdictional areas prohibiting the distribution of alcohol are scattered throughout the United States, primarily in the South and the Midwest. For instance, if someone possesses more than one quart of liquor or more than the equivalent of twenty-four 12-ounce containers of beer in a dry county in Texas, it is considered evidence of possession with intent to sell alcohol in a prohibited area. Of the 254 counties in Texas, 46 are "entirely dry" and another 169 counties are "partially dry." In Tennessee, the Jack Daniels Distillery is located in dry Moore County, while neighboring Coffee County, which houses the George Dickel Distillery, is "wet." Therefore, when taking a tour of the Jack Daniels facility, purchases and tasting are legally prohibited. A 45-minute drive away and customers can sample and buy George Dickel during a similar tour. These regions of the country are hold-outs from the Prohibition era: Counties that simply never re-legalized alcohol, or for reasons that are usually religious, decided to remain alcohol-free. There are also "dry areas" throughout the country that do not permit alcohol, including small towns in southern New Jersey and towns surrounding the Boston area in Massachusetts. Conversely, California has no dry counties.

The meanings attached to the concept of drugs are not just relative to people, time, and place, they are complex, multidimensional, and interrelated. More importantly, they can carry with them important, and at times questionable, social and policy implications. Therefore, defining and understanding drugs is not a simple matter that can be reduced to a one-dimensional approach.

FRAMES OF REFERENCE

Frames of reference are ways of looking at phenomena that guide our perceptions about drugs. Metaphorically speaking, just as the appearance of a picture may change depending on how it is framed, the same is true regarding the ways we view drugs. No particular framework stands apart as more correct than another; each brings a new level of understanding about the meaning of drugs. Taken together, different frames of reference offer an educated and holistic understanding of drugs. Three dominant frames of reference for studying drugs can be conceptualized as objective, subjective, and critical.

Objective Frame of Reference

Defining drugs objectively is akin to a scientific approach that provides information about material characteristics; it defines drugs as objects with definitive properties, actions, and effects. Objective definitions of drugs are empirical—they seek to describe with minimal bias what can be observed, measured, and quantified for study. An **objective frame of reference** is a pragmatic approach that typically seeks to distinguish drugs by their physical or chemical properties and/or actions through the use of a classification scheme. **Classification schemes** organize drugs by their common characteristics while also differentiating their more specific qualities from each other. While there are virtually hundreds of ways to classify drugs, three broad types of classification groups are widely recognized in the study of drugs: pharmacological, psychoactive, and legal.

PHARMACOLOGICAL DRUG DEFINITION AND CLASSIFICATION Pharmacology is the science that studies the chemical composition, characteristics, and actions of drugs. According to the **pharmacological definition of drugs** provided by the Food and Drug Administration, a drug constitutes:

> . . . articles intended for use in the diagnosis, cure, mitigation, treatment, or prevention of diseases in man or other animals; and articles (other than food) intended to affect the structure or any function of the body of man or other animals. (Federal Food, Drug & Cosmetics Act, 1938)

In the United States alone, over 500,000 prescription and over-the-counter (OTC) drugs and herbal and nutritional supplements fall under this definition. The broadest pharmacological classification separates drugs into prescription, OTC, herbal supplements, and nutritional

TABLE 1-1 Popular Sources for Pharmacological Drug Information

Publication	Types of Drugs Included	Information Provided
The United States Pharmacopoeia (USP)	Prescription drugs Over-the-counter drugs Herbal supplements	Generic, brand, chemical, international, FDA names; chemical structure; pharmacologic and/or therapeutic categories
Physicians' Desk Reference (PDR)	Prescription drugs	Manufacturer and product categories; generic and brand names; FDA-required usage information; clinical pharmacology; data on over 4,000 drugs; more than 2,000 cross-referenced photos
Physicians' Desk Reference for Over-the-Counter Drugs	Over-the-counter drugs Herbal supplements	More than 2,000 products within 144 categories in nonprescription drugs
PDR for Herbal Medicines	Herbal supplements Nutritional supplements	Indexed by common names and therapeutic category; dosages; effects; interactions; contraindications; precautions; adverse reactions; information on clinical trials
The Pill Book	Prescription drugs	Generic and brand names; FDA usage information; data on more than 1,500 drugs; 32 pages of actual-size photographs

supplements. The most specific pharmacological classification lists drugs alphabetically by their generic name (drugs may have many brand names but only one generic name). Drugs are often classified by a category name based on a general medical purpose and then by their chemical, generic, and brand names, respectively. For example: antibiotics (category name), penicillin (chemical name), amoxicillin (generic name), and Amoxil, Larotid, Trimox, and Wymox (brand names). A wide variety of publications are available for classifying, identifying, and detailing drugs. Such publications are indispensable for doctors, nurses, and pharmacists and also serve as valuable resources for law enforcement and court officials, social workers, psychologists, and substance use counselors. Table 1-1 lists and describes some of the most widely recognized publications of this type. Internationally, the most elaborate and widely used pharmacological classification system for drugs is the Anatomical Therapeutic Chemical (ATC) Classification System maintained by the World Health Organization (WHO). The ATC system categorizes drugs by the fourteen anatomic systems upon which drugs act.

PSYCHOACTIVE DRUG DEFINITION AND CLASSIFICATION **Psychoactive or psychotropic drugs** refer to substances that act upon the nervous system, specifically the central nervous system (CNS) or cerebrospinal axis to affect mind, moods, and/or behavior. The central nervous system is composed of the brain and the spinal cord which in turn include many neurochemicals. Psychoactive drugs act on these neurochemicals to elicit responses, typically altering mind and/or mood. Psychoactive drugs are often grouped into depressants, stimulants, narcotics, hallucinogens,

TABLE 1-2 Classification of Psychoactive Drugs

Type	CNS Effect	Drug Examples
Depressants/sedatives	Depresses central nervous system; reduces physical coordination; anesthetic effect	Alcohol, barbiturates, sedatives, tranquilizers
Stimulants	Stimulates or arouses the central nervous system; reduces appetite	Caffeine, nicotine, ritalin, ephedrine, amphetamines, cocaine
Narcotics	Slows central nervous system; analgesic or pain killing effect	Opium, morphine, heroin, dilaudid, codeine, methadone
Hallucinogens/ psychedelics	Distorts and alters sensory perceptions	Mescaline, psilocybin, PCP, LSD, inhalants
Cannaboids	Heightens sensory perception; mild euphoria	Marijuana, hashish
Antidepressants	Elevates mood levels	Sinequan, Tofranil, Prozac, Zoloft, Paxil

cannaboids, antidepressants, and antipsychotics. Table 1-2 provides an example of such a classification system and lists the central nervous system effects along with drug examples. However, it should be noted that this classification system of psychoactive drugs represents only one example. Some systems combine cannaboids with hallucinogens, or antidepressants and antipsychotics into one group called CNS or mood stabilizers. Other systems of classification isolate inhalants into their own specific group.

LEGAL DEFINITION AND CLASSIFICATION In the legal realm, drugs (particularly psychoactive drugs) are defined and classified by laws regulating or controlling their production, manufacture, export, import, distribution, trade, use, and possession. In approximately 140 countries, laws concerning the control of psychotropic drugs are guided by the **United Nations Single Convention on Narcotic Drugs**. The Single Convention is an international treaty among its signatory nations to limit to medical and scientific purposes more than one hundred drugs and to standardize national drug control laws. These drugs are classified into four schedules or tables. The schedules recommend a degree of legal control and are organized from the most to least restrictive based on therapeutic value and perceived harm or threat to individuals and public health. Table 1-3 summarizes each schedule by harmfulness, degree of control, and drug examples.

While the Single Convention requires signatory nations to follow its guidelines by creating laws regarding the control of these drugs, it does not mandate specific enforcement policies. Thus, enforcement varies widely among the signatory nations. For example, the Netherlands does not prosecute petty drug offenses and allows licensed shops to sell small amounts of cannabis for personal use. In some Asian countries, penalties for drug trafficking are the most severe; Singapore mandates the death penalty for trafficking 15 grams of heroin, 30 grams of cocaine, or 500 grams of marijuana. Considering this global continuum, the United States and many European countries are classified as having middle-range enforcement.

TABLE 1-3 UN Convention Schedule of Psychotropic Substances

Schedule	Harmfulness	Degree of Control	Examples of Drugs
I	High risk of abuse Serious threat to public health Little or no therapeutic value	Very strict Use prohibited except for scientific or limited medical purposes	Cannaboids, LSD, MDMA (ecstasy), mescaline, psilocybine
II	Risk of abuse Serious threat to public health Low/moderate therapeutic value	Less strict	Amphetamines, amphetamine-like stimulants
III	Risk of abuse Serious threat to public health Moderate/high therapeutic value	Available for medical use	Barbiturates
IV	Risk of abuse Minor threat to public health High therapeutic value	Available for medical use	Tranquilizers, analgesics, and some narcotics

Source: International Narcotics Control Board, 2005.

In the United States, psychoactive drugs are defined and classified by codified criminal statutes at federal, state, and local levels, with federal law taking precedent. That is, states can enhance restrictions, but typically cannot limit them. In defining drugs generally, the federal government adopts the FDA definition, but in classifying the legality of psychoactive drugs, they use the term **controlled substance** to refer to substances (excluding distilled spirits, wine, malt beverages, or tobacco) subject to federal control and punishment under the Controlled Substances Act of 1970 with amendments (Drug Enforcement Administration [DEA], 2005). The U.S. schedules take account of the following criteria in determining the status of controlled substances:

- actual or relative potential for abuse;
- scientific evidence of pharmacological effect;
- the state of current scientific knowledge;
- history and current pattern of abuse;
- the scope, duration, and significance of abuse;
- what, if any, risk there is to public health;
- psychic or physiological dependence liability; and
- whether the substance is an immediate precursor already controlled (DEA, 2005: 2–3).

While the FDA decides which drugs require a prescription, the responsibility for scheduling controlled drugs is assigned to the Office of the Attorney General in conjunction with the Drug Enforcement Administration (DEA) and decisions are based on research by the FDA and the Department of Health and Human Services. Table 1-4 summarizes the criteria of schedules and provides drug examples.

TABLE 1-4 U.S. Controlled Substance Act Classification of Drug Schedules, Criteria, and Drug Examples

Schedule	Criteria	Drug Examples
I	High potential for abuse No current accepted medical use in the United States Lack of accepted safety for use under medical supervision	Amphetamines, heroin, LSD, peyote, hashish, marijuana, mescaline, MDMA (ecstasy)
II	High potential for abuse Current accepted medical use in the United States with severe restrictions Abuse may lead to severe psychological or physical dependence Requires a written and signed prescription Prescription refills are prohibited	Opium, Percodan, dilaudid, cocaine, Demerol, methadone, methamphetamines, morphine, Ritalin
III	Lower potential for abuse than Schedule I and II drugs Current accepted medical use in the United States Abuse may lead to moderate or low physical dependence or high psychological dependence Requires an oral or written prescription Prohibits refilling prescriptions more than five times after the initial prescription	Barbiturates, paregoric, Vicodin, hydrocodone, codeine, anabolic steroids
IV	Low potential for abuse relative to Schedule III drugs Current accepted medical use in the United States Abuse may lead to limited physical or psychological dependence relative to Schedule III drugs Requires an oral or written prescription Prohibits refills more than five times after the initial prescription	Ativan, phenobarbital, benzodiazepines (Valium, Librium, Halcion), Darvon, Rohypnol
V	Low potential for abuse relative to Schedule IV drugs Current accepted medical use in the United States Abuse may lead to limited physical or psychological dependence relative to Schedule IV drugs	Cough syrups with codeine, Phenergan, Robitussin A-C, Lomotil

Source: Drug Enforcement Administration, 2005.

Drugs not scheduled under the Controlled Substance Act may still be subject to control by government and law enforcement agencies. For example, the use of ephedrine in herbal supplements for body building, weight loss, and enhanced physical performance was banned by the FDA in 2004. Additionally, the Methamphetamine Control Act of 1996 and the Methamphetamine Anti-Proliferation Act of 2000 classifies ephedrine as found in over-the-counter cold and allergy medicines as a primary chemical (precursor) used in the manufacture of methamphetamines. These Acts subject ephedrine to record keeping, reporting, registration, and import/export notification requirements under supervision of the DEA. Additionally, many states are currently passing legislation that places more intense restrictions on the sale of OTC products containing ephedrine, such as behind-the-counter monitoring and limiting amounts that can be sold at one time.

Alcohol is not defined or classified as a drug under the U.S. Controlled Substance Act or through the FDA but its production, distribution, trade, possession, and use is not without regulation and control by federal, state, and local laws. However, unlike other controlled psychoactive drugs, primary regulation of alcohol resides with the states rather than the federal government. The Twenty-First Amendment to the Constitution gives ultimate power to state governments to regulate and distribute alcohol within their borders. The federal government is limited to generally regulating the importation and interstate transportation of alcohol and sales and use of alcohol in the District of Columbia and on federal sites, such as military bases and national parks. The federal government however, has used financial pressures to influence state laws, including restricting funds for highway development in states that did not increase their minimum drinking age to 21. Not surprising, all states prohibit the use of alcohol, with few exceptions, by persons under the age of 21.

Since each state retains its own alcohol beverage agency and localities within states maintain their own alcohol governing boards, the laws governing alcohol in the United States vary from one geographical area to the next. The legal definition of alcohol generally refers to "intoxicating liquors" or beverages with greater than 0.5 percent alcohol content. In Mississippi however, the legal definition of alcohol refers to beverages with greater than 1 percent alcohol. Conversely, some states prohibit the sale of any beverage containing alcohol such as "nonalcoholic" or "near" beers with less than 0.5 percent alcohol content to persons under the age of 21. The patchwork of restrictions among localities often leads to confusion about what constitutes the meaning of alcohol as well as its legality.

Subjective Frame of Reference

A **subjective frame of reference** challenges us to question the authoritative nature of an objective point of view about drugs. It suggests definitions and classifications of drugs may not be devoid of personal interpretation and meaning. At times this frame of reference may raise as many questions about drugs as it answers. Do definitions and classification systems reflect the true nature of drugs or simply different points of view about drugs? If these systems reflect different points of view, whose point of view is reflected? How do these systems influence the way people think about drugs? The answers to these questions point to the importance of personal, cultural, and social experiences in defining drugs. Do the characteristics of drugs define the drug or do people define the characteristics of drugs? Some contend that "No combination of chemical properties distinguishes drugs from non-drugs; drugs basically share one characteristic: they have all been labeled as drugs" (Clinard & Meier, 1998, p. 225).

SUBJECTIVE EFFECTS OF DRUGS Pharmacologically, the chemical structure of substances defined as drugs is usually considered valid, but their chemical actions and effects often come under scrutiny. Many people experience drug effects subjectively. In other words, they experience the effects they expect or believe will occur. This is called the **placebo effect**. A placebo is a substance prepared to resemble a particular drug that actually contains some nonactive substance such as milk, sugar, or saline. In clinical trials of experimental drugs, placebos and the real substances are administered to research participants; the participants receiving the substances and the doctors administering the substances are unaware or "blind" as to who receives the real substance versus the placebo. In a typical study, there is a substantially large minority of participants (about 25 percent) who, after receiving a placebo, will report the expected effects of the drug being tested and, more interestingly, the effects are often physically observed and measured (Liska, 2004). That is, in some cases, the chemical action may not be as important as the subjective beliefs about the chemical action. Thus, the FDA mandates that before a drug is approved, pharmaceutical companies must not only establish the safety of a drug but prove its effectiveness is greater than a placebo.

Similarly, in a classic qualitative study of marijuana smokers, Howard Becker (1953) found many participants described their initial experiences with marijuana's effects as unpleasant. The participants who had continued use beyond their first encounter however related that they learned to perceive the effects as pleasurable through their associations with others who enjoyed smoking marijuana. Another study revealed that some participants reported they did not experience any effects during their initial use of marijuana. Most of these participants also admitted anticipating they would experience no effects during their first attempt (Hirsch, Conforti, & Graney, 1990). It is through such studies that the importance of the interaction between perceptions about drugs and their actual properties and effects is highlighted.

SUBJECTIVE DEFINITIONS AND CLASSIFICATIONS The subjective framework also suggests that criteria used to define and categorize drugs are affected by attitudes, impressions, and beliefs. Alcohol is categorized as a depressant in the classification of psychoactive drugs but legally it is treated different from most other psychoactive drugs. Indeed, many people do not consider alcohol a drug and some may even become indignant at the suggestion. Narcotics Anonymous (NA), a self-supporting 12-step organization devoted to helping addicts recover from addiction, specifically addresses such views about alcohol for its members. The introduction of the NA textbook which is read at the beginning of meetings states:

> Thinking of alcohol as different from other drugs has caused a great many addicts to relapse. Before we came to N.A. many of us viewed alcohol separately, but we cannot afford to be confused about this. Alcohol is a drug. We are people with the disease of addiction who must abstain from all drugs in order to recover (*Narcotics Anonymous*, 1988, p. 18).

Interestingly however, despite the fact that caffeine and nicotine are both classified as stimulants, these substances are often staples at NA meetings. In fact, a member is designated at each meeting to maintain a large pot of coffee and many members may be observed smoking outside.

A subjective framework often examines the logic used to form attitudes, impressions, and beliefs in defining and classifying certain substances as drugs but not others. Consider marijuana, for instance, in comparison with alcohol and nicotine using the legal criteria of the First Convention and the Controlled Substances Act. Does marijuana present a higher potential for abuse and dependency, less therapeutic value, or more harm for society than alcohol or nicotine? The answer is often negative. Nonetheless, marijuana remains classified as a Schedule I controlled substance; alcohol and nicotine are not classified as controlled substances. Similarly, even armed with contrary information, it becomes difficult for many people to put aside their own thoughts about the way they personally label these substances.

The subjective framework suggests socialization plays a large role in shaping the ways that people think about drugs as well as most other phenomena. Socialization is the process through which persons acquire their attitudes, impressions, and beliefs in concert with others. In other words, through interaction, people internalize shared standards about what is appropriate and what is not, and in time these standards guide their thoughts and behavior almost intuitively. These standards become a lens through which people view or interpret the world, in this particular case the world of drugs, and it becomes difficult to separate internal and external realities. The subjective framework does not suggest that people toss or disregard their standards, but instead that they take account of their significance in defining, classifying, and labeling drugs. The larger question remaining however examines the extent to which people actually participate in the societal definition of drugs. More succinctly, the question becomes, whose standards shape societal perception?

Critical Frame of Reference

The **critical frame of reference** asks us to think analytically and in a broader context than the objective and subjective frameworks. It takes a dialectic approach by looking at how the interactions between the objective and subjective approaches for defining, classifying, and labeling drugs translate into meanings that become shared, traditional, and institutionalized by society. Specifically, it looks at the processes of how subjective interpretations about drugs come to be understood as objective realities by members of society. The critical framework points toward the larger structural conditions and the historical, social, cultural, political, and economic institutions at work in shaping perceptions of drugs. Goode (1999) sums it up well with his often quoted contention that "a drug is something that has been defined by certain segments of the population as a drug" (p. 58). Therefore, the critical approach suggests the assumptions underlying the ways drugs and their effects are defined, classified, and labeled are not necessarily of individual making but of more powerful and dominant forces such as economic, moral, and political motives.

ECONOMIC MOTIVES The significance of therapeutic pharmaceutical drugs in improving the longevity as well as quality of our lives is well established. Vaccines prevent life-crippling and life-ending diseases. Antibiotics prohibit the growth or kill particular bacteria attacking our body system. Many other drugs, prescription or OTC, relieve the symptoms of many diseases and allow people to function normally when they might not otherwise be able. However, the majority of Americans have come to regard therapeutic drugs as "magic bullets" and American perceptions regarding "need" for these drugs are driven by the economic interests of the pharmaceutical industry (Liska, 2004). This is an extraordinarily powerful industry (as will be elaborated in Chapter Six) that, through billions of dollars in advertising has been able to convince the public that we need more and more drugs. By way of example, laxative commercials suggest if people do not have a bowel movement at the same time every day then they are "irregular"; and prone to becoming moody and sluggish. In reality, "regularity" for most people differs and may even vary for the same person with changes in diet, hydration, and exercise. The misconceptions about the need for laxatives, about which the FDA warns against regular or frequent use, results in Americans spending over $300 million on approximately 700 OTC laxative-related products annually (Liska, 2004).

MORAL MOTIVES In the case of psychoactive drugs, researchers from a critical framework suggest morality plays as large a part as profit in determining perceptions and legal policies. In a classic discussion about the role of morality in policy making, sociologist Howard Becker wrote: "Wherever rules are created and applied we should be alive to the possible presence of an enterprising individual or group. Their activities can properly be called 'moral enterprise' for what they are enterprising about is the creation of a new fragment of the moral constitution of society, its code of right and wrong" (Becker, 1963, p. 145). Becker and subsequent researchers form their conclusions based on historical analyses of legal policy formation. For example, the Eighteenth Amendment to the Constitution in 1919 made alcohol illicit until its repeal by the Twenty-First Amendment in 1933. The ban on alcohol during this period of time, known as the Prohibition, was the culmination of a movement spanning several decades of massive public rallying, publications, and political lobbying by groups such as the American Temperance Society, the Women's Christian Temperance Union, and many Protestant religious organizations. At the base of the Prohibition movement was a campaign espousing the moral threats and harms posed by alcohol. While the laws prohibiting alcohol did not last, many subsequent movements led by similar social groups or "moral entrepreneurs" opposing the legality of other drugs have been more successful, including those against marijuana (which, ironically, was legal during Prohibition).

POLITICAL MOTIVES Looking beyond business profit and ethics, other researchers using critical historical analyses point to political motives underlying the meanings attached to drugs, which often benefit some groups to the detriment of others. At the initiation of the Prohibition movement, the influx of newly arriving Irish Catholic immigrants presented different religious and cultural practices that were especially associated with alcohol and that were not much cared for by the already established Protestant communities. The Irish immigrants also posed a threat to the current order as an impoverished group often willing to labor for lower wages in order to earn a living, and they had a strong affiliation to the Catholic Church and its political agenda. The initial movement against alcohol has thus also been viewed by some researchers as a movement against Irish immigrants (Gusfield, 1963; Lender & Martin, 1987). Similar conclusions about other drugs, their affiliations to particular social groups, and policy considerations can be drawn through reviews of history.

DRUG USE, ABUSE, AND ADDICTION

The difficulties in defining drug use and its many dimensions are similar to those found in defining drugs themselves. In very broad terms, **drug use** refers to any consumption of a substance defined or labeled as a drug. This definition encompasses a rather large continuum of drug-using behaviors often bound by relative standards about what constitutes socially, medically, and legally approved drug use, deviant drug use, and compulsive drug use. The traditional concepts of drug use, abuse, and addiction have respectively been used to represent the points along this continuum. However, they are often used synonymously in everyday conversation, the media, and in drug-related literature despite their significant differences. Contemporary terms such as "substance abuse," "misuse," "harmful use," and "physiological and psychological dependence" are also quickly finding their way into common language about drug use. It is important to understand the different points along the spectrum of drug use, its terminology, and the contexts in which these terms are understood. Figure 1-1 illustrates the drug use continuum moving from total abstinence on one end to addiction or dependence on another. This continuum can assist in understanding the spectrum of drug use.

Drug Use

Drugs can be consumed through a variety of means referred to as **routes of administration**—the particular method in which a drug is ingested into the body. More specifically, it describes the course a drug takes toward entering the bloodstream. The different routes of drug administration are summarized in Table 1-5.

The way in which a drug is introduced into the body helps to determine the speed and intensity of its effect. For example, with oral ingestion it takes longer to feel the effects of drug than

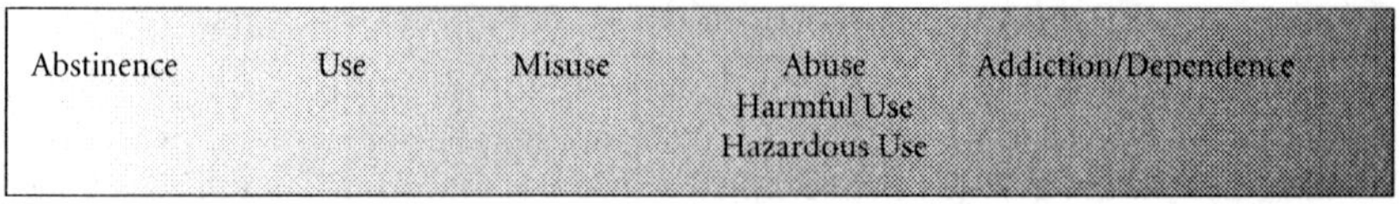

FIGURE 1-1 Drug Use Continuum.

with intravenous injection and inhalation. Therefore, drug use might constitute taking an ibuprofen or a hallucinogen, drinking a glass of wine, mainlining heroin, or inhaling gasoline fumes. And like drugs themselves, each of these behaviors carries connotations about what is considered appropriate and inappropriate relative to the situation in which the behavior takes place. Though reluctantly, many people would concede that taking ibuprofen can technically be considered drug use, albeit it is medically and socially appropriate drug use. However, members associated with the Church of Christian Science rely on healing through prayer and resist the use of modern medicines. As an additional example, those who agree drinking wine falls under the auspices of drug use may not so willingly agree that it does so when done during communion at a religious service. And many persons agree that taking hallucinogens is drug use, but what about its ceremonial use within the Church of Native Americans? How do we gauge the level of appropriateness for drug use?

Drug Abuse

The concept of **drug abuse** is relatively new. It has only been in the past century that officials have found it necessary to develop terminology to distinguish acceptable drug use from unacceptable drug use, short of compulsive or addictive behavior. Previously, drug use was widely tolerated and controlled by social convention unless it resulted in nonfunctional behavior and physical addiction. However, the rapid development of synthetic and semisynthetic drugs, governmentally and

TABLE 1-5 Routes of Drug Administration

Route of Administration	Description	Examples
Oral ingestion	Swallowed and absorbed into the bloodstream through the stomach or the small intestine	Drinking alcohol; swallowing pills
Injection (parenterally)	Injected by hypodermic needle intravenously or IV (into the vein), intramuscularly or IM (into the muscle), or subcutaneously (under the skin)	"Mainlining" heroin directly into veins; administering morphine through an IV line in the hospital
Inhalation	Inhaled through the mouth or nose and absorbed into the blood vessels of the lungs or nasopharyngeal region	Smoking cigarettes or marijuana; snorting cocaine; "huffing"
Transdermal (skin patch)	Worn on the skin and slowly absorbed into the bloodstream over a designated period of time	Nicotine, birth control, and morphine patches
Body orifice	Absorption into the bloodstream through drops in the nose, eyes, and ears, vaginal inserts, rectal suppositories	Ear, eye, and nose drops; suppositories for nausea/vomiting

The general criteria for a **substance abuse disorder**:

- A maladaptive pattern of substance use leading to clinically significant impairment or distress, as manifested by one (or more) of the following, occurring within a 12-month period:
- Recurrent substance use resulting in a failure to fulfill major role obligations at work, school, or home (e.g., repeated absences or poor work performance related to substance use; substance-related absences, suspensions or expulsions from school; neglect of children or household)
- Recurrent substance use in situations in which it is physically hazardous (e.g., driving an automobile or operating a machine when impaired by substance use)
- Recurrent substance-related legal problems (e.g., arrests for substance-related disorderly conduct)
- Continued substance use despite having persistent or recurrent social or interpersonal problems caused or exacerbated by the effects of the substance (e.g., arguments with spouse about consequences of intoxication, physical fights) (*DSM-IV*, 1994).

medically regulated protocols for drug use, and the proliferation of laws criminalizing the use of drugs led to a perceived need for middle-ground language in the spectrum of terminology about drug use.

INTERNATIONAL CLASSIFICATION OF DRUG ABUSE Internationally, the World Health Organization (WHO) guides and standardizes worldwide medical diagnoses in its *International Statistical Classification of Diseases and Related Health Problems (ICD) Manual.* The 1969 *ICD Manual* initially defined drug abuse as use of drugs that was either persistent or sporadically excessive and inconsistent with medical practice (World Health Organization [WHO], 1992). In its more current manuals, and in disagreement with the American Psychiatric Association, the WHO discontinued the term "abuse" due to its ambiguity and negative connotations in favor of the terms "harmful use" and "hazardous use" (United Nations Office for Drug Central and Crime Prevention [UNODCCP], 2000). The WHO also suggests the term **misuse** to replace "abuse" to describe the "use of a substance not consistent with legal or medical guidelines, as in nonmedical use of prescription medications" and to include substances other than psychoactives, including antidepressants, laxatives, steroids, analgesics, and antacids (UNODCCP, 2000, p. 45). The WHO also distinguished between "harmful use" of a substance, and "hazardous use" of a substance. **Harmful use** involves a pattern of psychoactive substance use that causes damage to health. The damage may be physical (e.g., hepatitis following injection of drugs) or mental (e.g., depressive episodes secondary to heavy alcohol intake). Harmful use commonly, but not invariably, has adverse social consequences (WHO, 1992). **Hazardous use** involves a pattern of substance use that increases the risk of harmful consequences (physical, mental, and/or social) for the user. The pattern of use is of public health significance despite the absence of any current disorder in the individual user (WHO, 1992).

U.S. CLASSIFICATION OF DRUG ABUSE In the United States, the American Psychiatric Association's *Diagnostic and Statistical Manual of Mental Disorders* (*DSM-I-IV*) establishes the standardized criteria that researchers and clinicians (physicians, psychiatrists, therapists, and counselors) rely on in diagnosing mental disorders. In the earliest editions of the manual, the *DSM-I* and *DSM-II*, alcohol and drug abuse were recognized solely as symptomatic of Sociopathic Personality Disturbances, now known as Antisocial Personality Disorder. In the 1970s and 1980s, the characterization of alcohol and drug abuse as a symptom of a pathological personality or deviant lifestyle was replaced by one identifying "problematic" alcohol and drug use as a condition in and of itself. Additionally, the concept of alcohol and drug abuse was replaced by the more inclusive term **substance abuse**, recognizing alcohol as well as other substances such as inhalants, caffeine, and nicotine as drugs. The revised *DSM-III* placed more emphasis on cultural and social factors in distinguishing abuse from the traditional two poles of use and dependence. The *DSM-III-R Training Manual.* in discussing the criteria for its newly formed diagnosis of Psychoactive Substance Abuse Disorders, specifically addressed the social and cultural distinctions between use and abuse:

> The use of certain psychoactive substances is considered normal in our society. For example, taking prescribed medication to relieve insomnia or pain is generally accepted practice. The recreational use of alcohol and the consumption of coffee, except among a few groups within our society, are also accepted behaviors. These practices lack the key elements that distinguish the Psychoactive Substance Abuse Disorders. To qualify as a disorder, the regular use of a psychoactive substance must lead to *culturally undesirable symptoms and maladaptive behaviors* (*DSM-III-R*, 1986, p. 97; emphasis in original).

The most current edition, the *DSM-IV*, recognizes the abuse potential for other substances and refers to these abuses as "Substance-Related Disorders."

LEGAL CLASSIFICATION OF DRUG ABUSE Among law enforcement and legal authorities, the terms "drug abuse" or "substance abuse" typically are the preferred terminology for drug use that is not medically, socially, or legally approved. The DEA considers drug abuse "when drugs are used in a manner or amount inconsistent with the medical or social patterns of a culture . . . [or] the use of [legal pharmaceuticals] outside the scope of sound medical practice" (DEA, 2005, p. 16). While this definition does not include drugs outside the Controlled Substance Act such as alcohol, tobacco, and inhalants, the DEA has begun to recognize and advocate education regarding the potential for harm, especially for minors, from the use of legal drugs. Any unsupervised or psychoactive drug use by minors, legal or illegal, is therefore also considered drug abuse.

Like drugs themselves, the standards among professionals about what constitutes abuse are not always consistent. From a mental and general health perspective, the focus is on recurrent patterns of use and their consequences or harm potential. From a legal perspective, the focus is

Goode's (2008) classification by use and legality:

Legal Instrumental Use: the use of either OTC drugs or prescription drugs for socially approved purposes such as taking No-Doz to stay awake while studying for an exam or Valium as prescribed to relieve anxiety.

Legal Recreational Use: the use of legal drugs for recreational or pleasurable purposes such as drinking alcohol at a party or a caffeine drink in the morning as a "pick-me-up."

Illegal Instrumental Use: the use of illegal drugs for socially approved purposes such as taking amphetamines to stay awake while studying for an exam or driving a long-distance truck.

Illegal Recreational Use: the use of illegal drugs for recreational or pleasurable purposes such as smoking marijuana at a party or to get high.

on the harmful nature of the drug being used. However, the daily excessive use of alcohol, cigarettes, and many OTC drugs over an extended period of time will almost always result in some type of health or other social consequence despite the use of such substances being legal. Conversely, one-time use of an illicit drug does not initiate a recurrent pattern of use for many individuals; however, for others, one-time use may result in severe consequences such as arrest, school expulsion, employment termination. The conflicts in distinguishing between use and abuse should be apparent. Much of this conflict, as well as the changes in nomenclature, appear to more accurately reflect the mission of the agency defining use, rather than the use itself. Therefore, Erich Goode (2008) suggests using the more neutral concept of "drug use" and then differentiating types of drug use by the goal of use (instrumental or recreational) and legality.

Drug Addiction

In further examining drug use on a continuum, total abstinence from drug use may mark the beginning of the spectrum and **drug addiction** the end point of this spectrum. Throughout most of human history, people who used drugs (particularly alcohol and opiates) habitually were considered sinners and/or criminals. In the late 19th century, physicians coined the term "addiction" to describe physiological dependence on drugs, and in the 1950s the WHO and the American Medical Association medicalized the condition by classifying alcoholism as a disease and treating physiological dependence on other drugs in much the same way. With this shift in ideology, the addict was now considered sick rather than evil. **Physiological dependence** represents the now classic model of addiction. It refers to a set of symptoms resulting from habitual and prolonged use of particular drugs: tolerance and physical withdrawal are most characteristic. **Tolerance** refers to the need for increasing amounts to achieve the same effects from a drug. Put differently, as some people use a drug continuously, they begin to tolerate its effects. **Withdrawal** occurs when a person uses large amounts of a certain drug for an extended period of time and then experiences a set of physical symptoms when use is reduced dramatically or stopped abruptly. For instance, during withdrawal from opiates such as morphine and heroin, the drug user will experience a set of symptoms including nausea, vomiting, diarrhea, muscle aches, fever, sweating, and insomnia. The only way to relieve the symptoms is to complete a withdrawal period usually lasting a few days to as long as 2 weeks or resume use of the drug.

The persistent use of many other drugs such as stimulants, hallucinogens, and marijuana do not culminate in physiological symptoms of addiction. However, some regular users of these drugs report an inability to easily stop taking the drugs for any length of time. Additionally, users who are withdrawn from physiological dependence, even for long periods of time, may return to drug use. Therefore, behavioral definitions of addiction based on psychological dependence were constructed to reflect such patterns. One such representative definition refers to addiction as "a behavioral pattern of compulsive drug use, characterized by overwhelming involvement with the use of a drug, the securing of its supply, and a high tendency to relapse after withdrawal (abstinence)" (Jaffe, 1975, p. 285). Here, the psychological obsession with the use of the drug, rather than physical symptomology, becomes the key for addictive use. For instance, a postsurgical patient using morphine for pain relief can become physically dependent on the drug but following withdrawal may not experience any further desire for the substance. Conversely, cocaine users may experience no obvious physical symptoms of withdrawal but continue drug use in order to relieve an overwhelming psychological obsession and a desire to alleviate an accompanying depression. Interestingly, many public and private insurance companies cover inpatient treatment only for physical drug dependency. As a result, some cocaine users seeking inpatient treatment will embellish reports of alcohol use in order to gain admission.

The WHO defines the concept of addiction in terms of dependence and incorporates both physiological and psychological factors:

> A cluster of behavioural, cognitive, and physiological phenomena that may develop after repeated substance use. Typically, these phenomena include a strong desire to take the drug, impaired control over its use, persistent use despite harmful consequences, a higher priority given to drug use than to other activities and obligations, increased tolerance, and a physical withdrawal reaction when drug use is discontinued (WHO, 1992, p. 6).

In looking specifically at drug addiction, there appears to be little disagreement among professionals such as doctors, psychologists, and addiction specialists about criteria for determining addiction or dependence. However, several questions arise when actually diagnosing someone with addiction. Who makes the decision about what constitutes acceptable amounts and periods of use, control over use, and harm to the user? Should the drug user or doctors, psychologists, addiction specialists, and criminal justice personnel make the decision? Professionals charged with making these types of decisions argue that denial or a lack of recognition about one's addiction and its effects is a large part of the psychological effects of addiction and that it is often necessary to convince the addict of his or her affliction. Some addiction treatment centers encourage friends and families to "help someone who doesn't want help" (Johnson, 1986). The A&E (Arts and Entertainment) network launched *Intervention*, a television show where families and friends team with a specialist to conduct planned, surprise confrontations of addicts to convince them to seek help. Similarly, addiction treatment and mental health professionals regularly assess misdemeanor and criminal offenders for court and correctional authorities. The assessments are often ordered whether or not the offense was drug related. The offenders are then required, usually at their own expense, to comply with recommendations that may include drug testing, inpatient or outpatient treatment, or self-help meetings, and failure to comply may result in confinement. If already confined, release time may be contingent on compliance with such recommendations. Most professionals and lay people alike agree that drug addiction is problematic for those dependent on drugs, their families and friends, and society in general. And in many ways this is correct. For instance, the Centers for Disease Control and Prevention (CDC) ranks cigarette smoking as the single most preventable cause, and excessive alcohol as the third leading cause, of premature death in the United States (Max, 2001). In addition, HIV is prevalent among many addicts who use drugs intravenously. Fewer individuals concur with how we should respond to drug addiction. Should it be addressed as a morality issue, a legal or policy issue, a medical issue, a personal issue, or an issue at all? The answers to these questions are not always clear though they have significant implications for all members of society.

Summary

- The definition of drugs is relative to the context in which it is defined, and is relative rather than absolute. "Drugs" carries with it many meanings, all dependent upon the context in which it is being understood.
- The meanings attached to the concept of drugs are not just relative to people, time, and place, they are complex, multidimensional, and interrelated. More importantly, they can carry with them important, and at times questionable, social and policy implications.

- Three dominant frames of reference for studying drugs can be conceptualized as objective, subjective, and critical. Defining drugs objectively is akin to a scientific approach that provides information about material characteristics; it defines drugs as objects with definitive properties, actions, and effects. Objective definitions of drugs are empirical—they seek to describe with minimal bias what can be observed, measured, and quantified for study. A subjective frame of reference challenges us to question the authoritative nature of an objective point of view about drugs. It suggests definitions and classifications of drugs may not be devoid of personal interpretation and meaning. The critical frame of reference asks us to think analytically and in a broader context, taking a dialectic approach by looking at how the interactions between the objective and subjective approaches for defining, classifying, and labeling drugs translate into meanings that become shared, traditional, and institutionalized by society. The critical approach suggests the assumptions underlying the ways drugs and their effects are defined, classified, and labeled are not necessarily of individual making but of more powerful and dominant forces such as economic, moral, and political motives.
- Drug use refers to any consumption of a substance defined or labeled as a drug. This definition encompasses a rather large continuum of drug-using behaviors often bound by relative standards about what constitutes socially, medically, and legally approved drug use, deviant drug use, and compulsive drug use. The traditional concepts of drug use, abuse, and addiction, respectively, have been used to represent the points along this continuum.
- The concept of drug abuse is relatively new. The 1969 *ICD Manual* defined drug abuse as use of drugs that was either persistent or sporadically excessive and inconsistent with medical practice. In its more current manuals, and in disagreement with the American Psychiatric Association, the WHO discontinued the term "abuse" due to its ambiguity and negative connotations in favor of the terms "harmful use" and "hazardous use." Among law enforcement and legal authorities, the terms "drug abuse" or "substance abuse" typically are the preferred terminology for drug use that is not medically, socially, or legally approved.
- Like drugs themselves, the standards among professionals about what constitutes abuse are not always consistent. From a mental and general health perspective, the focus is on recurrent patterns of use and their consequences or harm potential. From a legal perspective, the focus is on the harmful nature of the drug being used.
- Physiological dependence represents the now classic model of addiction. It refers to a set of symptoms resulting from habitual and prolonged use of particular drugs: tolerance and physical withdrawal are most characteristic. Tolerance refers to the need for increasing amounts to achieve the same effects of a drug. Withdrawal occurs when a person uses large amounts of a certain drug for an extended period of time and then experiences a set of physical symptoms when use is reduced dramatically or stopped abruptly.

Important Terms

Classification schemes
Controlled substance
Critical frame of reference
Drug abuse (substance abuse)
Drug addiction
Drug use
Dry county
Frames of reference
Harmful use
Hazardous use
Illegal instrumental use
Illegal recreational use

Legal instrumental use
Legal recreational use
Misuse
Objective frame of reference
Pharmacological definition of drugs
Physiological dependence
Placebo effect
Psychoactive (psychotropic) drugs
Routes of administration
Subjective frame of reference
Substance abuse (drug abuse)
Tolerance
United Nations Single Convention on Narcotic Drugs
Withdrawal

Critical Thinking Questions

1. Television news and talk shows regularly feature personal stories of different addictions, including gambling, food, sex, pornography, Internet, and even sports viewing. How are these addictions similar to and different from drug addiction? Why do you think these behaviors should be or should not be considered addictions?
2. You can find tobacco products for sale at almost any store carrying groceries or beer, whether it is your local grocer or your corner convenience store. But, how easy is it to find nicotine replacement products as found in gums, patches, and lozenges? For the most part, nicotine replacement products are considered medicine or pharmacy products and are not as readily accessible as tobacco products. How do you explain the differences in the sale of products containing nicotine?

Research Topics

1. Locate the "Important Product Information" on three over-the-counter drugs found in package inserts or through product Web sites. Examine the clinical studies for the use of placebos. Compare the effects of the actual drug and the placebo and discuss the implications.
2. Contact two local addiction treatment centers and interview their professionals about the types of assessment tools and procedures used to diagnose drug dependency. Compare and contrast the assessment tools and procedures used by each center.

Suggested Readings/Films

Abramson, John. (2005). *Overdosed America: The broken promise of American medicine.* New York, NY: Harper Perennial Press.

Coomber, Ross & South, Nigel (Eds.). (2004). *Drug use and cultural contexts: Beyond the West.* London: Free Association Press.

Liebman, Andrew (Producer and Director). (2003). *Dangerous prescription* [Film]. Available from PBS or can be viewed online at http://www.pbs.org/wgbh/pages/frontline/shows/prescription/view/

PART

I

Studying Drug Use

2

Creating the Problem of Drug Use

"The news media also create myths that come to shape our world"

—(RADFORD, 2003, P. 65).

OBJECTIVES:

When you have finished this chapter, you should be able to:

- Discuss how media sensationalism influences attitudes toward drugs and drug users
- Apply the tenets of a moral panic to the social problem of drugs
- Recognize how various types of drugs have been construed as a moral panic at various historical time periods
- Understand how the moral panic surrounding illicit substances impacts criminal justice policy

REAL LIFE

Many current drug prevention and education campaigns urge parents to talk to their kids about drugs, even calling parents the "anti-drug." While that tack may work for many families, it's way off the mark for others. Who introduces American youth to drugs? The common perception is that of reckless drug gangs pushing their drugs on bored, rebellious, or otherwise alienated youth. Yet the thrust is somewhat different. A survey of drug users in treatment found that one in five had been introduced to drugs by their parents, and drug users were nineteen times more likely to have been introduced to drugs by a family member than a professional drug dealer. And less than 1 percent were introduced to drugs by a professional dealer. Says David Rosenker, vice president of adolescent services at the Caron Foundation, a treatment program in Pennsylvania, "We already see it a lot: Baby boomer parents who are still using and still having a problem with their use. They're buying for their kids, smoking pot with their kids, using heroin with their kids." According to a study sponsored by the Center on Addiction and Substance Abuse at Columbia University, two-thirds of baby boomer parents who experimented with illegal drugs expect their own children to do the same, and many don't consider that a crisis. [This suggests that drug use may be better "solved" within families yet] "it's much easier to blame the 'other,'" the demonized and maligned drug dealers. After all, news reports of big drug busts of organized drug rings are sexy; they make good news footage, as do busy and loud predawn raids on crack houses . . . Again, our emotions lead us away from what's most effective (Radford, 2003, pp. 242–243).

DRUGS IN THE MEDIA

Attitudes toward which drugs are acceptable and which should be condemned are a social construct that changes significantly over time. Whereas today many jurisdictions have laws to regulate where one may smoke tobacco in public, prior to the 1970s, tobacco was widely used and lacked heavy legal regulation, despite the medical knowledge of its harmful effects. Why do we as a society embrace some drugs (caffeine, prescription substances, etc.) while engaging in a war against other substances (marijuana, cocaine, etc.)?

> One therapy drug such as Prozac becomes a vast commercial success, while another, nicknamed Ecstasy, is laden with sanctions just as severe as those surrounding heroin, though there is little evidence that Ecstasy is any more or less harmful than Prozac . . . One is proscribed, while its near chemical relation is prescribed, and quite lavishly (Jenkins, 1999, p. 3).

The media plays a major role in the development of public attitudes regarding drugs and drug users; in blurring and shifting the arbitrary boundary between those drugs we consider medicinal and those drugs we consider recreational. The **media** is a wide-ranging group of enterprises that include television, magazines, movies, documentaries, books, newspapers, advertising, information provided by the government, as well as information provided on the Internet. It is far beyond the scope of this text to discuss how each and every type of the media influences society's views on drugs. Instead, this chapter will focus on representations of drugs and drug users in the mainstream news media, including both television and newspapers.

Hysteria surrounding drugs has been a feature of American society for more than 200 years, beginning with the drug scares over alcohol in the late 18th century and continuing to today with drug scares over synthetic substances (Reinarman, 2008). Though there has been some rise and fall, since the 1960s the media has fairly consistently promoted fear of drugs and drug abusers. This is an incredibly "safe" political topic as there is no interest group that has a "pro-drug" agenda to counter this message. From an academic perspective, the concern is that panic and sensationalism have led the national agenda dictating drug policy, rather than rationality. "Misinformed about who uses drugs, which drugs people abuse, and with what results, we waste enormous sums of money . . . Federal drug enforcement, a $6 million expense in the 1960s, passed the $1 billion mark in the mid-1980s during Ronald Reagan's presidency and more than $17 billion during Bill Clinton's" presidency (Glassner, 1999, p. 131). What has resulted is a conservative, law-and-order approach to the drug issue: For decades an overwhelming majority of the public has accepted that a law enforcement solution is *the only* appropriate solution to the drug problem. Further, the way the drug issue is portrayed in the media hides structural problems of poverty, underemployment and unemployment, poor healthcare, poor education, racism, and a host of other macro-social problems. How did we reach this point?

"News events don't just come to be shown on television on their own; there are many steps involving judgment, selection, and interpretation between the actual, objective event and the version of it that the audience views or reads" (Radford, 2003, p. 66). Not everything reported on the news is important, and not everything of importance is reported on the news. The public however often believe that stories of significance are reported, as evidenced in the late anchorman Walter Cronkite's iconic sign-off: "That's the way it is." With regard to issues related to crime, in this case the relationship between drugs and crime, many of us watch news programs pretending that they provide enough information for us to understand the complex dynamics that are being presented. This, however, is impossible!

The media packages in short segments, really in sound bites, issues that are extremely complex, issues that take scientists years to unravel! "In the media, and particularly in prime-time television, every second counts. News reports are edited down to a few concise minutes (or seconds). Context and background essential to understanding the story are frequently left out due to time or space considerations. What is left is a bare-bones recitation of the basic facts as the reporter understands them" (Radford, 2003, p. 68). The news outlets therefore are left to essentially hit the highlights or as WINS news radio out of New York says: "give us 22 minutes, we'll give you the world." Clearly they cannot provide in-depth analysis when they are covering global news, including weather, sports, and traffic in a mere 22 minutes. What the public is often left with is a misunderstanding of the complexities of drugs, yet a firm belief that we are entirely informed. Ask anyone you know their opinion about drugs and crime, and each and every one of them will have an opinion about the nature of the drugs-crime connection (to be fully demystified in Chapter Nine), and likely an even stronger view about how to effectively "solve" this problem! However, what are these opinions based on, considering that they clearly cannot be based on the scant amount of in-depth information garnered in the mainstream news media?

Part of what leads to "sound bites" and lack of background information is the media's inclination toward sensationalism. "When the public is fed sensationalistic stories of celebrity stalkers, road rage, crack whores, and child molesters, they tend to forget about what needs to be done to make society a more humane and just place in which to live. In other words, the media serve the function of maintaining social control—that is, preventing the masses from demanding significant, meaningful social change" (Goode, 2008, p. 126). The media's use of this type of sensationalism and bias is revealed in several forms in the area of drugs: the number of users is exaggerated; the potential and actual harm caused by drug use both to the individual and to the larger society is overblown; the focus is on the gateway hypothesis, suggesting that those who engage in infrequent use of drugs such as marijuana will inevitably use "harder" drugs such as cocaine; the suggestion that addiction is almost immediate once an individual starts using an illicit substance, and the difficulty of overcoming addiction is overplayed as well as the idea that a drug that is popular in one locale will inevitably become popular throughout the United States, despite the lack of evidence toward this trend. Finally, criminal justice solutions are inaccurately portrayed as the only effective solution to this "epidemic." These biases can be seen across the decades.

THE CREATION OF A MORAL PANIC

Due primarily to intense media coverage of select illegal substances, the public has come to believe over the years that there have been "epidemics" of drug use. Citizens came to fear African Americans on cocaine, PCP (phencyclidine) users committing dangerous crimes, crack-using women and the potential harm they would cause to their babies, as well as the epidemic of date rape drugs. These media-driven sensations fueled a conservative approach to drug control. Well-known sociologist Stanley Cohen formulated the concept of a **moral panic** to refer to when:

> a condition, episode, person or group of persons emerges to become defined as a threat to societal values and interests; its nature is presented in a stylized and stereotypical fashion by the mass media; the moral barricades are manned by editors, bishops, politicians, and other right-thinking people; socially accredited experts pronounce their diagnosis and solutions; ways of coping are evolved or . . . resorted to; the condition then disappears, submerges or deteriorates and becomes more visible. Sometimes the subject of the panic is quite novel and at other times it is something which has been in existence long enough but suddenly appears in the limelight. Sometimes the panic passes over and is forgotten, except in folklore and collective memory; at other times it has more serious and long-lasting repercussions and might produce such changes as those in legal and social policy (Cohen, 1972, p. 9).

Using the concept of a moral panic to discuss drugs in society draws attention to the exaggerated and misdirected nature of societal fear and the misdirected policies that have been created as a result. Citizens respond based not on the *actual* harm of the substance but rather on the *symbolic* harm as portrayed in the media.

Best (2008) writes of a similar model in what he refers to as the "natural history of the social problems process," consisting of six steps: claimsmaking, media coverage, public reaction, policymaking, social-problems work, and policy outcomes (p. 18). The **claimsmaking** stage is when individuals or groups (often activists) recognize a condition as troublesome and suggest that something should be done to remedy this problem. These groups work to convince others of their message that change is needed. Such individuals, though often activists, may also be scientists, government officials, doctors, or other experts (Best, 2008). During the history of moral panics regarding drugs, as we will see through the examination of various examples, the claimsmaking process has involved government officials, doctors, as well as activists at different historical moments.

Once claimsmakers decide a social problem is worthy of attention, their natural choice is to seek out the media to garner a large audience and thereby increase the number of their supporters. As such, the second stage is media coverage which is where the creation of a moral panic really begins. The media has the power to create and reshape a problem and to influence how Americans perceive today's social issues. If you doubt that the media tells us what to think about (as opposed to what to think), consider this: A study examined print media coverage of the "drug crisis" and public opinion of this issue between 1985 and 1994. At some points during this period a mere one in twenty individuals viewed the drug crisis as the most important social problem in the United States, whereas at other times almost two in three individuals viewed the drug crisis as the most important social problem! The variation was explained solely by press coverage (Fan, 1996). During the 1980s, news began to blend with entertainment in the form of television shows termed *infotainment.* Such demonstrations showcased the war on drugs and satisfied the public's response to sensational television. Dramatic footage of law enforcement conducting drug raids occurred on all the major networks, further advocating the law-and-order solution to the drug problem. Examples of such shows are *Cops* or *Drug Enforcement Administration.* Stage three of the social-problem process is public reaction. Much of the public knows nothing of the "drug problem" except what they hear and see in the media; therefore, the media can have a profound and dramatic effect on public opinion and the public's view of reality.

Stage four is the realm of policymaking. While officials create and pass policy, it is the citizens and constituents who advise our policymakers about what is and is not important to us. "Policymakers respond to claimsmakers, media coverage, and public opinion" (Best, 2008, pp. 21–22). Recall however where we get our information—from the media. Especially with regard to issues related to crime, most Americans get their "reality" from the media, and based on this information we write letters to our congress people suggesting "solutions." The information provided in the media with regard to drugs and the link between drugs and crime lends itself to a very conservative "get tough on drugs" and "get tough on drug-crime" approach, rather than a rehabilitative or treatment approach. If the media is our main source of information about this social problem, we are likely to agree with these solutions and support politicians who advocate these solutions. Stages five and six are social-problems work and policy outcomes, respectively. These stages involve the implementation of policy changes and any responses to these new policies that are required, such as increased law enforcement (Best, 2008).

In a time of moral panic, links between drugs and serious crimes such as rapes or murders, although not commonplace, are perceived as "typical," and individuals using illicit substances, even a substance such as marijuana, are believed to be on a path of escalation to serious drug use and potential violence. In addition, police crack down on offenses that in the past may not have resulted in arrest or prosecution (petty offenses such as possession of paraphernalia or possession of small amounts of marijuana). This leads to the public perception that the rate of drug crimes is increasing as the police focus their attention on all types of drug offenses, thus driving up arrest rates. Additionally, the local media are more likely to report these events and place local crimes (no matter how minor) into the context of drug offenses occurring nationwide, leading yet again to the perception that the rate of these crimes is increasing, not only locally, but nationally as well—this further fuels the moral panic cycle. Or, the media may focus on local concerns, but portray them in such as way as to suggest they are a national problem. "A notorious example appeared in 1986 in the CBS television documentary *48 Hours on Crack Street.* This program presented the (then) essentially New York City problem of crack cocaine as if it were already a national epidemic, with vials littering the streets and parks of virtually every community across the country. Though largely spurious, this account had enormous influence in generating fears of a national crack epidemic" (Jenkins, 1998, p. 155). As a result, the public is led to believe that drug crimes are increasing. This belief is primarily a result of increased media coverage and increased police response, rather than a result of an *actual* increase in drug use rates or crime rates associated with drug use.

"Throughout the twentieth century the media helped foment a series of drug scares, each magnifying drug menaces well beyond their objective dimensions. From the turn of the century into the 1920s, the yellow journalism of the Hearst newspapers, for example, offered a steady stream of ruin and redemption melodramas. These depicted one or another chemical villain, typically in the hands of a 'dangerous class' or racial minority, as responsible for the end of Western civilization" (Reinarman & Duskin, 1998, p. 325). Moral panics surrounding specific drugs have been used in the past to displace citizens and to further marginalize groups of individuals.

> Anti-drug rhetoric has regularly drawn on a rather limited repertoire of images, which have successively been applied to many different drugs bearing no obvious connection. One familiar script suggests that a drug transforms a user into a soulless, drug-lubricated killing machine, a model variously applied over the years to cocaine, marijuana, PCP and methamphetamine. This concept is illustrated by tales of savage murders, sex attacks and mutilation, which acquire an urban legend quality as they are repeatedly retold in successive drug panics. If these earlier scripts are now known

> to have been thoroughly inaccurate regarding well-known substances like marijuana, is there any reason to suppose that they are likely to be truthful when applied to new or emerging menaces (Jenkins, 2003, p. 91)?

Another, perhaps unwitting, consequence of these moral panics has been the subsequent *increase* in the use of the *new* drug in question. According to Jenkins, who writes extensively on the social construction of social problems:

> The media ensure that the new drug gains a popularity it might never have acquired if it had simply been ignored. Instead, the substance is described in the most exaggerated terms, stressing its extremely powerful, pleasurable and enduring effects in a way that in other contexts would be seen as unabashed advertising. The media appear neither to know nor to care that such hyperbole can be counterproductive, encouraging drug users to add the new substance to their repertoires. The act of defining a new drug of choice, an ultimate high, a hot drug, may lead potential users to ask themselves why they are not sufficiently fashionable to have experienced it . . . The media have served as brilliantly successful public-relations workers, bringing local products to the national consciousness in a way that would excite huge professional envy if they were promoting soft drinks or fast food instead (Jenkins, 1999, p. 18).

A variety of examples of moral panics will be elaborated to illustrate the commonalities among these panics: The drug's use is portrayed as an epidemic on a national level, it is characterized as highly addictive, and the harm to both the user and those around the individual are exaggerated.

Marijuana as a Gateway Drug

Americans became aware of marijuana and its use in the early 1900s, despite the fact that it had been around for 7,000 years. Use of the substance was associated with immigrants such as Mexicans and Africans, as well as other Latino populations; therefore, the U.S. government viewed the use of marijuana as a negative and harmful habit. In response, the Federal Bureau of Narcotics (FBN) worked with state legislatures to expedite the passage of laws criminalizing the use of marijuana. This succeeded in part due to the invention of statistics by the FBN which were released to the media in order to sensationalize claims of harm associated with marijuana use. By the 1930s, states were enacting anti-marijuana laws on the heels of such sensationalized reports in the media: By 1937, all forty-eight states had such laws (Ksir, Hart, & Ray, 2008). At a congressional hearing, U.S. Commissioner of Narcotics Harry Anslinger was quoted as saying that "traffic in marihuana is increasing to such an extent that it has come to be the cause for the greatest national concern" (as cited in Ksir, Hart, & Ray, 2008, p. 372). This statement, however, was made without any scientific evidence that marijuana had become a widespread problem, but was based instead on myths linking violence and marijuana use. One such story appeared in the *American Magazine* in 1937:

> In Los Angeles, Calif., a youth was walking along a downtown street after inhaling a marijuana cigarette. For many addicts, merely a portion of a "reefer" is enough to induce intoxication. Suddenly, for no reason, he decided that someone had threatened to kill him and that his life at that very moment was in danger. Wildly he looked about him. The only person in sight was an aged boot-black [shoe-shiner].

> Drug-crazed nerve centers conjured the innocent old shoe-shiner into a destroying monster. Mad with fright, the addict hurried to his room and got a gun. He killed the old man, and then, later, babbled his grief over what had been wanton, uncontrolled murder. "I thought someone was after me," he said. "That's the only reason I did it. I had never seen the old fellow before. Something just told me to kill him!" That's marijuana (as cited in Ksir, Harx, & Ray, 2008, p. 372)!

Indeed, during this historical period, highly reputable journals published articles with reports of individuals driven to madness as a result of consumption of marijuana.

Through the decades the "weed of madness" stories declined and by the mid-1970s surveys identified that approximately 30 million people were in some way or another users of marijuana. Simultaneously, government agencies and their institutional vehicles continued to deliver the message of marijuana as a gateway drug, which had begun in the 1950s and continues by some researchers today. For example, the *Journal of the American Medical Association* provided the following statistic: Young people who engage in the use of marijuana are between two and five times more likely to advance to the use of harder drugs (Lynskey, Heath, Bucholz, Slutske, Madden, Nelson, Statham, & Martin, 2003). This finding was based on a study of 311 sets of twins, in which one twin used marijuana while the other twin did not. The authors also believed they found evidence of marijuana as a gateway drug, suggesting that marijuana is used by those individuals more likely to seek out new experiences, even if those new experiences are in violation of the law or existing social norms (Lynskey et al., 2003).

Conversely, the University of Pittsburgh Medical Center published very different findings on the gateway hypothesis based on a 12-year study of 214 males beginning when the subjects were between the ages of 10 and 12. When the boys reached age 22, the researchers categorized the individuals into three groups: "those who used only alcohol or tobacco, those who started with alcohol and tobacco and then used marijuana (gateway sequence) and those who used marijuana prior to alcohol or tobacco (reverse sequence)" ("Study Says Marijuana No Gateway Drug," 2006). This study determined that nearly a quarter of the study population (28 boys) who used both legal and illegal drugs at some point exhibited the reverse pattern of using marijuana prior to alcohol or tobacco, and those individuals were no more likely to develop a substance use disorder than those who followed the traditional succession of alcohol and tobacco before illegal drugs ("Study Says Marijuana No Gateway Drug," 2006). To further reinforce the findings, the Office of National Drug Control Policy stated that "many if not most users of hard drugs did use marijuana at some point in their life, however, these individuals also smoked cigarettes, and used alcohol as well as caffeine," which calls into question the notion of marijuana as a gateway drug (Abadinsky, 2008, p. 179).

Other reputable agencies like the Drug Policy Alliance Network (DPAN) purports that the perception of marijuana as a gateway drug is a myth. On their Web site, (www.drugpolicy.org/marijuana/factsmyths/), they state that most marijuana users do not use other illegal drugs. Interestingly, the DPAN also suggests that the gateway theory could have been mistaken for popularity: Since marijuana is the most popular drug in the United States, it is quite likely that users of less popular (and "harder") drugs have also used marijuana because such users would have already sought out the more easily accessible drugs. In order to further disprove the myth that marijuana is a gateway drug, one should consider the habits of marijuana users in the Netherlands, a country in which people aged 18 and older may legally purchase and consume marijuana. Since the 1970s, Dutch officials have worked to prevent any sort of gateway effect from the use of marijuana. In fact, they consider their policy a success because the increase in marijuana use has not been accompanied by an increase in the use of other drugs. In the Netherlands, the underage marijuana use rate is approximately 13.6 percent, compared to the underage marijuana use rate in the United States, which is typically about 38 percent (Morgan & Zimmer, 1995). The U.S. federal government however, is still holding out on squashing the gateway myth they created.

PCP and the Dangerous Criminal

PCP or phencyclidine was the most popular and most heavily used drug in American society from the mid-1970s through the early 1980s. This substance became fashionable to young people, both poor and middle class, and was associated with sensationalized reports of sexual conquests and liaisons. PCP also gained attention in the media, particularly in the Washington, DC area where use of the drug was believed to be the underlying reason for an increase in psychiatric commitments in 1973. By 1978, PCP was being discussed in congressional hearings as a new "national problem." It was at these hearings that PCP was described as "a deadly, mind-crippling, mind-altering drug, with the ability to induce psychotic and schizophrenic behavior . . . the King Cobra of all hallucinogens . . . [it] should be better known as hellfire" (Jenkins, 1999, p. 63). By the 1980s, the media had created an association between the use of PCP and the African American community, similar to mischaracterizations by the media of drugs like crack (Jenkins, 1999). Additionally, gangs were gaining attention across the country as they expanded in major U.S. cities, which fueled a media link between PCP and violence. A selection of news headlines from this time period illustrates the media spin in which PCP was framed:

- "Schizophrenia Epidemic Here Linked to Youths' Use of PCP"—headline in the *Washington Post*
- "Angel Dust: The Devil Drug That Threatens Youth"—headline in *Woman's Day* magazine
- "Angel Death"—headline in the *New York Times*
- "PCP: A Terror of a Drug"—headline in *Time* magazine (Jenkins, 1999, p. 64)

These headlines reveal the threatening nature of the drug and attempt to instill fear into society about its use; however, these headlines are merely a small sampling of the extraordinary hype surrounding PCP. Additional allegations in the media consisted of PCP releasing people's sexual reticence which led to assault and/or rape reports the suggestions that PCP could induce a person to commit crimes of violence against others or against themselves (including horrible tales of self-mutilation). Another legend stated that PCP users had superhuman strength (Jenkins, 1999).

All available research indicates that the media was the premier driving force behind these misrepresentations and exaggerations about PCP to the American public. An analysis of the substance and frequency of the media's PCP-related articles revealed that:

> . . . [t]he most repeated tale was that of self-removal of eyes which was cited 17 times during a three-year period. Different versions gave specific origins and identification. The victim was said to be a Baltimore college student, the son of a Massachusetts Congressman, a man in a mid-western city or a man from San Jose (Morgan & Kagan, 1980, p. 197).

By 1979, PCP became a popular recurring theme on fictional television dramas and news shows. One notable PCP-related television appearance was on *60 Minutes*. Journalist Mike Wallace presented his interview with Barry Braeske, who admitted to killing his parents and grandfather.

Police confirmed Braeske was under the influence of PCP at the time of the murders and this fact played in the media as the predominant motivating factor (Morgan & Kagan, 1980). Unfortunately, *60 Minutes* and some newspapers conveniently left out facts in the case that did not support the PCP-induced multiple-murder theory. These details revealed that Braeske's prime motivator was the collection of inheritance money (Morgan & Kagan, 1980). This is just one of many illustrations of deceptive journalism in which the myth of PCP-induced violence lives on through national publications and television reports.

It is important that society be educated that these horror tales are myths. It can be potentially very dangerous for myths to be believed as facts, because many people can be drawn to drugs such as PCP due to the hype generated by the media. Potential users know that there are people who have used PCP without disastrous results—this renders the media's version of "just say no" completely unbelievable (Morgan & Kagan, 1980). With that said, the media persisted during the 1970s and early 1980s in quickly reporting any crime of violence with a potential link to PCP use. Whether the link was myth or fact was irrelevant. This linkage has since been etched in society's mind and PCP users are forever associated with the commission of violence.

The Myth of the Crack Baby

The myth of a crack-baby epidemic started in the mid-1980s, and is considered to be a moral panic similar to the greater panic over drugs and their harmful effects. Rumors about babies having medical problems from maternal cocaine use started this myth, and the gossip circles believed that these babies' medical problems were due to drug-using mothers who engaged in the use of crack during pregnancy. Preliminary studies during this time consisted of a comparison between babies born to mothers who were known users of crack and babies born to drug-free mothers. The media extensively covered these studies and quickly publicized the findings. An example of what was reported to the public:

> Babies whose mothers were exposed to crack and powdered cocaine were, compared with those whose mothers were not exposed to drugs during pregnancy, more likely to be born premature, have a significantly lower birth weight, have smaller heads, suffer seizures, have genital and urinary tract abnormalities, suffer poor motor ability, have brain lesions, and exhibit behavioral aberrations, such as impulsivity, moodiness, and lower responsiveness (Goode & Ben-Yehuda, 1994, p. 216).

In addition, networks aired footage of infants screaming, allegedly in withdrawal from crack. Problematic however, was that the networks actually used footage of babies who were in withdrawal from heroin and portrayed it to the public as the "crack-baby epidemic." Physicians have determined that infants do not scream as the effects of crack or cocaine wear off, but instead sleep—this, however, would not have made for sensationalistic media (Sadofsky Baggins, 1998).

> *"The bright room is filled with baby misery; babies born months too soon; babies weighing little more than a hardcover book; babies that look like wizened old men in the last stages of a terminal illness, wrinkled skin clinging chicken bones; babies who do not cry because their mouths are full of tubes. . . . The reason is crack."*
>
> (Goode & Ben-Yehuda, 1994, p. 217)

As one can imagine these reports sparked outrage among society, and the innocence and purity of babies only heightened society's anger toward drug-abusing mothers for the potential harm they may cause to their offspring. With all of the media attention brought to this new social epidemic, it became a given that crack babies were an enormous health and social concern even though there were major flaws in these early studies. Early research lacked controls for other influential factors on newborns such as poor diet, and perhaps most notably, use of alcohol and/or tobacco products. Another glaring error of these studies was that they failed to conduct follow-up analysis on the growth and health of the newborns, meaning that such research could provide no long-term prognosis about the health of these children (Lyman & Potter, 2007). Nonetheless, these hasty and incomplete studies provided enough information to motivate state and federal legislators to enact policies which punished mothers for the use of crack and/or cocaine during pregnancy.

Additionally, media sources, such as the *New York Times* and the *Washington Post*, considered credible and truthful by the mass reading public, reported outrageous claims in the late 1980s including a quote by former federal drug czar, William Bennet, claiming that "one out of ten births results in the birth of a crack baby" (Goode & Ben-Yehuda, 1994, p. 217). Not surprisingly, there are no sources that can confirm this statistic. As a result of this claim and subsequent resulting headlines, the Department of Health and Human Services projected that due to the mass amounts of crack babies being born, society was incurring an insurmountable annual cost in the billions to medically treat crack babies (Jenkins, 1999). These myths resulted in severe implications: Medical professionals were now required by law to report pregnant drug users; babies were taken from their drug-using mothers and became wards of the state; and drug use during pregnancy was declared a criminal act with some states sentencing drug-using mothers to a maximum of 10 years for crack/cocaine use during pregnancy (Kappeler & Potter, 2005). Not only are these policies harsh, but they have been notoriously given to a demographic of poor black women addicted to crack/cocaine and unlikely to be able to obtain adequate prenatal care due to their lack of finances and lack of health insurance.

Similar to the media's initial portrayal of marijuana users, crack was routinely associated with minorities, and the public was led to believe a sensationalized link between minorities and crack which was a misrepresentation. "The crack scare demonized minorities. Half of all television news stories about drugs feature blacks as users or sellers, while only 32 percent of the stories feature whites. This is out of all proportion to the known patterns of drug use" (Kappeler & Potter, 2005, p. 197). The media's skewed reporting heavily influenced law enforcement's strategy and targets for the "crackdown" of crack and/or cocaine users. This is evident by looking at the statistics of prison occupants: The majority of convicted drug offenders were and still are African Americans, despite the fact that white and blacks *use* drugs at about the same rate!

To further substantiate the lunacy of the crack-baby scare, it must be noted that by the time the media and the government started heightening their crack-baby campaign, crack and cocaine use had stagnated across the United States. The National Institute of Drug Abuse reported that use of cocaine substances was declining for approximately four years prior to the media hype (Kappeler & Potter, 2005). Despite this sobering fact, the media struck with full force. One network that was particularly diligent in getting the message out about crack was NBC, as it ran approximately 400 televised reports concerning crack in the last six months of 1986 (Kappeler & Potter, 2005). The media and government exerted an excessive amount of energy on the crack-baby myth, despite the fact that research reveals no causal link between maternal cocaine use and poor fetal development. Further, there has been no detection of increased birth defects from pregnant women using cocaine (Kappeler & Potter, 2005). It appears that what leads to birth defects in babies are factors such as poor prenatal care, use of tobacco and alcohol (note these are legal drugs), poor nutrition, heredity, and other factors that non-drug-using women are exposed to merely by being pregnant on an increasingly polluted planet.

Designer Drugs as Rape Drugs

Designer drugs, such as fentanyl, MPTP, GHB (gamma-Hydroxybutric acid), rohypnol, and ecstasy, first gained popularity around the mid-1980s. These drugs are produced synthetically, can have a very powerful impact on the body, and altering the dosage by a small amount could have catastrophic effects. Such substances became referred to as "designer" because they were popular at the same time designer jeans were popular (Jenkins, 1999). This ingenious marketing of synthetic drugs was quite a success in upscale communities.

It soon became apparent that there were many variants of designer drugs available and very little knowledge as to which were lethal . . . this escalated hysteria concerning these substances which became labeled the "problem of the future" (Jenkins, 1999, p. 172). The hype spiraled into a greater level of awareness by 1985, due in large part to massive media coverage. Designer drug stories were broadcast in every prime-time slot from NBC's *Nightly News* to *A Current Affair*, with the majority of these reports focusing on extreme occurrences resulting from interactions with designer drugs (Jenkins, 1999). Almost five years later, synthetic chemists had developed a new designer drug called GHB. Referred to in the U.S. media as a "date rape drug," GHB received peak media attention after the death of celebrity River Phoenix in 1993. Though it was later revealed that Phoenix died due to other drugs, this did not remove GHB from the limelight. In the mid-1990s, *CNN* aired a report entitled "Trendy Drug Goes Club-Hopping . . . and Officials are Worried" which stated:

> Raves are to the '90s what disco was to the '70s—midnight-until-dawn dance-a-thons where the beat is techno. Apparently, it's not enough excitement for some revelers. GHB, or liquid ecstasy, is sweeping the club and bar scene. It's fairly easy to get and relatively cheap. But experts warn: It's also very dangerous . . . GHB was sold in health food stores until federal officials pulled it from the shelves in 1990. Some users compare the drug to drinking alcohol. But it can be dangerous when mixed with alcohol—especially beer . . . At least two people have reportedly died after consuming GHB, and emergency rooms around the country have reported a rise in cases linked to the drug. "As one goes to higher doses, it's very easy to get into trouble with it—coma, seizures. There are a couple of reports of respiratory arrest," pharmacist Gant Galloway said. "People have almost died, and would have without prompt medical attention" . . . GHB is so new, experts say, that few are aware of its danger. And at the raves, it's becoming the rage ("Trendy Drug Goes Club-Hopping . . . and Officials are Worried," 1996).

Various news reports also indicated that the market in which these synthetic drugs was in highest demand was among young Caucasian individuals. While GHB and rohypnol became quite popular in the 1990s, it was not reported early on that these drugs were being used for date rape. By 1996, the stories of drug use in the media increased steadily. The reports of the drug and its use as a date-rape drug escalated when *Newsweek* published a report entitled "Roofies: The Date-Rape Drug" in 1996. Various major newspapers followed with fear inducing headlines such as the San Francisco Chronicle's "Drug Zaps Memory of Rape Victims." While intense media coverage helped to spread panic regarding rohypnol and GHB, e-mail forwards were highly successful in this regard as well.

When the public became aware of designer drugs they were not yet classified as illegal substances due to legislation lagging far behind underground chemists' experimentation for the next high. Although legislation and law enforcement soon caught up with chemists with punitive laws for the use of rohypnol and GHB, the drugs continued to play as popular in the media. While an overwhelming number of the drug-related incidents occurred in the state of Florida, the media deceivingly exaggerated their coverage to lead the public to believe that such events were equally likely to occur in each of our backyards (Jenkins, 1999). Designer drugs continued to appear on a wide array of television shows from dramas like *Beverly Hills 90210* to adult cartoons such as *South Park.* Perhaps designer drugs became a true national social problem when discussed on the *Oprah Winfrey Show.* The program stated that "thousands of rapes" have occurred as a result of men slipping GHB into women's drinks. The problem, however, was that the show provided no supporting documentation of the immensity of this claim. After this episode aired on national television, GHB and rohypnol were forever labeled as rape drugs, and anyone found to be producing these synthetic drugs or using them were considered to be sex criminals (Jenkins, 1999). This stigma was exploited by the media even when there was no evidence of support. Hand in hand with these accounts were warnings for women. A Web site geared towards educating teenagers posted the following information:

> The drugs also make the victim act without inhibition, often in a sexual or physically affectionate way. Like most drugs, date rape drugs render a person incapable of thinking clearly or of making appropriate decisions. This makes for a very passive victim, one who is still able to play a role in what is happening but who will have no clear memory of what happened after-the-fact. Without any memory of events the victim is often unaware that they have even been raped, and if they are aware or have suspicions they make very poor witnesses ("Date Rape Drugs Explained and De-mystified" nd).

While these recommendations may be helpful, the media has effectively caused a moral panic specifically geared toward the female audience. These fear tactics were even employed by law enforcement, specifically the Santa Monica Rape Treatment Center which created a list of rules for women to follow in order not to fall victim to date rape. Unfortunately, these rules merely helped to create an unrealistic perception by women to see themselves as living in a state of sexual siege from predatory males who could be anywhere, just waiting to slip a roofie in their drink (Jenkins, 1999).

The Meth Explosion

Methamphetamines (meth) were first produced in the 1960s by pharmaceutical companies for medicinal purposes such as treating obesity, attention-deficit disorders, and narcolepsy. The drug soon gained popularity and was subsequently added to Schedule II of the Controlled Substances Act in 1971. By the late 1980s meth resurfaced, and according to the DEA use of meth had outpaced heroin and cocaine abuse in some areas of the United States. Meth became coined in the media as the "crack of the nineties," due to its cheapness and availability (Jenkins, 1999, p. 135). Likening meth use to crack use served a significant role in spreading the hype regarding meth, deceiving the public into believing that meth use was a nationwide epidemic, when in actuality the use of meth was found to be localized and only on the rise in Arizona, California, Hawaii, Oklahoma, and select areas in the Southwest (Jenkins, 1999).

Widespread arrests were made around the United States for the use of, importation of, and manufacturing of meth. Throughout the 1990s use of meth spread throughout the Midwest and was portrayed as an epidemic in the press about 1995. Additionally, major newspapers and television networks reported stories of meth abuse and destruction among families as a result of its use. Some articles included stories in which women had abandoned their familial responsibilities after becoming addicted to meth, while others reported on families producing the drug in their own home with children present. Media coverage of meth use also included some very serious accounts of violent acts which were reported as causally related to meth use, leading the public to believe that those under the influence of methamphetamines were more likely to be violent (Jenkins, 1999). Reports used catch phrases and dramatization to scare the public. For example, one report suggested: "The answer (concerning an upsurge in crime) is in the demonizing effects of methamphetamine on the 'normal' residents of the heartland" (Jenkins, 1999, p. 139).

The "meth problem" also gained attention when it was the topic of one of CBS's *48 Hours* shows. The segment provided footage of police storming a meth lab, while they discussed the potential risks involved with encountering individuals high on "speed" or "crank" (Jenkins, 1999). The perpetrators who were the subject of the report were almost always white and dwelling in a rural community, enhancing the image of a meth user as being "poor white trash"—the typical image repeated by a multitude of sources. Ironically, after several years of sensationalized reports in the media, statistics showed that the meth problem in the mid-1990s was no worse than what it had been five or ten years prior. It was then, and remained, a regional issue, primarily in the West and Southwest areas of North America (Jenkins, 1999).

By 1996, the DEA had effectively increased their raids on meth labs, leading President Clinton to announce that meth abuse was on the decline as a social problem (Jenkins, 1999). Contrastingly, other sources begged to differ, suggesting instead that meth use had spread throughout North America (Lyman & Potter, 2003). A likely reason that inspired people to use or manufacture meth was because the ingredients were accessible in most convenience stores, which allowed production costs to stay low and profits to stay high. In the short term, meth labs can be quite profitable until they get raided by federal and/or local law enforcement. The DEA reported that a day of production in a meth lab could result in approximately $50,000, sustaining an initial overhead investment of only $2,000 (Lyman & Potter, 2003). As a result of many of these factors, the media and government sources warned that meth would become the next national drug epidemic: They warned the public that it is a highly addictive substance, and because of its availability and low cost, it would be the next drug "explosion" of the nineties (Jenkins, 1999).

Ironically, the hype surrounding meth in the 1990s ended up being rather anticlimactic in comparison to the publicity crack use received in the 1980s. The height of public concern occurred during the congressional hearings concerning meth, wherein Congress presided over testimony concerning the profits of meth dealers and traffickers, and the dangers of the short- and long-term effects of meth use (Potter & Kappeler, 1998). The media paid an intense amount of attention to meth, and medical professionals testified at hearings regarding the harm and the risks of a drug so dangerous; it was believed it would define the decade (Potter & Kappeler, 1998). As the media attention slowly turned to the U.S. invasion of Kuwait, the "meth epidemic" faded from the spotlight. Statistics in 2006, however, reveal that "epidemic" may not have been the correct description as national use of methamphetamines are at a mere 2 percent of the population ("Meth Epidemic Just Media Hype," 2006).

Whether the subject of focus is marijuana as a gateway drug, PCP and the dangerous criminal, the myth of the crack baby, designer drugs as rape drugs, or the meth explosion, the importance of the media in highlighting these "problems" cannot be overstated. The media uses sound bites and sensationalism to distort the public's view of drug use, and consequently to distort our view of appropriate criminal justice responses to drug use and abuse. "A century from now historians may ponder this construction of drug demons just as they now ponder the burning of witches and heretics. But what is already clear is that a century's worth of scapegoating chemical bogeymen left even the very best journalists quite prepared to believe the very worst about drug users, especially inner-city addicts" (Reinarman & Duskin, 1998, p. 326). Until the media is prepared to offer a more balanced and contextualized approach to the issues surrounding drug use and abuse, American society is unlikely to be aware of (or support) a therapeutic, effective, and perhaps even non–criminal justice response to the drug issue.

Summary

- Attitudes toward which drugs are acceptable and which should be condemned are a social construct that changes significantly over time. The media plays a major role in the development of public attitudes regarding drugs and drug users in blurring and shifting the arbitrary boundary between those drugs we consider medicinal and those drugs we consider recreational.
- Hysteria surrounding drugs has been a feature of American society for more than 200 years, beginning with the drug scares over alcohol in the late 18th century, and continuing to today with drug scares over synthetic substances. Though there has been some rise and fall, since the 1960s the media has fairly consistently promoted fear of drugs and drug abusers. The way the drug issue is portrayed in the media hides structural problems of poverty, underemployment and unemployment, poor healthcare, poor education, racism, and a host of other macro-social problems.
- Due primarily to intense media coverage of select illegal substances, the public has come to believe over the years that there have been "epidemics" of drug use. Using the concept of a moral panic to discuss drugs in society draws attention to the exaggerated and misdirected nature of societal fear and the misdirected policies that have been created as a result. Citizens respond based not on the *actual* harm of the substance, but rather the *symbolic* harm as portrayed in the media. A similar model detailing the process of social problems involves six steps: claimsmaking, media coverage, public reaction, policymaking, social-problems work, and policy outcomes.
- By the 1930s, states were enacting anti-marijuana laws on the heels of sensationalized reports in the media: By 1937, all forty-eight states had such laws. Through the decades the "weed of madness" stories declined and by the mid-1970s surveys identified that approximately 30 million people were, in some way or another, users of marijuana. Simultaneously, government agencies and their institutional vehicles continued to deliver the message of marijuana as a gateway drug, which had begun in the 1950s and continues by some researchers today.
- PCP was the most heavily used drug in American society from the mid-1970s through the early 1980s. This substance became fashionable to young people, both poor and middle class, and was associated with sensationalized reports of sexual conquests and liaisons. PCP also gained attention in the media, particularly in the Washington, DC area where use of the drug was believed to be the underlying reason for an increase in psychiatric commitments in 1973. The media persisted during the 1970s and early 1980s to quickly report any crime of violence with a potential link to PCP use. Whether the link was myth or fact was irrelevant. This linkage has since been etched in society's mind and PCP users are forever associated with the commission of violence.
- The myth of a crack-baby epidemic started in the mid-1980s. These myths resulted in severe implications: Medical professionals were now required by law to report pregnant drug users; babies were taken from their drug-using mothers and became wards of the state; and drug use during

pregnancy was declared a criminal act with some states sentencing drug-using mothers to a maximum of 10 years for crack/cocaine use during pregnancy. Not only are these policies harsh, but they have been notoriously given to a demographic of poor black women addicted to crack/cocaine and unlikely to be able to obtain adequate prenatal care due to their lack of finances and lack of health insurance.

- Designer drugs first gained popularity around the mid-1980s. These drugs are produced synthetically, can have a very powerful impact on the body, and altering the dosage by a small amount could have catastrophic effects. When the public became aware of designer drugs they were not yet classified as illegal substances. While an overwhelming number of the drug-related incidents occurred in the state of Florida, the media deceivingly exaggerated their coverage to lead the public to believe that such events were equally likely to occur anywhere.
- Meth was coined by the media as the "crack of the nineties," due to its cheapness and availability. Likening meth use to crack use served a significant role in spreading the hype regarding meth and deceiving the public into believing that meth use was a nationwide epidemic, when in actuality the use of meth was found to be localized. Media coverage of meth use also included some very serious accounts of violent acts which were reported as causally related to meth use, leading the public to believe that those under the influence of methamphetamines were more likely to be violent.

Important Terms

Claimsmaking

Media

Moral panic

Critical Thinking Questions

1. Does the media portray the abuse of legal and illegal drugs differently? Through the use of examples, defend your position.
2. How might U.S. policies toward drugs be different if moral panics that demonized drug users and abusers were not created by the media?

Research Topics

1. Choose an illicit substance not discussed in this chapter and trace how the media have portrayed this substance and users of this substance during its height of popularity.
2. Write a two-page mock newspaper article regarding an illicit substance of your choosing and the individuals who use/abuse this substance. Write the article in a way that does not create a moral panic, does not demonize users, and in a way that may suggest a therapeutic as opposed to criminal justice solution.

Suggested Reading

Jenkins, Philip. (1999). *Synthetic panics: The symbolic politics of designer drugs.* New York, NY: New York University Press.

3

Explaining Drug Use

"It's about having a good time . . ."

—Palacios & Fenwick, 2006, p. 275.

OBJECTIVES:

When you have finished this chapter, you should be able to:

- Compare and contrast the general premises of biological, psychological, and sociological theories
- Explain two biological theories of addiction
- Understand the underlying assumptions for psychological personality traits and psychoanalytic theories of addiction
- Distinguish between positive reinforcement and negative reinforcement theories of addiction
- Distinguish micro-sociological and macro-sociological theories
- Understand the six primary sociological theories explaining drug-using behaviors

REAL LIFE

Substance abuse in the inner city is merely a symptom—and a vivid symbol—of deeper dynamics of social marginalization and alienation. Of course, on an immediately visible personal level, addiction and substance abuse are among the most immediate, brutal facts shaping daily life on the street. More importantly, however, the two dozen street dealers and their families that I befriended were not interested in talking primarily about drugs. On the contrary, they wanted me to learn all about their daily struggles for subsistence and dignity at the poverty line (Bourgois, 1995, p. 2).

The observation that drug use has been a part of human history is often overstated but it holds true. People throughout history have been taking drugs for many reasons, including therapeutic, religious, social, and recreational. Indeed, "there may be as many reasons for taking drugs as there are people who use them" (Inciardi & McElrath, 2004, p. 1). However, most of us are interested in learning why people deviate from social convention in their drug use, especially in the case of psychoactive drug use. Andrew Weil (1972) contends that humans have an innate drive to alter consciousness. He supports his idea with observations of young children whirling to the point of dizziness and hyperventilating themselves to almost unconsciousness, common daydreaming, and religious and spiritual leaders who seek higher experiences away from self. He argues psychoactive drug use is just another means to reach alternate states.

As touched on in Chapter One, Goode (2005) suggests we look at psychoactive drug use neutrally and examine purpose as one dimension of motivation. He differentiates between instrumental and recreational purposes for use. **Instrumental use** of substances might include taking drugs in order to stay awake to study or to work, or to improve athletic performance. Instrumental drug use is not for the purpose of intoxication, but to assist in achieving a goal. **Recreational drug use** refers to using substances to seek an altered state, typically some level of euphoria. Goode (2008) points out that instrumental use of drugs is often more acceptable in our society than recreational use. For instance, using amphetamines, even illegally, in order to be productive certainly is thought of differently than taking them to get high. Productivity certainly outweighs pleasure-seeking on a moral scale.

Theory seeks a systematic way to explain and to predict variation in drug-using behaviors, especially addiction. Why do some people use psychoactive drugs for pleasure or compulsively while others do not? Why do some people who use drugs become addicted while others do not become addicted? Are the answers found in the individual's biological or psychological makeup, or in society at large? Theories from three disciplines dominate discussions about drug use and addiction: biology, psychology, and sociology. And while each discipline approaches drug-using behaviors from a different perspective, no particular theory lays claim to complete understanding. That is, no one theory can explain all drug use in all circumstances. Table 3-1 gives a brief overview of how each discipline examines drug use and addiction.

As such, a theory may explain drug use extremely well under one condition, but may not apply if the circumstances are changed. In this chapter, some of the most important theories about drug use from biology, psychology, and sociology are examined.

TABLE 3-1 Overview of Disciplinary Perspective on Drugs

	Biological Theories	Psychological Theories	Sociological Theories
Overview	Examines the physiological influences that contribute to an individual's progression from drug use to addiction	Examines the psychodynamic processes and explains drug use and addiction in terms of individual characteristics and experiences	Examines drugs as embedded in the structural elements of society and focuses on the social environment of the user
Type	• Genetic predisposition • Metabolic and neurochemical change	• Personality trait • Reinforcement	• Social reaction • Social learning • Social control • Strain • Cultural deviance • Conflict

BIOLOGICAL THEORIES

Biological theories of addiction look specifically at the physiological influences that contribute to an individual's progression from drug use to drug addiction. Two theories dominate the literature about the biological foundations of addiction. The first theory contends that an inherent or genetic trait predisposes some individuals to addiction. The second sees addiction as an acquired metabolic or neurochemical condition resulting from the continued use of particular drugs.

Genetic Predisposition

Genetic predisposition theories propose that biological makeup, specifically the genetic structure of an individual, contributes to his or her susceptibility to addiction. These theories parallel medical theories about the genetic predisposition of a number of medical conditions. For example, physicians request a patient's medical history because a substantial amount of research suggests many conditions such as diabetes, heart disease, high blood pressure, and certain cancers have a genetic basis. Doctors use a family medical history in conjunction with many other mitigating factors to determine prevention, diagnostic, and treatment strategies. The same principles are thought to be at work for addiction. Studies about a genetic predisposition toward addiction are based primarily on research about the role of heredity in alcohol dependence. As discussed earlier, while drug addiction is generally treated as a medical condition by physicians and psychologists, alcoholism is officially recognized as a disease. Therefore, in reviewing research about alcohol dependence, one must be cautious in generalizing to addiction regarding other drugs.

Genetic Predisposition Theory suggests that the genetic structure of an individual contributes to his or her susceptibility to addiction

A preponderance of studies during the past fifty years have shown that individuals who have an immediate family history of alcohol dependence are between three and five times more likely than the general population to develop alcohol dependence (Schuckit, 1985). Many of these studies, however, do not account for the influence of environmental factors such as social, cultural, and interpersonal experiences. In an effort to separate genetic and environmental factors, researchers have conducted studies about alcohol dependence using twins and adoptees. In studies of twins, researchers compare identical or monozygotic (MZ) twins who share 100 percent of their genes with fraternal or dizygotic (DZ) twins who share 50 percent of their genes. While some of the findings are mixed, twin studies in general substantiate ideas about a genetic influence of alcohol dependence by showing MZ twins share higher rates of alcoholic symptoms than DZ twins, especially in the case of males (Heath, 1995; Heath & Martin, 1993; Pickens, Svikis, McGue, & LaBuda, 1995).

In other studies, researchers compare rates of alcohol dependence between adoptees with alcohol-dependent biological parents and adoptees with non-alcohol-dependent biological parents, both reared since or near birth in non-alcohol-dependent families. The assumption is that if a genetic predisposition to alcohol dependence is present then it will more likely be transmitted from the biological parent to the child; the environment of non-alcohol dependence serves as the control. The findings of these types of studies have been consistent in showing a higher rate of alcohol dependence, as much as four times greater, for those individuals with alcohol-dependent biological parents (Goodwin, Schulsinger, Hermansten, Guze, & Winokur, 1973; Cloninger, Bohman, & Sigvardsson, 1981).

While twin and adoption studies do suggest a genetic component for developing alcohol dependence, these studies are not without limitations. First, many of the samples are small. Second, many studies must be conducted over long periods of time and often findings are preliminary. Finally, while a genetic component appears likely, researchers have not been able to pinpoint exactly what biological mechanisms may lead to a predisposition toward alcohol dependence. As such, genetic theories should be interpreted cautiously. While such studies may indicate a genetic susceptibility, genetic theories also fail to adequately explain why the majority of individuals with this susceptibility do not develop alcohol dependence.

Molecular genetics researchers are beginning efforts to examine specific genetic codes to identify the propensity for alcohol dependence. Recently, the Collaborative Study on the Genetics of Alcoholism (COGA) teamed with the National Institute of Alcohol Abuse and Alcoholism (NIAAA) to attempt to isolate certain regions of chromosomes that may be connected to alcohol dependence. According to these researchers, the chance of determining a single gene linked directly to alcohol dependence is unlikely, but the possibility of a locating a combination of multiple genes leading to susceptibility toward alcohol dependence may be plausible in the next decade (NIAAA, 2000).

Heredity studies and molecular genetics promise both benefits and risks for those who may eventually be identified with a genetic predisposition toward alcohol dependence. Benefits and risks are similar to those associated with individuals being informed they have a genetic predisposition toward another medical condition. Primary benefits include creating better prevention programs, providing more accurate diagnoses, and improving intervention and treatment strategies. The most important benefit though, has been allowing individuals to make informed decisions in managing their health and quality of life. However, the risk of these decisions being taken from the individual and placed into the hands of authorities, as well as the risk of discriminatory practices may pose a real threat (WHO, 2004). Insurance companies regularly decline coverage for "preexisting conditions," and many individuals seeking genetic testing and counseling have concerns about being targeted as "at-risk" not just for disease but for the provision of medical coverage. Therefore, at this moment in history, being identified as "at-risk" lends itself to many other potential implications.

Metabolic and Neurochemical Change

Metabolic and Neurochemical Theories suggest addiction results when a specific drug causes a metabolic or neurochemical change in an individual leading to a visceral, chronic, and residual need for the drug

Metabolic and neurochemical theories explain addiction as a homeostatic response to the use of a specific drug. These theories postulate that the use of particular drugs for some people cause metabolic and neurochemical changes and that these changes lead to an almost visceral, chronic, and residual need for the specific drug much in the way diabetics need insulin to regulate their body functioning, or depressed individuals need antidepressants to balance their brain chemistry. Vincent Dole and Marie Nyswander (Dole, 1994) were the pioneers of this approach to addiction, and examined heroin addiction. In the 1960s, Drs. Dole and Nyswander worked with the Methadone Maintenance Research Program at Rockefeller University Hospital in New York. They conducted trial pharmacological studies using methadone maintenance for chronic intravenous heroin addicts who had proved difficult to treat due to high relapse rates even after controlled periods of abstinence. Methadone is an oral synthetic opioid medication that pharmacologically can substitute for other opioids to prevent withdrawal symptoms. Methadone does not produce the euphoric state of other opioids but allows users to function normally. It presents fewer long-term side effects and in sufficient doses blocks the usual euphoria of subsequent morphine or heroin use. Dole and Nyswander unexpectedly found that the majority of addicts maintained with methadone in their program not only abstained from heroin, but ceased much of their criminal behavior and became employed or enrolled in school. The results were particularly surprising due to the lack of psychiatric and psychological treatment provided for the rehabilitation of addicts.

These initial findings and their subsequent research on methadone maintenance for heroin addicts served as the foundation for suggesting the primacy of metabolic aspects of addiction. Dr. Dole summarized their position:

> A modern theory of narcotic addiction is that the compulsive (and quite specific) craving for narcotic drugs is a symptom of deficiency in function of the natural opiate-like substances in the brain. To be sure, sociological and psychological forces enter into the making of an addict, but these factors determine exposure—whether or not addictive drugs are available in the environment and whether a person chooses to experiment with them. In any person, with repeated exposure to a narcotic drug, the brain adapts and becomes pharmacologically dependent on a continuing input. In some susceptible persons—fortunately a minority of the population—the adaptation becomes fixed, and with repeated use a regular input of narcotic becomes a necessity. The experimenter has become an addict. From this perspective methadone maintenance is replacement treatment, compensating for impairment in function of natural opiate-like substances (Dole, 1994, pp. 1–4).

In the past several decades since the initiation of Dole and Nyswander's work, subsequent findings have not been as supportive of their ideas or of methadone maintenance in general (Goode, 2008). However, research has begun to show many psychoactive drugs may alter neurochemistry and physiology in a manner that would make long-term abstinence difficult after extended use. Researchers postulate that excessive drug use acts on neurochemical processes to the point where the brain and the body adapt to the drug's presence, and require the use of the drug, sometimes in larger dosages, to maintain normal neurochemical and physiological functioning (Robinson & Berridge, 2000). When the drug is withdrawn from the body, neurochemical and physiological impairment then occurs until the body can readjust its functioning without the drug. While the short-term physiological symptoms of withdrawal have been long recognized, the discovery of neurological links to addiction is relatively new and lends some support for Dole and Nyswander's original ideas about addiction and its treatment. This line of research suggests neurochemical recovery from the excessive use of some psychoactive drugs may extend beyond that of other shorter-term physiological symptoms of withdrawal (Hyman & Malenka, 2001). In the case of heavy cocaine users, researchers believe such users may not only experience short-term depression but may experience difficulty finding pleasure without chemical stimulation for long periods of time, leading to inevitable returns to drug use. Though varying in their specific neurochemical actions, excessive and long-term use of other drugs such as alcohol and nicotine are thought to produce similar processes and long-term neurochemical imbalances. In addition, metabolic and neurochemical theories suggest pharmacological remedies, or the use of alternate drugs, for addiction recovery. Because biological explanations seem "scientific" and "concise," we are sometimes drawn to such theories; however, drug use is a very complex issue that cannot be reduced to mere genetics.

PSYCHOLOGICAL THEORIES

Psychological theories of addiction turn attention to psychodynamic processes and explain addiction primarily in terms of individual characteristics and experiences. While psychological theories about addiction abound, they can be categorized into two groups: personality traits and reinforcement.

Personality Traits

Many psychologists and addiction treatment professionals deem personality characteristics primary in the addiction process. Similar to ideas about genetics and addiction, "characterological" models suppose that personality structures predispose individuals to drug dependency (Miller & Hester, 1995). In other words, certain personality traits lend themselves toward addiction, which is often referred to as an **addictive personality**. This type of personality is frequently associated with low self-esteem, insecurity, and anxiety, at times masked by depression or a sort of bravado. Various explanations for addictive personalities have been posited. In the past, some researchers speculated that personality was determined at birth and although this position lacks empirical support, many of us still accept some form of this principle. For instance, many of us rely on our parents' recollections of our personality as infants and children to explain our current disposition or marvel at television talk shows that reunite twins separated at birth, with a concentration on similarities in personality while ignoring the differences.

Psychologists with a more psychoanalytic bent argue that our individual experiences determine our personality makeup. According to a **psychoanalytical approach**, traumatic experiences such as physical and sexual abuse, neglect, and even mild family dysfunction can lead to attempts to medicate the resulting emotional problems (Bradshaw, 1988; Horney, 1964). The implications are that the emotional pain must be overcome through therapy for the addict to remain drug free after physiological withdrawal. Otherwise, the addict will return to chemical use for the same reasons that led him or her to use drugs in the first place. The research suggests many addicts have experienced abuse and dysfunction; however, research does not take note of the larger number of people who have had similar experiences and never turn to drugs.

> The Psychoanalytical Approach suggests that traumatic experiences such as physical and sexual abuse, neglect, and even mild family dysfunction can lead to attempts to medicate the resulting emotional problems

Reinforcement

Reinforcement theories are concerned with the transition from drug use to drug addiction, with special interest in explaining long-term addiction to street drugs. They are based on the classical behavioral theories of conditioning posed by Ivan Pavlov and B. F. Skinner. Pavlov was noted for his discovery that dogs salivated when they were presented with food and that when presented with another stimuli such as a bell ringing during feeding, the dog could be conditioned to salivate at the sound of the bell even without food present. In other words, the dog associated the sound of the bell with food, and this association produced the same physical response—salivation (Pavlov, 1927).

> Reinforcement Theories are based on classical behavioral theories of conditioning and are concerned with the transition from drug use to drug addiction, with a special interest in explaining long-term addiction to street drugs

Skinner (1938) was recognized for developing principles of operant conditioning or the use of reinforcements or consequences to modify behavior. **Positive reinforcement** occurs when a behavior is followed by pleasant stimuli and the behavior then increases. For instance, you may have trained an animal companion to sit and stay by providing treats following the desired behavior. You hope that through positive reinforcement your pet will repeat the behavior until it becomes habitual, and no longer needs to be reinforced. **Negative reinforcement** occurs when a behavior is followed by the removal of an aversive stimuli and the behavior also increases. In order to explain drug dependency, psychologists have used different variations of reinforcement theory. The general foundation for positive reinforcement is that the euphoric experience of drug use acts as a reward and thus increases the likelihood of continuing the behavior. For negative reinforcement the belief is that the discomfort or painful experience of withdrawal increases the likelihood of continuing drug use.

Lindesmith (1938) proposed what he termed a "sociological theory of drug addiction" based on the principles of negative reinforcement and social psychology. In his classic work, he contradicted the picture of addicts during the 1930s, particularly opiate addicts, as psychopaths seeking to chase highs or escape life stressors. He was vehemently opposed to the blame placed on the addict as morally or psychologically defective and weak. He argued that addicts had reached a point wherein their drug taking no longer resulted in euphoria but rather a type of normalcy. These individuals had come to recognize their plight as "dope fiends" and had begun to associate withdrawal, short- and long-term, through this lens of negative reinforcement. In short, he believed addicts used drugs habitually to avoid the psychological distress of withdrawal.

Alternately, theorists leaning toward a positive reinforcement model reject Lindesmith's findings. McAuliffe and Gordon (1974) argued that the primary motive for long-term addicts, again particularly opiate addicts, is to seek a euphoric state rather than to fight withdrawal. They found that addicts did not just maintain their addiction minimally but sought greater doses in order to experience a more intense high and that many of them expected positive effects from their drug use. Later, through interviews with long-term street addicts, McAuliffe (1982) found that the most common reason for returning to drug use was a desire for a euphoric high.

SOCIOLOGICAL THEORIES

Unlike biological or psychological perspectives on drug use, **sociological theories** approach the use of drugs as a phenomenon embedded in the structural elements of society. Sociologists assert that social and cultural factors influence our attitudes toward drugs, what is considered an illicit drug, what types of drugs are used by various groups of people, how we view drug users, as well as the significance of drug use as a problem in American society. Generally, sociological theories are less concerned with individual factors, and focus instead on the social environment of the drug user. Of the sociological theories addressed, social learning theory and social control theory place more emphasis on the individual than the other approaches. Many sociological theories are based on theories that explain criminal or deviant behavior in general. Theories may be **micro-sociological**, in that they focus on social interaction patterns in specific situations such as social reaction theory, social learning theory, and social control theory. Conversely, theories may be **macro-sociological**, in that they focus on structural issues that shape the whole of society such as **strain theory**, cultural deviance theory, and conflict theory. Table 3-2 provides an overview of the sociological approaches to drug use.

> Sociological Theories approach the use of drugs as a phenomenon embedded in the structural elements of society and believe that social and cultural factors influence our attitudes toward all elements of the drug issue

Social Reaction Theory

Social reaction theory, commonly known as labeling theory, asserts that some behaviors, and therefore the individuals who engage in such behaviors, are labeled negatively by society in general, and often by the criminal justice system. **Labeling** results in an individual being stigmatized by conventional society, which results in a negative reaction, which frequently fuels the individual's

TABLE 3-2 Overview of Main Points of Sociological Theories

Sociological Theory	Main Premise
Social reaction theory	Suggests that some people are labeled negatively by the larger society or those in the criminal justice system. This process of negative labeling results in the individual being shunned and treated differently by conventional society.
Social learning theory	Asserts that behavior is learned through human interaction. As such, individuals learn attitudes that are favorable or unfavorable to drugs from those in our close circle of friends.
Social control theory	Suggests that human behavior is controlled through close association with institutions and individuals. Examines how self-control and a commitment to conformity deter drug use.
Strain theory	Asserts that sharp divisions between the classes create an atmosphere of envy and mistrust that may lead to deviant behavior, including the use of drugs.
Cultural deviance theory	Asserts that deviance is the result of a combination of social disorganization in an environment and individual strain or frustration.
Conflict theory	Suggests that the powerful in society are able to assert their will over the poor. As applied to drugs this involves an examination of the disparate impacts of the war on drugs in different communities.

return to the behavior in question. Social reaction theory has its roots in the writings of George Herbert Mead and Herbert Blumer who suggested that the meaning we assign to events are shaped by our social and cultural experiences.

Social Reaction Theory suggests that some people are labeled negatively by the larger society or those in the criminal justice system; this negative labeling process results in the individual being shunned and treated differently by conventional society

With regard to drug use, labeling theorists assert that most individuals have engaged in temporary and exploratory experimentation with drugs. For most of us, experimentation with drugs is never revealed to the larger society; therefore, we do not regard our individual act as deviant. What happens, however, if our drug use is made public? What if our non-drug-using family and friends now know? What if our coworkers and boss know? Once our experimentation has been widely revealed and becomes labeled by others as a deviant activity, we too are labeled as deviant for being involved in this behavior. At this point we begin to view ourselves and our behavior as deviant. Often an individual will continue the behavior because he or she has internalized the deviant personality that other people expect.

The labeling process is as follows for drug use:

- An individual chooses to use drugs (social reaction theory does not attempt to explain the initial motivation for drug use, so the reasons could be varied).
- This person's behavior is brought to the attention of others or to the attention of the criminal justice system.
- If the substance is illicit, the likelihood of arrest is higher for those of a racial minority or of the lower class.
- Some of these individuals are officially labeled as deviant or as criminals.

- The labeled individuals are then viewed negatively by conventional society which does not accept or condone drug use.
- These individuals come to accept and internalize the negative label.
- Acceptance of the stigma leads to an association with others who have been similarly labeled, which often leads to further drug use.

Following this logic then, the likelihood of subsequent drug use could be decreased if society, and the criminal justice system, did not negatively label individuals. It is also important to note that class and race issues play a role in determining who is more likely to be labeled negatively. For example, a businessman who has three or four cocktails with clients over dinner is less likely to be negatively labeled than a construction worker who heads to the bar after work for three or four beers with friends to relax. Even more likely to get labeled is an inner city young man of a minority racial group who relaxes after work with his friends by smoking a joint.

Social reaction theory is important because it shifts the focus away from the question of why an individual uses drugs to society's reaction to the use of drugs by individuals. As such, labeling theorists attempt to address questions such as: Why are certain drugs legal and the use of these drugs is widely accepted in society, yet the use of other drugs is illegal and widely frowned upon by society? Why do some individuals who use illicit substances become negatively stigmatized and labeled, yet others engaging in the very same behavior avoid the societal stigma? How does the fact that we label individuals affect their lives and their choices for the future? As such, labeling theory raises some extremely interesting and important questions for dealing with drug use.

Social Learning Theory

Social learning theorists believe that behavior is learned from those closest to us. As we grow from children into adults we learn skills and behaviors through imitating others, trial and error, and positively reinforced behaviors. Just like we learn to hit a baseball from our father or from watching our favorite baseball player, or we learn to ride a bicycle from our older sister, we also learn attitudes that are favorable or unfavorable to drugs and how to experience drug use from those in our close circle of friends.

> Social Learning Theory asserts that criminal behavior is learned through human interaction

Edwin Sutherland (1939) used the term "differential association" to indicate that the key factor in whether or not an individual would engage in deviant behavior was the group of people with whom he or she associates. According to this theory, a person engages in deviant behavior when there are more favorable than unfavorable consequences to such behavior. It suggests that deviance, including drug use, is a learning process that can affect anyone in any culture, and that the skills and motives behind deviance are learned as a result of contact with values, attitudes, and definitions favorable of such behavior. As such, drug use would develop and continue if these "pro-deviant" values and behaviors are not matched or exceeded by conventional values and behaviors.

Rewards and punishments also play an important role in social learning theory. Whether specific behaviors are rewarded or punished in the group of people we are close with influences the type of behavior we continue in the future. For example, if the group of friends with whom you are closest are adamantly against drug use and would distance themselves from you if you decided to use drugs, this would likely influence your choices. If these friendships are truly important to you, the potential punishment of losing these friendships could be enough to keep you away from drugs. Conversely, if you are hanging around a group of people who regularly smoke marijuana and view it as socially acceptable, you will learn a definition from them that is favorable of drug use, making you more likely to participate in this rewarded behavior. Once a person has begun the use of drugs, continuation of the behavior involves identifying and maintaining contact with a seller, keeping the drug use hidden from those with unfavorable views of the behavior, and surrounding himself or herself with new friends who have a favorable attitude toward drug use. Social learning theorists also assert that an individual must "learn" to experience the effects of drug use as pleasurable. In a classic study on marijuana use, sociologist Howard Becker asserts:

> Marihuana-produced sensations are not automatically or necessarily pleasurable. The taste for such an experience is a socially acquired one, not different from acquired tastes for oysters or dry martinis. The user feels dizzy, thirsty; his scalp tingles; he misjudges time and distances. Are these things pleasurable? He isn't sure. If he is to continue marihuana use, he must decide that they are (Becker, 1963, p. 53).

As such, our friends and the influence of those we value become extremely important in defining the desirability of drugs. Therefore, the key for social learning theorists are the groups of people with whom you are closest. Prior to adolescence our parents are primary in the learning process, and once adolescence begins our friends become the most important. These individuals provide definitions of drugs that will either encourage your participation or your abstinence from drug use. Critics of social learning theory suggest the age-old "which came first, the chicken or the egg" question. Do you begin using drugs because you are hanging around friends who are supportive of drug use, or do you seek out drug-using friends once you have already begun using in order to surround yourself with like-minded individuals? Evidence suggests, however, that "the sequence of events in which deviant associations precede the onset of delinquent behavior will occur more frequently than the sequence of events in which the onset of delinquency precedes the beginning of deviant associations" (Akers & Lee, 1996, pp. 321–322).

Social Control Theory

Because deviance often results in rewards, **social control theorists** want to know why some people obey society's rules and others do not. They believe that self-control and a commitment to conformity deter deviant behavior. In other words, people's behavior is controlled by their attachment and association to conventional society. Applied to drug use, social control theorists would suggest that the vast majority of individuals would use drugs if it was not against the law or in violation of social norms.

> Social Control Theory suggests that human behavior is controlled through close associations with institutions and individuals

The dominant social control theorist is Travis Hirschi (1969) who believes that everyone is a potential deviant, but most people maintain control because they fear damaging relationships with those close to them. As such, Hirschi suggests that deviance and involvement in activities that are against social norms increases as an individual's bonds to society decrease. That is, the stronger our attachment to conventional society, the more likely it is that we will follow the rules. Hirschi (1969) outlined four main elements that serve to bond an individual to society:

- *Attachment* to family, friends, and the community builds respect for others and society's norms.
- If individuals have worked hard to *commit* to society, they are less likely to risk their position by engaging in deviance.

- Strong *beliefs* in honesty, morality, fairness, and responsibility keep individuals tied to conventional values, and less likely to violate norms.
- *Involvement* in conventional activities such as sports, community organizations, and social clubs leave little time for deviance.

The tighter these social bonds are to conventional society, the less likely an individual is to risk engaging in deviance, including the use of illicit substances. The empirical evidence for the validity of this theory is debatable and needs to be pursued further with a specific focus on drug use. Studies that have been conducted indicate that family and school act as important bonds for youth; however, social control theory fails to account for the important role of delinquent friends as a youth gets older.

Strain Theory

Robert Merton (1968) employed the concept of **anomie** to explain how the structural conditions precipitated by a capitalistic society, such as the United States, promote deviant behavior as a viable alternative to conventional behavior. According to Merton, anomie results from a disjuncture between culturally emphasized goals (such as wealth, status, and personal comfort) and the prescribed legitimate means (education and hard work) to attain these goals. The disjuncture is found between the *ideal* of the "American Dream," which suggests that all individuals have equal opportunity and access to the means for success, and the *reality* of a stratified, class-oriented system that does not provide equal opportunity and access to the means for success to all individuals, especially the lower class and minorities. The contradiction is compounded when the goals of material success are overemphasized and the legitimate means to reach these goals are underemphasized. Merton theorized that the anomic conditions arising from these conflicts lead to considerable strain or pressure for certain individuals and groups and that they respond by adapting based on their acceptance and/or rejection of societal goals and means (see Table 3-3 for a summary of Merton's framework of adaptation).

Strain Theory asserts that sharp divisions between the classes create an atmosphere of envy and mistrust that may lead to deviant behavior

In Merton's framework of adaptation, **retreatism** specifically addressed drug abuse and addiction. Retreatists are those individuals who repeatedly are unable to attain the culturally approved goals through legitimate means and who do not possess the capability to adopt illegitimate methods. In other words, access to legitimate and illegitimate means and therefore success, are all blocked for these individuals. They then adapt to the resulting strain by abandoning both the goals and means in order to "escape from the requirements of society" through drunkenness

TABLE 3-3 Overview of Merton's Adaptations to Strain

Adaptation	Goals of Society	Accepted Means of Attaining Goals
Conformist	Accept	Accept
Innovator	Accept	Reject
Ritualist	Reject	Accept
Retreatist	Reject	Reject
Rebel	Creates new	Revolts

or drug addiction. From Merton's standpoint, retreatists are dropouts from society: "persons who 'adjust' (or maladjust) in this fashion are, strictly speaking, in the society but not of *it.* Sociologically, these constitute the true 'aliens.' Not sharing the common frame of orientation, they can be included within the societal population merely in a fictional sense. In this category fall some of the adaptive activities of psychoticism, autists, pariahs, outcasts, vagrants, vagabonds, tramps, chronic drunkards, and drug addicts" (Merton, 1968, p. 277).

Beginning in the 1960s, Merton's explanation of retreatist behavior came under sharp criticism on several grounds. First, Merton's description of retreatists resembles a caricature of addicts as derelict skid row alcoholics and street junkies. However, many drug addicts lead productive and successful lives even when gauged under the strictest of American standards (such as former first lady, Betty Ford, an admitted addict). Further, studies of drug addicts, including street-based heroin addicts, depict a personally satisfying and demanding, albeit deviant, lifestyle rather than the passive escapist social world as described by Merton (Hanson, Beschner, Walters, & Bovelle, 1985; Preble & Casey, 1969). Second, Merton's theory reduces the complicated process of becoming a drug addict to the motivation for escape from social and economic pressure. As this chapter exemplifies, many physiological, psychological, and social or environmental factors appear to interact in the development of addiction. Finally, Merton assumes the inability to achieve success leads to addiction rather than examining how the consequences of addiction may lead to the inability to achieve success. Therefore, his theory may explain the effect rather than the cause.

While Merton's theory was all but rejected in the late 1980s, it has experienced a slight resurgence as contemporary theorists reconsider the impact of anomie on deviance (Messner & Rosenfeld, 2001). Researchers have reworked Merton's original concepts or have found other avenues of application. For example, Adrian (2003) suggests modes of adaptation other than retreatism can explain different aspects of drug-related behaviors. **Innovation** or the adoption of illegitimate means to attain the culturally approved goal of monetary success can offer an explanation for the individual who turns to drug dealing in the absence of legitimate channels. **Ritualism** or the participation in socially prescribed means without accepting the goals of success may be used to describe workers who strive to get through their workday routine in order to get home and enjoy their drug use. And **rebellion**, the substitution of alternative goals and means for conventional ones, may characterize the anarchic spirit of the hippie subculture of the 1960s, which adopted the ethos of "sex, drugs, and rock and roll" and "tune in, turn on, and drop out." Finally, **conformity** represents those who accept both the goals and means of conventional society. With regard to drugs, this would mean the use of only legal and socially accepted substances, such as alcohol.

Cultural Deviance Theory

> Cultural Deviance Theory asserts that deviance is the result of a combination of social disorganization in an environment and personal strain

Shaw and McKay (1972) popularized **cultural deviance theory** when they suggested that deviance was due to a combination of environmental social disorganization and personal strain. Specifically, their work purported that neighborhoods characterized by social disorganization, such as high rates of residential turnover and weak community ties, were more prone to developing delinquency or a subculture of individuals who engaged in delinquency. This subculture developed in response to the poor neighborhood conditions, which triggered feelings of hopelessness and strain in members of the community. Cultural deviance theorists assert that it is frequently members of the lower class who grow up in such a disorganized environment and create a subculture with their own rules and values that often clash with those of the conventional culture.

Applied to drug use, cultural deviance theory examines the drug subculture that is created in many neighborhoods due to the criminalization of drugs. In some respects this theoretical approach is similar to social learning theory in that individuals learn the norms of drug use from those within the subculture. The distinguishing structural factor of this approach, however, is that the individual's environment and the disorganization within that environment is important in explaining where and why subcultures develop.

Conflict Theory

Conflict theory finds its roots in the classic writings of Karl Marx (1848/1964) who viewed the development of an industrialized and capitalist society in terms of the struggles for economic resources. Marx saw capitalist society as divided among three classes:

- the bourgeoisie or the owners of the modes of production;
- the proletariat or laborers who provide the means of production; and
- the impoverished and socially marginal lumpenproletariat.

> Conflict Theory asserts that the powerful in society are able to assert coercive force against the poor and powerless through the illegality of specific drugs and the disproportionate application of these laws

Marx argued that the bourgeoisie, as owners of the modes of production, exploit the proletariat class and exert economic, political, and social domination in order to serve their own interests. Marx further contended that the proletariats allow this control and domination due to a false consciousness or an absence of collective recognition of their exploited plight. Marx attributed much of this false consciousness to alienation or an estrangement from society culminating from the powerlessness they felt over their work, earnings, and lives in general. In his writings with Friedrich Engels, Marx called for the inevitable development of a class consciousness and revolution in which the proletariats overthrow the powerful bourgeoisie to form a classless or communist society where resources are distributed equitably.

Marx wrote primarily as a political economist and activist and he addressed deviance only sporadically in his writings. Marx placed drug addicts and career criminals in the lumpenproletariat class and considered them the parasites of society, nonproductive and living off the work of others. While he expressed distaste for the most deviant, Marx saw deviance by the working proletariat as an outgrowth of the structure of an inequitable capitalist society. In this vein, Marx viewed deviance as a proletariat response to deplorable working and living conditions and law as a mechanism to maintain order and to protect and further the economic interests of the bourgeoisie.

More recently, Elliott Currie (1993) studied drug use from a conflict perspective. His work suggested that rates of drug use, specifically dependence on crack cocaine and heroin, may be higher in central urban areas due to lack of meaningful economic opportunities, and the resulting feelings of powerlessness. Prior to the 1980s, it was possible for most individuals to gain the skills and training required to sustain a household above the poverty line. Increasingly however, the gap between the rich and the poor is widening, leaving large numbers of individuals without access to employment sufficient to sustain a family. For some, the potential income opportunity from drug dealing seems like the only way out of poverty; for others, it is a quick way to attain the American Dream. Currie (1993) argued further that the war on drugs exacerbates these structural problems, leaving inner cities plagued with drug dependency. In many instances, these neighborhoods lack the political clout to lobby for resources for their communities that would decrease drug addiction, crime, and social disorganization. As such, individuals are left feeling demoralized and powerless to change the declining state of their community and they lack the resources to drive out the flourishing, and frequently violent, drug economy.

This theory provides a good explanation for hardcore drug use and dependency in the inner cities as well as a theoretical basis for explaining the discriminatory application of drug laws in the United States. Conflict theory has greater difficulty explaining middle- and upper-class drug use by individuals who are not structurally disadvantaged. Conflict theorists take the position that middle- and upper-class individuals use drugs experimentally, as part of social situations, or for the purposes of pleasure and most do not become dependent. Conflict theorists suggest that those most likely to become dependent are from structurally disadvantaged communities where issues of abuse have a greater negative impact on the community as a whole, rather than just on the individual.

Conflict theorists suggest radical changes to current drug policies. In order for drug policy to be effective in reducing abuse, widespread economic restructuring would be necessary to provide equal structural access to members of currently disadvantaged communities. This would mean that all citizens would have access to appropriate educational facilities, health care programs, meaningful economic programs, and the like. Needless to say, suggestions by conflict theorists are not widely supported by politicians who prefer more simplistic solutions to the problem of drug abuse. It is important to keep in mind that no theoretical explanation can provide an all-encompassing picture of why all types of people engage in drug use or abuse. Different theoretical approaches are used to explain different aspects of the issue, and no one theory perfectly explains all aspects of drug use. In addition, each theoretical approach necessarily has varied policy implications, or solutions for solving the overconsumption of drugs in society.

Summary

- Biological theories of addiction look specifically at the physiological influences that contribute to an individual's progression from drug use to drug addiction. Biological theories can be separated into genetic predisposition theories and metabolic and neurochemical theories.
- Genetic predisposition theories suggest that the biological makeup of an individual, specifically the genetic structure, contributes to his or her susceptibility to addiction. Metabolic and neurochemical theories assert that the use of a particular drug for some people causes changes that lead to an almost visceral, chronic, and residual need for the drug.
- Psychological theories of addiction explain addiction primarily in terms of individual characteristics or experiences. Psychological theories can be separated into personality traits theories and reinforcement theories.
- Psychological trait theories assume an individual's personality structure predisposes them to drug dependency. Psychoanalytic theories look toward traumatic experiences such as physical and sexual abuse, neglect, and even mild family dysfunction as leading to attempts to medicate the resulting emotional problems.
- Reinforcement theories are concerned with the transition from drug use to drug addiction

and are interested in explaining long-term addiction to street drugs.

- Sociological theories assert that social and cultural factors influence our attitudes toward drugs, what is considered an illicit drug, what types of drugs are used by various groups of people, how we view drug users, as well as the significance of drug use as a problem in American society.
- Micro-sociological theories focus on social interaction patterns in specific situations such as social reaction theory, social learning theory, and social control theory. Macro-sociological theories focus on structural issues that shape the whole of society such as strain theory, cultural deviance theory, and conflict theory.
- Social reaction theory asserts that some behaviors, and therefore the individuals that engage in such behaviors, are labeled negatively by society in general, and often by the criminal justice system. Labeling results in an individual being stigmatized by conventional society, which results in a negative reaction, which frequently fuels the individual's return to the behavior in question.
- Social learning theorists believe that behavior is learned from those closest to us; we learn attitudes that are favorable or unfavorable to drugs and how to experience drug use from those in our close circle of friends. Rewards and punishments also play an important role in social learning theory. Whether specific behaviors are rewarded or punished in the group of people we are close with influences the type of behavior we continue in the future.
- Social control theorists focus on why some people obey society's rules and others do not. They believe that self-control and a commitment to conformity deter deviant behavior. In other words, people's behavior is controlled by their attachment and association to conventional society. Applied to drug use, social control theorists would suggest that the vast majority of individuals would use drugs if it was not against the law or in violation of social norms.
- Strain theory uses the concept of anomie to explain how the structural conditions precipitated by a capitalistic society, such as the United States, promote deviant behavior as a viable alternative to conventional behavior. Anomie results from a disjuncture between culturally emphasized goals and the prescribed legitimate means to attain these goals.
- Cultural deviance theory suggests that deviance is due to a combination of environmental social disorganization and personal strain. Neighborhoods characterized by social disorganization, such as high rates of residential turnover and weak community ties, are more prone to developing delinquency or a subculture of individuals who engage in delinquency. This subculture develops in response to the poor neighborhood conditions, which triggers feelings of hopelessness and strain in members of the community.
- Conflict theory suggests that rates of drug use may be higher in central urban areas due to lack of meaningful economic opportunities, and the resulting feelings of powerlessness. In many instances, these neighborhoods lack the political clout to lobby for resources for their communities that would decrease drug addiction, crime, and social disorganization. As such, individuals are left feeling demoralized and powerless to change the declining state of their community and lack the resources to drive out the flourishing, and frequently violent, drug economy.

Important Terms

Addictive personality
Anomie
Biological theory
Conflict theory
Conformity
Cultural deviance theory
Genetic predisposition theory
Innovation
Instrumental drug use

Labeling
Macro-sociological theory
Metabolic theory
Micro-sociological theory
Negative reinforcement
Neurochemical theory
Positive reinforcement
Psychoanalytical approach
Psychological theory
Rebellion
Recreational drug use
Reinforcement theory
Retreatism
Ritualism
Social control theory
Social learning theory
Social reaction theory
Sociological theory
Strain theory

Critical Thinking Questions

1. Ask a fellow college student who uses drugs to elaborate his or her reasons for doing so. Ask an individual over the age of fifty who used drugs in his or her youth the reasons for doing so. Choose a theory that you think best elaborates their explanations. Defend your choices.
2. Which theory or theories align best with your own personal views in explaining drug use and addiction? Explain your answer.

Research Topics

1. If you were summoned to explain drug use to Congress and suggest potential policy solutions, what theoretical perspective would you use as the basis of your explanation and what policy recommendations would you provide? Write a position paper with relevant arguments supported by five academic sources.
2. Advocates of a harm reduction approach or one that advocates treatment and rehabilitation would most likely support which theory? Defend your position in a short paper.

Suggested Readings/Films

Boyle, Danny (Director). (1996). *Trainspotting* [Film]. Available from Miramax Home Entertainment.

Currie, Elliott. (1993). *Reckoning: Drugs, the cities, and the American future.* New York, NY: Farrar, Straus, and Giroux.

Preble, Edward, & Casey, John J. (1969). Taking care of business: The heroin user's life on the street. *The International Journal of Addictions, 4,* 1–24.

4

Researching Drug Use

"When I talk to people about statistics, I find that they usually are quite willing to criticize dubious statistics—as long as the numbers come from people with whom they disagree"

—(Best, 2004, p. xi–xiii.)

OBJECTIVES:

When you have finished this chapter, you should be able to:

- Understand the method by which drug use statistics are reported
- Recognize the three critical questions to ask when confronted with statistical data
- Evaluate the strengths and weaknesses of the surveys conducted to determine drug use trends
- Understand the extent of drug use
- Understand how drug use varies by age, gender, race/ethnicity, and geographical location
- Understand the dynamic elements of drug use through qualitative research

REAL LIFE

I wish to convey some idea of how my research subjects think about crime and offending. It was very difficult to decide what to relate that might be useful or lead people to think about things from a different perspective. The first problem that occurred to me when I started to consider the topic was that there is no single "criminal perspective" on crime. Since my particular areas of interest have been drug distribution and use, I count among my acquaintances—and sometimes my friends—hundreds of drug dealers and users. The opinions and attitudes of drug dealers and users vary as much as anyone else's, although there are some broad trends . . . I will share several lessons I have learned from the street level. Don't make assumptions about what people believe. I have learned—and continue to relearn with disturbing frequency—that it is not wise to make assumptions about people and then act on those assumptions. For example, I used to think that because police and drug dealers are adversaries they naturally dislike each other. Certainly, I have heard drug dealers rail about how aggressive policing has affected their business and how particular police officers seem to single them out for harsh (and, in their eyes, unjustified) treatment. I have also heard police officers complain about the "scourge" of drug dealing and talk about dealers and users as though they are subhuman. My conversation with the owner of a midsized crack business in Brooklyn illustrates another aspect of this issue. I had been eager to meet this individual, but I knew he was anxious about being "set up" by the police. I thought I might ease his fears about me by commiserating with him—by telling him about my own problems with a pair of officers in his precinct who had a history of abusive behavior. As I described my difficulties with these two officers, trying hard to establish my pedigree—my legitimacy—a funny grin came over his face. I finally stopped and asked what he found so amusing. He told me that one of the officers I had mentioned was a member of the paint ball team that he leads. I scratched my head and asked, "Now, let me get this right, Monday through Friday you shoot bullets at each other, but on Saturday and Sunday you shoot paint balls?!" "That's right," he said. He didn't seem to have any problem with the concept, but it took me a little while to digest what he had said and understand its implications. A general lesson was learned here: Don't make assumptions about what people believe. Assumptions can get you into trouble... The more I thought about what he told me, the more it made sense—sort of. In some ways, law enforcement officers and drug dealers are two sides of the same coin, and it should not be so surprising that they know each other so intimately. In many ways, selling drugs—or pursuing those who do—represents the major employment opportunity for youths from these neighborhoods. I know many dealers who have aspired to be law enforcement officers and many police officers who have "checkered" backgrounds (Curtis, 1999, p. 15–16).

As we continue in the United States to engage in a war on drugs, it is important to evaluate exactly what we know statistically about drug users and trends of drug use. Are we experiencing an epidemic of drug use? Are there significantly more drug users and are they getting younger and younger? The media would have citizens believe that the drug problem is out of control. Is this the truth? An examination of the studies conducted regarding drug use will give us a more accurate picture of who is using drugs, what types of drugs are being used, and the consequences of drug use in American society. While at some level drug use is a difficult social issue to measure because it is illegal, viewing these studies in combination will give us a fairly good idea of the dynamics of drug use. There are three basic ways that drug use statistics are reported:

- **Incidence** refers to the frequency of drug use.
- **Prevalence** refers to the number of individuals who engage in drug use.
- **Rates** illustrate the number of individuals using drugs per a specified unit of the population (for example per 1,000 people).

While reporting the number of individuals participating in drug use is a more dramatic method of illustration, reporting the rate takes into account increases or decreases in the population, thereby providing a more realistic picture of drug use. The goal of research on drug use should be to accurately portray patterns of use. There are several elements of research that may influence how large or small the drug issue may seem. For example, we may get a different picture of drug-use trends if we study those who are incarcerated, rather than members of the general public. We may get a different picture of drug-use trends if we study only metropolitan areas... how much will this tell us about drug use in rural locations throughout the United States? What if we only examine emergency room visits? Would this give an accurate portrait of drug use nationwide? What if we only survey a small number of people . . . can we then make statements about the larger American population? Methodologically there are many issues to consider when evaluating studies that examine drug use; however, an elaborate discussion of these concerns is beyond the scope of this book. Suffice it to say that it is important to study "everyday people" if we want to get an idea of how "everyday people" use drugs. An examination of drug use by those in emergency rooms or those arrested add another element to the story; however, these situations do not really represent the involvement of "everyday people" with drug use. Are we experiencing an epidemic of drug use never before seen in the United States as we are led to believe by many media images?

In 2001, Joel Best wrote an illuminating book entitled *Damned Lies and Statistics: Untangling Numbers From the Media, Politicians, and Activists.* In this book, he notes that much of the general public simply accept at face value the statistics presented to them in the media, because we are somehow led to believe that statistics are objective facts (Best, 2001). We see statistical graphs about the drug epidemic presented in news articles, we hear politicians drop figures about the number of young people on drugs, and we accept this as truth, believing that numbers are not to be questioned. Joel Best stresses that statistics are "products of our social arrangements" and are brought to our attention for particular purposes. He outlines the importance of asking ourselves three critical questions when viewing or hearing a statistic about a social issue: *Who* created the social statistics and how might their personal beliefs or professional affiliations influence the statistics? *Why* was the statistic created, or what is the purpose for which the statistic will be used? *How* was the statistic created, or what was the methodological design of the project? Together, answers to these three questions provide a solid foundation on which to evaluate the truthfulness (and usefulness) of statistics (Best, 2001). This is not to say that statistics cannot be used to prove anything and should not be trusted, it is merely a note that consumers of research must be diligent in evaluating statistics on social issues before accepting and passing these numbers on to others as hard-and-fast truth. "People create statistics: they choose what to count, how to go about counting, which of the resulting numbers they share with others, and which words they use to describe and interpret those figures. Numbers do not exist independent of people; understanding numbers requires knowing who counted what, why they bothered counting, and how they went about it" (Best, 2004, p. xi–xiii). Each type of study on illicit drug use has both advantages and disadvantages, and each gives a slightly different picture of the issue. Each source of information will be examined individually. Remember while reading to ask yourself: Who, how, and why? Referring to these questions will reveal a more accurate picture of drug-use trends.

GETTING THE NUMBERS FROM THE GENERAL PUBLIC

Drug Abuse Warning Network (DAWN)

The **Drug Abuse Warning Network (DAWN)** gathers data regarding substance use and data from medical examiners and coroners regarding drug-related deaths from hospital emergency room visits. This program began collecting data in 1972 and is sponsored by the Substance Abuse and Mental Health Services Administration (SAMHSA). The data collected by this program is not available through other sources, and it includes individuals who are not brought to the attention of law enforcement. For the collection of data, DAWN uses a representative sample of approximately 470 emergency rooms across the United States in addition to a random sample of 21 metropolitan hospitals. Patient charts for visits involving drug use are analyzed by medically trained personnel.

It is important to note that DAWN keeps track of the number of drug-related "incidents" that occur in participating emergency rooms, which does not necessarily correspond to the number of individuals using drugs. Not all drug users will utilize emergency rooms, and some drug users will visit an emergency room on more than one occasion. It is frequently assumed then, that while the sample in these studies can be generalized to emergency room visits nationally, DAWN findings more accurately present a portrayal of hard drug users as opposed to recreational users (Drug Abuse Warning Network [DAWN], 2002). DAWN researchers collect information about the type of drug(s) used as well as demographic information about the patient and the reasons surrounding the emergency room visit. Figure 4-1 illustrates that in 2004, cocaine was the drug responsible for most emergency room visits.

The reasons surrounding emergency room visits are varied as demonstrated by the graph in Figure 4-2. It is noteworthy, however, that 35 percent of the patients listed a reason for their emergency room visit that was not the subject of examination by researchers, or the patient failed to provide any explanation for their visit to the hospital.

A case is considered "drug abuse" if:

The case involves one of the following:

- illegal drug use;
- legal drug use without adhering to the directions; or
- inhalation of a nonpharmaceutical substance

and

the rationale for substance use was:

- dependence on drugs;
- attempt to commit suicide;
- recreational use; or
- achievement of psychic effects (DAWN, 2002).

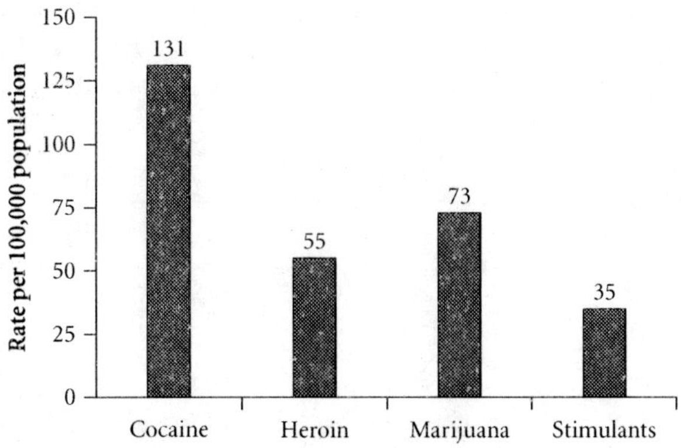

FIGURE 4-1 Illicit Drugs Involved in Emergency Room Visits, 2004.

Source: Drug Abuse Warning Network, 2006.

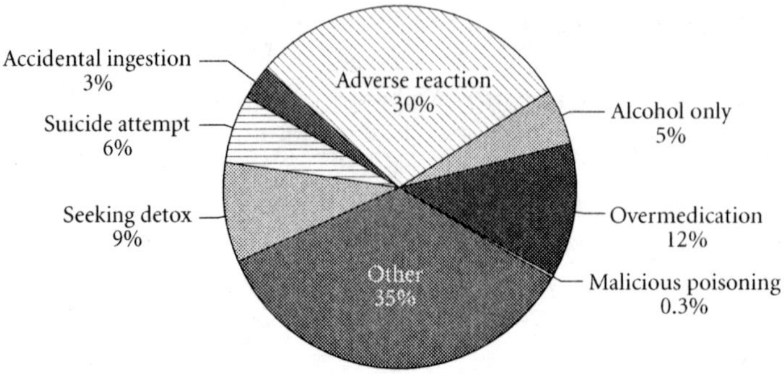

FIGURE 4-2 Drug-Related Emergency Room Visits by Type of Case, 2004.
Source: Drug Abuse Warning Network, 2006.

In addition to emergency room visits, DAWN collects data from medical examiners and coroners in approximately 140 jurisdictions, representing 43 metropolitan areas in the United States. The data is collected through the examination of medical examiner or coroner reports that elaborate on deaths that were a result of drug use. Data collected from medical examiners or coroners are not based on representative samples, and therefore do not provide a picture of drug-related deaths that can be generalized nationally or even generalized to the specific metropolitan areas in which the samples are collected (DAWN, 2002). Table 4-1 uses state-level data to determine the number of deaths due to misuse of drugs or drug-related suicides per 1,000,000 in the population in the six states in which DAWN collects data.

DAWN collects data annually that gives us the ability to track health trends related to drug use over time, which is a major advantage of this research. Additionally, the data collected by this initiative is not available elsewhere, which makes it a unique contribution to our understanding of drug use. In interpreting the findings of DAWN, however, be aware that the data represents immediate drug-related health problems and cannot provide estimates of the prevalence of drug use in the United States, or the effects of chronic drug use on an individual. As well, the individual drug user who utilizes emergency room facilities is certainly not representative of the typical drug user. In addition, overconsumption of alcohol may result in violent incidents or alcohol-induced accidents which are not reported in DAWN statistics. In this research, alcohol use is reported only when in conjunction with other drugs. The sole use of alcohol that may result in assaults, domestic problems, or vehicular manslaughter, for example, is not included in this survey. This effectively minimizes our understanding of the relationship between alcohol use and physical harm (DAWN, 2002).

TABLE 4-1 Drug-Related Deaths per 1,000,000 Population, 2003

State	Drug Misuse Deaths	Drug-Related Suicide Deaths
Maine	88.1	17.6
Maryland	126.5	3.8
New Hampshire	87.8	20.2
New Mexico	161.6	19.2
Utah	138.6	19.1
Vermont	119.5	22.6

Source: Drug Abuse Warning Network, 2005.

Monitoring the Future (MTF)

Every year since 1975, the **Monitoring the Future** (**MTF**) survey has been conducted nationally on a sample of high school students. In the 2005 survey discussed here, approximately 49,300 students in 8th, 10th, and 12th grades participated. The survey is administered by researchers at the Institute on Survey Research at the University of Michigan. Normally, students respond to the paper survey during a class session, after proper parental approval has been obtained. Students are requested to self-report their use of drugs at four different time periods: across their lifetime; in the past year; in the past month; and daily use. In addition, students provide their views on the availability of drugs, risks involved with drug use, and their general approval or disapproval of substance use.

Figure 4-3 gives an overview of the percentage of 8th, 10th, and 12th graders who have used any illicit substances over their lifetime. This data is presented over time to provide an overview of drug use among students across a 30 year period beginning in 1975. The most recent MTF survey included the following noteworthy findings:

- In the year preceding the survey, the use of any illicit substance had decreased approximately 33 percent for 8th graders, almost 25 percent for 10th graders, and 10 percent for 12th graders.
- As of 2005, the lifetime reporting rates for use of illicit substances were 21 percent for 8th graders, 38 percent for 10th graders, and 50 percent for 12th graders.
- The use of illicit substances peaked for high school students in 1996 and 1997 and has been declining since.
- Use of cocaine, crack, heroin, and crystal methamphetamine remained steady in 2005.
- The survey reports a very modest increase among 12th graders of the use of sedatives, OxyContin, and inhalants in the preceding 12 months (Johnston, O'Malley, Bachman, & Schulenberg, 2006).

Monitoring the Future (MTF) is of limited use not only because it excludes those students not present on the day the survey is conducted, but more importantly because it excludes the high

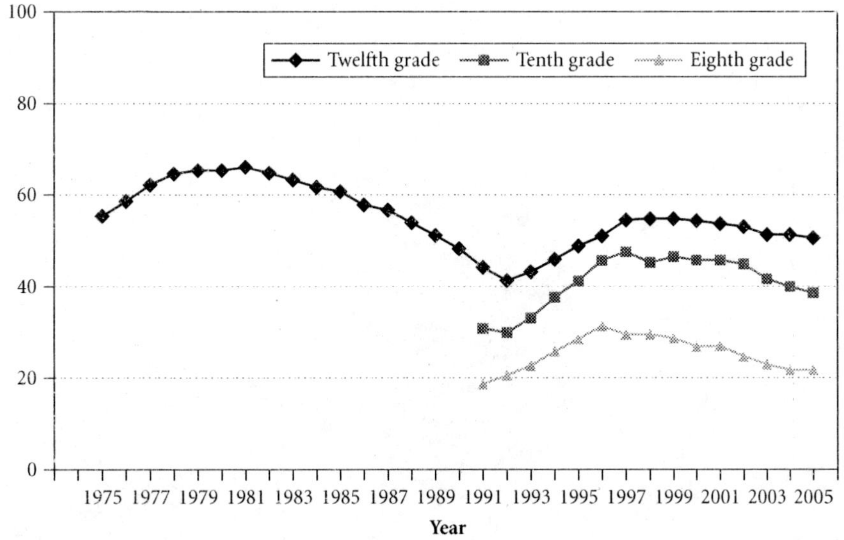

FIGURE 4-3 Percentage of 8th, 10th, and 12th Graders Who Have Used Any Illicit Drug Across Their Lifetime

Source: Johnston, O'Malley, Bachman, & Schulenberg, 2006.

school dropout population. Because researchers hypothesize drug use to be higher among dropouts and students with sporadic attendance, MTF is often viewed as an underestimation of drug use. Conversely, however, MTF includes a very large and fairly representative sample of high school students in the United States, and is conducted yearly, thereby giving a very good picture of substance use among students.

National Survey on Drug Use and Health (NSDUH)

The **National Survey on Drug Use and Health (NSDUH)** was formerly the National Household Survey on Drug Abuse (NHSDA). This project has collected data since 1971, with the project conducted annually beginning in 1992. The NSDUH attempts to be inclusive of all age groups; studies a general population; and includes household residents, noninstitutional living facility residents, and civilians residing on military bases. Groups excluded from this survey include military personnel and institutionalized populations, such as those in hospitals and prisons. The NSDUH involves face-to-face interviews with approximately 70,000 individuals ages 12 and older across the United States. Participants are asked to self-report their involvement with illicit drugs. The survey includes questions regarding the frequency of drug use, how recently participants have used illicit substances, attitudes toward drug use, as well as demographic information. Information is obtained in this study for illicit use of nine categories of drugs: marijuana, cocaine, heroin, hallucinogens, inhalants, nonmedical use of pain relievers, tranquilizers, stimulants, and sedatives.

Major findings include:

- Approximately 19.7 million Americans self-reported illicit drug use in the month prior to the survey, representing 8.1 percent of the population ages 12 and older.
- The rate of illicit drug use in the month prior was 7.9 percent in 2004, 8.2 percent in 2003, and 8.3 percent in 2002, indicating very little fluctuation in the overall rates of drug use.
- In 2005, marijuana was used by 74.2 percent of those self-reporting illicit drug use.
- Among those reporting illicit drug use in the month prior, 54.5 percent used marijuana only, 19.6 percent used marijuana in combination with another illicit substance, and 25.8 percent used an illicit substance other than marijuana (see Figure 4-4).
- Marijuana, with 14.6 million users in the month prior, was the most commonly used illicit substance (Substance Abuse and Mental Health Services Administration [SAMHSA], 2006).

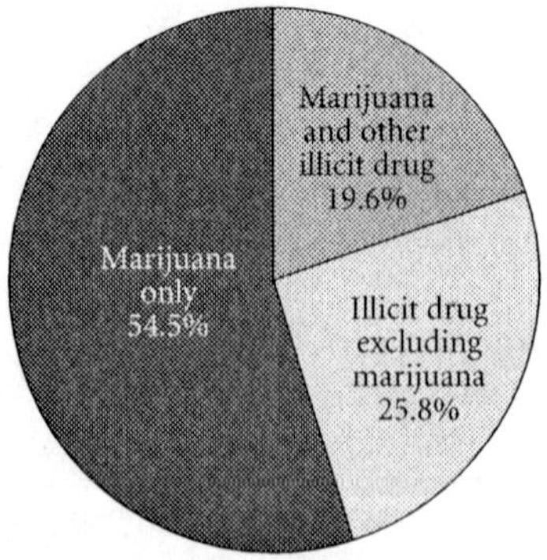

FIGURE 4-4 Types of Illicit Drugs Used in the Past Month by Users Aged 12 or Older, 2005

Source: Substance Abuse and Mental Health Services Administration (SAMHSA), 2006.

The NSDUH is clearly the most powerful measurement currently available to examine the prevalence of drug use. While it does not include individuals who are institutionalized or homeless, it otherwise provides an excellent representative and generalizable examination of drug use in the United States. When examining these studies, do keep in mind that there are methodological problems or flaws with every study that has been conducted on drug use. These flaws should be considered when evaluating the accuracy of findings; however, methodological imperfection is an inevitable part of social science and should not be used as an excuse to dismiss relevant research.

GETTING THE NUMBERS FROM THOSE ARRESTED

Arrestee Drug Abuse Monitoring (ADAM)

The **Arrestee Drug Abuse Monitoring Program (ADAM)** is a project that randomly selects recently arrested individuals and conducts interviews and urinalysis within 48 hours of booking to assess their involvement with drugs. Interviews are conducted four times a year over a period of 1 to 3 weeks at thirty-nine different sites across the United States. The selection sites are primarily metropolitan areas; however, a handful of less populated areas are included as well. Interviews are confidential and delve into the types of drugs used by the arrestees, the frequency of drug use, as well as the specifics of where and how drugs were acquired. The interviews deal specifically with five types of illicit substances: cocaine (crack and powder), marijuana, opiates, methamphetamine, and PCP. Male subjects are chosen randomly; however, females are chosen on an availability basis due to the significantly lower number of female arrestees. Because women are chosen based on availability, this raises questions about whether the study findings can be generalized for the larger population of women who are arrested.

Across all sites collecting data, the major findings include:

- Use of at least one of the five illegal drugs ranged from 52 percent to 80 percent
- Use of marijuana ranged from 29 percent to 57 percent
- Use of cocaine, either crack or powder, ranged from 11 percent to 49 percent (Arrestee Drug Abuse Monitoring Program [ADAM], 2003)

As illustrated in Table 4-2, gender differences on all drugs except marijuana are minimal. The ADAM report is useful for explicating the relationship between drugs and crime which will be elaborated in Chapter Nine, but note here that median drug use among those arrested is very high.

TABLE 4-2 Median Percentage Drug Test Results by Gender, 2000

Type of Drug Used	Male	Female
Cocaine, opiates, marijuana, methamphetamine, or PCP	64.2	62.5
Marijuana	40.9	26.7
Cocaine	30.9	33.1
Opiates	6.5	7.2
Methamphetamine	1.6	3.0
PCP	0.3	0.0

Source: Arrestee Drug Abuse Monitoring, 2003.

Because ADAM collects data quarterly, drug use can be tracked over time, which is certainly an advantage of this study. Another major advantage of this survey approach is that participant honesty is encouraged by the inclusion of urinalysis. Conversely, however, the only participants in this study are arrestees which may not be representative of the larger group of drug users in the United States that do not come to the attention of law enforcement. In addition, though ADAM uses cities geographically spread throughout the country, the primary focus of the study initially was in metropolitan areas, with smaller cities being added only in the later years of this program. This raises questions about the generalizability of the study. Can statements be made about drug-use trends of the American public in general when we have studied only those arrested in primarily urban locations? Due to funding issues, the ADAM program ended in 2004, though it was reinstated in 2008.

WHAT DO THE NUMBERS TELL US?

Extent of Drug Use

As discussed earlier, findings about the extent and demographics of drug use will vary by the type of research study conducted and the methodology used in the research. This section elaborates the general trends in nationwide drug use through a discussion of a combination of different studies. It will become clear from analyzing the information provided that drug use affects individuals of all incomes, races, classes, genders, ages, and lifestyle groups, though trends change as these demographics vary. Detailed information about specific drugs is provided in later chapters, though some specific use trends by drug are overviewed here to give a brief analysis of the larger issue. As Figure 4-5 demonstrates, approximately 2.9 million individuals used illicit substances for the first time in 2005, with pain relievers and marijuana being the primary drugs of choice.

Studies reveal that the rate of illicit drug use has stayed fairly stable over the past several years. Current users are identified as those admitting to drug use in the past 30 days. In 2005, approximately 8 percent of the population, or 19.7 million people, were considered current users. Of these individuals, 74 percent were using marijuana. Nine million people were current users of

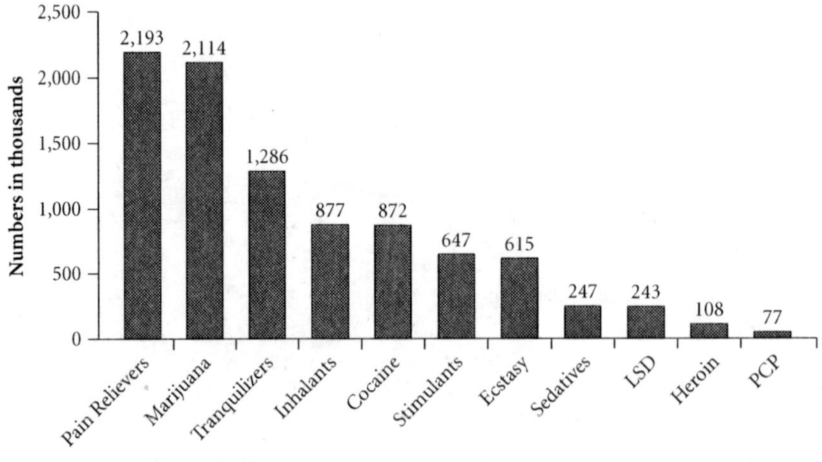

FIGURE 4-5 Number of New Illicit Drug Users in the Past Year, Aged 12 and Older, 2005

Source: Substance Abuse and Mental Health Services Administration (SAMHSA), 2006.

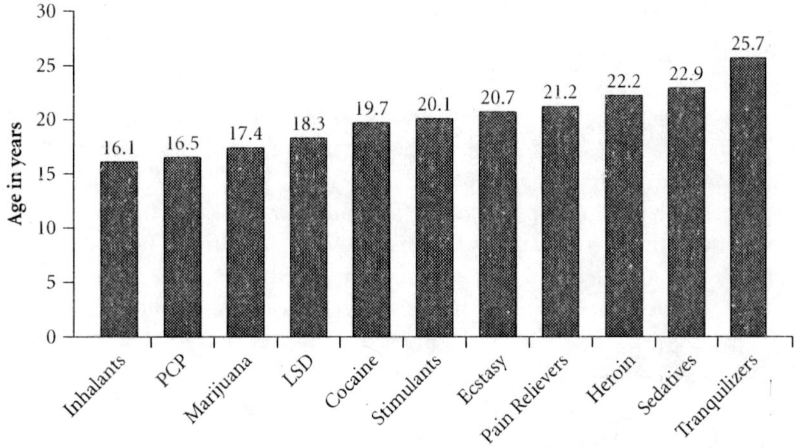

FIGURE 4-6 Mean Age for First Use of Illicit Drugs by Past Year Initiates Ages 12-49, 2005

Source: Substance Abuse and Mental Health Services Administration (SAMHSA), 2006.

other illicit drugs, with the largest percentage using drugs such as pain relievers, tranquilizers, stimulants, and sedatives for nonmedical purposes. Most new users of illicit substances were under the age of 18 and the majority were female. The average age of first-time marijuana use was 17.4, and for pain relievers the average age of onset was 21.2 (see Figure 4-6).

First-time use trends for marijuana have remained relatively stable over the past three years. In 2005, 2.1 million individuals aged 12 and older used marijuana for the first time (see Figure 4-7) with most of these individuals under the age of 18. Indeed, the Monitoring the Future report found that in 2005, 41 percent of those in 8th grade, 73 percent of those in 10th grade, and 86 percent of those in 12th grade had "easy access" to marijuana (Johnston, O'Malley, Bachman, & Schulenberg, 2006).

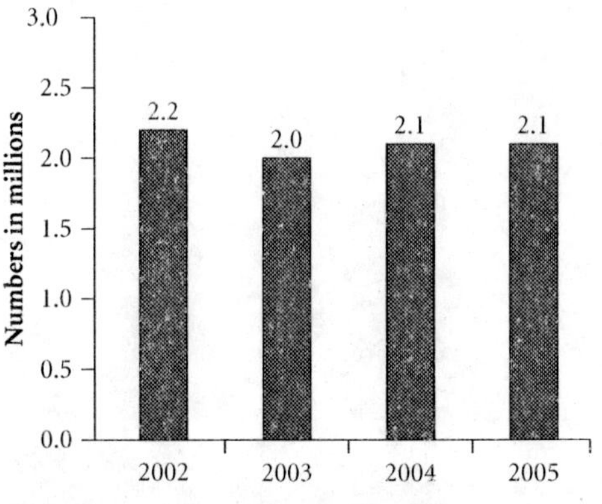

FIGURE 4-7 Past Year Marijuana Initiates Aged 12 and Older, 2002–2005

Source: Substance Abuse and Mental Health Services Administration (SAMHSA), 2006.

This usage trend by age exists for many other illicit substances as well:

- The use of cocaine has remained stable since 2002 with 2.4 million current users. In 2005, there were 872,000 new users, with the average age of first use being 19.7 years. The number of crack users in 2005 was 682,000 which was a slight, but insignificant, increase from 2004.
- For heroin there were approximately 136,000 users and 108,000 individuals admitted to using heroin for the first time in 2005.
- With regard to hallucinogens, including LSD and ecstasy, 1.1 million people admitted use in the month prior to the survey, consistent with data from 2003 and 2004. Similarly, 953,000 people admitted to use of hallucinogens for the first time in the past year.
- Inhalants were the substance with the lowest average initiation age of 16.1 years. In 2005, there were 877,000 new inhalant users with 72 percent of those under the age of 18.
- From 2002 to 2005, rates of methamphetamine use over the lifetime (range of 4.3 percent to 5.3 percent) and past year (range of 0.5 percent to 0.7 percent) decreased. Since 2002, the number of monthly users has remained stable; however, the number of individuals dependent on methamphetamine increased significantly from 164,000 in 2002 to 257,000 in 2005 (SAMHSA, 2006).

Conflicting News Headlines:

The Meth Menace: Easy & Addictive Drug Is Creeping Up Social Ladder (Fenner & Moore, 2006)

Teen Drug Use Declines 23 Percent in Five Years: Marijuana, Meth Use Drop Sharply (PR Newswire, 2006)

Profiles of Drug Users

Rates of drug use vary by age, gender, race/ethnicity, and geographical location. Each of these demographics will be elaborated to provide a profile of the "typical" drug user.

AGE Among youths ages 12 to 17, the rate of illicit drug use increases with age. At ages 12 or 13, the rate of illicit drug use in the past month was approximately 3.8 percent; at ages 14 or 15, the rate rose to 8.9 percent; at ages 16 or 17, the rate rose further to approximately 17 percent (see Figure 4-8). The highest rate of illicit drug use was approximately 22 percent among those

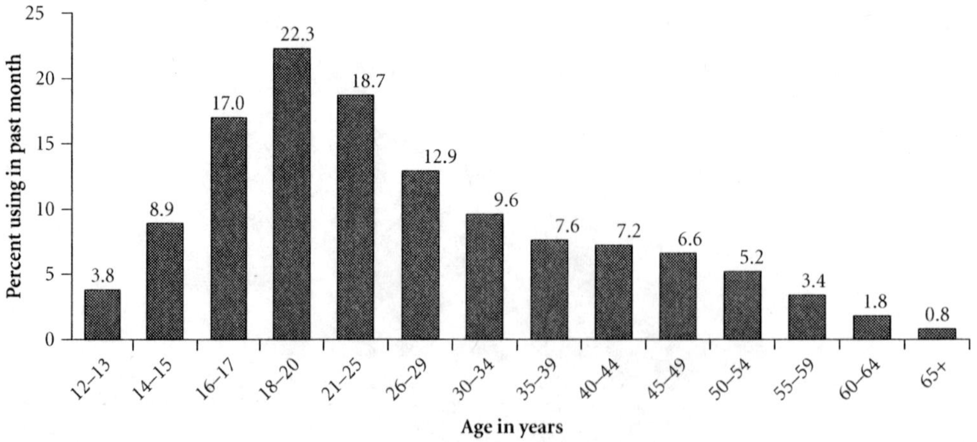

FIGURE 4-8 Past Month Illicit Drug Use Among People Aged 12 or Older, by Age, 2005

Source: Substance Abuse and Mental Health Services Administration (SAMHSA), 2006.

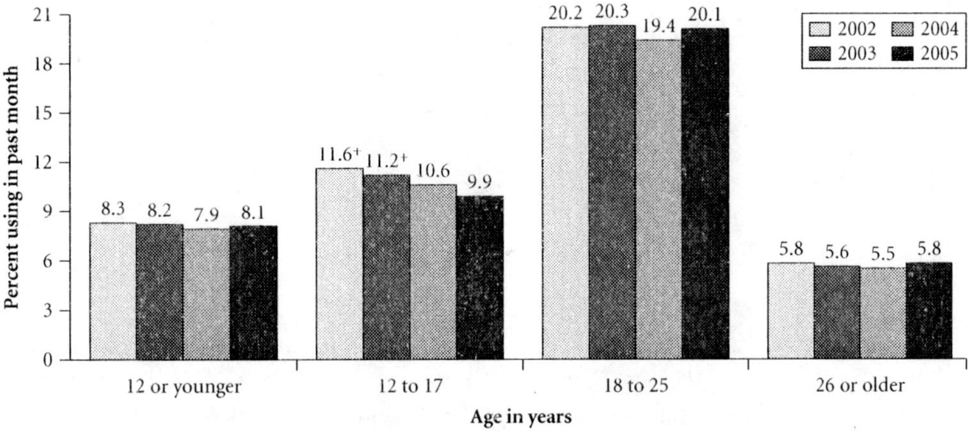

FIGURE 4-9 Past Month Illicit Drug Use Among People Aged 12 or Older, by Age, 2002–2005
Source: Substance Abuse and Mental Health Services Administration (SAMHSA), 2006.

aged 18 to 20. The rate then declined slightly to 18.7 percent among those aged 21 to 25, and declined further with increasing age. These trends persisted across time as illustrated in Figure 4-9.

A person's age also influenced their choice of illegal substance. Figure 4-10 illustrates trend data for choice of illicit substance in the past month among those aged 12 to 17. In 2005, 9.9 percent of youths aged 12 to 17 were current illicit drug users. Overwhelmingly, the choice of drug among this age group was marijuana which was used by 6.8 percent of youths in 2005, followed by 3.3 percent involved in the nonmedical use of prescription drugs. The rate of illicit drug use among this age group was significantly lower in 2005 than in 2002, thus demonstrating an overall downward trend in current drug-use rates among those aged 12 to 17.

The rate of current use of illicit drugs was the highest among young adults aged 18 to 25, and this trend repeats itself over time. In 2005, the rate of current use was 20.1 percent, with 16.6 percent involved in marijuana use, followed by 6.3 percent involved in the nonmedical use of prescription drugs. These trends are represented in Figure 4-11. Rates of use among this age group have remained fairly stable over time except for a significant increase in the use of cocaine from

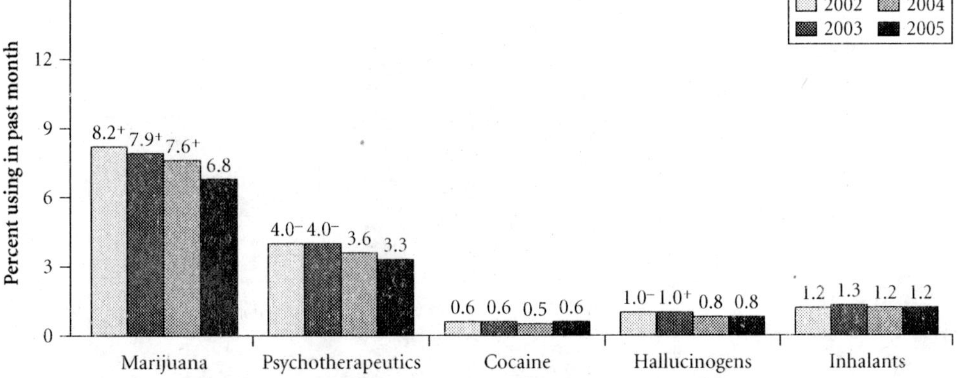

FIGURE 4-10 Past Month Selected Illicit Drug Use Among People Aged 12 to 17, 2002–2005
Source: Substance Abuse and Mental Health Services Administration (SAMHSA), 2006.

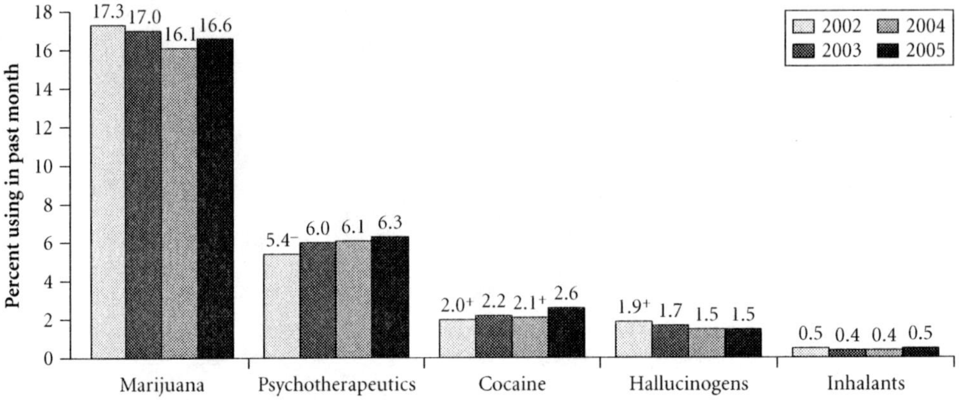

FIGURE 4-11 Past Month Selected Illicit Drug Use Among People Aged 18 to 25, 2002–2005

Source: Substance Abuse and Mental Health Services Administration (SAMHSA), 2006.

2004 to 2005. This age range represents the college-aged population (typically ages 18 to 22); however, studies indicate that the use of drugs among college students is no higher than the use of drugs among those in the same age group who are not attending college. The only exception to this trend is an increase in the use of methamphetamines among full-time college students between 2004 and 2005. This phenomenon was not found among those of the same age range who were not attending college.

Once individuals reach the age of 26 and beyond, drug-use rates once again decline. In 2005, the current illicit drug-use rate among those aged 26 or older was 5.8 percent, with 4.1 percent involved in marijuana use, and 1.9 percent involved in the nonmedical use of prescription drugs. Less than 1 percent of individuals in this age group are involved in the use of cocaine, hallucinogens, or inhalants. These trends have remained fairly stable over the years. The exception to this trend was the rate of current illicit drug use over time by those aged 50 to 59 as represented in Figure 4-12. Those aged 55 to 59 have experienced a significant increase in

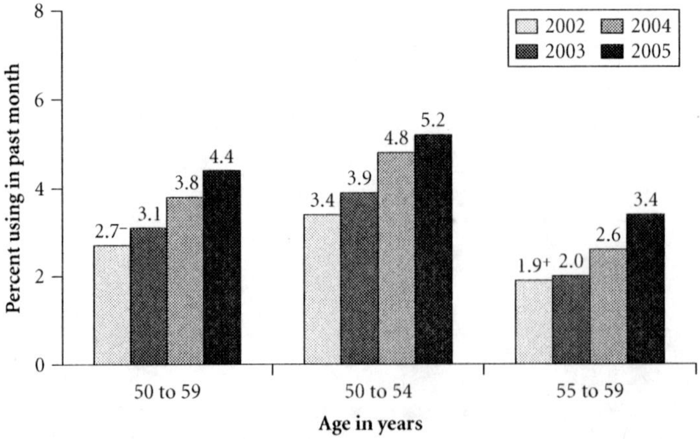

FIGURE 4-12 Past Month Illicit Drug Use Among People Aged 50 to 59, 2002–2005

Source: Substance Abuse and Mental Health Services Administration (SAMHSA), 2006.

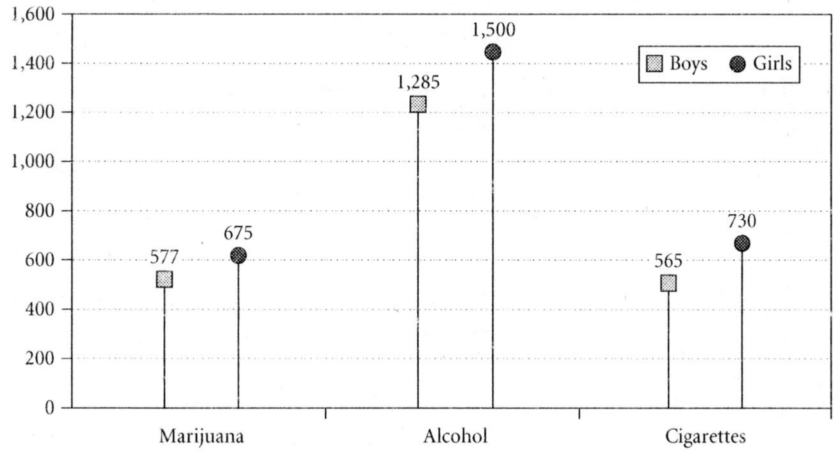

FIGURE 4-13 Number of New Users, Ages 12-17 by Gender, 2004

Source: Substance Abuse and Mental Health Services Administration (SAMHSA), 2005.

drug-use rates, likely explained by a cohort effect. The individuals in this age group were part of the baby boom era, which has consistently experienced a higher rate of lifetime drug use than other cohorts (SAMHSA, 2006).

GENDER In 2005, males (10.2 percent) continued to be more likely to report current illicit drug use than females (6.1 percent), with males almost twice as likely to be involved in marijuana use. Rates of drug use between the genders equalize for the nonmedical use of prescription drugs (SAMHSA, 2006). With regard to new users of illicit substances, however, recent research indicates that girls are gaining ground on boys (see Figure 4-13). Findings demonstrate that new users of marijuana, alcohol, and cigarettes are more likely to be girls than boys (Office of National Drug Control Policy [ONDCP], 2006). By way of example, over the past several years:

- In 2002, 895,000 teenage girls started using marijuana.
- In 2003, 657,000 teenage girls started using marijuana.
- In 2004, 675,000 teenage girls started using marijuana.
- In 2004, 1,500,000 teenage girls started using alcohol.
- In 2004, 730,000 teenage girls started smoking cigarettes (ONDCP, 2006).

Studies of young female drug users reveal that there are different motivating factors for drug use, including excessive concerns regarding physical appearance and weight issues, low self-esteem, physical and/or sexual abuse, the early onset of puberty, peer pressure, anxiety, stress, and perhaps most commonly, depression. Young females may use substances in an attempt to increase self-esteem, reduce tensions, or deal with social problems or anxieties.

RACE/ETHNICITY Trends also remained stable in 2005 regarding race/ethnicity and current illicit drug use. Asians continued to have the lowest rate of drug use (3.1 percent), followed by 7.6 percent of Hispanics, 8.1 percent of Caucasians, 8.7 percent of Native Hawaiians or Other Pacific Islanders, 9.7 percent of African Americans, and 12.8 percent of American Indians or Alaskan Natives. Among those aged 12 to 17 reporting current illicit drug use, 3.3 percent were Asian, 9.4 percent were Hispanic, 10.1 percent were Caucasian, 11.0 percent were African American, and 19.2 percent were American Indians or Alaskan Natives (SAMHSA, 2006).

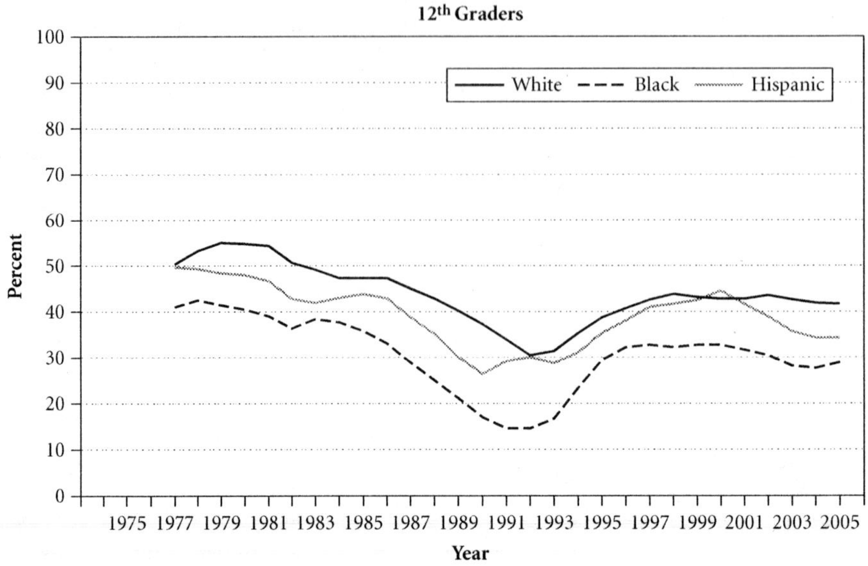

FIGURE 4-14 Trends in Annual Prevalence of Illicit Drug Use by Race/Ethnicity of 12th Graders, 1977–2006

Source: Johnston, O'Malley, Bachman, & Schulenberg, 2006.

The Monitoring the Future project, a study of 8th, 10th, and 12th graders, examined differences between the three largest racial/ethnic groups: whites, African Americans, and Hispanics. Findings of this study were contrary to the study discussed above and instead found that at all three grade levels, African Americans had a substantially lower rate of drug use than whites. As presented in Figure 4-14, Hispanics had rates of drug use that fell between whites and African Americans, usually closer to the rates of whites. By 12th grade, Hispanics had the highest rate of use for crack, heroin, ice (crystallized and smoked methamphetamine), and rohypnol, with rates of methamphetamine and steroid use roughly the same as that of whites (Johnston, O'Malley, Bachman, & Schulenberg, 2006). As discussed earlier in this chapter, statistical discrepancies between these two studies are due to methodological differences. The types of questions and the population under study have an influence on findings. As a critical consumer of research, these differences should be considered in your analysis of the "typical" drug user.

GEOGRAPHICAL VARIATION Drug use trends also vary by where a person lives in the United States. For those aged 12 and older, current illicit drug use in 2005 was 9.0 percent in the West, 8.9 percent in the Northeast, 7.5 percent in the South, and 7.5 percent in the Midwest (SAMHSA, 2006). These findings were reinforced by those of the Monitoring the Future Project (Johnston, O'Malley, Bachman, & Schulenberg, 2006). Regardless of region of the country, some studies have indicated that drug-use rates were higher in metropolitan areas than in nonmetropolitan areas, as evidenced in Table 4-3 (SAMHSA, 2006). This finding, however, is not consistent from study to study, with findings from the Monitoring the Future Project demonstrating greater decline of drug use in urban areas, thereby leaving nonurban areas with higher rates of use among youth (Johnston, O'Malley, Bachman, & Schulenberg, 2006).

TABLE 4-3 Current Drug-Use Rate by Location Type, Aged 12 and Older, 2005

Type of Location	Rate of Current Drug Use in Percentage
Large metropolitan county	8.4
Small metropolitan county	8.4
Nonmetropolitan county	6.9
Nonmetropolitan, urbanized county	7.8
Nonmetropolitan, less urbanized county	6.5
Nonmetropolitan, very rural	5.1

Source: Substance Abuse and Mental Health Services Administration (SAMHSA), 2006.

In addition to regional differences, generally those aged 12 to 17 experienced specific differences with regard to marijuana use over time. In the Northeast, Midwest, and South, youth involvement in use of marijuana in the past month decreased between 2002 and 2005. In the West, marijuana use rates among this age group increased from 2002 through 2004, before experiencing a decline in 2005 as presented in Figure 4-15 (SAMHSA, 2006).

With regard to other illicit substances, the epidemic of cocaine use in the early 1980s was much more pronounced in the West and Northeast regions of the United States. The South and West have typically experienced lower rates of alcohol use among youth, with rates of cigarette smoking lowest in the West. Finally, while ecstasy use in the late 1990s was primarily a Northeastern phenomenon, by 2000 the popularity of the drug had spread to the remaining regions of the country (Johnston, O'Malley, Bachman, & Schulenberg, 2006).

What does drug use look like outside of the United States? Let's look at the case of marijuana use. There are an estimated 162 million people who have used marijuana during their lifetime. Of these individuals, 10 percent progress to daily use for at least a portion of their lives, and 20 to 30 percent use on a weekly basis. Rates of marijuana use in the United States are very similar to countries such as New Zealand, Australia, England, and Wales. In Canada, use rates are

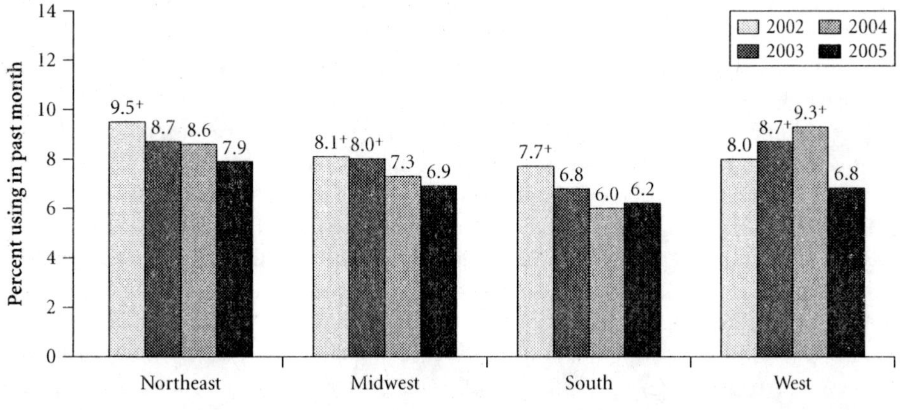

FIGURE 4-15 Past Month Marijuana Use Among People Aged 12–17 by Geographic Region, 2002–2005

Source: Substance Abuse and Mental Health Services Administration (SAMHSA), 2006.

TABLE 4-4 Annual Percentage of the Population Aged 15–64 Using Cannabis in the Past Year Selected by Country

Country	% of the Population Using Cannabis
Canada, 2004	16.8
New Zealand, 2001	13.4
Australia, 2002	13.3
United States, 2004	12.6
England and Wales, 2004	10.8
France, 2002	9.8
Switzerland, 2003	9.6
Netherlands, 2001	6.1
Mexico, 2002	1.3

Source: United Nations Office on Drugs and Crime, 2006.

slightly higher, and rates are slightly lower in countries such as France, Switzerland, and the Netherlands (as demonstrated in Table 4-4). Compiling data from a wide range of sources and countries suggests that about 14 percent of those admitting to marijuana use in the past 12 months are daily users, suggesting that approximately 22.5 million people worldwide use marijuana daily (United Nations Office on Drugs and Crime [UNODC], 2006).

LOOKING DEEPER: QUALITATIVE RESEARCH

Rather than asking people in a survey or in a relatively brief interview their involvement with drugs, **qualitative participant observation research** takes a much deeper look into the world of drug use. This type of research involves participation with a group of individuals and a description of the world as seen through the eyes of the participants. Researchers gain access to a population they are interested in studying and spend a considerable amount of time with these individuals, observing and usually to some extent participating in their activities. Rather than providing a picture of the prevalence of drug use, qualitative research provides in-depth exploration of why people use drugs, how they get involved with drug use, why they stay involved with drug use, and how drug use impacts their social world. Snapshots of drugs users were illustrated in many classic qualitative projects in the 1950s and 1960s such as Howard Becker's (1953) *Becoming a Marihuana User* and a project that changed existing views of drug use entitled *Add Center Project Final Report: The World of Youthful Drug Use* (Blumer, Sutter, Ahmed, & Smith, 1967).

One of the purposes of qualitative research is to reach the hidden populations that are not included in traditional methods of research. As discussed earlier, with various types of surveys it is important to keep in mind many methodological considerations: What, if anything, can a specific study tell us about the larger population? In the case of qualitative research, the goal is to provide an in-depth portrait of a group of individuals. This portrait, however, cannot be generalized to other people in the population . . . it cannot even be generalized to other users of that particular drug. Qualitative research is excellent for explaining, in greater depth, the issue under study; however, keep in mind that qualitative research cannot provide a generalizable understanding of drug use in America. Using key informants and word of mouth, qualitative researchers gain access to individuals who would not likely be included (or agree to participate) in surveys on drug use.

For example, a qualitative study of female drug users in Atlanta provides information that may not appear in survey responses. The purpose of this study, named **Project FAST**, was to identify the impacts of drug use on women and to explore how social surroundings influence habits of use. Almost all of the women in the study revealed an ongoing tension between their drug use and their role as a mother . . . a tension they do not believe exists for men who are not primary caregivers. Women also spoke of their susceptibility to abuse, much of which stems from engaging in prostitution or sex-for-drug exchanges to support their drug use. In addition, women are found to play a subordinate role in the drug world, and are cautious of revealing the truth of their drug habits due to the fear of repercussions, such as the custodial loss of children or retaliation from dominant men (Sterk-Elifson, 2005). This detailed, contextualized information would have been difficult, if not impossible, to obtain from traditional survey methodologies.

Summary

- There are three basic ways that drug-use statistics are reported. "Incidence" refers to the frequency of drug use. "Prevalence" refers to the number of individuals who engage in drug use. "Rates" illustrate the number of individuals using drugs per a specified unit of the population.
- Critical questions to ask when viewing or hearing a statistic about a social issue are: *Who* created the social statistic and how might their personal beliefs or professional affiliation influence the statistic? *Why* was the statistic created, or what is the purpose for which the statistic will be used? *How* was the statistic created, or what was the methodological design of the project?
- The Drug Abuse Warning Network (DAWN) gathers data regarding substance use and data from medical examiners and coroners regarding drug-related deaths from hospital emergency room visits and is sponsored by the Substance Abuse and Mental Health Services Administration (SAMHSA). Findings indicate that in 2004, cocaine was the drug responsible for the most emergency room visits.
- The Monitoring the Future (MTF) survey gathers data nationally from a sample of high school students and is administered by researchers at the Institute on Survey Research at the University of Michigan. Students self-report their involvement with drugs and provide their views on the availability of drugs, risks involved with drug use, and their general approval or disapproval of substance use. As of 2005, MTF reports that 21 percent of 8th graders, 38 percent of 10th graders, and 50 percent of 12th graders have used an illegal substance at some point in their lives.
- The National Survey on Drug Use and Health (NSDUH) studies a general population of all ages using face-to-face interviews regarding self-reports of drug use, including questions regarding frequency of use, how recently participants have used illicit substances, and attitudes toward drug use. Approximately 19.7 million Americans self-reported illicit drug use in the month prior to the survey, with 74 percent reporting the use of marijuana.
- The Arrestee Drug Abuse Monitoring Program (ADAM) conducts interviews and urinalysis on randomly selected recent arrestees at varied sites across the United States. Questions delve into the types of drugs used, the frequency of drug use, and the specifics of where and how drugs were acquired.

- Research reveals that approximately 2.9 million individuals used illicit substances for the first time in 2005, with pain relievers and marijuana being the primary drugs of choice.
- The rate of illicit drug use has stayed fairly stable over the past several years.
- Among youths aged 12 to 17, the rate of illicit drug use increases with age. The highest rate of drug use is among those aged 18 to 25, and drug use declines as individuals reach age 26 and beyond.
- Males continue to be more likely to report current illicit drug use than females, though recent research indicates that among new users of marijuana, alcohol, and cigarettes young females outnumber young males.
- Trends regarding race and ethnicity have remained fairly stable with regard to drug use, with some studies showing African Americans with lower levels of use than Caucasians.
- Drug use continues to be generally higher in the West and Northeast than the South and Midwest, though it varies by specific drug. Researchers dispute whether drug-use rates are higher in metropolitan or rural areas of the country.
- Globally, the United States has drug-use rates similar to New Zealand, Australia, England, and Wales, with higher rates found in Canada and lower rates in France, Switzerland, and the Netherlands.
- Qualitative participant observation research takes a deeper look into the world of drug use and involves participation in a group of individuals and a description of the world through their eyes. This type of research provides an in-depth exploration of why people use drugs, how they get involved with drug use, why they stay involved with drug use, and how drug use impacts their social world.

Important Terms

Arrestee Drug Abuse Monitoring Program (ADAM)
Drug Abuse Warning Network (DAWN)
Incidence
Monitoring the Future (MTF)
National Survey on Drug Use and Health (NSDUH)
Prevalence
Project FAST
Qualitative participant observation research
Rates

Critical Thinking Questions

1. Many of the statistics presented in this chapter are a result of government funded and/or collected data. Address the three questions Joel Best (2001) indicates should be explored when presented with statistics. How might critical consideration of these three questions influence our interpretation of government statistics about drug use? How do these statistics contribute to our understanding of drug use as a social problem?
2. Qualitative participant observation provides a much different view of drug use than quantitative surveys or interviews. Discuss how you think our views toward drugs and drug users may be different if we relied primarily on information provided by qualitative research.

Research Topics

1. Locate data regarding drug-use statistics for a specific drug from three different data sources discussed in this chapter. Compare the findings for various age groups and elaborate potential reasons for the discrepancies.
2. Find an article that deals with the qualitative examination of drug use. After reading the article, find a quantitative study that deals with use of the same drug. Elaborate the differences between the two studies and discuss whether or not there are findings in the qualitative article that would be difficult to obtain from conducting a survey.

Suggested Readings

Becker, Howard S. (1953). Becoming a marihuana user. *American Journal of Sociology, 59,* 235–242.

Best, Joel. (2001). *Damned lies and statistics: Untangling numbers from the media, politicians, and activists.* Berkeley, CA: University of California Press.

Blumer, H., Sutter, A., Ahmed, S., & Smith, R. (1967). *Add center project final report: The world of youthful drug use.* Berkeley, CA: University of California Press.

Curtis, Richard. (1999). The ethnographic approach to studying drug crime. In *Looking at crime from the street level: Plenary papers of the 1999 conference on criminal justice research and evaluation—Enhancing policy and practice through research* (NCJ 178260). Washington, DC: U.S. Department of Justice.

PART

II

Classifying Drug Use

5

Legal Drugs

"A miracle drug is any drug that will do what the label says it will do"

—(Hodgins, 1981, p. 266).

OBJECTIVES:

When you have finished this chapter, you should be able to:

- Elaborate the role of the FDA in drug regulation
- Discuss basic pharmacology, use trends, benefits/consequences, and current issues with regard to caffeine
- Discuss basic pharmacology, use trends, benefits/consequences, and current issues with regard to tobacco
- Discuss basic pharmacology, use trends, benefits/consequences, and current issues with regard to alcohol
- Discuss basic pharmacology, use trends, benefits/consequences, and current issues with regard to inhalants
- Discuss basic pharmacology, use trends, benefits/consequences, and current issues with regard to herbal supplements
- Discuss use trends and benefits/consequences with regard to diet drugs

REAL LIFE

Lesly's journey to stop smoking:

> Three years ago I was a desperate woman. I was desperate to quit smoking—I was desperate to smoke. I was sick to death of smoking—I loved to smoke. I hated how I smelled—I loved the smell of my smokes. I hated the burn holes, fears, sickness—I loved the rituals. I hated being told I should quit—I *knew* I should quit. Most of all—I was sick and tired of being sick

and tired, and I hated feeling stupid. Bottom line. So—I jumped off the teeter-totter and jumped in . . . with both feet. I clung desperately to the lifelines thrown to me and I held on with all my might through the storms (heck, more like hurricanes) that followed. I held on with both hands and all my heart to one thing that a man who was one of my dearest friends told me. He told me this: "You *think* you love to smoke and you *think* it is so important to your happiness, but when you quit (and I know you will), you will find out that all that happiness associated with smoking is a lie. It's a cheap carnival trick. It is nothing more than smoke and mirrors." Guess what? He was right! There is not one thing in my life that I can't do better without a cigarette hanging out of my mouth . . . one of my greatest sorrows is that he died before I found the courage to quit smoking. Quitting is hard—it takes effort, determination and commitment, but it *can be done.* You need to be brutally honest with yourself, though, and you cannot quit by continuing to smoke. You have to stop! Not one—not one puff and no excuses. There is a sign in my gym that motivates me. I'll try to recreate it for you.

The Ten Steps to Success

Try

Try again

Try harder

Try tomorrow

Try thinking about what has worked in the past

Try and ask someone who has done it

Try and figure out what is not working

Try it a different way

Try it once more

Don't stop trying!

The longest journey has to start with one simple, tiny step. I took my first step three years ago today, and I have never regretted it" ("Lesly's Three Year Smoke Free Milestone," 2009).

ROLE OF THE FDA IN DRUG REGULATION

What does it mean to have the "FDA stamp of approval"? Recall that in the United States, the **Food and Drug Administration (FDA)** is solely responsible for approving what products can legally be prescribed or sold as medicine and for regulating their safety. The FDA may approve a drug and then recall it later thus labeling it legal and appropriate for medical use at one point in time and then illegal and not appropriate for medical use at a later time (which is what happened to the painkiller Vioxx in 2004 after studies revealed that it increased the risk of heart attack and stroke in those taking this medication). The motto of the FDA is "Protecting and Promoting *Your* Health" (emphasis in FDA motto), and the mission according to the Web site is:

> The FDA is responsible for protecting the public health by assuring the safety, efficacy, and security of human and veterinary drugs, biological products, medical devices, our nation's food supply, cosmetics, and products that emit radiation. The FDA is also responsible for advancing the public health by helping to speed innovations that

> make medicines and foods more effective, safer, and more affordable; and helping the public get the accurate, science-based information they need to use medicines and foods to improve their health (http://www.fda.gov/AboutFDA/CentersOffices/default.htm).

Every new drug must pass through a series of stages prior to approval. First, the drug manufacturer must demonstrate that the drug is therapeutically effective in animal tests and that it demonstrates the potential to be therapeutically effective in humans. Second, tests are conducted on humans to demonstrate the effectiveness and safety of the drug. The testing period of a drug (after its development) averages 15 months in the United States, 7.8 months for medications deemed "priority." Finally, a New Drug Application (NDA) (which averages 100,000 pages in length) including all prior documentation regarding testing and effectiveness, is submitted, and based on this information the FDA evaluates risks and benefits of approving the drug for market, or defers the decision until after additional testing is conducted. In 2002, seventy-eight new drugs were approved by the FDA, of which seventeen had never previously been marketed in the United States, and thirteen were authorized for sale over the counter without a prescription. Additionally, approvals were given for 321 generic versions of drugs previously marketed (www.fda.gov/).

Perhaps one conflict of interest is that the FDA is permitted to collect user fees from companies that seek approval of their drugs. An extensive amount of time and resources is put into the development of a drug, so by the time the FDA is considering its approval the pressure is really on from the standpoint of the manufacturer to "donate" as much as is necessary to "encourage" approval. By that point the drug company has invested up to 15 years of research time and up to $500 million (Liska, 2004). Even after the FDA approves a drug for market, unforeseen side effects can come to light, as in the case of Vioxx. Once they do, the FDA normally requests a voluntary recall by the manufacturer. If the company fails to comply, the FDA has the power to initiate legal action to compel a product recall. So while the FDA is trying to protect the public from dangerous drugs, there are some gaps in their mission: "A surprising number of older prescription medicines have been around for so long that they have never been vetted by the agency. Officials have promised for decades that they would catch up with these products. But dozens, perhaps hundreds, still remain" ("What's Behind an F.D.A. Stamp?" 2008). In addition:

> . . . just last year, the F.D.A. announced that it would force off the market many unapproved products containing hydrocodone, a popular and addictive narcotic often used as a cough suppressant. Many of these products had not been inspected or approved by the agency, and some had labels stating they could be used in children as young as 2, although such products had never been approved for use in preschool children. Even some products with F.D.A. approval have very little evidence that they work [because when they were] . . . approved . . . decades ago, its standards were far lower than they are today. Some of the medicines in these products have never proved effective in children, and children have, in rare cases, been harmed by them ("What's Behind an F.D.A. Stamp?" 2008).

Perhaps the most difficult situation facing the FDA recently is adverse reactions to approved drugs.

> The agency received nearly 500,000 such reports last year, but most were false alarms. Figuring out which signal real safety issues is difficult. In the past the agency typically said little or nothing about its suspicions of safety issues until top officials concluded

> that they were real. But several years ago, a midlevel drug safety officer concluded in a report that studies of antidepressants showed that the drugs caused an increase in suicidal behaviors or thoughts in children and teenagers. Top officials suppressed the report and refused to allow the official to testify before an expert committee. A year later, a more thorough study confirmed the risk. When news of the earlier report leaked, the agency was severely criticized. Top agency officials promised to be more open about potential drug risks. [Now] the F.D.A. . . . sen[ds] out public health advisories about potential drug problems and [has also] created a consumer information Web site . . . However, a drug's appearance on the list does not mean that the F.D.A. has concluded that the medicine is particularly risky. Rather, it shows that safety officials have some reason to suspect a problem ("What's Behind an F.D.A. Stamp?" 2008).

These advisories are likely to be even more confusing to the public as the FDA is essentially saying "this drug *may* be a problem, we're not entirely sure, we *may* be in the process of investigating." This is problematic.

The FDA is also responsible for monitoring the business known as **quackery**. This is a business worth more than $27 billion per year (Liska, 2004) and promotes useless remedies as "cures" for medical ailments. These products are touted on billboards, in magazines, and most commonly on paid-for-television advertisements, and the easy targets are seniors, though women are frequently targeted with weight-loss scams as well. The FDA lists the most commons forms of quackery or health care frauds as:

- Cancer fraud, which involves herbal cancer treatments with no proven benefits, such as Hoxsey Cancer Treatment and black salves;
- HIV/AIDS fraud, which promise quick fixes to the disease;
- Arthritis fraud, which involves about $2 million of the total spent in this area by consumers on treatments not proven to be effective;
- Bogus dietary supplements, such as vitamins, minerals, amino acids, herbs, and animal extracts, which make outrageous claims such as "eat all you want and lose weight";
- Weight-loss fraud, which is an area of increasing concern to the FDA as many products contain dangerous ingredients and make claims that are intentionally misleading;
- Sexual enhancement product fraud, which involves drugs that are not FDA approved for the treatment of erectile disorders and which claim to solve this medical problem;
- Diabetes fraud, which involves products claiming to significantly drop blood sugar in a short period of time or eliminate insulin resistance; however, these claims have not been proven; and
- Influenza (flu) scams, which involve the selling of counterfeit or contaminated flu shots (Food and Drug Administration [FDA], 2009).

According to the FDA Web site, to avoid health care scams there are several things that a consumer should be wary of, including:

- claims that a product is a quick, effective cure-all or a diagnostic tool for a wide variety of ailments
- suggestions that a product can treat or cure diseases
- promotions using words such as "scientific breakthrough," "miraculous cure," "secret ingredient," and "ancient remedy"

- text with impressive-sounding terms such as "hunger stimulation point" and "thermogenesis" for a weight-loss product
- undocumented case histories by consumers or doctors claiming amazing results
- limited availability and advance payment requirements
- promises of no-risk, money-back guarantees
- promises of an "easy" fix
- claims that the product is "natural" or "nontoxic" (which doesn't necessarily mean safe) (FDA, 2009).

Though the FDA has had difficulties and made mistakes, it is an organization that is essential. Without an organization to oversee the safety, efficacy, and security of drugs, consumers would be at the mercy of quacks.

CAFFEINE

Caffeine, in the form of tea and coffee, is the most widely used psychoactive drug in the world (Gahlinger, 2001). Caffeine is considered a recreational drug, meaning it is a substance taken for pleasure and consumed for nonmedical purposes. It is a central nervous system (CNS) stimulant that is presently so domesticated that many people own coffeemakers, teapots, and other devices used to extract caffeine from plant products, and enjoy caffeine-containing beverages and foods within their homes on a regular basis. Caffeine is found in coffee, tea, maté (a hot beverage that is popular in the South American, Arabic, and Portuguese cultures), kola nuts, and cocoa. It is also found in soft drinks, chocolate, over-the-counter (OTC) cough and cold medications, herbal remedies, stimulants (caffeine pills), and weight-loss pills. Caffeine is naturally present in over sixty trees and plants cultivated by humans. For example, guarana, an Amazonian vine, contains enough caffeine to stimulate the CNS at a similar intensity to that of cocaine (Liska, 2004).

Pharmacology and Effects

After oral consumption, caffeine is absorbed from the gastrointestinal tract, and it reaches the brain quickly as it has the ability to pass through the blood–brain barrier. Peak blood levels are reached approximately 30 minutes after consumption. The half-life of caffeine varies significantly, ranging from 2.5 to 7.5 hours. Caffeine is distributed equally in total body water, making the concentration of caffeine consistent throughout the body. Caffeine is metabolized by the liver, and is excreted mostly by the kidneys. Minimal levels of caffeine are also excreted in saliva, semen, breast milk, and feces (Maisto, Galizio, & Connors, 2008).

Caffeine blocks the brain's receptors for adenosine, which is a neurotransmitter that causes behavioral sedation and drowsiness by preventing the release of other neurotransmitters. Consumption of caffeine in small doses, such as two cups of coffee per day (approximately 150 milligrams of caffeine), has been shown to have mood-elevating effects. However, larger doses tend to have negative effects, causing restlessness, nervousness, excitement, insomnia/disturbed sleep, flushed face, muscle twitching, rapid heart beat, increased urination, cardiac irregularities, and gastrointestinal irritation. Caffeine may also initiate anxiety or panic attacks in those susceptible to such disorders (Maisto, Galizio, & Connors, 2008). Even in moderate doses, caffeine consumption can be hazardous to one's health. It can negatively affect heart rate, heart rhythm, blood vessel diameter, coronary circulation, blood pressure, and other bodily functions. As caffeine affects the region of the brain that regulates breathing, tremors or shakiness may also result. In extremely large doses, caffeine can be toxic and have potentially fatal results. Researchers' estimates of fatal doses vary: Some estimate between 3 and 8 grams of caffeine (the equivalent of thirty to eighty cups of coffee at one time) may prove fatal, whereas others estimate that a fatal dose consists of 10 grams (the equivalent of seventy to one hundred cups of coffee at one time) (McKim, 2007). Extremely high doses of caffeine result in convulsions and respiratory failure, which can cause death. These effects, however, are extremely rare.

Historical Trends of Consumption

Consumption of caffeine dates back to ancient times. Many stories have been created in various cultures to explain the origination of beverages made from plants containing caffeine. During the 3rd century BC, tea began to gain global popularity. Tea was first cultivated in China, and then traded with the English. The English distributed tea all over the world as the British Empire spread. The popularity of tea slowly grew and eventually became an essential aspect of global politics. Specifically, the American Revolution and wars in China started over issues surrounding the trade of tea (Gahlinger, 2001). Coffee beans were first cultivated in Ethiopia around AD 600. Coffee was initially consumed by chewing the beans, then later through the infusion (blending) of coffee leaves. It was not until the 14th century that coffee beans were roasted and ground to make a hot drink. Some Eastern societies initially deemed coffee to be the "brew of the devil." For example, coffee was thought to be contrary to the spirit of the Koran in 16th-century Egypt, and coffee consumption was therefore prohibited. Prohibitions were eventually repealed, and by 1551 coffee had become popular in Asia Minor, Syria, and Persia (Inciardi, 2002). It eventually became known as the "wine of Islam" and was traded in Europe, resulting in the creation and popularity of coffee houses. This popularity spread to America as Americans rebelled against the British tradition of drinking tea and high taxes on tea. Further, the powerful American influence on global trade helped promote the popularity of coffee in countries all over the world (Gahlinger, 2001).

Coffee and tea account for the majority of caffeine consumed, with an average American adult consuming approximately 200 to 300 milligrams of caffeine per day (approximately three to four cups of coffee) compared to the global average of 70 milligrams (Maisto, Galizio, & Connors, 2008). This is a widespread habit, with about 90 percent of the world's adult population consuming caffeine on a regular basis (Abadinsky, 2008). Coffeehouses have gained popularity among individuals of all backgrounds and cultures, and they have become places for socializing. This can be problematic as caffeine is highly addictive.

Benefits/Consequences

Caffeine dependence may result in individuals who consume as little as 100 milligrams per day (the equivalent of one cup of coffee). Psychological dependence on caffeine, known as **caffeinism**, is characteristic of heavy use and preoccupation with caffeinated products. Tea contains less caffeine than coffee, making those who consume tea less likely to develop caffeine dependence than those who drink coffee. Those with caffeinism commonly experience agitation, anxiety, and heart palpitations. Caffeine withdrawal may occur when caffeine intake is abruptly ceased among individuals who consume caffeine heavily on a regular basis. Withdrawal symptoms include restlessness, irritability, shakiness, headache, inability to work and concentrate effectively, and lethargy, with headache being the most common symptom. These withdrawal symptoms may last as long as 1 week (Ksir, Hart, & Ray, 2008).

Caffeine stimulates the cerebral cortex (the center for thought processes), resulting in more rapid and clearer thinking, greater sensitivity to stimuli, better physical coordination, increased motor activity, and the diminishment of drowsiness and fatigue. These effects are noticeable subsequent to the consumption of approximately 150 to 250 milligrams of caffeine, the equivalent of about two cups of coffee (Inciardi, 2002; Liska, 2004). Caffeine also stimulates the spinal cord and the area of the brain that controls breathing, resulting in increased respiration. Heart muscles are stimulated which increases the heart's efficiency in pumping blood; however, in some individuals the excitement of the heart muscles manifests itself in an irregular heartbeat (Liska, 2004).

Though there are few medical benefits of caffeine, it is a vasoconstrictor (meaning it constricts blood vessels), and some studies have demonstrated its effectiveness in the treatment of migraine headaches, whereas other studies have found caffeine to be a "trigger" in the onset of migraines. Also, studies have shown that caffeine may enhance the effects of OTC analgesic (pain-relieving) medications, such as aspirin and ibuprofen (Liska, 2004). Studies have shown that coffee may decrease the risk of diabetes. Tea, specifically green tea, is a good source of antioxidants, and it has been shown to reduce the risk of cancer, heart disease, and high cholesterol (Mosher & Akins, 2007).

Many individuals who consume moderate levels of caffeine do not experience significant health effects and quite the opposite, welcome the stimulation. However, individuals with health issues, including heart problems or ulcers, are at risk for increased morbidity when they choose to consume products that contain caffeine. (Liska, 2004). It is believed that those who consume more than 300 milligrams of caffeine per day may experience health problems, including increased risk for heart disease and pregnancy complications. Studies suggest that caffeine increases blood pressure and the risk for cardiac disease, and it has been shown to accelerate loss of bone density in postmenopausal women. Further, in individuals with caffeinism, caffeine has caused abnormal behavior, including sensory disturbances, mild delirium, and excitement (McKim, 2007). Research has shown mixed results regarding the effects of caffeine on pregnancy. Previously, it was commonly believed that caffeine bore no harmful prenatal consequences. However, more recent research has shown caffeine consumption may be correlated with increased risk for miscarriage, the retardation of fetal growth, and low birth weight (Liska, 2004; McKim, 2007). Newborns with mothers who consumed extremely large amounts of caffeine during pregnancy

No Time for Sleep: Caffeine Pills as a Quick Fix

Though caffeine in concentrated tablet form has been available for decades, it has become popular in the United States in recent years. Caffeine pills, such as NoDoz and Vivarin, contain between 100 and 350 milligrams of caffeine per tablet. In addition to taking caffeine pills as instructed, some individuals dissolve the tablets in liquid, such as coffee, and consume the resulting syrup. If ten or more tablets are consumed at once, the poisonous effects of extreme caffeine consumption, including convulsions, respiratory failure, and death, may occur. It has been found that the combination of caffeine with other stimulants can be extremely harmful. A popular caffeine supplement used to boost energy is Ripped Fuel, which contains caffeine-packed guarana (a plant), as well as ephedrine, another CNS stimulant. Ripped Fuel has been connected to the death of a 15-year-old female soccer player from California. The combination of guarana and ephedrine in particular has been associated with negative side effects, including chest pain and tightness, irregular heartbeat and heart attack, and tightness in the throat. (Liska, 2004).

may exhibit symptoms of caffeine withdrawal after birth, including vomiting, irritability, and jitters (McKim, 2007). The consequences of caffeine consumption in children are largely unknown. One study concluded that American children (ages 1 to 5) had the highest intake of caffeine per kilogram of body weight. Due to their body weight, one soft drink consumed by a child has the same effect that four cups of coffee have on an adult (Liska, 2004).

Americans consume more than 100 billion doses, or 5000 tons, of caffeine annually. Data from the National Institute of Mental Health reveal that 82 percent of Americans drink coffee and 52 percent drink tea. Of coffee drinkers, 45 percent consume three or more cups each day (Liska, 2004). This makes caffeine an extremely profitable industry—even larger than the tobacco industry (McKim, 2007)! Caffeine is an established, and legal, aspect of American culture, and indeed much of the globe. Further, it seems overall to be a relatively safe drug if consumed in moderation. Cases of extreme overuse and death are relatively rare. Caffeine is the only "cradle to grave" psychoactive substance, meaning that caffeine is the only psychoactive substance used nonmedically by individuals of all ages, in all stages of life.

NICOTINE/TOBACCO

Nicotine is a mood-altering drug. It is a volatile alkaloid found in tobacco leafs. Nicotine is known to occur naturally only in tobacco and is partly destroyed when cigarettes are burned. On average, there are 8 to 10 milligrams of nicotine in each cigarette, of which only 1 to 3 milligrams are inhaled by the user (approximately 1 milligram every ten puffs). A 40 to 60 milligram dose of nicotine is toxic, and a 60 milligram dose has been known to kill a human. Smoking tobacco, through cigars, cigarettes, or pipe tobacco, is the most common way in which nicotine is used, though users may also consume smokeless tobacco, popular primarily among adolescent males. Hookahs (water pipes) are also used to smoke (usually flavored) tobacco (shisha). Tobacco can also be consumed in the form of bidis, which are flavored cigarettes made in India that do not have filters. Bidis have more nicotine and tar than regular cigarettes, and are popular among American teens (Gahlinger, 2001; Liska, 2004).

Street Terms for Nicotine/Tobacco

- butts
- chew
- dip
- coffin nails
- cancer sticks

Pharmacology and Effects

Nicotine stimulates nicotinic receptors throughout the nervous system. Stimulation of these receptors in the peripheral nervous system causes the release of adrenaline (epinephrine) within the adrenal gland, resulting in increased heart rate and blood pressure. The release of adrenaline, however, does not have a significant effect on the CNS, as it cannot pass the blood–brain barrier. The nicotine in tobacco and other unidentified ingredients in tobacco smoke create higher dopamine levels (Liska, 2004). When tobacco is chewed, nicotine is absorbed into the membranes within the mouth. When nicotine consumed orally passes through the liver during digestion it is metabolized at a very fast rate, and therefore very little nicotine reaches the rest of the body (McKim, 2007). The absorption and distribution of nicotine through the body occur best when nicotine is inhaled into the lungs. When tobacco is smoked, high concentrations of nicotine are inhaled and absorbed within the lungs (though membranes in the mouth also absorb nicotine from tobacco smoke). Because of the high concentration of nicotine in the lungs, it has no chance to dissipate. Therefore, nicotine is absorbed within the lungs and carried to the heart, and then blood containing nicotine circulates through the blood and reaches the brain (McKim, 2007). Once inside the brain, nicotine remains there for approximately 30 minutes and then moves to the liver, kidneys, salivary glands, and stomach. It is metabolized by the liver and excreted by the kidneys. Moreover, according to McKim (2007), "nicotine crosses most barriers, including the placenta, and may be found in the sweat, saliva, and milk of nursing women" (pp. 200–201).

According to the Surgeon General of the United States, the biological and behavioral factors that contribute to nicotine addiction are similar to those that determine heroin and cocaine addiction (Grilly, 2006). Nicotine excites the brain and may cause tremors; increased respiration; increased blood pressure and heart rate; nausea and vomiting; increased peristalsis and activity of the intestines; diarrhea; reduction in urine flow; lower circulating plasma levels; and elevated concentration of free fatty acids in the blood. Tobacco smoke/nicotine may cause heart disease, lung disease, cancer, as well as problems during pregnancy (McKim, 2007). Nicotine dependency is predisposed by genetic factors and strongly associated with alcohol addiction. Further, those addicted to nicotine are more likely than nonusers to experience depressive or anxiety disorders. It was previously thought that depression preceded nicotine dependency; however, a recent study of adolescent smokers revealed that depressive symptoms developed after approximately 1 year of tobacco use (Grilly, 2006).

Historical Trends of Consumption

The origins of tobacco are American. Aboriginal North and South Americans used the drug heavily: Cave drawings from Mayan temples indicate Native American priests and shamans used large amounts of tobacco in rituals focused on curing illness and predicting the future. Columbus noted that the natives of San Salvador appreciated dried tobacco leaves and smoked cigars when he landed there in 1492. Rodrego de Jerez, one of the explorers, began smoking and was imprisoned during the Inquisition for his "devilish habit" (McKim, 2007). Jean Nicot, French Ambassador to Portugal, sent seeds to the French royal family, as he was convinced they were medically useful. Nicotine was eventually named after him. The English were the last of the Europeans to catch on to tobacco use, but they played a large role in enhancing its popularity. The English brought tobacco from the West Indies to Europe, and tobacco was later cultivated in the English colonies of America and distributed through trade. Tobacco use spread. It was first thought to be a "wonder cure," then it became popular for recreational purposes (McKim, 2007).

Global estimates reveal that approximately half of all men in the world (47 percent) smoke, compared to 12 percent of women. Each day, 15 billion cigarettes are consumed. Though tobacco use has been declining in industrialized countries, it has been increasing by 1.4 percent per year in developing countries. If these trends continue, roughly 85 percent of smokers will be from poor, developing countries by the mid-2020s (McKim, 2007). Many current smokers report they began smoking during adolescence. Studies have shown a number of indicators that predict adolescent smoking in the United States, including being a white male, having a positive attitude toward smoking, having low self-esteem and/or concerns regarding body weight, perceiving low internal control over life, experiencing high anxiety, having parents who smoke or parents who permit smoking, having the perception that smoking has positive benefits, having low expectations for school achievement, having easy access to tobacco, and having a number of friends who smoke (Grilly, 2006). In the United States, tobacco use peaked in the 1960s (at which point 40 percent of adults were smokers), and has been declining since as a result of educational campaigns and advertising restrictions. Now, nationally, about 25 percent of adults smoke. However each day, approximately 3,000 new individuals under the age of 18 begin smoking (Grilly, 2006). Smoking is also prevalent among individuals who abuse other drugs. For example, in one study, 90 percent of those being treated on an inpatient basis for alcoholism were smokers (Bien & Burge, 1990). Psychosocial rewards for smoking include peer acceptance and the feeling of identifying with a role model (Grilly, 2006). However, aside from these factors, researchers are unsure as to what reinforces tobacco use because one's initial experience with nicotine tends to be unpleasant. Approximately one-third to one-half of individuals who try cigarettes become habitual smokers (McKim, 2007).

As early as 1604, arguments over the medical usefulness and potential harmfulness of tobacco were made. This came as a result of the very high public demand for tobacco, which caused a great deal of concern within the English government. King James I wrote an essay entitled "A Counterblaste to Tobacco," which argued that tobacco filled the body with "soote," citing autopsies of smokers as proof (McKim, 2007). Over 200 research studies have shown strong evidence that nicotine is addictive. Many smokers exhibit compulsive use, and once an individual is dependent, attempts to cease use often fail. Relapse to tobacco addiction is common. Withdrawal may occur within a matter of hours following an individual's last cigarette. Withdrawal symptoms include tobacco cravings; irritability; headache; increased hunger; decreased heart rate; sleep problems; gastrointestinal disturbances; drowsiness; and impairment of concentration, psychomotor performance, and judgment. In an attempt to quit, individuals may try a variety of nicotine replacement therapies, such as nicotine gum, patches, nasal sprays, and inhalers, which nearly double the likelihood of quitting (Grilly, 2006). Some individuals experience negative side effects, including nasal, throat, and mouth irritation, with the inhalers and nasal sprays. No significant side effects have been found with the use of nicotine gums and patches. The patch has proven most successful as compliance is easier than with the gum, and it has fewer and less-serious side effects than the gum and the inhaler. In addition to nicotine replacement therapies, Zyban (originally Wellbutrin, an antidepressant), has been proven effective in aiding the cessation of tobacco dependency (McKim, 2007).

Benefits/Consequences

Talking to a smoker, one would expect to find many perceived benefits of smoking which produce a calming effect, including increased happiness and lowered levels of anxiety. While tobacco does have the ability to alleviate negative affective states (such as sadness, anger, anxiety, and boredom) that are caused either internally by depression or social withdrawal, or externally within the individual's environment, this is *only* when nicotine is used in a minimal amount (0.01mg/kg). Higher amounts (0.04 mg/kg), typical of most smokers, produce negative effects, and the consequences of tobacco use are high (McKim, 2007).

Smokers who average one pack per day pay approximately $1,000 per year for their habit. In addition to the cost of tobacco, users face potential health costs for treatment of emphysema, cardiovascular dysfunction, lung cancer, and other diseases caused by smoking. Though smokeless tobacco is less harmful than smoking tobacco, it too is dangerous and is associated with oral and pharyngeal cancers, dental and gum issues, and cardiovascular problems resulting from increased blood pressure and heart rate. Evidence shows that smoking on a daily basis prior to the age of 18 results in irreversible, lifelong damage to DNA and the lungs (McKim, 2007).

Tobacco use also results in adverse second-hand consequences. Tobacco use during pregnancy may result in a baby with low birth weight, increased risk of death during the first year of life, and low scores on standardized tests of physical function during childhood. Further, non-smokers who live in the same residence with smokers are at four times the risk of suffering a heart attack than those living in a smoke-free environment. Our furry companions, including cats and dogs, have also been known to suffer the negative effects of second-hand smoke (McKim, 2007). Unlike individuals using other types of drugs who "mature out" of use as they age or enter new life stages (e.g., marriage, parenthood), very few smokers mature out of tobacco use. Quitting occurs only with relentless determination, and frequently does not result in a loss of interest in smoking, making it all the more difficult for an individual to stay away from the habit.

Sociological and Legal Issues

The approximate annual cost of tobacco abuse to American society is $157 billion. In terms of treatment, healthcare, and lost worker productivity, this amount translates to $7 per pack of cigarettes sold (CDC, 2002). Nicotine is the most addictive substance Americans encounter. Approximately one-third of serious smokers become addicted as compared to 25 percent of heroin users, 15 percent of cocaine and alcohol users, 11 percent of amphetamine users, and 9 percent of marijuana users (Liska, 2004). Approximately 64 million Americans currently smoke. Of those between the ages of 12 and 17, roughly 4.5 million individuals smoke: These individuals are about twelve times more likely to use illicit drugs and twenty-three times more likely to heavily consume alcohol than nonsmoking individuals in the same age group. Among people in the 18 to 25 age group, the smoking rate is at 40 percent (Liska, 2004). Statistics reveal that lung cancer has surpassed heart disease as the leading cause of smoking-related deaths in the United States. At least one-third of cancer deaths in the United States are the result of smoking (which translates to 160,000 deaths per year or 440 deaths per day). Additionally, about 425,000 individuals in the United States die each year from nicotine- and tobacco-related diseases, including stroke, heart attack, and emphysema (Liska, 2004).

For various political and economic reasons, tobacco has never really been considered a drug, despite the fact that it contains an addictive active ingredient, namely nicotine. Because it is not considered a drug (or medicine) it is largely unregulated in the United States and in other industrialized countries. Tobacco is also not considered a consumer product, and therefore cannot be regulated by the U.S. Consumer Product Safety Commission. Beginning in 1994, the Food and Drug Administration (FDA) began requesting that cigarettes be regulated as drugs. The FDA's arguments before Congress, however, largely failed as the tobacco industry has a significant lobby group. In 1997, however, things changed somewhat and the FDA was given authority to decrease the access to and the appeal of tobacco products to minors. Further, sales of tobacco to individuals under age 18 were, at that time, made illegal on the federal level.

In March 2009, the U.S. Supreme Court left in place an award of $79.5 million to a smoker's widow. This ended a battle that had raged for 10 years over the large award. The Supreme Court's ruling let stand a ruling made by the Oregon Supreme Court against Philip Morris, USA, in favor of Mayola Williams. Ms. Williams, in 1999, was able to convince a jury that Philip Morris should be held liable for misleading the public into thinking cigarettes were not addictive or dangerous. The Supreme Court justices initially agreed to review judgment made by the Oregon court, then changed their minds, letting the Oregon court's ruling stand without further explanation ("Supreme Court Clears $79.5M Award for Smoker's Widow" 2009).

In June 2009, President Barack Obama signed the Family Smoking Prevention and Tobacco Control Act. Hailed as a bill to protect children from the dangers of cigarettes, the President said this of the bill:

> Today, thanks to the work of Democrats and Republicans, healthcare and consumer advocates, the decades-long effort to protect our children from the harmful effects of tobacco has emerged victorious. Today, change has come to Washington. This legislation will not ban all tobacco products, and it will allow adults to make their own choices. But it will also ban tobacco advertising within a thousand feet of schools and playgrounds. It will curb the ability of tobacco companies to market products to our children by using appealing flavors. It will force these companies to more clearly and publicly acknowledge the harmful and deadly effects of the products they sell (http://www.democracynow.org/2009/6/12/headlines#5).

This legislation, however, has been criticized by many public health officials, who argue that it was created with the interests of the tobacco companies in mind (and indeed it was drafted in part by one of America's leading cigarette companies, Philip Morris). Michael Siegel, public health professor at Boston University, suggested:

> This is a huge victory for big tobacco. This basically is going to institutionalize cigarettes forever. This is going to give the federal government's seal of approval to cigarettes. Basically, the FDA is being asked to look the other way. For every other product that the FDA regulates, if it finds that that product is killing people, it takes the product off the market immediately (http://www.democracynow.org/2009/6/12/headlines#5).

So tobacco remains a huge cash crop in the United States and one that is not subjected to a significant amount of government regulation, despite the overwhelming data that implicates it in serious and significant health issues. The same is true for alcohol.

ALCOHOL

Street Terms for Alcohol

- booze
- brews
- hard stuff
- hooch
- juice
- sauce

Alcohol is a potentially dangerous recreational drug whose use is widely accepted socially and culturally, and is even incorporated into some religious practices. Though it is regulated by the government, it is not a controlled substance; therefore, there are few restrictions governing its use and sale. There are three types of alcohol, including rubbing alcohol (isopropyl alcohol), wood alcohol (methyl alcohol), and alcoholic beverages (ethanol). Isopropyl and methyl alcohol are normally not purposely consumed, as they are highly toxic. There are three major types of alcoholic beverages: beer, wine, and hard liquor (distilled spirits). Beer and wine are fermented and can reach a maximum alcohol content of 15 percent. Hard liquor is distilled in a process to increase the alcohol content (Maisto, Galizio, & Connors, 2008).

Pharmacology and Effects

Alcohol is a CNS depressant which is absorbed in lipid membranes. It then disturbs the normal chemical actions within these membranes by entering their internal structures and altering their configuration (Maisto, Galizio, & Connors, 2008). This results in ineffective neural impulses.

Alcohol can be absorbed by the body prior to being digested. In humans, alcohol is rapidly and completely absorbed in the small intestine after it leaves the stomach. Following absorption, alcohol is carried by an individual's blood to all of the body's tissues. Blood alcohol concentration (BAC) is the amount of alcohol in an individual's blood. BAC is dependent on an individual's body weight; therefore, women tend to reach a higher BAC with less alcohol than their male counterparts who have higher body weight.

Historical Trends of Consumption

Alcohol use dates back thousands of years. Some authors state that the accidental creation of wine (fermentation of berries/fruit juice) dates back to the Stone Age. Researchers believe that the first beers originated in Egypt between 6000 BC and 5000 BC. Specifically, the ancient Egyptians created an acidy beer called "boozah." As well, distilled alcohol was created in China in 1000 BC, and distilled spirits eventually reached Western Europe around AD 800. Many early European societies referred to alcohol as the "water of life." However, historically it has been considered a double-edged sword, as many societal problems were attributed to the excessive consumption of alcoholic beverages (Maisto, Galizio, & Connors, 2008).

Alcohol became an important part of culture and life in colonial America, to the point of excessive consumption. Taverns became the center of society, as they were social and political places of business and pleasure. America became known as a "country of drunkards." By 1830, the average American adult consumed approximately five alcoholic beverages per day, making the per capita rate 7 gallons of pure alcohol per year (Maisto, Galizio, & Connors, 2008). In the mid 1800s several states (starting with Maine in 1851) outlawed alcohol, but its use remained widespread. The movement toward prohibition started to gain momentum in 1874 with the formation of the National Prohibition Party, and gained further popularity with the formation of the Anti-Saloon League in 1895 which supported only political candidates who advocated prohibition.

"The temperance ideology differed from the modern alcoholism movement in that it maintained that alcohol is inevitably dangerous for everyone. That is, some people might believe they can drink moderately, but it is only a matter of time before they encounter increasing problems and completely lose control of their drinking. As strange as it seems to us today, the temperance message thus was that alcohol is inevitably addicting, in the same way that we now think of narcotics" (Peele, 1995, p. 37).

> Around 1908, just as the Anti-Saloon League was preparing for a broad state-by-state drive toward national prohibition, a number of businessmen contributed the funds essential for an effective campaign. The series of quick successes that followed coincided with an equally impressive number of wealthy converts, so that as the movement entered its final stage after 1913, it employed not only ample financing but a sudden urban respectability as well. Substantial citizens now spoke about a new discipline with the disappearance of the saloon and the rampaging drunk. Significantly, prominent Southerners with one eye to the negro and another to the poorer whites were using exactly the same arguments (Wiebe, 1967, pp. 290–291).

These efforts were extremely successful: By 1913, 50 percent of U.S. citizens resided in "dry" states (Lyman & Potter, 2007). During the Temperance Movement, social problems were blamed on excessive alcohol consumption, leading to national Prohibition in 1920. Many big industry businessmen, including Henry Ford, Andrew Carnegie, and John D. Rockefeller, morally and financially supported the Temperance Movement, as they felt sober employees would be more productive employees. Prohibition resulted in law officials becoming corrupted and widespread disrespect for the law. Many violated Prohibition, and violent crime increased. Prohibition was repealed in 1933, and individual states were given significant power to regulate the sale and consumption of alcohol thereafter. Mississippi was the last state to repeal Prohibition in 1966 (Lyman & Potter, 2007).

In terms of medical and/or therapeutic uses, alcohol is used as an ingredient in some medical products, including cough syrups, dermatological products, and liniments. Ethanol sponges are used to alleviate fever because ethanol cools as it evaporates. Alcohol is also, at times, injected near nerves to relieve chronic pain. Alcohol, in small amounts, can also be found in mouthwash and shaving cream. Occasionally, alcohol before meals is recommended to the elderly and those recovering from an illness or disability to build appetite and stimulate digestion. However, alcohol consumption in the elderly places an increased burden on the liver. Alcohol is excreted from the blood at a slow rate, and the BAC levels in the elderly are 30 to 40 percent higher than in younger users drinking the same amount (Liska, 2004).

Socially and culturally, alcohol has always been an important part of social occasions, such as marriages, religious ceremonies, births, funerals, and the like. As with trends for other types of drug use, the rate of alcohol use rises and falls over time; however, in the United States the effects of alcohol are far worse than those of illegal drugs. Alcohol misuse results in approximately 200,000 deaths per year, whereas misuse of illegal drugs results in about 8,000 deaths per year (Liska, 2004). Additionally, approximately 36 million Americans are affected by familial alcoholism, and are subsequently vulnerable to the damaging psychosocial effects of alcohol, including divorce, violence, poverty, displaced children, and family violence (Liska, 2004).

Individuals who abuse alcohol may become physically dependent. Habitual alcohol users develop a tolerance, meaning they must consume increasingly greater amounts of alcohol to obtain the desired effects. Hangovers are common and are considered to be mild withdrawal symptoms, occurring between 4 and 12 hours following the highest level of BAC achieved. Hangovers are caused by the body's readjustment to a state of sobriety. Hangover symptoms include headache, dizziness, involuntary muscle twitching, nausea, vomiting, rapid heart rate, insomnia, anxiety, fatigue, and thirstiness. Such effects may result in lost productivity (such as missed work days) as well as unsafe driving. Additionally, alcohol can be acutely or chronically toxic, resulting in a host of health problems (Gahlinger, 2001). Treatment options for alcoholism include support groups, such as Alcoholics Anonymous (AA); prescription treatment with medications, such as Antabuse, which induce sickness if an individual consumes alcohol while taking this medication; behavioral therapy; and a community reinforcement approach, which promotes the learning of socially acceptable skills such as job training and bolsters social support networks. Additionally, addicts are taught relapse prevention that focuses on the realization of social cues to drink, and provides training in coping skills.

Benefits/Consequences

Studies have shown that long-term moderate drinkers are actually healthier than those who abstain entirely from alcohol consumption. It is thought that a moderate level of alcohol intake increases the body's production of high-density lipoproteins which remove cholesterol from artery walls. Some studies also show that moderate drinking is correlated with lower risk for cardiovascular and coronary diseases; however, more research is needed regarding the benefits of long-term moderate drinking (Gahlinger, 2001).

Conversely, there are many negative consequences of alcohol consumption. These negative impacts include increased urination, warming and reddening of the skin, increased appetite, nausea, vomiting, and short-term memory loss in the form of "grayouts" (partial loss of memory) or "blackouts" (complete loss of memory) with no loss of consciousness. At a BAC of 0.05 percent or more, alcohol has sensorimotor effects, including impaired vision, decreased pain sensitivity, decreased reaction time, inability to maintain a "steady state" (such as walking a straight line), and severely hindered coordination (such as necessary to drive a motor vehicle).

Long-term consequences of chronic, heavy alcohol use include weight gain; impaired brain functioning; heart disease; a weakened immune system; cancers of the mouth, throat and liver; and other problems of the liver, including fatty liver, alcohol hepatitis, or cirrhosis. In addition, alcohol can have severe negative impacts on pregnancy, and result in fetal alcohol syndrome, which can cause severe problems for a child. A safe level of alcohol consumption during pregnancy has not been established, and it is therefore generally recommended that pregnant women abstain from drinking entirely.

At extremely high doses, alcohol can cause unconsciousness, depressed circulatory and respiratory functions, as well as death. Research on alcohol poisoning showed individuals who consumed 500 milligrams of alcohol per 100 milligrams of blood died within a couple of hours. As well, studies have shown correlations between alcohol use and increased violence toward others and oneself. Other studies have shown that alcohol, in small doses, increases libido in men; however, in larger doses, alcohol decreases sexual arousal and performance in men (Maisto, Galizio, & Connors, 2008).

Sociological and Legal Issues

In the 1980s, Congress requested the Transportation Department hold back federal highway money from states that did not set the drinking age at 21, and by 1988, the uniform minimum legal drinking age across the United States became 21. Studies consistently indicate that over 60 percent of Americans drink alcohol. In the United States, 13 percent more men than women drink, and the presence of alcohol dependence is three times higher in men than women. The most significant social problems associated with alcohol are from its misuse. The federal government banned the sale of alcohol to Native Americans from 1802 through 1953, which resulted in pattern binge drinking and socially devastating effects that are not present in populations in which alcohol has always been legal and available. As such, the problems of alcohol abuse and dependence are magnified in the Native American population. Among the larger U.S. population, alcohol dependence is the third leading health problem, following only cancer and heart disease.

In 1970, Congress passed the Comprehensive Alcohol Abuse and Alcoholism Prevention, Treatment, and Rehabilitation Act, which recognized alcoholism as a disease and called for rehabilitative treatment. It also established the National Institute on Alcohol Abuse and Alcoholism (NIAAA). In terms of legalities, there is no consistent BAC level considered to be the legal level of intoxication across the United States. However, in the 1990s Congress required that all states lower the legal BAC level to 0.08, otherwise they would lose federal funds for highways. Many groups recommend that it be nationally set to 0.05. A wide variety of citizen groups, including Mothers Against Drunk Driving (MADD) and Students Against Drunk Driving (SADD) have promoted awareness about the dangers of drunk driving, and have successfully pushed for harsher punishments for individuals who drive while impaired.

Party Time: Binge Drinking by College Students

Many researchers have noted that there exists a "culture of alcohol" among undergraduate college students in that alcohol consumption is a cultural aspect of college social life that is passed down to each new generation of college students. Drinking games among college students, such as beer pong and flip cup, have become popular in recent years, and promote heavy drinking. **Binge drinking** (also known as episodic heavy drinking) is considered five drinks for men and four drinks for women in less than 2 hours (Abadinsky, 2008). In a 2001 survey, results revealed that 81 percent of female college students and 79 percent of male college students admitted drinking alcohol within the last year. Of these individuals, 41 percent of the females and 49 percent of the males admitted to binge drinking. This trend does not apply across all campuses: Students attending religious and commuter schools, as well as predominantly African American colleges, on average, consume less alcohol. Research has shown that students most likely to heavily consume alcohol are first-year Caucasian students who are athletes and/or members of a fraternity or sorority (Maisto, Galizio, & Connors, 2008). Heavy drinking among college students is associated with "accidental death, injury, assault, unwanted and unprotected sex, drunk driving, vandalism, suicide, and academic problems" (Maisto, Galizio, & Connors, 2008, p. 194). Heavy alcohol consumption in college, however, is not significantly correlated with alcohol problems later in life, but it has been found to result in a multitude of problems while the individual is a student.

INHALANTS

Inhalants consist of a wide variety of chemicals that individuals self-administer in order to produce psychoactive effects. Such substances typically include:

- Volatile solvents: these are liquids that vaporize at room temperature and are typically found in glues, sprays, paint products, cleaning fluids, correction fluid, hair spray, nail polish, and other commercial products.
- Fuels: these include butane and propane, and typically involve inhaling gasoline or propane fumes from butane lighters, propane tanks, or refrigerants.
- Propellants/Aerosols: contained in pressurized aerosol spray cans such as hair spray, cooking spray, deodorant, or fabric-cleaning sprays.
- Anesthetics: ether was one of the first inhalants to be used for its psychoactive effects, but whipped cream propellant, nitrous oxide (a.k.a. laughing gas), and volatile anesthetics (i.e., ether or chloroform) are also used.
- Nitrates: these are chemicals typically used for sexual enhancement, and are sold in small sealed bottles or small glass containers called "snappers" or "poppers." These bottles are then cracked open and inhaled (McKim, 2007).

Because these chemicals are very different from one another, each of them has different effects on humans when inhaled.

Pharmacology and Effects

Chemicals are almost always inhaled in their gaseous states, though in rare cases, they are ingested in their liquid forms. **Sniffing** occurs when chemicals are inhaled through the nose; **huffing** occurs when chemicals are inhaled through just the mouth, or the mouth and nose. Some substances, such as adhesives, are inhaled from paper bags, whereas other substances, such as fuels, are inhaled from plastic bags. Pressurized gases are inhaled from balloons. Aerosols or propellants may be inhaled either from a bag, or sprayed directly into the mouth and nose. These substances are quickly and entirely absorbed by the lungs, and rapidly reach the brain.

The concentration of these chemicals within the blood is equivalent to their concentration in the air that is inhaled. Concentration of the chemical within the blood therefore, decreases quickly when an individual stops sniffing or huffing. Intoxication can last for a few hours if the chemical is self-administered continuously over a period of time. The blood carries the chemical to tissue, with fatty tissues, such as the brain and liver, receiving the highest concentrations of the chemicals. After the substance passes through the body, metabolism occurs within the liver (McKim, 2007).

Most solvents have the effects of depressants. Generally, small doses of inhaled solvents stimulate motor activity. Larger doses result in initial stimulation, then a decrease in activity. Behavioral effects vary depending on the type of solvent inhaled, and these effects include head jerking, ataxia, falling, paralysis of the legs, aimless scratching, and physical weakness/exhaustion. Some solvents have effects that are opposite of depressants, and include CNS excitation, hyperactivity, and convulsions. At high doses, solvent inhalation can cause unconsciousness and death (McKim, 2007).

Users typically report the effects of inhalants as being similar to those of alcohol consumption. Some users report visual and auditory hallucinations. Solvents can irritate the eyes, nose, and throat, and cause coughing and wheezing. Those who sniff/huff solvents may experience headache, slurred speech, disorientation, and weakness. Prolonged exposure can lead to severe motor limitations, leading to depressed reflexes, seizure, coma, and/or death. Long-term effects of inhaling solvents and other chemicals include nosebleeds, nasal ulcers, short-term memory loss, cognitive impairment, tremor, loss of hearing and smell, weight loss, emotional instability, depression, and staggering. Some evidence exists that sniffing/huffing causes irreversible damage to the nervous system and some long-term users exhibit psychotic behavior (McKim, 2007).

Street Terms for Inhalants

whippets
poppers
snappers
air blast
moon gas
oz
poor man's pot
bolt
boppers
bullet rush
Satan's secret
buzz bomb
shoot the breeze
snotballs
Texas shoe shine
highball
thrust
hippie crack
toilet water
huff
toncho
laughing gas
locker room

Historical Trends of Consumption

Reports of deliberate inhalation were nonexistent before 1959. In this year, school children were arrested in Colorado and Arizona for sniffing glue. These stories and others were reported in newspapers around the country, and incidences of deliberate inhalations rose. By the 1960s, solvent sniffing became widespread. It is believed that a report entitled "The Consumers Union Report on Licit and Illicit Drugs" written in 1972 as well as media coverage of sniffing incidents brought attention to the hazards of inhalation of chemical substances, which incidentally increased the popularity of sniffing/huffing. By the end of the 1960s, an estimated 5 percent of Americans admitted to sniffing glue at least once before graduating from high school. Anti-glue sniffing legislation was passed in thirteen states by 1968 (Maisto, Galizio, & Connors, 2008).

In the 1970s, an anti-inhalation campaign against sniffing the contents of aerosol cans was waged. Public service announcements and warnings from experts were made via the media and within schools. Similar to the effect of publicity regarding solvent and glue sniffing, these measures only made sniffing substances from aerosol cans more popular. Solvent and aerosol sniffing is still popular today. In the 1990s, gasoline sniffing also became popular, and it remains so currently. In 2001, some officials referred to solvent sniffing as having reached epidemic proportions (Maisto, Galizio, & Connors, 2008).

It is currently unclear as to whether tolerance develops among those using inhalants, but dependence can occur following frequent use. Treatment of those who use inhalants is typically difficult and unsuccessful. No existing treatment modalities have proven significantly useful with inhalant users thus far, though inpatient treatment has been the most successful. Those who abuse inhalants typically do not volunteer for treatment, and are usually mandated or referred by legal or social service systems. Such users also typically have a variety of other life problems, including familial, financial, social, or behavioral issues, which often complicate treatment (Maisto, Galizio, & Connors, 2008).

Benefits/Consequences

Some inhalants, such as nitrous oxide, can be safely used medically to alleviate the pain and anxiety associated with minor medical procedures. In addition, there is little risk involved with the use of nitrous oxide if it is administered properly. In addition to the negative health consequences already discussed, chronic use of inhalants can result in permanent brain damage. Many inhalants are extremely toxic, and can result in death after just one use; "sudden sniffing death" is due to the resulting irregular heartbeat. Several inhalant users have also suffocated not only from lack of oxygen due to the inhalation of chemicals, but also from asphyxiation associated with the use of plastic bags while huffing. Other deaths associated with inhalants result from accidents such as falling from sniffing in an unsafe place such as a rooftop or being burned while trying to inhale flammable substances. Finally, long-term inhalation of gasoline and the resulting inhalation of lead can cause leukemia or certain types of cancer. Gasoline inhalation has also been associated with anorexia and seizure (Maisto, Galizio, & Connors, 2008).

Sociological and Legal Issues

The highest use of inhalants is reported among 8th graders, with usage rates steadily dropping among 10th and 12th graders. Researchers assert that inhalants are most popular among children and adolescents because inhalants are quite often the only substances readily available to individuals in this age group that produce psychoactive effects. Legally, many jurisdictions have prohibited the sale to children of substances that could be used as inhalants, though this has not been successful in decreasing the rates of inhalant use. There are so many substances that could potentially be used as inhalants that it would be unreasonable to expect retail stores to anticipate the risk of countless everyday household items (e.g., forbidding a teenage girl from buying hairspray or deodorant in an aerosol can because of its potential for being an inhalant). Further, it has been shown that when the sale of certain inhalants, such as glues that contain toluene, to children is prohibited, rates of use of other substances subsequently increase (e.g., gasoline or aerosol sprays) (Maisto, Galizio, & Connors, 2008).

HERBAL SUPPLEMENTS

Herbal supplements include naturally occurring substances, such as plant leaves or nuts, that have (or are thought to have) various health benefits, and that may have psychoactive effects. In many cases, these supplements have been used culturally and/or religiously by native peoples for hundreds of years. In most cases they are considered food products, and therefore are not regulated by the FDA. In recent years, many globally available herbal supplements have gained increasing popularity within the United States. There are hundreds of herbal supplements that exist and are currently sold in the United States. Listed below are some of the most common types:

- DHEA (Dehydroepiandrosterone): a naturally secreted hormone produced by the adrenal glands, it is believed to prevent a number of illnesses, including heart disease, cancer, diabetes, and obesity, and is thought to have anti-aging effects. No proof exists supporting any of these assertions; however, DHEA may have mood-enhancing effects.
- Ephedra/Ma huang: a number of plants within the ephedra plant species are used as herbal supplements as they contain the naturally occurring stimulant ephedrine. Products containing ephedrine were marketed as energy boosters before they were banned from being sold over the counter in 2004. High doses of this supplement are thought to have effects similar to ecstasy, but such doses have been linked to stroke, heart attack, and death.
- Ginkgo biloba: extracted from ginkgo tree leaves, this supplement has been shown to increase concentration and memory specifically in Alzheimer patients, and some studies point to its effectiveness with healthy individuals as well.
- Kava: a plant indigenous to the southern Pacific Islands, which is usually consumed as tea. Kava has effects similar to those of depressants and is thought to promote relaxation and euphoria, but also talkativeness. Kava is becoming increasingly popular in the United States.
- Salvia: is indigenous to southern Mexico and is a potent hallucinogen that is typically eaten or smoked. It is slowly becoming popular in the United States, and is currently illegal in thirteen states. Salvinorum A, the active ingredient, is the most potent naturally occurring hallucinogen; its hallucinogenic effects last approximately 1 hour.
- Saint-John's-wort (Hypericum): is indigenous to Europe; this drug is considered to have depression-fighting and sleep-aiding effects, yet these effects have not been proved empirically. Saint-John's-wort may be unsafe as it has the potential to interact negatively with other drugs (Maisto, Galizio, & Connors, 2008).

Pharmacology and Effects

The pharmacology and effects of herbal supplements of course vary depending on each substance. Some are eaten (e.g., betel nuts), some are consumed in drink form (e.g., kava), and others are taken in pill form as dietary supplements (e.g., ginkgo biloba). When mixed with other substances, some of these drugs can be dangerous. For example, ginkgo biloba thins the blood, which promotes circulation. However, when mixed with other substances that reduce blood clotting, such as aspirin, ginkgo can be dangerous. In large amounts, ephedra can produce effects similar to MDMA. Kava can cause diarrhea, loss of appetite and weight loss, weak

Herbal Supplements: Placebo or Real Effects?

Effects of herbal supplements vary. Research points to the effectiveness of some herbal remedies, such as valerian and melatonin (which are sleep aids). However, many herbal supplements, such as Saint-John's-wort, have not been proven effective in treating depressive symptoms. Further, those that are ineffective may not only fail to deliver whatever effects they promise but may also have harmful side effects. Reports regarding Saint-John's-wort provide conflicting results. One study found it to be more effective than a placebo; however, a large-scale study conducted in 2001 found Saint-Johns-wort to be ineffective in relieving depression (Maisto, Galizio, & Connors, 2008).

vision, and skin problems such as yellow skin, ulcers, or rashes (Maisto, Galizio, & Connors, 2008). Due to lack of testing and regulation, many of the side effects of herbal supplements are unknown.

Historical Trends of Consumption

Historical trends of use vary by herbal supplement. Many supplements have been used culturally and religiously for hundreds of years within the regions where they are naturally grown. Popularity of supplements within the United States has grown markedly since the early 1990s. This was caused in part by The Dietary Supplement Health and Education Act of 1994, which established herbal supplements as food products rather than drugs (Maisto, Galizio, & Connors, 2008). As such, the FDA does not require that these supplements meet strict drug standards, and manufacturers or producers are not required to publish information regarding harmful side effects on product packaging. Other countries, such as Germany, market herbal supplements as drugs. Therefore, the supplements in Germany must meet strict safety standards, unlike in the United States. As such, as Americans search for "cures" for what ails them, many turn to these supplements in hopes of finding their answer.

Though some studies point to the effectiveness of certain herbal supplements in treating various illnesses (such as Saint-John's-wort for depression), most herbal supplements have not been studied enough to exert empirical evidence of effectiveness. Little is known about the side effects and dangers of most supplements, as supplements are not regulated. This can be very problematic. Many feel that herbal supplements are safe because the ingredients are "naturally" occurring substances. Use of these substances is therefore fairly widespread. However, substances found in nature (i.e., substances derived from plants, which include, e.g., cocaine, mescaline, nicotine) are not always safe.

Sociological and Legal Issues

In 1992, the herbal supplement market was valued at $3.5 billion; in 1995, the value rose to $11 billion; and in 2003, the value was $19 billion. By 2003, the herbal supplement market was as large as the OTC medicine market. According to the American Association of Poison Control Centers, there were 6,914 reports of adverse effects related to the use of herbal supplements in 1998, as compared to 17,132 reports in 2007 (National Poison Data System [NPDS], 2008). This shows the rising popularity of herbal supplements. The Dietary Supplement Health and Education Act, which was passed in 1994, rescinded the FDA's authority to control herbal and other organic supplements. Such supplements, as long as their manufacturers do not make any claims to prevent, treat, or cure any diseases or illnesses on the packaging, are not considered drugs and therefore are not regulated by the FDA for safety and efficacy. Producers are therefore not required to print the possible side effects on product labels (Maisto, Galizio, & Connors, 2008). Some of these substances have been banned due to side effects. Following the death of professional baseball player Steve Bechler, the FDA investigated and then banned OTC sale of products containing ephedrine. Due to its harmful side effects and increasing popularity in the United States, salvia is now illegal in thirteen states.

DIET DRUGS

The only FDA-approved diet drugs are prescription **amphetamines** (which include Benzedrine, Dexedrine, and methamphetamine), which are typically prescribed as a part of short-term weight-loss regimens. There are no FDA-approved OTC weight-control drugs; though a number of herbal/dietary supplements claiming to have weight-loss effects exist.

Prescription antiobesity drugs are split into three categories:

- Sympathomimetic-amine type: stimulate the CNS and increase metabolism, and therefore pose the highest potential for amphetamine abuse because CNS stimulation produces euphoria
- Seratonin-release type: result in decreased appetite
- Lipase-blocker type: inhibit fat digestion/absorption

Most diet pills (including all of those available by prescription) belong to a class of drugs called amphetamines, which are synthetic drugs. Some popular amphetamines used for weight-loss purposes include Fen-Phen (no longer on the market), Xen-Phen, Xenical, and Meridia.

Products containing phenylpropanolamine (PPA) were marketed as weight-loss drugs beginning in the 1970s. However, in 2000, the FDA published a study that found women taking PPA increased their risk of having a hemorrhagic stroke. The FDA requested that all PPA-containing products be withdrawn from the market, a process that was completed by 2001. Dexatrim is an example of a weight-loss drug that originally contained PPA. In 2001, after PPA products had been removed from the market, Dexatrim was remarketed with ephedra, until ephedra was banned in 2004. Dexatrim was then remarketed again with a green tea extract (McKim, 2007). The marketing of many other products as diet drugs, such as benzocaine-containing gum, starch blockers, and products containing cholecystokinin (CCK, a hormone that decreases food consumption), has been banned by the FDA in recent years. Laxatives have also been marketed as weight-loss drugs, though their use is unsafe and not endorsed by the FDA. Amphetamines are a class of drugs that stimulate metabolism and result in increased energy. Amphetamines used to suppress appetite bring about the release of norepinephrine and serotonin. Seratonin-specific amphetamines have been removed from the market, as they have been shown to cause heart problems. Amphetamine overdose causes seizures, irregular heartbeat and/or heart failure, and can result in permanent brain damage or death.

Historical Trends of Consumption

Use of amphetamines as appetite suppressants for weight-loss purposes became widely popular between the 1950s and the 1970s. Legal production of amphetamines in the United States totaled 3.5 billion tablets in 1958, 10 billion tablets in 1970, and 12 billion in 1971. In the 1950s, fifty doses of amphetamines were produced for every adult and child in the United States; 20 percent of all prescriptions written were for amphetamines. Over 20 million prescriptions were written for amphetamines per year (mostly for weight-loss purposes) in the United States during the 1960s, reaching 31 million amphetamine prescriptions in 1967 (McKim, 2007). Beginning in the 1970s, as the justifiable medical uses of amphetamines slowly declined due to spreading knowledge of their harmful side effects and abuse potential, their availability on the market decreased. Later, fenfluramine and phentermine were developed and sold individually, and were then combined in the 1990s to create Fen-Phen. Fen-Phen instantly became popular and was used by those wishing to lose weight (including individuals not overweight to begin with). Over 6 million people used Fen-Phen, because it was extremely effective in aiding weight loss; however the weight quickly would be regained following termination of use (McKim, 2007). A variety of other drugs quickly became Fen-Phen "replacements" after Fen-Phen was removed from the market when its use was linked to heart damage.

Those who consume medical doses of amphetamines are unlikely to develop dependence and withdrawal symptoms as such doses are usually below 60 milligrams. Those who abuse amphetamines, either by exceeding their prescribed doses, or by obtaining and consuming the pills illegally, may develop tolerance and withdrawal symptoms. After several days of moderate to heavy use, individuals ceasing consumption of amphetamines usually experience a crash, characterized by depressive symptoms and hunger. Amphetamine withdrawal symptoms include depression (for some to the point of suicidal ideation), inability to experience pleasure, periods of long or troubled sleep, muscle and abdominal pain, hunger, slowed response time, anxiety, and fatigue. Additionally, psychological dependence on amphetamines is common and overpowering among abusers as the drug produces energy and euphoria which is craved once the drug leaves the individual's system (McKim, 2007). Despite these potential side effects, the U.S. market for diet pills exceeds $200 million annually.

Dieting to Size Zero: Eating Disorders Among Teen Girls

According to the Centers for Disease Control and Prevention, as of 2008 approximately two-thirds of Americans are overweight, many of whom are clinically obese. Roughly 14 percent of children suffer from childhood obesity. Obesity is not only a health issue, but becomes a psychosocial issue for overweight children who are teased and socially ostracized because of their weight. Conversely, media images of women, including actresses and models, have become increasingly thinner over the past several decades. These social trends are realized by teenage girls who develop eating disorders such as anorexia nervosa and bulimia in their quest to maintain a dangerously low weight to meet social standards of "beauty." In doing so, they risk serious health consequences. The Centers for Disease Control and Prevention research reveals that between 15 and 25 percent of teenage girls have symptoms severe enough to warrant clinical evaluation for an eating disturbance (CDC, 2008).

Benefits/Consequences

The appeal of amphetamines is for weight loss, yet studies have shown that they are only minimally effective as a part of short-term weight-loss regimens. An additional benefit, though an illicit benefit, is that amphetamines have been used to enhance sexual activity, specifically in that they delay/prolong orgasm. In terms of consequences, frequent overuse of amphetamines may result in depression, lethargy, heart disease, and psychosis. Long-term use of high doses of amphetamines results in damage to the CNS, specifically "damage to the nerve endings of serotonin and dopamine neurons" (Gahlinger, 2001, p. 220). This can eventually manifest in movement or mood disorders, such as Parkinson's disease or depression.

Summary

- The Food and Drug Administration (FDA) is solely responsible for approving what products can legally be prescribed or sold as medicine and for regulating their safety. The FDA may approve a drug and then recall it later, thus labeling it legal and appropriate for medical use at one point in time and then illegal and not appropriate for medical use at a later time.
- The FDA is also responsible for monitoring the business known as quackery which promotes useless remedies as "cures" for medical ailments. These products are touted on billboards, in magazines, and most commonly on paid-for-television advertisements, and the easy target is seniors, though women are frequently targeted with weight-loss scams as well.
- The consumption of caffeine dates back to ancient times. This is a widespread habit, with about 90 percent of the world's adult population consuming caffeine on a regular

basis; however this can be problematic as caffeine is highly addictive.

- According to the Surgeon General of the United States, the biological and behavioral factors that contribute to nicotine addiction are similar to those that determine heroin and cocaine addiction. Global estimates reveal that approximately half of all men in the world smoke, compared to 12 percent of women. Each day, 15 billion cigarettes are consumed. While tobacco use has been declining in industrialized countries, it has been increasing by 1.4 percent per year in developing countries. If these trends continue, roughly 85 percent of smokers will be from poor, developing countries by the mid-2020s.
- The approximate annual cost of tobacco abuse to U.S. society is $157 billion. Nicotine is the most addictive substance Americans encounter. Approximately one-third of serious smokers become addicted. Statistics reveal that lung cancer has surpassed heart disease as the leading cause of smoking-related deaths in the United States. At least one-third of cancer deaths in the United States are a result of smoking.
- Socially and culturally, alcohol has always been an important part of social occasions; however, the effects of alcohol are far worse than that of illegal drugs in the United States. Alcohol results in approximately 200,000 deaths per year, whereas illegal drugs result in about 8,000 deaths per year. Additionally, approximately 36 million Americans are affected by familial alcoholism, and are subsequently vulnerable to the damaging psychosocial effects of alcohol, including divorce, violence, poverty, displaced children, and family violence.
- Reports of deliberate inhalation were nonexistent before 1959. By the 1960s, sniffing solvents became widespread. In the 1990s, sniffing gasoline also became popular, and remains so today. In 2001, some officials referred to solvent sniffing as having reached epidemic proportions.
- Many herbal supplements have been used culturally and religiously for hundreds of years within the regions where they are naturally grown. Popularity of supplements within the United States has grown markedly since the early 1990s. Manufacturers are not required by the FDA to meet strict drug standards, nor are they required to publish information regarding harmful side effects on product packaging. Many feel that herbal supplements are safe, as their ingredients are "naturally" occurring substances.
- The appeal of amphetamines is for weight loss, yet studies have shown that they are only minimally effective as part of short-term weight-loss regimens. In terms of consequences, frequent overuse of amphetamines may result in depression, lethargy, heart disease, and psychosis.

Important Terms

Alcohol	Caffeinism	Inhalants
Amphetamines	Food and Drug Administration (FDA)	Nicotine
Binge drinking	Herbal supplements	Quackery
Caffeine	Huffing	Sniffing

Critical Thinking Questions

1. Discuss how American culture contributes to the use of at least one type of drug discussed in this chapter.
2. Create an ideal Food and Drug Administration that you believe could more effectively regulate the drug industry.

Research Topics

1. Research the government agency in charge of drug regulation in another industrial country. Compare this agency's effect on drug safety in that nation to the role of the FDA in the United States.
2. Choose one herbal supplement currently on the market. Research the claims made by the company regarding the product's effects on the consumer. Track down empirical studies that have tested whether these claims are true. Also research the popularity of this product in terms of profitability for the company.

Suggested Readings

Knapp, Caroline. (1997). *Drinking: A love story.* New York, NY: Dial Press.

The Tobacco Papers. (July/August,1998). *The Multinational Monitor, 19*(7&8). Retrieved from http://multinationalmonitor.org/mm1998/98july-aug/toc.html

6

Medical Drugs

A fan and St. Louis Cardinal supporter reacts to the admission by Mark McGwire that he was using performance-enhancing drugs while playing baseball: "It's like when you find out your favorite grandfather didn't turn in his income taxes . . . You didn't like him any less, but you squint at him and look at him a little funny because you wish he wouldn't have done that"

—(McGwire is Testing a Loyal Baseball Town 2010).

OBJECTIVES:

When you have finished this chapter, you should be able to:

- Elaborate the growth of the pharmaceutical industry
- Discuss basic pharmacology, use trends, benefits/consequences, and current issues with regard to ADD/ADHD drugs
- Discuss basic pharmacology, use trends, benefits/consequences, and current issues with regard to drugs related to both female and male sexuality
- Discuss basic pharmacology, use trends, benefits/consequences, and current issues with regard to HIV drugs
- Discuss basic pharmacology, use trends, benefits/consequences, and current issues with regard to drug use in sports

REAL LIFE

Starting in the late 1990s, Barry Bonds used a variety of performance-enhancing drugs over a period of five seasons in an event that eventually grew into an enormous scandal. Written about in a book published in 2006 entitled *Game of Shadows,* authors and reporters Mark Fainaru-Wada and Lance Williams chronicle Bonds's persistent doping.

For instance, the authors write that by 2001, when Bonds broke Mark McGwire's single-season home-run record (70) by belting 73, Bonds was using two designer steroids referred to as the Cream and the Clear, as well as insulin, human growth hormone, testosterone decanoate (a fast-acting steroid known as Mexican beans) and trenbolone, a steroid created to improve the muscle quality of cattle. Bay Area Laboratory Co-Operative (BALCO) tracked Bonds's usage with doping calendars and folders—detailing drugs, quantities, intervals, and Bonds's testosterone levels—that wound up in the hands of federal agents upon their September 3, 2003 raid of the Burlingame, California business. Depending on the substance, Bonds used the drugs in virtually every conceivable form: injecting himself with a syringe or being injected by his trainer, Greg Anderson, swallowing pills, placing drops of liquid under his tongue, and, in the case of BALCO's notorious testosterone-based cream, applying it topically. According to the book, Bonds gulped as many as twenty pills at a time and was so deeply reliant on his regimen that he ordered Anderson to start "cycles"—a prescribed period of steroid use lasting about three weeks—even when he was not due to begin one. Steroid users typically stop usage for a week or two periodically to allow the body to continue to produce natural testosterone; otherwise, such production diminishes or ceases with the continued introduction of synthetic forms of the muscle-building hormone. Bonds called for the restarting of cycles when he felt his energy and power start to drop. If Anderson told Bonds he was not due for another cycle, the authors write, Bonds would tell him, "F—off, I'll do it myself" ("Bonds Exposed," 2006).

THE GROWTH OF THE PHARMACEUTICAL INDUSTRY

Historically, the pharmaceutical industry looked much different than it does today. Many medicines were obtained through trade with England; however, following the Revolutionary War, the United States saw the emergence of its own patent medicine industry. This industry was the first to take advantage of widespread marketing via the growing United States press. So-called patent drugs were actually unpatented, and their contents were, therefore, kept unpublished. "Patent drugs" containing opium (e.g., Dover's Powder, Mrs. Winslow's Soothing Syrup, McMunn's Elixir) were popular and available throughout America by the late 18th century. Opium-containing medicines were marketed as treatments for a variety of ailments, including teething, general pain, cough, fever, cholera, baldness, and cancer. These medicines were made with both imported opium and poppies that were legally grown domestically. The medical profession endorsed the use of such medicines at the time (Gahlinger, 2001). Other medicines containing cocaine, heroin, and morphine were also popular. Cocaine was widely used as an unregulated substance within the patent industry. Heroin also gained support from the medical community as a treatment for the cough and chest pain commonly experienced by those suffering from pneumonia and tuberculosis, and it was also marketed as an over-the-counter patent drug. Morphine was discovered in the early 1800s and became the most popular and effective pain reliever available. It was unregulated and consumed via injection. Sears, Roebuck and Co. even sold needle and syringe kits for the self-administration of morphine (Inciardi, 2002).

The Proprietary Medicine Manufacturers and Dealers Association was founded in 1881 to advocate for producers of unpatented "patent drugs." This group contested disclosure laws while drugs containing opium and other illicit drugs were sold in large amounts to an unknowing public. "As to the number of different varieties of patent medicines available, an 1804 New York catalog listed some ninety brands of elixirs; an 1857 Boston periodical included almost six hundred; in 1858 one newspaper account totaled over fifteen hundred patent medicines; and by 1905 the list had stretched to more than twenty-eight thousand" (Inciardi, 2002, p. 19). By the early 1900s, the medical community was beginning to learn of the long-term effects of the various unregulated medicines available to the American public. Many patent drugs were extremely dangerous, as the public combined substances such as morphine, heroin, and cocaine with alcohol. The American Medical Association (AMA) discontinued the advertisement of questionable medicines in its journal and launched an investigation of the patent medicine industry. Their study results were then shared with and published by the muckraking press, who attacked the patent industry with publications such as *The Great American Fraud: A Series of Articles on the Patent Medicine Evil* written in 1905.

Shortly thereafter, several laws were passed, which established new standards for drug quality and safety, thereby forming the foundation for current policy. In 1906, as a response to these shocking media items, the Pure Food and Drug Act was passed which set quality standards and packaging and labeling rules. This brought about an end to the patent industry. Further, the Harrison Act was passed in 1914, which made cocaine and opiate drugs illegal—in turn creating a black market for these substances. Even before the passage of the Pure Food and Drug Act and the Harrison Act, patent drug use had declined as religious and social stigma had emerged surrounding the use of such substances. Not long after, the Food, Drug, and Cosmetic Act of 1938 created the Food and Drug Administration (FDA), which sought to put an end to the promotion and sale of unsafe drugs. The Kefauver-Harris Drug Amendments were added in 1962, which required drug producers to prove the effectiveness of their products before they were to be marketed and sold.

The Pharmaceutical Industry Today

The United States and New Zealand are the only countries that permit pharmaceutical companies to advertise products to consumers directly, called **direct-to-consumer advertising** (DTC). The amount of print and electronic media advertisements for prescription drugs in the United States has significantly increased since its beginning in the 1980s. In fact, pharmaceutical companies spend almost twice as much on advertising than they do on research and development, and this trend has been accelerating (Gagnon & Lexchin, 2008). In 1997, $1 billion was spent by pharmaceutical companies on DTC advertising (Huh & Langteau, 2007), compared to $4.2 billion in 2005 (U.S. General Accounting Office [GAO], 2006), with television advertising taking up the bulk of this marketing effort. Increasingly, however, the Internet is becoming an avenue for advertising for pharmaceutical companies. Drugs advertised directly to consumers are typically those that sell the best for the company (GAO, 2002). Studies estimate an increase in sales of approximately $2 for every $1 spent on advertising (GAO, 2006).

The FDA is charged with regulating DTC advertising under the Federal Food, Drug, and Cosmetic Act (FFDCA). Their guidelines require that advertisements must not be misleading or false, must not omit material facts about the drug, and must present a fair balance between risk and effectiveness of the drug. From the 1950s to about the early 1980s, pharmaceutical companies focused their advertising efforts on physicians as there existed a traditional doctor–patient relationship in which most individuals wholeheartedly trusted the advice proffered by their physician (Donohue, Cevasco, & Rosenthal, 2007). In the early 1980s, pharmaceutical executives realized that the traditional doctor–patient relationship had evolved, primarily due to the consumer's rights movement and the patient's movement. These movements had consumers/patients taking a more active role in their health and brought about the advent of direct-to-consumer advertising. The FDA released guidelines for these advertisements in 1985 and was assigned the task of monitoring any violations. The FDA, however, has been lax in regulating the messages sent to the American public via these advertisements. FDA investigators have 2 to 11 weeks to issue notices to pharmaceutical companies who violate advertising regulations, which is problematic as most advertisements run for only approximately 1 month. As such, the advertisement may be aired for its full broadcast course as intended before the FDA takes action to address violations. This means the pharmaceutical company will have gained any "benefit" from their advertisement before the FDA has had a chance to respond to a violation.

Direct-to-consumer advertising is not without controversy. The Pharmaceutical Research and Manufacturers of America (PhRMA), which represents pharmaceutical research and biotechnology companies, suggests that DTC advertising is successful in educating consumers about health and potential treatment options. In this way, according to PhRMA, this type of advertising is actually empowering for consumers (Pharmaceutical Research and Manufacturers of America [PhRMA], 2005). These advertisements encouraged "important doctor–patient conversations about health that might otherwise not have happened" (PhRMA, 2005). Do physicians agree with this assessment? Though many doctors were initially very skeptical, recent studies have shown that their attitudes are becoming more positive (Morris, Gadson, & Burroughs, 2007). Some studies suggest that physicians believe DTC advertising has prompted patients to seek medical care (Robinson, Hohmann, Rifkin, Topp, Gilroy, Pickard, & Anderson, 2004), while other studies are mixed and suggest that only about half of doctors surveyed believe such advertisements result in better doctor–patient discussion or patient awareness (Rados, 2004). From a patient perspective, knowledge of a drug and the condition it treats can provide empowerment and make a patient feel less embarrassed to discuss the condition during a doctor consultation. Advocates of DTC advertising also suggest that advertising facilitates competition, which results in lower drug prices for the consumer (Huh & Langteau, 2007).

Perhaps the main detractor from DTC advertising is the American College of Physicians, which argues that this approach undermines the trust relationship between a doctor and patient and creates a demand for drugs unnecessarily (Huh & Langteau, 2007). Critics argue that this type of advertisement has resulted in the "overprescription of drugs for conditions people weren't even aware of . . . [and] has resulted in massive profits for the industry by preying on consumers' emotions" ("Ads Spur Urge For Drugs," 2008). Opponents suggest that the advertisements do not provide enough knowledge to patients in short commercial segments so that in a doctor visit, the physician is required to spend time explaining why the drug that patients think would be perfect for them is in fact entirely inappropriate. Research reveals, however, that when doctor–patient visits involve a discussion of a drug a patient saw advertised on television, the physician prescribes the drug 40 percent of the time. In over half of these cases, doctors claim to having prescribed the drug to accommodate the request of the patient (Metzl, 2007).

In addition to the money spent on direct-to-consumer advertising, pharmaceutical companies spend billions of dollars promoting their drugs to doctors. In fact, companies spend on average $3 billion per year more promoting their drugs to doctors than to potential patients, resulting in an expenditure of nearly $8 billion a year (GAO, 2006). It makes sense to target advertising to physicians as they are the ones who ultimately write the prescriptions, and studies estimate that every dollar spent on advertising in medical journals results in $5 worth of sales, while every dollar spent on sponsoring a professional meeting or educational event for a doctor results in about $3.50 worth of sales ("The Payoff," 2007).

Over the years a number of pharmaceutical companies have been convicted of criminal practices, though none of the pharmaceutical executives have ever been imprisoned for illegal business acts. For example, various companies have been charged with acts such as profiting illegally from keeping low-priced generic cancer prescriptions from becoming available; conspiring with medical professionals to charge patients insured by the government for free drug samples, or for overcharging government insurance companies for specific prescriptions; and using foreign, unapproved materials in their drugs to cut costs, among other offenses. One potential reason for lack of serious penalties may be that because it is one of the largest and most profitable industries in the United States, the pharmaceutical industry has influence over national politics. The industry spent $500 million on lobbying between 1997 and 2002. Further, in 2002 more than $30 million was spent by various pharmaceutical companies on congressional campaigns (Mosher & Akins, 2007).

In order to reach the market and gain FDA approval, prescriptions must be proven effective and safe in clinical trials. These studies are paid for and conducted by the pharmaceutical companies themselves, and therefore can be biased as the companies stand to profit if the studies produce positive results. Indeed, many pharmaceutical companies have been found to conceal negative side effects of drugs. "It is estimated that more than 125,000 Americans die from drug reactions and mistakes each year, making pharmaceutical drugs the fourth leading cause of death after heart disease, cancer, and stroke" (Mosher & Akins, 2007, p. 351). As such, it is questionable as to whether the FDA is fulfilling its mission to protect public health. One of the main arguments behind questioning the effectiveness of the FDA is that some scientists serving on FDA panels have financial conflicts of interest in pharmaceutical companies. Can these individuals really be objective when making decisions regarding the safety of drugs going to market? As such, many argue that the production of pharmaceuticals in the United States appears to be geared more toward profit than public health and safety, a phenomenon not found in many other industrialized nations.

The Controversy over Canadian Drugs

The cost of prescription drugs in the United States is higher than in almost every other country in the world. Beginning in the 1990s, prices have increased significantly. Unlike the United States, the cost of prescriptions in Canada is regulated by the government. Canadian drugs are cheaper than drugs manufactured in the United States, which has resulted in many Americans purchasing prescription drugs from Canadian companies either via the Internet or from Canadian stores established within the United States. In 2003, Americans spent roughly $1 billion on Canadian drugs (Mosher & Akins, 2007). In response, the American pharmaceutical companies, who lost money when consumers purchased Canadian drugs, launched advertisement campaigns that questioned the safety of Canadian medications. Some of these campaigns suggested that Canadian drugs are actually imported from other foreign countries, thereby making them unsafe. Ironically, the pharmaceutical industry in the United States is the world's leading importer of foreign drugs. The arguments regarding the efficacy of Canadian prescription drugs are therefore an attempt by the American pharmaceutical industry to maintain incredibly high prices for prescription drugs, rather than an attempt to ensure public health (Mosher & Akins, 2007).

In addition to advertising, U.S. pharmaceutical companies pressured the FDA to enforce already-existing laws which ban the importation of foreign (in this case Canadian) drugs into the United States. Though the pharmaceutical companies and the FDA claim to question the safety of Canadian drugs, not one case exists in which an individual was harmed by a Canadian drug. Also, Health Canada (the Canadian equivalent of the FDA) imposes safety standards and regulates drugs just as strictly as the FDA. Why is there such a difference in cost however, considering the medicines are the same?

Street Terms for Pharmaceutical Drugs

- skittles
- trail mix
- pharm party
- parachuting
- smurf snot
- smurf coke

In the United States, brand-name prescription drugs are patented under trade names for 20 years. The company that produces a brand-name drug can sell privileges to make and distribute the drug under a generic name to another company. Countless brand-name medications are not available as generics as they fall under patent protection. Some generic drugs cost approximately 25 percent of the price of their brand-name equivalents. According to a study completed by the University of California at Berkeley, generic medications sell on average for 30 to 80 percent less than their trade-name counterparts (Mosher & Akins, 2007). Canada has historically had a shorter patent length, meaning that drugs could move to generic availability sooner—and therefore be sold to the public at a decreased cost more quickly. In 1987, however, Canada moved to a 20-year patent as well, indicating that drug prices there will slowly begin to rise. Generic drugs must meet the same standards the FDA has for their trade-name counterparts in terms of ingredients, making them an effective and financially savvy alternative for the American public who save over $1 billion per year by purchasing generic drugs (Mosher & Akins, 2007).

DRUGS USED IN THE TREATMENT OF ATTENTION DEFICIT HYPERACTIVITY DISORDER (ADHD)

Attention Deficit Hyperactivity Disorder (ADHD) (as well as Attention Deficit Disorder—ADD) are syndromes associated with inattention, poor school performance, distractibility, misbehavior, peer conflict, and conflict with authority. Although the causes of ADHD are unknown, studies have shown that the expression of ADHD symptoms is due, in part, to genetic factors. It is believed ADHD is caused by deficiencies within catecholamine-rich areas of the prefrontal cortex of the brain. Some children outgrow the symptoms of ADHD once they undergo puberty, though approximately one-third of individuals continue to experience ADHD symptoms throughout adulthood. Drugs that treat ADHD are central nervous system (CNS) stimulants such as methylphenidate (e.g., Ritalin and Concerta) and amphetamines (e.g., Adderall) (Ksir, Hart, & Ray, 2008). Ritalin is the most frequently prescribed stimulant in the United States.

Pharmacology and Effects

It is not fully understood how stimulants effectively treat the symptoms of ADHD. One theory is that amphetamines and methylphenidate (Ritalin) enhance catecholamine activity within the brain, thereby reducing the catecholamine deficits that are thought to be associated with the disorder (Ksir, Hart, & Ray, 2008). The positive effects of Ritalin last for only 4 hours, which means that many children have to take a second dose to get through the school day. However, Concerta has an extended-release formula which lasts for 12 hours. The effects of these drugs are often dramatic, as described in a conversation between college students:

MICHELLE: The few times I took Ritalin, I got the pills from a boyfriend whose parents were psychiatrists. He didn't have Attention Deficit Disorder (ADD), but mom and dad were willing to write him a prescription so he could stay up nights to cram for exams. I was 17, and figured if someone's highly educated and expert parents would casually hand him a drug, then it had to be safe. The first time I tried Adderall wasn't much different—this time, the source was a friend who got the drug from a roommate with a prescription. Look, I wasn't a habitual drug user. But I was driven to do well in school, and couldn't see my way through all the papers, tests and projects on two or three hours of sleep a night. That is, until I encountered my friends' little pills. Sometimes they were free, and sometimes a single pill could cost as much as seven or eight dollars. Whatever the cost, the returns were amazing.

JESSE: The whole time you're on it, you just feel like that's the way things are supposed to be. You feel like it's gotten you normal.

MICHELLE: That's Jesse Anderson, a friend of mine who used Adderall for the first time in a college study group. Someone gave it to him, and he thought, "Sure, why not."

JESSE: I remember everyone sitting around and thinking, "You know, maybe we all have ADD, because this stuff makes me feel great, like I don't feel weird. I feel like I want to do my work."

MICHELLE: You can pop a pill at midnight, he says, write a 10-page paper in a few hours and still have time to clean your room and catch breakfast before your 8 a.m. class. And though transactions in these stimulants aren't always in the open, they don't carry the same stigma as many recreational drugs. Jesse knows a lot of people who won't touch marijuana—but it doesn't take much for them to chow down Adderall without a prescription.

JESSE: Because it's made by a company, it comes in a nice pre-packaged way. They're not going to sell anything to millions of kids that's going to kill them. It seems relatively safe. ("Black Markets for ADD Drugs Exist on College Campuses," 2006)

The neat little packaging and ease of getting these stimulants, however, belies the serious health consequences of these substances.

Historical Trends of Consumption

ADHD was previously referred to as "childhood hyperactivity" and "minimal brain dysfunction" (MBD), and was characterized by a child's inability to sit still and learn at school, despite the fact that children receiving this diagnosis had an average or above-average IQ. The American Psychological Association (APA) originally referred to this disorder as Attention Deficit Disorder (ADD) in the *Diagnostic and Statistical Manual of Mental Disorders* (*DSM*), yet in the most recent edition (*DSM-IV-TR*), it has been renamed Attention Deficit Hyperactivity Disorder (ADHD). The APA made this change to formally recognize the strong correlation between inattention and hyperactivity, though not all children with ADHD exhibit hyperactive behaviors (Ksir, Hart, & Ray, 2008).

In 1937, Charles Bradley was the first to discover that stimulants actually have calming effects on hyperactive children. Ritalin was sold in Switzerland beginning in the 1950s to treat ADHD, and the FDA approved Ritalin for sale in the United States in 1961. Prescription Ritalin use increased from 150,000 children using the drug in 1970 to 900,000 children using it in 1990. Although, as a group, children with ADHD are more likely to abuse substances as adults, research indicates that male children affected by ADHD who have been treated with stimulants are actually less likely to abuse substances as adults than those male children affected by ADHD who did not receive drug therapy (Maisto, Galizio, & Connors, 2008). The majority of stimulant medications are prescribed for ADHD patients by pediatricians as opposed to psychiatrists. In the present managed-care environment in the United States, insurance seldom covers family therapy, so children tend to receive only medication rather than psychological treatment and therapy for the possible underlying causes of their behavioral symptoms. In addition to stimulant drug treatment, physicians are currently exploring non-stimulant drugs (such as Strattera and Provigil) to treat ADHD as it is thought that these drugs present a minimal abuse potential and fewer side effects (Maisto, Galizio, & Connors, 2008).

With regard to potential for tolerance of Ritalin and similar drugs, a tolerance does not develop in children treated for ADHD, and there is a large population on which to gather data. In 2004 alone, 29 million prescriptions were written for stimulants to treat ADHD and 23 million of these prescriptions were for children ("Report of Ritalin Risks Prompts a Federal Study," 2005). The rate at which adults are diagnosed with ADHD is also increasing: Approximately 1.5 million individuals in the United States between 20 and 64 years of age are currently taking stimulant medication prescribed to treat ADHD (Maisto, Galizio, & Connors, 2008).

In addition to youths taking stimulants with a prescription, these drugs are taken by many without a prescription. During the 1990s, emergency room admissions for Ritalin abuse among children between the ages of 10 and 14 skyrocketed from a mere 40 admissions in 1990 to 400 admissions in 1995. Interestingly, the 1995 statistic of 400 admissions for Ritalin abuse was identical to the number of admissions for cocaine abuse by children in the same age group (Maisto, Galizio, & Connors, 2008). Ritalin is sometimes referred to as "kiddie cocaine" because those who abuse this drug frequently crush and snort it. Additionally, some may dissolve crushed pills in a liquid and drink the drug. When used recreationally, Ritalin produces a high for only a short period of time and as the effects wear off, users experience withdrawal symptoms that include depression and loss of memory and concentration. As such, it is occasionally mixed with heroin, cocaine, or both to produce stronger effects. Many college students admit to abusing Ritalin to stay awake in order to study, though it has also been misused for its euphoric effects, and to suppress appetite in order to lose weight.

Benefits/Consequences

Although the mechanism by which stimulants operate is not fully understood, they have been shown to improve school performance and reduce unruly behaviors in children through the improvement of attention and the suppression of hyperactivity. They are, however, associated with several negative side effects in children, including loss of appetite, weight loss, insomnia, and delays in physical growth (including height and weight suppression). To counteract the growth delays, many children are instructed to cease taking stimulants for several months (what doctors refer to as a "drug holiday" over the summer months) to allow them to have growth spurts and "catch up" physically (Ksir, Hart, & Ray, 2008; Maisto, Galizio, & Connors, 2008). When used recreationally rather than under a physician's care, stimulants can cause heart attack, stroke, racing heart, nausea, headaches, appetite suppression, abdominal pain, and sleep interruption ("Report of Ritalin Risks Prompts a Federal Study," 2005). Long-term abuse may also result in paranoid psychosis, an effect similar to that of long-term methamphetamine abuse.

Sociological and Legal Issues

In 2004, Americans spent over $3 billion on medications prescribed to treat ADHD—money spent primarily on Ritalin, which has been classified as a Schedule II drug under the Controlled Substances Act (Ksir, Hart, & Ray, 2008). The symptoms of ADHD, including fidgeting, inattention, and restlessness, are behaviors exhibited by all children and adults. For this reason, many argue that these behaviors do not indicate a child should be diagnosed (or labeled) with a syndrome and prescribed medication. However, these behaviors are more severe in some children than in others, and for some youths it can affect their learning and school performance. But the question for many critics is: Are doctors overmedicating our children and stifling what was historically considered normal childhood explorative behavior? Attention deficit hyperactivity disorder is about three times more common in boys than in girls: Roughly 10 percent of boys and 3 percent of girls have been diagnosed with ADHD in the United States (Ksir, Hart, & Ray, 2008). There is no standard test for ADHD, so physicians make an ADHD diagnosis after evaluating an individual's symptoms. Many feel that physicians are prescribing Ritalin to children who meet several symptoms of ADHD but do not meet all of the diagnostic criteria. Further, many feel prescription drugs such as Ritalin take a Band-Aid approach by solely treating symptoms as a first method of attack rather than addressing underlying issues with psychotherapy. An additional criticism is the lack of truly long-term data regarding potential health impacts of stimulant use for those being treated with medication. What is clear, however, is that much of the American public has embraced stimulants such as Ritalin as a quick-fix to the hyperactivity and attention deficit problems of our youths.

DRUGS RELATED TO FEMALE SEXUALITY

Birth control (also known as anovulatory agents, oral contraceptives, and "the pill") is an orally administered medication that prevents pregnancy. Birth control pills are taken once per day, and are nearly 100 percent effective, making them the most effective form of pregnancy prevention available. Birth control pills contain synthetic progestin, which is modeled after the naturally occurring hormone progesterone. Progesterone is the female pregnancy hormone that stops the production of hormones which bring about ovulation. The pill fools the body into thinking it is pregnant, and also makes the lining of the uterus thinner, thereby making it less accessible to a fertilized egg. Estrogen is also present in "combination birth control pills," which helps to prevent breakthrough bleeding, or "spotting." The levels of estrogen in birth control prescriptions has decreased from when estrogen was first added to pills in the 1960s, as higher levels of estrogen are correlated with higher risks. Pill manufacturers are exploring new pill options, referred to as Mini-Pills, that contain only progestin and no estrogen, which is thought to be less harmful. Many birth control medications are available in 28-day regimens, which include 21 pills containing hormones, and 7 placebo pills (or no pills at all). Menstruation takes place during the 7 days when placebo pills or no pills are taken. In addition to once-daily pills, birth control is also available in monthly or quarterly injections, patches, and intrauterine devices (IUDs). Emergency contraceptive medication is also available. Commonly referred to as the "morning after pill," this medication is taken shortly following intercourse to prevent pregnancy from occurring, and is not intended for routine use.

As women age, **hormone replacement therapy** (HRT) is commonly used to treat the symptoms of menopause, which include irregular menstruation, fatigue, depression, mood changes, decreased libido, anxiety, insomnia, hot flashes, and night sweats (www.imaginis.com). HRT provides the body with hormones once the body's creation of these hormones has naturally slowed. Delivery of hormones is cyclical and can be via patch, tablet, cream, gel, or rarely, via injection. This type of treatment is used primarily to provide short-term relief over a period of 12 to 24 months from the symptoms of menopause.

Historical Trends of Consumption

The first oral contraceptive was Enovid (norethynodrel), which was approved for sale in the United States in 1960. Since that time, manufacturers have developed many variations of the pill, each containing varying levels of progestin, or progestin and estrogen, as well as IUDs, and contraceptive injections and patches. An emergency contraceptive pill has been prescribed in the United States since the 1970s. The proportion of women between the ages of 15 and 44 using some form of birth control rose from 56 percent in 1982 to 62 percent in 2002. Of those using a contraceptive, 31 percent chose the birth control pill and remained on this method for an average of 4.8 years (CDC, 2004). Hormone replacement therapy in the form of Premarin (made from pregnant mare's urine) became available in the United States in the early 1940s and remains a popular HRT option to this day. Estimates of the percentage of women receiving one of the many forms of HRT vary widely and are extremely difficult to obtain due to lack of research in this area of drug use.

Benefits/Consequences

The most obvious benefit of the birth control pill is the prevention of pregnancy, and in the case of emergency oral contraceptives, this is especially important when a woman is sexually assaulted. Other benefits of oral contraception include protection against ovarian cancer and endometrial cancer. There are, however, many potential negative side effects which are experienced by approximately 40 percent of women using the pill. These negative side effects are so severe that one in four women actually stop taking the pill as a result. Minor negative side effects of the pill include weight gain, nausea, vomiting, dizziness, breast tenderness, irregular menstruation, headache, and depression. Major negative side effects include blood clots which can result in stroke, hypertension, increased cholesterol, vitamin B6 deficiency, and certain types of cancer. Additionally, smokers who take the pill are at increased risk for heart attack and circulatory problems (http://www.webmd.com/sex/birth-control/birth-control-pill).

With regard to HRT, the benefit is the reduction in symptoms associated with menopause. There is also some indication that HRT may help lower the risk for colon cancer and reduce the number of bone fractures; however, there are many potential adverse side effects to this type of treatment (http://www.imaginis.com/breasthealth/hrt.asp). Minor negative side effects include bloating, nausea, breast tenderness, vaginal bleeding, fluid retention, weight gain, depression, and migraines. Studies have indicated, however, that there are some very serious potential negative side effects of HRT, including increased risk of endometrial cancer (cancer of the lining of the uterus), breast and ovarian cancers, heart attack and stroke, and blood clots (http://www.imaginis.com/breasthealth/hrt.asp). Given all these potentially very serious side effects, how did HRT become so popular? In 2009, court records revealed that Wyeth pharmaceutical company (maker of Premarin) funded ghostwriters to author twenty-six scientific papers published between 1998 and 2005 supporting the use of HRT. These articles were published in respected medical journals such as *The International Journal of Cardiology* and *The American Journal of Obstetrics* and touted the benefits of these types of therapies, while downplaying the risks. These articles undoubtedly played a role in the rise in prescriptions for HRT, including Premarin. In fact, Wyeth had sales of nearly $2 billion in 2001 from hormone drugs ("Medical Papers by Ghostwriters Pushed Therapy," 2009). The apparent consensus about the successes of HRT disintegrated in 2002 after a federal study of more than 160,000 women was abruptly stopped when research revealed a link between specific types of hormones and increased risks for stroke, heart disease, and breast cancer, as well as dementia in older women. The findings of this study were replicated in an even larger study of women in the United Kingdom. As a result of these disturbing results, the number of American women participating in HRT has declined by about 50 percent ("Medical Papers by Ghostwriters Pushed Therapy," 2009).

Sociological and Legal Issues

Premarin is a type of HRT drug made from PREgnant MARes' urINe. It is a drug that has helped its manufacturer, Wyeth pharmaceutical, make a significant amount of money, though it has not been without controversy. (Interestingly, Wyeth is somewhat used to controversy as it was also the manufacturer of Fen-Phen, the diet drug that caused severe medical complications which resulted in several civil lawsuits).

> The history of Premarin is entangled in a fascinating story of human intrigue involving ingenuity, influence, controversy, animal rights, competition, money, protection of stockholders, government regulatory power, patient rights, emotions, greed, power, personal and professional freedom, state rights, and perhaps even, ultimately, constitutional issues. As the saga of Premarin evolves it no doubt will continue to be one of the more interesting and compelling stories of the practice of pharmacy (Vance, 2007, p. 1).

Annual revenues for Premarin are approximately $1.2 billion, which accounts for about 13 percent of Wyeth's sales worldwide. Globally, this one drug holds 75 percent of the supplement market for estrogen and costs patients on an HRT regimen about $400 per year (www.premarin.org).

Aside from the medical complications caused by HRT, another controversy, brought to light by animal-rights and animal-welfare activists, is the treatment of pregnant mares used for the production of Premarin (and the resulting foals). Most farms for the collection of mare urine (termed PMU farms) are located in the prairie provinces in western Canada, with a few also located in North Dakota and Minnesota. On the approximately 500 PMU farms, mares enter in September and remain tethered in a narrow stall until March or April. A mare's urine is collected "with a rubber cup positioned over her vulva to collect the urine flow. The cup is held in place by overhead supports and a partial body harness. The tether and collection apparatus greatly restrict movement, and the mare is unable to turn around or take more than a step or two in any direction. If the tether is too short, she may even be unable to lie down comfortably" (http://www.hsus.org/horses_equines/issues/the_facts_about_premarin.html). Estimates indicate there are about 50,000 mares on the farms, which result in the births of about 40,000 foals each year (http://www.hsus.org/horses_equines/issues/the_facts_about_premarin.html). Animal activists have a number of concerns, including: the confinement of mares for nearly 6 months of their 11-month pregnancy, the lack of exercise provided to otherwise active animals, the lack of interaction between mares and other horses, the lack of adequate bedding and lack of insulation from the cold northern winter, and the lax veterinary care provided for serious illness or injury that results to mares or foals (http://www.hsus.org/horses_equines/issues/the_facts_about_premarin.html). An equally pressing concern is what happens to mares that are no longer "productive" and to the foals of PMU mares? While mares are used for several years, provided they continue to become pregnant, once their usefulness in creating urine has expired, the demand for them expires as well. These horses are typically difficult to handle as they are untrained, which means there are few individuals waiting to purchase or adopt them. Foals remain with their mothers for nursing for about 3 or 4 months (rather than the usual 6-month nursing period for horses), then there are several options: The farmer may keep a few female foals for PMU production, or the farmer may sell the foal as a riding horse or breed the horse for later sale, but the reality is that there is a surplus of horses in comparison to individuals seeking a horse. The result is that thousands of foals are sent to feedlots to live without shelter until they reach a desirable market weight. From there they are sent (as are the unproductive mares) to the slaughterhouse, where they are killed and their carcasses are shipped to Europe and Asia for human consumption (http://www.hsus.org/horses_equines/issues/the_facts_about_premarin.html).

DRUGS RELATED TO MALE SEXUALITY

Though approximately 43 percent of women experience sexual dysfunction compared to 31 percent of men, the aphrodisiac industry remains geared toward the male population (Lauman, Paik, & Rosen, 1999). Only recently have companies begun to create products to treat **female sexual dysfunction**, which includes symptoms of decreased sexual desire and arousal, inability to orgasm, and pain during sexual intercourse. Conversely, men have a variety of options, including Viagra, Cialis, and Levitra for erectile dysfunction (ED). All of these drugs encourage the relaxation of smooth muscle and therefore allow a man to more easily attain and maintain an erection. With a 50 percent rate of success, Viagra begins working about 1 hour after it is taken, and its effects can last up to 5 hours. Levitra is similar in the time it takes to work, and the duration of effectiveness. Referred to as "the weekender," Cialis starts to take effect in a short 30 minutes, and its effects can last for approximately 36 hours (Mosher & Akins, 2007).

As stated by a professor of medicine to a sociology professor: "Pretty soon, we won't even have to have sex. We'll just take a pill instead"
(Loe, 2004, p. 169)

Historical Trends of Consumption

Viagra was approved for use in the United States by the FDA in 1998. Its effects were discovered accidentally, as it was originally created to treat angina. Following its extreme popularity, other ED drugs were created and marketed. By the middle of 2002, Viagra sales reached over $1.3 billion annually (Mosher & Akins, 2007). In the United States alone, nearly 10 million men had been prescribed Viagra by 2003(Loe, 2004). While use crosses all age, economic, ethnic, and sexual-orientation lines, the majority of Viagra users are white, heterosexual, middle- to upper-class men over the age of 40. On a global scale, seven tablets are dispensed every second, making Viagra the number one treatment for ED (Loe, 2004). In addition to treating ED in those attempting to achieve "normal" sexual functioning, many use ED drugs recreationally in an attempt to enhance their already "normal" sexual functioning. Viagra has come to be known as the "phallic enabler" and the "Pfizer riser." Statistics show that Viagra use tripled between 1998 and 2002, which upholds the suggestion that it is being used by many recreationally, in addition to those using it to treat a medical disorder (Mosher & Akins, 2007).

Benefits/Consequences

Those consuming sexual enhancement drugs for medical purposes (as opposed to a growing number of individuals who consume them recreationally) can experience what society defines as "normal" sexual functioning, which for many is an obvious and profound benefit. Minor adverse side effects of ED drugs are headache, upset stomach, facial flushing, blurred vision, or sensitivity to light. More serious side effects include a sudden decrease or loss of either vision or hearing (Mosher & Akins, 2007). As well, ED drugs have been blamed for an increase in venereal disease as men seek out prostitutes after consuming the drug, or engage in other types of risky sexual behavior. Additionally, men who take Viagra with illegal drugs such as ecstasy (on the street called sextasy) or methamphetamine often experience painful and prolonged erections, or create highly dangerous drug cocktails (Loe, 2004).

A Hard Pill to Swallow: Clinical Trials of Male Birth Control Pills

The creation of a birth control pill for men that would render them infertile only while using the drug has proven difficult. Women ovulate once per month, but men produce sperm all year long. The biggest breakthrough in fertility control drugs for men so far has been gossypol, which works by reducing sperm count. This drug has been shown to prevent pregnancy without having a negative effect on libido, but one dangerous adverse side effect is irreversible and permanent sterility in some men. Some minor negative side effects include nausea, lack of appetite, and inability to sweat. Some studies have found gossypol to be 99.89 percent effective. Gossypol is not sold in the United States because as it has not yet been approved by the FDA.

(LISKA, 2004).

Sociological and Legal Issues

The use of ED drugs has been linked with negative social consequences in addition to health risks. Some researchers suggest that men who consume Viagra are more likely to cheat on their spouses, which may be in part because the spouses of those on ED drugs are bothered by their partners' newly enhanced sexuality, and are unwilling to "keep up" with their partners' increased libido (Mosher & Akins, 2007). In fact, these women have been termed "Viagra wives."

> Since Viagra's debut, "normal sex" in America is more and more narrowly defined and difficult to achieve . . . Pharmaceutical ads and medical experts tell us that erectile dysfunction, especially the "mild" form, is common for millions of men . . . , but not normal. Likewise, female sexual dysfunction is constructed as common for millions of women . . . , but not normal. Normal for males, as defined by Pfizer Pharmaceuticals and its experts, is having a consistently hard and penetrative penis, feeling eighteen again, and never having to worry about occasional problems with erections. More recently, we have heard that normal for women means sexually desirous, easily aroused, fully lubricated, and orgasmic. With such elevated standards, normal sex in the Viagra era probably requires medical or pharmaceutical intervention (Loe, 2004, pp. 19–20).

Is it realistic or desirable to live in a society where "normal" sexual functioning *requires* medical intervention for many individuals, and leaves many others feeling unsatisfied and abnormal? Studies show that while ED drugs are still extremely popular, some of the initial appeal may have worn off: In the past 5 years, millions of American men have requested a prescription for Viagra from their physician; however, only about 50 percent of them have requested a refill (Loe, 2004). The lesson learned may be that great sex does not always solve self-esteem or relationship problems, and indeed in many instances it can create further problems.

HIV DRUGS

Human Immunodeficiency Virus (HIV) is the virus that causes Acquired Immunodeficiency Syndrome (AIDS). HIV can be transmitted when the blood, semen, or vaginal secretions of an infected individual come in contact with an uninfected individual's broken skin or mucous membranes. HIV can also be transmitted from a mother to her child during pregnancy or while breastfeeding. If an individual tests positive for HIV, he or she may or may not develop AIDS, which is a syndrome that weakens the immune system, resulting in the decrease of certain cells, and increased susceptibility to cancers and infections. Treatment of HIV is difficult and the disease spreads at an extremely fast rate. By way of example, "10 billion new HIV virus particles can be replicated daily in an infected human" (Liska, 2004, p. 64). Also, the virus produces strains that are resistant to drug treatment.

Current treatment mechanisms for HIV/AIDS involve the use of one of four classes of antiretroviral drugs:

- Reverse transcriptase (RT) inhibitors which include:
  - Nucleoside reverse transcriptase inhibitors (NRTIs)—These drugs are synthetic nucleoside analogs that prevent the virus from making copies of itself and growing.
  - Non-nucleoside reverse transcriptase inhibitors (NNRTIs)—These drugs are similar to NRTI drugs in that they prohibit the replication of HIV, yet they take less time to be processed by the body because they are chemically pre-activated and do not have to be biologically activated.
- Protease inhibitors (PIs)—These drugs inhibit the production of the protein protease. Without this protein coating, the virus cannot leave a host cell, thus inhibiting the survival of the virus.
- Entry and fusion inhibitors—These drugs keep the virus from entering a host cell by hindering the virus from fusing with the cellular membrane.
- Integrase inhibitors—These drugs block the enzyme integrase, which HIV uses to incorporate viral genetic material into a host cell.

Beginning in the mid-1990s, these drugs were combined to create drug "cocktails" (a combination of drugs taken together), in order to more aggressively fight AIDS. Compliance with drug regimens is difficult and many patients are noncompliant, because drug therapy often involves multiple doses of multiple medications per day. Other types of medications are currently being developed and studied. For example, drugs are being explored that will bolster depleted immune functioning and research is being conducted into possible vaccines (Liska, 2004). Many physicians and researchers have noted the positive and safe effects of marijuana use in treating the nausea, appetite loss, pain, and anxiety associated with AIDS, and testified to these findings at a public hearing before the United States Drug Enforcement Agency (DEA) in 1986. In 1988, the DEA overruled an order by Francis L. Young, DEA administrative law judge, to change marijuana from a Schedule I drug to a Schedule II Controlled Substance. As a result, marijuana is not currently used as a treatment for AIDS.

Historical Trends of Consumption

AIDS was first clinically named as a new and distinct syndrome in 1981. Symptoms of immunosuppression were reported by a growing number of homosexual men at this time, resulting in the unusual diagnoses of pneumocystis carinii pneumonia (PCP) (5 cases in Los Angeles) and Kaposi's sarcoma (KS) (26 cases in New York and California). These reports were strange, as these diagnoses were never seen among healthy young men prior to the early 1980s. The occurrence of these diagnoses, in addition to the occurrence of other opportunistic infections among individuals with inexplicable immune dysfunction came to be known as AIDS. Further research by the Centers for Disease Control and Prevention determined that the first cases of AIDS in the United States probably occurred in 1977 (Liska, 2004). The majority of individuals who initially acquired AIDS were homosexual, and so AIDS was originally thought to be caused by some unknown aspect of the male homosexual lifestyle, at that historical juncture characterized by promiscuity and an alarmingly high rate of sexually transmitted diseases (Liska, 2004). In the early 1980s however, the National Institutes of Health revealed that AIDS is caused by the human T-cell lymphotropic virus, type III.

Speculation continues to this day surrounding the original sources of AIDS, with many researchers believing it may have been central Africa. One theory states AIDS may have existed for years in remote villages and did not spread rapidly because of strict social mores. Urbanization eventually brought about a new social climate which promoted the spread of AIDS and other sexually transmitted diseases in recently developed African cities. Another theory states that HIV originated within the African green monkey species, mutated, and then infected humans. Green monkeys were frequently shipped to Haiti and kept as pets in male brothels, and it was rumored by some that homosexual American males vacationing in Haiti became infected and brought the virus to the United States. There have also been theories about AIDS being a manmade virus intended for genocide purposes, whereas some Soviet theories postulate that AIDS was created during experiments at the Pentagon. All of this however remains speculation.

Regardless of the origin, AIDS remains a serious concern that impacts a large number of individuals each year. Every year, about 40,000 Americans are newly infected with AIDS; about half of these individuals are under the age of 25. Of all individuals with AIDS in the United States, 77 percent are male and 23 percent are female, 42 percent are African American, 36 percent are Caucasian, and 20 percent are Hispanic (Hanson, Venturelli, & Fleckenstein, 2006). Currently, about 40 million individuals are HIV positive worldwide and 900,000 of these individuals are American. As of 2003, about 350,000 Americans have died of AIDS (Liska, 2004). Those most at risk for contracting AIDS are:

- Men with a history of multiple homosexual or bisexual partners
- Injection drug users and their sexual partners
- Heterosexuals with multiple partners
- Infants born to HIV-infected women
- People who receive contaminated blood products for transfusions or treatment of blood disorders (Hanson, Venturelli, & Fleckenstein, 2006, pp. 510–511)

Risk for men is primarily from sex with other men (54 percent of male AIDS cases) or injection drug use (23 percent of male AIDS cases), whereas risk for women is from heterosexual encounters (68 percent of female AIDS cases) and injection drug use (30 percent of female AIDS cases) (Hanson, Venturelli, & Fleckenstein, 2006). To treat individuals with AIDS most effectively, highly active antiretroviral treatments (HAART) are used to reduce the number of HIV/AIDS-related fatalities and reduce the spread of the virus.

Benefits/Consequences

Administrators of HAART aim to prevent the virus from spreading to more blood cells within an individual who has already been infected, in essence suppressing HIV and bolstering the immune system. HAART gives the immune system an opportunity to strengthen, therefore protecting the body from acquiring opportunistic infections. Adverse side effects include nausea, vomiting, abnormal fat allocation, irregular metabolism of lipids and glucose, and loss of bone density. Such drugs are extremely expensive, costing approximately $10,000 to $12,000 annually (Hanson,

Venturelli, & Fleckenstein, 2006). Drug combinations that comprise HIV/AIDS treatments have become less effective as the virus develops resistance to the medications. Although HAART can suppress HIV, there is no cure, so an individual infected with HIV can still transmit the virus to another individual—there is no cure for AIDS!

Desperate for a cure, many of those infected with the AIDS virus turn to any treatment proposed to be a cure. AIDS patients have been duped by dishonest vendors into purchasing amino acids, garlic and herbal remedies, acupuncture and meditation sessions, snake venom, enemas, and colonics and participating in holistic healing rituals.

> One patient is taking 100 pills a day; another spends $600 a month for food supplements, $300 for acupuncture sessions, $250 for colonics, and $500 for sessions with a holistic doctor. Many patients travel to Mexico to purchase investigational drugs not sold in the United States. Although no one can advise a patient whose life is threatened to avoid a purported cure, one can advise that unscrupulous dealers are all too ready to fleece the easily deceived person with bogus alternative therapies. Furthermore, we must consider the power of the placebo effect when we take any drug (Liska, 2004, p. 67).

The FDA actually responded to this situation by establishing the AIDS Health Fraud Task Force Network.

Sociological and Legal Issues

As already indicated, many HIV infections (in addition to infections of hepatitis C) are caused by the sharing of dirty needles among intravenous drug users and unprotected sex. Statistics demonstrate that one drug user infected with HIV can conceivably expose one hundred other individuals to HIV (Lyman & Potter, 2007). Early research uncovered that diabetic intravenous drug users were far less likely to become infected with HIV/AIDS than nondiabetic drug users. It was determined that the reason for this was access to new and clean hypodermic needles. States subsequently began providing needle exchange programs (NEPs) to drug users in 1992. The basic purposes of NEPs are as follows:

- Distribute clean and sterile needles to individuals currently using drugs intravenously
- Actively promote the return of used ("dirty") needles from injection drug users in order to have control over the manner in which these needles are discarded
- Provide counseling and health education to the drug-using community in an attempt to positively change their behavior (Lyman & Potter, 2007)

Currently, all fifty states have legislation that approves NEPs. Interestingly, New Jersey (the state with the highest number of HIV cases) was the last state to adopt needle-exchange legislation in 2006. Needle exchange has been a controversial undertaking, as many people feel the legal distribution of clean needles to drug users sends the message that state governments not only support, but facilitate, drug use. For this reason, in 1998 President Clinton chose not to lift a 1989 ban on federal financial support of NEPs, despite reports from government researchers which stated such programs prevented the spread of HIV/AIDS without encouraging drug use (Lyman & Potter, 2007). Programs such as these have been operating in countries such as England, the Netherlands, Sweden, and Australia since the mid-1980s with great success. Needle exchange however runs counter to the United States' criminal justice response to drugs, instead falling into a harm-reduction approach.

DRUGS IN SPORTS

The sporting world has been rocked by the recent BALCO scandal under federal investigation, in which it was alleged that high-profile athletes were given steroids in exchange for endorsements of legitimate nutritional supplements. Jose Canseco (2006) recently wrote an apparent expose entitled *Juiced: Wild Times, Rampant 'Roids, Smash Hits, and How Baseball Got Big*, which captured the public's imagination as a best seller. Controversy shrouds the images of both current and past sports heroes; President George W. Bush discussed steroids in his State of the Union addresses, and the government began a new war on drugs in locker rooms across America.

For centuries, societal pressures on women to conform to constructed femininity have been the focus of sociological discussion. Only recently however, have scholars begun to recognize the pressures on men to achieve physical perfection (Pope, Phillips, & Olivardia, 2000). Men in American society are inundated with media images of physical dominance, all part of today's constructed masculinity wherein muscles are larger than ever in history and men are regularly exposed to messages encouraging them to build the perfect body. In reality, however, as in the case of women starving themselves to attain the perfect media-image physique, it is virtually impossible for an average man to achieve this benchmark without the assistance of supplements. We have become a society of enhancements, and ironically the supplements used to create the perfect body often need to be countered with pharmaceuticals to enhance sexual performance, leaving men in a quandary about outward physical perfection alongside many adverse consequences, both physical and emotional. **"Doping"** is the term used most commonly to describe the use of performance-enhancing drugs. Examples of such drugs are:

Street Terms for Steroids

Arnolds
gym candy
pumpers
roids
stackers
weight trainers
gear
juice

- CNS stimulants (such as ephedrine, caffeine, or amphetamines) which incite the CNS to elevate blood pressure and heart rate, thereby making the user more alert, focused, and aggressive
- Anabolic proteins which increase the supply of oxygen in the blood and are used to enhance stamina and endurance
- Anabolic steroids which build protein and other bodily tissue and spur the production of red blood cells and muscle
- Beta-blockers which work to slow an individual's heart and may be beneficial depending on an athlete's sport of choice
- Pain relievers which permit an individual to "work past the pain"
- Diuretics which help maintain an individual's weight
- Hormones, such as the human growth hormone (hGH), which are used to help grow muscle and are typically taken via injection
- Drugs that mask the presence of other drugs

Masking agents come in various forms and aim to hide the presence of drugs that are not permitted in an athlete's system as per the rules of the competition. Examples of masking agents are diuretics (which cleanse the system of the drug by flushing it out in one's urine), probenecid (which prevents drugs from being released into one's urine), and fruit pectin (which is believed to hide the presence of drugs, though it has not been proven effective) (Hanson, Venturelli, & Fleckenstein, 2006;

Liska, 2004). Additionally, other legal drugs may be used to increase energy or endurance, such as complex B vitamins or over-the-counter decongestants.

Historical Trends of Consumption

Various substances, such as figs, mushrooms, herbs, and sesame seeds, have been consumed historically since ancient times in attempts to enhance athletic performance. The use of performance-enhancing drugs increased during the late 19th century and thereafter. Specifically, during the late 1800s, unwitting horses and competitive jockeys took part in "doping" to obtain an edge. Anabolic steroids were initially developed for the German Nazi Army in the 1930s, and use of these drugs among competitive athletes began in Russia in the 1950s. Stimulant use among other athletes became popular in the 1950s and 1960s, and the result was the start of drug testing at Olympic Games in 1968. In 1976, drug detection methods were improved to allow detection of almost any drug within an individual's system (Mosher & Akins, 2007). Individuals intent on using drugs adapted to these methods, and the use of hormones (e.g., hGH) became popular in the last decade, both due to increased attention of law enforcement on steroids as well as the difficulty in detecting hormones during drug screens.

According to the DEA, approximately 1 million individuals in the United States use steroids, most of whom participate in bodybuilding activities or are adolescents attempting to impress peers by enhancing their physical appearance (Hanson, Venturelli, & Fleckenstein, 2006). Among the youth population, data from the nationwide Monitoring the Future (MTF) study indicates that about 3 percent of high school students have used anabolic steroids at least once (Johnston, O'Malley, Bachman, & Schulenberg, 2006). Of the steroids available in the United States, between 85 and 90 percent are imported from Mexico and over half are counterfeit. This is, however, an extremely profitable business, making from $300 to $400 million annually (Mosher & Akins, 2007). Those who use steroids illegally take between 10 and 200 times the therapeutic/medical doses.

> Users take nonmedical anabolic-androgenic steroids in *cycles,* periods of use lasting 6 to 12 weeks or longer. "Stacking these drugs means taking more than one at a time, which is common. The use of different steroids taken singly but in sequence is called "cycling." To avoid developing tolerance to a particular steroid ("plateauing"), athletes often stagger the various drugs, sometimes taking them in overlapping patterns or alternately. Users often move from a low daily dose at the beginning of a cycle to a higher dose, then reduce their use toward the end of the cycle ("pyramiding")" (Hanson, Venturelli, & Fleckenstein, 2006, p. 476).

This process may work to enhance both the positive and negative effects of the drugs.

Benefits/Consequences

If there were not a variety of benefits, drug use in sports would not be as prevalent as it is today. These benefits include (if steroids are taken in high enough doses with a very strict diet and intense training regimen) significant increase in muscle mass as well as significant increase in muscle strength. Much of this effect will dissipate when drug use stops, therefore many individuals develop not a physical addiction to performance-enhancing drugs, but a psychological addiction to the advantage that these drugs provide. Additionally, many users experience a euphoria or high, resulting in increased energy, concentration, and alertness (Hanson, Venturelli, & Fleckenstein, 2006).

There are, however, many and significant negative side effects of performance-enhancing drugs. As anabolic steroids are chemically similar to testosterone, these drugs can have androgenic effects on both male and female users. Stunted growth may occur in children and teenagers. Men can develop testicular atrophy, baldness, "man breasts," decreased sperm production, difficulty urinating, high blood pressure, impotence, high cholesterol, heart attack, increased risk for liver problems, and kidney disease. Women may also experience kidney, liver, and cardiovascular issues; loss of body curves; problems with menstruation; and develop a deeper voice, irreversible baldness, and an enlarged clitoris. Increased aggressiveness has been present in select instances, but violent mood swings (known in the media as "'roid rages") have not been supported in the research and are therefore yet another example of a moral panic (Hanson, Venturelli, & Fleckenstein, 2006). More research is needed regarding long-term adverse effects of chronic steroid use, because existing evidence points to a correlation between use and prostate and liver cancer. These effects are less likely with injected drugs (as compared to oral drugs, which are more toxic to the liver); however, intravenous steroid use raises the risks associated with dirty needles.

Sociological and Legal Issues

The federal Anabolic Steroids Act, passed in 1990, prohibits the manufacture, distribution, illegal use, and possession of anabolic steroids. Such acts are criminal offenses punishable by 1 to 10 years in prison. The use of drugs (all types of performance-enhancing drugs) has become big news in recent years: The NCAA (National Collegiate Athletic Association) performs random drug screens on collegiate athletes (divisions 1 and 2 football as well as track and field), in addition to performing drug screens prior to all championship and bowl games. Additionally, the Supreme Court has ruled that public schools can drug screen athletes without violating their constitutional rights.

On the Olympic stage, many athletes have been stripped of their medals after it was discovered they consumed drugs that violated game rules (winners are tested within an hour following competition). The International Olympic Committee (IOC) has prohibited the use of amphetamines, various other stimulants (including excessive amounts of caffeine), narcotics, anabolic steroids, analgesics, diuretics, and beta-blockers. In fact, an athlete using medicines to treat a cold could test a false positive for amphetamines. Despite regular drug testing, athletes continue to use performance-enhancing drugs as evidenced by the fact that twenty-four athletes were disqualified from the 2004 Olympics for the use of steroids. It was during 2004 that the use of steroids in professional sports, including major league baseball and professional football, became a regular media topic. A company called BALCO distributed designer steroids to a number of professional athletes marketed as "supplements," which were, at the time, not detectable by the drug screening methods in place. Some athletes tied to the use of BALCO products included Barry Bonds, Mark McGwire, Rafael Palmiero, Jason Giambi, and Bill Romanowski. During this major federal investigation it was suggested by the media that between 50 and 85 percent of major league baseball players used steroids. Of course this is speculation, but for years athletes have been looking for advantages in the form of sleek swimsuits, high-tech running shoes, the most sophisticated snowboards—this is just another way for many of them to enhance their athletic performance.

Summary

- Historically, the pharmaceutical industry looked much different than it does today. "Patent drugs" containing opium were popular and available throughout America by the late 18th century. Other medicines containing cocaine, heroin, and morphine were also popular.
- In 1906, the Pure Food and Drug Act was passed, which set quality standards and packaging and labeling rules. This brought about an end to the patent industry. Further, the Harrison Act was passed in 1914, which made cocaine and opiate drugs illegal—in turn creating a black market for these substances.
- The United States and New Zealand are the only countries that permit pharmaceutical companies to advertise products to consumers directly. In fact, pharmaceutical companies spend almost twice as much on advertising as they do on research and development, and this trend has been accelerating; drugs advertised directly to consumers are typically those that sell the best for the company.
- The FDA is charged with regulating DTC advertising under the Federal Food, Drug, and Cosmetic Act (FFDCA). Their guidelines require that advertisements must not be misleading or false, must not omit material facts about the drug, and must present a fair balance between risk and effectiveness of the drug.
- The cost of prescription drugs in the United States is higher than in almost every other country in the world. Beginning in the 1990s, prices have increased significantly. Canadian drugs are cheaper than drugs manufactured in the United States, which has resulted in many Americans purchasing prescription drugs from Canadian companies, either via the Internet or from Canadian stores within the United States.
- Attention Deficit Hyperactivity Disorder (ADHD) (as well as Attention Deficit Disorder—ADD) are syndromes associated with inattention, poor school performance, distractibility, misbehavior, peer conflict, and conflict with authority. Stimulants effectively treat the symptoms of ADHD, although it is not fully understood how.
- Ritalin was sold in Switzerland beginning in the 1950s to treat ADHD, and the FDA approved Ritalin for sale in the United States in 1961. Prescription Ritalin use increased from 150,000 children using the drug in 1970 to 900,000 in 1990. In 2004 alone, 29 million prescriptions were written for stimulants to treat ADHD and 23 million of these prescriptions were for children.
- Birth control pills are an orally administered medication that prevents pregnancy. Birth control pills are taken once per day, and are nearly 100 percent effective, making them the most effective form of pregnancy prevention available.
- As women age, hormone replacement therapy (HRT) is commonly used to treat the symptoms of menopause, which include irregular menstruation, fatigue, depression, mood changes, decreased libido, anxiety, insomnia, hot flashes, and night sweats. HRT provides the body with hormones once the body's creation of these hormones has naturally slowed. The apparent consensus about the successes of HRT disintegrated in 2002 after a federal study of more than 160,000 women was abruptly stopped when research revealed a link between specific types of hormones and increased risks for stroke, heart disease, and breast cancer, as well as dementia in older women.
- Though approximately 43 percent of women experience sexual dysfunction, compared to 31 percent of men, the aphrodisiac industry remains geared toward the male population. Only recently have companies created products to treat female sexual dysfunction, which includes symptoms of decreased sexual

desire and arousal, inability to orgasm, and pain during sexual intercourse. Conversely, men have a variety of options, including Viagra, Cialis, and Levitra for erectile dysfunction (ED). By the middle of 2002, Viagra sales reached over $1.3 billion annually.

- Human Immunodeficiency Virus (HIV) is the virus that causes Acquired Immunodeficiency Syndrome (AIDS). Current treatment mechanisms for HIV/AIDS involve the use of one of four classes of antiretroviral drugs. Beginning in the mid-1990s, these drugs were combined to create drug "cocktails" in order to more aggressively fight AIDS. Compliance with drug regimens is difficult and many patients are noncompliant, as drug therapy often involves multiple doses of multiple medications per day. Every year, about 40,000 Americans are newly infected with HIV, with about half of these individuals under the age of 25. Of all individuals with AIDS in the United States, 77 percent are male and 23 percent are female.
- "Doping" is the term most commonly used to describe the use of performance-enhancing drugs. Stimulant use among athletes became popular in the 1950s and 1960s, and the result was the start of drug testing at Olympic Games in 1968. In 1976, drug detection methods were improved to allow detection of almost any drug within an individual's system. Individuals intent on using drugs adapted to these methods, and the use of hormones (e.g., hGH) became popular in the last ten years. According to the DEA, approximately 1 million individuals in the United States use steroids, most of whom participate in bodybuilding activities or are adolescents attempting to impress peers by enhancing their physical appearance.

Important Terms

Attention Deficit Hyperactivity Disorder (ADHD)
Birth control
Direct-to-consumer advertising (DTC)
Doping
Female sexual dysfunction
Hormone replacement therapy (HRT)

Critical Thinking Questions

1. Compare and contrast the approach to drugs that address male and female sexuality. How might this be different if women were in charge of research and development of pharmaceuticals?
2. Is the prescription of Ritalin merely providing a Band-Aid solution to children with ADD/ADHD? Should these children be left to "normal childhood exploration"? Should they be treated with therapy? Should there be an alternate solution? Discuss your position.

Research Topics

1. Should performance-enhancing drugs be banned in professional sports or should athletes be permitted to use supplements to enhance their abilities? Defend your position.
2. Research the prevalence of HIV/AIDS and the availability of treatment in Africa in comparison to the treatment available in the United States. Write a short paper taking a position on whether or not you believe U.S. pharmaceutical companies have a moral obligation to assist African countries with serious HIV/AIDS epidemics.

Suggested Readings/Films

Adams, Samuel Hopkins. (1905). *The great American fraud: A series of articles on the patent medicine evil.* San Francisco, CA: P.F. Collier & Son.

Gaviria, Marcela (Director). (2001). *Medicating kids: Frontline* [Documentary]. Available from PBS—Available online at: http://www.pbs.org/wgbh/pages/frontline/shows/medicating/

Loe, Meika. (2004). *The rise of Viagra: How the little blue pill changed sex in America.* New York, NY: New York University Press.

7

Illegal Drugs

"Crack's addictive quality has led to the rapid establishment of a crack culture and makes it easy to maintain a clientele. The belief in the community is that crack addiction is immediate and permanent. Once you try crack, it is said, you're always "chasing the ghost"—the high that you get the first time is so intense that you can never achieve it again, but the desire to do so is strong enough that you keep pursuing it. One drug dealer told me that he has never seen anybody walk away from crack permanently, even if a user gets off it for two years, he said, the right drug dealer can easily hook him again by talking to him in the right way."

—(ANDERSON, 1999, P. 121)

OBJECTIVES:

When you have finished this chapter, you should be able to:

- Discuss basic pharmacology, use trends, and benefits/consequences with regard to marijuana
- Discuss use trends and the benefits/consequences with regard to opiates
- Discuss basic pharmacology, use trends, benefits/consequences, and current issues with regard to hallucinogens/psychedelics such as LSD, psilocybin, peyote, ecstasy, and PCP
- Discuss use trends, benefits/consequences, and current issues with regard to methamphetamine
- Discuss use trends and benefits/consequences with regard to cocaine

REAL LIFE

From *Code of the Street: Decency, Violence, and the Moral Life of the Inner City* by Elijah Anderson:

> Strikingly, they [crack dealers] may even become customers themselves—it is easy enough to become hooked by trying it once. Through the posturing required to prevail in the street life,

many young people come to feel invincible, or they develop a profound need to show others they feel this way. And the power that accrues to dealers compounds the sense that they can control anything, even a crack cocaine high. In these circumstances they become "the man." Sometimes such a dealer does manage crack off and on for a couple of years. Getting high now and then, he feels he is handling it, but, as the wiser dealers say, there is a fine line between handling it and having it handle you. At some inopportune moment he may be suddenly overcome with an insatiable need for the drug. Such a person is said to be "jonesing" for it; he is filled with such an intense desire for a high that he loses control of his actions. The predator becomes the prey—a common occurrence (Anderson, 1999, pp. 115–116).

MARIJUANA

Marijuana (sometimes also spelled marihuana) is by far the most commonly used illicit drug as well as the largest cash crop in the United States (Gahlinger, 2001). It is a preparation of leafs from the cannabis plant that is most typically smoked; it can be consumed in the form of a marijuana cigarette (joint) or rolled in cigar paper (blunt). It can be mixed with hashish (another preparation of the cannabis plant) and smoked in a pipe (usually a water pipe or bong), or mixed with hash oil and heated so users can inhale the fumes. There are various types of cannabis plant species, including:

- *Cannabis sativa* which is from Asia but now grows worldwide. It grows as a weed in the United States and Canada, and fibers from this species are used to make hemp rope.
- *Cannabis indica* is grown worldwide, including in the United States, and it is popular for its psychoactive resins.
- *Cannabis ruderalis* is mostly grown in Russia, and does not grow in the United States.

The potency of the plant depends not only on genetics but also on environmental conditions such as weather and moisture level (Goldberg, 2006; Mosher & Akins, 2007). There are three types of marijuana that grow in the United States:

- *Indian hemp* (more commonly called ditchweed) is the most common, and it grows in the wild and has little value on the market because the THC (delta-9-tetrahydrocannabinol, explained in the next section) level averages about 0.14 percent. It is most commonly used as "filler" with more expensive marijuana.
- *Commercial grade* is the type of marijuana typically sold on the street with an average THC level between 5 and 8 percent.
- *Sinsemilla* (meaning "without seeds" in Spanish) is the most potent and therefore the most profitable, and represents about 25 percent of marijuana available on the street and has an average THC level between 8 and 12 percent (Lyman & Potter, 2007).

Street Terms for Marijuana

grass
pot
weed
bud
Mary Jane
dope
indo
hydro
ganja
Acapulco gold
reefer
Thai sticks
Maui wowie

Growing, purchasing, or using any of the above types of marijuana is, of course, illegal and laws do not distinguish between grades of illicit substances; however, the grade determines the potency, and therefore profit margin for the seller.

Pharmacology and Effects

There are sixty-six substances, known as cannabinoids, uniquely found within cannabis plants. THC is one of these substances. It is the THC that produces psychoactive effects in users. Most THC-containing resin is concentrated within the flowering tops and leafs of the marijuana plant, whereas very little is contained within the stalks. There are various preparations of cannabis leafs, including charas and hashish, which consist of THC-containing resin that has been removed from the plant; ganja, which contains dried out flowered tops of the plant; and bhang, which is a powder made from the leftover parts of the plant once the top has been removed. Bhang is typically added to beverages and food. Hash oil, which is extracted when the plant is boiled in alcohol and the resin evaporates off the plant and forms a dark oily material, is another preparation (Goldberg, 2006; Mosher & Akins, 2007).

When marijuana is smoked, THC is absorbed by the blood which flows to the brain and the rest of the body. THC can reach the brain within seconds, with the user beginning to feel the effects within several minutes. The peak effect occurs about 30 minutes after smoking and the high usually lasts for about 2 hours (Goldberg, 2006). When THC is eaten, it is absorbed at a much slower rate, with effects occurring in about 90 minutes to a couple of hours and lasting up to 12 hours. Much of orally ingested THC is metabolized in the liver, with very little reaching the brain (Goldberg, 2006; Mosher & Akins, 2007). THC may remain in the body of a heavy user for 2 or 3 weeks, and if given a drug test, a casual user may test positive 3 days after marijuana use (Goldberg, 2006). The potency of marijuana has greatly increased in the last 40 years, and this increase in potency is attributed mostly to the discovery and implementation of improved growing conditions.

Historical Trends of Consumption

The use of the cannabis plant is mentioned in Chinese writings as early as 2737 BC, and in Muslim writings as early as AD 1000. The use of marijuana spread to Europe in the 19th century when French soldiers brought hashish home from Egypt, historically to be used for medical purposes, most typically as a pain reliever (Ksir, Hart, & Ray, 2008). Additionally, hemp fibers were used for rope and clothing; when America declared independence, about 90 percent of all clothes in the nation were made from hemp (Gahlinger, 2001).

Marijuana did not become popular as a drug in the United States, until the late 1920s, though there were some reports of Mexican immigrants using it in the early 1920s. In fact, the Mexican laborers are actually thought to be the first to call cannabis marijuana and to smoke the leafs. (Ksir, Hart, & Ray, 2008). Marijuana use came to be associated with minority ethnic groups, artists (specifically jazz musicians), and crime, and by 1936, all states had laws regulating its use and sale. Increasing unsubstantiated reports were published in newspapers across the country that linked marijuana use with crime and violence. A 1936 movie entitled *Reefer Madness* added to public hysteria, and the result was an increasing fear of the drug. This fear was eventually transferred to other drugs.

For many years, however, marijuana has been the most widely used drug in the United States, and it is the third most recreationally used drug following tobacco and alcohol. Presently there are 14.5 million American marijuana users (i.e., individuals who have used marijuana within the past 30 days), which represents 6.1 percent of the American population 12 years of age and older (globally, 4 percent of the population uses marijuana). Approximately 20 million individuals have used marijuana in the last year, with 25 percent of these individuals using it upwards of once per week (Ksir, Hart, & Ray, 2008). Marijuana is a drug that is very easy to obtain, with 78 percent of high school students reporting that it is available at their school (Ksir, Hart, & Ray, 2008). Easy availability notwithstanding, organizations such as Partnership for a Drug Free America

The Origins of 420

420 is a concept that has various meanings for marijuana users, but it is most often seen as a term used to express collective identity. "420" is printed on drug paraphernalia and t-shirts, is mentioned in printed magazines such as *High Times*, and is included in song lyrics. 420 is an international code used as a symbol for marijuana use and the marijuana subculture. Only insiders (users) typically understand its significance. (For example, it is used in apartment advertisements or singles advertisements to express that marijuana use is accepted (e.g., "420 friendly").) Consequently, April 20 (4/20) at 4:20 pm has become the "pot-smokers holiday." Additionally, the time 4:20 pm is considered a good time of day to "take a break" and smoke marijuana.

Origins of this term are unclear. Many believe it was started by the "Waldo Family," a group of high school students from San Rafael, California, who would gather at 4:20 pm to smoke marijuana. Steve Waldo, a student, would use the expression "420 Louie" to remind other students to join them. This group was then apparently popularized by fans of the Grateful Dead.

Another theory of the origin of 420 is that it was the code used by Los Angeles police officers to communicate marijuana smoking in progress. 420 is also rumored to be the address of the Grateful Dead's home.

Among users, what is found to be most important is not necessarily the actual origin of the term, but the collective feeling of community it evokes, and the conversations the term spurs among insiders regarding the history and sociology of marijuana use.

have turned their attention to other illicit substances and have not created an anti-marijuana public service announcement since 2005. This is primarily due to statistics that show a decline in marijuana use among teenagers and a growing fear that they are using prescription drugs at an increased rate. Marijuana use peaked in the United States between the 1960s and 1970s, and steadily declined thereafter through the early 1990s, peaking again in the late 1990s. A recent Monitoring the Future (MTF) study shows that marijuana use among youth has been declining for a decade, and among youth who have used in the past 30 days, use has declined 25 percent since 2001 ("Pot No Longer Focus of Anti-Drug Campaigns," 2009). Combining youth with the adult population and examining lifetime use rates, one-third of all Americans have experimented with marijuana at some point in their life (Ksir, Hart, & Ray, 2008).

A user does not develop a physical dependence on marijuana, however, regular, significant use can result in a tolerance to marijuana's cognitive effects (Ksir, Hart, & Ray, 2008). Research does suggest that users can become psychologically dependent on marijuana: "the perceived need for the drug is believed to be responsible for compulsive use and dependence" (Goldberg, 2006, p. 246). The *Diagnostic and Statistical Manual for Mental Disorders (DSM)* does not recognize withdrawal from marijuana; however, some clinical studies have found that mild withdrawal symptoms are sometimes present in individuals who cease use after several consecutive days of regular use. These withdrawal symptoms include negative mood, disturbed sleep, lowered food intake, and possibly aggressiveness which lasts between 4 and 12 days (Mosher & Akins, 2007). If an individual consumes an excessive amount of marijuana orally, he or she will recover within several hours without medical attention: No human has ever died from a marijuana overdose and the lethal dose for humans has not yet been officially established (Ksir, Hart, & Ray, 2008).

Despite its widespread use, there are approximately 700,000 people arrested every year for marijuana use in the United States, which amounts to one individual every 45 seconds (Ksir, Hart, & Ray, 2008). One of the reasons marijuana is prosecuted by the criminal justice system is because it is considered by many to be a gateway drug, meaning individuals who use marijuana are more likely to progress to using more serious illicit drugs. Research shows that:

> even in heaviest usage marijuana does not lead to heroin or any other drug. Many junkies smoked marijuana before they tried opiates, but few marijuana users take narcotics. Many junkies also drank alcohol heavily before they discovered heroin, sometimes at a very young ages, yet no one argues that alcohol leads to heroin. The reason, of course, is that alcohol enjoys general social approval, while marijuana is a "bad" drug and so invites false attributes of causality (Weil & Rosen, 1998, p. 120).

As elaborated in greater detail in Chapter Two, the "gateway hypothesis," therefore, has more to do with media representation than factual evidence.

Benefits/Consequences

Individuals use cannabis recreationally for the euphoria it creates, and some indicate that it improves creativity and appreciation of art (Ksir, Hart, & Ray, 2008). As well, many users experience increased relaxation, which can lead to sleepiness. There are, however, other established benefits of cannabis. In 1972, it was determined that marijuana is successful in treating glaucoma, as it reduces the pressure in one's eye, and in 1975, research revealed that THC decreased nausea in cancer patients receiving chemotherapy and elevated patients' appetites, thereby facilitating weight gain. It can also be used by AIDS patients to rouse their appetite (Ksir, Hart, & Ray, 2008). By 2007, thirteen states (Alaska, California, Colorado, Hawaii, Maine, Michigan, Montana, Nevada, New Mexico, Oregon, Rhone Island, Vermont, and Washington) had passed legislation allowing individuals to use marijuana for medical reasons as long as they had permission from their physicians. Issues surrounding the medicinal use of marijuana are not without controversy and will be elaborated in Chapter Fourteen in a larger discussion of legalization of drugs.

Negative consequences of cannabis use include reddening of the eyes, dry mouth and throat, mild paranoia, hallucinations, and increased appetite. Less-experienced marijuana users typically incur panic, anxiety, and/or paranoid feelings. Marijuana use also slows cognitive performance (Mosher & Akins, 2007). Though studies on the effects on one's ability to drive have yielded inconsistent results, most point to an impairment from marijuana consumption, making it a matter of great concern that between 60 and 80 percent of users admit to sometimes driving while high (Liska, 2004). Use of cannabis is associated with short-term memory disruption called **temporal disintegration** in which the ability to remember and coordinate information is lost. For example, individuals under the influence may stop speaking mid-sentence because they forgot what they were going to say. Also observed in individuals who use marijuana is **amotivational syndrome,** which is characteristic of changes in lifestyle and personality, and includes decreases in motivation and ambition. Individuals with amotivational syndrome are unlikely to accomplish conventional goals, including educational accomplishment. Of greater concern, particularly in the eastern United States, is the practice of adding other illicit drugs (such as cocaine or PCP) to joints, which may cause a wealth of negative side effects depending on the types of drugs added. It has been found recently that embalming fluid (a street name of PCP) is also frequently added to marijuana, which produces immediate psychiatric effects following consumption.

OPIATES

The term "opiates" (also referred to as "opioids" or "narcotic analgesics") refers to a group of drugs (including both synthetic and natural substances) that contain chemical properties resembling opium, or one of its active ingredients, that are typically used for the reduction of pain and to induce sleep. Technically, **opiates** are naturally occurring from the opium poppy plant and are used in manufacturing the depressants morphine, codeine, and heroin; whereas **opioids** are synthetic drugs with characteristics of opiates (Gahlinger, 2001). For this section, however, opiates will refer to both natural and synthetic substances.

Opium is a natural drug that comes from the sap of the poppy plant, which originated in Asia. Though there are 250 species of poppies, only 2 of these produce opium, the active ingredients in which are morphine and codeine. **Heroin** is a semi-synthetic drug made by combining vinegar with morphine. It is available as a powder or tar, which is injected, snorted, or smoked, and is almost 10 times more potent than morphine. Popular synthetic opiates include Demerol (which is similar to morphine), methadone, and oxycodone (sold legally with a prescription as Percocet or Percodan and sold illegally on the street as OxyContin) (Gahlinger, 2001; Ksir, Hart, & Ray, 2008). Opiates work by affecting opioid receptors in the brain. The body produces natural opioids known as endorphins, most of which are produced and secreted by the pituitary gland to produce a natural feeling of well-being. Opiates block pain messages from areas like the spinal cord that communicate them to the brain.

Historical Trends of Consumption

The use of the opium poppy for medical and recreational purposes among ancient Middle Eastern populations has been documented since 5000 BC. As Islam spread, opium use was brought to India and China by traders, with the Chinese being the first to smoke opium. Opium was traded in Europe as well, and became popular initially as a medicine, but then became available to the general public. Morphine became available in the 19th century, but was not as widely available as opium as it was used strictly for medical purposes: In fact, morphine was the first drug ever to be extracted from a plant (Gahlinger, 2001). The first large-scale war over a drug (other than alcohol) was the first Opium War (1839–1842), fought in China over trade in opium, with a second war following in 1856 (Abadinsky, 2008). The first U.S. legislation to control opium was passed in 1868, when opium addiction started to become a social problem in the United States. Opium was consumed at a greater rate in the United States than in European countries, and was available mostly as patent medicines. Morphine was also used heavily by Civil War soldiers to treat battlefield injuries (Abadinsky, 2008; Gahlinger, 2001; Hanson, Venturelli, & Fleckenstein, 2006). Attitudes started to change in the mid-1870s when the economy started to take a downturn and employment started to rise. Cities started to prohibit opium dens "not because of health concerns as such, but because it was believed that the drug stimulated coolies into working harder than non-smoking whites" (Latimer & Goldberg, 1981, p. 208). Eventually the United States needed to ally with China against the Japanese and tariffs were then added to the opium that was brought into the United States. All that ended, however, in 1914, when the Harrison Act became law and opium use became illegal. Marketed in the early 1900s as being more effective than morphine and causing less nausea and vomiting, heroin was claimed by the Bayer Company to be nonaddictive. By the early 1920s, however, it was associated with crime, and in 1924, it was banned in the United States. As with morphine among the military, about 10 to 15 percent of U.S. soldiers used heroin during the Vietnam War (Gahlinger, 2001; Hanson, Venturelli, & Fleckenstein 2006; Ksir, Hart, & Ray, 2008).

In the United States, 1.26 million individuals abuse opiates monthly, and 2.45 million Americans have tried heroin. Heroin users typically used injectable heroin through the 1980s, after which the use declined, becoming popular again in the 1990s. When injected, heroin's effects occur in approximately 10 seconds (Gahlinger, 2001). In the 1990s, however, heroin was typically snorted or smoked due to the fear among users of acquiring HIV/AIDS. These methods of consumption typically take about 15 minutes to take effect. Opiates remain in a user's system for approximately 4 days (Gahlinger, 2001). Among 500,000 to 1 million American heroin addicts, about 100,000 receive methadone maintenance treatment from the approximately 800 methadone clinics in operation in the United States. Most opiate abuse occurs with prescribed opiates, and codeine, morphine, and oxycodone are all available by prescription. Forty-five percent of the world's legal (medical) opiate supply is consumed in the United States (Goldberg, 2006; Ksir, Hart, & Ray, 2008). Legally available oxycodone (given with a prescription as Percocet or Percodan) provides long-term pain relief, and is referred to on the street as "hillbilly heroin," as it was first used in rural areas of America. Its abuse is most common in rural Maine, Pennsylvania, Virginia, West Virginia, and Kentucky, and among a population that experiences high unemployment and high rates of chronic illness (Mosher & Akins, 2007). All statistics suggest, however, that although heroin receives quite a bit of publicity, about 98 percent of the American population have never tried the drug, and the use rates for other opiates are quite low as well (Ksir, Hart, & Ray, 2008).

Benefits/Consequences

One benefit of opiates is the treatment and management of pain. The effects of opiates like morphine are experienced differently by people who have persistent pain, with these individuals not normally experiencing the "high" described by users who have no pain. For recreational users, benefits include euphoria, muscle relaxation, and a sense of relief. One user describes a heroin high:

> This is the key to a heroin high. Nothing matters . . . when one is high on smack, one looks at the outside world and only has one thought: Who . . . (cares)? You feel as if you've been wrapped in the most pleasing, warm, and comfortable blanket in the world. At high doses, you fall in and out of consciousness, and getting this "nod" is what the veteran user prays for every time he shoots up: to sleep the sleep of angels is the ultimate goal of the heroin addict (Drugs, Youth & the Internet, 2002, p. 23).

Another benefit is that some artists and authors who have used opium claim it induces increased sensitivity and creativity (Gahlinger, 2001). Users take the drug for the sense of euphoria and the feeling of relaxation it induces. Overall, opiates have very few long-term health consequences and as such, many opiate addicts can actually lead normal and even very successful lives. Many famous and accomplished individuals, including Benjamin Franklin, have been opiate addicts.

There are, however, drawbacks to opiate use. Aside from the health drawbacks, one potential consequence of use is the cost: For example, a heroin habit costs between $30 and $100 per day, compelling many users to alter other aspects of their life or even to resort to illegal behavior

Methadone Maintenance: The Long and Short of It

Methadone is used to treat heroin addiction because it prevents heroin withdrawal symptoms. It is administered orally and its effects last up to 24 hours. Because of this, it is administered in a clinic setting and therefore not given to addicts to be used on their own. Further, methadone is a heroin antagonist, meaning those receiving methadone will not experience a euphoric high should they simultaneously use heroin. Methadone is not an effective treatment on its own and should always be paired with psychological treatment. Methadone maintenance has been shown to reduce illness and death related to drug use, crime, as well as the transmission of HIV/AIDS. Some individuals remain on methadone treatment indefinitely; others are slowly weaned off methadone, however, there is an 80 to 90 percent relapse rate among those weaned (Gahlinger, 2001).

in order to pay for this habit (Ksir, Hart, & Ray, 2008). The mild negative side effects typically are nausea and vomiting, profuse sweating, constricted pupils, constipation, and a decrease in sex hormone production. Abuse of opiates can also result in psychiatric symptoms, high doses can result in convulsions, or a comatose state with depressed breathing that typically causes death. Health consequences resulting from heroin use include constipation and increased susceptibility to cancer. Because heroin is usually injected intravenously, the user also incurs the risk of acquiring HIV and hepatitis. Additionally, the purity of heroin can vary from 0 to 99 percent, increasing dramatically the risk of accidental overdose and death (Gahlinger, 2001; Hanson, Venturelli, & Fleckenstein, 2006; Ksir, Hart, & Ray, 2008).

Both physical and psychological opiate dependence occurs with continued use, with perhaps the psychological dependence being the most difficult to address (Ksir, Hart, & Ray, 2008). Withdrawal symptoms appear within 24 and 72 hours and can last up to 10 days. Withdrawal symptoms include teary eyes, runny nose, sweating, yawning, irritability, muscle cramps, insomnia (which can last for days), vomiting, and diarrhea (resulting from constipation while on the drugs). Tolerance to opiates develops, however; after a period of nonuse, individuals can actually lose their tolerance. Overdose or death frequently results when individuals use the drug in large amounts after a period of nonuse, at which point their tolerance has been lost (Gahlinger, 2001; Ksir, Hart, & Ray, 2008).

HALLUCINOGENS/PSYCHEDELICS

Hallucinogens, also known as psychedelics, phantastica, and psychotomimetics (meaning it mimics psychosis), is a complex group of drugs consisting of over ninety naturally occurring plants and even more synthetic substances that produce a variety of consciousness-altering effects. These drugs produce sensory disturbances, and some even cause schizophrenia-like psychosis (Mosher & Akins, 2007). Each hallucinogen produces different effects; however, many side effects appear to be similar to natural psychosis. Not all hallucinogens cause hallucinations per se, making the name of this group of drugs somewhat misleading.

There are four general types of hallucinogens:

- Serotonergic hallucinogens, which include lysergic acid diethylamide (LSD), psilocybin (found in some mushrooms) and mescaline (peyote cactus). Effects include hallucinations and other forms of altered consciousness. These drugs affect serotonin transmission within the brain, which affects an individual's mood.
- Methylated amphetamines, which includes MDA and MDMA (ecstasy) and produces little or no sensory effects but alters mood and consciousness.
- Anticholinergic hallucinogens, which include naturally occurring substances such as atropine and scopolamine found in plants. These drugs act on cholinergic synapses in the brain and put users in a trancelike daze, and individuals come off these drugs with little or no memory of this daze.
- Dissociative anesthetics include phencyclidine (PCP) and ketamine which produce effects similar to surgical anesthetics, yet the user remains semiconscious. These drugs act on a receptor in the brain that affects glutamate, a neurotransmitter (Liska, 2004).

Hallucinogenic plants were first discovered by early Central and South Americans, and Africans. Many of these plants were considered sacred and used in religious and cultural ceremonies. The use of hallucinogens in the United States and in European countries did not become popular until the 1960s. The most widely known hallucinogens are ecstasy, LSD, PCP, psilocybin (found in mushrooms), and peyote (mescaline).

LSD

LSD (lysergic acid diethylamide) was created by Albert Hoffman in Switzerland in 1938 as a medical drug. Animal testing proved commercially fruitless, and the drug was put aside until 1943 when Hoffman gave the drug a second look. While working, he accidentally spilled some of the substance on his hand and experienced a dreamlike high. Further tests were completed, and LSD was distributed to psychologists and psychiatrists, who were urged to prescribe the drug in combination with psychotherapy (Mosher & Akins, 2007).

Serotonergic hallucinogens, such as LSD, mimic natural serotonin, and thereby activate serotonin receptors within the brain. LSD is extremely potent, possibly the most potent psychoactive drug known: Two gallons of LSD would be enough to make the entire U.S. population trip. LSD is usually consumed orally in the form of a gel, a tablet, or from a paper blotter. LSD is rapidly absorbed, and its effects become apparent between 20 and 60 minutes following consumption. The high typically lasts between 8 and 12 hours, and can be detected in urine for up to 72 hours following use. Effects on the user include pupil dilation; increased temperature and sweating; increased heart rate and blood pressure; visual and auditory hallucinations; depersonalization, where users can "step outside" of themselves; distortion of time; and a greater ability to empathize (Gahlinger, 2001; Liska, 2004; Mosher & Akins, 2007). Psychological reactions vary from person to person, but generally intensify whatever mood an individual is in before taking the drug.

Street Terms for Hallucinogens

- acid
- blotter acid
- window pane
- dots
- mellow yellow
- lucy in the sky with diamonds
- Alice
- Bart Simpsons
- blue heavens
- Chinese dragons

> Psychedelics do not necessarily produce any particular mood or state of mind. They act as intensifiers of experience. If you take them when you are elated, they make you superelated. If you take them when you are depressed, they make you superdepressed. If you take them with a friend you feel totally comfortable with, they may deepen your friendship. If you take them with someone you feel uncomfortable with, they may intensify that discomfort to an unbearable degree (Weil & Rosen, 1998, p. 110).

As such, the hallucinogens can have very unpredictable effects, depending on how much of the drug was consumed, an individual's mood, their expectations, as well as the surrounding environment.

Historically, LSD has been used for a variety of purposes. The U.S. military began experimenting with LSD in the late 1940s, exploring it as a brainwashing substance and possible chemical weapon. Beginning in the 1950s, the CIA launched a research program called MK-ULTRA in which they administered LSD into the food/beverages of unaware subjects, and then spied on their subsequent activities and behaviors (including their sexual actions). The U.S. Army also conducted research studies from 1956 through 1967, in which LSD was administered to at least 585 soldiers and 900 civilians. Generally, those who are unaware that they have been given LSD may experience extreme negative consequences, including believing that they are in fact going crazy. For example, biochemist Frank Olson suffered an acute panic attack and committed suicide 2 weeks after the CIA secretly put LSD in his drink (his family was compensated $750,000 by the government for his death) (Hanson, Venturelli, & Fleckenstein, 2006; Ksir, Hart, & Ray, 2008; Mosher & Akins, 2007). LSD and other LSD-like hallucinogens have also been used psychotherapeutically in the past, though these uses are no longer accepted. Additionally, LSD was previously used in the United States to treat alcoholism, and it has been used as an effective painkiller for terminal cancer patients.

Among the general population, LSD was popularized in America in the 1960s by Timothy Leary, a former Harvard psychologist, who started a religion called the League of Spiritual Discovery in which the use of LSD was a sacrament. LSD was primarily popular among individuals in the hippie subculture and was promoted by many musical artists at the time (including the Grateful Dead, Jimi Hendrix, and the Beatles). After its initial explosion in the 1960s, LSD use declined throughout the 1970s and 1980s, then spiked once more (as did other hallucinogenic drugs) in the 1990s. The peak year was 1996, at which time almost 9 percent of high school seniors reported using LSD within the past year. Use has since declined: In 2005, just under 2 percent of high school seniors reported LSD use within the past year. In total, approximately 15 million Americans have used LSD at least once in their lives (Goldberg, 2006).

LSD does not result in physical dependence, and there are no withdrawal symptoms that result from use. However, tolerance develops quickly with LSD and repeated daily doses are no longer effective after 3 or 4 days. As well, cross-tolerance exists among LSD, mescaline, and other serotonergic hallucinogens (Ksir, Hart, & Ray, 2008). Additionally, even after an individual stops use, there may be consequences: Approximately 30 to 60 percent of all heavy LSD users experience flashbacks to hallucinogenic trips that occurred possibly years before (termed **hallucinogen persisting perception disorder**) (Ksir, Hart, & Ray, 2008). Other negative side effects are "bad trips," characterized by acute paranoia and induction of a psychotic state, which may possibly lead to self-harm, harm to others, and long-term psychiatric illness or suicide.

Street Terms for Psilocybin

- Alice
- boomers
- magic mushrooms
- musk
- shrooms

Psilocybin

Like LSD, **psilocybin** is a serotonergic hallucinogen which mimics natural serotonin, and thereby activates serotonin receptors within the brain. More commonly referred to as "magic mushrooms" or "shrooms," there are about one hundred mushroom species containing psilocybin that grow in the United States, Mexico, and Europe. Historically, mushrooms containing psilocybin were used by the Aztecs in ritual as far back as 1000 BC (Gahlinger, 2001). In the late 1950s, LSD creator Albert Hofmann isolated the psychedelic property of these mushrooms, and their use increased on college campuses in the early 1960s until LSD became more popular (Goldberg, 2006). Synthetic psilocybin was also manufactured by pharmaceutical companies during the late 1950s and early 1960s for psychiatric use until it was outlawed in 1965 (Gahlinger, 2001). Mushrooms containing psilocybin are eaten whole, or a brew/beverage such as a tea is created with the mushrooms. Potency of psilocybin is far less than LSD (about 1 percent as potent), and its effects begin within 30 minutes of consumption and last between 4 and 6 hours (Mosher & Akins, 2007). Effects include pupil dilation, increased temperature and sweating, increased heart rate and blood pressure, visual and auditory hallucinations, as well as feelings of relaxation and euphoria (Liska, 2004; Mosher & Akins, 2007). As described by one user:

> The first time I shroomed everything looked like it was made of plastic, like everything could be folded up or something. Whatever somebody told me, I would believe it to be true. Like if I was drinking a beer and someone told me it was tequila, I would taste tequila (Hanson, Venturelli, & Fleckenstein, 2006, p. 367).

A more religiously interpreted description is provided below:

> It permits you to see . . . vistas beyond the horizons of this life, to travel backwards and forwards in time, to enter other planes of existence, even (as the Indians say), to know God . . . Not unnaturally what is happening to you seems freighted with significance, beside which the humdrum of everyday life seems trivial. All these things you see with an immediacy of vision that leads you to say to yourself, "Now I am seeing for the first time, seeing direct, without the intervention of mortal eyes" (Wasson, 1963, pp. 39–40, as cited in Mosher & Akins, 2007, p. 106).

When consumed in larger doses, time is distorted, the user can be easily distracted as well as open to suggestion, as his or her ability to concentrate is impaired (Goldberg, 2006). As with LSD, psychological effects vary by person, depending upon the dose, his or her mood, expectation, and the environment. The greatest dangers from the use of magic mushrooms are mistaking poisonous mushrooms for ones with psilocybin, or purchasing mushrooms on the black market and instead receiving another drug, most typically LSD or PCP (Gahlinger, 2001). Statistics regarding current use of psilocybin are lacking, perhaps due to the difficulty in obtaining mushrooms as compared to other illicit substances. In terms of physical danger, a fatal overdose of psilocybin has never been reported (Goldberg, 2006).

Street Terms for Peyote

- cactus
- dry whiskey
- half moon
- hikuri

Peyote

Peyote is a cactus that grows in northern Mexico and Texas. The entire cactus is psychoactive; however, the most powerful psychoactive ingredient is called mescaline and is found in the top of the plant. The use of peyote within the Native American Church (NAC) for religious purposes is protected by the First and Fourteenth Amendments. The consumption of peyote buttons is actually considered a sacrament among individuals in the NAC. Peyote "buttons" have been used by those indigenous to North America for thousands of years, but were banned by the Spanish as the "work of the Devil" in 1620 (Mosher & Akins, 2007). Use continued among the natives and a very small number of recreational users (Ksir, Hart, & Ray, 2008). It is consumed orally in the form of cactus buttons, with many users consuming between five and ten buttons (containing a total of up to 800 mg of mescaline). The effects begin 30 to 120 minutes after consumption and last between 10 and 14 hours and are similar to LSD and psilocybin; they include euphoria, visual and auditory hallucinations, pupil dilation, and increased pulse (Ksir, Hart, & Ray, 2008). Unlike the other two substances, however, peyote buttons frequently result in nausea and vomiting. One user reports "I ate one but three days ago, was violently sick for twenty-four hours" (Ksir, Hart, & Ray, 2008, p. 351). Tolerance develops quickly with the use of peyote, and cross-tolerance exists among LSD, mescaline, and other serotonergic hallucinogens. In terms of withdrawal, only mild symptoms which include fatigue and anxiety are produced. As with psilocybin, black market availability of peyote is low compared to other illicit substances; what is sold is most typically a hallucinogen other than peyote (Hanson, Venturelli, & Fleckenstein, 2006). There is a lack of statistics regarding the use of peyote.

Street Terms for Ecstasy

- MDMA
- ecstasy
- XTC
- E
- X
- beans
- Adams
- hug drug
- disco biscuit
- go
- Adam
- hug
- love drug

Ecstasy

The club/rave scene began in Europe in the 1980s, and subsequently gained extreme popularity in the United States in the 1990s. Rave subculture is characterized by all-night parties at clubs or empty/abandoned buildings or fields, with light shows, "techno" music, and illicit drug use. Club drugs typically include ecstasy, methamphetamine, Ritalin, ketamine, LSD, or GHB (gamma-Hydroxybutric acid). Methylenedioxyamphetamine (MDMA) is one of 200 drugs from the methylenedioxyamphetamine (MDA) group. The term **"ecstasy"** is typically used to refer to all drugs belonging to the MDA family.

MDMA is a designer synthetic drug, which bears the street names ecstasy (or XTC) and the "love drug." Many considered it to be the club/rave drug of choice, though research reveals that LSD is actually used more frequently at parties (Mosher & Akins, 2007). Though the number of raves has declined since the late 1990s, the popularity of ecstasy has continued to increase. Ninety percent of the world's supply of MDMA is manufactured in the Netherlands and Belgium, and then distributed worldwide by Israeli organized crime groups. Approximately 2 million pills are trafficked weekly from Europe to the United States, with a dose of ecstasy selling for between $10 and $20 (Hanson, Venturelli, & Fleckenstein, 2006). Approximately 10,000 doses of MDMA were consumed in 1976 in the entire United States, but by 1985, it was estimated that 30,000 doses were consumed in one major U.S. city alone per month. By 2001, almost 12 percent of high school seniors reported having tried ecstasy; however, use rates have declined since that time. Overall, it is estimated that approximately 8 million people have tried ecstasy (Goldberg, 2006). MDMA was not made illegal until 1985 and in 2003 The RAVE Act (Reducing America's Vulnerability to Ecstasy) was passed, which makes it illegal to attain a building for the purpose of consuming drugs. Under the RAVE Act, the owners do not necessarily have to be involved with raves or the sale of illicit drugs to be subject to the harsh punishments provided.

Ecstasy is a synthetic drug available on the street as either a white powder, or in the form of brightly colored tablets sometimes featuring small pictures or symbols. It is typically administered orally, though occasionally it is crushed and snorted. Effects begin about 1 hour after consumption, peak at about 1.5 hours, and last for between 6 and 8 hours (Hanson, Venturelli, & Fleckenstein, 2006). MDMA works by releasing serotonin and dopamine. Physical effects include pupil dilation, grinding of the teeth, inability to sleep, loss of appetite, and increased blood pressure, heart rate, temperature, and muscle tension. In most users MDMA produces delightful psychological effects that include euphoria characterized by psychological and emotional warmth, increased closeness with others, more intensely experienced physical sensations, and increased emotionality and empathy—this is how the drug got its street name ecstasy (Ksir, Hart, & Ray, 2008; Mosher & Akins, 2007). It is a unique drug that is sometimes referred to as a "hallucinogenic amphetamine" because it has properties similar to both amphetamines and mescaline (Valentine, 2002). MDMA was created in 1912 as an appetite suppressant, though it is not used for this purpose anymore. It is currently being studied to determine if it has any medical value in treating posttraumatic stress disorder and anxiety in cancer patients. MDMA is also thought to facilitate communication, and as such it is advocated by some as a potential psychotherapeutic tool. Interestingly, it was explored by the CIA in the 1940s as a truth drug (Gahlinger, 2001; Mosher & Akins, 2007).

There are, however, many potential negative consequences to ecstasy use. In 2000, there were over 4,000 emergency room admissions related to MDMA use: MDMA can cause dehydration, heat exhaustion/heatstroke, heart attacks, seizures, strokes, and kidney failure. Toxic doses do not necessarily have to be large; many have died after taking low doses. Many negative drug effects are due to increased body temperature, which is intensified by increased physical activity (e.g., dancing) and high environmental temperatures (e.g., in small, densely populated clubs). As well, use is associated with sexual risk-taking behaviors (Goldberg, 2006). MDMA use results in withdrawal symptoms including muscle and abdominal pain, increased appetite, chills, lack of energy, and at times depressive feelings and suicidal tendencies (Weil & Rosen, 1998). The risk of potential physical dependence on MDMA is much lower than that of many other drugs; however, it has been noted that some users do use the drug compulsively because of the euphoric effects it produces. Long-term consequences of MDMA use may include brain damage, cognitive defects, depressed mood, insomnia, and memory problems; however, more research is needed on the long-term effects of MDMA use as many individuals studied used more than one illicit substance, making it difficult to separate out the effects of MDMA (Gahlinger, 2001).

PCP

Unlike the previously discussed hallucinogens which produce similar effects of euphoria and in many cases mental clarity, PCP (phencyclidine) users tend to experience mental confusion and a separation from reality (Ksir, Hart, & Ray, 2008). **PCP** is a dissociative anesthetic which acts on a receptor in the brain that affects glutamate (a neurotransmitter) to produce effects similar to surgical anesthetics, yet the user remains semiconscious. PCP was created in 1956 and was historically used as an anesthetic for animals and is still used for this purpose in countries other than the United States.

> Marketed under the name Sernyl, PCP was used originally with humans as an anesthetic. It was considered desirable for surgery, because patients remained awake yet were unable to recall their experiences because of the amnesia that PCP produced. Moreover, it had no adverse effect on circulation, heart rate, or respiration. However it was discontinued by 1965 because of undesirable effects including agitation, delirium, and disorientation. Once the effects wore off, patients became unmanageable, confused, and disassociated from nearby surroundings. PCP later was used in veterinary medicine but has been largely replaced by similar drugs such as ketamine (Goldberg, 2006, p. 270).

Street Terms for PCP

- embalming fluid
- wack
- ozone
- angel dust
- dust
- crystal
- rocket fuel
- loveboat
- zombie dust
- peace pill

PCP became popular as a street drug in the 1970s, and in the 1980s roughly 20 percent of high school students had tried this drug. As of 1978, however, it was illegal to produce PCP. Beginning in the 1990s, use had significantly declined (to less than 1 percent of high school seniors in the preceding 12 months) as its serious effects had been widely publicized (Goldberg, 2006; Hanson, Venturelli, & Fleckenstein, 2006; Ksir, Hart, & Ray, 2008).

PCP takes effect in under 15 minutes when smoked or injected, but it takes effect roughly 2 hours following oral consumption. The high lasts from 4 to 6 hours; however, a user can remain confused for up to 24 hours following consumption (Goldberg, 2006). Users do not develop a tolerance and there are no withdrawal symptoms, though users can experience flashbacks. In PCP users, unlike in users of other hallucinogens, flashbacks are not psychological, but actual chemical reactions that result from drug residue in the body (Gahlinger, 2001). One dose of PCP can result in a positive drug test 2 weeks later, and heavy PCP users test positive for up to 4 weeks after their last use (Gahlinger, 2001). Effects of PCP include rapid eye movement, blurred vision, slurred speech, hyperactivity/aggression or catatonia, and "K-holes" which involve distortions in body perception. These effects typically last several hours, but can last days/weeks. In small doses, users feel relaxed, numb, may depersonalize or have distorted body images, experience slow reaction time, confusion, and sudden mood swings (Goldberg, 2006). Between 50 and 80 percent of PCP users experience bad trips, characterized by paranoia or depression, during which they must be "talked down" or require medical attention and/or physical restraints (Ksir, Hart, & Ray, 2008). Serious adverse side effects include coma, seizures, respiratory failure and death, or psychosis which may persist for months.

Street Terms for Methamphetamine

- speed
- meth
- crystal meth
- chalk
- ice
- crystal
- crank
- tweak
- uppers
- black beauties
- glass
- biker's coffee
- methlies quick
- poor man's cocaine
- chicken feed
- shabu
- stove top
- trash
- co-fast
- yaba
- yellow bam

METHAMPHETAMINE

Psychomotor stimulants (also referred to as uppers, speed, or sympathomimetics) include natural and synthetic substances that produce effects in the body similar to those of adrenaline. These substances are used for both recreational and medical purposes. Amphetamines are synthetic stimulants, which are mixtures of d-amphetamine and l-amphetamine isomers, and were also mentioned in Chapters Five and Six as they can be used to treat ADHD and obesity.

This section will focus specifically on **methamphetamine** (meth), a synthetic drug that can be created using legal substances. Methamphetamine is extremely easy to create and can be done by anyone who possesses a detailed recipe. "With $500 worth of chemicals, laboratory glassware, and a rudimentary knowledge of chemistry, an outlaw chemist can easily produce a pound of methamphetamine worth $20,000 to $30,000" (Abadinsky, 2008, p. 142). Ingredients include many common items, including pseudoephedrine, which is an ingredient of many over-the-counter (OTC) cold medicines. Meth labs pose serious health risks, as they produce toxic waste and noxious fumes. Also, because a lot of meth ingredients are flammable, meth labs also pose a high risk of explosion. Meth is sold illegally in paste, tablet, powder, or crystal form (Gahlinger, 2001).

When snorted or consumed orally, stimulants take action in 10 to 15 minutes, as opposed to 30 seconds when injected intravenously. When crystal meth in particular is smoked, it takes effect in less than 30 seconds. Most stimulants produce an almost immediate rush upon administration, and even though drug levels within the body remain high for some time thereafter (with effects lasting between 4 and 12 hours), users crave more to feel the initial rush again. Subsequent rushes are typically not as satisfying as the first (Gahlinger, 2001; Liska, 2004; Mosher & Akins, 2007).

Stimulants are thought to affect monoamine neurotransmitters within the brain. Specifically they block the reuptake of dopamine, norepinephrine, and serotonin, while also largely increasing the release of dopamine. This produces increased neurotransmitter activity. In the long-term, monoamines become diminished and actually result in a decrease in dopamine, which is why chronic stimulant use causes depression and movement disorders such as Parkinson's Disease (Mosher & Akins, 2007).

Historical Trends of Consumption

Amphetamines were first developed in the 1800s, yet were not explored for medical use until the 1920s. They were first marketed as a nasal spray to treat low blood pressure and asthma. Abuse became widespread, and OTC sale of these drugs was made illegal in 1959. Amphetamines have been used to treat colds, sinus problems, narcolepsy, obesity, and ADHD. The drugs were also used by soldiers during World War II to increase endurance, which resulted in widespread amphetamine abuse following the war. Amphetamines were also given to factory workers to increase productivity after the war. This practice was eventually found to be ineffective due to the effects stimulants have on mood as well as the exhaustion that results when the drugs wear off (Abadinsky, 2008; Gahlinger, 2001).

Methamphetamine was created in Japan in 1919, and was also used widely during World War II. In fact, Hitler was addicted to methamphetamine and reportedly used it 8 times per day. Methamphetamine was used in the 1960s to treat heroin dependence and has also been used to treat obesity, but this drug is no longer used medically due to the very high abuse potential. Although it has been used illicitly in America since before the 1960s, it did not become popular until the 1980s and 1990s (Gahlinger, 2001). During the 1980s and 1990s, meth use was prevalent among working-class white males and within the biker subculture. Indeed, during the 1980s, meth was was distributed primarily by the motorcycle group the Hell's Angels, and the street term "crank" actually originated from this group, as the drug was typically kept in motorcycle crank bags. Meth is now considered to be a club drug and is more popular among young adults, and next to marijuana, it is the most-used drug across the globe (Abadinsky, 2008). Most meth users are white individuals between 25 and 35 years of age, and while usage is distributed almost equally between men and women, females make up a large portion of patients receiving treatment for meth dependence. As of 2003, just over 12 million Americans admitted to trying meth at least once in their life (Goldberg, 2006).

Benefits/Consequences

The initial rush felt by stimulant users when methamphetamines are first administered is comparable to an orgasm. This euphoric feeling is what makes these drugs so appealing. One dealer described the appeal of meth this way: "At first we give it away. Then the addicts will do anything to get more" (Reding, 2009, p. 7). Moderate doses of stimulants produce mood elevation and euphoria, increased sociability, talkativeness, alertness, and arousal. As well, strength and endurance are increased. Some individuals use stimulants because they reportedly enhance sexual activity (Goldberg, 2006; Ksir, Hart, & Ray, 2008).

Negative consequences include several days without eating or sleeping, as these drugs decrease appetite and prevent sleep. Additionally, stimulants increase blood pressure, heart rate, blood flow to the brain, and body temperature, and cause sweating and pupil dilation. The effects of meth are most severe when the drug is administered intravenously. When methamphetamine and amphetamines are taken in large doses, users may develop psychotic symptoms including paranoid delusions known as "speed bugs" under which users believe there are bugs crawling under their skin and they scratch compulsively to try to get the bugs out. The term for these symptoms is "stimulant psychosis." Compulsive behavior, such as body rocking, also results. Meth use results in tooth decay and tooth loss (termed "meth mouth") and brain damage that may be permanent. Research has yet to determine if abstinence helps to return normal brain function. Other effects include respiratory problems and anorexia, hallucinations, and irritability (Abadinsky, 2008; Mosher & Akins, 2007). Death from amphetamine overuse is rare. However, the phrase "speed kills" does hold some validity as stimulant psychosis often leads to violence. High doses of methamphetamine can induce seizures, convulsions, and cardiovascular collapse. If immediate medical attention is not received, overdose can result in permanent brain damage or death (Abadinsky, 2008; Goldberg, 2006; Ksir, Hart, & Ray, 2008).

Amphetamines have a high potential for abuse and meth use has resulted in more emergency room visits and deaths than any other club drug. Acute tolerance results during extensive use, but typically dissipates within a day. Users continue to take amphetamines multiple times chasing their initial high, however each subsequent time the drug is used the high has a lesser effect. Chronic tolerance also builds, resulting in the need for extremely high doses. Although withdrawal symptoms are not as severe as with other drugs, use does result in physical as well as psychological dependence. Withdrawal symptoms generally consist of a let down following the high, which includes depression, lethargy, insomnia, and decreased appetite. The depression can be severe enough to result in suicidal ideation or actual suicide attempts (Abadinsky, 2008; Goldberg, 2006; Ksir, Hart, & Ray, 2008; Liska, 2004).

Sociological and Legal Issues

The number of meth labs seized in the United States increased dramatically in the 1980s, from 88 in 1981 to 652 in 1989. However, the numbers then decreased in the early 1990s, only to rise again. This temporary drop in seizures is thought to be due to the passage of the Chemical Diversion and Trafficking Act of 1988, which put a lot of the chemicals (including phenyl-2-propanone) needed to make meth under the control of the federal government. However, newer recipes were created for meth which included, for example, cold medicines in the mid- to late 1990s. This resulted in a significant rise in the number of labs targeted: For example, the DEA's Cleanup Program was responsible for cleaning up 446 meth labs in 1991, compared to 10,100 in 2004, with the major increase beginning in the mid-1990s (Drug Enforcement Administration [DEA], 2005). The DEA began funding state and local cleanup of meth labs in 1998. Figure 7-1 reflects the number of cleanups funded by the DEA by state in 2004. This figure does not, however, reflect cleanups that were funded by state or local law enforcement. The states of California, Washington, Missouri, and Kentucky specifically report high levels of meth lab cleanups funded by state and local resources (DEA, 2005).

The Comprehensive Methamphetamine Control Act was passed in 1996 to regulate the large-scale manufacture and sale of meth, which resulted in the creation of smaller "kitchen" meth labs, which are much more difficult for law enforcement personnel to detect and control.

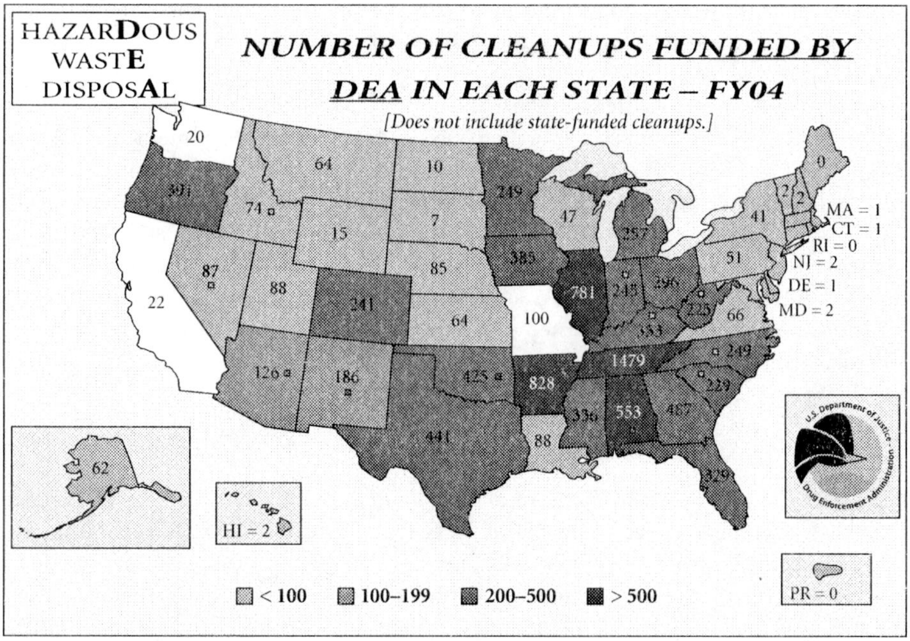

FIGURE 7-1 Number of Cleanups Funded by DEA in Each State in 2004 (not including state-funded cleanups)

Source: Drug Enforcement Administration, 2005.

> Labs could be anything from a house with a fairly complex setup in the basement to a guy and his wife single-batching in a Johnny on the Spot behind the dugout at the Sports Complex. No matter where the labs were, though the . . . police were exposed to the toxic waste and the harmful fumes while wearing nothing more than their regular uniforms. As recently as the late 1990s, . . . the police [in some towns], unsure of what to do, let labs burn. Other times, knowing how much it would cost to clean them up, the police burned the labs themselves. Anecdotally across the nation, cancer rates among first-responders to meth disasters have been climbing since the 1980s. Bill Ruzzamenti, a former DEA agent and the current director of the Central Valley High Intensity Drug Trafficking Area (HIDTA) in California, likes to tell the story of how he smelled so bad after dismantling superlabs in San Diego during the 1990s that his wife would have to hose him down in the garage and burn his clothes. Still, said Ruzzamenti, the stench of ether and what smelled like cat urine would be so thoroughly soaked into his hands that they'd have to throw their phone away each month: the receiver and keypad stunk too bad to keep using (Reding, 2009, pp. 130–131).

The result was the DEA and the Environmental Protection Agency collaborating in the early 2000s to create standardized protocol for law enforcement in charge of dismantling meth labs, no matter how big or small.

> The wastes found at a laboratory site may weigh from a few pounds to several tons. Chemicals and wastes include solvents, reagents, precursors, by-products, and the drug products themselves. Many of these wastes are reactive, explosive, flammable,

> corrosive, and/or toxic. On rare occasions, low level radioactive material has been seized at a clandestine drug laboratory (DEA, 2005, p. 15).

The risks of cleanup are therefore both acute and chronic, which illustrates the need for specialized training for law enforcement in charge of meth lab cleanup. Production of meth additionally poses significant environmental hazards as meth producers contaminate the local environment by dumping chemical wastes into water sources or burying it (Abadinsky, 2008). In an effort to restrict the sale of products that can be used to create meth in such kitchen labs, photo identification is now required to purchase many cold medicines that contain pseudoephedrine, a common ingredient of meth. This effort has been successful in curtailing the private manufacture of meth, but now users once again have returned to relying on the illegal trafficking of purer and higher quality meth from Central America.

COCAINE

Cocaine is an illicit stimulant drug derived from a natural substance (the coca leaf). Cocaine is available as "street cocaine," which is white powder that can be snorted or injected intravenously. Freebasing cocaine is also popular, which is a method in which cocaine is heated and the fumes are inhaled. **Crack**, another form of cocaine made by dissolving base cocaine in alkaline solution (i.e., baking soda), is also smoked. Cocaine is derived from the coca bush/tree which grows in the Andean regions in Bolivia, Peru, and Ecuador. Coca paste is made when the leafs are mashed in alkali. It is then made into cocaine, or the coca paste can be consumed as is by adding it to tobacco or marijuana and smoking it (Gahlinger, 2001).

Street Terms for Cocaine

- coke
- snow
- flake
- blow
- nose candy
- snowball
- tornado
- wicky stick
- perico
- yayo
- black rock

The pharmacology of cocaine is largely similar to other stimulants, such as amphetamines. However, cocaine is metabolized more quickly than other stimulants and its effects diminish within 20 to 80 minutes after use. Cocaine can be detected in one's urine for up to 3 days following use. Cocaine stimulates the brain by blocking the reuptake of dopamine, norepinephrine, and serotonin. Cocaine is among the most powerful pharmacological reinforcers; the drug is overwhelmingly irresistible, meaning first time users typically cannot help but use it again. The effects of cocaine use depend largely on the route of administration.

Historical Trends of Consumption

It is estimated that use of the coca bush dates back several thousand years. It was first used by the native people of Bolivia, Peru, and Ecuador, namely the Incas. The leaf was used for religious, medicinal, and work-related purposes, and it was thought to be a gift from the gods. The Spanish Conquistadores arrived in the Andean region during the 16th century and, although they themselves considered use of the plant to be a vice and refused to use it, they permitted its use among the natives as they felt it helped the Incas to work harder. The Spanish began to regulate the plant, and the coca leaf was used as money in trade transactions. The coca plant was not popular in Europe until the 1800s, when curiosity grew resulting from several accounts of the plants' effects on European naturalists traveling in South America. By the 1850s, European scientists who had been studying the plant were able to isolate the active ingredient from the leafs (Gahlinger, 2001; Ksir, Hart, & Ray, 2008).

Sigmund Freud first became popular following his work on cocaine. He wrote *On Coca*, in which he argued that cocaine could be used as an anesthetic and even an aphrodisiac, in addition to its medical value for treating depression and neuroses, syphilis, morphine and alcohol dependence, indigestion, and asthma. Almost all of Freud's postulations were incorrect, and a period of widespread cocaine abuse resulted (Hanson, Venturelli, & Fleckenstein, 2006; Ksir, Hart, & Ray, 2008). Freud, in his later publications, was not as supportive of the use of cocaine, but at that point the drug was widely available not only by medical prescription but also in the form of patent medications that could be bought almost anywhere. The drug also became available in beverage form in Coca-Cola and Mariani's Coca Wine (Hanson, Venturelli, & Fleckenstein, 2006; Ksir, Hart, & Ray, 2008; Mosher & Akins, 2007). Cocaine dependence and the risk of overdose/death eventually became apparent, and the number of cocaine-related deaths grew in the late 1800s; the popularity of cocaine subsequently declined by the early 1900s. The first U.S. policy that addressed cocaine control was the Harrison Act of 1914. Although this law was written primarily to control opiates, cocaine was also included.

Cocaine came back into fashion in the 1970s when the drug was somewhat rare and difficult to obtain. As such, it was considered the drug of choice among wealthy athletes and movie stars, many of whom injected the drug intravenously, or snorted it through rolled $100 bills.

> By publicizing and glamorizing the lifestyle of affluent, upper-class drug dealers and the use of cocaine by celebrities and athletes, all forms of mass media created an effective advertising campaign for cocaine, and many people were taught to perceive cocaine as chic, exclusive, daring, and nonaddicting. In television specials about cocaine abuse, scientists talked about the intense euphoria produced by cocaine and the compulsive craving that people (and animals) develop for it. Thus, an image of cocaine as being extraordinarily powerful, and a (therefore desirable) euphoriant was promoted (Wesson & Smith, 1985, p. 193).

When availability increased and prices dropped, patterns of use shifted, as more people were able to obtain large amounts of the drug. Smoking cocaine became popular, and the use of crack emerged and was deemed a national crisis in the media by the mid-1980s. Approximately 6 million Americans used cocaine in the 1980s.

Crack is cheaper to produce than freebase cocaine. It is more affordable for users because of its potency; only small crack "rocks" are needed at a time to obtain a high. As such, economically disadvantaged individuals are able to use crack (although an addict's habit can still cost between $100 and $200 per day) (Abadinsky, 2008). Once crack was introduced, it produced dependence and strong cravings, and cocaine became a major health issue in the United States. The criminal justice system and legislators responded, instituting laws with penalties for crack about one hundred times as severe as for powder cocaine (in the form of the Anti-Drug Abuse Act of 1986)—laws that disproportionately targeted the African American population. Use peaked in 1986, when about 4 percent of high school seniors admitted to trying crack and just under 13 percent admitted to using cocaine. Those numbers then declined, reaching a low of 1.5 percent for crack use and 3.1 percent for powder cocaine use in 1992. Since then, use rates have increased slightly: In 2005, 1.9 percent of high school seniors admitted to using crack and 5.1 percent admitted to using powder cocaine. Overall, less than 2 percent of the U.S. population has ever used crack cocaine (Maisto, Galizio, & Connors, 2008).

The media link cocaine use and distribution to crime and violence, as street gangs pretty much control the drug's market. Cocaine-related disputes result in a number of violent urban acts, including drive-by shootings. More globally, Columbian cartels have historically provided almost all of America's illicit cocaine, despite the fact that the United States has spent over $5 billion in recent years in an attempt to eliminate Latin American drug sources. U.S. efforts reduced Columbian production of cocaine, but production rates have subsequently become higher in Bolivia and Peru (Hanson, Venturelli, & Fleckenstein, 2006).

Benefits/Consequences

Legal cocaine can be used medically as a local anesthetic, and was actually the first local anesthetic ever used for surgery, as it reduces both pain and bleeding. It is still used today on rare occasions, usually for facial surgeries. Used illicitly, individuals consume cocaine for the rush experienced following administration which is reportedly extremely euphoric and pleasurable. However, a crash occurs only 10 to 20 minutes later and leaves users craving more. Similar to other stimulants, moderate doses of cocaine produce mood elevation and euphoria, increased sociability, talkativeness, alertness, and arousal (Abadinsky, 2008; Gahlinger, 2001). There are, however, many negative side effects.

Effects of cocaine use include dilated pupils, constriction of the blood vessels, and increased body temperature, blood pressure, heart rate, and respiration. Cocaine produces insomnia and is an appetite suppressant; therefore, many users go for long periods of time without sleeping and eating. Many students attempt to pull "all-nighters" with the help of cocaine and other stimulants. When these drugs are used while studying, state-dependent learning may occur, and the individual may not be able to retain or access the information stored once he or she is no longer under the influence of the drug. These drugs can negatively influence an individual's ability to complete complex tasks (Abadinsky, 2008; Gahlinger, 2001; Liska, 2004). The effects of cocaine use depend largely on the route of administration. Overdose, fatalities, dependence, and cocaine-induced psychosis are more common when cocaine is inhaled intranasally or smoked, but less common when it is injected intravenously. Those who use freebase cocaine can have bleeding in the lungs, chest pain, and chronic cough; powder cocaine and crack can result in the buildup of fluid within the lungs; and those who administer cocaine intranasally experience inflammation and tissue damage within the nose. Even moderate cocaine use can cause serious heart problems, including palpitations and inflammation of the heart, while large amounts can result in respiratory failure, convulsions, cardiovascular collapse, liver damage, and death (Abadinsky, 2008; Gahlinger, 2001; Liska, 2004). An additional side effect of cocaine use is that when a cocaine addict has no more money to spend on drugs, sexual favors may be performed in return for a score which can result in the spread of HIV. An addict explains:

> "The purpose of this drug," she continues sipping from a bottle of beer, "becomes a sexual thing for the male more than it does the female. Being that the females have no dealing connections of any kind—in the sense of selling it, I mean; they are not behind the scales—their only means of getting it is either to have money or to use their bodies. If they don't work for a living or have a sugar daddy, they use their bodies. So it is really a force thing. The sexual thing is a forceful thing because the men say, 'If you don't give me sex, I won't give you the drug'" (Williams, 1992, p. 115).

A further, long-term consequence is that use may result in diminished dopamine levels which affect an individual's normal ability to experience pleasure and may result in depression.

Cocaine is often used in combination with other substances (e.g., opiates and alcohol), as this may enhance the high experienced. These combinations, however, dramatically increase the risk of overdose and death. In 1990, there were over 80,000 cocaine-related emergency room visits: in 2005, this number increased to 125,000. By this point, cocaine accounted for 20 percent of all drug-related emergency room visits—higher than all other illicit drugs (Maisto, Galizio, & Connors, 2008). Acute tolerance results during cocaine use; users continue to administer the drug multiple times in an effort to continue to experience the initial rush, though each time the rush has a lesser effect. This acute tolerance dissipates usually within 1 day, at which point the strong effects of the first high can be experienced all over again. Chronic tolerance and dependence also develop with continued use. Withdrawal symptoms include anxiety, irritability, discomfort and muscle aches, hunger, lethargy, chills, tremors, and exhaustion (Abadinsky, 2008; Gahlinger, 2001; Hanson, Venturelli, & Fleckenstein, 2006; Liska, 2004). Perhaps most notably, "cocaine blues" is a typical characteristic of withdrawal. Heavier use results in a more severe crash than moderate use, and therefore a deeper depression, which can be an incentive for many addicts to continue using.

Summary

- Marijuana is by far the most commonly used illicit drug as well as the largest cash crop in the United States. It did not become popular in the United States as a drug until the late 1920s, though there were some reports of Mexican immigrants using the drug in the early 1920s. Marijuana use came to be associated with minority ethnic groups, artists (specifically jazz musicians), and crime, and by 1936, all states had laws regulating its use and sale.
- There are 14.5 million American marijuana users (i.e., individuals who have used marijuana within the past 30 days), which represents 6.1 percent of the American population 12 years of age and older. Approximately 20 million individuals have used marijuana in the last year, with 25 percent of these individuals using it upwards of once per week. Combining youth with the adult population and examining lifetime use rates, one-third of all Americans have experimented with marijuana at some point in their life.
- A user does not develop a physical dependence on marijuana, however, regular, significant use can result in a tolerance to marijuana's cognitive effects.
- Despite its widespread use, there are approximately 700,000 people arrested in the United States every year for marijuana use, which amounts to one individual every 45 seconds. One of the reasons marijuana is prosecuted by the criminal justice system is because it is considered by many to be a gateway drug, meaning individuals who use marijuana are more likely to progress to using more serious illicit drugs.
- By 2007, 13 states (Alaska, California, Colorado, Hawaii, Maine, Michigan, Montana, Nevada, New Mexico, Oregon, Rhone Island, Vermont, and Washington) had passed legislation allowing individuals to use marijuana for medical reasons as long as they had permission from their physicians.
- Negative consequences of cannabis use include reddening of the eyes, dry mouth and throat, mild paranoia, hallucinations, increased appetite, and slowed cognitive performance. Less-experienced marijuana users typically incur panic, anxiety and/or paranoid feelings.
- Opiates are a group of drugs (including both synthetic and natural substances) that

contain chemical properties resembling opium or one of its active ingredients. They are typically used for the reduction of pain and to induce sleep. Popular synthetic opiates include Demerol, methadone, and oxycodone.

- The first U.S. legislation to control opium was passed in 1868, when opium addiction started to become a social problem in the United States. Opium was consumed at a greater rate in the United States than in European countries, and was available mostly via patent medicines.
- In the United States, 1.26 million individuals abuse opiates monthly, and 2.45 million Americans have tried heroin. Heroin users typically used injectable heroin through the 1980s, then use declined, becoming popular again in the 1990s. When injected, heroin's effects occur in approximately 10 seconds. In the 1990s, however, heroin was typically snorted or smoked due to the fear among users of acquiring HIV. These methods of consumption typically yield effects in about 15 minutes.
- The mild side effects of opiates typically are nausea and vomiting, profuse sweating, constricted pupils, and constipation, and decreased sex hormone production. Abuse can also result in psychiatric symptoms, high doses can result in a comatose state with depressed breathing that typically causes death, and convulsions. Because heroin is usually injected intravenously, it also poses the risk of the user acquiring HIV/AIDS and hepatitis. Additionally, the purity of heroin can vary from 0 to 99 percent, increasing significantly the risk of an accidental overdose and death.
- Hallucinogens are a complex group of drugs consisting of over ninety naturally occurring plants and even more synthetic substances that produce a variety of consciousness-altering effects. These drugs produce sensory disturbances, and some even cause schizophrenia-like psychosis. Each hallucinogen produces different effects. The most widely known hallucinogens are ecstasy, LSD, PCP, psilocybin (found in mushrooms), and peyote (mescaline).
- LSD mimics natural serotonin, and thereby activates serotonin receptors within the brain. LSD is extremely potent, possibly the most potent psychoactive drug known: Two gallons of LSD would be enough to make the entire U.S. population trip. In 2005, just under 2 percent of high school seniors reported LSD use within the past year. LSD does not result in physical dependence, and there are no withdrawal symptoms that result from use. However, tolerance develops quickly with LSD and repeated daily doses are no longer effective after 3 or 4 days.
- Psilocybin is a serotonergic hallucinogen which mimics natural serotonin, and thereby activates serotonin receptors within the brain. More commonly referred to as "magic mushrooms" or "shrooms," there are about one hundred mushroom species containing psilocybin that grow in the United States, Mexico, and Europe. Potency is far less than LSD, and effects begin within 30 minutes and last between 4 and 6 hours.
- Peyote is a cactus that grows in northern Mexico and Texas. The entire cactus is psychoactive; however, the most powerful psychoactive ingredient is called mescaline and is found in the top of the plant. The use of peyote within the Native American Church (NAC) for religious purposes is protected by the First and Fourteenth Amendments. The effects begin 30 to 120 minutes after injection and last between 10 and 14 hours and are similar to LSD and psilocybin.
- MDMA is a designer synthetic drug, which bears the street name ecstasy, the popularity of which has continued to increase since the late 1990s. Approximately 2 million pills are trafficked weekly from Europe to the United States, with a dose of ecstasy selling for between $10 and $20. In 2000, there were over 4,000 emergency room admissions

related to MDMA use: MDMA can cause dehydration, heat exhaustion/heatstroke, heart attacks, seizures, strokes, and kidney failure. Toxic doses do not necessarily have to be large; many have died after taking low doses. Many negative drug effects are due to increased body temperature, which is intensified by increased physical activity and high environmental temperatures. As well, use is associated with sexual risk-taking behaviors.

- PCP is a dissociative anesthetic which acts on a receptor in the brain that affects glutamate (a neurotransmitter) to produce effects similar to surgical anesthetics, yet the user remains semiconscious. PCP became popular as a street drug in the 1970s, and in the 1980s roughly 20 percent of high school students had tried this drug. Beginning in the 1990s, use had significantly declined as its serious effects had been widely publicized.
- Methamphetamine is a synthetic drug that can be created using legal substances. Most stimulants produce an almost immediate rush upon administration, and even though drug levels within the body remain high for some time thereafter, users crave more to feel the initial rush again. Subsequent rushes are typically not as satisfying as the first. Although it has been used illicitly in America since before the 1960s, meth did not become popular until the 1980s and 1990s. During the 1980s and 1990s, its use was prevalent among working-class white males and within the biker subculture. It is now more popular among young adults, is considered to be a club drug, and next to marijuana is the most-used drug across the globe. As of 2003, just over 12 million Americans admitted to trying meth at least once in their life.
- Cocaine is an illicit stimulant drug derived from a natural substance and on the street is available as a white powder that can be snorted or injected intravenously. Freebasing cocaine is also popular, which is a method in which cocaine is heated and the fumes are inhaled. Crack, another form of cocaine made by dissolving base cocaine in alkaline solution, is smoked.
- Cocaine became popular in the 1970s when it was considered the drug of choice among wealthy athletes and movie stars. When availability increased and prices dropped, patterns of use shifted as more people were able to obtain large amounts. Smoking cocaine became popular, and the use of crack emerged and was deemed a national crisis in the media by the mid-1980s. Approximately 6 million Americans used cocaine in the 1980s.
- Crack is cheaper to produce than freebase cocaine. It is more affordable for users because of its potency; only small crack "rocks" are needed at a time to obtain a high. As such, economically disadvantaged individuals are able to use this drug. Once crack was introduced, which produced dependence and strong cravings, cocaine became a major health issue in the United States. Legislators responded, instituting laws with penalties for crack about one hundred times as severe as for powder cocaine—laws that disproportionately targeted the African American population.

Important Terms

Amotivational syndrome
Cocaine
Crack
Ecstasy
Hallucinogen persisting perception disorder
Hallucinogens (psychedelics)
Heroin
LSD
Marijuana
Methamphetamine
Opiates
Opioids
PCP
Peyote
Psilocybin
Psychedelics (hallucinogens)
Temporal disintegration

Critical Thinking Questions

1. On which drugs should law enforcement concentrate their efforts? Defend your position.
2. Should any of the drugs discussed in this chapter be available for recreational use? Why or why not?

Research Topics

1. Choose one of the drugs discussed in the chapter and research how it was used historically and how attitudes have changed over time. Interview an individual over the age of 50 and an individual in his or her early 20s about their attitudes toward this drug. Discuss the reasons for the differences or similarities.
2. Choose one of the drugs discussed in the chapter and conduct further research into the historical and current medical applications of this substance. Make a brief presentation regarding your findings.

Suggested Readings

Reding, Nick. (2009). *Methland: The death and life of an American small town.* New York, NY: Bloomsbury.

Williams, Terry. (1992). *Crackhouse: Notes from the end of the line.* New York, NY: Penguin Books.

PART III

The History and Effects of Drug Use

8

A Legal History of Illicit Drugs in America

"We have been following essentially the same Drug Prohibition policy for many decades, and it has given us the worst of all worlds."

—(Gray, 2001, p. 1)

OBJECTIVES:

When you have finished this chapter, you should be able to:

- Understand the historical development of the drug control policy in the United States
- Understand the purpose of drug control legislation
- Discuss the types of controls created by the major pieces of drug legislation
- Understand the policy of recent presidential administrations on drug control
- Recognize the role of race in the formation of drug control legislation
- Understand the varied policies regulating illicit and legal drugs in the United States

REAL LIFE

Kay Tanner, Age 56, Serving 10 Years for Conspiracy to Traffic Cocaine:

> The night before Christmas Eve, my front door was rammed in and approximately fifteen fully armed DEA and police invaded my home. This was all related to my tenants that had moved. I was handcuffed and interrogated for eight hours about people I didn't even know. I was threatened with arrest and they tore my house apart looking for evidence. I was not arrested as they found nothing they were looking for. I was later indicted for one count of Conspiracy to Traffic Cocaine. Conspiracy does not require any evidence. All you need is testimony by a government witness, which is bought with plea bargains. There were two

witnesses who faced twenty year sentences and got only 12–18 months for their testimony. I was convicted for having knowledge of my tenants' actions by hearsay only. I have lost my home and spent all of my money defending myself, trying to undo this nightmare. Prison is about loneliness and despair. About mothers and grandmothers without their families, most of which were victims themselves. Victims of their husbands, boyfriends, or poorly chosen friends. Now they are victims of the federal government with no hope in sight (Norris, Conrad & Resner, 1998, p. 11).

THE EARLY ROLE OF LEGISLATION

The first use of a substance to alter an individual's mental status can be traced to an alcoholic drink produced in 8000 BC, with various wines and beer appearing as early as 6000 BC, and opium use beginning in 4000 BC. For a variety of reasons in a variety of historical locales, mind-altering substances appear to be a part of human culture. Throughout history, the use of various drugs, at one point including the use of caffeine (widely embraced in our society today), has been targeted as problematic to society.

Though concerns regarding alcohol and its potentially negative effects on society were strong by the mid-19th century, the use of other drugs during this period was widespread for both medicinal and recreational purposes. Alcohol use was viewed by many in society as the cause of negative personal and family relationships, a weakening economic base of the United States, and it was shunned by some for religious reasons. Other drugs, however, were not regulated prior to the 20th century and could be formulated and sold by anyone, due to the lack of legal controls. Use of drugs was considered an individual decision and responsibility, and even physicians endorsed the liberal use of drugs such as morphine and heroin. Starting in the 20th century, however, a slew of laws were passed to control the use and distribution of most drugs in the United States.

> *If people let government decide what foods they eat and what medicines they take, their bodies will soon be in as sorry a state as are the souls of those who live under tyranny . . . A society that will trade a little liberty for a little order will lose both, and deserve neither.*
>
> —THOMAS JEFFERSON

Early Anti-Opium Legislation

One of the first drug laws passed was against opium use, in San Francisco in 1875. A large number of Chinese immigrated to the West to build the railroads and mines; however, after the depression of the 1890s hit, this population was deemed a threat to other laborers. Western states such as California put an end to immigration from China; and laws against opium, the use of which was associated with the Chinese population, were used to legally control Chinese immigrants. Such legislation did not apply to medicines that were opium based and beneficial to Americans, but applied only to opium dens frequented by the Chinese. This pattern of creating legislation to control groups perceived as threats to mainstream society is evident in other areas of drug control policy as well.

During this time, cocaine, like opium, was an ingredient in a variety of popular medications advocated by pharmaceutical companies. By the late 1800s, however, medical practitioners had become aware of the potential of cocaine to cause serious dependency, and therefore it was considered a drug of social concern. The perceived association between cocaine and uncontrollable violence by African Americans directed at the white community contributed to increased social control and oppression of blacks. Based entirely on rumor, stories proliferated in the South of black men with impenetrable strength, so much so that .32 caliber bullets were thought to be insufficient to control these "superhumans" (which apparently led many police departments in the South to switch to .38 caliber weapons) (Musto, 1999). Vilification of African Americans based on a drug scare is a part of the same pattern of control used against the Chinese. Indeed, later in history the penalties for crack versus powder cocaine demonstrate again the use of legislation to control a specific segment of the population.

> *"If the Chinaman cannot get along without his 'dope,' we can get along without him"*
> (American Pharmaceutical Association 1902 as cited in Levinthal, 2008, p. 37).

Passage of Drug Legislation in the U.S.

1906	Pure Food and Drug Act
1914	Harrison Narcotic Act
1937	Marihuana Tax Act
1951	Boggs Act
1956	Narcotic Control Act
1961	Single Convention of Narcotic Drugs
1963	Community Mental Health Centers Act
1966	Narcotics Addict Rehabilitation Act
1968	Mental Health Centers Act
1970	Comprehensive Drug Abuse Prevention & Control Act
1970	Drug Abuse Education Act
1970	Racketeer-Influenced and Corrupt Organizations Act
1973	New York Rockefeller Drug Laws
1974	Narcotic Addict Treatment Act
1979	Model Drug Paraphernalia Act
1979	Marijuana Section of Rockefeller Drug Laws Repealed
1984	Comprehensive Crime Control Act
1984	Comprehensive Forfeiture Act
1986	Anti-Drug Abuse Act
1986	Mandatory Minimum Laws
1988	Anti-Drug Abuse Act (expanded)
1990	Crime Control Act
1994	Crime Bill
1994	First "Three Strikes" Law in California
1996	Proposition 215 in California (medical marijuana)
1998	Higher Education Act
2000	Substance Abuse & Crime Prevention Act (California)

The Pure Food and Drug Act of 1906

The purpose of the **Pure Food and Drug Act** of 1906 was to inform consumers of the ingredients in medicines and packaged food in an attempt to make these products safer. This legislation required the industry to provide a label listing ingredients that could be harmful to consumers, such as cocaine, cannabis, opiates, or alcohol. Advocacy for this act took approximately 25 years and met strong opposition from the medicine industry. The real impetus to this act was a book called *The Jungle* written by Upton Sinclair in 1906. *The Jungle* elaborated the bestial and filthy conditions in the meat packing industry of Chicago. The public was outraged and sales of meat quickly fell by almost 50 percent. An investigative report authorized by President Roosevelt confirmed the horrific conditions described by Sinclair and later that year the Pure Food and Drug Act was passed.

The Harrison Act of 1914

Still concerned about the effects of opium consumption, a group of thirteen nations called the **Shanghai Opium Commission** met in 1909 to devise a plan for the international control of narcotics. No definitive plans resulted, so 2 years later, a group of twelve nations met at The Hague in the Netherlands to further the discussion. An international effort at narcotics control, termed the **Hague Convention** of 1912, was agreed upon, though it was not immediately enacted. One of the results of this convention was an international obligation to domestic narcotics control, demonstrated by the United States in the passage of the **Harrison Narcotics Act.**

Passed in December 1914, the Harrison Narcotics Act used taxation and regulation to limit drug use. The Department of the Treasury was responsible for enforcing the act, which essentially required any individual who prescribed or distributed drugs to purchase tax stamps and register with the government. An individual in possession of drugs without a prescription was considered to be in violation of the act. Punishment for violating the act was not to exceed $2000 and/or 5 years in prison. One notable fact regarding the passage of this act was the minimal attention given during the congressional debates to the so-called evils of drugs or the apparent link between drugs and crime.

Effectively, the Harrison Act criminalized drugs unless prescribed by a physician for a few clearly defined medical purposes. During this period, most physicians were of the belief that the prescription of morphine or heroin to drug addicts for maintenance purposes was in line with the Hippocratic Oath under which physicians are bound to alleviate suffering. There was ambiguity in the Harrison Narcotics Act, however, regarding the acceptability of medical maintenance for opiate addicts. The practice of prescribing morphine or heroin for medical maintenance was deemed illegal in 1919 by the Supreme Court in *Webb v. United States.* Doctors were wary of prescribing opiates for maintenance treatment, and enforcement of the Harrison Act resulted in the arrest of approximately 30,000 doctors. Approximately 3,000 physicians served prison time, and by 1925, all municipal clinics that provided maintenance for addicts were closed. Some believe that the Harrison Narcotics Act had an influence on addiction rates, with estimates of addiction to illegal drugs at approximately 500,000 in 1920 and between 40,000 and 50,000 in 1945 (Lyman & Potter, 2003). This figure can be somewhat misleading, however, as one of the consequences of the act was the substitution of legal alternatives such as barbiturates, which enjoyed immense popularity before the nonmedical dangers of these drugs were widely recognized. So, while the number of addicts of illegal drugs declined dramatically, there was a parallel increase in the number of addicts of legal substances.

Unintentionally, the Harrison Act also contributed to the development of an underground subculture of drug use. Once a substance becomes illegal, users must continue to find drugs on a regular basis, and avoid detection by law enforcement in the process. The Harrison Act resulted in a dramatic increase in the cost of drugs such as heroin, which rose from $6.50 per ounce on the street to approximately $100 per ounce after this legislation was enacted (Musto, 1999). Thus the result was a group of individuals either using or selling drugs that cultivated relationships with other law violators. This criminal subculture was (and remains) a direct response to the criminalization of drugs.

The Marihuana Tax Act of 1937

Just as with many other drugs, marijuana use has been documented throughout history. In 1850, the *United States Pharmacopeia* recommended the use of marijuana for ailments such as rheumatism, hysteria, insanity, and asthma, to name a few. The Harrison Act of 1914 left out the regulation of marijuana, with the federal government wanting the individual states to deal with marijuana control. By 1930, sixteen states, specifically western states where marijuana use was associated with Mexican laborers, passed legislation prohibiting the use or possession of marijuana.

While Mexican immigrants arrived in the United States to work difficult jobs on U.S. farms, the beginning of the Great Depression rendered immigrants unwelcome and their association with violence and marijuana use became commonplace (similar to the Chinese immigrants and opium earlier in history). During the same time period, a series of articles appeared in a New Orleans newspaper linking the use of marijuana to heightened crime rates. In the late 1930s, the Federal Bureau of Narcotics, under the commission of Harry Anslinger, sought federal regulation of marijuana and mounted a scare campaign alleging numerous dangerous side effects. The Bureau of Narcotics was initially not that concerned with marijuana and its side effects: "this publicity tends to magnify the extent of the evil and lends color to an inference that there is an alarming spread of the improper use of the drug, whereas the actual increase in such use may not have been inordinately large" (Becker, 1963, p. 138). However, when it came time to mount a campaign against marijuana, the potential effects were greatly exaggerated by the government to gain support for criminalization, despite the fact that many studies conducted at the time found no support for the potential addiction to marijuana or any association with aggressive behavior. In 1937, the **Marihuana Tax Act** was passed. This act was modeled after the Harrison Narcotics Act and required a special tax of $100 per ounce for all marijuana transactions. The required tax stamps were rarely issued, effectively making the substance illegal. Marijuana was regulated by this law until the passage of the Controlled Substances Act of 1970.

POLITICS AND THE WAR ON ILLICIT DRUGS

Politicians have garnered public support and political benefit from the passage of "get tough" laws that, for the most part, consider all illegal substances in one broad category. Both the Boggs Act in 1951 and the Narcotic Control Act in 1956 paved the way for increasingly strict sentences for drug offenses. These acts served to invoke mandatory minimum sentences for offenses involving both marijuana and narcotics and dramatically increased sentences. For example, under the Narcotic Control Act a first offense was punishable by 2 to 10 years, a second offense by 5 to 20 years, and a third offense by 10 to 40 years. In addition, the sale of heroin to a minor was punishable by 10 years to life with a possible death sentence.

In the 1960s, several laws were passed that increased the role of the federal government in drug regulation and treatment. In 1961 the United Nations adopted the **Single Convention of Narcotic Drugs** which served to establish a regulatory schedule for psychotropic drugs and monitor licit pharmaceuticals. In addition, federal assistance was provided to treatment centers with the passage of the Community Mental Health Centers Act in 1963. Further support was provided with the 1966 Narcotics Addict Rehabilitation Act, which provided support to community treatment programs and mandated a federal treatment program. This 1966 act permitted the courts to order commitment for drug treatment as an alternative to prison.

Just prior to Nixon's presidency, the Federal Bureau of Narcotics merged with the Bureau of Drug Abuse Control to form the **Bureau of Narcotics and Dangerous Drugs** under the control of the Department of Justice. The Bureau has a wide variety of drug control goals, such as protecting communities, limiting drug use, and controlling crime and drug-related violence, with the specific intent of stifling the growth of criminal organizations. While there are a variety of laws related to drug offenses, such as paraphernalia laws, conspiracy laws, forfeiture laws, and racketeering laws, to name a few, there are three main categories of laws related to drugs that can be identified:

- Use or possession laws prohibit individuals without a valid prescription from possessing illegal substances in their home, car, or on their person
- Manufacturing laws prohibit the production of illegal substances
- Distribution laws prohibit the sale, transportation, or storage of illegal substances

Many state and federal agencies are in charge of enforcing these laws. In the 1960s, the Federal Bureau of Narcotics was concerned primarily with the illegal importation of drugs to the United States, and its powers included its officers' ability to carry firearms and issue arrest and search warrants. In the mid-1960s, the **Bureau of Drug Abuse Control** (BDAC) was created to focus on the diversion of drugs from legal channels to illegal enterprise. Just prior to the Nixon administration, the U.S. Department of Justice was charged with the enforcement of federal laws related to drugs, resulting in the dismantling of both the Federal Bureau of Narcotics and the Bureau of Drug Abuse Control.

NIXON ADMINISTRATION (1969–1974)

When President Richard Nixon took office, public opinion polls revealed that drugs were a major public concern. The use of illicit substances had increased markedly during the 1960s and the baby boom generation entered the period of their life in which drugs and crime are most common (ages 15 to 24). In fulfillment of his "law and order" focus as president, Nixon declared a "total war against dangerous drugs" in 1969, with a federal budget of $86 million dedicated to the drug issue. For the first time in history, prisons were filled with drug offenders (predominantly marijuana offenders) and threats were made to end all foreign aid to countries that could not control drug trafficking (Abadinsky, 2008). For example, during this period much of the heroin in the United States came from Turkey and the Nixon administration took steps to end aid to Turkey if they failed to stop their export of opium to the United States. In the short term, this strategy worked to lower rates of heroin use; however, Mexico soon replaced Turkey as the source of American heroin and the government turned its eradication programs to Mexico. Also under Nixon's command, a major piece of legislation, the Comprehensive Drug Abuse Prevention and Control Act, was passed.

Comprehensive Drug Abuse Prevention and Control Act

Passed in 1970, the **Comprehensive Drug Abuse Prevention and Control Act** (also called the **Controlled Substances Act**) sought to revise and give uniformity to drug control policy. The act provided for methods to decrease the availability of dangerous drugs, set procedures for controlling a substance and established criterion for the requirements of control, and elaborated on any obligations of the United States resulting from international treaties. The Comprehensive Drug Abuse Prevention and Control Act placed all regulated substances into one of five schedules (discussed in Chapter One), which were based on the medical use of the drug, potential for abuse, and safety or risk of addiction. This act placed drug control under federal jurisdiction and became the foundation of U.S. drug regulation. Similar legislation has been enacted in most industrialized nations. The act also involved some bureaucratic changes that resulted in the formation of the Drug Enforcement Administration (DEA).

Creation of the DEA

The Comprehensive Drug Abuse Prevention and Control Act of 1970 shifted responsibility for drug enforcement from the Treasury Department to the Department of Justice, where the DEA was created. In 1973, to fight the war on drugs, the **Drug Enforcement Administration (DEA)** was formed to collect and disseminate information related to drug intelligence, and to investigate drug-related events. The mission of the DEA is:

> to enforce the controlled substances laws and regulations of the United States and bring to the criminal and civil justice system of the United States, or any other competent jurisdiction, those organizations and principal members of organizations, involved in the growing, manufacture, or distribution of controlled substances appearing in or destined for illicit traffic in the United States; and to recommend and support non-enforcement programs aimed at reducing the availability of illicit controlled substances on the domestic and international markets (http://www.usdoj.gov/dea/agency/mission.htm).

Specifically, the DEA is responsible for:

- The investigation of interstate and international controlled substance laws
- The investigation of drug gangs
- Working with American and foreign officials to collect, analyze, and disseminate drug intelligence information
- The enforcement of forfeiture laws when property is linked to drug trafficking
- The enforcement of the Controlled Substances Act
- Linking various levels of law enforcement in order to maximize investigative efforts
- Working with American and foreign officials to reduce drug availability through programs such as crop eradication and crop substitution
- Working with organizations such as the United Nations regarding international drug control programs (http://www.usdoj.gov/dea/agency/mission.htm).

The mission and responsibilities of the DEA are global and the organization therefore plays an integral role in the collection of drug-related intelligence. The creation of the Drug Enforcement Administration remains to this day the hallmark of Nixon's war on drugs.

Treatment as Anti-Drug Strategy

Though the Nixon Administration certainly placed emphasis on the creation of legislation to control drug use, it was also the first time the federal government allocated funds for drug treatment, primarily in the area of harm reduction. Harm reduction programs involve both drug substitution programs and maintenance approaches, both which have a long history. The idea is to provide addicts with legal access to substances that would otherwise be obtained illegally. The rationale is to limit the risk of medical complications such as overdose, remove the motivation for addicts to involve themselves in crime to support a drug habit, and to encourage drug users to be productively involved in society. As discussed earlier in this chapter, morphine maintenance clinics were widespread at the start of the 20th century; however, these clinics were closed due to the pressure of law enforcement. Such programs, specifically methadone maintenance programs, made a resurgence during the Nixon administration due to the proliferation of heroin addicts.

Methadone maintenance programs are used to wean heroin users through the prevention of withdrawal symptoms. Treatment involves hospitalization and daily doses of methadone, which are gradually increased to a point of stability. The idea is that once methadone is stable (usually at 100 milligrams per day) the addict will no longer desire heroin and can move to the outpatient phase and become a productive member of society once again. Such programs do not attempt to withdraw the patient from methadone, but instead see social rehabilitation as more important than the medical cure of addiction.

As with other harm reduction programs, the goal of maintenance programs is to limit the complications of drug use, and to encourage the user to desist from crime and join the ranks of the productive citizenry. Nixon was committed to treatment as a major factor in reducing society's drug problem, and had allotted two-thirds of the federal anti-drug budget for such programs. Indeed, by the end of 1973, methadone maintenance programs across the United States enrolled approximately 80,000 heroin addicts and crime rates in cities with methadone maintenance programs were decreasing (Musto, 1999). Treatment also included psychotherapy or counseling on an inpatient basis as well as other inpatient detoxification programs. Another element of Nixon's war on drugs was prevention, which included research and education. Shortly after Nixon's 1972 reelection, however, the tide began to turn away from treatment and education toward harsh penalties for drug-law violations.

Beginning of the "War on Drugs"

President Nixon officially declared the first "War on Drugs" in 1971 and this was followed 2 years later with one of the harshest drug laws in the United States in New York state, spearheaded by Governor Nelson Rockefeller. This began the movement away from treatment and toward the punishment of drug users. **Rockefeller Drug Laws** created mandatory minimum sentencing laws that were intended to crack down on high-level drug offenders. Under these laws, offenders were sentenced based entirely on the amount of drugs sold or possessed, with no consideration for the offender's circumstances or role in the drug industry. What resulted was that many offenders sentenced under these laws were punished more severely than individuals convicted of rape or manslaughter. Nixon followed the Rockefeller Drug Laws with the creation of punitive federal legislation with a similar foundation. These actions began decades of severe punishment of drug users.

Of particular note is that the Rockefeller Drug Laws greatly impacted minority communities, both during the Nixon administration and long afterward. New York's population hovers around 23 percent African American or Latino; however these groups comprise 93 percent of those incarcerated for drug felonies. Between 1990 and 2002, New York City experienced an 882 percent increase in arrests for marijuana, including a 2,461 percent increase for marijuana possession offenses. While African Americans represent approximately 14 percent of marijuana users in New York City, they represent 30 percent of those arrested for marijuana violations (King & Mauer, 2005). Though Rockefeller laws were somewhat tempered by the 2004 Drug Law Reform

Act which created a determinate system of sentencing and reduced mandatory minimum sentences for nonviolent felony drug offenses, the pattern of discrimination repeated itself in many states. For example, in Maryland between 1996 and 2001, of all African American offenders 64 percent were sentenced on drug violations, and an astounding 81 percent of individuals sentenced for drug offenses were African American (King & Mauer, 2002). An overwhelming amount of scholarly research indicates that racial minorities do not partake in the use of drugs with any more frequency than do whites. Nevertheless, the coexistence of race and a lower class position leave many minorities more visible to law enforcement, giving the misperception of higher levels of drug involvement. This results in disproportionate arrest and prosecution. Of all drug prisoners in state facilities until 2002, 56 percent were African American and 23 percent were Hispanic (King & Mauer, 2002). By 1983, similar laws with mandatory minimum sentencing had been passed in forty-nine states. Rockefeller Drug Laws represented the new era in drug enforcement that was unfolding: punishment was to be the primary "deterrent" to drug use.

FORD ADMINISTRATION (1974–1977)

The presidency of Gerald Ford was replete with issues of greater national and international concern than drug use: unemployment, inflation, and the energy crisis were of prominent concern. Though the Narcotic Addict Treatment Act was passed in 1974, the Ford administration had minimal interest in the drug problem and throughout Ford's presidency the federal budget slowly shifted from a focus on treatment to a focus on enforcement. In 1975, the Domestic Council Task Force on Drug Abuse prepared a paper entitled *White Paper on Drug Abuse,* wherein interesting findings were documented that indicated that all drugs are not equally dangerous, and that all drug use is not equally destructive. The paper further noted the unlikely possibility of containing and limiting the adverse consequences of drug use. Despite these findings, the shift from treatment to enforcement occurred and the imbalance between treatment and punishment continued, perhaps spawned by the resurgence in the use of heroin across the United States.

CARTER ADMINISTRATION (1977–1981)

In 1972, the National Commission on Marijuana and Drug Abuse, appointed by President Nixon, recommended the decriminalization of small amounts of marijuana used for personal consumption. By 1978, eleven states decriminalized the use and possession of marijuana. This position was advocated by President Carter who believed that penalties for the use or possession of drugs should not be more damaging that the use of the substance itself. As such, the attitude of tolerance present under Gerald Ford for the presence of drugs in society continued under President Carter.

Though there are many arguments in favor of drug decriminalization, proponents of this position believe strongly that the criminalization of drugs is the result of a historic moral opposition to drug use and the subsequent over-application of criminal law. The result is the overburdening of the criminal justice system through the arrest, prosecution, and imprisonment of nonviolent offenders that costs billions of dollars per year. The notion of decriminalization is to treat the possession of a specific amount of a substance as a civil matter for which citizens would not be incarcerated. This notion of decriminalization would allow law enforcement to refocus its efforts on high-level drug dealers and traffickers. In addition, it is purported by most public-health experts that substance abuse would best be resolved through the use of a variety of medical and social services; as opposed to a prison term. This is the essence of the harm reduction model, in which the goal is to reduce the harm that results from both drug use and current drug policies.

Decriminalization would result in proportional penalties for the recreational act of substance use that even drug authorities assert can never be entirely eliminated. As part of a harm reduction approach, during the Carter administration the marijuana section of the Rockefeller Drug Laws was repealed, which eliminated draconian sentences for marijuana sale and possession.

As the 1970s closed and the 1980s began, public attitudes shifted toward drug use, especially drug use among youth. Parents groups grew in strength and number and focused their attention on the effects of drug use on adolescent users as well as on the family as a whole. Most parents groups did not agree with the notion that "some" drugs and "some" drug use were acceptable, but instead stressed that both users and nonusers were endangered by the use of all drugs (including alcohol). Such groups supported, and were delighted, with the election of Ronald Reagan in 1981.

THE REAGAN YEARS (1981–1989)

The tide turned once again to harsh control of illegal substances under the presidency of Ronald Reagan. This began when the Congress passed the **Department of Defense Authorization Act**, which permitted the involvement of military forces in drug interdiction efforts. In 1982, President Reagan officially declared a war on drugs, which began a period of rapid incarceration for drug offenses and the allotment of billions of dollars for construction of new prisons. Of the drug budget, an overwhelming percentage was dedicated to stopping drugs before they entered the United States, which meant dramatic increases in foreign aid to countries such as Bolivia, Colombia, Ecuador, Peru, and Mexico. The increased foreign aid to these countries was to provide an incentive for the reduction of drug production. When some countries engaged in a half-hearted attempt at drug control, military intervention was the next step (e.g., military intervention in Nicaragua and Afghanistan). Reagan's war on drugs quickly became an international conflict.

South Florida Drug Task Force Formed 1982

Miami citizens lobbied the federal government in response to increasing violence believed to be drug related. President Reagan responded with the creation of the South Florida Drug Task Force headed by George Bush. The task force mobilized against drug traffickers by combining agents from the DEA, Customs, FBI, ATF (Alcohol, Tobacco, and Firearms), IRS, Army, and Navy. Reagan later created regional task forces elsewhere in the country.

While the responsibilities of the DEA are solely related to the drug trade, other federal agencies are also involved in the drug war. In 1982 the **Federal Bureau of Investigation (FBI)** was designated concurrent jurisdiction for drug-law enforcement, with its primary responsibility focused on organized crime as related to the drug trade. Both the DEA and the FBI enforce the Controlled Substances Act, though the FBI is more concerned with related offenses such as Continuing Criminal Enterprise (CCE) violations or Racketeer-Influenced and Corrupt Organizations (RICO) violations.

In 1984, the **Comprehensive Crime Control Act** permitted the DEA to dictate a substance as illegal for a period of 12 months without review by the current government. In addition, this act served to increase bail and sentences as well as federal authority to asset forfeiture for individuals convicted of felony drug offenses. This same year a Comprehensive Forfeiture Act was passed which allowed for the seizure of assets related to the drug industry.

Nancy Reagan: "Just Say No"

The importance of Reagan's war on drugs was hit home in 1986 by the death of Len Bias, a basketball star from the University of Maryland. At the young age of 22, Len Bias was chosen to play for the Boston Celtics, and less than 48 hours later died of a cardiac arrhythmia associated with a cocaine overdose. A mere 8 days later, Don Rogers, a 23-year-old football player for the Cleveland Browns, also died of a cocaine overdose. This sparked even greater interest in the devastating consequences of drug use on a community.

The war on drugs was further fueled by Nancy Reagan's "Just Say No" campaign. Funded by corporate and private donations, the campaign was geared primarily toward white, middle-class children and sought to prevent their involvement in drugs. Despite the efforts of Reagan's wife Nancy to educate the public about the dangers of drugs, the Reagan administration was characterized by the slashing of social programs and the increase of enforcement efforts to eradicate drugs.

Anti-Drug Abuse Act of 1986

In 1986, the **Anti-Drug Abuse Act** was passed which had a significant impact primarily on the mass incarceration of minority group members for drug possession offenses. The Anti-Drug Abuse Act allotted $1.7 billion to fight the drug problem: $97 million was ear-marked for the construction of new prisons, $200 million was to be used for drug education, and $241 million was to be used for treatment. The allotment of funds made it clear that the approach toward drugs was firmly enforcement related, with education and treatment playing a very tangential role.

Perhaps the most consequential part of this law was the imposition of a mandatory minimum sentence of 5 to 40 years for cocaine possession. To trigger this mandatory minimum sentence, one needed to possess 500 grams of powder cocaine or 5 grams of crack cocaine. Despite crack being the least-used illicit substance, the sentencing guidelines under the Anti-Drug Abuse Act specifically targeted the possession and sale of crack cocaine by lower-class and minority individuals. Because minorities are over-represented among the poor, the case of laws regarding crack cocaine versus powder cocaine is illustrative of the intersections of discrimination by class and race.

> *"Most of the attacks upon white women of the South are the direct result of the cocaine-crazed Negro brain . . . Negro cocaine fiends are now a new Southern menace"*
> (New York Times, February 8, 1914 as cited in Levinthal, 2008, p. 37).

The wide discrepancy in federally mandated sentences for crack cocaine versus powder cocaine illustrates a class and racial bias in the criminal justice system. Minorities are primarily prosecuted for crack offenses, whereas whites are primarily prosecuted for powder cocaine offenses (Human Rights Watch, 2000). Though the sentencing discrepancy between crack cocaine and powder cocaine offenses have closed slightly since the passage of the Anti-Drug Abuse Act of 1986, the gap was significant in creating current disproportionate minority confinement. Approximately two-thirds of those charged with powder cocaine offenses were white, while an overwhelming proportion of those charged with crack offenses were minority group members. Statistics such as these overwhelmingly illustrate the disproportionate arrest and confinement of lower-class minorities despite research by the Department of Health and Human Services reporting that less than 1 percent of young African Americans had used crack cocaine in their lifetime, compared to 4.5 percent of whites (Barak, Leighton, & Flavin, 2007). It readily becomes apparent that increased social control of this group of individuals has been accomplished through the use of drug-related laws that are enforced with vigor in low-income, minority neighborhoods. While drug laws may be superficially equal and not discriminatory in intent, the consequences of applying "get tough" legislation in fighting the war on drugs has been unprecedented incarceration of the poor and minorities as well as a significant increase in the number of women under the control of the criminal justice system. Assumptions based on race, class, and gender stereotypes have created and perpetuated moral panics that fuel support for the drug war. Examples of sentencing are illustrated in Table 8-1.

TABLE 8-1 Trafficking Penalties by Select Types of Drugs and Offense Number, 2007

Drug	Quantity	First Offense	Second Offense
Cocaine	500–4999 grams mixture	Not less than 5 years, and not more than 40 years. If death or serious injury, not less than 20 or more than life. Fine of not more than $2 million if an individual (that is, if trafficking drugs alone), $5 million if not an individual (that is, if the person is involved in trafficking drugs with the aid of others).	Not less than 10 years, and not more than life. If death or serious injury, life in prison. Fine of not more than $4 million if an individual, $10 million if not an individual.
Cocaine base (crack)	5–49 grams mixture	Not less than 5 years, and not more than 40 years. If death or serious injury, not less than 20 or more than life. Fine of not more than $2 million if an individual, $5 million if not an individual.	Not less than 10 years, and not more than life. If death or serious injury, life in prison. Fine of not more than $4 million if an individual, $10 million if not an individual.
Heroin	100–999 grams mixture	Not less than 5 years, and not more than 40 years. If death or serious injury, not less than 20 or more than life. Fine of not more than $2 million if an individual, $5 million if not an individual.	Not less than 10 years, and not more than life. If death or serious injury, life in prison. Fine of not more than $4 million if an individual, $10 million if not an individual.
LSD	1–9 grams mixture	Not less than 5 years, and not more than 40 years. If death or serious injury, not less than 20 or more than life. Fine of not more than $2 million if an individual, $5 million if not an individual.	Not less than 10 years, and not more than life. If death or serious injury, life in prison. Fine of not more than $4 million if an individual, $10 million if not an individual.
Methamphetamine	5–49 grams pure or 50–499 grams mixture	Not less than 5 years, and not more than 40 years. If death or serious injury, not less than 20 or more than life. Fine of not more than $2 million if an individual, $5 million if not an individual.	Not less than 10 years, and not more than life. If death or serious injury, life in prison. Fine of not more than $4 million if an individual, $10 million if not an individual.

TABLE 8-1 (continued)

Drug	Quantity	First Offense	Second Offense
PCP	10–99 grams pure or 100–999 grams mixture	Not less than 5 years, and not more than 40 years. If death or serious injury, not less than 20 or more than life. Fine of not more than $2 million if an individual, $5 million if not an individual.	Not less than 10 years, and not more than life. If death or serious injury, life in prison. Fine of not more than $4 million if an individual, $10 million if not an individual.
Marijuana	1,000 kg or more mixture; or 1,000 or more plants	Not less than 10 years, not more than life. If death or serious injury, not less than 20 years, not more than life. Fine not more than $4 million if an individual, $10 million if other than an individual.	Not less than 20 years, not more than life. If death or serious injury, mandatory life. Fine not more than $8 million if an individual, $20 million if other than an individual.
Marijuana	100–999 kg mixture; or 100–999 plants	Not less than 5 years, not more than 40 years. If death or serous injury, not less than 20 years, not more than life. Fine not more than $2 million if an individual, $5 million if other than an individual.	Not less than 10 years, not more than life. If death or serious injury, mandatory life. Fine not more than $4 million if an individual, $10 million if other than an individual.
Marijuana	more than 10 kg hashish; 50–99 kg mixture; more than 1 kg of hashish oil; 50–99 plants	Not more than 20 years. If death or serious injury, not less than 20 years, not more than life. Fine $1 million if an individual, $5 million if other than an individual.	Not more than 30 years. If death or serious injury, mandatory life. Fine $2 million if an individual, $10 million if other than individual.
Marijuana	1–49 plants; less than 50 kg mixture	Not more than 5 years. Fine not more than $250,000 if an individual, $1 million if other than individual.	Not more than 10 years. Fine $500,000 if an individual, $2 million if other than individual.
Hashish	10 kg or less	Not more than 5 years. Fine not more than $250,000 if an individual, $1 million if other than individual.	Not more than 10 years. Fine $500,000 if an individual, $2 million if other than individual.
Hashish Oil	1 kg or less	Not more than 5 years. Fine not more than $250,000 if an individual, $1 million if other than individual.	Not more than 10 years. Fine $500,000 if an individual, $2 million if other than individual.

Source: U.S. Drug Enforcement Administration Web site, 2007.

Created under the guidance of the U.S. Department of Health and Human Services, the **Substance Abuse and Mental Health Services Administration (SAHMSA)** was established with the motto "A Life in the Community for Everyone." SAHMSA is "based on the premise that people of all ages, with or at risk for mental or substance use disorders, should have the opportunity for a fulfilling life that includes a job/education, a home, and meaningful personal relationships with friends and family" (www.samhsa.gov). SAHMSA uses action-oriented methods to strive toward this mission with a focus on prevention and early intervention programs that exist in local communities.

Gender discrimination is another adverse consequence of the "get tough" drug legislation that was part of the Anti-Drug Abuse Act of 1986. The war on drugs' criminalization of women's involvement hinges on the notion that female offenders have transgressed mainstream society's definitions of appropriate gender and maternal roles. Women's involvement in the drug trade can frequently be attributed to economics, as opposed to personal addiction. The feminization of poverty has resulted in women seeking alternative sources of income as decoys or drug couriers ("mules") who import or transport drugs. The risks of this employment "choice" are high, often resulting in mandatory minimum sentences for first offenses.

In the late 1980s, the media-driven crack-baby epidemic led the public to believe that children born to crack-addicted mothers would face educational and social obstacles that were insurmountable. This scenario fueled gender and racial discrimination in the war on drugs, as an overwhelming majority of mothers portrayed in the media to have given birth to crack babies were of a racial or ethnic minority. The impression that the birth of crack babies was an epidemic resulted in the passage of laws that criminalized drug use during pregnancy. Such a legal response, however, dissuaded some women from seeking prenatal care and drug treatment. In addition, maternal drug-abuse laws were enforced primarily on minority women: African American and Latino women represented approximately 80 percent of those subject to prosecution (King & Mauer, 2002). Though research from the National Institute of Drug Abuse indicated that early medical reports regarding the long-term effects of being born crack addicted were overstated, the stereotype of the drug-abusing African American or Latino mother remains in the eyes of many Americans. At the close of 1999, more than 80 percent of the women in prison for drug offenses were sentenced using mandatory minimum sentencing laws (King & Mauer, 2002). The Anti-Drug Abuse Act was further expanded in 1988.

Anti-Drug Abuse Act of 1988

The issue of drug abuse was a major concern in the 1988 presidential campaign, and shortly thereafter greater regulations were included in an expansion of the Anti-Drug Abuse Act. The following regulations were included:

- It became a federal offense to distribute drugs within 100 feet of a park, youth center, playground, swimming pool, or video arcade
- Penalties were doubled for the deliberate involvement of juveniles
- A life sentence became mandatory for an individual conducting a continuing criminal enterprise involving drugs
- Warning labels were to be provided on all alcoholic beverages and money was allotted to the states to address the issue of driving while intoxicated
- The federal death penalty was reinstituted for significant drug traffickers
- Asset forfeiture was permitted for those individuals arrested for drug violations
- Drug Free Workplace guidelines set provisions for employers to perform drug testing

- Drug-Free School guidelines were included that provided information about penalties and available treatment and established the parameters of drug testing in schools
- Any commission or ordering of a homicide in conjunction with a drug-related felony was grounds for the death penalty
- Penalties for drug possession included the loss of federal benefits (including student loans) for a period of 1 year for a first offense and 5 years for a second offense
- If drug-related activity occurred in or near public housing, the individual and his or her family was to be removed from government housing

In addition, the Anti-Drug Abuse Act required annual presidential evaluation of countries producing or transporting drugs and the labeling of cooperating countries as "anti-drug allies" in the war on drugs. Unless granted a waiver by the president, countries that were lacking in cooperation with the American drug war were to face possible trade sanctions, loss of foreign aid, and opposition from the United States to loans from international lending institutions.

The Anti-Drug Abuse Act has had an enormous impact on drug policy in the United States. This act has been the impetus for mass incarceration of drug offenders and a big push in the growth of the prison industrial complex. As shown in Chapter Four on drug-use trends, however, the United States has not experienced a similar dramatic decrease in the number of individuals admitting to drug use. One of the main elements of the Anti-Drug Abuse Act of 1988 was that **asset forfeiture** was permitted for those individuals arrested for drug violations. According to the Web site of the Department of Justice, the primary goal of the asset forfeiture program is "to employ asset forfeiture powers in a manner that enhances public safety and security. This is accomplished by removing the proceeds of crime and other assets relied upon by criminals and their associates to perpetuate their criminal activity against our society. Asset forfeiture has the power to disrupt or dismantle criminal organizations that would continue to function if we only convicted and incarcerated specific individuals" (www.usdoj.gov/jmd/afp/). There are two categories of forfeiture: criminal and civil. In a criminal forfeiture, the government can seize property as punishment after the owner of the property has been convicted of a crime. In a civil forfeiture, the interested or charged party is the property, as opposed to the owner of the property. The property is presumed guilty until the owner can demonstrate proof of innocence in court.

Supreme Court Cases Related to Asset Forfeiture:

Calero–Toledo v. Person Yacht Leasing Co. 1974 determined that owners who are innocent may have their property forfeited with no compensation in civil proceedings.

Libretti v. United States 1995 held that the requirement of a court to ascertain a factual basis for a guilty plea does not extend to forfeiture.

The Comprehensive Crime Control Act established two forfeiture funds: First, the U.S. Department of Justice would receive forfeitures from agencies such as the DEA and the FBI; and second, the U.S. Department of the Treasury would receive forfeitures from agencies such as the Coast Guard. Forfeiture funds could be used for a wide variety of purposes, including payments to informants, the construction of prisons, as well as general law enforcement functions. In addition, while the previously seized assets were given entirely to the federal government, local law enforcement agencies benefited from new forfeiture laws and were now permitted a share of the net proceeds from forfeitures in which they assisted. It should be no surprise that shortly after the act was passed, the number of forfeitures and value of assets seized increased dramatically. For example, the Department of Justice Assets Forfeiture Fund was $27 million in 1985 and grew to $644 million in 1991. This increase translated into a large sum of money allotted to both state and local law enforcement. In 2006, just over $941 million worth of assets were seized, up from $833 million in 2005 (www.usdoj.gov/jmd/afp/). Critics argue that the lucrative nature of forfeiture laws creates a situation in which property seizure itself becomes the goal, rather than preventing drug-related criminal organizations. Though criminal forfeiture can remove profit from the illicit trade in narcotics, and therefore serve a very important purpose, civil forfeiture laws currently undermine civil liberties, and negatively impact the integrity of the criminal justice system. As such, many critics argue for the abolition of civil forfeiture laws in which the presumption of guilt runs counter to fundamental due process guarantees of the criminal justice system.

THE FIRST BUSH ADMINISTRATION (1989–1993)

The Anti-Drug Abuse Act of 1988 established the creation of the **Office of National Drug Control Policy** (ONDCP). According to the ONDCP Web site, the purpose of the organization is "to establish policies, priorities, and objectives for the Nation's drug control program. The goals of the program are to reduce illicit drug use, manufacturing, and trafficking, drug-related crime and violence, and drug-related health consequences. To achieve these goals, the Director of ONDCP is charged with producing the **National Drug Control Strategy**. The Strategy directs the Nation's anti-drug efforts and establishes a program, a **budget**, and guidelines for cooperation among Federal, State, and local entities" (www.ondcp.gov). The director of the ONDCP is appointed by the president and acts as the "drug czar" for the United States.

> In January of 1990, President Bush proposed the addition of an extra $1.2 billion to the war on drugs, which included a 50 percent increase in military spending.

The 1990 National Drug Control Strategy recommended a $2.2 billion increase in drug-control funding to a total of $7.9 billion. This money was dedicated to:

- Increasing the role of the Department of Defense and military involvement in drug warfare
- The expansion of the criminal justice system at all levels (police, courts, and corrections)
- Examine the development of incarceration alternatives such as boot camps
- Begin a vigorous crop eradication program against domestically grown marijuana
- Promote and expand drug-free workplace policies in the private and public sectors
- Increase the emphasis on drugs as a foreign policy concern and target international production and trafficking sources, including the enhancement of border operations
- Enhance and expand intelligence gathering both domestically and internationally

President Bush was committed to the "get tough" approach on drugs that gained popularity under the Reagan administration.

These policies continued to have a negative impact on racial and ethnic minorities at both the federal and state levels. Drug raids were conducted in black communities and involved mass arrests and the ransacking of many homes. Such raids were given names such as Memphis' Operation Invincible, New York's TNT, and Operation Clean Sweep. For many critics, the Bush administration continued years of threats to the civil liberties of African Americans under the guise of protecting society from harm. The promises of "zero tolerance" continued to erode race relations in the United States and did little to decrease the number of drug users. Additionally, the surplus of money dedicated to the war on drugs came from cuts in federal programs aimed at low-income families and juvenile justice assistance.

THE CLINTON YEARS (1993–2001)

President Clinton's first term in office involved a fairly laissez-faire attitude toward drugs and the governmental offices designed to control illicit substances, as evidenced by an 83 percent decrease in the staff of the Office of National Drug Control Policy. After all, Clinton grew up during a period of increasing drug tolerance and admitted during his first presidential campaign that he had tried marijuana in college. This approach shifted, however, during the difficult race for his second term. Republicans used the issue of drugs to attack the Democratic platform, and so Clinton adopted a "get tough" approach toward drugs. He dramatically increased federal spending on drug control (from $1.5 billion in 1989 to $18.5 billion in 2000), continued heavy-handed tactics in Central and South American countries in attempts to increase drug interdiction efforts, and continued the legacy of past presidents with minimal focus on the reduction of demand for drugs. In addition, drug policies and enforcement during this period (and after) were largely focused on marijuana (see Figure 8-1).

During President Clinton's second term in office, there were unusual ballot measures that arose to present an attack on federal drug policy. These measures were state-level propositions that would make currently illicit substances available to those for whom they were prescribed. The major ballot was Proposition 215 in California, which dealt with the medical use of marijuana. This Proposition passed and permitted the use of marijuana for any individual with either written or oral permission from a physician. Keep in mind that legally federal legislation always trumps state legislation; therefore, Proposition 215 in favor of medical marijuana was primarily intended as a symbolic initiative to illustrate changes in the public's attitudes toward drugs. Changes in the public's attitudes were also illustrated by organizations such as the American Civil Liberties Union which took a public stance in favor of drug decriminalization on the grounds that the criminalization of drugs results in more harm than use of illicit substances. Though the foundation for decriminalization took place in the late 1960s, the harsh drug laws of several consecutive administrations were leading the public to question

Civil Asset Forfeiture Reform Act 2000: The Reform Act requires the government to have much stronger evidence of wrongdoing before a person's property can be seized. The burden of proof has been raised from "probable cause" to "a preponderance of the evidence" that the property is linked to a crime. Further, this act shifts the burden of proof to the federal government . . . the government must now prove in court that the property was involved in crime instead of the property owner needing to prove the opposite.

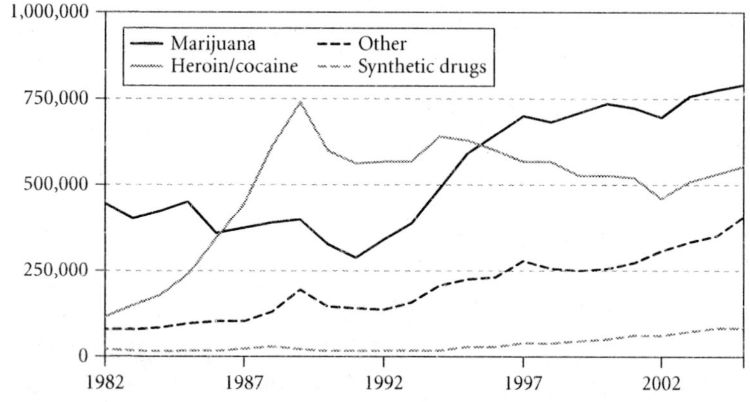

FIGURE 8-1 Number of Arrests by Drug Type, 1982–2005

Source: FBI, 2006.

federal drug policy. The public seemed polarized: those who support "get tough" measures and believe that drug use is a serious problem in society, and those who support harm reduction measures and believe that the criminal justice response to drug use is disproportionate to the offense. The government was in the former camp.

In 1995, the administrators of federal sentencing guidelines, the U.S. Sentencing Commission which was created in the mid-1980s, recommended the revision of mandatory minimums related to drug offenses. The commission issued a report acknowledging the racial and ethnic disparities in the sentencing of crack versus powder cocaine. The commission suggested reducing the discrepancy between the sentencing for the two substances, which would necessarily reduce the racial disparity of drug sentences. For the first time ever, Congress and the Clinton administration decided to override the recommendation of the U.S. Sentencing Commission. The Commission further explained in a 1997 report to Congress:

> while there is no evidence of racial bias behind the promulgation of this federal sentencing law, nearly 90 percent of the offenders convicted in federal court for crack cocaine distribution are African-American while the majority of crack cocaine users are white. Thus, sentences appear to be harsher and more severe for racial minorities than others as a result of this law. The current penalty structure results in a perception of unfairness and inconsistency (U.S. Sentencing Commission, 1997, p. 8).

The disparity of sentencing is illustrated in Figure 8-2.

The U.S. Sentencing Commission issued a report to Congress in 2007, which was the fourth time it made the same plea for a reduction in the sentencing disparity between crack and powder cocaine. The recommendation once again went unheeded.

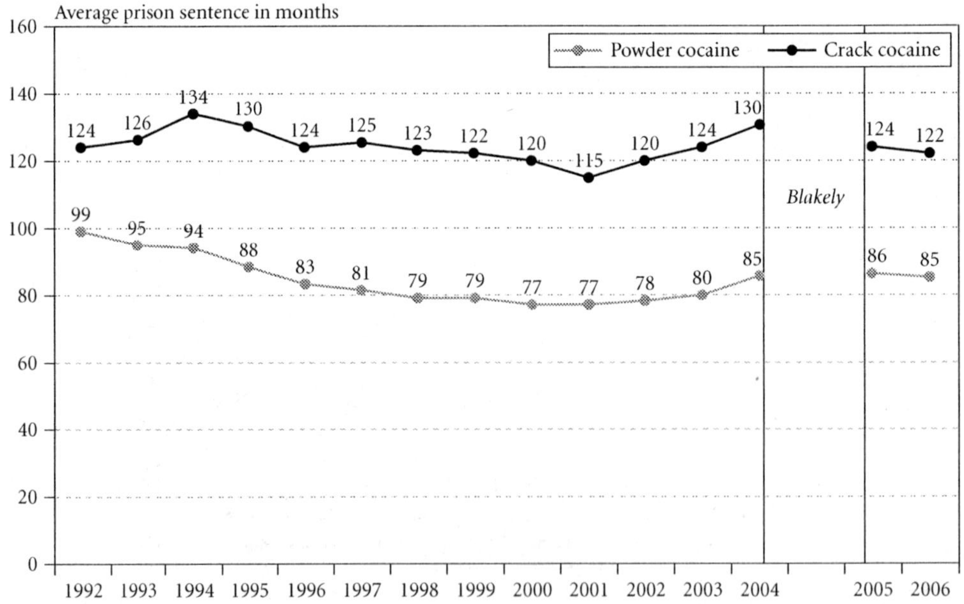

FIGURE 8-2 Trends in Prison Sentences for Powder Cocaine and Crack Cocaine Offenders, 1992–2006
Source: U.S. Sentencing Commission Report, 2007.

There were a handful of other laws put forward under Clinton's presidency that added further restrictions for drug offenders. A provision of the Federal Welfare Reform Act of 1996 indicates that an individual convicted of a felony drug offense may be denied federal benefits, such as food stamps, for the duration of his or her life. This provision clearly disproportionately impacts the poor and minorities (who are over-represented among the poor) and interestingly is not a provision that applies to other serious offenders, such as murderers. At the state level, similar provisions are commonplace. In 1998, two laws were altered that affected drug offenders. The Anti-Drug Abuse Act required public housing agencies to evict a tenant if the tenant or a member of his or her family was involved in a drug-related offense. This policy was challenged in the Supreme Court by four elderly individuals who were evicted from public housing due to the drug involvement of a family member. Though none of these individuals were evicted based on personal use or possession of an illicit substance, the Supreme Court upheld the evictions in a 2002 ruling, arguing that a tenant must be able to control the activities of other household residents, or they become a risk to other residents of the housing facility. Finally, the Higher Education Act included a provision in 1998 that required those applying for financial assistance to answer a question regarding their involvement with illicit substances. An individual who fails to respond to the question or who has a drug conviction (including for marijuana possession) can be denied financial assistance to pursue education. As with the restriction of welfare benefits, this type of restriction applies to no other type of offender. As such, an individual convicted for possession of marijuana could be legally denied welfare assistance and student aid; however, an individual convicted for murder would be considered for welfare benefits and financial aid to attend college. The relationship between these types of restrictions on those convicted for drug offenses and the deterrent impact of such policies is nonexistent, and it seems as though these provisions are simply further impedance to positive participation in society.

THE SECOND BUSH ADMINISTRATION (2001–2009)

When George W. Bush entered office he had a difficult road ahead with regard to drug policy: In the previous two administrations, drug interdiction allocation had risen 1200 percent; punishment for drug offenses was often greater than for murder; the prison population had increased dramatically due to mandatory minimums, with the biggest increase in possession offenses (see Figures 8-3 and 8-4), yet the rate at which individuals used drugs in the United States remained about the same.

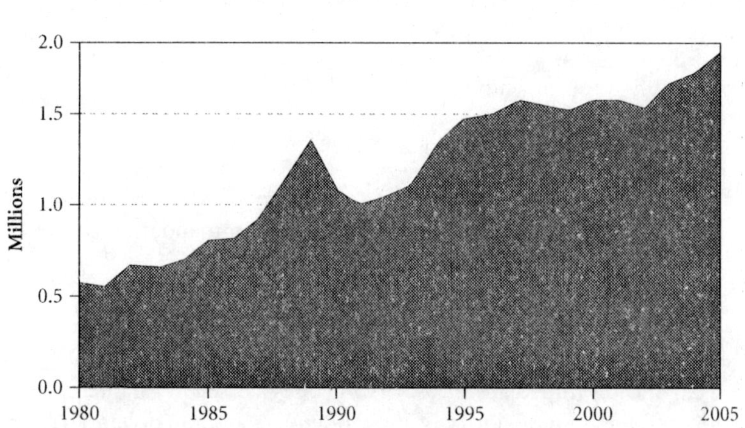

FIGURE 8-3 Drug Abuse Violation Arrests, 1980–2005
Source: FBI, 2006.

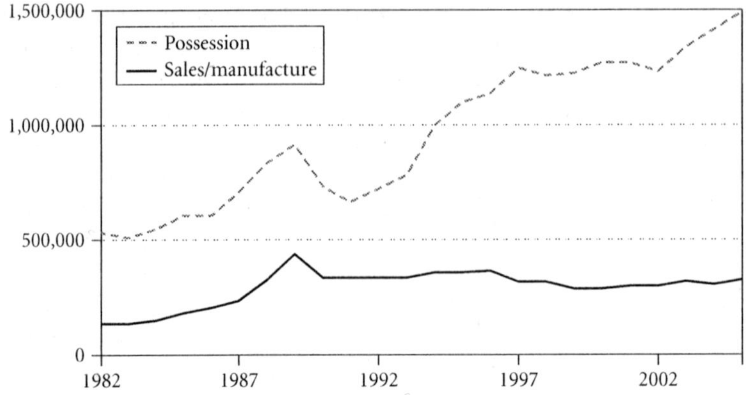

FIGURE 8-4 Arrests by Type of Drug Law Violation, 1982–2005

Source: FBI, 2006.

Further, after the events of September 11, 2001, the war on terrorism took precedence over the war on drugs. For many in politics, these two wars quickly merged into one: In 2002, Colombia was provided $650 million in funding to combat drug trafficking and terrorism. Domestically, one of the responses of President George W. Bush was a plan to help drug addicts. In August of 2003, Bush "announced a 3-year, $600 million federal treatment initiative to help addicted Americans find needed treatment from the most effective programs, including faith-based and community-based organizations. This new investment will make treatment available to help 300,000 more Americans combat their addiction over the next 3 years, by providing vouchers to individuals identified as needing assistance" (www.georgewbush.com).

President Bush on drug education, treatment, and enforcement: "We must stand with our families to help them raise healthy, responsible children. And when it comes to helping children make right choices, there is work for all of us to do. One of the worst decisions our children can make is to gamble their lives and futures on drugs. Our government is helping parents confront this problem with aggressive education, treatment and law enforcement" (2004 State of the Union address to joint session of Congress January 20, 2004).

The work of organizations like the American Civil Liberties Union and the U.S. Sentencing Commission continue to oppose the harsh and racially disparate sentences handed down for drug offenses. Many states are attempting to remove mandatory minimum sentences and there seems to be a greater focus on treatment than in the recent past. In fact, in December of 2007, the U.S. Supreme Court returned discretion regarding sentencing to federal judges in an attempt to reduce sentencing disparity between crack cocaine offenses and powder cocaine offenses. The recommendation of the U.S. Sentencing Commission to equalize crack cocaine and powder cocaine sentences that was put forward in spring of 2007 was applied retroactively, which permitted federal judges to shorten the sentences of previously convicted crack cocaine offenders. Approximately 19,500 drug offenders are eligible for early release over the next 30 years due to these changes, and as of April 2008, about 1500 drug offenders were eligible for immediate release. As will be discussed in Chapter Nine, it is important to note that the overwhelming majority of these offenders are nonviolent and were serving disproportionately excessive sentences due only to a racial bias in the law and its application.

In historic precedent, in New York the Rockefeller Drug Laws were repealed in 2009.

> [I]t has been blindingly clear for some time that mandatory minimum sentences are too inflexible, too blunt, to deal with nonviolent offenders. The laws ought to have been repealed years ago . . . New York was one of the first states to impose mandatory sentences, and it is among the last to repeal them. The state will save money in reduced prison expenses—it costs nearly $50,000 a year to keep a drug offender in prison—although that is hardly the only reason repeal should be welcomed. Judges will have the discretion to send nonviolent offenders to treatment and give them a chance to get clean and rebuild their lives. The offenders, it should be noted, will have to plead guilty in order to be eligible for the treatment option. In other words, going for treatment will not give them a blank slate—their arrest and their guilty plea will be on the record. If they fail to follow treatment guidelines, prison remains an option. The new drug laws provide funds to expand treatment centers and support drug courts, which have been found to be extremely effective when judges have the flexibility to deal with nonviolent offenders not as hardened criminals, but as drug users in need of intervention ("Finally: New York Repeals Rockefeller Drug Laws," 2009).

This is definitely a move away from the "get tough" approach the United States had adopted toward drugs and drug offenders in recent decades. Lessons from other nations show that drug courts and drug treatment are more appropriate avenues to reduce the likelihood of seeing these offenders again in the criminal justice system.

CONSEQUENCES OF POLITICS AND THE WAR ON ILLICIT DRUGS

The Office of National Drug Control Policy's (ONDCP) Executive Summary for 2006 indicates a 2007 federal budget of $12.7 billion for reducing illegal drug use, an increase of $80.6 million from 2006. This is in addition to the approximately $28 billion total state budgets, bringing spending for the war on drugs to approximately $40 billion per year. The ONDCP budget, however, does not appear to fall in line with its stated priorities, which are:

- Priority I Stopping use before it starts
- Priority II Intervening and healing America's drug users
- Priority III Disrupting the market.

In 2007, just over $4 billion (reduced slightly from 2005 and 2006) will be devoted to Priorities I and II combined. The remaining two-thirds of the budget will be dedicated to disrupting the market through the use of programs such as the Andean Counterdrug Initiative which provides counterdrug support to Afghanistan, the Secure Border Initiative for border protection and increased customs patrol presence, the Cleaning Up Methamphetamine Laboratories program, as well as financial support of the DEA (www.ondcp.gov).

Aside from the economics of the prison industrial complex at the state and federal levels, the number of arrests for drug offenses more than tripled from 580,900 in 1980 to 1,846,400 in 2005. Government studies reveal that over half of those imprisoned on federal drug offenses are street-level dealers or transporters, about one-third are mid-level dealers, and approximately 11 percent of federal offenders are high-level dealers (Federal Bureau of Investigation [FBI], 2006). On the state level, 58 percent of drug offenders have no history of either violence or high-level drug activity, and one-third has been convicted only of a drug-related crime (King & Mauer, 2002).

In addition to the expanding prison population, it is also important to recognize the types of offenses for which individuals are receiving lengthy prison terms. During the period from 1990 to

2002 there was an increase in drug arrests; 450,000 individuals were arrested. Of these arrests, 82 percent were for marijuana charges, and 79 percent of marijuana offenses were for possession only. As such, results indicate that nearly half of the drug arrests per year are for marijuana, with a mere 6 percent resulting in a felony conviction. To pursue such vigorous incarceration policies toward marijuana, the United States spends an estimated $4 billion annually on arrest, prosecution, and incarceration (King & Mauer, 2005). Research indicates that the increases in arrests do not correspond to a decrease in the use of illegal substances. As such, the dramatic increase in marijuana arrest rates can be attributed only to selective law enforcement decisions, which have disparate impacts on the lower-class and racial minorities as well as on the female population.

The current American political system rewards politicians who approach crime with a "get tough" attitude and this fuels the fire of ever-increasing spending on the prison industrial complex. This has been true for decades, as illustrated in a 1986 *U.S. News and World Report* editorial:

> Easily the most prominent beneficiary of the drug furor is Ronald Reagan. Just weeks ago the president seemed trapped in a thicket of thorny problems. For now at least, all that has been changed. Other issues have not gone away, but they have been pushed to the back burner, providing Reagan with much needed breathing room and a chance to do what he does best—rouse the troops in a campaign summoning the traditional American values so key to his popularity (Baum, 1996, p. 236).

What has resulted from decades of drug war are two distinct drug problems as elaborated by Currie (1993): a problem for those with money, and a different problem for those without money. Currie sums up the drug problem in affluent communities as "by no means insignificant, and it has caused more than its share of personal tragedies. But it is a *manageable* problem, and it has been steadily decreasing for several years, for reasons unrelated to the war on drugs" (Currie, 1993, p. 3, emphasis in original). The problem of drugs among the poor, however, "has grown malignantly in the face of the drug war—and it is much further from solution than it was when that war began" (Currie, 1993, p. 3). The drug war has been fought vehemently, though policy decisions often reflect prejudices rather than realities and too frequently lack empirical foundation.

Summary

- Though concerns regarding alcohol and its potentially negative effects on society were strong by the mid-19th century, the use of other drugs during this period was widespread for both medicinal and recreational purposes.
- One of the first drug laws passed was against opium use in San Francisco in 1875. The pattern of creating legislation to control groups perceived as threats to mainstream society (e.g., Chinese immigrants and African Americans) is evident in other areas of drug control policy as well.
- The perceived association between cocaine and uncontrollable violence by African Americans directed at the white community contributed to increased social control and oppression of blacks.
- The purpose of The Pure Food and Drug Act of 1906 was to inform consumers of the ingredients in medicine and packaged foods in an attempt to make these products safer. This legislation required the industry to provide a label listing ingredients that could be harmful, such as cocaine, cannabis, opiates, or alcohol.

- Passed in December 1914, the Harrison Narcotics Act used taxation and regulation to limit drug use. Effectively, the Harrison Act criminalized drugs unless prescribed by a physician for a few clearly defined medical purposes.
- Though initiatives to prohibit alcohol have existed since the United States was settled, the early 19th century brought a burgeoning temperance movement. In the mid-1800s several states (beginning with Maine in 1851) outlawed alcohol; however, its use remained popular.
- In 1937, the Marihuana Tax Act was passed. This Act was modeled after the Harrison Narcotics Act and required a special tax of $100 per ounce for all marijuana transactions. The required tax stamps were rarely issued, effectively making the substance illegal.
- The three main categories of law related to drugs are: use or possession laws, manufacturing laws, and distribution laws.
- The war on drugs was first declared during the Nixon administration and many laws were passed, including the Comprehensive Drug Abuse Prevention and Control Act, as well as the Rockefeller Drug Laws. The DEA was created, and some funds were devoted to harm reduction strategies.
- The Ford administration had other issues of national and international concern to address, however, the imbalance between treatment and enforcement for drug issues continued.
- The Carter administration took the position that penalties for the use or possession of drugs should not be more damaging that the use of the substance itself. As such, the attitude of tolerance for the presence of drugs in society under President Gerald Ford continued under President Carter.
- Reagan invigorated the enforcement of drug laws by relaunching the war on drugs. Many very strict drug laws were passed, including the Anti-Drug Abuse Act of 1986 and revisions in 1988, which created mandatory minimum sentences for drug offenses.
- The administration of George Bush established the ONDCP and continued the dedication to strict enforcement of drug laws that were often disparate in their treatment of racial minorities.
- President Clinton's first term in office was fairly laissez-faire with regard to drugs; however, pressure from Republicans during the reelection period resulted in a dramatic change for his second term. Of particular importance was the overriding of the recommendations by the U.S. Sentencing Commission which sought to minimize the racial impact of drug legislation.
- The presidency of George W. Bush merged the issues of drugs and terrorism and funds were dedicated to the prevention of both. Within the United States, President Bush set out a plan to dedicate more funds to treatment of addicts and return somewhat to a harm reduction model.

Important Terms

Anti-Drug Abuse Act
Asset forfeiture
Bureau of Drug Abuse Control (BDAC)
Bureau of Narcotics and Dangerous Drugs
Comprehensive Crime Control Act
Comprehensive Drug Abuse Prevention and Control Act (Controlled Substances Act)
Controlled Substances Act (Comprehensive Drug Abuse Prevention and Control Act)
Department of Defense Authorization Act
Drug Enforcement Administration (DEA)
Federal Bureau of Investigation (FBI)
Hague Convention
Harrison Narcotics Act
Marihuana Tax Act

Office of National Drug Control Policy (ONDCP)
Pure Food and Drug Act
Rockefeller Drug Laws
Shanghai Opium Commission
Single Convention of Narcotic Drugs
Substance abuse and Mental Health Services Administration (SAHMSA)

Critical Thinking Questions

1. Discuss the social dynamics that influenced policies toward drug use in the 1960s, 1970s, and 1980s.
2. Elaborate the significance of race and class in the war on drugs.

Research Topics

1. Choose a specific drug and outline the history of the development of moral panic with regard to this drug. Provide as many specific examples as possible regarding myths that were purported to demonstrate that this drug was extremely harmful. Then address the reality of the potential harm caused by this substance.
2. Select and locate the text of a specific piece of legislation discussed in this chapter. Once you have outlined the main controls provided by this piece of legislation, contextualize this law through a discussion of the social dynamics of the period leading up to its passage.

Suggested Readings

Erlen, Jonathon, and Spillane, Joseph F. (Eds.). (2004). *Federal drug control: The evolution of policy and practice.* New York, NY: Haworth Press.
Lusane, Clarence. (1991). *Pipe dream blues: Racism and the war on drugs.* Boston, MA: South End Press.
Peele, Stanton. (1995). *Diseasing of America.* San Francisco, CA: Jossey-Bass.

9

Drugs and Crime

"Murder Weed Found Up and Down Coast ~ Deadly Marihuana Dope Plant Ready for Harvest that Means Enslavement of California Children"

—HEADLINE FROM THE *LOS ANGELES EXAMINER*, NOVEMBER 5, 1933

OBJECTIVES:

When you have finished this chapter, you should be able to:

- Elaborate the relationships between drugs and various types of crime
- Understand the theoretical explanations for a drugs-crime link
- Understand the relationships between drugs and various types of crime
- Explain the structure of the illicit drug trade
- Discuss current trends in domestic and global drug trafficking
- Understand the domestic trafficking of methamphetamine
- Understand the global trafficking of cocaine and the role of organized crime
- Understand the role of women in the drug economy

REAL LIFE

Segment from "My Bloody Life" by Reymundo Sanchez:

> I lit up a joint, drank half a bottle of wine as if it were water, and grabbed the shotgun . . . I pumped the shotgun and moved to the side door of the van. Pebbles was looking out the window and instructing me as to what corner the Vicelords were standing on. Suddenly the van stopped and Hercules yelled "Now!" I jumped out, ran toward the northeast corner, and

opened fire. I did just as Hercules had instructed: pump and shoot, pump and shoot. People were screaming and running all over the place. I ran up on the curb and saw a couple of people pleading for mercy as they bled to death. Some guy came running out from the back of a car. I reacted by turning toward him and pulling the trigger. The shots hit him in the back and head; he fell forward and lay there motionless. I ran back inside the van and slammed the door . . . For some reason the incident did not affect me . . . I felt relaxed and proud of myself. Maybe it was the weed and wine . . . I really didn't know what the difference was and I didn't care. What was important was that I had proved myself (Sanchez, 2000, pp. 88–89).

BELIEVING IN A DRUGS-CRIME LINK

As a reminder from Chapter Eight, the Harrison Narcotics Act was passed in December 1914 and used taxation and regulation to limit drug use. The act essentially required any individual who prescribes or distributes drugs to purchase tax stamps and register with the government. An individual in possession of drugs without a prescription was considered in violation of the act. Effectively, the Harrison Act criminalized drugs unless prescribed by a physician for a few clearly defined medical purposes, and unintentionally this act contributed to the development of an underground subculture of drug use. Once a substance becomes illegal, users must continue to find drugs on a regular basis, and avoid detection by law enforcement in the process. Thus the result is a group of individuals either using or selling drugs who cultivate relationships with other law violators. This criminal subculture is a direct response to the criminalization of drugs. Therefore, for many scholars, the passage of the Harrison Act was the point in history during which law-abiding citizens were turned into criminals.

The moral panics surrounding various drugs (elaborated in Chapter Two) illustrate the historic and current perceived relationship between crime and drugs, usually thought to be among a minority population, such as the Chinese, Mexicans, or African Americans. Much of the public believes that if the pervasive use of drugs is significantly reduced, so too will the crime rate be significantly reduced. This notion is rooted in the high crime rates of the 1960s when policymakers sought to link crime to drugs. The importance of myth in understanding the relationship between drugs and crime is elaborated in the following:

> Myth is a body of lore regarded as roughly true. It implies collective fantasy, drawing its fabulous plots from notions based more on traditions and convenience than on fact. Myth guides conduct by orienting, sustaining, or suppressing aspects of social behavior. The chronicle of our nation, from its earliest pages, reflects a noticeable dependence on myth in its perception and understanding of the use of drugs for the enhancement of pleasure or performance. Remarkably, this phenomenon seems to persist despite any contradictions by science and logic . . . it is generally believed, for example that all drug users are degenerate and dependent people; that heroin and cocaine are the most dangerous substances on earth; that PCP is a Jekyll and Hyde drug that immediately changes mild-mannered users into raving maniacs; that crack is at the base of all inner-city problems; that the use of marijuana invariably leads to heroin addiction . . . (Inciardi, 2002, p. 167).

The relationship between crime and drugs, however, is much more complicated than simply "drugs cause crime," and usually falls into one of three categories (see also Table 9-1):

- **Drug-defined crimes**, which include the sale and/or possession of an illegal substance;
- **Drug-related crimes**, which include violent behaviors induced by the properties of a drug or illegal activity that occurs to further a drug habit; and
- **Crimes associated with drug use**, which include crimes that may have occurred while an individual was under the influence of an illegal substance, but the crime was not a direct result of drug use (Walker, 2006).

In fact, the Department of Justice itself views the drug-crime link as complex, suggesting that "for some individuals drug use is independent of their involvement in crime . . . these people may continue to commit crimes even if drugs were unavailable" (Bureau of Justice Statistics [BJS], 1992, p. 2). Nevertheless, the fear of a relationship between drugs and crime led to the creation of the National Institute on Drug Abuse in 1974.

Examination of the literature does reveal a connection between drugs and crime: Those who use drugs (including alcohol) are more likely to be involved in criminal behavior than those who do not use drugs. But why? Does using drugs cause involvement in crime? Or is it the reverse: Does involvement in criminal activity lead one to use drugs? Or, are involvement in crime and use of drugs the result of some other factor? Much existing research suggests that drug use does not precipitate involvement in crime, but does impact the extent of crime, the types of crime, and the duration one is involved in crime. Since the 1920s, these questions have been researched and debated by scholars.

TABLE 9-1 The Relationship Between Drugs and Crime

Relationship	Definition	Examples
Drug-defined crimes	Violations of laws prohibiting or regulating the possession, use, distribution, or manufacture of illegal drugs	Drug possession or use; marijuana cultivation; methamphetamine production; sale of illegal substances
Drug-related crimes	Offenses in which a drug's pharmacologic effects contribute; offenses motivated by the user's need for money to support continued use; and offenses connected with drug distribution itself	Violent behavior resulting from drug effects; stealing to get money to buy drugs; violence against rival drug dealers
Crimes associated with drug use	Drug use and crime are common aspects of a deviant lifestyle; the likelihood and frequency of involvement in illegal activity is increased because drug users and offenders are exposed to situations that encourage crime	A life orientation with an emphasis on short-term goals supported by illegal activities; opportunities to offend resulting from contacts with offenders and illegal markets; criminal skills learned from other offenders

Source: Bureau of Justice Statistics, 1992.

ILLUSTRATING A DRUGS-CRIME LINK

Recall from Chapter Four that the Arrestee Drug Abuse Monitoring Program (ADAM) is a project that randomly selects recently arrested individuals and conducts interviews and urinalysis within 48 hours of booking to assess their involvement with five types of illicit substances: cocaine (crack and powder), marijuana, opiates, methamphetamine, and PCP (phencyclidine). Across all sites collecting data, findings revealed that use of at least one of the five illegal drugs ranged from 52 percent to 80 percent, use of marijuana ranged from 29 percent to 57 percent, and use of cocaine (either crack or powder) ranged from 11 percent to 49 percent (Arrestee Drug Abuse Monitoring Program [ADAM], 2003). As illustrated in Table 9-2, gender differences in usage of all other drugs except marijuana are minimal. The ADAM report is useful for elaborating the relationship between drugs and crime, as median drug use among those arrested is quite high. This does not mean, however, that the use of an illegal substance "causes" an individual to engage in crime.

Though the ADAM reports median findings are based on drug test results, other surveys conducted in state and federal correctional facilities ask inmates about their use of drugs during the commission of an offense. These findings are also illustrative:

- Thirty-two percent of state prisoners and 26 percent of federal prisoners admitted being under the influence of drugs while committing their most recent offense
- Fifty-six percent of state prisoners were considered dependent upon drugs or alcohol
- In 1996, just over half of convicted jail inmates admitted being under the influence of drugs while committing a violent offense against an intimate victim (BJS, 2007).

Keep in mind that many studies do not separate those individuals arrested for drug-defined offenses (like drug possession) from those arrested for drug-related offenses (such as burglary or assault). Chapter Eleven will address specifically the demographics of those arrested for drug-defined offenses, but here we will elaborate the relationship between drug use and drug-related offenses, including property crime, violent crime, and domestic violence.

Violent Crime and Alcohol Consumption

Studies have demonstrated that a large proportion of violence occurring in the United States is associated with the consumption of alcohol. The relationship between violent crime and alcohol reveals that individuals consuming alcohol are involved in at least half of the reported assaults

TABLE 9-2 Median Percentage Drug Test Results by Gender, 2000

Type of Drug Used	Male	Female
Cocaine, opiates, marijuana, methamphetamine, or PCP	64.2	62.5
Marijuana	40.9	26.7
Cocaine	30.9	33.1
Opiates	6.5	7.2
Methamphetamine	1.6	3.0
PCP	0.3	0.0

Source: Arrestee Drug Abuse Monitoring Program, 2003.

and homicides. Additionally, prior to a violent episode, alcohol consumption is high in both assailants and victims (Murdoch, Pihl, & Ross, 1990). Additionally, approximately 20 percent of violent victimizations involve a victim who believes the offender was under the influence of alcohol (BJS, 1998). Figure 9-1 elaborates the relationship between alcohol consumption and rape/sexual assault, robbery, aggravated assault, and simple assault as revealed in a BJS Report in 1998.

Another study examining the relationship between violent crime and alcohol, the Drug Relationships in Murder Project, was conducted in 1984 in New York State. A total of 268 homicide offenders were interviewed extensively in order to understand the role of drugs in the commission of murder. Overwhelmingly, the substance used immediately preceding the homicide was alcohol, with 58 percent of alcohol users believing that alcohol use influenced the commission of their crime. One respondent suggested:

> Alcohol kept me from being self conscious, so I couldn't monitor my behavior. Whatever feelings stirred up were unrestrained. No inhibitions, no thinking about what I'm doing, on automatic. Feel something, then just do it. If not drunk, I would have thought of the consequences ahead of time. If not drunk, it wouldn't have happened (Spunt, Goldstein, Brownstein, Fendrich, & Langley, 1994, p. 151).

This study illustrates one potential relationship between alcohol and homicide.

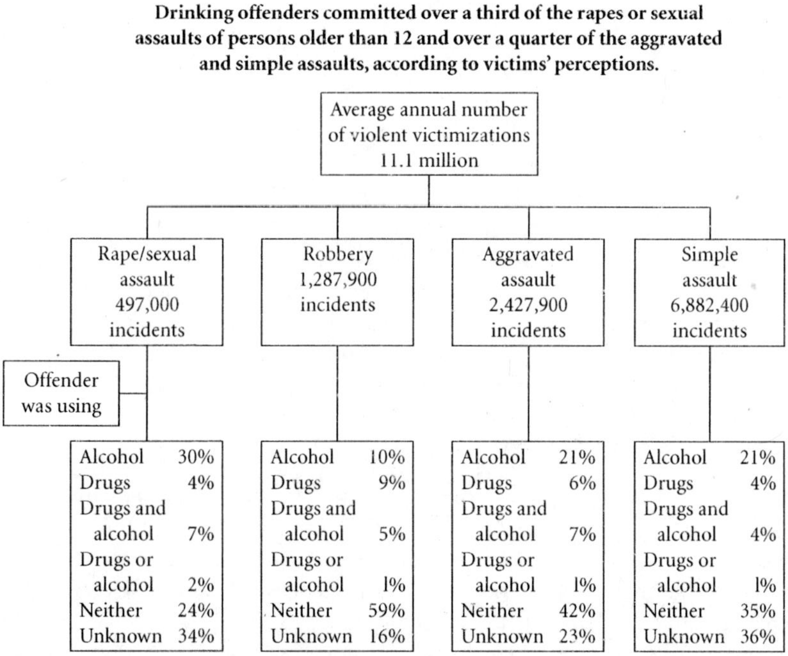

FIGURE 9-1 Relationship Between Alcohol Consumption and Violent Crime, 1998.
Source: Bureau of Justice Statistics, 1998.

Over the past 10 years, public and scholarly interest in juvenile crime has increased dramatically. Though associations between youth, violence, and illicit substances abound in the literature (Fagan, 1989; Reiss & Roth, 1993), the association between youth, violence, and alcohol is less well researched. It was the topic, however, of an ethnographic study conducted in the late 1970s (Burns, 1980):

> Accompanied by an ethnographer during an evening of drinking, four young European-American males from a working-class neighborhood in Boston were brought closer by their displays of aggression. While they had been deferential at local bars to elder drinkers, they ran amok in the "adult entertainment" sections of the city. Their aggressive behavior included "loud conversation, good-natured wrestling, piling into a car, speeding, verbal boasting, verbal threatening, raucous comments, verbal disparagement, being rowdy, yelling, screaming, arguing, putting a fist through a store window, fighting, bottle crashing, threatening with a gun, and sexual aggressiveness." The more beers the boys consumed, the more aggressive they were (Hamid, 1998, p. 149).

A study by Hunt and Laidler (2001) examined the role of drinking in gang behavior generally, and specifically the relationship between violence and alcohol consumption. Drinking is endemic to most gang activity and frequently is done to maintain group cohesiveness and increase social cohesion. Overwhelmingly, those in African American and Latino gangs admit to engaging in alcohol consumption at least sometimes in the process of cruising, hanging out with the group during the day or night, or attending group parties. Additionally, African Americans (55 percent) and Latinos (44 percent) admit to sometimes using alcohol prior to engaging in a fight, as well as after a gang fight (African Americans 87 percent; Latinos 77 percent). This is one example that confirms an association between youth, violence, and alcohol consumption (Hunt & Laidler, 2001).

Other researchers point to more of a socialization effect, suggesting that there is little empirical evidence between intoxication and aggression. Some scholars argue that it is not the actual psychopharmacological effects of alcohol that result in violence. What is more important is the *belief* that one is intoxicated. This learned and socially acceptable response to alcohol may lead to an increase in aggression as individuals attribute, or blame, their behavior on alcohol, subsequently allowing themselves to preserve their own social standing and self-image while acting against social norms (Briddel, Rimm, Caddy, Dorawitz, Sholis, & Wunderlin, 1978). The relationship between alcohol and aggression remains complex, with alcohol resulting in violence in some situations and not others, and in some cultures but not others, lending support to the notion that drug use is often used as an "excuse" for inappropriate behavior.

Domestic Violence and Drugs

Historically, an association between domestic violence and drugs, specifically alcohol, has been widely accepted and perpetuated by the media, literature, and popular song. The belief has existed for centuries that drugs alter judgment and release a person's inhibitions, often resulting in family violence. The findings, however, are not entirely clear. Domestic violence is a significant social problem that affects between 17 percent and 39 percent of male/female couples each year, with approximately 6 percent experiencing severe violence (Caetano, Vaeth, & Ramisetty-Mikler, 2008). Some studies find a clear and consistent relationship between drugs and domestic violence, and other studies find merely a weak association. For example, the most frequently cited studies are Bard & Zacker (1974), which found only a slight association, versus Wolfgang's (1958) study, which found drinking commonplace among victims of family violence.

According to a report by the BJS (2006), the relationship between intimate/domestic violence and alcohol is significant: Roughly 42 percent of victims of domestic violence between 2001 and 2005 reported that drugs or alcohol were involved at the time of their abuse. Other research, however, shows that the effects of drugs and alcohol on the likelihood of violence in a relationship depend heavily on the dynamics of each couple, and the presence of other various psychosocial stressors (Jung, 2001). A study conducted on a large, representative sample in the 1980s that sought to examine the relationship between alcohol consumption and the likelihood of familial violence indicated a strong link between alcohol abuse and assault on an intimate partner. Though men who were heavy drinkers had significantly higher rates of committing a familial assault, it is important to note that approximately 80 percent of this group of male heavy drinkers never committed a single act of domestic violence (Kantor & Straus, 2003).

The types of violence may also vary depending on the presence or absence of drugs and alcohol. Women and men with alcohol abuse problems experience a higher rate of both moderate and severe domestic violence than individuals in community control samples who do not use drugs or alcohol. Further, if a male aggressor is under the influence of alcohol, the severity of the domestic violence, and therefore the likelihood that his female partner will become physically harmed, increases (Caetano, Vaeth, & Ramisetty-Mikler, 2008). Over 60 percent of couples that include a male entering substance abuse treatment have some history of domestic violence (Fals-Stewart & Clinton-Sherrod, 2009). Some studies have also found that the amount of alcohol consumed plays a role in the presence of violence, specifically that binge drinkers who become heavily intoxicated are more likely to be abusive (Jung, 2001). In a longitudinal study of a community sample of adults in California, researchers found that "drug problems in adulthood were associated with a lifestyle of criminal behavior that included drug crimes, poor adherence to societal norms, and a lack of supportive social networks for drug problems," which supports the correlation between substance abuse and criminal behavior (Newcomb, Galaif, & Carmona, 2001, p. 191). However, "whether drug problems precede criminality or criminal behaviors precede drug problems continues to be debated" (Newcomb, Galaif, & Carmona, 2001, p. 185).The bottom line is that what emerges from the family violence literature is a multidimensional relationship between intimate violence and the use of drugs and/or alcohol that requires significantly more scholarly investigation.

EXPLAINING A DRUGS-CRIME LINK

In elaborating the relationship between drugs and crime, Goldstein (1985) has offered three useful explanations: psychopharmacological, economic–compulsive, and systemic.

Psychopharmacological Explanations

Psychopharmacological explanations suggest that drugs induce psychological and physical reactions that increase the likelihood of users getting involved in crime. It is believed that use of some drugs result in users becoming irritable, excitable, irrational, or detached and these reactions may lead to violence. Furthermore, psychopharmacological models suggest that individuals under the influence of drugs may be more susceptible to victimization than an individual who has complete control. These beliefs have provided the basis for moral panics surrounding various drugs, including the "drug crazed, super strong cocaine addict." Empirical evidence to support this position, however, is scarce. Indeed, one problem with psychopharmacological explanations is that urinalysis testing can detect some drugs in a person's system for up to 2 months: This leaves much to debate as to whether the drug had a direct influence on the criminal behavior of the individual being tested. Even with drugs that have a reputation for being associated with violence (such as crack), it is unclear whether the violence is a result of the drug or another factor. Indeed in the case of crack, violent tendencies are also observed during withdrawal (Levinthal, 2008).

Most studies suggest that a psychopharmacological response to drugs is rare and when it does occur it is most frequently associated with alcohol consumption, as was discussed in relation to domestic violence (White & Gorman, 2000). Therefore, research finds that "intoxication does not consistently lead to aggressive behavior . . . [there is] only limited evidence that consumption of alcohol, cocaine, heroin, or other substances is a direct, pharmacologically based cause of crime" (Fagan, 1990, p. 243). It is important to remember that the pharmacological response to a substance occurs within a social context. If the biological response to a substance such as alcohol was predictable, we would expect to see similar responses across individuals. Instead, there are many varieties of drunks: some become violent or belligerent, while others become gregarious and amorous. These individual differences indicate that social context has much to add to a psychopharmacological understanding of drugs.

Economic–Compulsive Explanations

Scholars advocating an **economic–compulsive explanation** for the drug-crime link suggest that drug users engage in various types of crime (which may result in violence) in order to financially support their drug habit. This explanation is rooted in the assumption that drugs are expensive and addicting, and that once addicted an individual must somehow obtain the finances to support his or her habit. This explanation was advocated by Commissioner Anslinger in 1951:

> It is well established that a larger proportion of the pickpocket artists, the shoplifters, the professional gamblers and card sharks, the confidence men operating fake horse races or fake stock sale schemes, the "short con" men such as the "shortchange artists" or the coin matchers, are addicted to the use of narcotic drugs (as cited in Inciardi, 2002, p. 183).

Based on recent data (see Table 9-3), there is some support for this theoretical explanation, with up to 30 percent of prisoners admitting to engaging in crime to earn money to buy drugs.

TABLE 9-3 Percent of Prison/Jail Inmates Who Committed an Offense to Earn Drug Money

Offense	Local Jail Inmates (2002)	State Prisoners (2004)	Federal Prisoners (2004)
Total	16.4	16.6	18.4
Violent	8.0	9.8	14.8
Property	26.9	30.3	10.6
Drugs	24.8	26.4	25.3
Public order	5.2	6.9	6.8

Source: Bureau of Justice Statistics, 2006; Bureau of Justice Statistics, 2007.

A study of incarcerated parents revealed that mothers in state prison (32 percent) were more likely than fathers (19 percent) to admit to committing a crime to get drugs or to earn money to purchase drugs (BJS, 2007).

A 1967 study of heroin addicts revealed that property crimes in an area increased with an increase in the rates of heroin addiction and crimes against people decreased. It was suggested that as an addiction to heroin developed, individuals would concentrate their efforts on activities to monetarily support their habit (Finestone, 1967). This association between drug use and property crime (as opposed to crimes against people) was supported in a variety of other research studies (Inciardi & Chambers, 1972). In fact, a survey conducted in 2004 of inmates in state prison revealed that 39 percent of property offenders reported being under the influence of drugs at the time of their offense (BJS, 2007).

Though drug use may not initiate involvement in crime, it does influence the amount of individual criminal activity. Using longitudinal data, research has demonstrated significant decreases in criminal involvement during periods of abstinence from drugs such as heroin, and spikes in criminal involvement during periods of heavy drug use (Ball, Rosen, Flueck, & Nurco, 1981). For example, a study of crack users revealed that 59 percent of participants engaged in 6,669 robberies over a period of 1 year, most of which were committed to secure money to purchase drugs (Inciardi, 1990). There is evidence to suggest that this may be explained by economic–compulsive explanations because substances like heroin and cocaine are relatively expensive and many users are unemployed or underemployed. Indeed, as drug prices increase, so does the level of property crime. From a policy perspective this means that decreasing the drug supply increases the cost of drugs on the street, which in turn has the potential to result in increased property crime rates.

Systemic Explanations

Systemic explanations of the drug-crime connection suggest that the illegal nature of substances and the underground economy surrounding drug trafficking and distribution results in crime as dealers must "settle scores" on their own without legal protection. Some scholars use this explanation as the basis to advocate a decriminalization or legalization position, suggesting that it is the illegal nature of the substance that leads to involvement in criminal activity. This position is supported by the spike in crime that occurred during Prohibition. Systemic explanations purport that the business of drugs results in crimes such as territorial violence, efforts at debt collection, and disputes over the quantity/quality of drugs.

Empirical testing of Goldstein's (1985) classifications of the relationship between drugs and crime has tended to support systemic explanations for a drug such as crack (Goldstein, Brownstein, & Ryan, 1992), but provides less support for other types of drugs (Lattimore, Trudeau, Riley, Leiter, & Edwards, 1997). In 2005, 4 percent of the 14,860 homicides reported in the Uniform Crime Reports were considered drug related (BJS, 2007). As well, some research suggests that use of drugs sustains one's involvement in crime by interfering with their ability to mature or grow out of the crime stage. Ethnographers purport that "the subcultural values that emerge in street-drug-using cultures encompass crime as a means to obtain drugs and as a cultural value itself in opposition to the straight world of legitimate low-paying jobs . . . using drugs and criminal behavior become well integrated within the cultural/social role of the street-drug user" (McBride & McCoy, 2003, p. 110). As such, the use of drugs is a central part of the subculture that exists on the street, making both crime and drug use part of a generally deviant lifestyle.

What becomes evident is that there is no clear and consistent relationship between drugs and crime that has been established in the literature, despite hundreds of scientific studies addressing this relationship. What emerges instead is a dynamic view: In some instances a psychopharmacological approach provides the best explanation and in other instances an economic–compulsive or systemic explanation may be more appropriate. Crime usually results from a confluence of factors, and the use of drugs is only one of many factors that may lead to involvement in criminal activity. So, while there is certainly some relationship between drugs and crime, the extent and exact nature of that relationship remains open to debate and further investigation.

THE ILLICIT DRUG TRADE

Estimates regarding the amount of money spent annually on drugs abound and vary dramatically. While the value of an illicit market is extremely difficult to assess, the trafficking and distribution of drugs is an enormously profitable endeavor by any estimate. The United Nations Office on Drugs and Crime estimated the world narcotics trade in 2005 at approximately US$320 billion (United Nations Office on Drugs and Crime [UNODC], 2007). The drug trade can be divided into various stages from production through distribution, including:

- Cultivation and manufacturing occur throughout the globe in various circumstances, depending on the type of substance;
- Drugs are then imported to the United States by drug traffickers through various routes, again depending on the cultivation and manufacture location of the substance;
- Wholesale distribution then occurs wherein large quantities of the substance are sold to a wholesaler;
- Finally, distribution at the retail level occurs, which involves the sale of smaller quantities of the substance to various street-level dealers.

At both (or either) the wholesale distribution and retail distribution levels, the substance may be adulterated or "cut" (mixed with other substances) in order to increase profit. The transits of different types of drugs will be clarified with two examples in this chapter.

Generally, retail distribution of drugs involves one of two models. In the **freelance model** of drug distribution, dealers who work independent of any large-scale drug organization sell as part of a "cash only" business. Typically, dealers have a variety of buyers, some they see on multiple occasions for regular or semi-regular sales, and other customers whom they see only once, for example at a concert or nightclub. In the **business model** of drug distribution, retail-level sales are organized hierarchically and drugs are "fronted" as opposed to being paid for immediately. The center of this model is a crew boss who obtains drugs from a wholesaler and then divides the supply among a variety of street-level dealers called "runners." This model is described as follows:

> Runners most often are young (aged fourteen to twenty-three) males recruited from inner-city neighborhoods. Each crew boss may have as many as 20 runners working under his direction. Runners are assigned to work at a particular street location, sell only at a given price, and then hand over all of the money to the crew boss. As the drugs are sold, the money flows up the chain, from runners, to crew boss, and back to the wholesaler. Prices are agreed upon before the drugs are fronted. At the end of the day, each runner is paid in money or drugs for his or her work. To avoid rip-offs and robberies, each crew is guarded by an armed lieutenant who supervises several street sellers. Crack dealing organizations located in many urban neighborhoods best exemplify the business model of street dealing . . . Members of urban street gangs in the United States, such as the Crips and Bloods, are often involved in the business model of street dealing, working both as runners and crew bosses (Levinthal, 2008, pp. 306–307).

Depending on the type of drug and the distribution model, the origination and routes of drug trafficking vary. Additionally, the level of organization or decentralization of people trafficking in the illicit substance varies (as will be seen later in this chapter in a discussion of the involvement of organized crime in the cocaine trade). Keep in mind, however, that the drug business is a global business just like any other, and therefore benefits the global economy and the economy of the nation involved in the trade. Indeed, complete elimination of the illicit drug trade would decimate the economic viability of many countries in which legal industries are not nearly as profitable. The trade in drugs, just like the trade in other goods, has become global in recent decades as trade zones have expanded and capitalism has spread across the world. (Table 9-4 gives a brief overview of drug trafficking to the United States).

The specific trafficking route varies from drug to drug, and even from year to year, in response to law enforcement initiatives. Goode (2008) elaborates three drug trafficking models.

- Marijuana provides the most illustrative example of the **pure agricultural model**. A drug produced using this type of model involves minimal manufacturing and no synthetic production. The drug is harvested and consumed in nearly its natural state.
- Drugs such as methamphetamine and LSD provide an example of the **pure chemical model**. A drug produced using this type of model is created synthetically from start to finish, and does not have an agricultural product as its origin.
- Heroin and cocaine are examples of the **mixed model**, which describe an agriculturally grown substance that is then synthesized into a chemical for consumption. "The mixed model can be depicted by an hourglass shape; it requires funneling the produce of many farms to a fairly small number of labs, through high-level to lower-level dealers. Hence, the user relies on both the grower and the manufacturer with chemical know-how to obtain a usable drug" (Goode, 2008, p. 363).

These three models elaborate the production of an illicit substance and may indicate trafficking patterns as well. For example, drugs such as cocaine and heroin could not reasonably be grown in the United States, and therefore must be imported from countries in which the opium plant or the coca plant grow. Marijuana, conversely, is amenable to growth either indoors or outdoors,

TABLE 9-4 Brief Guide to Drug Trafficking

Illicit Substance	Trafficking Overview
Cocaine	Most coca cultivation takes place in Colombia, Bolivia, or Peru, and Mexican criminal organizations are responsible for importation and distribution in the United States
Hallucinogens	Most LSD in the United States is manufactured in laboratories in northern California; MDMA originates primarily from Europe and is trafficked into the United States; PCP is produced and distributed by street gangs in California
Heroin	The four major sources of heroin to the United States are the Golden Triangle of Southeast Asia; the Golden Crescent of Pakistan, Afghanistan, Turkey, and Iran; Mexico; and South America
Marijuana	Most outdoor cultivation takes place in California, Hawaii, Washington, Oregon, Tennessee, and Kentucky; foreign sources for marijuana are primarily Mexico and recently Canada
Methamphetamine	Large-scale production is based in Mexico and California

which influences the trafficking routes to U.S. consumers. Trafficking patterns are illustrated in this chapter through examples using methamphetamine and cocaine.

DOMESTIC DRUG TRAFFICKING

Domestic trafficking of drugs developed into a booming business at the end of the 20th century as demand from the consumer continued to climb. Research suggests that trafficking organizations reflect a degree of hierarchy and stages of "career advancement" similar to legitimate businesses.

> Each level of the hierarchy has a definitive job description and level of responsibility to assure smooth operation. Like those in legitimate businesses, drug dealers rely on their knowledge to train new recruits and tend to organize, plan, and execute their ventures in ways similar to legitimate businesspersons. Those with the highest degree of responsibility earn the most profit, those with less responsibility tend to earn the least. In short, a dealer's occupational involvement takes the form of a career with methods of entry, levels of advancement, and retirement phases similar to those found in most legitimate work environments (Vannostrand & Tewksbury, 2006, p. 316).

But why would an individual choose this illegal "career path" as opposed to legitimate employment? Interviews with dealers reveal a confluence of motives, including financial gain, a desire for status or power that is often motivated by greed, or a need to support their own drug habit.

Some dealers enter into drug sales primarily due to financial need and the belief that legitimate, lucrative employment opportunities are unavailable. For example, one participant in a study of drug dealers said:

> The money is one reason that got me motivated because I wasn't working and I was trying to make ends meet. Trying to take care of my responsibilities. Then, I started to work. It was like, "I don't have to work. I can make more in a day [dealing] than what I would for a whole week doing this" (Vannostrand & Tewksbury, 2006, p. 318).

Though some individuals enter drug dealing to earn a living they believe cannot be earned in a legitimate business, others are motivated by greed and drawn to the luxuries that are often associated with higher-level drug dealing. For example:

> I can't say that I was forced. My family always had money. I was never broke, I was never hungry . . . The people I hung around with kind of caught on to me. I guess I was just a spoiled brat, or whatever. I started hanging around guys that was dealing and they would show me all this money and all this stuff . . . Money started coming so fast! . . . It just grabs you, takes you (Vannostrand & Tewksbury, 2006, p. 319).

Still others enter the world of drug dealing for the perceived status:

> People gave you more respect [as a dealer]. They looked at you better. You could just feel the difference . . . It's a real big difference (Vannostrand & Tewksbury, 2006, p. 319).

Whatever the motivation for entering a lifestyle that involves drug dealing, the mechanics of the business parallel legitimate business practices in the selection of buyers that are willing and able

Case Study:

Methamphetamine in the United States

Surveys of American high school students reveal that the use of methamphetamine dropped approximately 37 percent between 2002 and 2006. Among the adult population, meth use decreased approximately 20 percent. In 2004, the National Survey on Drug Use and Health determined that approximately 1.4 million Americans used meth in the previous 12 months, and 583,000 are regular users that reported use in the past month (www.dea.gov/concern/meth.html#6). Despite these figures, however, local and state agencies continue to report high levels of concern regarding this illicit substance. The "meth threat" began in the early 1990s primarily in western states and has since spread east, though the impact of methamphetamine is much less in the Northeast region than in other areas of the country. The expansion eastward of methamphetamine was significant in states such as Arkansas, Illinois, Indiana, Kansas, and Missouri, which experienced large increases in trafficking and abuse (especially in rural areas) between the late 1990s and 2004 (www.dea.gov/concern/methmhtml#6). As evidenced in Table 9-5, the Pacific states, West Central states, and Southwest view meth as the greatest drug threat in the region, with local and state agencies in the Great Lakes area and the Southeast considering it a significant problem as well (UNODC, 2007).

TABLE 9-5 Greatest Drug Threat (in Percent) by Region, Reported by Local and State Agencies, 2006

Region	Meth	Marijuana	Cocaine	Heroin	Pharmaceuticals
Florida/Caribbean (FL, Puerto Rico, United States Virgin Islands)	12.7	9.5	75.6	0.0	0.4
Great Lakes (MN, WI, Northern IL, MI, IN, OH, KY)	27.6	17.1	39.4	8.6	6.5
Mid-Atlantic (PA, MD, DE, WV, VA, DC)	3.9	15.0	54.7	19.9	4.2
New England (ME, NH, VT, MA, CT, RI)	1.9	15.5	33.2	37.6	9.3
New York/New Jersey (NY, NJ)	1.6	25.9	47.0	18.5	4.9
Pacific (AK, HA, American Samoa, Northern Mariana Islands, Guam, WA, OR, ID, NV, Northern and Central CA)	92.2	4.1	2.7	0.0	0.6
Southeast (LA, MS, TN, AL, GA, SC, NC)	36.3	3.0	54.7	0.9	4.3
Southwest (OK, TX, NM, AZ, Southern CA)	74.6	6.3	16.2	1.3	0.6
West Central (MT, WY, UT, CO, ND, SD, NE, KS, IO, MO, AR, and Southern IL)	76.8	3.5	17.6	1.4	0.3

Source: U.S. Drug Enforcement Agency, 2006.

to pay, a preference for certain methods and locations for transactions, and a variety of techniques used to both identify and avoid law enforcement. Some of these parallels can be seen in the production and trafficking of methamphetamine in the United States.

According to the United Nations Office of Drug Control (UNODC) (2007) report, most indicators suggest that domestic production of methamphetamine has been declining in recent years, due to a variety of factors, one of which is the war on drugs. During 2006, a total of 5,395 federal defendants were sentenced in U.S. courts for meth-related charges, and 98 percent of these cases were for trafficking in methamphetamine (http://www.whitehousedrugpolicy.gov/drugfact/methamphetamine/index.html).

One of the main ways to limit the production of amphetamine-type stimulants (ATS) is the seizure and dismantling of clandestine labs. Overwhelmingly, both domestically and globally, the laboratories producing meth are primarily small, improvised kitchen-type labs. These labs are a very American production enterprise; 95 percent of global meth labs dismantled by law enforcement are located in the United States. While historically labs were located primarily in the west and southwest, now meth labs have been located and dismantled in every state, including Alaska. Most large super-labs, however, remain in California (UNODC, 2007). There are varied and significant consequences to the production of methamphetamine and to the property surrounding a meth lab. For example, for every pound of meth produced, between 5 and 6 pounds of hazardous waste is produced, which negatively impacts water supplies, farmland, and vegetation. Cleanup of these areas is expensive for local jurisdictions and the impacts in some areas are so severe that an area of land may remain unusable for decades (UNODC, 2007). In addition, the Hazardous Substances Emergency Events Surveillance (HSEES) system that assesses data on health consequences reveals that meth production frequently results in injuries to people involved in production. Over a span of less than 4 years between 2000 and 2004, HSEES reported 558 events in which meth production resulted in injuries to 947 individuals (www.whitehousedrugpolicy.gov/drugfact/methamphetamine/index.html).

The United States has curtailed the availability of pseudoephedrine, which is used to manufacture methamphetamine. In 2006, the **Combat Methamphetamine Epidemic Act** of 2005 (CMEA) was passed as part of the Patriot Improvement and Reauthorization Act of 2005. The CMEA required a variety of actions by merchants involved in the sale of ephedrine, pseudoephedrine, and phenylpropanolamine, including:

- A record of the name and address of each party purchasing these products must be retained for 2 years;
- Proof of identity must be provided at the sale;
- Any suspicious payments or missing regulated products must be reported to the Attorney General;
- These products must be sold behind the counter or otherwise restricted from public access; and
- Daily sales must not exceed 3.6 grams.

Additionally, most states have laws restricting pseudoephedrine sales, and Oregon goes so far as to require a prescription for purchase. Regulations on substances involved in the production of methamphetamine have decreased the number of kitchen labs throughout the United States considerably.

Another factor contributing to the decline of domestic meth production has been the rising production in a growing number of super-labs in Mexico. There were ten super-labs dismantled in Mexico in 2002, eighteen in 2004, and thirty-four in 2005. In fact, Mexican authorities suggest that of the methamphetamine produced in that country, 99 percent is eventually exported to the

United States (UNODC, 2007). Increasing seizures of meth along the U.S.-Mexico border also point to an increase in trafficking, which began in approximately 2002. Though originally drug trafficking organizations in Mexico transported most of their product into California, production in the interior of Mexico has increased dramatically, which has altered the smuggling routes east to Arizona and southern Texas (www.dea.gov/concern/meth.html#6). Mexico-based traffickers are frequently well organized, which poses an increasing challenge to law enforcement officers.

The Role of Women in the Drug Economy

The role of women in the drug economy has historically been thought of as somewhat peripheral with men often viewing women as unable to handle high-level responsibilities in the drug world due to the possibility of violence. However, some scholars argue that in the crack cocaine market of the 1980s and beyond, women became more involved:

> While women were consigned secondary, gender-specific roles in . . . [drug] businesses in the past, the size and seemingly frantic activity of the current drug markets has made possible for women in new ways to participate in street networks. Their involvement in drug selling at high income levels defies the gendered norms and roles of the past, where drug dealing was an incidental income source often mediated by domestic partnerships . . . the expansion of drug markets in the cocaine economy has provided new ways for women to escape their limited roles, statuses and incomes in previous eras (Fagan, 1994, p. 210).

Though Fagan found women earning relatively high incomes in drug dealing compared to the past, another study that interviewed women in New York City revealed conflicting findings.

> During the entire three years of fieldwork, including the interviews with the larger group of over 200 women, we did not discover any woman who was a business owner, and just one worked as a manager. The highly structured nature of the market in Bushwick, coupled with its kin-based organization, mitigated against personal or intimate sexual relationships between female drug users and higher-level male operatives. To the limited extent that they participated in drug selling, women were overwhelmingly concentrated at the lowest levels. They were almost always used as temporary workers when men were arrested or refused to work, or when it was "hot" because of police presence (Maher & Daly, 2006, p. 141).

Therefore, this study found that the sexism that proliferated in the underground drug economy of the past remained a factor to exclude women from the most profitable areas of the drug economy. In a study conducted over a 6-year period in the 1990s, drug traffickers caught transporting drugs through Heathrow Airport were analyzed. Approximately 27 percent of the sample were women involved in the high-risk role of courier. Compared to the men in the study, women were usually smuggling a greater weight and value of drugs and were more likely to carry Class A substances. The results of this study, therefore, lend credence to the position of gender inequity in the drug economy (Harper, Harper, & Stockdale, 2002).

While research continues to find conflicting results regarding the role of women in the drug business, statistics indicate clearly that the number of women arrested and sentenced to prison for drug offenses has increased significantly beginning in the mid-1980s. For example, the U.S. Department of Justice estimates that 3.2 million women were arrested on felony drug convictions in 1998, representing 17 percent of all drug arrests (BJS, 1999). The harsh sentencing policies and mandatory minimum laws for drug offenses that will be elaborated in detail in Chapter Eleven impact women significantly, despite the fact that many of them have no prior criminal record. So while scholars have conflicting views of the role of women in the global drug economy, the punishments for women are not in debate.

GLOBAL DRUG TRAFFICKING

Some global drug trafficking concerns fall under the purview of **INTERPOL** is the largest international police organization in the world, with 187 member countries. INTERPOL works within existing laws by attempting to prevent international crime, including global drug crime. According to its Web site, the primary drug-control role of INTERPOL is to:

> identify new drug trafficking trends and criminal organizations operating at the international level and to assist all national and international law enforcement bodies concerned with countering the illicit production, trafficking and abuse of cannabis, cocaine, heroin, and synthetic drugs by:
>
> - collecting and analysing data obtained from member countries for strategic and tactical intelligence reports and disseminating these reports to the concerned countries;
> - responding to and supporting international drug investigations;
> - helping to co-ordinate drug investigations involving at least two member countries;
> - organizing operational working meetings between two or more member countries where INTERPOL has identified common links in cases being investigated in these countries;
> - organizing regional or global conferences on specific drug topics, the aims of which are to assess the extent of the particular drug problem;
> - exchange information on the latest investigative techniques; and
> - strengthen co-operation within law enforcement communities (http://www.interpol.int/Public/Drugs/default.asp).

Many of INTERPOL's activities are reported on by the UNODC which monitors drug activity globally among the 187 member states. This office reported 1.5 million drug seizures in 2005. Cannabis constituted 57 percent of the seizure cases in 2005, followed by opiates (17 percent), and then amphetamine type stimulants (10 percent). Approximately half of the ATS seizures reported globally were for methamphetamine (UNODC, 2007). Though coca products, primarily cocaine, accounted for only 9 percent of seizure cases globally in 2005, this illicit substance will be the focus of further elaboration of global drug trafficking in the following case study.

The Role of Organized Crime

Perhaps the primary interest in drugs for any criminal organization is the enormous profit potential. Though for the public there is often a mental association between organized crime and drug trafficking, how common is the involvement of organized criminals in the global transportation of drugs? In some instances, drug trafficking is carried out by large, highly organized, highly structured groups; in other instances, drug trafficking is carried out by small, flexible,

Case Study:

Cocaine

The UNODC estimates that globally approximately 14 million people use cocaine in any given year, with the highest prevalence rate in North America (6.4 million users), followed by West and Central Europe (3.9 million users). While demand for cocaine has not expanded in North America, European demand has increased significantly over the past 10 years (UNODC, 2007). The global market in cocaine, including total production, total amount of cocaine intercepted, and total available for potential consumption, has remained fairly stable from 1994 through 2004. Much of the global supply of coca bush comes from Colombia (54 percent), Peru (30 percent), or Bolivia (16 percent), with minimal fluctuation in the number of hectares cultivated over the past several years, and minimal fluctuation in the potential production of cocaine in these three countries (UNODC, 2007). Though there were successes in the reduction of cultivation beginning in 2000, the reduction in cultivation did not translate to a decline in the production of cocaine. Coca yields have improved in recent history due to greater knowledge and skill regarding production, as well as the use of fertilizers and pesticides. This has resulted in the relative stability of cocaine production globally (UNODC, 2007). Beginning in 2000, there has been a marked increase in seizures of cocaine. International law enforcement increased the interception rate for cocaine from 24 percent in 2000 to almost double (42 percent) in 2006. Additionally, there has been an increase in the number of countries reporting seizures of cocaine, which numbered 45 in 1980 and as of 2005 had risen significantly to 131 nations (UNODC, 2007). Globally, the largest seizures were in South America (51 percent), followed by those in North America (27 percent) (UNODC, 2007). More specifically, the largest cocaine seizure in 2005 was made in Colombia. Additionally, 99 percent of the 5,737 clandestine laboratories that were dismantled for producing cocaine in 2005 were in Bolivia, Colombia, or Peru. This demonstrates that much of the cocaine production process is located very close to the areas of cultivation. Indeed, the UNODC finds no indications of large-scale coca cultivation and production outside of Bolivia, Colombia, and Peru.

There were a significant number (27.4 percent) of seizures of cocaine in the United States as well, due to cooperation among law enforcement that permits the interception of trafficking routes. It should be understood that cocaine trafficking in 2005 was much more global than in 1980, as evidenced by the number of countries reporting seizures during this time period. Currently, 80 percent of countries that report seizing some illicit substance report cocaine among the drugs confiscated (UNODC, 2007). Though cocaine is making its way around the globe, five countries (Colombia, the United States, Venezuela, Spain, and Ecuador) accounted for almost three-quarters of cocaine seizures in the world in 2005 (UNODC, 2007). Colombia, the United States, Venezuela, and Spain have topped the list of significant cocaine seizures for years; however Ecuador is new to the list, perhaps indicating a new trafficking route. Because Ecuador is a southern neighbor to Colombia, this would be a good shipment route for traffickers.

The main trafficking route of cocaine is from Colombia to the United States. The U.S. Interagency Assessment of Cocaine Movement reported in 2005 that approximately half of the cocaine transported to the United States came by way of the eastern Pacific, and 38 percent was

(*Continued*)

transported along the coasts of Central American nations. Shipments by boat tend to be large and point to a highly organized group behind the transport due to the risks of having boats seized in asset forfeiture proceedings. Currently Mexico is the primary intermediate country for cocaine trafficking, with American authorities estimating that at minimum three-quarters of the cocaine in the United States enters via Mexico and is transported to southern Texas, southern California, Arizona, and western Texas. Prior to 2005, almost half of the cocaine entering the United States did so through the Caribbean, however, by 2005 this route constituted less than 10 percent. As well, in the 1980s direct air shipments from Colombia to the United States were used for trafficking, however, this method was used for less than 1 percent of shipments in 2005; in fact, only 11 percent of cocaine entered the United States via air in 2005 (UNODC, 2007). The movement in cocaine is frequently linked to Mexican organized-crime groups, which began replacing Colombian criminal groups approximately 15 years ago in the southern and mid-western regions of the United States. Law enforcement initiatives suggest that Colombian organized crime remains in charge of cultivation, production, and even some initial transport, but Mexican groups have all but taken over the trafficking and distribution required for American street-level sales. For example, Mexican trafficking organizations use Atlanta as a hub for cocaine to eastern markets, such as Florida and northeastern states. For the immediate future, it is likely that production levels will remain stable and Colombia will remain the prominent country in terms of cocaine production. Due to continued pressure from law enforcement and continued cooperation among agencies, trafficking routes will likely change as criminal enterprise responds to the constraints of interdiction efforts (UNODC, 2007).

temporary associations. The problem is that the extent of involvement of each type of group is unclear. What is clear to criminologists is that the traditional, highly structured type of organized crime that much of the public associates with the mob is an outdated view of organized crime. Increasingly, an organized-crime enterprise is associated with a network of knowledgeable individuals who work within a structure that is quite flexible. It has recently been purported that:

> Organised crime groups are becoming increasingly heterogeneous and dynamically organised in structural terms, moving toward loose networks rather than pyramidal monoliths . . . While there are criminal groups organised along the homogeneous and hierarchical lines, many groups are in practice loose networks of relatively independent members that coalesce around one or more prominent criminals. These networks take up tasks of varying structure, length and complexity according to the demand and concrete profits (UNODC, 2007, p. 171).

This change in organized crime has impacted the trafficking and distribution of illegal drugs as well. For example, groups involved in trafficking illicit substances are now often involved in the movement of more than one type of contraband, and may also be involved in transporting legal goods. As well, whereas ethnic links were historically paramount, many recent groups involve ethnically diverse individuals, or "contract" with other organized-crime groups or street gangs for certain parts of the trafficking and distribution process.

The movement of cocaine at all stages of the trafficking chain has traditionally been run by highly organized groups, dubbed "cartels" during the 1980s. During this period, the Cali Cartel was believed to be responsible for approximately 80 percent of trafficking in cocaine to the United States, which made this organization a target for law enforcement. Strategies such as seizing of assets and extraditing and imprisoning leadership resulted in the dismantling of this single significant organization. It was replaced by numerous lower-profile groups or "baby cartels." Prior to entering the trafficking chain, the growth of the coca leaf is highly decentralized in order to conceal the plant from law enforcement activities such as aerial spraying programs and manual eradication. In 2005, there were approximately 68,600 households in Colombia involved in the cultivation of coca (UNODC, 2007). Two-thirds of these households were also involved in processing the coca leaf to create a cocaine base. From this point forward, the business becomes more centralized. A laboratory is required to convert cocaine base into cocaine hydrochloride and these labs are normally under the purview of organized crime. From this point, the product must be consolidated, which requires a large amount of organization. The cocaine then makes its way, via a variety of transportation routes discussed earlier, to the United States.

At some point prior to reaching American borders, most of the cocaine enters the possession of Mexican groups for distribution in the United States. Even in a climate of relatively loose organization (compared to the large "cartels" of the past), the trafficking of cocaine is enormous business. The U.S. National Drug Intelligence Agency estimates the wholesale value of cocaine in the United States at approximately US$12 billion per year. Retail value of cocaine exceeds this estimate by three to five times. This enormous profit in part explains the violence in Mexico as criminal syndicates fight for key border crossings. This competition for the drug market resulted in at least 1,400 murders in Mexico in 2006 (UNODC, 2007). The huge amount of drugs seized during law enforcement raids points to highly organized groups dominating the trafficking of drugs in Mexico. Once the drugs are in the United States, however, trafficking is the primary responsibility of Americans. Indeed, of the 11,787 individuals arrested for the federal trafficking of cocaine in 2004, 75 percent were American citizens (UNODC, 2007). Thus, while less centralized than in the past, the trafficking of cocaine to the United States remains under the control of relatively large organizations as evidenced by both large seizures worth hundreds of millions of dollars, and the low use rate among the populations in countries traversed as drugs move to the destination where they will be worth the highest values.

Summary

- A criminal subculture remains a direct response to the criminalization of drugs, and for many scholars the passage of the Harrison Act was the point in history during which formerly law-abiding citizens were turned into criminals.
- The relationship between crime and drugs is much more complicated than "drugs cause crime," and usually falls into one of three categories:
  - Drug-defined crimes, which include the sale and/or possession of an illegal substance;
  - Drug-related crimes, which include violent behaviors induced by the properties of a drug or illegal activity that occurs to further a drug habit; and
  - Crimes associated with drug use, including crimes that may have occurred while an individual was under the influence of an illegal substance, but the crime was not a direct result of drug use.
- The ADAM report is useful for elaborating the relationship between drugs and crime as median drug use among those arrested is very high, however, this does

not mean that the use of an illegal substance "causes" an individual to engage in crime.

- Studies have demonstrated that a large proportion of violence occurring in the United States in associated with the consumption of alcohol, however, the relationship between alcohol and aggression remains complex, with alcohol resulting in violence in some situations and not others, and in some cultures but not others, lending support to the notion that drug use is often used as an "excuse" for inappropriate behavior.
- Historically, an association between domestic violence and drugs and alcohol has been widely accepted and perpetuated by the media, literature, and popular song; however, what emerges from the family violence literature is a multidimensional relationship between intimate violence and the use of drugs and/or alcohol that requires significantly more scholarly investigation.
- Three classifications of the relationship between drugs and crime have been offered by Goldstein (1985):
  - Psychopharmacological models provide explanations for drug-related crimes, suggesting that drugs have psychological and physical reactions that increase the likelihood of users getting involved in crime;
  - The economic–compulsive explanation for the drug-crime link suggests that drug users engage in various types of crime (which may result in violence) in order to financially support their drug habit; and
  - Systemic explanations of the drug-crime connection suggest that the illegal nature of substances and the underground economy surrounding drug trafficking and selling results in crime as dealers must "settle scores" on their own without legal protection.
- Though the value of an illicit market is extremely difficult to assess, the trafficking and distribution of drugs is an enormously profitable endeavor by any estimate, estimated in 2005 at approximately US$320 billion.
- The drug trade can be divided into various stages from production through distribution, including: cultivation and manufacturing, import to the United States, wholesale distribution, and distribution at the retail level.
- Retail distribution of drugs involves of one two models: the freelance model or the business model.
- There are three drug trafficking models: the pure agricultural model, the pure chemical model, and the mixed model.
- Dealers enter into the business for motives including financial gain, a desire for status or power that is often motivated by greed, or a need to support their own drug habit.
- Most indicators suggest that domestic production of methamphetamine has been declining in recent years, due to a variety of factors, one of which is the war on drugs.
- The role of women in the drug economy has historically been thought of as somewhat peripheral with men often viewing women as unable to handle high-level responsibilities in the drug world due to the possibility of violence.
- Much of the global supply of coca bush comes from Colombia, Peru, or Bolivia, with minimal fluctuation in the number of hectares cultivated over the past several years and minimal fluctuation in the potential production of cocaine in these three countries.
- What is clear to criminologists is that the traditional, highly structured type of organized crime that much of the public associates with the mob is an outdated view of organized crime, and increasingly an organized-crime enterprise is associated with a network of knowledgeable individuals who work within a structure that is quite flexible.

Important Terms

Business model
Combat Methamphetamine Epidemic Act (CMEA)
Crimes associated with drug use
Drug-defined crimes
Drug-related crimes
Economic–compulsive explanations
Freelance model
INTERPOL
Mixed model
Psychopharmacological explanations
Pure agricultural model
Pure chemical model
Systemic explanations

Critical Thinking Questions

1. Discuss the portrayal of a drugs-crime link presented in the media. Is this representation supported by scholarly research?
2. Elaborate the constrained role of women in the drug economy.

Research Topics

1. Examine drug use rates and crime rates in the state in which you live. Discuss the type of relationship between drugs and crime that is supported by your findings.
2. Choose a drug other than cocaine or methamphetamine and research its trafficking route to the United States.

Suggested Readings

Gaines, Larry K., & Kraska, Peter B. (Eds.). (2003). *Drugs, crime, & justice: Contemporary perspectives.* Prospect Heights, IL: Waveland Press.

Kelley, Margaret S. (Ed.). (2006). *Readings on drugs and society: The criminal connection.* Boston, MA: Allyn & Bacon.

National Institute of Justice (NIJ). (2003). *Toward a drugs and crime research agenda for the 21st century* (No. 194616). Washington, DC: National Institute of Justice.

United Nations Office on Drugs and Crime (UNODC). (2007). *World drug report* (ISBN 978-92-1-148222-5). Sweden: United Nations Publication.

10

Drugs and Other Collateral Damage

—Lauren M. Caravaglia, MSW, LSW

"Man's natural character is to imitate; that of the sensitive man is to resemble as closely as possible the person whom he loves. It is only by imitating the vices of others that I have earned my misfortunes."

—Marquis de Sade

(as quoted on www.RandomTerrain.com)

OBJECTIVES:

When you have finished this chapter, you should be able to:

- Understand the effects drug and alcohol abuse have on an individual's personal social functioning, health, and well-being
- Explain how substance abuse affects the family system
- Understand the effects alcohol and drug use have on an individual's ability to parent effectively
- Describe the consequences of alcohol consumption during pregnancy, including both the negative health effects experienced by the fetus as well as the potential consequences faced by the mother
- Explain the effects parental substance abuse has on children, and how the substance abuse affects the children later in life once they have become adults
- Elaborate on the effects that drugs have on community life

REAL LIFE

A case study discussed in an article entitled *Co-dependency: A Paradoxical Dependency:*

> At 13, Jim was an average student, attractive, popular among his peers, athletic, and extroverted, but because his father was an alcoholic, Jim lived two lives. At home he was lonely and terrified over what others might find out about his family. Jim was depressed, filled with shame and doubt, guilty for wrongs never committed, and deeply resentful. Unable to discuss the fear, anger, or any of the other normal emotions he was feeling, Jim turned to alcohol and drugs. Twelve years later, Jim entered treatment for chemical dependency, where for the first time he learned that the family rules operating while he was growing up were largely responsible for his inability to face his own personal problems constructively. In an effort to compensate for these unhealthy rules, Jim had developed a pattern of perfectionism, compulsive overworking, and destructive dependency in his interpersonal relationships, in addition to his alcoholism (Subby & Friel, 1984, p. 35).
>
> "I come from a family that had an alcoholic and a binge drinker in it. Drinking and smoking helped kill my grandfather at age 69 and also helped kill my abusive first stepfather who died at the age of 45. It also took many years for me to overcome the flashbacks from my childhood. I lived it. I know the truth. Drinking has no place in the home."
>
> —DUANE ALAN HAHN, AS QUOTED ON WWW.RANDOMTERRAIN.COM

Drug and alcohol use do not exist in a vacuum. On the contrary, substance abusers not only face personal consequences to their health and social well-being, their use also affects the people around them both on a micro and macro level. This chapter will explore the various effects drug and alcohol use have on an individual, on the family system, and on communities.

INDIVIDUAL EFFECTS

Substance abuse results in a number of personal consequences. The following sections detail how substance dependency disrupts the social functioning and overall health and well-being of drug and alcohol abusers.

Spiritual Problems

Research has shown that spirituality and religiosity play a role in both the prevention and treatment of substance abuse disorders. It has been found that those who pursue treatment and remain clean and sober are more likely to have strong spiritual or religious beliefs, which they cite as their motivation to cease using drugs (Califano & Sheehan, 2002). Further, those who attend treatment programs with a spiritual base, such as 12-step programs like Alcoholics Anonymous (AA), are more likely to find success in treatment and have lower levels of relapse (Califano & Sheehan, 2002). According to one study, "adults who do not consider religious beliefs important are more than one and a half times more likely to smoke, more than three times likelier to binge-drink, almost four times likelier to use an illicit drug other than marijuana and more than six times likelier to smoke pot than those adults who believe that religion is important" (Califano & Sheehan, 2002, p. 9). This research further recommends that clergy and religious figures obtain more training in substance abuse and become more involved in treatment efforts, and additionally that health care professionals recognize the importance of spirituality and religion in drug treatment (Califano & Sheehan, 2002).

Financial Problems and Homelessness

Financial issues and subsequent homelessness have been found to be severe problems among substance abusers. A 34-year-old homeless man in the United Kingdom named Keith describes his view on homelessness and drugs:

> When you're homeless, you're drawn more to drugs, it's inevitable really. It's the only way you can cope with being homeless, with rough sleeping, and stuff like that. It's there all the time; it's just the norm. You begin to just think you're just doing a normal thing (McNaughton, 2008, p. 182).

Another homeless individual in the United Kingdom, a 26-year-old woman, gives her perspective:

> [In homeless accommodation] you want to shelter yourself . . . hide away, "I'll just get through it, keep your head down" but then you end up, as I say, like it could be drinking or it could be taking drugs . . . just to escape it [the experience of homelessness]. People do turn to the streets, and the drugs, because they're meeting other people who don't care about themselves (McNaughton, 2008, p. 182).

There is a very high representation of those who are substance dependent, most often abusing alcohol and cocaine, in the current homeless population. Though there is an established correlation between substance abuse and homelessness, it is debated whether substance abuse results in homelessness, or homelessness results in substance abuse (Eyrich-Garg, Cacciola, Carise, Lynch, & McLellan, 2008).

Homelessness is a significant social problem, as it is estimated that approximately 3.1 percent of the total U.S. population has been homeless at least once in the last five years (Eyrich-Garg, Cacciola, Carise, Lynch, & McLellan, 2008). Substance abuse problems are extremely high among the homeless population, in addition to other psychosocial concerns, including "mental health, physical health, legal and employment problems" as well as lack of social supports (Eyrich-Garg, Cacciola, Carise, Lynch, & McLellan, 2008, p. 831). Approximately 62 percent of homeless individuals have some history of substance abuse, and as many as 45 percent have used drugs within the last year (Eyrich-Garg, Cacciola, Carise, Lynch, & McLellan, 2008). In a small qualitative study conducted in the United Kingdom, it was found that substance abuse could be "(1) a form of escape from the material reality of marginalization and isolation [the homeless experience]; (2) a form of assimilation to the environment and social networks they had; or (3) a means to cope with prior trauma in their lives, psychologically" (McNaughton, 2008, p. 177).

The majority of homeless individuals in the United States have either a high school education or some kind of trade skill, but fail to utilize these personal resources for issues related to their substance dependency. A national study of substance abusers in treatment found that over 60 percent of homeless individuals do have some type of legitimate, legal income, such as Social Security disability insurance, averaging between $500 and $700 monthly, but they remain homeless nonetheless (Eyrich-Garg, Cacciola, Carise, Lynch, & McLellan, 2008). "The addicted homeless spend most of their money on substances; the more money they acquire, the more (or higher quality) substances they purchase, thus sustaining their homelessness" (Eyrich-Garg, Cacciola, Carise, Lynch, & McLellan, 2008, p. 832).

Health Effects

Alcohol and drug use can result in a multitude of negative physical and mental health effects for users. As illustrated in previous chapters, most people who use drugs and alcohol develop tolerance, which means that over time more and more is needed to achieve the desired euphoric effects of their drug of choice. Increased use puts individuals at risk for overdose, and subsequently, death (Liska, 2004). Further, suddenly discontinuing use of alcohol or drugs is also associated with severe health effects. After prolonged and/or heavy use, a sudden cease in use can result in withdrawal syndrome, causing users to experience withdrawal symptoms such as irritability, nausea, jitters, and headache (Jung, 2001). For drugs considered central nervous system (CNS) depressants, such as alcohol, withdrawal typically causes hyperexcitability, whereas withdrawal from CNS stimulants, such as cocaine, causes depression and lethargy (Jung, 2001). For some drug users, depending on rates of previous use, sudden withdrawal can be fatal (Liska, 2004).

Research has shown that alcohol abuse can lead to a number of negative physiological effects. Alcohol, particularly beer, tends to be high in calories. Therefore, many who regularly drink heavily will typically skip meals and instead consume only alcohol. This can cause health-related problems such as malnutrition and related illnesses (Inciardi, 2002). Those who binge drink are at increased risk for experiencing blackouts or alcohol poisoning, which can lead to death (Liska, 2004). Alcohol can cause problems with the gastrointestinal tract and kidneys, and is known to cause cirrhosis of the liver, which affects about 10 percent of alcoholics (Liska, 2004). Recent studies also suggest that alcohol may play a role in the development of certain types of cancer, including liver, stomach, breast, and various types of oral cancer (Liska, 2004).

In addition to alcohol, many illicit drugs frequently result in negative physiological effects as well. For example, cocaine use has been noted to result in heart problems, seizure, and stroke (Liska, 2004). Heroin, one of the most dangerous and addictive illicit substances, has "a high abuse liability and dependency potential. At overdose levels heroin can produce coma, shock, and, ultimately, respiratory arrest and death" (Inciardi, 2002, p. 101). Heroin abuse has claimed the lives of many, including a number of famous entertainers such as Jimi Hendrix, Janis Joplin, Jerry Garcia of the Grateful Dead, Sid Vicious of the Sex Pistols, and Brad Nowell of Sublime (Inciardi, 2002).

In addition to physical consequences, substance abuse is also frequently associated with mental health problems. Long-term alcohol abuse has been shown to have a significant impact on the psychological well-being of users, and often results in depression and anxiety (Centers for Disease Control and Prevention [CDC], 2007). In fact, 40 percent of psychiatry-related hospital admissions per year are a result of alcohol use (Liska, 2004). Those individuals who are dependent on alcohol are also at increased risk of committing suicide: "Alcoholics have a suicide rate 6 to 15 times greater than that of the general population and alcoholic depression is the number one cause of suicide in the United States" (Liska, 2004, p. 221). Similarly, cocaine use has been noted to cause depression and paranoia (Liska, 2004).

In addition to the physiological and psychological effects of drugs and alcohol, substance use can also result in irresponsible behavior that threatens an individual's general health and well-being. Substance use is typically associated with risk-taking behavior. For example, those under the influence of alcohol are more likely to participate in unprotected sex, which can lead to the acquisition of sexually transmitted diseases and unwanted pregnancy (CDC, 2007). Alcohol use has also been shown to increase the risk of accidental injury and death: "Alcohol accounts for 11 million accidental injuries each year" (Liska, 2004, p. 221). According to the Centers for Disease Control and Prevention (CDC) (2007), such alcohol-related accidental injuries can be caused by events such as motor vehicle accidents, drowning, or burns.

Employment Problems

According to a U.S. Department of Labor report (2009), 75 percent of active drug users, almost 80 percent of heavy alcohol users, and 60 percent of those diagnosed as having a substance use disorder were employed in 2007. Studies on how substance abuse relates specifically to employment have been mixed. Some studies have shown no significant relationship between drug abuse and employment rates, though these studies have found that drug abuse over a considerable period of time does reduce earnings (Schmidt, Zabkiewicz, Jacobs, & Wiley, 2007). Conversely, studies focusing on substance abuse and long-term chronic unemployment reveal that substance abuse may actually affect productivity and ability to retain employment.

> These studies suggest that substance use may have more impact on the capacity to keep a stable job than on the capacity to get one in the first place. Numerous studies show that longer periods of unemployment, and especially episodic, unsteady employment patterns, are strongly associated with increased alcohol and drug consumption and related problems. Furthermore, work performance has been found to decline with substance use over time. Illicit drug use, in particular, has been associated with high rates of job turnover and decreased tenure (Schmidt, Zabkiewicz, Jacobs, & Wiley, 2007, p. 1070).

Though illicit drug use is associated with higher rates of job turnover, results have been mixed regarding alcohol use and work productivity. Though some research suggests that drinking considerably lowers work productivity, it has been found in other studies that moderate use of alcohol may, in fact, increase work productivity (Schmidt, Zabkiewicz, Jacobs, & Wiley, 2007).

According to the National Drug Intelligence Center (NDIC), on-the-job intoxication is extremely hazardous and puts the employee, coworkers, and other individuals at risk of injury or harm. "Economically, businesses often are affected because employees who abuse drugs sometimes steal cash or supplies, equipment, and products that can be sold to get money to buy drugs. Moreover, absenteeism, lost productivity, and increased use of medical and insurance benefits by employees who abuse drugs affect a business financially" (National Drug Intelligence Center [NDIC], 2006, np). One important limitation regarding the existing research on substance abuse and employment is that it often focuses only on men. More research is needed to determine how substance abuse impacts women's employment (Meara, 2006).

FAMILY EFFECTS

> "Mid pleasures and palaces, though we may roam,
> Be it ever so humble, there's no place like home.
> But there is the father lies drunk on the floor,
> The table is empty, the wolf's at the door,
> And mother sobs loud in her broken-back'd chair,
> Her garments in tatters, her soul in despair."
>
> NOBIL ADKISSON, *RUINED BY DRINK* [C. 1860]

Parental Influence

Consider the following information, published by the Substance Abuse and Mental Health Services Administration (SAMHSA) in their 2009 National Survey on Drug Use and Health Report:

> Over 8.3 million children (11.9%) lived with at least one parent who was dependent on or abused alcohol or an illicit drug during the past year. Of the children living with a substance abusing parent, almost 7.3 million (10.3%) lived with a parent who was dependent on or abused alcohol, and about 2.1 million (3.0%) lived with a parent who was dependent on or abused illicit drugs. About 5.4 million children under 18 years of age lived with a father who met the criteria for past year substance dependence or abuse and 3.4 million lived with a mother who met the criteria (Substance Abuse and Mental Health Services Administration [SAMHSA], 2009, np).

The following sections provide insight into the impact of substance abuse on parenting. Substance abuse significantly affects an individual's ability to parent appropriately and responsibly, and act in the best interest of his or her child(ren). Both the federal as well as state governments have reacted to this concern by enacting child welfare legislation that pertains to substance abusing parents.

EFFECTS OF SUBSTANCES ON PARENTAL CAPACITY IN RELATION TO CHILD WELFARE "Alcohol and drugs have blown away the topsoil of family life and reshaped the landscape of child abuse and neglect in America" (Califano, 1999, p. 11). Parental substance abuse has been shown to increase the risk of the occurrence of child abuse and neglect. Put very simply, "substance abuse and addiction can destroy the natural instinct of parents to love and care for their children" (Califano, 1999, p. 12). Research shows that the majority of children abused or neglected by a substance abusing parent are under the age of five, which is particularly detrimental as a wealth of social development and bonding should be occurring for children during this stage in life. Sadly, "the addicted parent sometimes sees the child as an obstacle to getting drugs," and rather than nurture and care for the child, the child is either met with hostility or simply pushed aside while the parent pursues his or her addiction (Califano, 1999, p. 11). Parents are likely to act more aggressively toward their children while under the influence of alcohol or drugs, and subsequently commit acts of physical, verbal, psychological, or sexual child abuse (Jung, 2001). Studies suggest there is evidence that alcohol plays a role in the occurrence of **battered child syndrome**, which is defined by the Office of Juvenile Justice and Delinquency Prevention as "the collection of injuries sustained by a child as a result of repeated mistreatment or beating" (Office of Juvenile Justice and Delinquency Prevention [OJJDP], 2002, p. 1).

> Children whose parents abuse drugs and alcohol are almost three times likelier to be physically or sexually assaulted and more than four times likelier to be neglected than children of parents who are not substance abusers. The parent who abuses drugs and alcohol is often a child who was abused by alcohol- and drug-abusing parents (Califano, 1999, p. 10).

Further, it can be said that the occurrence of child abuse and substance abuse is cyclic. Sadly, those who experience abuse as children, particularly females who are sexually abused, in turn are more likely than the general population to abuse alcohol or drugs as adults and develop other significant psychosocial problems. In a recent study, adult women who experienced physical or sexual abuse exhibited "physical symptoms, depression, anxiety, somatization, and low self-esteem. They were more likely than the general population to be abusing drugs or alcohol, and more likely to have attempted suicide and to have had a psychiatric [hospitalization]" (Jung, 2001, p. 377). When a substance dependant parent exposes a child to substance use, the parent is essentially modeling behavior that the child is then at risk of one day imitating. Studies have demonstrated that children of parents who drink heavily are more likely to develop similar drinking behaviors as adults (Jung, 2001).

Lawmakers have recognized the dangers associated with exposing children to substance abuse. Exposing a child to drug-related activity, including for example, using, manufacturing, and selling drugs in the presence of a child, is considered an illegal activity punishable by law in twenty-five states (U.S. Department of Health and Human Services, 2009). In four states, any adult who commits such an offense could be charged with child endangerment, and in several states manufacturing and distributing drugs in the presence of children is considered a felony. In addition to legal charges, such offenses also warrant referral to Child Protective Services (CPS) (U.S. Department of Health and Human Services, 2009). Many child welfare systems are greatly challenged by cases of substance abusing parents. The goal of CPS is typically to provide whatever supportive services are necessary to strengthen the family system and maintain natural families (U.S. Department of Health and Human Services, 2009). However, many professionals are realizing that substance abusing parents lack motivation to attend treatment. Further, those parents who are actually motivated to change typically need a significant amount of time to rehabilitate, which is precious time that can be considered lost to a developing child who needs constant nurturance and a stable home environment (Califano, 1999). This illustrates a need for:

> comprehensive treatment that is timely and appropriate, especially for substance-abusing mothers . . . to prevent further child abuse and neglect. Treatment must be part of a concentrated course that would include mental health services and physical health care; literacy, job and parenting skills training; as well as socialization, employment and drug-free housing. Since most fathers have walked out on their responsibilities, such treatment must be attentive to the fact that most of these parents are women (Califano, 1999, p. 12).

According to the Centers for Disease Control and Prevention (CDC) (2009b), children with FAS may have the following characteristics:

- Abnormal facial features, such as a smooth ridge between the nose and upper lip (this ridge is called the philtrum)
- Small head size
- Shorter-than-average height
- Low body weight
- Poor coordination
- Hyperactive behavior
- Difficulty paying attention
- Poor memory
- Difficulty in school (especially with math)
- Learning disabilities
- Speech and language delays
- Intellectual disability or low IQ
- Poor reasoning and judgment skills
- Sleep and sucking problems as a baby
- Vision or hearing problems
- Problems with the heart, kidneys, or bones (CDC, 2009b)

FETAL ALCOHOL SYNDROME (FAS) AND GENERAL IMPLICATIONS Consumption of alcohol during pregnancy can cause a number of problems for a developing fetus.

Specifically, exposure to alcohol can affect fetal growth, cause damage to the developing brain, and result in low birth weight (CDC, 2009b). The most severe consequence of drinking while pregnant is **Fetal Alcohol Syndrome**, or FAS, a disorder caused by exposure of a fetus to alcohol, which results in a variety of both physical and psychological issues. FAS is characterized by growth and CNS problems, permanent birth defects, heart and limb defects, as well as behavioral problems and learning disorders later in life. In some severe cases, FAS can cause fetal death (CDC, 2009b).

Those children who are born with FAS experience physical birth defects including abnormal facial features, such as small eyes and eye openings, a thin upper lip, and a smooth philtrum (the area just above the upper lip, which is typically grooved). Many individuals with FAS also tend to have a flat mid-face, a short nose, and an underdeveloped jaw (CDC, 2009b). In addition, some with FAS develop a disorder called microcephaly, which affects neurological development by impeding brain growth. Those with microcephaly tend to have a smaller than average head circumference. As children with FAS mature into adults, many remain below average height and weight and experience hearing and vision problems.

In addition to physical defects, those with FAS are more likely to experience developmental delays and learning disabilities, exhibit maladaptive behaviors, and become diagnosed with psychiatric disorders (CDC, 2009b). Those with FAS are also more likely to become involved in crime, and have higher levels of unemployment and lower levels of education than the general population (CDC, 2009b). Fortunately, there are protective factors that have been found to produce positive outcomes for individuals with FAS, which include early diagnosis, enrollment in early intervention and special education programs, and a stable and healthy home environment (CDC, 2009b).

Not all fetuses that are exposed to alcohol develop FAS. In fact, only 35 percent of women diagnosed with alcohol-related disorders actually give birth to children with FAS (Sadock & Sadock, 2003). According to the CDC, research shows that the occurrence of FAS in the United States is somewhere between 0.5 and 2.0 in every 1,000 live births (CDC, 2009a). As per the CDC, there is no specific amount of alcohol considered safe to consume during pregnancy nor is there a specific time during pregnancy when it is considered safe to drink. For these reasons, the U.S. Attorney General strongly suggests that women abstain entirely from consuming alcohol during pregnancy (CDC, 2009b).

Sadly, the CDC reports that FAS is the most frequently occurring and totally preventable cause of mental retardation and birth defects in the United States. As illustrated in Figure 10-1, the rates of drinking among pregnant women did not substantially change between 1991 and 2005, fluctuating just above and below 10 percent for this 14-year period. Estimates from 2005 to 2006 show that approximately 12 percent of pregnant women reported using alcohol during that time period (Harrison & Sidebottom, 2009). This lack of substantial change in drinking rates among pregnant women points to the need for community education and prevention campaigns to inform women of the dangers of consuming alcohol while pregnant. Unfortunately, many may consume alcohol prior to even knowing they are pregnant, which is why it is also important for doctors to educate female patients, whether pregnant, planning to get pregnant, or simply within childbearing years, about the dangers of drinking during pregnancy.

LAWS RELATED TO DRUG USE/ABUSE AND PREGNANCY. Recent studies have shown that approximately 4 percent of pregnant women report using illicit substances during pregnancy, which means between 200,000 and 400,000 children born each year are prenatally exposed to illicit substances (Schempf & Strobino, 2008; Harrison & Sidebottom, 2009). The most frequently

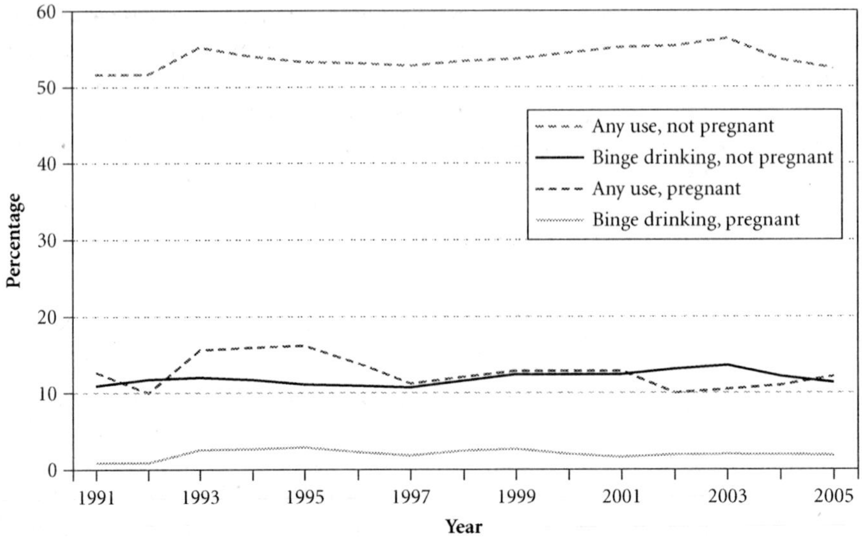

FIGURE 10-1 Average Percentage of Women

Source: Centers for Disease Control and Prevention, 2009a.

abused illicit drug during pregnancy is marijuana, followed by cocaine, and then opiates (Schempf & Strobino, 2008). Exposing a fetus to illicit drugs during pregnancy can have deleterious effects on fetal growth and weight gain, and can cause low birth weight, premature birth, or miscarriage. Further, some babies born to drug-using mothers suffer from withdrawal symptoms following birth, which can include tremors, convulsions, irritability, and difficulty sleeping and feeding. In considering these dangerous effects, prenatal exposure to drugs is considered in some states to be a form of child abuse or neglect.

There are a number of laws that address drug use during pregnancy. On the federal level, The Child Abuse Prevention and Treatment Act (CAPTA) requires that each state's CPS agency follow up on reports of newborns who were prenatally exposed to illicit substances. The way in which each state's CPS agency then handles prenatal drug exposure varies. The CPS agencies typically work to establish a plan of care for the newborn to ensure that he or she has a safe and stable home environment, though plans of care vary based on the situation (U.S. Department of Health and Human Services, 2009). In some cases, exposing a child to prenatal substance abuse is grounds for removal and termination of parental rights following the baby's birth. This usually occurs when the mother shows no motivation to stop using. In other cases, CPS agencies work with mothers and families to implement supportive services and drug treatment, and the newborn remains with his or her biological family (U.S. Department of Health and Human Services, 2009).

Care must be taken in handling cases of prenatal drug exposure. Punitive laws that require the separation of a mother from her child at birth can have a negative effect on mother/child bonding. Many things should be taken into consideration when making the decision to remove a newborn from his or her mother, including the mother's willingness to attend drug treatment; her interest in, attachment to, and appropriateness with the child; and the availability of social support, such as another family member or significant other to help care for the child. If CPS finds the mother to be unfit, relative care is typically pursued first, followed by foster care if there are no other options (Helfer, Kempe and Krugman, 1997). The majority of CPS agencies are required to become involved only after the substance-exposed fetus is born. However, there are some states in which CPS agencies intervene prior to the baby's birth and refer the substance abusing mother for drug treatment. Several states, but not all, address the requirement of CPS to intervene in cases of children who were prenatally exposed to drugs within their statutes. Only twelve states and the District of Columbia actually list prenatal exposure to drugs and alcohol within their legal definitions of child abuse and neglect (U.S. Department of Health and Human Services, 2009).

Financial Problems

In addition to poverty and high cost of living, family dysfunction has been shown to contribute to economic instability and homelessness among families (Wood, Valdez, Hayashi, & Shen, 1990). Substance abuse, in particular, has been correlated with financial hardship and family homelessness. In a California study, researchers found that many homeless families, most frequently consisting of single mothers and two to three children, reported that substance abuse had played some role in their family's financial hardship and subsequent homelessness. Further, many of the mothers of these homeless families were found to have grown up in homes in which their parents abused drugs or alcohol. In addition to a history of substance abuse, some other factors found to contribute to family homelessness included a history of domestic violence, child abuse, mental illness, and lack of social support (Wood, Valdez, Hayashi, & Shen, 1990).

There are government assistance programs available to families facing economic hardship, but such programs are frequently only available to single parent families that fall under a certain income level. One such program is known as Temporary Aid to Needy Families (TANF). Recent estimates show that approximately 20 percent of mothers receiving TANF are substance abusers (Meara, 2006). It has been found in general that substance abusing recipients of public assistance are more likely to exhibit "welfare cycling" (going on and off welfare over time as a result of an inability to obtain or keep steady employment) than non–substance abusing recipients (Schmidt, Zabkiewicz, Jacobs, & Wiley, 2007). However, these studies have focused on general assistance programs, and very little research has been done specifically on substance abusers who receive TANF (Meara, 2006).

The longer a mother receives TANF, the less likely she is to seek employment and come off welfare. Research has found that, when other factors are controlled for, substance abuse was found to have no significant impact on the amount of time women received TANF, the probability of coming off TANF to obtain employment, the amount of time women stayed off TANF to work, or the probability of reentering the TANF system after loss of employment (Schmidt, Zabkiewicz, Jacobs, & Wiley, 2007). Substance abusing TANF recipients are more likely to lack basic literacy and job training skills than other women on welfare: This lack of skills, rather than the substance abuse itself, subsequently affects this population's ability to find and keep jobs (Meara, 2006). It has been found that those mothers who do leave the TANF system, whether substance abusers or not, frequently find only short-term employment with very minimal earnings, which typically results in continued economic hardship for families (Meara, 2006; Schmidt, Zabkiewicz, Jacobs, & Wiley, 2007). Very little is known, at this point in time, about substance abusing mothers receiving TANF and their ability to come off welfare and obtain employment; for this reason, more research is needed to inform treatment and intervention efforts. "Some research suggests that employment might play a complementary role in substance abuse treatment" (Meara, 2006, p. 231). Better understanding of the link between substance abuse among female welfare recipients and the ability to obtain employment would lead to the creation of informed policy and effective treatment programs, which could subsequently result in multiple social benefits such as lowered spending on welfare programs and substance abuse.

Divorce

Divorce is a much more common occurrence than most people realize. Almost half of all first marriages in the United States end in divorce, the majority of which are among couples under the age of 30 (Collins, Ellickson, & Klein, 2007). Substance abuse is one factor among many that has been shown to lead to divorce. In fact, 11 percent of divorced individuals report that substance abuse was at least partly responsible for the breakup of their marriages. Of the various types of substance abuse, alcohol abuse is the most frequently cited as contributing to divorce (Collins, Ellickson, & Klein, 2007). In a longitudinal study of young adults on the west coast, researchers found that frequent alcohol intoxication among married 23-year-olds was likely to result in divorce by age 29 (Collins, Ellickson, & Klein, 2007).

In a study on how drug use affects the quality of intimate relationships, it was determined that drug use resulted in the "deterioration of both women's and men's relationship stability and quality over time" (Newcomb, 1994, p. 473).

> Among women, poly-drug use led to decreased satisfaction, increased relationship trouble, and increased divorce . . . High frequency of alcohol predicted more sexual dissatisfaction. Cannabis use led to less perceived support from one's partner and less relationship satisfaction. Cocaine use was associated with a decrease in cohesion . . . [and] earlier poly-drug use increased later trouble in a relationship (Newcomb, 1994, p. 473).

Substance abuse increases the likelihood that couples will become dissatisfied in their relationships, which contributes to increased risk for divorce. As such, it has been found that divorced individuals in the United States have higher rates of alcohol and drug abuse than married individuals (Collins, Ellickson, & Klein, 2007). Further, following divorce, substance abuse rates may increase as divorcees encounter difficulty coping with the end of their marriages. Some studies have found that after divorce occurs, alcohol abuse increases (Jung, 2001).

Adult Children of Alcoholics

> "Alcoholism isn't a spectator sport. Eventually the whole family gets to play."
>
> —Joyce Rebeta-Burditt, as quoted on www.RandomTerrain.com

Children who grow up in alcoholic households are at an increased risk of developing various types of psychological problems as adults. While growing up in a dysfunctional family, children of alcoholics (COAs) learn to react to their parents' drinking in a number of ways; some withdraw, some may experience anger and resentment, many blame themselves and experience low self-esteem, and some try to take on the role of mediator (Jung, 2001). As a result of a childhood in an alcoholic household, those children who grow up to become **Adult Children of Alcoholics (ACOAs)** frequently exhibit sixteen general characteristics, namely:

> fear of losing control; fear of intense feelings; an overdeveloped sense of responsibility; feelings of guilt when they stand up for themselves; inability to relax and have fun; harsh self-criticism; denial; difficulty with intimate relationships; living life as a victim; compulsive behavior; the tendency to confuse pity and love; fear of abandonment; the tendency to view issues in black and white terms; the development of stress related illness (for example, migraine or stress headaches, irritable bowel syndrome, ulcers, etc.); delayed feelings of grief surrounding losses; and a tendency to react rather than to act in stressful situations (Asper, 2006, pp. 1–2).

Adult Children of Alcoholics are also at increased risk for developing alcoholism, and abusing illicit substances during adolescence and adulthood (Jacob, Windle, Seilhamer, & Bost, 1999; Jung, 2001). However, it is important to note that each ACOA has a unique experience, as having an alcoholic parent may impact some more profoundly than others.

Why then, do some ACOAs develop alcoholism and significant psychopathology while others do not? The development of psychological and substance abuse disorders depends largely on the child's home situation and the presence of protective factors while the child is maturing.

> All alcoholic parents do not have the same severity of alcoholism, or the alcoholism does not lead to divorce or a splitting of the family in all cases. The age of the child when the parent develops alcoholism, the child's relationship in general with parents, the size of the family, and other forms of parental psychopathology are added factors that might prove important in determining how detrimental the alcoholism of a parent is on the mental health of the children (Jung, 2001, p. 387).

Further the presence of a supportive, nonalcoholic parent, sibling, relative, friend, or mentor may help to ameliorate the effects of growing up in an alcoholic household.

Similar to AA, where recovering alcoholics can obtain support from peers, there are groups in which ACOAs and other individuals who are coping with an alcoholic family member or friend can turn to for support from peers who share similar experiences. The Adult Children of Alcoholics World Service Organization, Inc. (http://adultchildren.org) holds meetings in various countries throughout the world not just for ACOAs but also for other adults who have had a dysfunctional family experience and can identify with the agency's purpose and mission. ACOAs may also attend Al-Anon (http://www.al-anon.alateen.org/) meetings, in which any adult who has been affected by someone else's drinking is welcome. Also, adolescent COAs have the option of attending Alateen (http://www.al-anon.alateen.org/alateen.html), a similar group available to teenagers whose lives have been affected by the drinking of a parent or other loved one. Al-Anon and Alateen are faith-based groups that follow the same 12-step tradition as AA.

Codependency

Families that include an alcohol abusing member quite often develop unusual and maladaptive behaviors in an effort to cope with the alcoholism. Without realizing it, many spouses, children, siblings, and parents develop responses to their family member's drinking that actually reinforce the addiction, often times despite their desires to cease alcohol use (Jung, 2001). The term

Characteristics of codependent people are:

- An exaggerated sense of responsibility for the actions of others
- A tendency to confuse love and pity, with the tendency to "love" people they can pity and rescue
- A tendency to do more than their share, all of the time
- A tendency to become hurt when people don't recognize their efforts
- An unhealthy dependence on relationships. The codependent will do anything to hold on to a relationship; to avoid the feeling of abandonment
- An extreme need for approval and recognition
- A sense of guilt when asserting themselves
- A compelling need to control others
- Lack of trust in self and/or others
- Fear of being abandoned or alone
- Difficulty identifying feelings
- Rigidity/difficulty adjusting to change
- Problems with intimacy/boundaries
- Chronic anger
- Lying/dishonesty
- Poor communications
- Difficulty making decisions (Mental Health America, 2009).

codependency describes the reciprocal relationship between an alcoholic and a nonalcoholic in which the nonalcoholic unintentionally supports and even encourages the alcoholic's drinking (Jung, 2001). In other words, codependents inadvertently become accomplices or enablers of the alcohol abuse. For example, an individual may exhibit codependent behavior by denying there is an alcohol problem within his or her family and making excuses for the alcoholic's behavior. Further, many family members exhibit codependent behavior by assuming the various roles of the alcoholic as he or she becomes impaired and is unable to carry out his or her familial duties. An example of this would be an 11-year-old child cooking dinner for her younger siblings while both of her parents become intoxicated. Though codependency was originally used to describe the effects of alcoholism, the concept has been applied more recently to various other forms of substance abuse, addictions, and dependencies.

Though codependents act with good intentions, namely taking care of the substance abuser, they typically suffer personally as a result of repressing their feelings and ignoring their own needs, which is why codependents are frequently referred to as "martyrs." "By continually adjusting and reacting to the alcoholic's drinking, but without success, the codependent suffers a loss of self-esteem and experiences a mixture of depression, helplessness, and self blame" (Jung, 2001, p. 392). Codependents subsequently develop a number of maladaptive personality characteristics, which may include, for example, the need to be in control, the need to feel approval from others, and avoidance of feelings of abandonment (Mental Health America, 2009). Similar to Al-Anon and ACOA groups, there is also a Codependents Anonymous (CoDA) (http://www.codependents.org) fellowship in which codependents can meet with peers who share similar experiences for support.

In looking at the family unit from the **systems perspective**, in which the operation of a family as a system depends on the successful functioning of its various parts, a family that includes a substance abuser may develop codependent behaviors as a result of the family's desire to maintain balance and equilibrium. Substance abuse becomes the focus of all family encounters, to which everyone must adapt; these adaptations frequently result in dysfunctional behaviors. Many family systems are resistant to change, so rather than confront the substance abuse, many family members make sacrifices to simply cope with its occurrence (Jung, 2001). The concept of codependency has been criticized, specifically by those who view the issue from a feminist perspective, for blaming and stigmatizing the victim (Gordon & Barrett, 1993; Peled & Sacks, 2008). Additionally, there is a lack of empirical evidence about the nature of codependency and a need for more research to validate what is mostly anecdotal evidence that exists presently (Jung, 2001).

COMMUNITY EFFECTS

A police officer in a northeastern metropolitan community describes the struggle of dealing with the community impacts of drugs:

> Okay, what happened was the big dealers took over. They just spread out in the [housing projects] . . . What they do is that they go in and they pay the [tenant's] rent and buy the groceries for everybody in a [particular] building and they set up house. They set up lookouts on the roof and on the stairs . . . We couldn't do anything [about] it, and they took over all of [the housing projects]. [Tenants] shut up and wouldn't talk. I mean let's face it, a mother that's got three or four kids on welfare and you know just barely has enough to eat and someone's going to come in and say keep [quiet], I'll give you $2,000 a week or $1,000 a week, who wouldn't say yes (Stevens & Capitman, 2005, p. 283)?

Disorganization

The presence of drug abuse and drug trafficking networks can be absolutely devastating to community life. The consequences of drug culture most seriously impact minority urban communities. "Inner-city drug profiteering promotes a street subculture of social disorganization characterized by violence, crime, and the loss of life, social ties, and physical space" (Stevens & Capitman, 2005, p. 279). Many researchers refer to the drug epidemic as a "social disaster" to convey the seriousness of the myriad of consequences faced by drug-affected communities (Stevens & Capitman, 2005). Residents of drug-affected neighborhoods typically report significant feelings of loss, which include both loss of collectivity and community cohesion, as well as physical loss, such as the deterioration of community structures and shared spaces. These losses have affected the general well-being of community members, who, as a result of their unsafe environment, resort to isolation (Stevens & Capitman, 2005).

It is important to note the effects drug networks have on rates of violence and crime in communities. In the 1980s and 1990s, with the rise of the crack market in many urban communities, drug-related violent crime sharply increased. "As the crack markets waned during the 1990s, levels of violence also subsided. But illegal drug use and drug trafficking continue to flourish and fuel violent crime in many cities" (Martinez, Rosenfeld, & Mares, 2008, pp. 846–847). In examining Miami neighborhoods, findings revealed that drug activity was strongly correlated with increased levels of neighborhood violence and crime, specifically aggravated assault and robbery (Martinez, Rosenfeld, & Mares, 2008).

Drugs can also wreak havoc on the economic stability of communities. Drug abuse "severely burdens federal, state, and local government resources and, ultimately, the taxpayer" (NDIC, 2006, np). It is estimated that the total cost of drug abuse to the United States in 2002 was $180.9 billion (NDIC, 2006). Drug use can also result in a number of public health issues for communities, including increased rates of HIV/AIDS, which in turn also leads to increased health care costs. Methamphetamine laboratories in particular, often created by users and dealers within their own homes or abandoned structures can put community members including children, police, and other officials at serious risk as they pose severe health threats including injury and death (NDIC, 2006).

Police Corruption

Drug-related police corruption is another impact drug use may have on communities. According to the U.S, General Accounting Office (GAO), the specific extent to which drug-related police corruption exists is unknown as there is no federal-level collection of data on such cases. Though little is known about the extent of the problem, it has been determined that drug-related police corruption is typically more involved than other types of police corruption. Specifically, officers involved in drug-related corruption are much more likely to "be actively involved in the commission of a variety of crimes, including stealing drugs and/or money from drug dealers, selling drugs, and lying under oath about illegal searches" rather than taking a passive role and simply allowing crime to take place (U.S. General Accounting Office [GAO], 1998, p. 3). Drug-related corruption is also frequently associated with the use of excessive force or police brutality. Police officers involved in drug-related crime frequently commit such crime for money, power, and street justice (GAO, 1998).

The GAO found that drug-related police corruption is typically accompanied by a "code of silence" in which officers are extremely reluctant to report any foul play by a fellow officer (GAO, 1998, p. 4). Another factor contributing to police corruption is a lack of managerial supervision. It has been found that younger and less educated officers are more likely to engage in illegal drug activity (GAO, 1998). "In addition, on-the-job opportunities to commit illegal acts; inadequate training, particularly integrity training in the police academies and on the job; police brutality; and pressures arising from an officer's personal neighborhood ties [are] also believed by some sources to be associated with drug-related police corruption" (GAO, 1998, p. 4).

Case Study:

The Rampart Scandal

One of the most extensive cases of drug-related police corruption, known as the Rampart Scandal, occurred in an anti-gang unit of the Los Angeles Police Department (LAPD) known as the Community Resources Against Street Hoodlums (CRASH) unit, which patrolled the Rampart community of Los Angeles. Throughout the late 1990s, the officers within this unit were involved in a number of criminal actions brought to light by one of their fellow officers, Rafael Perez. On August 25, 1998, Officer Perez was arrested for stealing 6 pounds of cocaine from a police evidence room. Perez later pleaded guilty to theft, and in order to receive a reduced sentence, provided information to authorities about other police officers in the CRASH unit involved in a multitude of illegal activities (Public Broadcasting Services, 2008). Several other officers were subsequently indicted for offenses that ranged from murder to drug charges. Further, countless convictions of drug dealers and other individuals were later overturned due to the extensive police misconduct that had taken place in the Rampart district (Drug Policy Alliance Network, 2009).

A Board of Inquiry was assembled, and it issued a report with various recommendations for the LAPD in 1999. The police commission also formed an independent review panel which made further findings and recommendations in 2000 based on the events of the Rampart scandal (Public Broadcasting Services, 2008). The CRASH unit was finally disbanded in 2000.

Summary

- Research has shown that a correlation exists between substance use and criminal behavior, which can lead to various legal problems for substance users. Almost half of U.S. prisoners report they were under the influence of alcohol or drugs when they committed the crime for which they are incarcerated. Substance abuse may possibly cause increased aggression, but more research is needed on this topic. There are various protective factors that can reduce the likelihood of substance abuse, and therefore involvement in subsequent criminal activity and legal issues.
- Spirituality and religiosity have been shown to play a role in the prevention and treatment of substance abuse disorders. Those with strong religious or spiritual beliefs are more likely to enter treatment and remain sober than those with no religious or spiritual beliefs.
- There is a strong correlation between substance abuse (most often alcohol and cocaine abuse) and financial problems, which may lead to homelessness. Over 60 percent of the homeless population has some substance abuse history. It is unknown whether substance abuse results in homelessness, or homelessness results in substance abuse. Most substance abusing homeless individuals have either a high school education or trade skills but do not utilize these resources effectively because of their substance dependency. Also, many substance abusing homeless individuals do have legitimate income, but spend their money on their drug habits, which sustains their homelessness.
- Alcohol and drug use can cause a number of physical and mental health problems for users. Extensive use can lead to overdose. Abruptly ceasing use can also pose a threat to the well-being of the individual abusing drugs, as sudden removal of a substance from an abuser could cause withdrawal syndrome. Substance use is typically associated with risk-taking behavior, which puts drug abusers at risk for accidental injury and the acquisition of sexually transmitted diseases.
- Research findings on the effects of alcohol and drug use on employment are mixed. Some studies have found that alcohol and drug use have no significant effect on employment, whereas other studies that have focused on substance abuse and patterns of long-term unemployment have shown that illicit drug abuse reduces productivity and increases job turnover. There is mixed evidence about the effects alcohol consumption, in particular, has on job productivity. Substance abuse in the workplace is dangerous, and increases the risk of on-the-job injury and economic consequences for businesses. More research is needed on the topic of substance abuse and employment, as most existing research on this topic is biased in that it focuses predominantly on men.
- Almost 12 percent of children in the United States grow up in homes with at least one substance abusing parent. Substance abuse has a significant impact on an individual's ability to parent responsibly and effectively. Substance abusing parents are more likely to abuse and act aggressively toward their children. Alcohol, in particular, has been shown to play a role in the occurrence of battered child syndrome. Those children who are abused are in turn more likely to abuse drugs and alcohol, and experience significant psychological and psychosocial problems as adults. Substance abuse can also play a negative role in successful child development.
- In some states, adults can be charged with a felony or with child endangerment for exposing a child to illegal drug activity. Child Protective Service (CPS) agencies have difficulty working with substance abusing parents because many parents lack motivation to rehabilitate, and those who are willing to

undergo treatment need a significant amount of time to rehabilitate.

- Fetal Alcohol Syndrome (FAS) is a disorder caused by exposure of the fetus to alcohol that results in a variety of both physical and psychological issues. FAS is characterized by growth and CNS problems, permanent birth defects, heart and limb defects, as well as behavioral problems, learning disorders, and psychological and psychosocial problems later in life. FAS is the most frequently occurring and totally preventable cause of mental retardation and birth defects in the United States. There is no amount of alcohol considered safe to consume during pregnancy, nor is there a specific time during pregnancy when it is safe to drink. Rates of alcohol consumption among pregnant women have remained stable in the last two decades, pointing to a need for more community education on the dangers of drinking while pregnant.
- The Child Abuse Prevention and Treatment Act (CAPTA) requires that each state's CPS agency follow up on reports of newborns who were prenatally exposed to illicit substances. The way in which each state's CPS agency then handles prenatal drug exposure varies depending on the specific situation. Most states become involved only after the baby is born. Few states list prenatal drug exposure within their legal definitions of child abuse and neglect.
- Substance abuse has been correlated with financial hardship and family homelessness. Research has shown that approximately 20 percent of those families who receive welfare in the form of Temporary Aid to Needy Families (TANF) include substance abusing mothers. More research is needed to determine how substance abuse affects TANF recipients, specifically focusing on their ability to eventually obtain employment and come off welfare.
- Divorce occurs in half of all first marriages in the United States. Substance abuse is one factor among many that has been shown to lead to divorce. Of all types of substance abuse, alcohol is most frequently cited as contributing to divorce. Drug use has been shown to deteriorate relationship quality over time by increasing marital dissatisfaction in a number of ways. Some studies suggest that substance abuse increases following divorce as well.
- Adult Children of Alcoholics (ACOAs) develop significant psychopathology as a result of growing up in homes with alcoholic parents. The extent to which ACOAs develop psychological and psychosocial problems as a result of parental alcohol abuse depends largely on the extent of the alcohol abuse in the home as well as the presence of protective factors. There are various 12-step groups available to ACOAs, which they can attend to network with and obtain support from individuals who share similar experiences.
- Codependency describes the reciprocal relationship between a substance abuser and a non–substance abuser in which the non–substance abuser unintentionally supports and even encourages the substance abuse. Codependents frequently suffer as a result of continual self-sacrifice, and develop a number of maladaptive personality characteristics. According to the systems perspective, codependency within a family may be a result of the family's desire to maintain balance and equilibrium.
- Drug abuse and trafficking can have devastating effects on community life. Predominately urban minority communities are affected by drug culture. The drug epidemic has been described as a "social disaster," and can result in community violence, crime, economic hardship, and public health concerns. Community members can experience feelings of multiple losses, including loss of community cohesion and physical loss of community structures. Drug presence results in increased isolation and a decreased sense of community.
- One potential effect drug presence can have on communities is drug-related police

corruption. Drug-related police corruption varies from other forms of police corruption in that officers are more likely to become involved in criminal activity rather than passively allow crime to occur. The extent to which drug-related police corruption occurs is unknown, as there is no collection of such data at the federal level. One of the most extensive cases of drug-related police corruption is the Rampart Scandal, which occurred in Los Angeles in the late 1990s.

Important Terms

Adult Children of Alcoholics (ACOAs)
Battered Child Syndrome
Codependency
Fetal Alcohol Syndrome (FAS)
Systems perspective

Critical Thinking Questions

1. Discuss the myriad of effects one individual's substance abuse has not only on that individual but also on the individual's family and community.
2. Elaborate on the experiences of children who grow up with a substance abusing parent. How does parental substance abuse affect these children later in life? What type of treatment and social support programs do you think could ameliorate the effects of parental substance abuse?

Research Topics

1. What drug and alcohol treatment programs are available in your community? Do these treatment programs focus only on individual rehabilitation or do they include couple and family components as well? How effective are these treatment programs?
2. How have communities near you been affected by drugs? Discuss economic, family, and community cohesion consequences, and what these communities are doing to fight the drug epidemic.

Suggested Readings

Conyers, B. (2003). *Addict in the family: Stories of loss, hope and recovery.* Center City, MN: Hazelden.

Deaton, W. (1994). *Drinking and drugs in my family: A child's workbook about substance abuse in the family.* Alameda, CA: Hunter House, Inc.

Enderson, L. (2006). *Addiction: A personal story.* Simi Valley, CA: Bennett Deane Publishing.

Pelzer, D. J. (1995). *A child called 'it': One child's courage to survive.* Deerfield Beach, FL: Health Communications, Inc.

PART

IV

Controlling Drug Use

11

U.S. War on Drugs

"In the final analysis, what legislators and other politicians need to better understand is that we cannot legislate our way out of the drug problem by passing mandatory sentencing and asset forfeiture laws, we cannot police our way out of the drug problem by further expanding narcotic enforcement activities both domestically and internationally, and we cannot build our way out of the drug problem by constructing more penitentiaries and prison cells."

—(INCIARDI, 2008, P. 321)

OBJECTIVES:

When you have finished this chapter, you should be able to:

- Elaborate on incarceration trends for drug offenses
- Discuss the varied impacts of drug laws on race and gender
- Discuss the types of asset forfeiture as well as the advantages and disadvantages of this drug war strategy
- Understand the types of interdiction policies and the federal agencies involved in interdiction efforts
- Understand the advantages and disadvantages of eradication policies
- Discuss the role of certification policies in the war on drugs
- Understand varied types of street level enforcement in the drug war

REAL LIFE

Scott Walt, Age 39, Serving 24.5 Years for Conspiracy to Possess Marijuana with Intent to Distribute:

> [The agent] stated to me, "We want to search your house. If we have to get a warrant we will bust your doors down, put guns to your wife and children's heads and tear your f—ing house apart, or you can sign this waiver and we'll be nice." Well I signed the waiver . . . They found no drugs, no scales, no ledgers, nothing! They took financial records, a cell phone, our home phone and address book, and $7,350 in our bedroom. My wife was a team leader for Mary Kay Cosmetics and her office was in our home. She asked, "Why are you taking the money." They said, "drug proceeds." We shook our heads in disbelief . . . At sentencing the government wanted a fine of $250,000 . . . The judge said, "No fine; enough is enough." This man is getting far too much time, murderers receive less. If it weren't for the book, (he held up the sentencing guidelines), I would not be sentencing him to this. We'll all be dead and his marriage will be over. "Enough is enough!" (Norris, Conrad, & Resner, 1998, p. 54).

Valerie Johnson, Age 33, Serving 10 Years, 1 Month for Possession with Intent to Distribute Crack Cocaine:

> I was charged as a first-time offender. I have been given 121 months and five years supervised release for only 87.8 grams of cocaine base. If I would have been charged with just cocaine I would have gotten 24 months. When I was in one prison, I had a roommate who killed her daughter and she is doing less time than me—a non-violent, low-level offender. That bothers me. My grandmother, 74, said to me the other day, "Baby, you can tell me what you really did, we'll still love you." They think I killed someone or something. It's so hard to explain this to them, they just don't understand. It's just not fair (Norris, Conrad, & Resner, 1998, p. 20).

The American war on drugs is based on an ever-changing, cultural reaction to a substance, rather than to an actual threat of individual or social harm. Public perceptions of drugs are socially constructed and change based on many factors discussed in Chapter Two. One of the main factors motivating the war on drugs is the intensity of media campaigns detailing community devastation at the hands of drugs addicts and drug dealers, and resulting pressure on politicians to once and for all win this war. The drug war involves an expanding prison industrial complex; a series of "get tough" measures written into the law; an inundation of drug war rhetoric; and discriminatory treatment based on class, race, and gender. The costs of this war have been high and have frequently resulted in violence, crime, corruption, devastation of social bonds, the destruction of inner-city communities, and the exponential growth in the number of minorities and women incarcerated.

As a reminder, Chapter Eight detailed the creation of "get tough" laws throughout history that have primarily considered all illegal substances in one broad category. Though the Boggs Act in 1951, the Narcotic Control Act in 1956, and the ratification of the United Nations Single Convention of Narcotic Drugs in 1961 paved the way for increasingly strict sentences for drug offenses, Richard Nixon dramatically expanded anti-drug efforts and officially declared a War on Drugs. The federal budget for drug prevention and law enforcement increased from $150.2 million in 1971 to $654.8 million in 1973 under Nixon's guidance (Inciardi, 2002). Though Nixon's drug war included moderate financial support for treatment programs, this was dismantled with Ronald Reagan's re-declaration of the War on Drugs in the 1980s. Nancy Reagan popularized the "Just Say No" campaign, and abstinence as a solution was moved center-stage. These and similar campaigns increased public support for anti-drug efforts and were followed in the mid-1980s by several legal measures that served to increase federal authority to seize assets, create mandatory minimum sentences, and require annual presidential evaluation of global drug activities. All of these crime control measures served to dramatically increase the number of individuals incarcerated and fueled the growth of the prison industrial complex. The Office of National Drug Control Policy's (ONDCP) Executive Summary for 2006 indicated a 2007 federal budget of $12.7 billion for reducing illegal drug use, an increase of $80.6 million from 2006. This is in addition to approximately $28 billion in state budgets, which results in drug war spending of about $40 billion per year. This chapter will detail the tools of the drug war, including:

- Incarceration;
- Asset forfeiture;
- Interdiction;
- Eradication;
- Certification; and
- Street-level enforcement.

CONTROL OF DRUGS BY INCARCERATION

Recall from the discussion of drugs and crime in Chapter Nine that the relationship between crime and drugs is much more complicated than simply "drugs cause crime." There are usually three separate categories that elaborate the relationship:

- Drug-defined crimes, which include the sale and/or possession of an illegal substance;
- Drug-related crimes, which include violent behaviors induced by the properties of a drug or illegal activity that occurs to further a drug habit; and
- Crimes associated with drug use, including prohibited behavior that may have occurred while an individual was under the influence of an illegal substance, but the crime was not a direct result of drug use (Walker, 2006).

When discussing how drugs are controlled through the use of incarceration, the focus here is specifically on drug-defined crimes such as drug possession or use, drug cultivation or production, or the sale of prohibited substances.

According to the FBI, the number of arrests for drug offenses more than tripled from 580,900 in 1980 to 1,846,400 in 2005. Government studies reveal that over half of those imprisoned for federal drug offenses are street-level dealers or transporters, about one-third are mid-level dealers, and approximately 11 percent of federal offenders are high-level dealers (Federal Bureau Investigation [FBI], 2006). During the period from 1990 to 2002 there was an increase in drug arrests of 450,000 individuals. Of these arrests, 82 percent were for marijuana charges, and 79 percent of marijuana offenses were strictly for possession. These numbers represent an increase of 113 percent in marijuana arrests between 1990 and 2002, while overall arrests decreased by 3 percent, and arrests for other drugs increased by only 10 percent. As such, analysis indicates that nearly half of drug arrests per year are a result of marijuana, with a mere 6 percent resulting in a felony conviction. Figure 11-1 illustrates the average length of imprisonment by drug type and

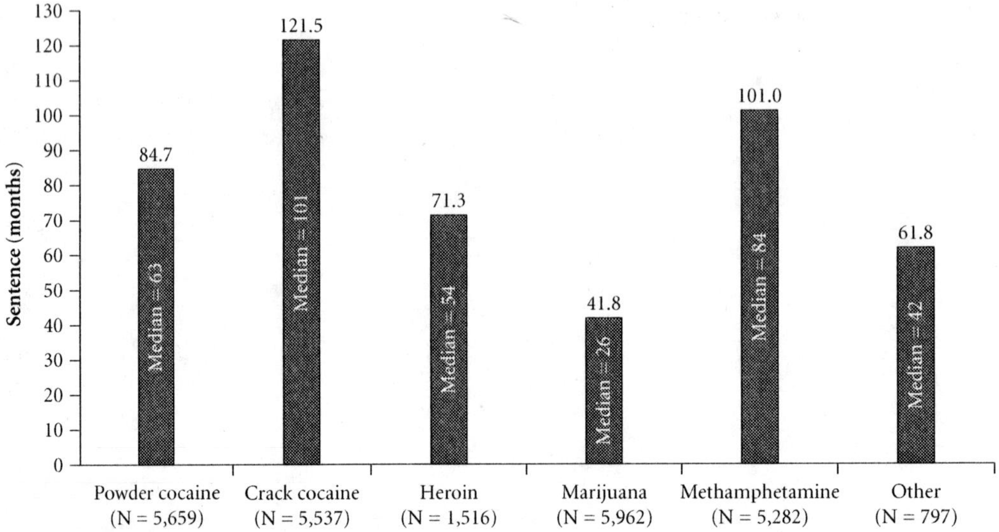

FIGURE 11-1 Average Length of Imprisonment by Drug Type, 2006.

Source: U.S. Sentencing Commission, 2007.

Table 11-1 illustrates the percentage of offenders receiving a mandatory minimum sentence by drug type in the year 2006.

To pursue such vigorous incarceration policies toward marijuana, the United States spends an estimated $4 billion annually on arrest, prosecution, and incarceration (King & Mauer, 2005). As was noted earlier, however, increases in arrests do not follow an increase in the use of illegal substances as many assume. Furthermore, the shifting of law enforcement resources to a focus on marijuana is not in line with any substantiated decrease in the use of other drugs. That is, law enforcement has not shifted its focus to marijuana control because of a decrease in the use of other "harder" drugs. As such, the dramatic increase in marijuana arrest rates can be understood only as the result of selective law enforcement decisions.

TABLE 11-1 Offenders Receiving Mandatory Minimum Sentences by Drug Type, 2006

Drug Type	Number of Cases	5-Year Mandatory Minimum, Percent	10-Year Mandatory Minimum, Percent
Cocaine, crack	5,623	32.2	46.0
Cocaine, powder	5,841	27.2	51.3
Heroin	1,576	26.4	38.1
Marijuana	6,423	31.6	11.0
Methamphetamine	5,395	23.5	56.3
Other	956	6.3	7.7
TOTAL	25,814	27.8	38.7

Source: U.S. Sentencing Commission, 2007.

Adverse Impacts by Race

"Drug policy has from the beginning been driven, in part, by a deep-seated nativist fear about the moral, political, social, and economic implications of an ever larger, polyglot, urban mass of people whose skin color or ethnic heritage differs from that of the dominant group" (Ryan, 1998, p. 228). Race is intimately connected to the consequences of the war on drugs. A case in point is New York's Rockefeller Drug Laws, which were enacted in 1973. These laws created mandatory minimum sentencing requirements intended to crack down on high-level drug offenders. Sentencing was based entirely on the amount of drugs sold or possessed, with no consideration to the offender's circumstances or role in the drug industry. What resulted was that many offenders sentenced under these laws were punished more severely than individuals convicted for more serious offenses such as rape or manslaughter. Rockefeller Drug Laws had great impacts on minority communities. The population of New York was 23.2 percent African American or Latino; yet these groups comprised 93 percent of those incarcerated for drug felonies. In New York City between 1990 and 2002, there was an 882 percent increase in arrests for marijuana, including a 2,461 percent increase for marijuana possession offenses. Though African Americans represented about 14 percent of marijuana users, they were 30 percent of those arrested for marijuana violations (King & Mauer, 2005).

In 2004, the Rockefeller laws were somewhat tempered by the Drug Law Reform Act, which created a determinate system of sentencing and reduced mandatory minimum sentences for nonviolent felony drug offenses. The pattern of racial discrimination with regard to drug laws, however, repeats itself throughout the United States. Table 11-2 illustrates the ethnicity of drug offenders for each drug type in a study conducted in 2006 by the U.S. Sentencing Commission. Arrest rates of minorities remain high despite an overwhelming amount of scholarly research indicating that racial minorities do not partake in the use of drugs with any more frequency than whites. In addition, recent research suggests that minorities are more likely to be detained until arraignment on drug charges, more likely to be convicted, and more likely to receive a jail sentence than whites (Golub, Johnson, & Dunlap, 2007).

The drug war initiated the widespread search for drugs, and not surprisingly drugs were overwhelmingly found where law enforcement exerted their primary search efforts: in low-income, minority neighborhoods where use and dealing are the most visible due to lack of privacy, thus sale of drugs occurs in public settings. Despite crack being the least-used illicit substance in

TABLE 11-2 Race of Drug Offenders by Select Drug Type, 2006

Drug Type	Number of Cases	White, Percent	Black, Percent	Hispanic, Percent	Other, Percent
Cocaine, crack	5,619	9.3	81.0	8.6	1.1
Cocaine, powder	5,830	14.7	27.0	57.0	1.2
Heroin	1,574	11.1	27.4	60.5	0.9
Marijuana	6,399	26.7	10.8	59.3	3.2
Methamphetamine	5,391	53.6	1.7	38.6	6.2
Other	950	51.7	19.9	12.6	15.8
TOTAL	25,763	25.8	29.2	41.7	3.2

Source: U.S. Sentencing Commission, 2007.

the United States, the drug war specifically targeted possession and sale of crack by lower-class and minority individuals. Because minorities are over-represented among the poor, the case of laws regarding crack cocaine versus powder cocaine is illustrative of the intersections of discrimination by class and race. Wide discrepancy in federally mandated sentences for crack cocaine versus powder cocaine existed in the criminal justice system for years with adverse consequences, specifically for African Americans who constituted 81 percent of offenders arrested for crack cocaine offenses in 2006 (see Table 11-2). The sentencing disparity initially specified that 5 grams of crack cocaine would earn an offender the same 5-year mandatory minimum sentence as 500 grams of powder cocaine, and approximately 70 percent of crack defendants are sentenced to mandatory prison terms. This 100:1 sentencing gap was significant in creating disproportionate confinement of African Americans. Historically, approximately two-thirds of those charged with powder cocaine offenses were white, though recently the Hispanic population has been prominent in the arrest rates for powder cocaine (see Table 11-2). The disproportionate rates of arrest and sentencing were despite research by the Department of Health and Human Services, which suggested that less than 1 percent of young African Americans had used crack cocaine in their lifetime, compared to 4.5 percent of whites (Barak, Leighton, and Flavin, 2007).

On December 10, 2007, the Supreme Court issued a 7–2 ruling in *Kimbrough v. U.S.* that allows judges to utilize their discretion when imposing drug sentences. This landmark case highlights the racial disparity in drug laws and provides the foundation for significant change. After the Supreme Court ruling, the U.S. Sentencing Commission voted to make this guideline retroactive beginning March 3, 2008. The application of the decision retroactively makes approximately 19,500 inmates eligible for a sentence reduction on average of just over two years. It must be clear, however, that these guidelines do not have any impact on mandatory minimum penalties, which must be addressed through the actions of Congress. Congressional action has started with the introduction of the Drug Sentencing Reform and Kingpin Trafficking Act of 2007. This act, put forward by Senator Joseph Biden, would equalize penalties for crack and powder cocaine, and shift the efforts of federal enforcement to high-level traffickers.

RACIAL PROFILING An issue of much controversy for the past decade has been that of racial profiling. Allegations that minorities, specifically African Americans and Hispanics, are targeted disproportionately as compared to whites in traffic stops have been supported in a wide range of scholarly research. Indeed, the phrase "driving while black" is commonly used to refer to this phenomenon. In the case of drug smugglers, law enforcement agents create drug courier profiles which are designed to weed out the "type" of person who typically transports drugs. In 1989, the U.S. Supreme Court ruled in *United States v. Sokolow* that such a profile could provide a foundation to "reasonably" suspect a specific individual of drug smuggling. In this particular case, a young African American male purchased two airline tickets from Honolulu to Miami for a 48-hour jaunt. The tickets were paid for in cash, the young gentleman did not check any baggage, and travelled under a false name. These elements were used to create a profile of him as a potential drug courier. The man was stopped at the airport in Honolulu and a drug-detection dog indicated the presence of an illicit substance. After a search, enforcement officers found more than 1,000 grams of cocaine in his carry-on bag. In this case, it seems clear that there were circumstances beyond the race, ethnicity, or national origin to suspect this individual of drug trafficking. The difficulty with permitting profiling, however, is that some law enforcement personnel use race, ethnicity, or national origin as the *sole* basis for a profile. When race, ethnicity, or national origin is the only factor used to establish a profile, this practice is referred to as **racial profiling.** From studies discussed earlier, it is clear that members of racial/ethnic minority groups are no more likely to be users or traffickers of drugs than members of the white population, so using race as a basis for a profile creates both legal and ethical dilemmas. This was apparent to former President Bush, who in 2003 prohibited all federal agencies from using racial and ethnic profiling for drug investigations.

Adverse Impacts by Gender

Gender discrimination is another adverse consequence of the drug war. Criminalization of women involved with drugs is frequently attributed to economics, as opposed to personal addiction. High poverty rates among women have resulted in their seeking income in the drug world as decoys or drug couriers (mules) that import or transport drugs. The risks of this employment "choice" often result in mandatory minimum sentences for women with no prior criminal record (Logan, 2003). As can be seen in Table 11-3, however, women comprise a relatively small number of offenders arrested on drug charges.

The media-driven "crack baby epidemic" of the late 1980s led the public to stereotype women of a racial or ethnic minority, who were portrayed as the overwhelming majority of "crack mothers." The impression that this was an epidemic resulted in the application of laws to criminalize drug use during pregnancy. The first person ever convicted for delivering a drug-addicted child was Jennifer Johnson in 1989. Johnson, a young, poor, African American mother in Florida, received a sentence of 15 years, including 14 years of probation for the impact of crack cocaine on her newborn child. Cases such as these were commonplace in the late 1980s and early 1990s, with twenty-four states bringing similar charges during this timeframe (Logan, 2003). This legal response, however, dissuaded many women from seeking prenatal care and/or drug treatment. An overwhelming number of these convictions were eventually overturned, however, charges continue to be filed against women who are abusing drugs during their pregnancy, a decision supported by a large percentage of the public (Logan, 2003). Organizations such as the American Medical Association have a contrary opinion: "the current policy of prosecuting women who use drugs during pregnancy is irrational because it does not further the state's purpose of preventing harm to infants . . . drug addiction is an illness, which like any illness, is not due simply to a failure of individual willpower" (Lieb & Sterk-Elifson, 1995, p. 693). Other tactics used by law enforcement with pregnant women include "protective incarceration" wherein a drug-using pregnant woman is imprisoned or otherwise confined to protect her unborn child or a policy by hospitals in many states that test pregnant women suspected of drug abuse and then report them to either the police or Child Protective Services (CPS). Further, maternal drug-abuse

TABLE 11-3 Gender of Offenders Arrested by Select Drug Type, 2006

Drug Type	Number of Cases	Male Percent	Female Percent
Cocaine, Crack	5,623	91.1	8.9
Cocaine, Powder	5,837	90.0	10.0
Heroin	1,576	84.9	15.1
Marijuana	6,417	87.3	12.7
Methamphetamine	5,394	84.1	15.9
Other	956	84.0	16.0
TOTAL	25,803	87.8	12.2

Source: U.S. Sentencing Commission, 2007.

laws are enforced primarily on minority women: African American and Latino women represented approximately 80 percent of those subjected to prosecution, despite the lack of differences in drug-use rates across race and ethnic lines. At the close of 1999, more than 80 percent of the women in prison for drug offenses were sentenced using mandatory minimum sentencing laws, and approximately 70 percent of those women were mothers (Inciardi, 2002). This has significant and adverse effects on the children's emotional and psychological well-being as well as on those individuals who assume guardianship responsibilities and incur financial costs for supervising the children of incarcerated women. Perhaps most notably, the psychological impact on the children remains for many years and disrupts their developmental maturity.

In an analysis of discrimination in the war on drugs, it is evident that race, class, and gender are inextricably intertwined as racial minorities are disproportionately represented among the poor. Drug-related laws, enforced with vigor in low-income, minority neighborhoods are used to accomplish increased social control of racial minorties. Though drug laws may be superficially equal and not discriminatory in intent, the consequences of applying such legislation in fighting the war on drugs has been unprecedented incarceration of the poor and minorities as well as a significant increase in the number of women under the control of the criminal justice system. Assumptions based on race, class, and gender stereotypes have created and perpetuated moral panics that fuel support for the drug war.

CONTROL OF DRUGS BY ASSET FORFEITURE

In use since biblical times and wrought with controversy is the control of criminal activity through **asset forfeiture**, which involves the government seizing property that is believed to be the result of crime, including a person's real estate, cars, boats, or planes, as well as cash. This procedure serves the following goals according to the President's Commission on Model State Drug Laws (1993, p. A-29): "(1) removes financial incentive to engage in illegal activity; (2) restores economic integrity in the marketplace; and (3) compensates society for economic damages suffered due to illegal activity by rededicating forfeited property to socially beneficial uses." Asset forfeiture began to be applied to the war on drugs under the 1970 Comprehensive Drug Abuse Prevention and Control Act. This act permitted the forfeiture of any and all property believed to be used in relation to drug activity. Amendments to this act in 1978 expanded the boundaries so the forfeiture of all cash profits from trafficking in drugs as well as all assets purchased with money earned from drugs was permitted. The 1984 amendment to the Comprehensive Drug Abuse Prevention and Control Act further expanded the boundaries to include all profits or property that was used or *may* be used in drug activity, regardless of how minor the offense (including simple possession). In 1986, the Anti-Drug Abuse Act was amended to include a greater number of offenses that could trigger forfeiture; in 1990, still more offenses were added; and in the 1992 Amendment yet more offenses were added to the list.

There are two basic types of forfeiture: criminal and civil. **Criminal asset forfeiture** occurs simultaneously with a criminal charge. If the defendant is found guilty, the property in question is forfeited; in a plea agreement, forfeiture of property can often be used to decrease the criminal punishment of a defendant. The standard of proof in criminal asset forfeiture is the same "proof beyond a reasonable doubt" as required in a criminal trial and the burden is on the prosecution to establish guilt. Conversely, **civil asset forfeiture** has no relationship to a criminal charge and indeed often proceeds without any criminal charge ever to follow. The property is seized and forfeited irrespective of the guilt or innocence of the property owner. The standard of proof, as in other civil proceedings, is "preponderance of the evidence." There are three types of civil asset forfeitures: summary forfeiture, administrative forfeiture, and a civil judicial proceeding.

1. A **summary forfeiture** is when illegal property is seized by law enforcement on the grounds that one cannot "own" something that is illegal. For example, police seize a bag of marijuana from an individual upon arrest. This person cannot later claim "ownership" of this substance and request its return, as marijuana is illegal. This type of forfeiture is not intended to financially penalize an individual.
2. An **administrative forfeiture** is when law enforcement seizes possessions that can be moved, but are not illegal, and are believed to be somehow associated with drugs or a drug enterprise. This would include cash, or vehicles, but not something like real estate (because it cannot be physically moved). The owner of these possessions is then given a specified period of time in which to contest the seizure. This is perhaps the most controversial type of forfeiture because the burden is on the owner to secure and pay for an attorney to contest the seizure in a civil proceeding. If a small amount of cash and a vehicle worth approximately $10,000 were seized by law enforcement, an individual (whether guilty or not) may not contest the forfeiture simply because it would cost almost the value of the goods in order to attempt to have them returned. As such, a basic cost-benefit analysis by those impacted by an administrative forfeiture can result in many uncontested forfeitures. In addition, property is often used as a mechanism to encourage plea bargaining. For example, if the individual in question agrees not to contest the forfeiture, the prosecutor will reduce the charges or not file charges at all.
3. A **civil judicial proceeding** is when a civil proceeding is brought against a defendant prior to the seizure of his or her property. This procedure is normally reserved for possessions that cannot be easily moved (such as real estate). If the defendant loses the civil proceeding or fails to contest the proposed forfeiture, then the property is seized by law enforcement.

According to the Web site of the Drug Enforcement Administration (DEA) (www.dea.gov), the highlights of seizures in 2005 included the following:

- $1.9 billion from drug traffickers, consisting of $1.4 billion in assets and $477 million in illicit substances;
- $21.6 million in a combination of cash and property was seized from traffickers involved in the illegal sale of prescription drugs on the Internet; and
- "Operation Wildlife," which targeted methamphetamine producers, resulted in the seizure of 56 meth labs, 200,000 pseudoephedrine tablets, 123 weapons, 28 cars, and approximately $255,000 in cash.

> *"On October 2, 1992, the Los Angeles County Sheriff's Department and agents shot Malibu, California, millionaire Donald Scott to death in his own home during a raid from five federal law enforcement agencies. Officials had obtained a warrant to search for marijuana cultivation on the property, but many believe the search was motivated by a desire to seize the expensive ranch on which Scott and his wife resided. A report of the Ventura County District Attorney concluded that the police lied to obtain the warrant. When they served it in the middle of the night, Scott's wife ran downstairs to hear what the commotion was about, and when Scott appeared at the top of the stairs brandishing a gun, he was shot. The details as to why Scott was shot were not made clear."*
>
> (Worrall, 2003, p. 275).

So where do all these assets go? This is where the controversy behind asset forfeiture occurs: Though state laws vary widely, most states (and federal statutes) permit the proceeds to be given back to law enforcement to further fund the war on drugs. The value of assets seized raises legal, ethical, and constitutional questions regarding the role of forfeiture in the execution of the drug war.

Advantages

Because most law enforcement agencies are permitted to keep at least some of the proceeds garnered from asset forfeiture, those involved in the prosecution and enforcement activities of the legal system usually regard this policy as positive. Proceeds from forfeitures assist with the funding of future drug control activities, thereby arguably saving taxpayer money. As well, those in favor of asset forfeiture provisions contend that civil forfeitures occur frequently without an accompanying criminal charge because the forfeiture of property can be used as a bargaining chip in the plea process, which in the end saves the prosecutor's office money, as well as contributing to the law enforcement fund. Those who support asset forfeiture further contend that an individual who has assets seized in an administrative forfeiture or assets that may be seized in a civil judicial proceeding have legal recourse to challenge this action, thereby making this strategy perfectly legitimate.

Disadvantages

Critics of asset forfeiture argue that this policy amounts to "policing for profit" as law enforcement has a financial incentive to pursue drug dealers and traffickers. Financial gain has not been the traditional motive of the criminal justice system, and indeed a mere fraction of individuals who have goods seized are ever charged criminally for a drug-related offense (Hyde, 1995). Critics argue that due to forfeiture provisions law enforcement purposefully targets individuals with cash as opposed to those with property for arrest: For example, a drug buyer who would have cash, as opposed to a drug dealer who would have drugs. In addition, it is difficult for property owners who have been subject to seizure to prove a negative in court: the property owner must prove that he or she is not involved in drugs or that the piece of seized property was not purchased with drug earnings. There are many ethical questions raised about law enforcement when the system benefits financially from policing. This begs the question: Are the most harmful offenders being pursued? Or are the most potentially profitable offenders being pursued? In addition, the use of informants has created a significant amount of controversy with regard to asset forfeiture because the informant receives a percentage (sometimes as much as one-quarter) of the assets seized.

Regulation of asset forfeiture comes under the Civil Asset Forfeiture Reform Act (CAFRA) of 2000, which, compared to past legislation, is much less burdensome on the property owner. This is federal legislation however, and therefore does not dictate state forfeiture policy. Despite changes, however, critics still contend that "courts have allowed the use of hearsay, circumstantial evidence, tips from anonymous informants, and even information obtained *after* an initially illegal seizure to meet the probable cause burden" (Worrall, 2003, p. 277; emphasis in original). The Civil Asset Forfeiture Reform Act of 2000 does make some significant changes to federal forfeiture laws, including:

- The burden is now on the government, as opposed to the property owner, to prove that the goods were subject to legitimate forfeiture;
- The government must demonstrate a significant connection between crime and property;
- If goods are seized that would cause an individual undue financial hardship, provisions now exist for the property to be returned to the owner pending a court decision;
- Counsel is provided for poor property owners and individuals who pay for counsel and successfully challenge a seizure are awarded money for reasonable attorney fees;
- No bond is required to contest a seizure unless an individual's interest is deemed frivolous, in which case the court can impose a fine;

- An "innocent owner defense" is now available, but must be demonstrated by the property owner using preponderance of the evidence as the standard of proof (this would be useful, for example, if you lend your car to a friend who is pulled over, drugs are found in his possession, and your car is seized: in this case you could mount an "innocent owner defense" if you could demonstrate that you had no knowledge of this activity); and
- If a property owner is successful in court and the property has been damaged by law enforcement, the owner has the right to sue the federal government for financial compensation (Worrall, 2003).

Though the Civil Asset Forfeiture Reform Act of 2000 made some noteworthy changes at the federal level, its drawback is that it is not applicable to states, and a wide variety of offenses that are subject to forfeiture remain under this new legislation. Thus, though this reform demonstrated movement in the right direction, it only minimally decreased controversy surrounding this tool of law enforcement in the war on drugs.

CONTROL OF DRUGS THROUGH SUPPLY REDUCTION

Recall from earlier in the chapter that the Office of National Drug Control Policy's (ONDCP) Executive Summary for 2006 indicates a 2007 federal budget of $12.7 billion for reducing illegal drug use, in addition to about $28 billion from state budgets, for a total in spending of about $40 billion per year. This budget, however, does not appear to fall in line with the stated priorities of the ONDCP. As provided on its Web site, the priorities of the ONDCP are:

- Priority I Stopping use before it starts;
- Priority II Intervening and healing America's drug users; and
- Priority III Disrupting the market (www.ondcp.gov).

In 2007, just over $4 billion was devoted to Priorities I and II combined. The remaining two-thirds of the budget was dedicated to disrupting the market through the use of programs such as:

- The Andean Counterdrug Initiative;
- Providing Afghanistan counterdrug support;
- The Secure Border Initiative for U.S. border protection and increased customs patrol presence;
- The Cleaning Up Methamphetamine Laboratories program; and
- Financial support for the DEA (www.ondcp.gov).

These strategies are carried out primarily through the interdiction or eradication of illicit substances.

Interdiction Policies

One of the major ways to control the supply of drugs is through **interdiction** policies. Interdiction is the attempt to stop drugs from entering the United States via air, land, or water. This is a formidable task as drug smugglers can be quite creative in their methods of transporting drugs. Smugglers have transported animals such as snakes or dogs, surgically implanted with balloons of drugs across the border; smugglers fashion drugs to look like statues or vegetables; smugglers create secret compartments in planes, boats, or cars to store drugs; smugglers may implant drugs in the thighs or buttocks of humans; or they may use "mules" for transport. A **mule** is typically a female who may be forced into smuggling drugs by threats of harm to her family, or who enters the drug business for a quick financial profit. A mule may swallow up to fifty drug-filled condoms, take a plane to her destination, and then use a laxative to hasten retrieval of the illicit substance. The potential side effects can be catastrophic as a ruptured condom may result in a serious drug overdose, or even death. In addition, as discussed earlier, female drug smugglers are subject to mandatory minimum sentences for trafficking which can lead to more than 10 years in prison for a woman with no prior record. This has a trickle-down effect on families, especially if the woman is the primary caregiver to children. Due to heightened airport security, humans carrying drugs and transport of drugs in creative ways by car (specifically over the Mexican border) have become common methods of drug movement.

Most foreign marijuana entering the United States is smuggled from Mexico (and much of the cocaine entering the United States is transported through Mexico), making Mexico a focus of interdiction efforts. Seizures of marijuana on the southwest border have remained stable at approximately 1.1 million kilograms per year since 2001 (www.dea.gov). This is a dramatic difference from the statistics regarding marijuana smuggled from Canada. Though law enforcement contends there has been an increase in smuggling from Canada of high potency marijuana, primarily due to Asian drug organizations within Canada, seizures still hover at less than 10,000 kilograms per year on average, indicating that this is a very small percentage (approximately 3 percent) of the marijuana being trafficked into the United States (www.dea.gov).

INVOLVED FEDERAL AGENCIES To stop the movement of drugs into the United States, a variety of federal agencies are involved, including the DEA, the U.S. Coast Guard, the U.S. Customs and Border Protection Agency, and the U.S. military. In concert, these federal entities patrol the land, air, and water for illicit substances.

The DEA is perhaps the most responsible for enforcing drug laws, as this is the only federal agency with this enforcement as its sole responsibility. The DEA works both domestically and abroad on covert operations to identify and apprehend drug traffickers, cooperate with foreign governments to apprehend offenders outside of the United States, collect intelligence, train law enforcement personnel in other nations regarding how to best fight the war on drugs, and other functions to minimize drug trafficking. Of all federal agencies, the DEA is the only one whose agents have the power to arrest individuals for drug offenses.

The U.S. Coast Guard leads water interdiction efforts with a focus on the Gulf of Mexico, the Caribbean, and the Eastern Pacific. They have the authority, without probable cause, to detain and search all vessels within 12 miles of the U.S. border and this agency is responsible for a significant amount of cocaine seizures each year (see Table 11-4).

The U.S. Customs and Border Protection Agency is responsible for border protection and for keeping illicit substances from crossing the U.S. border, specifically at the entry points with Mexico and Canada. In 2004, Customs and Border Protection was responsible for more than 56,000 seizures, resulting in almost 2.2 million pounds of various illicit substances (www.dbp.gov). This agency has a Marine Branch which monitors near-shore vessels; as well as an Air Branch, which can force suspicious planes from the sky. Like the U.S. Coast Guard, the U.S. Customs and Border Protection Agency does not require probable cause and can search a person, a container, or any type of vehicle at whim.

The U.S. military is also very active in the interdiction of illicit substances both at home and abroad. Domestically, the military works with other federal and state agencies to assist with operations such as intelligence gathering, observation of offenders, assessment of environments in which drugs are produced, as well as training of law enforcement in tactical skills for anti-drug efforts. Military personnel are not however, permitted to search or arrest those involved with drugs, as this is left to the cooperating agency. The involvement of the military in the war on drugs has been encouraged by the status of the drug war in the media as an overwhelming problem, as stated by a politician

TABLE 11-4 U.S. Coast Guard Drug Seizures by Year

Year	Number of Events	Number of Vessels	Number of Arrests	Marijuana Seizures (in pounds)	Cocaine Seizures (in pounds)	Value of Cocaine in US$ Billion
2007	65	37	188	10,385	238,040	n/a
2006	64	23	200	9,059	234,337	3.1
2005	87	66	364	10,026	303,662	9.7
2004	104	71	326	25,915	242,435	7.7
2003	65	56	283	14,059	136,865	4.4
2002	58	40	207	40,316	117,780	3.5
2001	65	30	114	34,520	138,393	4.5
2000	92	56	204	50,463	132,480	4.4
1999	118	74	304	61,506	111,689	3.7
1998	129	75	297	31,390	82,623	3.0
1997	122	64	233	102,538	103,617	4.0
1996	36	41	112	42,063	44,462	1.1
1995	44	34	56	40,164	33,629	1.3
1994	67	28	73	33,895	47,333	1.8

Source: U.S. Coast Guard, (http://www.uscg.mil/hq/g-o/g-opl/Drugs/Statswww.htm)

in a Congressional meeting: "this is a war that requires the increased use of our military to protect our nation from being destroyed by the deadliest menace of drugs that have inundated every city, town and school" (Subcommittee on Crime, 1985, p. 44). Similarly, the Committee on Armed Services (1988, p. 112) suggested: "There is no greater threat to the survival of our society than drugs. If the present condition continues, we will no longer be free independent citizens but people entwined and imprisoned by drugs. The military forces of this country must become more involved."

On foreign soil the U.S. military provides some of the same functions as it does domestically, and works to prop up the strength of law enforcement or military personnel in drug-producing nations. Specifically in Latin America, the U.S. military employs Tactical Analysis Teams (TATs) wherein military personnel work together with DEA agents and military teams in the host nation to gather intelligence and outline operations. Critics of TATs suggest that the American military may be training foreign troops with a history of human rights violations against the citizens, which may pose an ethical dilemma for the United States and the involvement of this nation in the war on drugs beyond the borders. As long as the drug problem globally is viewed as such a threat to our well-being as individuals in a democratic society, virtually any policy, or the involvement of a variety of government agencies, seems morally appropriate in order to fight this demon.

SUCCESS Evidence suggests that interdiction has not been very successful. Despite increased seizure of illicit substances, drugs continue to be readily available on the streets. Indeed, some estimates suggest that all levels of law enforcement succeed in the interdiction of a mere 10 to 15 percent of the total supply of illegal drugs (Walker, 2006). This position is reinforced by statistics that demonstrate the increase in global production of drugs alongside increased interdiction efforts. Given the vast U.S. border and the evolving creativity and organization of smugglers, the challenges for law enforcement should not be surprising.

Eradication Policies

Eradication policies are aimed at minimizing the cultivation and production of drugs, primarily on foreign soil. This involves the destruction of crops such as coca plants, marijuana plants, and opium poppies using the assumption that a decrease in the crop production would result in the higher cost of the drug to the consumer, which would serve to decrease use. The Andean Counterdrug Initiative mentioned above is one program financed by the U.S. government that eradicates coca plants in Colombia. Crop eradication can be either done manually or with the use of herbicides. **Manual crop eradication** involves removing the plants from the ground and destroying them, usually by burning. This process is undertaken most frequently by either regional law enforcement (often trained by the U.S. military in such techniques) or employees of private security corporations. **Herbicide eradication** most frequently involves spraying herbicides from a small plane onto the crops below.

DOMESTIC ERADICATION One of the main goals of the DEA is the suppression of marijuana on U.S. soil, which led to the creation of the Domestic Cannabis Eradication/Suppression Program. Marijuana is widely used in the United States and can be grown in this country, unlike opium or cocaine, which must be trafficked into the United States. A marijuana eradication program started in California and Hawaii in 1979 and by 1985 had expanded to include the entire nation. The DEA supports law enforcement efforts at the state and local level and shares intelligence and technology in order to maximize eradication. The Domestic Cannabis Eradication/Suppression Program claims more than 8,300 arrests and the seizure of assets worth more than $55 million since its inception in 2000 through 2006 (www.dea.gov). Table 11-5 illustrates seizures by year from this program.

Indeed, this program partly measures its success by the changes growers are making in response to increased law enforcement. Though large outdoor cannabis facilities are most advantageous from a production standpoint, growers have been forced to move toward indoor growth and hydroponics to hide from the authorities.

FOREIGN ERADICATION Strong opposition to U.S.-backed efforts toward coca eradication exists in both Peru and Bolivia. Insurgents in these countries are powerful and often backed by the populace. In Bolivia, coca production brings greater profit than all legal exports combined, and in Peru's

TABLE 11-5 Seizures by Year, Domestic Cannabis Eradication/Suppression Program

Year	Indoor	Outdoor	Total
2006	400,892	4,830,766	5,231,658
2005	270,935	3,938,151	4,209,086
2004	203,896	2,996,225	3,200,121
2003	223,183	3,427,923	3,651,106
2002	213,040	3,128,800	3,341,840
2001	236,128	3,068,632	3,304,760
2000	217,105	2,597,798	2,814,903

Source: Drug Enforcement Agency, (http://www.dea.gov).

Upper Huallaga Valley no less than 60,000 families depend on this crop for their financial survival. Peru's President Fujimori attempted to battle the drug producers by shooting down planes suspected of drug trafficking, and with U.S. financial assistance, to teach Peruvian farmers crop substitution with coffee. Despite these efforts, after only 4 years drug traffickers had reopened old transportation routes, created new transportation routes, and production of coca had rebounded (Vargas, 2002).

> In both Bolivia and Peru, the failure of coca control is not a temporary aberration but a function of culture, tradition, and the weakness and poverty of underdevelopment. These basic social conditions render effective enforcement against coca impossible. Widespread corruption in the enforcement agencies, the judiciary, and elsewhere in government is endemic. Indeed, the central governments do not necessarily control major portions of the coca-growing countryside, where the traffickers rule like feudal lords (Wisotsky, 1987, p. 57).

In countries with no viable cash alternative, eradication of illicit crops results in immense social unrest and poverty.

DISADVANTAGES One of the main problems with eradication policies is that growers of these plants simply relocate, which means destroying the existing plants or crops on a new plot of land for growing coca plants, marijuana plants, or opium poppies. This has had serious environmental consequences in South America where erosion in mountainous regions and deforestation of the rain forest have been unintended consequences of eradication policies, as growers continuously search for new areas of land to exploit.

Another serious criticism of crop eradication policies revolves around the fact that aerial crop spraying kills both the intended plants as well as plants that the indigenous population may be growing for their own livelihood and sustenance. This has the potential to cause significant disruption of the local economy in already depressed rural areas. Some poor families in Latin American and South American countries have few other avenues for income than to cultivate coca and poppies. This has the potential to cause revolt by peasant farmers when their income is destroyed by crop spraying, which has been the case in Colombia on multiple occasions. The government of Peru decided to try an alternate strategy in an attempt to avoid farmer revolt after crop eradication. Peruvian officials, with financial support from the United States, paid farmers who voluntarily destroyed their coca crops, and the government also advocated for the growth of alternative crops (Vargas, 2002). No military or police personnel were involved in this endeavor because the goal was to avoid conflict between farmers and officials. The difficulty with such a plan is that the alternative crops that succeed in a climate such as that found in Peru are not nearly as financially lucrative as growing coca plants. This makes for difficult decisions for farmers trying to support their families in a very poor nation.

ADVANTAGES Advocates of crop eradication counter environmental critiques of this procedure by suggesting that the production of coca is far more harmful to the environment than the herbicides used in crop spraying. Coca production can result in soil erosion, water contamination may result from the improper or careless use of chemical fertilizers, and toxic chemicals are involved in processing the leaf into cocaine paste (Vargas, 2002). As such, this method is perceived as a viable option to reducing the illicit drug supply.

SUCCESS The success of crop eradication programs is debatable. Some countries, such as Bolivia, report dramatic decreases in the amount of land used to grow coca plants and attribute this decrease to crop eradication programs. Looking at the big picture, however, the implementation of crop eradication policies and policies that encourage crop substitution have had little impact on the global production of either cocaine or opium. So, while production may decline in Bolivia, there often occurs a corresponding increase in another location, such as Colombia. This is called the "**balloon effect**," which basically suggests that the "problem" (in this case, drug production) simply relocates if pushed out of one area. For example, under the pressure of the U.S. government, Turkey dramatically curtailed its opium production in the 1970s, with a rise in opium production seen immediately afterward in Mexico and Southeast Asia (Farrell, 1998). Nevertheless, the American government continues to financially support crop eradication programs, despite their questionable results on a global scale.

Certification Policies

A lesser known way to control drugs in other nations is through the **certification** process. Beginning in 1986, the United States started evaluating the level at which foreign countries were cooperating with the anti-drug position of the United States. Every year the president compiles a list of countries involved in the production or transport of illicit substances. Countries are then categorized as:

- Cooperative with the anti-drug position of the United States, and therefore "certified";
- Uncooperative with the anti-drug position of the United States, and therefore "decertified"; or
- Uncooperative with the anti-drug position of the United States, but "certified" nevertheless because the country in question is involved in a vital U.S. interest (Mosher & Akins, 2007).

Decertified countries are penalized, with the withholding of all U.S. aid. In addition, the World Bank and International Monetary Fund both have U.S. representatives on their boards who are required to vote against a request for loans from all decertified nations. These penalties remain in effect until the country is officially "certified" once again.

CONTROL OF DRUGS THROUGH STREET-LEVEL ENFORCEMENT

Street-level enforcement, involving federal, state, and local agencies, is also an integral aspect of drug control. Working in multijurisdictional taskforces, law enforcement at all levels works to share intelligence and techniques to apprehend drug offenders. Goals of street-level drug enforcement include (Moore & Kleiman, 2003):

- Reduction of violence that occurs in combination with organized drug activity;
- Minimization of crime commission by drug users;
- Improvement of the health of drug users;
- Prevention of youth from experimenting with drugs; and
- Restoration of community well-being through the reduction of drug activity.

To accomplish these goals, the police engage in a variety of strategies, including knock and talk, undercover enforcement, and the use of informants.

One street-level method is **knock and talk** in which law enforcement will arrive at the home of a suspected drug offender. For a variety of reasons there may not have been probable cause to obtain a search warrant, so officers use the element of surprise and knock on the door. They request permission to enter the home after identifying themselves and begin asking questions and asserting allegations about drug offenses. Often the offense the officers allege is much more severe than the offense they actually suspect is occurring, and in an effort to "prove their innocence," the homeowners consent to a search of the home. Studies indicate that in an overwhelming number of instances in which this strategy is used, offenders waive their right to privacy and consent to a search of their home, where drugs are often found (Levinthal, 2008).

Other types of street-level enforcement involve officers working undercover. In an **undercover buy** an undercover officer seeks to purchase drugs and the seller is arrested either immediately or after a period of monitoring by law enforcement. A similar approach is the **controlled buy** in which a monitored undercover informant purchases drugs and the seller is then arrested either immediately or after a period of surveillance. In a **reverse sting**, an undercover officer acts as a drug dealer and drug users are arrested after making a purchase. Critics of the reverse sting argue that it targets the personal user, as opposed to the more harmful drug dealer or traffickers.

Regardless of the intensity of the enforcement effort against drugs, the actions of the community are extremely important in reducing the problems associated with drug use and drug dealing in a neighborhood. If community members respond simply by staying indoors and summoning police assistance for drug-related offenses, enforcement efforts often will not be very successful as drug crimes are difficult to investigate because many community members are unwilling to testify. If community members respond more aggressively through the creation of anti-drug programs and other types of overt messages that drugs are not welcome in the neighborhood, this approach (in combination with law enforcement) can be highly successful (Moore & Kleinman, 2003). It is often very difficult for a community to reclaim their neighborhood from street-level drug dealing and associated drug activity. Street-level enforcement can be problematic because the police can arrest far more individuals for drug offenses than the criminal justice system can reasonably process. Conversely, however, street-level enforcement can be an important step in restoring hope and quality of life to neighborhoods wrought with drug activity.

> *"The areas that are safe rarely hear a police siren. Those that have yielded to the drug trade are criss-crossed by racing patrol cars with sirens blaring. The reason that little policing sometimes produces safe communities while heavy policing sometimes fails to do so is simply that success in confronting drug trafficking depends as much (or perhaps more) on the community's self-defense than on official police effort. Where community will and capacity for self-defense are strong, a little official policing goes a long way to keep the neighborhood free of drugs. Where it is weak, even heavy doses of official policing will not get the job done."*
>
> (Moore & Kleiman, 2003, p. 252)

By most accounts, the war on drugs has been a failure as drug production has not significantly decreased and neither has drug use. The war on drugs has been a success for many politicians, however, and can serve to "distract" the public from more complicated social issues. If we measure success in terms of politics, the war on drugs may well be considered successful; however, if we measure the war on drugs in terms of production and use of illicit substances, the results have been a dismal failure. The war on drugs and the ability of law enforcement to significantly decrease the global flow of drugs and drug-use rates is seriously hampered by a variety of factors. To begin, the trafficking and smuggling of drugs is an enterprise with billions of dollars in profit and one that spans the globe. Should law enforcement personnel be successful in reducing drug production in one country, the "balloon effect" suggests that another country simply takes over, making minimal global change in drug production statistics. This business is also a major employer, with traffickers spending their profits in the legal market, thus stimulating the economy—especially in countries where drugs are a major part of the economic system. A major barrier to "winning" the war on drugs is the enormous border of the United States and the millions of visitors and cargo that require monitoring which makes interdiction strategies very difficult. This translates to a very low risk of a drug smuggler getting caught—a reality that most drug smugglers understand, as evidenced by an in-depth study of traffickers. A response regarding the likelihood of being caught trafficking drugs into the United States included the following: "I can tell you, you can do it all the times you want, and we cannot get caught. Well if we break down, okay, if we get unlucky, like there happens to be a cop right there when you're coming in you know, those chances you always got that" (Decker & Chapman, 2008, p. 137). This perception of minimal risk also has smugglers returning to trafficking even after receiving a prison term:

> So an imaginary person. This imaginary person will probably go to it again because you got to figure this. This person—the system does not work. He's not a shoemaker. He's not a doctor. He doesn't know how to build houses, but yet he knows how to smuggle and he's very good in the logistics and he's very good with people. So chances are he's going back to it. (Decker & Chapman, 2008, pp. 139–140)

The above factors, combined with the violence that can accompany the trade in drugs, pose significant challenges to law enforcement. More and more it seems a reality that a country "without illicit drugs" is a utopian fantasy.

Summary

- The American war on drugs is based on an ever-changing, cultural reaction to a substance, rather than to an actual threat of individual or social harm. The drug war involves an expanding prison industrial complex; a series of "get tough" measures written into the law; an inundation of drug-war rhetoric; and discriminatory treatment based on class, race, and gender. The costs of this war have been high and have frequently resulted in violence, crime, corruption, devastation of social bonds, the destruction of inner-city communities, and the exponential growth in the number of minorities and women incarcerated.
- The Office of National Drug Control Policy's (ONDCP) Executive Summary for 2006 indicates a 2007 federal budget of $12.7 billion for reducing illegal drug use, an increase of $80.6 million from 2006. This is in addition to approximately $28 billion in state budgets, which results in spending of about $40 billion per year.
- According to the FBI, the number of arrests for drug offenses more than tripled from 580,900 in 1980 to 1,846,400 in 2005. Government studies reveal that over half of those imprisoned on federal drug offenses are street-level dealers or transporters, about one-third are mid-level dealers, and approximately 11 percent of federal offenders are high-level dealers.
- Race is intimately connected to the consequences of the war on drugs. A case in point is New York's Rockefeller Drug Laws which were enacted in 1973 and created mandatory minimum sentencing requirements intended to crack down on high-level drug offenders.
- Wide discrepancy in federally mandated sentences for crack cocaine versus powder cocaine existed in the criminal justice system for years with adverse consequences, specifically for African Americans who constituted 81 percent of offenders arrested for crack cocaine in 2006. On December 10, 2007, the Supreme Court issued a ruling that allows judges to utilize their discretion when imposing drug sentences.
- In 1989, the U.S. Supreme Court ruled in *United States v. Sokolow* that a drug courier profile could provide a foundation to "reasonably" suspect a specific individual of

drug smuggling. In 2003, former President Bush prohibited all federal agencies from using racial and ethnic profiling for drug investigations.

- High poverty rates among women have resulted in their seeking income in the drug world as decoys or drug couriers (mules) that import or transport drugs. The risks of this employment "choice" are high, often resulting in mandatory minimum sentences for women with no prior criminal record.
- The media-driven "crack baby epidemic" of the late 1980s led the public to stereotype women of a racial or ethnic minority who were portrayed as the overwhelming majority of "crack mothers." Tactics to control pregnant women include "protective incarceration" wherein a drug-using pregnant woman is imprisoned or otherwise confined to protect her unborn child, and a policy by hospitals in many states that test pregnant women "suspected" of drug abuse and then report them to either the police or CPS. Maternal drug-abuse laws were enforced primarily on minority women.
- Asset forfeiture began to be applied to the war on drugs under the 1970 Comprehensive Drug Abuse Prevention and Control Act. This Act permitted the forfeiture of any and all property believed to be used in relationship to drug activity. Amendments continued to expand forfeiture provisions through 1992.
- Asset forfeiture can be criminal or civil, and there are three types of civil asset forfeitures: summary forfeiture, administrative forfeiture, and a civil judicial proceeding. Because most law enforcement agencies are permitted to keep at least some of the proceeds garnered from asset forfeiture, those involved with the prosecution and enforcement end of the legal system usually regard this policy as positive. Critics of asset forfeiture argue that this policy amounts to "policing for profit" as law enforcement often has a financial incentive to pursue drug dealers and traffickers.
- One of the major ways to control the supply of drugs is through interdiction, which is the attempt to stop drugs from entering the United States via air, land, or water. To stop the movement of drugs into the United States, a variety of federal agencies are involved, including the DEA, the U.S. Coast Guard, the U.S. Customs and Border Protection Agency, and the U.S. military. In concert, these federal entities patrol the land, air, and water for illicit substances.
- The DEA is perhaps the one most responsible for enforcing drug laws, as this is the only federal agency with enforcement of drug laws as its sole responsibility. The DEA works both domestically and abroad on covert operations to identify and apprehend drug traffickers, cooperate with foreign governments to apprehend offenders outside of the United States, collects intelligence, trains law enforcement personnel in other nations regarding how to best fight the war on drugs, and other functions to minimize drug trafficking.
- Evidence suggests that interdiction has not been very successful. Despite increased seizure of illicit substances, drugs continue to be readily available on the streets.
- Eradication policies are aimed at minimizing the cultivation and production of drugs on foreign soil. This involves the destruction of crops such as coca plants, marijuana plants, and opium poppies using the assumption that a decrease in the crop production would result in higher cost of the drug to the consumer, which would serve to decrease use.
- One of the main problems with eradication policies is that growers of these plants simply relocate, which means destroying the existing plants or crops on a new plot of land for the growth of coca plants, marijuana plants, or opium poppies. The success of crop eradication programs is debatable. Some countries, such as Bolivia, report dramatic decreases in the amount of land used to grow coca plants and attribute this decrease to crop eradication programs. Looking at the big picture, however, the implementation of crop eradication policies and policies that encourage crop substitution have had little impact on the global production of either cocaine or opium.

- A lesser known way to control drugs in other nations is through the certification process, which involves the U.S. president compiling a list of countries involved in the production or transport of illicit substances. Decertified countries are penalized with the withholding of all U.S. aid.
- Street-level enforcement, involving federal, state, and local agencies, is also an integral aspect of drug control. Working in multijurisdictional taskforces, law enforcement at all levels works to share intelligence and techniques to apprehend drug offenders. Methods involved include: knock and talk, undercover buys, controlled buys, and reverse stings.

Important Terms

Administrative forfeiture
Asset forfeiture
Balloon effect
Certification
Civil asset forfeiture
Civil judicial proceeding
Controlled buy
Criminal asset forfeiture
Eradication
Herbicide eradication
Interdiction
Knock and talk
Manual crop eradication
Mule
Racial profiling
Reverse sting
Summary forfeiture
Undercover buy

Critical Thinking Questions

1. What are some of the potential adverse consequences of U.S. involvement in foreign nations in the war on drugs? How does this impact the United States? How does this impact the foreign nation in question?
2. The American Prosecutors Research Institute has a publication entitled *Beyond Convictions,* which is supportive of forfeitures. Conversely, organizations such as Forfeiture Endangers American Rights (FEAR) or the American Civil Liberties Union are against forfeitures. Examine the Web sites or publications by these groups with regard to asset forfeitures and then indicate and defend your position on this issue.

Research Topics

1. Choose a country in South America or Latin America and research the involvement of the United States in this country's drug policy. Prepare a report to present to the class.
2. Select a town/city in your state and research community efforts to decrease drug use and drug dealing. Present this information along with a discussion of rates of drug use in this location.

Suggested Readings

Campbell, Nancy D. (2000). *Using women: Gender, drug policy, and social justice.* New York, NY: Routledge.

Gray, James P. (2001). *Why our drug laws have failed and what we can do about it.* Philadelphia, PA: Temple University Press.

MacDoun, Robert J., & Reuter, Peter. (2001). *Drug war heresies: Learning from other vices, times, and places.* Cambridge: Cambridge University Press.

Kraska, Peter B. (2003). The military as drug police: Exercising the ideology of war. In Larry K. Gaines and Peter B. Kraska (Eds.), *Drugs, crime, & justice: Contemporary perspectives* (2nd ed., pp. 288–308). Prospect Heights, IL: Waveland Press.

Sadofsky Baggins, David. (1998). *Drug hate and the corruption of American justice.* Westport, CT: Praeger Press.

12

U.S. Drug Control Through Prevention

"Just Say No" – DARE motto.

OBJECTIVES:

When you have finished this chapter, you should be able to:

- Discuss how drug use is prevented through education, public service announcements, drug testing, and zero tolerance policies
- Understand the types of drug education and their effectiveness
- Elaborate the role of public service announcements in affecting drug use
- Understand the role of drug testing in schools and the workplace and its impact on drug usage
- Recognize the controversy of zero tolerance policies in the war on drugs

REAL LIFE

The following is part of an interview with an individual who had consumed herbal tea and a diuretic in an attempt to pass a drug test required for preemployment screening:

> It tasted bad. But I did that and took a diuretic. Plus I drank lots of water before the test. Between all that water and the diuretic, I had to piss constantly. I must have pissed gallons. Well, I'm sure I pissed as much as I took in. I had to piss all the time. So me and some other job applicants were loaded into a van and were driven *very* slowly by this old guy who was taking us to the testing lab. We went so slow, I had to ask him to stop along the way so that I could piss. Then, as soon as we got to the lab, I walked in and said "Where's the bathroom?" everyone had to have known what I was doing. But, I passed the test. And you know, the ironic thing about that is I had only been using marijuana and I got tested for a job selling used cars (Tunnell, 2004, p. 119; italics in original).

Preventing individuals from using drugs is one strategy of a multipronged approach to reduce (and ideally eliminate entirely) drug use in the United States. As a part of this strategy, the government and other anti-drug organizations use educational programs, public service announcements, drug-testing policies, as well as zero tolerance policies. Just as with other aspects of drug war policy, prevention strategies are replete with myths and misinformation, and frequently do not meet their intended goal of reduced rates of drug use.

PREVENTION THROUGH EDUCATION

Drug education has existed in the United States since the lessons were provided by the Women's Christian Temperance Union in the late 1800s. These early programs, like many current education programs, used scare tactics to discourage individuals from drug use. One "health lesson" of the Women's Christian Temperance Union suggested that initial moderate amounts of alcohol would quickly lead to a great appetite for alcohol and regular drunkenness (Moilanen, 2004). Other early drug education efforts were highly ideological, and perhaps the most well-known is the now cult-classic film *Reefer Madness.* The film was originally entitled *Tell Your Children* and put out in 1936 by the Federal Bureau of Narcotics. The film was intended as an educational piece on the potential consequences of marijuana use among high school students, including suicide, rape, hit-and-run, and general madness. In the 1970s, however, it became a satirical comedy and inspired an off-Broadway musical in 2001—hardly the effect intended by the federal government! Current advertisement by the Office of National Drug Control Policy (ONDCP) advocates similar ideological themes and purports that the only way to truly avoid the spell of drug addiction is by never using or experimenting with drugs, as advocated by the "Not Even Once" slogan of The Meth Project (Moilanen, 2004; www.themethproject.org). A significant amount of money is put into anti-drug educational efforts: In 2005, the federal government provided $611 million to the Department of Education for this purpose (Caulkins, Pacula, Paddock, & Chiesna, 2004). It is suggested that for each dollar devoted to school-based drug prevention programs, there is a net savings of $5.60 from a reduction in drug use (Caulkins, Pacula, Paddock, & Chiesna, 2004).

Drug prevention has been dominated by three educational models: the information model, the affective model, and the social influence model.

- The **Information Model** suggests that when you inform youth of the potential hazards of using drugs, they will use that information to avoid harm. This model purports that information leads to negative attitudes regarding drugs, which results in avoidance of drug use (Ellickson, 1995). The information model may involve anti-drug videos and public service announcements or lectures by former drug addicts that detail the horrors of drug addiction (Cohen, 1996). This model most typically involves scare tactics and talks *at* students with little opportunity for youth engagement or questioning. Critics of this model suggest that not all the consequences of drug use are negative (or nobody would continue to use drugs) and this should be considered in the creation of educational programs (Cohen, 1996).
- The **Affective Model** suggests that youth with high levels of self-esteem will avoid the use of drugs (Cohen, 1996). As such, the goals are to improve communication, self-image, decision making, problem-solving abilities, and abilities to interact within a group of young individuals in order to keep youth away from involvement with drugs (Ellickson, 1995). Many programs that use the affective model apply principles of social control theory and work to build stronger social bonds between youth and mainstream society. An example of this model is a program called Families That Care: Guiding Good Choices (formerly called

Preparing for the Drug-Free Years), which seeks to strengthen family bonds and reduce risk factors such as lack of parental monitoring and communication, inconsistent or severe discipline, or parental drug use.

- The **Social Influence Model**, also referred to as the drug resistance education model, suggests that youth are extremely susceptible to peer pressure and must be taught the skills to make rational decisions to avoid the use of drugs (Cohen, 1996). The premise of this model is that once youth are armed with rational decision-making skills, they can resist the temptations, both internal and external, and not succumb to drug use. The most common example of this type of model is the DARE program.

Irrespective of the educational model employed, **primary prevention programs** are built on the foundation that individuals are less likely to engage in drug use and abuse if the positive aspects of their life are enhanced and risk factors for drug use are diminished. Factors that increase a youth's likelihood of drug use include: failure at school, rebellion against authority, lack of social skills, low self-esteem, a family history of substance use or abuse, lack of adequate parental supervision, availability of drugs in the community, peers that use or abuse substances, a poor economic situation, or community attitudes that are favorable to drug use (see Figure 12-1 for an

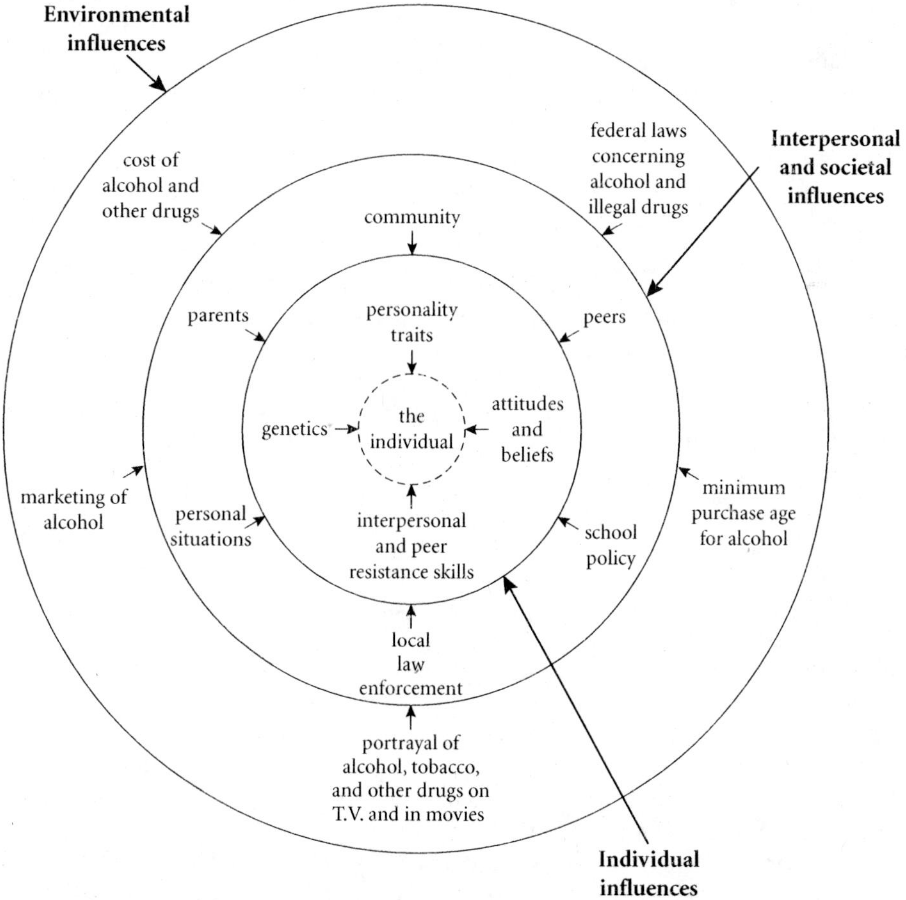

FIGURE 12-1 Factors That Can Influence the Likelihood of Substance Use

Source: Department of Health and Human Services, 1989.

illustration of some of these variables). These factors predispose young people to engage in substance use or abuse and require them to be more resilient in order to resist the pressures associated with drugs. Once an individual begins using drugs, the focus becomes early identification of use and intervention before use of drugs turns into abuse and addiction: this is termed **secondary prevention.**

Drug Abuse Resistance Education (DARE)

The most common educational program in the United States is the school-based **Drug Abuse Resistance Education (DARE)** program, developed in 1983 by the Los Angeles Police Department (LAPD). The program was initially geared toward 5th and 6th grade students and advocated the notorious "Just Say No" to drugs motto. It also encouraged self-esteem, taught drug education, stress management techniques, and how to resist peer pressure. The funds for DARE come from a nonprofit organization, and in 1993, the cost was estimated at $700 million per year (Wysong, Aniskiewicz, & Wright, 1994). Since the 1980s, however, DARE has been significantly expanded. According to the DARE Web site, its mission is to:

> provide children with the information and skills they need to live drug-and-violence-free lives. The mission is to equip kids with the tools that will enable them to avoid negative influences and instead, allow them to focus on their strengths and potential. And, that's exactly what D.A.R.E. is designed to do. Additionally, it establishes positive relationships between students and law enforcement, teachers, parents, and other community leaders. Every youngster should have the opportunity to grow-up healthy, safe, secure, and equipped with the skills needed to succeed in life (www.dare.com).

The program is now at work in 75 percent of schools across the United States, and in forty-three countries, beginning in kindergarten and continuing through grade 12. The focus is not singularly on drugs anymore, but includes gangs and violence as well (www.dare.com). Costs are now estimated at just over $1 billion per year (Shepard, 2001).

Is all this money well spent? On its face, DARE seems like a very positive type of community policing. It engages law enforcement with youth and would seem to have a positive impact—but the question is: Does it lead to lower rates of substance abuse by youth? DARE officials would, of course, indicate that this program is highly successful. Ninety-seven percent of those teaching DARE rate it as "good" to "excellent," and 93 percent of parents who have children participating in the program believe it contributes to drug avoidance (Moilanen, 2004). In addition, officers teaching DARE continually offer anecdotal "proof" of the effectiveness of the program's success.

But what do independent evaluations reveal about the effectiveness of DARE? Almost all of the scientific evidence suggests that this program has no impact on substance abuse rates—and indeed, there is some research to suggest a counterproductive effect on drug-use rates. A study which followed youth in Colorado for 3 years after their involvement with a DARE program found no statistically significant impact from DARE on the youth (Dukes, Ullman, & Stein, 1997). A study in Illinois comparing students 5 years after their involvement with DARE with a group of similarly aged students who had not been involved with DARE actually found higher rates of drug and alcohol use among those individuals who had been involved with DARE (Rosenbaum & Hanson, 1998). A review of DARE data between 1987 and 1992 in Indiana found no reduction in drug use (Wysong, Aniskiewicz, & Wright, 2003). Perhaps most damaging are studies by the U.S. General Accounting Office (GAO) (2003), the Surgeon General's Office, and the National Academy of Sciences, all of which indicate that the DARE program has been ineffective in its reduction of drug use among youth (Wright, 2001). The program continues, however, because it is *perceived* as successful:

> The adults rightly perceive that most children who go through DARE do not engage in problematic drug use. Unfortunately, these individuals may not realize that the vast majority of children, even without any intervention, do not engage in problematic drug [use] . . . That is, adults, may believe that drug [use] among adolescents is much more frequent than it actually is. When children who go through DARE are compared to this "normative" group of drug-[using] teens, DARE appears effective (Lynam, Milich, Zimmerman, Novak, Logan, Martin, Leukefeld, & Clayton, 1999, p. 593).

Given that drug-use statistics discussed earlier reveal that is it extremely common, almost normative, for youth to experiment with drugs prior to graduating from high school, it should come as no surprise that many youth do not respond well to the "Just Say No to Drugs" message purported by DARE.

According to Rosenbaum (2007), the DARE message has been compromised because educators fail to delineate between *use* and *abuse* of drugs, and instead insist that "all use is abuse." They provide inaccurate information and use scare tactics, and they lack a comprehensive set of tools that would assist users in reducing harms that may be associated with the use of drugs. When youth realize that DARE educators are misleading them about marijuana being a gateway drug or exaggerating the risks that are associated with drug experimentation, they are likely to reject the entire anti-drug message, even the parts of the anti-drug message that are true! This is illustrated in the case of a heroin addict detailing how she became addicted:

> When I was in high school they had these so-called drug education classes. They told us if we used marijuana we would become addicted. They told us if we used heroin we would become addicted. Well, we all tried marijuana and found we did not become addicted. We figured the entire message must be b.s. So I tried heroin, used it again and again, got strung out, and here I am (Rosenbaum, 1999, p. 1).

It is possible that DARE participation may have the effect of increasing drug use: "More often than not, lectures, pamphlets and film strips that [exaggerate the dangers of drugs] stimulate curiosity, make the prohibited substances look more attractive to young audiences, and make authorities appear ridiculous" (Weil & Rosen, 1998, p. 3). Is it any surprise that youth would question the information provided by a DARE officer who suggests as "fact" that "when a person smokes marijuana, half of their brain cells are erased forever" (Rosenbaum, 2001, p. 26)? It has been well documented for decades that educational efforts with regard to drug prevention are not successful (Wald & Hutt, 1972), yet the government continues to fund such endeavors. Interestingly, research reveals that those who presumably know the most about drugs—physicians—have a substantial drug abuse problem ("Death Highlights Drug's Lethal Allure to Doctors," 1995; "The Junkie in the O.R.," 2006).

Given the evidence suggesting the ineffectiveness of DARE, some critics advocate teaching youth *safety* about drugs and drug use and trying to prevent drug *abuse* among youth. This approach to drug education would educate about the effects of drugs and the varied risks associated with using drugs, and teach youth how to minimize harm. This approach recognizes that youth experiment with drugs, both illegal and legal, and instead of fighting against what is viewed as inevitable experimentation, focuses on reduction of harm during this period of experimentation by trying to prevent youth from moving from *use* to *abuse* of substances (Rosenbaum, 2007). Advocates of this approach suggest that this method would also focus on delaying the average age of first drug use, reducing dangerous ways of using drugs such as mixing various types of drugs and bingeing at weekend parties on drugs, and would caution youth against using unknown substances (Skager, 2001). While Great Britain and the Netherlands have adopted such progressive programs, the funding just does not exist in the United States, as guidelines instituted by the federal government permit the funding of drug education programs only if they advocate an abstinence-only platform (Rose, 2002). Reviews of drug education programs reveal that the "best" programs involve the following (Shin, 2001):

- A significant number of educational hours over a period lasting at least 3 years;
- Involvement of peers;
- A focus on resisting peer influence, improving life skills, and other social influences;
- Recognition that a change in attitudes is important; and
- Involvement of a variety of parties, including peers, parents, as well as the community, in changing attitudes regarding drugs.

The "no" approach clearly has not been working in the United States—perhaps it is time to focus on the "know" approach?

Students Against Drunk Driving/Prom Promises

Students Against Destructive Decisions (SADD), formerly known as **Students Against Drunk Driving** is a nationwide peer organization which seeks to prepare young adults to make responsible decisions for the prevention of underage alcohol and drug use and drunk or impaired driving. SADD was founded by Robert Anastas, a coach and health educator in Wayland, Massachusetts, in 1981. SADD was one of the first peer groups to focus on student leadership and was considered by many to be groundbreaking in its teaching methods. SADD not only educates young adults about the implications of engaging in illegal consumption of drugs and alcohol but it does so while explicitly avoiding the frequently used scare tactics to deliver these messages. The organization also provides guidance on choosing not to drive in situations where alcohol and/or drugs have been consumed, and provides an extracurricular component to deter drug use. SADD has local chapters throughout the United States and Europe, and their Web site provides a calendar of upcoming events that students can participate in instead of engaging in activities such as underage drinking or illicit drug use. SADD's goal is to inform and empower young adults to make positive decisions in their life, and the organization has about 350,000 members across the United States with chapters spanning from middle schools, to high schools, and even colleges ("Teens and SADD: Organization Helps Kids Make Positive Choices," 2008).

Students Against Destructive Decisions became popular in the 1980s and 1990s but was not without its critics. SADD was criticized for accepting funding from entities within the alcohol beverage industry and for provisions included in their "Contract for Life." The Contract for Life was an agreement that members of SADD could execute with their parents/guardians which ensured that their parents/guardians would provide safe transportation home in the event that their child was under the influence of alcohol/drugs. Some critics contend that this provision effectively implies parental acceptance of underage alcohol or drug consumption. In response,

SADD has refused any additional moneys from the alcohol beverage industry and has changed their Contract for Life language to a "no-use" clause concerning alcohol and contraband ("Students Against Destructive Decisions SADD," 2001). The organization now reinforces in their materials that "SADD does not condone safe rides programs in which sober teens offer their intoxicated or drug-impaired friends a safe ride home. SADD promotes a 'No Use' policy for alcohol and other drugs" (http://www.sadd.org/howtoformchapter.htm). How effective SADD is in actually preventing underage alcohol and drug consumption remains to be seen; however, it does seem that students exposed to their message generally have a positive attitude geared toward avoiding the practice of drinking or using drugs and then driving ("Students Against Destructive Decisions SADD," 2001). Another method of prevention among students is the Prom Promise.

The **Prom Promise** is a pledge that some students around the United States have taken to not consume alcohol or drugs on their prom night. It is a nationwide movement that began around 1990. A typical Prom Promise reads similar to the following:

> I, ______________________ hereby promise to behave responsibly before, during and after ______________________'s Prom.
>
> Date: ____________________
>
> I commit to an alcohol and drug free prom night because I care about my fellow students, my community, and myself.
>
> Signed by: ______________________
>
> Student: ______________________
>
> Parent: ______________________
>
> Principal: ______________________
>
> I WANT TO LIVE. I want to laugh, listen to great music and dance. I want to have an absolutely great time at prom. The day after, I will relive it, hour by hour, with my friends. I want to remember it. All of it. I will not use alcohol at prom (http://www.promgirl.com/prom-guide/prom-promise).

In 2007, Mothers Against Drunk Driving (MADD) sought to create a program that would send an anti-drug/alcohol message to students more than once or twice per year, and created THINK. This is also a program that is pledge-based, but focuses on additional popular party times throughout the high school year such as Friday night sporting events, spring break, homecoming, and other times of the year when school is not in session. Many teachers, parents, principals, and students feel good about participating in these programs because they find that it aids in combating the problem of student drug or alcohol use (www.madd.org). Though the research as to the effectiveness of such programs is debatable, it is a method to open the lines of communication between youth and adults regarding the risks of drug and alcohol use as well as the dangers of consuming drugs and then driving.

Public Service Announcements

Sponsored primarily by the ONDCP with about a $180 million per year advertising budget, **public service announcements** advocate anti-drug attitudes and behaviors on television or radio spots, print or billboard advertisements, or other similar advertising locales. Announcements typically use an integrated approach to work toward the prevention and reduction of illicit drug use among youth, and seek to support parents in their efforts to keep youth drug free. The ONDCP campaign was initiated by Congress in 1998, though prior to that there were public service announcements funded by nonprofit organizations such as Partnership for a Drug-Free America (PFDFA). Two main ONDCP campaigns geared toward preventing teen drug use are entitled "Above the Influence," and "Parents: The Anti-Drug." The "Above the Influence" campaign urges youth to find factors in their own life that can keep them above the peer pressure and influence of those who may try to encourage them to use drugs. It focuses on the positive power of sports, art, music, or academics in keeping youth away from illicit substances: in keeping them "above the influence" of drugs. The campaign "Parents: The Anti-Drug" recognizes that youth drug-use rates are declining and focuses on the potential abuse of prescription and over-the-counter drugs that can be most easily obtained at home. As such, the motto of this campaign is "Teens don't need a drug dealer to get high," and puts center-stage the role of parents in preventing teen drug use.

More recently, an organization called The Meth Project has been receiving attention for its public service announcements. The organization was formed in 2005 by a businessman in Montana who sought to prevent the use of methamphetamine in that state. According to the organization's Web site: "The Meth Project's core message, Not Even Once, speaks directly to the highly addictive nature of meth. Every day, people are faced with the decision to try meth. Many perceive benefits in using the drug, but little-to-no risk. This is the root of the problem. The goal of the Meth Project is to arm teens and young adults with the facts about methamphetamine so that they can make well-informed decisions when presented with the opportunity to try it" (www.methproject.org). To get this message across The Meth Project utilizes billboards, radio advertisements, and television advertisements that are graphic and disturbing. In one public service announcement, a woman is bloodied and hunched over, the following caption written below her: "My mother knew I'd never hurt her, then she got in the way" ("Meth Ads Talk to Teens in Spanish," 2009). In another announcement, a filthy urinal is portrayed above the caption, "No one thinks they'll lose their virginity here. Meth will change that" ("Meth Ads Talk to Teens in Spanish," 2009). Another ad of a jail cell has the caption, "No one thinks they'll spend a romantic evening here. Meth will change that" (Meth Ads Talk to Teens in Spanish," 2009). Since its inception in 2005, The Meth Project has expanded its mission to Arizona, Colorado, Hawaii, Idaho, Illinois, and Wyoming (www.methproject.org).

Studies analyzing the effectiveness of thirty different public service announcements produced by ONDCP and PFDFA indicated mixed results. There were some public service announcements that youth believe may result in a lower likelihood of drug use, other advertisements that had no effect on the likelihood of drug use, and six of the thirty advertisements had a negative impact on the likelihood of drug use, meaning that they had the potential to encourage use, rather than discourage use (Fishbein, Hall-Jamieson, Zimmer, von Haeften, & Nabi, 2002). This same research revealed that the most effective public service announcements dealt with "harder" drugs, like methamphetamine and heroin. Another study, focusing on anti-drug public service announcements between 1999 and 2002 dealing specifically with marijuana, revealed that the ads may lead to the perception that drug use is more common among youth than it is in reality, and may have the counterproductive effect of increasing the number of people who use marijuana later in life (Hornik et al., 2002).

YOUR BRAIN ON DRUGS Partnership for a Drug-Free America (PFDFA) is a nonprofit organization which has been integral in the prevention and treatment of drug use among youth in the United States. Long before the government started a public service announcement media campaign, PFDFA became well-known for their "This Is Your Brain on Drugs" campaign of the 1980s. Also known as "The Fried Egg Story," the Partnership's Web site (www.drugfree.org) describes this campaign as:

> the most widely-shown television message of any created by the Partnership for a Drug-Free America in its 20-year history. The initial and lasting response to this message has been incredible, as it delivers a simple yet strong anti-drug message that has been embraced by the public and turned into *the* slogan for the drug prevention movement. In the mid-1980s, attitudes regarding drug use evolved from "acceptable and harmless" to "addictive and dangerous." In 1987, the Fried Egg television message exploded into popular culture to catalyze a developing social perception, and reinforce the new belief that drugs were a growing problem in our country . . . Fried Egg's sharp message earned the Partnership a great deal of recognition . . . This spot can now be seen in the Museum of Television Broadcasting and the Smithsonian. More than any other single TV message, the Fried Egg put the Partnership—and its mission—in the public eye (www.drugfree.org).

PFDFA was created in 1986 and since then has been a major player in the advertising business. In fact, in the late 1990s they were the second largest advertiser in the United States, with only McDonald's advertising more! PFDFA advertises on the radio, television, in newspapers, on buses, taxis, billboards, and in bathroom stalls, to name only a few locations. Several years ago both PFDFA and the ONDCP were criticized by scholars for their lack of attention to the abuse of prescription drugs and over-the-counter drugs by youth, and this criticism (which was very true at the time) may have resonated with the organizations. Though PFDFA corporate sponsorship remains fairly heavy in terms of pharmaceutical company contributions, they now have an educational campaign designed to reduce and prevent youth from experimenting with prescription and over-the-counter medications (as does ONDCP). Nothing in their arsenal has been as powerful, however, as their "This Is Your Brain on Drugs" campaign of the 1980s.

DRUGS AS TERRORIST SUPPORT **Narcoterrorism** is a type of terrorism in which terrorist groups are involved directly in the cultivation, manufacture, transportation, and/or distribution of illicit substances. According to the Drug Enforcement Administration (DEA), an organization involved in narcoterrorism is a group involved in drug trafficking in order to further fund their terrorist activities. After the September 11, 2001 attacks on the United States, the ONDCP unveiled a series of multimillion dollar advertisements linking drug use in the United States to the support of terrorists in other countries. The advertisements said: "I helped murder families in Colombia—it was just innocent fun." "I helped a bomber get a false passport—all the kids do it." "I helped blow up buildings—my life, my body." The advertisements typically ended with: "Drug money supports terror. If you buy drugs, you might too" ("Strong Views, Pro and Con, on Ads Linking Drug Use to Terrorism," 2002). This was a scare tactic that hit many Americans at their emotional core; but was it true? In February

2002 during Super Bowl XXXVI, the federal government spent $3.5 million on advertisement time during kick off in what became known as the "terror war campaign" (http://www.narcoterror.org/ondcpads.htm). Most previous ONDCP advertisements had focused on how drug use harms the users themselves: this was a major leap to suggest that American drug money could fuel foreign attacks on Americans. But the ad did not stand alone; it was part of a $10 million campaign that included radio and newspaper spots as well as educational materials distributed to middle and high schools. The message was to be spread far and wide.

Also launched in 2002 was a traveling exhibit entitled *Target America: Opening Eyes to the Damage Drugs Cause* sponsored by the ONDCP, the Center for Substance Abuse Prevention, the National Institute on Drug Abuse, the National Guard, and PFDFA. Like the ONDCP advertisements, the goal of the traveling exhibit was to "explore and educate the public about the connections between drug trafficking and terrorism in the months following September 11, 2001" (www.targetamerica.org). The exhibit was expanded in 2004 with more physical displays encouraging teachers, parents, and students to begin conversations about how each individual can help solve the drug problem (www.targetamerica.org). Though there was evidence to suggest a link between drugs and terrorism in countries such as Afghanistan and Colombia when these advertisements were produced (and links that continue to this day), it is unlikely that youth smoking marijuana were going to believe that they were supporting narcoterrorism with their illicit purchase. Indeed, at that time it was unlikely that their marijuana purchase (the most frequently used substance) was supporting terrorism: Ironically, it is currently far more likely that a youth's purchase of marijuana is supporting terrorism by a Mexican drug cartel than when these ONDCP ads were in production!

What is clear in drug prevention education strategies is that a "one size fits all" approach has not been successful! "Strategies which are adequate for preventing experimentation among those at low risk of engaging in serious antisocial behaviors may be wholly inadequate for preventing initiation and use by those who exhibit a 'deviance syndrome.' On the other hand, well-founded strategies for preventing drug abuse among those at highest risk for abuse may be inappropriate for those at risk of only becoming experimental users" (Hawkins, Lishner, & Catalano, 1987, p. 78). The goals and targets of these goals, therefore, need to be explicitly clear if drug-use rates are to be lowered. "If the goal of prevention is to prevent serious maladaptive behavior associated with drug abuse in adolescence, then it may be desirable from an etiological perspective to focus prevention efforts on those youth who manifest behavior problems, including aggressive and other antisocial behaviors during elementary grades. On the other hand, if the goal is to prevent experimentation with drugs, or to delay the age of experimentation in the general population, such highly focused efforts may be inappropriate" (Hawkins, Lishner, & Catalano, 1987, p. 80). So the question becomes: Are we trying to prevent drug *use* or drug *abuse*? When the government attempts to design programs to prevent both, aimed at multiple populations, what results are programs that serve to prevent drug use in no population, but merely cost the taxpayers a significant sum of money. By all estimates, universal school-based programs can show only modest reductions in drug or alcohol use—in the realm of approximately 2 percent—but with only 30 hours or so of education, what can be expected ("What Kind of Drug Use Does School-Based Prevention Prevent?" 2002)?

PREVENTION THROUGH DRUG TESTING

Since the 19th century, law enforcement has been conducting crude forms of drug testing, such as slurred speech tests to assess alcohol intoxication or looking for pupil constriction to assess for narcotic use. Other simple or observational tests can include looking for needle tracks, examining a person's motor skills, such as walking a straight line or standing on one foot, or reciting common phrases such as the alphabet. The first biochemical test for drugs was created in the 1920s in response to the prohibition of alcohol and is today referred to as the **"breathalyzer"**, which analyzes one's breath for the presence of alcohol (Ackerman, 1995). This was not, however, the beginning of full-fledged drug testing, which did not begin on a systematic basis until the late 1980s with the creation of the Drug Use Forecasting System (DUF) (renamed in 1997 as the **Arrestee Drug Abuse Monitoring System—ADAM**). More scientific tests, such as hair follicle, urine, and blood, can now be used to test for a vast array of drugs. Within law enforcement, the Federal Bureau of Prisons tests for both prescription and illicit substances, and post-conviction drug testing is frequently a requirement for individuals on probation as well as for those on parole and those due for community release. However, one does not need to have come to the attention of law enforcement to be required to take a drug test.

> **"Soldier's Disease"**
>
> This was the term used to refer to military personnels' addiction to morphine. Morphine was used without regard for the potentially addictive consequences as analgesic for battle wounds. When soldiers returned from the Vietnam War heroin addicted, the government began sporadic drug testing. In 1980, a study revealed that just over one-quarter of Navy personnel under the age of 25 admitted using drugs (Ackerman, 1995). No rigorous drug testing occurred however until tragedy struck in 1981. A fighter jet crashed on the deck of a nuclear aircraft carrier and fourteen people were killed, and forty-eight others were injured. Investigative efforts revealed that six of those killed had used illegal substances within the past month (Ackerman, 1995). The Department of Defense responded by instituting mandatory urinalysis drug testing throughout the armed forces, with the Navy instituting the most rigorous testing procedures of all branches and performing approximately 1.8 million tests per year (Ackerman, 1995).

Increasingly, more and more segments of the population are succumbing to drug testing—from sports, to the military, to the workplace, to the school. In the workplace, problems of alcohol and drug abuse have been of some concern since the 1960s as it impacted absenteeism and on-the-job accidents. The movement to on-the-job drug testing, however, has not been the result of increased public concern: Research in the early 1990s suggested that a mere 0.3 percent of employers believed drugs at the workplace were a significant problem, with another 8 percent considering drug in the workplace a moderate problem (Zeese, 1997). Instead, the push came from public anxiety about drug use, aggressive marketing by drug-testing companies, and government regulations and policies requiring testing (Zeese, 1997, p. 1.2). Private industry did not really embrace drug testing until the 1980s, when the transportation and utilities industries were the first to follow the lead of the military. What opened the door was the signing of an executive order by President Reagan in 1986, which created the **Drug-Free Federal Workforce** goal. Reagan claimed that:

> Drug use is having serious adverse effects upon a significant proportion of the national work force and results in billions of dollars of lost productivity each year . . . Federal employees who use illegal drugs, on or off duty, tend to be less productive, less reliable, and prone to greater absenteeism than their fellow employees who do not use illegal drugs. The use of illegal drugs, by Federal employees impairs the efficiency of Federal departments and agencies, undermines public confidence in them, and makes it more difficult for other employees who do not use illegal drugs to

> perform their jobs effectively. The use of illegal drugs, on or off duty, by Federal employees also can pose a serious health and safety threat to members of the public and to other Federal employees (Drug Free Federal Workplace, 1986).

This Executive Order (No. 12564) mandated drug testing for federal agencies, but set the stage for private corporations to pursue this same agenda. In addition, both state and federal governments offered financial incentives for corporations to join the war on drugs and drug test potential and/or current employees (Zimmer & Jacobs, 1992). Currently, drug testing usually occurs as part of one of the following:

- Screening of applicants *prior* to their hire at a place of employment;
- Random drug testing of current individuals at a place of employment;
- Drug testing of a specific individual at a place of employment if there is *reasonable suspicion* that he or she is engaging in drug use;
- Postaccident drug testing when an individual has been involved in an on-the-job accident; or
- Regularly scheduled testing (also called periodic testing), which is conducted in employment sectors such as law enforcement and typically involves advance notice and goes hand-in-hand with a physical examination.

In the late 1980s, about 21 percent of companies drug tested employees, compared to almost 85 percent in 1993. Approximately 18 percent of Fortune 500 companies drug tested employees in the mid-1980s, compared to 40 percent by the early 1990s (Zeese, 1997). Drug testing also varies dramatically by the size of the organization. Of corporations with more than 1,000 employees, approximately 71 percent drug test and 42 percent test for alcohol; of corporations with between 50 and 99 employees, approximately 40 percent drug test and 16 percent test for alcohol; and of corporations with fewer than 50 employees, only 2 percent drug test and none report testing for alcohol (Hartwell, Steele, French, & Rodman, 1996). It is ironic then that of those admitting current illicit drug use, more than half work at a place of business with fewer than 25 employees—the very place least likely to test for drugs (SAMHSA, 1997)! Overall, 62 percent of private sector employees work at an organization that tests for drugs and 33 percent work at an organization that tests for alcohol (Tunnell, 2004).

The goals of a company that drug tests its employees are varied, and may include (Hanson, 1993):

- Identifying those individuals using drugs within the company
- Deterring potential users from drug use
- Improving worker morale within the company
- Increasing productivity
- Decreasing accidents in the workplace
- Improving cost-effectiveness within the company

In an interview, a corporate spokesman described the goals of drug testing from his perspective:

> I think one issue that a company has to consider is that it has become pretty much a standard business practice and particularly in manufacturing to do pre-employment testing. If you don't do that, then you have a chance of getting all the other rejects. Everybody that has tested positive will come here and say, "Hey, they don't test us over there," And that may just be a mental impression of what would happen. The

> other thing is that we take a very aggressive approach in safety. It's a pretty proven fact that people that are under the influence of either illegal drugs or even abusing prescription drugs and/or alcohol, it impairs their decision process and their mental process of making logical decisions. Sometimes, particularly in an industrial setting, you have to react rather quickly to a situation that's happened. If you're mentally impaired or not ready to make that decision, it could put you in a very hazardous situation. And I think the second thing, as part of that, is drug use in our society has gotten to be so big of a problem that employers are having to do it to protect themselves. It becomes a safety issue. Unfortunately you have to do this to protect yourself because it's become very rampant in the society that we live [in] (Tunnell, 2004, p. 26).

Is there a research to demonstrate the effectiveness of drug testing at achieving any (or all) of the above goals?

There is some research to suggest that workplace drug tests are useful for identifying those individuals using drugs within the company—this should be obvious (Hanson, 1993). With regard to drug tests deterring drug use, research suggests that there may be a slight deterrent effect, but this is modest at best (Lange, Cabanilla, Moler, Frankenfield, & Fudala, 1994). One concern of drug testing is that of lowered worker morale, because low morale can negatively impact productivity as well as rates of absence and accidents. Generally, however, studies find that workers support drug testing, provided that the testing procedures and results are strictly confidential (LeRoy, 1991). While commonsense would seem to dictate that drug users are less productive, have more accidents at work, and therefore cost the company money, the research in each of these regards is inconclusive—despite the fact that the ONDCP estimated on-the-job productivity losses in 2000 at $110.5 billion due to drug use (Office of National Drug Control Policy [ONDCP], 2001)! Some studies suggest findings in line with "commonsense" and suggest lowered productivity due to drug use (Zwerling, Ryan, & Orav, 1990; Zwerling, Ryan, & Orav, 1992), whereas others suggest that drug users are just as productive as nonusers, that the impact of drug testing on accidents wanes over time, and that the cost-effectiveness of drug testing is exaggerated (Anglin & Westland, 1989; Shepard & Clifton, 1998; Swena & Gaines, 1999). It seems, however, that this is another case of moral panic with productivity loss statistics misrepresented and repeated over and over in the media, in corporations' promotional literature, and by politicians, until it took on a life of its own (Tunnell, 2004). Ignored was commentary on the data by the National Academy of Sciences which purported "the data . . . do not provide clear evidence of the deleterious effects of drugs other than alcohol on safety and other job performance indicators" (Normand, Lempert, & O'Brien, 1994, p. 107).

Compared to the workplace, school-based drug testing is rare, though endorsed by the federal anti-drug strategy. In the 2004 State of the Union address, President George W. Bush proposed $23 million in additional funds for schools wanting to use drug testing as one tool to "save children's lives." Despite the extra money, prevalence of these programs remains fairly low:

> In the 2005–06 school year, 5 percent of public schools reported performing drug testing on athletes and 3 percent reported doing so for students in other extracurricular activities. A higher percentage of public high schools than middle or primary schools reported performing drug tests on students: 13 percent of high schools reported performing drug tests on athletes, compared to 7 percent of middle schools and 1 percent of primary schools (National Center for Education Statistics, 2009).

A study conducted to evaluate the effectiveness of drug testing in reducing youth drug-use rates focused on 76,000 students between 1998 and 2001. This study found absolutely no significant difference between the rates of drug use in schools that tested for drugs compared to schools that did not test for drugs (Yamaguchi, Johnston, & O'Malley, 2003). Schools that choose to drug test, however, find this a very costly endeavor. For example, an Ohio school drug tested 1,473 students in one year, for a total cost of $35,000! Of the almost 1,500 students, only 11 tested positive for drugs (Rosenbaum, 2004). So, if the effectiveness of drug testing is highly debatable, should this policy continue given all the controversy?

The two main controversies in the area of drug testing are reliability and constitutionality. Without going into the chemical details of how the tests are conducted, drug tests hold reasonably high potential for false positives. This was the topic of a *Seinfeld* episode entitled "The Showerhead" in which Elaine tested positive for opium after eating poppy seed muffins the day before (Ackerman, 1996) a drug test. The potential for this occurring is taken so seriously by the Federal Bureau of Prisons that inmates released on furlough are required to agree to a condition stating: "It has been determined that consumption of poppy seeds may cause a positive drug test which may result in disciplinary action. As a condition of my participation in community programs, I will not consume any poppy seeds or items containing poppy seeds" (Federal Bureau of Prisons Form BP-S291(52)). Because the consequences of a false positive can be so severe, including arrest, disqualification from employment, the military, sports, and so on, a more specific test, and one with a greater degree of reliability, is *usually* conducted before action is taken. This, however, is not always the case. Another problem is that only blood tests (and in the case of alcohol, breathalyzers) test immediate (and current) use of drugs. All other drug tests measure past use of drugs—with hair analysis able to test whether or not drugs have been consumed within the past 12 months or even longer! Research reveals that when drugs are involved in workplace accidents, the most likely drug involved is alcohol: yet workplace drug testing rarely involves breathalyzers or blood tests which would assess alcohol intoxication.[1]

The greatest objection has been to the privacy and constitutional issues raised by drug testing. The Fourth Amendment guarantees against the right of unreasonable search and seizure of one's person, and many would argue that a drug test is a clear violation of this constitutionally guaranteed right. But has the court agreed? Drug testing is definitely a search and seizure—seizing bodily fluids (usually under the watchful eye of a monitor to ensure that the urine is not tampered with or switched with someone else's "clean" urine), and then it is searched for the presence of illicit substances. So the courts had to decide, is this process reasonable? In essence, the courts have decided:

- If the state has a compelling interest (which usually involves the well-being of the community), even without suspicion, mandatory drug testing is permitted—this means that public-sector workers can be tested, as can students participating in extracurricular activities at school
- Mandatory drug testing programs without any cause for testing are not permitted
- Drug testing due to suspicion is permitted

[1] Random and preemployment drug and alcohol testing is required by the following agencies: the Department of Defense, the Department of Energy, Federal Aviation Administration, Federal Highway Administration, Federal Railroad Administration, the National Aeronautical and Space Administration, the Nuclear Regulatory Commission, and the Urban Mass Transportation Administration.

- Both private and public employers can legally require drug screening as a condition of employment
- Schools are permitted to conduct drug testing without suspicion of any student involved in any school-based extracurricular activity, from sports to choir to the chess team

In essence, the courts have decided that drug tests are "in the category of 'administrative searches' that meet 'special needs' of the government in relating to safety, security or workplace management. Then by 'balancing' the rights of the individual against the needs of the government, it is ruled that the drug-testing programs . . . are not unreasonable searches" (Gilliom, 1994, p. 86).

What has resulted in response to the rapidly growing drug-testing industry is the detox industry—an industry that preys on those desperate to beat the drug test.

> Products range from $24.95 for Klear Carbo Drink, touted as "perfect for concert goers and very light users," to $99.00 for Never Fail Urine Cleanser, which is "perfect for daily users, no matter what you use," all the way up to $153.00 for All Drugs Follicle Cleanse, an "all drug removing shampoo kit" that is "perfect for those of you that partake in a little more than marijuana." The product making the most blatant claims is After Burner Hair Shampoo, which, according to the Web site, is "a revolutionary new way to rid the hair shaft of toxins such as THC (marijuana), cocaine, amphetamines, methamphetamines, opiates (heroin), etc" (Tunnell, 2004, p. 87).

These "flush drugs" or "wash-out regimens" are advertised online as well as in the magazine for marijuana connoisseurs, *High Times*. This industry, however, manipulates the gullibility of individuals and makes blatantly deceptive claims about their products. The Web sites provide anecdotal "evidence" from allegedly satisfied customers and works on the same "I'll give it a chance and keep my fingers crossed" premise that the weight-loss industry does. According to empirical research, however, the multimillion dollar per year detox industry has "no good scientific foundation" and has "been found to be unreliable" (Gieringer, 1992, p. 4).

PREVENTION THROUGH "PROTECTION"

Preventing drug use through "protection" policies involves primarily what is known as **zero tolerance**. These are policies that trigger the suspension or expulsion of students in possession of drugs on school grounds. First popular as part of the 1980s war on drugs, zero tolerance was expanded in 1994 under the Safe and Drug-Free Schools Act, and an overwhelming percentage of schools have implemented zero tolerance policies for both alcohol and drugs (both illicit and prescription). In addition to drug testing (which remains somewhat rare in middle and high schools), drugs are most frequently located through the use of drug-sniffing dogs, used by 61 percent of American high schools (National Center for Education Statistics, 2009). The application of zero tolerance policies, however, has run out of control. Take for example the following case:

> When a Fairfax County mother got an urgent call from school last month reporting that her teenage daughter was caught popping a pill at lunchtime, she did not panic. "It was probably her birth-control pill," she thought. She was right. Her heart dropped that afternoon in the assistant principal's office at Oakton High School

> when she and her daughter heard the mandatory punishment: A two-week suspension and recommendation for expulsion. "I realize my daughter broke a rule . . . [but] the punishment does not fit the crime" . . . Health advocates say that harsh penalties for students who take birth-control pills at school conflicts with a campaign schools are waging against teen pregnancy. A small portion of school health clinics across the country distribute birth-control pills to teens. But in Fairfax, even carrying the pills in a backpack is counted among the most serious offenses in the Student Responsibilities and Rights handbook. During two weeks of watching television game shows and trying to keep up with homework online, the Fairfax teen, an honor student and lettered athlete, had time to study the handbook closely. If she had been caught high on LSD, heroin or another illegal drug, she found, she would have been suspended for five days. Taking her prescribed birth-control pill on campus drew the same punishment as bringing a gun to school would have ("Birth-Control Pill Lands Fairfax Girls 2-Week Suspension," 2009).

This case is not an isolated incident, and students have been suspended across the United States for possession of Advil, Tylenol, and Alka-Seltzer; suspended for "distribution" for sharing Midol or asthma inhalers; or suspended for alcohol use for swallowing instead of spitting out mouthwash (Skiba & Peterson, 1999; "Zero Tolerance Policy Lacks Flexibility," 1999). Though statistics of the number of students suspended or expelled are very difficult to unearth, Berkeley researcher Joel Brown uses 1997 national data, "the only year for which national statistics are available," to reveal that "more than 177,000 students were suspended or expelled for drug, alcohol or tobacco violations. Eighty percent of those students, or about 136,000 kids, were suspended for more than five days or expelled. That ranked drug related reasons second only to physical fights as a reason for school discipline . . . [Brown continues], young people are removed from mainstream education for drugs nearly three times more often than they are removed for weapons, and ten times more often than the number of young people removed for carrying firearms" (Brown, 2001 as cited in "Zero Tolerance Policies in Schools Under Attack," 2001). In addition, "minorities are two to three times [more] likely to be suspended than white kids. Males [are] four times as likely as females. Just for the record, a kid who's been suspended is statistically at high risk of dropping out of school" ("Zero Tolerance Policies in Schools Need to End," 2009). Those who remain in school face further challenges in pursuing higher education if drug offenses have been a part of their history.

In 1998, the Higher Education Act was amended to restrict the eligibility of those convicted of certain drug charges for federal financial study aid, referred to as the Aid Elimination Penalty. Estimates reveal that this penalty impacts approximately 20,000 students who are denied Pell Grants each year, and an additional 30,000 to 40,000 students who are denied student loans due to drug convictions ("Drug Law Denies Aid to Thousands," 2005). This is in addition to an untold number of potential students who simply do not apply because they are aware of the restrictions imposed upon them due to their conviction. In 2006, this law was scaled back somewhat so that if an individual is convicted for a drug offense while receiving student financial aid, they will lose their eligibility (for 12 months for a first possession offense, 24 months for a second possession offense, and indefinitely for a third drug offense). Under the revision, however, if an individual receives a drug conviction while not enrolled in higher education, and therefore not receiving taxpayer support, they are eligible to apply for such aid. This revision to the law will be most beneficial to nontraditional students who wish to enter college and improve their life after receiving a drug conviction. The unfairness of the Aid Elimination Penalty was articulated in a *New York Times* editorial:

> By narrowing access to affordable education, the federal government further diminishes the prospects of young people who are already at risk of becoming lifetime burdens to society. Members of Congress are understandably hesitant to cast votes that might brand them as being "soft on crime." But it doesn't take a genius to see that barring young offenders from college leads to more crime—not less. Student aid was never intended for use as a law enforcement weapon. Any attempt to employ it that way will inevitably yield perverse and unfair results (as cited in Students for Sensible Drug Policy [SSDP], 2006, p. 6).

In March 2006, the American Civil Liberties Union and Students for Sensible Drug Policy (SSDP) filed a lawsuit in federal court challenging the constitutionality of the remaining penalty. The lawsuit alleges that this penalty violates the Fifth Amendment's double jeopardy clause as it punishes individuals twice for the same offense. The lawsuit also charges that the penalty is in violation of the Fifth Amendment's guarantee of equal protection because it designates a class of people (those individuals with drug convictions) as unworthy of educational financial assistance. The District Court upheld the penalty as constitutional and the case was filed with the U.S. Court of Appeals in April 2007 (*SSDP v. Spellings*).

There has been however a recent ruling that may suggest that the courts are pulling back the discretion of administrators and the blanket policy of zero tolerance that has existed to this point.

> In October 2003, after obtaining an unverified tip from another student that eighth grader Savana Redding might have ibuprofen and finding none in her backpack, Safford Middle School assistant principal Kerry Wilson asked a school nurse and administration assistant to search Savana in the nurse's office. The two women had Savana take off her shoes and socks, then her shirt and pants. They then directed her to pull out her bra and pull open her panties to see if she was hiding any pills. None were found ("Court Says Strip Search of Child Illegal," 2009).

Almost 6 years later, the U.S. Supreme Court in an 8–1 ruling declared that school administrators overstepped their bounds and violated the girl's privacy. The justices noted a clear distinction between searching the locker or backpack of a student and requiring the student to remove his or her clothes. Justice David Souter suggested that "'a reasonable suspicion of danger' regarding the contraband sought and a belief that it could be in the student's underwear [is necessary] before making 'the quantum leap from outer clothes and backpacks to exposure of intimate parts'" ("Court Says Strip Search of Child Illegal," 2009). Justice Ruth Bader Ginsburg further added: "Wilson's [the assistant principal] treatment of Redding [the student] was abusive and it was not reasonable for him to believe that the law permitted it" ("Court Says Strip Search of Child Illegal," 2009). Though this ruling protecting the privacy of youth barring sufficient evidence is promising, it remains to be seen if it will be the beginning of scaled-back zero tolerance policies.

Summary

- Early drug education programs, like lessons from the Women's Christian Temperance Union in the late 1800s and the film *Reefer Madness* in the 1930s used scare tactics to discourage individuals from drug use. This trend continues today with slogans like "Not Even Once" and "Just Say No."
- Drug prevention has been dominated by three educational models: the information model (informs youth of the potential hazards of using drugs, and they will use that information to avoid harm), the affective model (youth with high levels of self-esteem will avoid the use of drugs), and the social influence model (teach youth the skills to make rational decisions so they can avoid drug use).
- The most common educational program in the United States is the school-based DARE program, which advocated the notorious "Just Say No" to drugs motto to youth from kindergarten through grade 12. It also encouraged self-esteem, drug education, stress management techniques, and how to resist peer pressure.
- Almost all of the scientific evidence suggests that DARE has no impact on substance abuse rates, and indeed, there is some research to suggest a counterproductive effect on drug-use rates. The program continues, however, because it is *perceived* as successful.
- Public service announcements advocate anti-drug attitudes and behaviors using an integrated approach to work toward the prevention and reduction of illicit drug use among youth, and seek to support parents in their efforts to keep youth drug-free.
- Studies analyzing the effectiveness of thirty different public service announcements produced by the ONDCP and PFDFA indicated mixed results. There were some public service announcements that youth believed may result in a lower likelihood of drug use, other advertisements that had no effect on the likelihood of drug use, and six of the thirty advertisements had a negative impact on the likelihood of drug use, meaning that they had the potential to encourage use, rather than discourage use. Research revealed that the most effective public service announcements dealt with "harder" drugs, like methamphetamine and heroin.
- Increasingly, more and more segments of the population are succumbing to drug testing—from sports, to the military, to the workplace, to the school. In the workplace, problems of alcohol and drug abuse have been of some concern since the 1960s as it impacted absenteeism and on-the-job accidents. Private industry did not really embrace drug testing until the 1980s, then the transportation and utilities industries were the first to follow the lead of the military.
- Currently, drug testing usually occurs as part of one of the following: screening of applicants *prior* to their hire at a place of employment; random drug testing of current individuals at a place of employment; drug testing of a specific individual at a place of employment if there is *reasonable suspicion* that he or she is engaging in drug use; postaccident drug testing when an individual has been involved in an on-the-job accident; or regularly scheduled testing (also called periodic testing) which is conducted in employment sectors such as law enforcement and typically involves advance notice and goes hand-in-hand with a physical examination.
- There is some research to suggest that workplace drug tests are useful for identifying those individuals using drugs within the company; however, drug testing has only a slight deterrent effect on usage rates.
- Compared to the workplace, school-based drug testing is rare, occurring in about 5 percent of public high schools for athletes

and 3 percent of public high schools for students in other extracurricular activities. A study conducted to evaluate the effectiveness of drug testing found absolutely no significant difference between the rates of drug use in schools that tested for drugs compared to schools that did not test for drugs.

- Controversy surrounds the issue of drug testing with regard to reliability and constitutionality. The greatest objection has been to the privacy and constitutional issues raised by drug testing. The Fourth Amendment guarantees against the right of unreasonable search and seizure of one's person, and many would argue that a drug test is a violation of this right. The courts have generally decided however that if the state has a compelling interest, even without suspicion, mandatory drug testing is permitted; mandatory drug-testing programs without any cause for testing are not permitted; drug testing due to suspicion is permitted; both private and public employers can require drug screening legally as a condition of employment; and schools are permitted to conduct drug testing without suspicion of any student involved in any school-based extracurricular activity.
- Zero tolerance policies result in the suspension or expulsion of students for use, possession, or distribution of drugs while on school grounds, and currently result in a significant number of youth being disciplined, increasing their likelihood of dropping out.
- In 1998, the Higher Education Act was amended to restrict the eligibility of those convicted of certain drug charges for federal financial study aid, referred to as the "Aid Elimination Penalty." Estimates reveal that the penalty impacts approximately 20,000 students who are denied Pell Grants each year, and an additional 30,000 to 40,000 students who are denied student loans due to drug convictions. This was somewhat revised in 2006.

Important Terms

Affective Model
Arrestee Drug Abuse Monitoring (ADAM) system
Breathalyzer
Drug Abuse Resistance Education (DARE)
Drug-Free Federal Workforce
Information Model
Narcoterrorism
Partnership for a Drug-Free America (PFDFA)
Primary prevention programs
Prom Promise
Public service announcements
Secondary prevention
Social Influence Model (drug resistance model)
Students Against Destructive Decisions (SADD)
Students Against Drunk Driving
Zero tolerance policies

Critical Thinking Questions

1. Given the controversies surrounding the issue of drug testing, especially the potential consequences of falsely testing positive, under what circumstances and in what situations do you advocate drug testing? Would you work for an organization that conducts random drug screening without suspicion? If you operated an organization, would you implement a policy of random drug screening without specific suspicion? Defend your position.
2. Design a mock drug education program for youth ages 14 through 16, keeping in mind the disadvantages of current educational models. Why do you think your model might work better than what is currently implemented?

Research Topics

1. Locate drug education material from your middle school or high school. Critique the program in light of what you have learned in this chapter, elaborating both advantages and disadvantages. Discuss how the program influenced your decision to engage or abstain from drug use.
2. Interview a Republican and a Democrat regarding their position on drug testing, and the potential controversy surrounding this topic. Elaborate in a short paper the differences between the two individuals' positions, and how each aligns with the general position of the courts on this controversial issue.

Suggested Readings/Films

Gasnier, Louis (Director). (1936). *Reefer Madness* [Film]. (Available from Motion Picture Ventures).

Tunnell, Kenneth D. (2004). *Pissing on demand: Workplace drug testing and the rise of the detox industry.* New York, NY: New York University Press.

13

U.S. Drug Control Through Treatment

"Treatment and prevention programs are frequently required to show that they are cost-effective, a standard never imposed on drug enforcement"

—(MacCoun & Reuter, 1997, p. 47)

OBJECTIVES:

When you have finished this chapter, you should be able to:

- Discuss the use of drug courts in the United States as a diversion from traditional criminal justice
- Elaborate the varied aspects of pharmacological treatment and its effectiveness, including a discussion of methadone maintenance
- Explain the varied aspects of residential treatment and its effectiveness
- Discuss the use of outpatient treatment to treat drug/alcohol addiction and its effectiveness
- Elaborate the prevalence and effectiveness of anonymous self-help treatment programs such as Alcoholics Anonymous and Narcotics Anonymous
- Explain the history and current use of prison-based and compulsory treatment programs and the effectiveness of these programs

REAL LIFE

Faye from Indianapolis, Indiana, entitles her story of addiction "I Thought I Knew:"

> I just relapsed after 75 days of sobriety. I know 75 days isn't long at all in the scheme of things, but, it was a damned good start. I have been drinking since I was 11. Adopted at birth, my biological mother gave me away to my adoptive parents whom she met in a bar.

> So I was passed from one alcoholic to two others before I was even brought upon this earth. My life has been typical of an alcoholics' life. Married 3 times (two divorces)—Present husband also an alcoholic. Four children in varying stages of fallout from my addiction. Rehab, AA, prayer, abstinence, then ALWAYS that relapse. This time I really thought I was onto something. I detoxed, I lived 5 weeks at an Assisted Living facility, I went to meetings, I completed an IOP [outpatient] program and followed it up with one-on-one counseling. I made new friends, I read the literature, hell, I even MEMORIZED part of the 12 steps. Yes, folks, I was going to make it this time!!! This time was DIFFERENT! This time I knew how to do it. I had the tools, the desire, and the motivation. The only problem is, I forgot to tell the addict inside me that I was in control this time. So she waited patiently for me to weaken. She laid back and snickered while I sat in meetings and made excuses for why I was only attending one or two a week. She haunted my sleep with dreams of intoxication. She laughed out loud when I began to allow my life to come before my sobriety. And she was beside herself with glee when, last Saturday, having had a fight with my husband, I went to buy cigarettes, and came home with a twelve pack of beer. Needless to say, I drank the beer and went to get more, drank it, and drove drunk and bought a case, which I drank most of on Christmas day, to the immeasurable delight of my children. Thank God, my husband was there to help me polish off the case, or it might have turned into a much worse Christmas than it was (if that's possible). And so, here I am, standing on the edge of hell, ready to dive in AGAIN, disgusted with myself, scared, disappointed, angry, embarrassed, and, infinitely sad. I just read the story by the lady named *x* who passed away earlier this year. And, what scared me the most is how much of me I saw in her writings—So, if anyone reads this, please pray for me . . . I don't want to die drunk . . . (http://www.anonymousone.com/story52.htm).

Prevention of drug use can be primary, secondary, or tertiary. **Primary prevention** is the foundation of drug education programs and is designed to prevent the use of drugs before use begins. **Secondary prevention** programs are implemented once an individual starts using drugs and the focus of these programs is on early identification of use and intervention before the use of drugs becomes an addiction that derails an individual's life. **Tertiary prevention** is directed at those individuals already addicted to drugs and is focused on rehabilitative efforts and the road to sobriety. Though there are many different types of treatment, there is also the issue of cost: Should we consider the financial aspects in addition to the harm reduction strategies?

> Keeping people in prison is expensive. It costs the state of Texas more than $14,000 (at the low end) to house an inmate in a state jail facility for a year and, on average, more than $16,000 per year to house an inmate in a Texas prison. According to the Texas Department of Criminal Justice's 2007 annual review, it costs more than $2 billion per year to incarcerate felons—79.4% of the agency's budget. The cost might be understandable if it were being spent to house violent offenders who pose a real risk to society. But the fact is that a large chunk of that money is actually being spent to house low-level, nonviolent drug offenders. Keeping those folks out of state jails and prisons could save the state . . . as much as $500 million over just five years. That's the goal of Senate Bill 1118, the so-called Treatment Works bill . . . which would divert from prison and state jail offenders charged with third-degree felony or misdemeanor drug possession. These defendants instead would be put into community supervision and, importantly, drug treatment—at an average cost of just $3,241 per person. The drug treatment costs would be paid by the individual, if possible, meaning the state would have to provide drug-treatment funding for roughly 60%

> of offenders eligible for the diversion. But that cost pales in comparison to the costs associated with keeping low-level drug offenders in jail: As of Aug. 31, 2008, there were more than 19,000 inmates in Texas facilities for drug possession, which costs, on average, more than $260 million a year . . . And the bill contains extra motivation for offenders to stay out of jail. If successful in treatment, a defendant can ultimately ask a judge for nondisclosure of the original charge, which helps individuals land and keep employment, access funding for education, and stay clean . . . [Studies show that] $1 spent on treatment actually saves $4 to $7 in costs related to addiction. Given the money involved and the lives in the balance, getting people out of jail and into treatment makes perfect sense . . . ("Reefer Madness: Treatment Works," 2009).

This chapter will discuss the use of drug courts in the treatment of drug offenses as a public health concern as well as the various types of treatment methods, including pharmacological, residential, out-patient, anonymous self-help, prison based, and faith based.

DRUG COURTS

An increasing drug problem in the late 1960s was cause for public concern. The National Institute of Drug Abuse (NIDA) and federal law enforcement responded with an initiative named **Treatment Alternatives to Street Crime (TASC)**, which would break the link between addiction and crime that was believed to be occurring. TASC linked treatment and the criminal justice process and was the beginning of the movement toward the creation of drug courts. In the mid-1980s, Florida State Attorney Janet Reno was displeased at the number of felony drug cases and commissioned a study into possible alternatives. It was determined that:

> The traditional adversarial system of justice, designed to resolve legal disputes, is ineffective at addressing AOD [alcohol and other drug] abuse. Moreover, many features of the court system actually contribute to AOD abuse instead of curbing it: Traditional defense counsel functions and court procedures often reinforce the offender's denial of an AOD problem . . . Moreover, the criminal justice system is often an unwitting enabler of continuing drug use because few immediate consequences for continued AOD use are imposed (Office of Justice Programs [OJP], 1997, p. 6).

Born from this was America's first drug court in Dade County, Florida, in 1989, which was designed to be a judicially supervised program to aid in the treatment of drug abuse for individuals who had committed a drug-related offense (Nolan, 2001). **Drug courts** treat an individual's drug offense as not just a concern for the criminal justice system but also as a public health issue. Program organization and scope varies by state, but the similarity is the collaboration between the criminal justice system, the treatment community, and other social service institutions to aid referred individuals. There are ten key components to drug courts that are standard, irrespective of the day-to-day practice of how the drug court is operated. These ten key components are:

1. Drug courts integrate alcohol and other drug treatment services with justice system case processing.
2. Using a non-adversarial approach, prosecution and defense counsel promote public safety while protecting participants' due process rights.
3. Eligible participants are identified early and promptly placed in the drug court program.

4. Drug courts provide access to a continuum of alcohol, drug, and other related treatment and rehabilitation services.
5. Abstinence is monitored by frequent alcohol and other drug testing.
6. A coordinated strategy governs drug court responses to participants' compliance.
7. Ongoing judicial interaction with each drug court participant is essential.
8. Monitoring and evaluation measure the achievement of program goals and gauge effectiveness.
9. Continuing interdisciplinary education promotes effective drug court planning, implementation, and operations.
10. Forging partnerships among drug courts, public agencies, and community-based organizations generates local support and enhances drug court program effectiveness (OJP, 2008, p. 18).

While each state bases its program on the model developed in Dade County, there are vast differences across courts in terms of who is eligible to participate, when in the criminal justice process the defendant is admitted to the drug court program, when types of agencies work in collaboration with the court to offer treatment, and the penalties for noncompliance. There were nearly 2,150 drug courts as of 2007, with these specialized courts present in every state (OJP, 2008). (See Figure 13-1 for the distribution of drug courts across the United States).

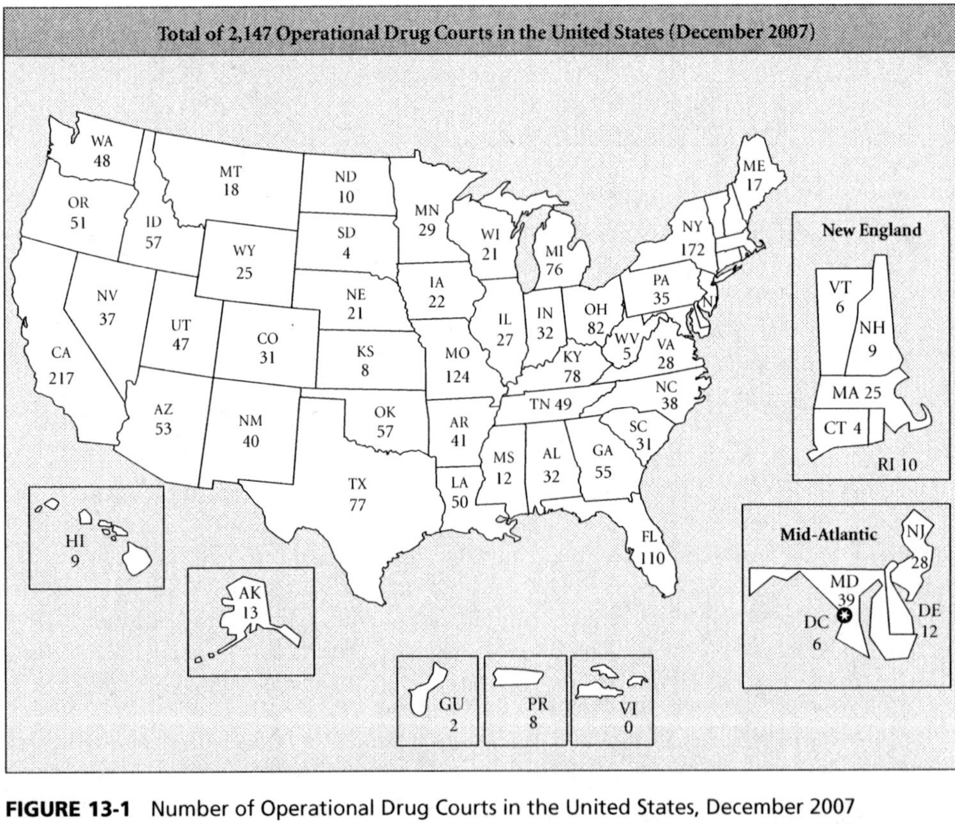

FIGURE 13-1 Number of Operational Drug Courts in the United States, December 2007

Source: Office of Justice Programs, 2008.

The treatment plan is typically determined by the judge, the prosecuting attorney and the defense attorney, a representative from probation, as well as a treatment official.

The plan generally consists of three phases. Phase one involves detoxification, where the user's dependence on the drug is removed. Phase two is a stabilization period that focuses on treating the psychological addiction the user has to the substance. Phase three involves assisting the individual in seeking community resources that will help him or her succeed, such as education, job training, and housing. Phase three also involves strategies that encourage the user to remain drug free, such as continuation of treatment groups (OJP, 2000). In its entirety the process is typically designed to last 12 months; however, it often lasts much longer, as drug addiction is difficult to overcome for many individuals.

> Treatment has been shown to work—if substance abusers stick with it; however, between 80 and 90 percent of conventional drug treatment clients drop out before 12 months, the period generally found to be the minimum effective duration. By providing a structure that links supervision and treatment, drug courts exert legal pressure on defendants to enter and remain in treatment long enough to realize benefits. More than two-thirds of participants who begin treatment through a drug court complete it in a year or more—a six-fold increase in retention compared with programs outside the justice system (OJP, 2006, p. 1).

The incentive for offenders to participate is that successful completion of the program usually results in dismissal of the criminal charge or the defendant having the arrest expunged. Failure to conform to the guidelines of treatment may result in mandated community service, a short jail term, or mandated increased involvement in treatment. Indeed, many offenders serve more time in jail proceeding through a drug court program than if they had simply been adjudicated. This is because every time the individual fails to complete the requirements of the treatment program, they *could* be sent to jail: "[i]f you add up all those short periods of incarceration you would find that in some cases it exceeds the time they would actually serve" (Nolan, 2001, p. 56).

Frequently the atmosphere of a drug court is different from a traditional court. For example, Judge Stanley Goldstein worked in a drug court in Miami from its beginning in 1989 until he retired 10 years later. His approach was part tough love, part encouragement. This is evidenced by reading portions of what he said in a 1995 drug court session:

> This is a two part program. First is to get you off drugs. Second is to teach you how to live in this world. The first lesson you learn is to follow the rules . . . Let me tell you guys something. I told almost everyone of you when you came in here, there ain't no other way. Any other way out of here and you lose. You stay being a junky: you lose, I win. You die: I win, you lose. You burn your brain out: you lose, I win. Forget about it. You hate me, want to get even with me? Quit using drugs, and get yourself a good job. Then you get even with me. I love you. I want everyone here to beat me into the ground with goodness (Nolan, 2001, pp. 9–10).

Judge Goldstein worked in a criminal court prior to moving to drug court and said this about his work: "It never made me feel like I did anything . . . I was taking one jackass off the street, and that was all" (Nolan, 2001, p. 10). About drug court he said:

> I walk out of this program almost everyday and feel like I have accomplished something. If I save one guy a day I'm happy. It took me awhile to realize that you can't

> save everybody. Some of them just ain't got it . . . Some people I praise. Some people I try to insult. Some people, I'll try anything, anything that might work (Nolan, 2001, pp. 10–11).

This perspective illustrates the varied approach that drug courts take from the traditional approach of the criminal justice system. In studies of effectiveness, this approach has proven beneficial.

Research suggests that drug courts are effective in reducing involvement in criminality for those individuals who successfully finish the program (OJP, 2006). Additionally, a program like drug court contributes significantly to reducing court congestion as courts are relieved of the burden of the large number of drug-related offenses. These benefits are accrued at significant cost savings to the system: to divert a defendant to drug court costs between $1,200 and $3,500 depending upon their treatment regimen compared to an average incarceration cost of $5,000 (OJP, 1999). A longitudinal study of drug courts in and around Portland, Oregon, revealed a 30 percent reduction in crime over 5 years. Most astonishingly, the crime reduction benefit of the drug court program was still present 14 years after initial arrest (Finigan, Carey, & Cox, 2007)! In sum "[r]esearch verifies that no other justice intervention can rival the results produced by drug courts. Drug courts are demonstratively effective. According to over a decade of research, drug courts significantly improve substance abuse treatment outcomes, substantially reduce crime, and produce greater cost benefits than any other justice strategy" (OJP, 2008, p. 2). As such, drug courts have demonstrated that treatment is far more successful an approach to drug addiction than criminal justice sanctions.

How an individual theoretically explains substance abuse (discussed in Chapter Three) influences one's choice of treatment. For example, if you believe that drug abuse is a biological disease, you may be inclined to support a pharmacological treatment option. Goals of treatment also vary: some treatment modes advocate total abstinence from all drug use, whereas other treatment modes advocate controlled social use, wherein an individual can use moderate amounts of the substance so long as they are able to control the amount used (this is most typical for alcohol as it is the only legal recreational substance in the United States). Substance abuse that is left untreated costs the United States approximately $165 billion each year (Garrett, Stanton, Landau, Hbaciewica, Brinkman-Sull, & Shea, 1999). Estimates suggest that well over 7 million Americans need treatment for their substance abuse addiction, yet only a fraction of these (just over 1 million)

An example of drug court statistics from New Jersey, 1996 to January 2003:

- Over 2,600 non-violent substance abusing offenders have entered New Jersey's adult drug court pilot programs
- The current roster of drug court participants statewide is approximately 1,500
- Over 120 participants have graduated from drug court and have been successfully discharged from probationary supervision
- Almost 350 participants have celebrated their "commencement" from the supervision of a drug court judge, but remain under probationary supervision until they are eligible to graduate from the program
- Approximately 32 percent of individuals enrolled in the program have been terminated for non-compliance and sentenced to a custodial term
- The cumulative rate of retention since the program began in New Jersey in 1996 is 64 percent
- Thirty-one drug-free babies were born to previously addicted female participants (http://www.judiciary.state.nj.us/criminal/crdrgct.htm)

receive treatment each year, primarily due to lack of resources dedicated to these programs (Substance Abuse and Mental Health Services Administration [SAMHSA], 2004). In considering methods of treatment, there are a variety of options, and treatment modes are frequently used in combination with one another.

Regardless of the treatment approach, research over 20 years has demonstrated fundamental principles that are at work in *effective* drug treatment programs. These thirteen principles are:

1. Addiction is a complex but treatable disease that affects brain function and behavior.
2. No single treatment is appropriate for everyone.
3. Treatment needs to be readily available.
4. Effective treatment attends to multiple needs of the individual, not just his or her drug abuse.
5. Remaining in treatment for an adequate period of time is critical.
6. Counseling—individual and/or group—and other behavioral therapies are the most commonly used forms of drug-abuse treatment.
7. Medications are an important element of treatment for many patients, especially combined with counseling and other behavioral therapies.
8. An individual's treatment and services plan must be assessed continually and modified as necessary to ensure that it meets his or her changing needs.
9. Many drug-addicted individuals also have other mental disorders.
10. Medically assisted detoxification is only the first stage of addiction treatment and by itself does little to change long-term drug abuse.
11. Treatment does not need to be voluntary to be effective.
12. Drug use during treatment must be monitored continuously, as lapses during treatment do occur.
13. Treatment programs should assess patients for the presence of HIV/AIDS, Hepatitis B and C, Tuberculosis, and other infectious diseases as well as provide targeted risk-reduction counseling to help patients modify or change behaviors that place them at risk of contracting or spreading infectious diseases (National Institute on Drug Abuse [NIDA], 2008, pp. 2–5).

With regard to the prevalence of treatment programs, in 1990 there were approximately 16,000 facilities across the country, 55 percent of which were residential, 30 percent of which were outpatient, and 15 percent of which were methadone maintenance. As of 2001, there were only 14,000 treatment facilities for substance abuse and the vast majority of these were outpatient programs (Inciardi, 2008).

PHARMACOLOGICAL TREATMENT

Historically, the use of drugs to treat drug abuse was common, and is termed **pharmacological treatment**. Freud used cocaine experimentally to treat opiate abuse, opium was used as a treatment for alcohol addiction, and addiction was viewed as a medical problem and a medical condition. In the early 1900s, the U.S. Public Health Service opened hospitals to detox users from drugs (Goldberg, 2006). Detoxification in and of itself, however, is not pharmacological treatment: There are some drugs from which untreated withdrawal can result in death; therefore, a medical withdrawal is necessary. Detox is then followed by a form of treatment, one option of which is pharmacological treatment. This type of treatment uses drugs to counteract the symptoms of withdrawal from narcotics as a form of therapy usually (but not always) in combination with a particular form of behavioral therapy rehabilitation. A former hard-core alcoholic for more than 30 years, named Kent, describes his addiction:

> It's like a little kid wanting a piece of candy. You see it, you want the taste of it . . . You can be by yourself, and all of a sudden get even a hint of alcohol, just the smell of it, and say, Oh, I need a drink. That sensation is not something you can get rid of ("With Anti-Addiction Pill, No Urge No Craving," 2009).

Currently, Kent says he is not at all tempted, thanks to a prescription medication named naltrexone. This is one of many anti-addiction drugs changing the traditional approach to rehabilitation.

Naltrexone is used both to block the effects of opiates and to treat alcohol dependence. Studies on its effectiveness show that it is almost twice as effective as a placebo in preventing relapse in alcoholics over a 12-week treatment period. Side effects of naltrexone include nausea, sweating, light-headedness, irritability, and anxiety (Goldberg, 2006). A study named "COMBINE" which pairs naltrexone with cognitive-behavioral therapy showed promising results as patients were more likely to remain drug-free ("With Anti-Addiction Pill, No Urge No Craving," 2009). Another drug used to treat alcoholism is disulfiram (commonly known as antabuse), which causes individuals to become violently ill if they consume alcohol. Other side effects of disulfiram include dizziness, nausea, fatigue, restlessness, blurred vision, difficulty breathing, and lowered blood pressure, all of which can last for up to 2 weeks after the drug treatment is stopped (Goldberg, 2006). Studies on the effectiveness of disulfiram have been questionable but typically indicate that it is most effective when used in combination with psychosocial therapy (Finn, 2004). Another current method of pharmacological treatment is methadone treatment or methadone maintenance, which will be elaborated below. Methadone programs are used to treat opiate addictions and studies in the United States on effectiveness of such programs show a reduction in heroin use, a reduction in HIV transmission rates, and a reduction in criminal activity (Centers for Disease Control and Prevention [CDC], 2003). Researchers have noted that methadone maintenance has made a "real and beneficial contribution to reducing the social and individual costs associated with addiction" (Anglin & McGlothlin, 1985, pp. 274–275). Pharmacological treatment is also used for nicotine addiction in the form of nicotine replacement therapies (such as the transdermal patch, nicotine gum, nasal spray, vapor inhaler, and lozenge) as well as the non-nicotine replacement treatment, bupropion (Zyban). Each of these pharmacotherapies has been shown in studies to decrease an individual's craving for nicotine and in many cases decrease actual use of nicotine (Ksir, Hart, & Ray, 2008).

Some experts suggest that pharmacological treatments target the *effect* of a particular drug but "do nothing to counteract the effects of craving and over learned drug-seeking behavioral responses that frequently lead [an individual] to relapse" (Harwood & Myers, 2004, p. 11). Other experts are concerned that addicts who go through pharmacological programs make them too "comfortable," which may increase the individual's chance of relapsing or simply holding over their fix until they can afford their next high. Although many studies have demonstrated the effectiveness of the pharmacological approach, established rehabilitation models have been exceedingly slow to incorporate the use of medication in their treatment plans.

> At Hazelden in Minneapolis, Minnesota, a small proportion of patients receive anti-addiction drugs, but medical director Dr. Kevin Clark says the traditional model—based on intensive therapy and the 12 steps popularized by Alcoholics Anonymous—is still best. "It is a disease of the brain, but it's a multifaceted disease. It has a spiritual component, a behavioral component to it," says Clark. "Our experience tells us that

> having the network of support and recovery is what really makes the difference." John Schwarzlose, executive director of the Betty Ford Center, echoes that but takes a more stringent approach. No patients at Betty Ford receive anti-addiction drugs as part of treatment ("With Anti-Addiction Pill, No Urge No Craving," 2009).

Conversely, some experts believe that the use of chemicals to assist individuals with their substance abuse can draw addicts to seek treatment and increase their chances of successfully completing treatment (Abadinsky, 2008). These experts believe that addiction is more than simply a failure of an individual's willpower, and is a medical disease that can often be assisted by pharmacological treatment.

Case Study:

Methadone Maintenance

One type of pharmacological treatment is the use of methadone to treat opiate addiction. **Methadone maintenance** was first started in the United States over 30 years ago and is a treatment that has been used more extensively since that time in European countries. Methadone is a synthetic opiate administered orally whose effects are longer lasting (up to 24 hours) than other opiates used illicitly, such as heroin and morphine. There are several benefits from a harm reduction standpoint for opiate users receiving methadone treatment, including:

- Methadone is administered in a clinical setting and not given to users to take at their discretion. Administration is, therefore, medically monitored. Daily clinical methadone use decreases illicit intravenous heroin use (i.e., no use of dirty needles), and therefore lowers the incidence of the spread of HIV/AIDS.
- Because the effects of methadone are longer lasting than other opiates, those receiving the treatment are less likely to experience withdrawal, and therefore cravings. Therefore, users are less likely to attempt to obtain heroin/other opiates by any means necessary. This in turn is believed to decrease the rate of drug-related crime (i.e., theft, prostitution, etc.) (Liska, 2004).

The United States however, compared to its European counterparts, has not embraced this strategy. In 2004, less than 20 percent of heroin addicts in the United States were on methadone treatment compared to about 60 percent of the heroin addict population in the Netherlands (Liska, 2004; MacCoun & Reuter, 2001).

Research on the efficacy of methadone maintenance as a treatment for heroin addiction began in the late 1950s at Rockefeller University. It was found that methadone relieves the many symptoms of withdrawal (such as depression and anxiety), and addicts can use methadone maintenance as an inexpensive way to avoid withdrawal as it is provided for free or at a very minimal cost in clinics. Users of heroin are likely to build a tolerance to heroin, and therefore increase their dose to achieve a high, which can be very dangerous because there is a very fine line between a heroin high and a heroin overdose. Those on methadone are stabilized at the same dose over an extended period of time, and some users can eventually be entirely weaned off the drug. Those who begin **methadone treatment** with the goal of being drug-free are usually weaned within 3 weeks. If the treatment extends past that point, it is considered methadone maintenance—where individuals are "maintained" on methadone so they will not engage in heroin (or other opium) use. Studies show that

(Continued)

approximately 80 percent of individuals quickly weaned from methadone (i.e., in less than 6 months) are likely to relapse, so there is logic to a maintenance period (Liska, 2004).

Those who receive methadone do not experience the high that is typically associated with heroin; methadone simply stops a user's withdrawal symptoms. As well, methadone is a heroin antagonist or blocker, so if addicts use heroin while on a methadone program they will not experience a high either. The physical negative effect of methadone treatment is that there is a withdrawal when stepping down from heroin to methadone that the user must manage (Liska, 2004). From a psychological standpoint, the user must deal with the stigma attached to continued opiate use. This stigma is why many Americans are opposed to methadone maintenance therapy and frequently object to the opening of new clinics; they advocate a position of drug abstinence instead. From a treatment perspective, methadone should be paired with psychological counseling: in countries such as France, Germany, and Sweden, this was the sole preferred method of treatment until the mid-1990s when methadone treatment was finally accepted (MacCoun & Reuter, 2001).

Switzerland tried a variation on methadone treatment beginning in 1994 when they opened a heroin maintenance clinic as part of a 3-year trial program to deal with the significant heroin problem and high rates of HIV infection. This is how the program worked:

> Each addict could choose the amount he or she wanted and inject it in the clinic under the care of a nurse up to three times a day, seven days a week. The drug could not be taken out of the clinic. Sixteen small clinics were scattered around the country, including one in a prison. Patients had to be over 18, have injected heroin for two years and have failed at least two treatment episodes. In fact, most of them had more than ten years of heroin addiction and many treatment failures. They were among the most troubled heroin addicts with the most chaotic lives (MacCoun & Reuter, 2005, pp. 266–267).

Though the program had its critics, it had much success:

> By the end of the trials, more than 800 patients had received heroin on a regular basis without any leakage into the illicit market. No overdoses were reported among participants while they stayed in the program. A large majority of participants had maintained the regime of daily attendance at the clinic; 69 percent were in treatment eighteen months after admission. This was a high rate relative to those found in methadone programs. About half of the "dropouts" switched to other forms of treatment, some choosing methadone and others abstinence-based therapies. The crime rate among all patients dropped over the course of treatment, use of nonprescribed heroin dipped sharply and unemployment fell from 44 to 20 percent (MacCoun & Reuter, 2005, p. 267).

After the trial period ended, the government of Switzerland approved an expansion to permit the program to continue.

There is little research evaluating the effectiveness of methadone programs. As in the Switzerland study, some research finds these programs quite successful, whereas other research in Europe finds high levels of dropout and criminality (MacCoun & Reuter, 2001). Studies in the United States show a reduction in heroin use, a reduction in HIV transmission rates, a reduction in criminal activity, and a reduction in societal costs as it is much more fiscally effective to treat an individual with methadone therapy or maintenance than it is to send them to prison (CDC, 2003).

RESIDENTIAL TREATMENT

Organizations that employ the **residential treatment** approach are often referred to as the therapeutic community (TC). The goal of residential treatment programs focuses on the resocialization of people into a life without drugs. Subscribers to the TC approach believe that "drug abuse is a disorder of the whole person; the problem is the person, not the drug, and the *addiction* is only a *symptom* and not the essence of the disorder" (Nielsen & Scarpitti, 1997, p. 280). These programs typically isolate patients from the outside world and encourage them to engage in group activities with other residents to promote a drugless existence. Additionally, these types of treatment programs focus on increasing patients' responsibility to themselves and to others. Most residential programs involve responsibilities such as job assignments and chores; in addition to counseling, however, there are a few residential programs that are more "spa-like." The latter are the type of treatment programs that cater to the rich and/or famous. These spa-like facilities unfortunately are known to offer poor aftercare treatment and/or follow up, which may be one contributing factor to celebrities revisiting these facilities again and again (Abadinsky, 2008). Some of these programs employ medication-assisted withdrawal in collaboration with behavioral therapy, whereas others are based on a 12-step approach free of any drug consumption, such as the widely known Alcoholics Anonymous (AA) and Narcotics Anonymous (NA). One of the most profound aspects of these treatment programs is that they are often run by recovering addicts (as are AA and NA) who can identify with the residents and their problems. One of the main goals of residential treatment is the formation of a conventional and productive individual.

> The primary aims of therapeutic community are a global change in lifestyle reflecting abstinence from illicit substances, elimination of antisocial activity, increased employability, and prosocial attitudes and values. A critical assumption in TCs is that stable recovery depends upon a successful integration of these social and psychological goals. The rehabilitative approach, therefore, requires multidimensional influences and training that, for most clients, can only occur after an extended period of living in a 24-hour residential setting (De Leon, 1986, p. 69).

Such programs advocate mutual trust and total resocialization of the addict. As such, treatment is very structured, typically occurs in groups, and can sometimes be confrontational. These programs are based around the idea that an individual is always a "recovering" addict because no matter how long someone has been drug-free, it remains a struggle.

It is difficult to determine how successful or unsuccessful residential programs are in preventing future drug/alcohol use because of all the complexities, including varying types of programs and varying types of addicts. Critics conclude that many drug abusers who would fail these programs are eliminated in the stringent interview process that often requires highly motivated individuals. Some research has found that "those who enter the therapeutic community with a greater degree of mental health, with limited or no attachment to a criminal subculture, and with employment skills are obviously better equipped to deal with a post program experience" (Abadinsky, 2008, p. 255). Contrastingly, other research suggests that inpatient residential programs have produced evidence of dramatic and positive results despite the many personal problems impacting clients, their long histories of deviant lifestyles, their long absences from medical care, and a lack of support for clients' rehabilitative efforts in their communities (Kappeler & Potter, 2005, p. 208). Because ideally residential programs are to last for an extended period of time (12 to 24 months), they have a very high dropout rate: those who complete a residential treatment program, however, have the highest success rate of any of the drug treatment programs (Goldberg, 2006).

OUTPATIENT TREATMENT

Outpatient treatment programs can vary in their intensity; however, they all maintain the same goal of sustaining a drug-free lifestyle. The less intense outpatient programs are more educationally focused and can be beneficial to individuals who may not have a life-crippling addiction, but still struggle with substance abuse. The more intense outpatient programs are heavily focused on educating the addict, but they also strive to provide patients with a supportive environment and guidance in recommending additional supportive resources to assist in treatment. These programs frequently use the 12-step method, and patients are strongly encouraged to attend AA or NA meetings in conjunction with their outpatient therapy. Outpatient programs are offered daily after work or after school to accommodate patient and family schedules. People who use these programs usually have family obligations and/or are employed, making a residential treatment plan difficult. Intensive outpatient programs can also be offered daily for approximately 6 or 7 hours, with the individual going home at the end of the treatment session. The daily program is for patients who need a higher regimented schedule in order to continue their rehabilitation successfully (Cole & James, 1975).

Outpatient programs frequently attempt to examine the underlying problems which led to the substance abuse in order to personalize treatment for maximum success. Part of the curriculum of outpatient programs involves attending group therapy, which helps build a larger support network for patients extending beyond their family. Many patients are uplifted by sharing their addiction struggles (Abadinsky, 2008). Additional assistance from outpatient programs can include individual counseling, career development assistance, referrals to specific support groups, and other supportive measures depending on the needs of the clientele. Periodic meetings with an individual counselor are scheduled to revaluate patient progress and adjustments to the patient treatment regimen are made if necessary. For many individuals, an outpatient program is not the first course of treatment, as the user has often completed a residential treatment program and is in a sense "graduating" to outpatient treatment (Soyka & Schmidt, 2009).

Recent research has discovered that outpatient treatment is an effective setting for alcohol-dependent patients who remain with the program through its completion (Soyka & Schmidt, 2009). It appears that outpatient treatment works for individuals who cannot financially afford a residential program or who for lifestyle reasons (such as employment or family commitments) cannot dedicate themselves full time to a residential program. Outpatient programs are most successful if the patient is serious and motivated about becoming drug free. Additionally, those with an extensive social support network are more likely to succeed long term. A major advantage of outpatient treatment programs is that they are less costly than residential programs, and therefore less-advantaged users who need help have a better chance of getting it in an outpatient program. Another benefit is that outpatient programs can be helpful to users at different stages in their recovery program, so outpatient treatment in this aspect is more versatile than other types of treatment programs (Wallace & Weeks, 2004). Some research suggests that this type of treatment is less effective than other modes because the individual is more likely to return to an environment that condones the use and abuse of substances (Goldberg, 2006). This is one reason why patients need to be highly motivated for outpatient treatment to be successful.

ANONYMOUS SELF-HELP TREATMENT

Alcoholics Anonymous (AA) and Narcotics Anonymous (NA) are two of the more famous voluntary 12-step **anonymous self-help treatment** methods for drug abusers. Other self-help groups endorsed by the federal and/or local government are Al-Anon (for family and friends of alcoholics), Adult Children of Alcoholics, Chemically Dependent Anonymous, and Marijuana Anonymous. Those following a traditional 12-step approach abide by the following:

1. We admitted we were powerless over alcohol—that our lives had become unmanageable.
2. Came to believe that a Power greater than ourselves could restore us to sanity.
3. Made a decision to turn our will and our lives over to the care of God as we understood Him.
4. Made a searching and fearless moral inventory of ourselves.
5. Admitted to God, to ourselves, and to another human being the exact nature of our wrongs.
6. Were entirely ready to have God remove all these defects of character.
7. Humbly asked Him to remove our shortcomings.
8. Made a list of all persons we had harmed, and became willing to make amends to them all.
9. Made direct amends to such people wherever possible, except when to do so would injure them or others.
10. Continued to take personal inventory and when we were wrong promptly admitted it.
11. Sought through prayer and meditation to improve our conscious contact with God as we understood Him, praying only for knowledge of His will for us and the power to carry that out.
12. Having had a spiritual awakening as the result of these steps, we tried to carry this message to alcoholics, and to practice these principles in all our affairs (http://www.alcoholicsanonymous.org/).

The hallmark of AA and NA is a treatment goal of complete abstinence. Drug and alcohol users are viewed as biologically different from other individuals and therefore they cannot engage in the use of substances in a controlled way (Ksir, Hart, & Ray, 2008). Additionally, their "road to recovery" is a lifelong journey and addicts are always "recovering," as a reminder of their disease. When attending AA or NA, members' personal information is kept strictly confidential. Only first names are used at meetings, and this rule of anonymity is often what draws individuals to reach out to such a self-help program. Members usually attend about four meetings a week for the first 5 years or so and then attend meetings as needed once they are able to navigate the world without drugs or alcohol. These programs preach that effective treatments for addictions are more complex than simply maintaining sobriety and advocate strongly the role of continued peer support in the recovery process. Part of the recovery process is a sponsor system, wherein each recovering individual has someone they can turn to, day or night, when they are in need of support or advice. This sponsor is a recovering addict who has successfully navigated the 12-steps and can now assist someone else in doing so. "Members usually give of themselves without reservation; exchange telephone numbers with newcomers; come to help at any hour when a fellow member is in crisis; are free with tips on how to avoid that first drink" (Robertson, 1988, p. 47). This peer support is of the utmost importance.

> *"A man falls into a hole so deep he can't get out. A doctor walks by, and the man calls for help. The doctor writes a prescription, tosses it into the hole, and walks on. A priest walks by, and the man tries again. The priest writes a prayer, tosses it into the hole, and walks on. Finally a friend walks by, and again the man asks for help. To his surprise, the friend jumps in with him. 'Why did you do that?' the man asks. 'Now we're both in the hole.' 'Yes,' the friend responds, 'But I've been in this hole before, and I know the way out'"*
> (Clay, 2004, p. 1).

Many of these programs seek to discover what an individual's addiction is attempting to conceal, such as an emotional trauma or painful memory. It is also about taking responsibility. Both AA and NA:

> attempt to instill the substitution of more adaptive attitudes to replace habitual dysfunctional ones. The extreme use of denial and projection of responsibility for chemical dependency onto other people, circumstances, or conditions outside oneself is an example of a target behavior strongly challenged in the substance abuse self-help group. The familiar opening statement of "I'm an alcoholic and/or drug addict" epitomizes the concrete representation that defense mechanisms of projection and denial run counter to the group culture and norms (Spitz, 1987, p. 160).

Programs such as NA and AA are nondenominational but religious, as they rely on a higher power and believe they must undoubtedly surrender to this higher power in order to maintain sobriety. In fact, courts have ruled that what occurs at AA meetings is similar to what occurs between clergy and parishioner, and as such prisoners cannot be mandated to attend AA or NA due to its religious orientation (Abadinsky, 2008; Goldberg, 2006). Secular individuals have the option of joining less popular self-help groups such as Secular Organizations for Sobriety (SOS) or Rational Recovery (RR). These nonreligious programs advertise that they provide a set of tools or life skills for people to maintain sobriety and live their life successfully without the use of mind-altering substances.

In addition to the traditional self-help programs of AA and NA, corporations and business-minded individuals have exploited this approach and created an entire industry of books, DVDs, CDs, and seminars to "cure" people of their addictions based on their spin on the philosophy of self-help. Online booksellers such as Amazon have an entire category, known as "self-help," for people seeking to anonymously cure themselves of ailments from depression to substance abuse. Unfortunately, it can be quite difficult for addicts to successfully kick their habit alone with the use of a self-help approach, as it takes a highly motivated individual to do so. Self-help groups, however, can bring together individuals with common problems, and they can provide a unique system of support that can assist in overcoming substance abuse and maintaining sobriety.

Self-help groups like AA and NA rely on intimate meetings in which people share their experiences. It is through this experience that the members form a bond and a support network to help each other live drug and alcohol free. There are six factors that make AA and NA successful as models of recovery:

1. Mutual sharing by members, which provides solutions to alcohol- [and drug-] related problems and helps alleviate guilt by showing members that others have acted irrationally also.
2. Provision of a regular support group of individuals working toward the goal of abstinence.
3. Frequent and regular meetings to help members structure their time.
4. Availability of AA [and NA] as an adjunct to other treatments, such as counseling and psychotherapy.
5. Absence of membership fees and nondiscrimination by race, sex, or socioeconomic status.
6. Establishment of comprehensive goals covering the emotional, behavioral, and spiritual life of the members (Fields, 2010, p. 333; as identified by Lawson, Peterson, & Lawson, 1983).

Though it is difficult to gauge the success of self-help programs, it remains clear that effectiveness is directly tied to the individual's commitment and ability to maintain a consistent level of support within their network. Though AA has over 50,000 registered branches across the United States, the organization's approach has historically been criticized by professionals because it preaches total abstinence and lacks recent research to support its effectiveness (though there were several studies in the 1970s that indicated AA programs were useful in ceasing alcohol consumption) (Armor, Polich, & Stambul, 1978; Bateman & Peterson, 1971; Delbanco & Delbanco, 1995). One reason there is minimal research regarding the effectiveness of AA and NA programs is because they rely on anonymity: It is difficult to assess program success among a group of people when there are no records of members! Despite the need for current empirical research, many of the substance abuse programs now in existence are based in some way on the 12-step model of AA, lending significant credence to its approach.

PRISON-BASED AND COMPULSORY TREATMENT

All prison-based drug treatment programs are considered **compulsory treatment** "based on the philosophy that most drug addicts are not intrinsically motivated to seek treatment, or to stay in treatment once being admitted, and hence must be forced to do so for their own benefit but especially the benefit of the community" (Faupel, Horowitz, & Weaver, 2004, p. 396). That is, compulsory treatment programs are not ones that an individual enters into voluntarily, but a treatment program that is forced upon an individual, for example, in place of a prison sentence. As such, critics of **prison-based treatment** argue that such programs are inherently ineffective because the commitment and motivation of the addict is lacking (Hartjen, Mitchell, & Washburne, 1981). Despite this criticism, involuntary programs have a reasonably long history in American criminal justice.

Early criminal justice endeavors regarding drug treatment occurred in the 1930s. "Farms" were opened in Kentucky (1935) and Texas (1938) for addicts who came in contact with the criminal justice system to experience treatment, including physical withdrawal, individual and group counseling, as well as job counseling (Abadinsky, 2008). These programs waned due to lack of conclusive proof of their effectiveness until the 1960s. The **California Civil Addict Program** was started in 1961, which involuntarily committed (mostly) narcotics addicts in order for them to receive treatment. This program was administered by the Department of Corrections (DOC) and was essentially a diversion method as individuals were provided with this treatment as an alternate to imprisonment. So for example, if John Doe was a drug-involved offender sentenced to 18 months for his crime, rather than serve it in jail, he would serve his time in the California Rehabilitation Center run by the DOC. This facility was medium security and could accommodate about 800 females and 4,000 males (Abadinsky, 2008). Treatment in these programs was geared toward recognizing that each individual user had individual treatment needs, but was based on a community model that involved mostly group, but also some individual, therapy (Anglin & Hser, 1990). In 1972, the TASC program was started, which provided for nonviolent offenders to be referred to drug/alcohol treatment facilities in the community either to supplement another criminal justice sanction or in place of a criminal justice sanction. TASC programs had been established in eighteen states by 1988, and since then similar programs have been established across the nation (Tonry & Wilson, 1990). An individual's progress in the program is monitored, and an individual who fails to meet the requirements faces further sanctions by the criminal justice system.

Of the drug-involved offenders arrested and imprisoned, the vast majority are in need of treatment that is long-term and residential. As such, in the 1980s, the number of treatment beds and programs in correctional facilities began to increase. This realization culminated in the passage of the Residential Substance Abuse Treatment for State Prisoners (RSAT) Act in 1994. This Act provided funds to local and state correctional facilities for treatment programs. The type of treatment best suited to individuals for whom drug use and abuse has led to crime is a program that is intensive and separate from other aspects of prison life. Prison-based treatment is a process that takes place over a period of at least 12 months, wherein individuals are segregated from prison culture and instilled with pro-social values to recover from their drug abuse (Inciardi, 2008). Such a program usually involves the following:

> During the early phase of treatment, the major clinical thrust involves observation and assessment of client needs and problem areas. Orientation to the prison [therapeutic community] procedures occurs through individual counseling, encounter sessions, and seminars. Clients are given low-level jobs and granted little status. During the later phase of treatment, residents are provided opportunities to earn higher-level positions and increased status through sincere involvement in the program and hard work. Encounter groups and counseling sessions are more in-depth and focus on the areas of self-discipline, self-worth, self-awareness, respect for authority, and acceptance of guidance for problem areas. Seminars take on a more intellectual nature. Debate is encouraged to enhance self-expression and to increase self-confidence (Wexler & Williams, 1985, p. 224).

Following treatment in prison, the individual then typically engages in a "transitional" TC while simultaneously involved in a work release program. This stage exposes the individual to some of the negative experiences that may have led to drug use initially, and treatment is used to counteract these negative influences. In the final stage, the individual may or may not be on parole and therefore under community supervision, but he or she will still be involved in outpatient counseling and/or group therapy sessions in order to reinforce his or her drug-free lifestyle (Inciardi, 2008). Research findings have clearly demonstrated that offenders who are involved with drugs and who participate in a program that includes (1) prison-based treatment, (2) a transitional treatment while on work release, and then (3) outpatient treatment once they are in the community have much lower rates of recidivism and drug relapse over the short- and long-term compared both to individuals in other treatment programs and to individuals receiving no treatment at all (Inciardi, Martin, Butzin, Hoopoer, & Harrison, 1997). In fact, "when compared with those who receive no treatment at all, the chances are three times greater for remaining drug free and arrest free" (Inciardi, 2008, p. 321). To answer the criticism regarding the lack of voluntariness of these programs: Research shows that those "forced" into treatment by the criminal justice system remain in a program longer than those who voluntarily enter treatment, which increases their chances of remaining drug free (Anglin & Hser, 1990; Young 2002). This translates to safer communities. Unfortunately, in the war on drugs, treatment has taken a backseat and as funding is cut, program effectiveness surely decreases as well: "treatment is only as good as the programs to which clients are sent" (Inciardi, 2008, p. 321). The United States needs to reevaluate its "get-tough" approach and turn an eye to other nations and their strategies of harm reduction.

Summary

- Primary prevention is the foundation of drug education programs and is designed to prevent the use of drugs before use begins. Secondary prevention programs are implemented once an individual starts using drugs and the focus of these programs is on early identification of use and intervention before the use of drugs becomes an addiction that derails an individual's life. Tertiary prevention occurs and is directed at those individuals already addicted to drugs and is focused on rehabilitative efforts and the road to sobriety.

- America's first drug court was in Dade County, Florida, in 1989; it was designed to be a judicially supervised program to aid in the treatment of drug abuse for individuals who had committed a drug-related offense. These courts treat an individual's drug offense as not just a concern for the criminal justice system but also as a public health issue. There were nearly 2,150 drug courts as of 2007, with these specialized courts in every state.
- The treatment plan in drug court generally consists of three phases: (1) detoxification; (2) stabilization; and (3) assisting the individual in seeking community resources. In its entirety the process is typically designed to last 12 months; however, it often lasts much longer.
- Treatment has been shown to work—if substance abusers stick with it; however, between 80 and 90 percent of conventional drug treatment clients drop out before 12 months, the period generally found to be the minimum effective duration. By providing a structure that links supervision and treatment, drug courts exert legal pressure on defendants to enter and remain in treatment long enough to realize benefits.
- Research suggests that drug courts are effective in reducing involvement in criminality for those individuals who successfully finish the program. Additionally, to divert a defendant to drug court costs between $1,200 and $3,500 depending upon their treatment regimen compared to an average incarceration cost of $5,000.
- Substance abuse that is left untreated costs the United States approximately $165 billion each year. Estimates suggest that well over 7 million Americans need treatment for their substance abuse addiction, yet only a fraction of these (just over 1 million) receive treatment each year, primarily due to lack of resources dedicated to these programs.
- Pharmacological treatment is the use of drugs to treat drug abuse. This type of treatment uses drugs to counteract the symptoms of withdrawal from narcotics as a form of therapy usually (but not always) in combination with a particular form of behavioral therapy rehabilitation.
- One type of pharmacological treatment is the use of methadone to treat opiate addiction. Methadone maintenance treatment was first started in the United States over 30 years ago and is a treatment that has been used more extensively since that time in European countries. Methadone is a synthetic opiate administered orally whose effects are longer lasting (up to 24 hours) than other opiates used illicitly, such as heroin and morphine.
- The goal of residential treatment programs is the resocialization of people into a life without drugs. These programs typically isolate patients from the outside world and encourage them to engage in group activities with other residents to promote a drugless existence. Additionally these type of treatment programs focus on increasing patients' responsibilities to themselves and to others. Some of these programs employ medication-assisted withdrawal in collaboration with behavioral therapy, while others are based on a 12-step approach free of any drug consumption, such as the widely known Alcoholics Anonymous and Narcotics Anonymous.
- It is difficult to determine how successful or unsuccessful residential programs are in preventing future drug/alcohol use because of all the complexities, including varying types of programs and varying types of addicts. Critics conclude that many drug abusers who would fail these programs are eliminated by the stringent interview process that often requires highly motivated individuals.
- Outpatient treatment programs can vary in their intensity; however, they all maintain the same goal of maintaining a drug-free lifestyle. The less intense outpatient programs are more educationally focused and can be beneficial to individuals who may not have a life-crippling addiction, but still struggle with substance abuse. The more intense

outpatient programs are heavily focused on educating the addict, but they also strive to provide patients with a supportive environment and guidance in recommending additional supportive resources to assist in treatment. These programs also frequently use the 12-step method, and patients are strongly encouraged to attend AA or NA meetings in conjunction with their outpatient therapy.

- Recent research has discovered that outpatient treatment is an effective setting for alcohol-dependent patients who remain with the program through its completion. It appears that outpatient treatment works for individuals who cannot financially afford a residential program or who for lifestyle reasons cannot dedicate themselves full time to a residential program. Outpatient programs are most successful if the patient is serious and motivated about becoming drug free. Additionally, those with an extensive social support network are more likely to succeed in the long term.
- Alcoholics Anonymous (AA) and Narcotics Anonymous (NA) are two of the more famous voluntary 12-step self-help organizations for drug abusers. The hallmark of AA and NA is a treatment goal of complete abstinence. Drug and alcohol users are viewed as biologically different from other individuals, and therefore they cannot engage in the use of substances in a controlled way. These programs preach that effective treatments for addictions are more complex than simply maintaining sobriety and advocate strongly the role of continued peer support in the recovery process. Part of the recovery process is a sponsor system, wherein each recovering individual has someone they can turn to, day or night, when they are in need of support or advice.
- Though it is difficult to gauge the success of self-help programs, it remains clear that effectiveness is directly tied to the individual's commitment and ability to maintain a consistent level of support within their network. Though AA has over 50,000 registered branches across the United States, the organization's approach has historically been criticized by professionals because it preaches total abstinence and lacks recent research to support its effectiveness (though there were several studies in the 1970s that indicated AA programs were useful in ceasing alcohol consumption).
- Compulsory treatment programs are not ones that an individual enters into voluntarily, but a treatment program that is forced upon an individual, for example, in place of a prison sentence. As such, critics of prison-based treatment argue that such programs are going to be inherently ineffective because the commitment and motivation of the addict is lacking.
- Prison-based treatment is a process that takes place over a period of at least 12 months, wherein individuals are segregated from prison culture and instilled with pro-social values to recover from their drug abuse. Following treatment in prison, the individual then typically engages in a "transitional" TC while simultaneously involved in a work release program. In the final stage, the individual may or may not be on parole and therefore under community supervision, but he or she will still be involved in outpatient counseling and/or group therapy sessions in order to reinforce his or her drug-free lifestyle.
- Research findings have clearly demonstrated that offenders who are involved with drugs participate in a program that includes prison-based treatment, a transitional treatment while on work release, then outpatient treatment once they are in the community have much lower rates of both recidivism and drug relapse over the short- and long-term compared both to individuals in other treatment programs or individuals receiving no treatment.

Important Terms

Anonymous self-help treatment
California Civil Addict Program
Compulsory treatment
Drug courts
Methadone maintenance
Methadone treatment
Outpatient treatment
Pharmacological treatment
Primary prevention programs
Prison-based treatment
Residential treatment
Secondary prevention programs
Tertiary prevention programs
Treatment Alternatives to Street Crime (TASC)

Critical Thinking Questions

1. Given that there is not much current research to support the effectiveness of self-help programs such as AA or NA, why do you think these are so popular in comparison with the other methods of treatment discussed?
2. How might the criminal justice system be impacted if all drug offenders were diverted to drug court and mandated treatment? How do you think this would impact the crime rate? Support your argument.

Research Topics

1. AA and NA usually have an "open" portion of their meeting for the first 45 minutes or so. Attend one of these meetings in your community. Discuss with the class how you think this venue for treatment may contribute to an individual's sobriety from drugs and/or alcohol.
2. Sit in on a drug court session. Prepare a brief research paper detailing the effectiveness of drug courts in your state with your impressions from attending drug court. Do you think this is a viable alternative to traditional criminal justice system processing?

Suggested Readings

Nolan, James L. Jr. (2001). *Reinventing justice: The American drug court movement.* Princeton, NJ: Princeton University Press.

Office of Justice Programs (OJP). (2008). *Painting the current picture: A national report card on drug courts and other problem-solving court programs in the United States.* Washington, DC: U.S. Government Printing, Office. Retrieved September 2, 2009, from http://www.ndci.org/sites/default/files/ndci/PCPII1_web%5B1%5D.pdf

14

Alternative Approaches

"The message this country is really sending the rest of the world is that we in the U.S. are simply unable to stop our people from using these drugs, so the rest of the world must stop their people from producing them."

—(Mosher & Akins, 2007, p. 394).

OBJECTIVES:

When you have finished this chapter, you should be able to:

- Discuss the effects of U.S. drug control policy on other nations
- Elaborate the advantages and disadvantages of a legalization perspective
- Explain the advantages and disadvantages of a decriminalization perspective
- Discuss harm reduction and the advantages and disadvantages to this approach

REAL LIFE

The relationship between drug decriminalization and HIV:

> The use of illicit drugs must be decriminalised if efforts to halt the spread of Aids are to succeed, one of the world's leading independent authorities on the disease has warned. In an unprecedented attack on global drugs policy, Michele Kazatchkine, head of the influential Global Fund to Fight Aids, Tuberculosis and Malaria, has [said] that without a radical overhaul of laws that lead to hundreds of thousands of drug users being imprisoned or denied access to safe treatment, the millions of pounds spent on fighting HIV and Aids will be wasted. Kazatchkine will use his keynote speech at the 20th International Harm Reduction Association conference [in April 2009] in Bangkok to expose the failures of policies which treat addiction as a crime. He will accuse governments of using what he calls "repressive" measures that deny addicts human rights rather than putting public

health needs first. He will argue that governments should fully commit to the widespread provision of harm reduction strategies aimed at intravenous drug users, such as free needle exchanges and providing substitutes to illicit drugs, such as methadone. "A repressive way of dealing with drug users is a way of facilitating the spread of the [HIV/Aids] epidemic," Kazatchkine said. "If you know you will be arrested, you will not go for treatment. I say drug use cannot be criminalised. I'm talking about criminalising trafficking but not users. From a scientific perspective, I cannot understand the repressive policy perspective." He condemns policymakers who argue that, because drug users frequently turn to crime to fund their habit, it justifies making it a criminal justice issue. Harm reduction both helps the addict and wider society and reduces the need to commit crime, he said. Alex Stevens, a senior research fellow specialising in drugs and criminalisation at the University of Kent, [concurs:] "In many countries, serious human rights infringements are committed in the name of fighting drugs," he said. "These include the use of the death penalty for drug offences, compulsory treatment regimes that include methods (such as physical beatings) that are akin to torture, and, for example in the USA, depriving convicted drug law offenders of the right to vote." Stevens said that, while the UK was ahead of many other countries on harm reduction, its tendency to criminalise drug users could undermine its efforts. What is needed, [according to Stevens] . . . is a total rethink of drugs policies. "What I'm saying is that government's function is to protect their citizens. This is why harm reduction should be supported by all governments everywhere ("Curb Aids and HIV by Decriminalising Drugs, Say Experts," 2009).

EFFECTS OF U.S. DRUG CONTROL POLICY ON OTHER NATIONS

Recall that the drug policy in the United States presently is that of prohibition, meaning that the creation, distribution, sale, and use of drugs are illegal and severely punishable. The logic behind U.S. drug policy is that drug use poses a threat not only to individuals but to society as a whole and must therefore be prevented. Further, it is believed that drug use will be deterred by harsh legal standards. Prior to the 1900s, drug laws were entirely delineated by individual states. In the early 1900s, federal drug laws began to emerge, but were fragmented. By 1969 however, things started to come together: President Richard Nixon called for a war on drugs to address growing public concern regarding the increase in drug use among adolescents and college students, and the perceived social ill of heroin addiction. This was the start of a plethora of drug laws and drug enforcement that continues to incarcerate masses of people to this day.

In 1970, the Controlled Substances Act was passed, which set out to fuse and strengthen the federal laws already in existence. This act addressed control, penalties, prevention, and treatment, and also called for research on addiction. In addition, it developed a ranking system of five schedules in which drugs could be classified by their level of dangerousness (refer to Chapter One for more information on the scheduling of drugs). Additional federal legislation in the 1980s and 1990s (i.e., the 1984 and 1990 Crime Control Acts, and the 1986 and 1988 Anti-Drug Abuse Acts) called for harsher sentencing and mandatory sentencing for drug offenders and increased efforts toward prevention and treatment, including school-based drug education.

But how does the approach of the United States toward illicit substances impact other nations? The prohibitionist attitude of the United States toward drugs does not stop at the border, and therefore has had an enormous impact on other countries as the U.S. government lays blame at their doorsteps for our drug problems. For example, in 1969 President Nixon initiated

Operation Intercept in an effort to decrease the supply of marijuana entering the United States from Mexico. This operation lasted a mere 20 days as the impact on border passage was so severe that it virtually stopped all traffic! This is one short-term example; however, on a larger scale the United States has financially impacted countries that were unwilling to encourage the same prohibitionist attitude in their own nation.

The Foreign Assistance Act of 1971 allowed for monetary aid to other countries for the purpose of controlling the creation and trafficking of drugs. It also called for the halting of foreign monetary assistance and/or military assistance to countries that were not actively taking steps to control the creation and distribution of illicit drugs (Gouvis Roman, Ahn-Redding, & Simon, 2005). Additionally, the Anti-Drug Abuse Act of 1986 called for the withholding of federal aid to other countries if the U.S. President did not confirm that the other county had "cooperated with the United States, or [has] taken the appropriate steps to prevent drug production, drug trafficking, and drug-related money laundering" (Gouvis Roman, Ahn-Redding, & Simon, 2005, p. 26). A subsequent amendment to this act required that countries sign a treaty prior to the receipt of federal aid stating they would cooperate with U.S. drug enforcement efforts.

The war on drugs in America became the initiative and justification for the United States to take military action against several countries. During Operation Just Cause in 1989, the United States invaded Panama for a number of reasons, including the fact that Panama had become a site for trafficking drugs into the United States. Plan Colombia, initiated in 2000, was a $1.3 billion aid package for the purpose of eliminating coca farms and combating illegal drug traders in Colombia, which is also a site for heavy trafficking of illegal drugs.

> Colombia's efforts to attack the drug trade have been hampered over the years by the activities of insurgent guerillas and paramilitary groups that control the country's drug-producing regions. Moreover, organized drug cartels run the international aspects of Colombia's drug trade. For years a vicious circle has existed—the money produced by the drug trade enriches the outlaw groups, which generate violence and corruption in government, which threaten the country's democratic institutions. The backbone of Plan Colombia was supplying thirty Blackhawk and thirty-three Huey helicopters for the Colombian Army and police forces, as well as almost $600 million to train and equip three Colombian Army battalions for antidrug operations. This plan had numerous critics in addition to the Criminal Justice Policy Foundation—even in the U.S. Congress (Inciardi, 2008, p. 267).

A part of Plan Colombia involved the crop spraying of coca farms, which was heavily criticized by environmentalists for "harming the health of thousands," causing "irreparable damage to the Amazon rain forest," and creating "up to one million refugees" with the fumigation (Livingston, 2004, p. 123). The end result was a **balloon effect** that had no impact on drug production: Though there was a minor decline in coca production in Colombia, there were increases in Bolivia and Peru, which compensated, resulting in a stable market (United Nations Office on Drugs and Crime [UNODC], 2007). What did result were significant increases in poverty for Colombian farmers. Spraying coca farms frequently also resulted in the chemical spraying of nearby crops. Additionally, the United States has provided only a small amount of funds to teach farmers how to grow alternative crops—the markets for which are very small—essentially resulting in a decline of 90 percent of their potential yearly income ("Taking The Side of the Coca Farmer," 2002)!

More recently, the Merida Initiative, which was signed in 2008, is an agreement among the United States, Mexico, and other Central American countries to address drug trafficking. This initiative is deemed necessary because "roughly 90 percent of all the cocaine consumed in the

United States transits Mexico. The country is also the largest foreign supplier of marijuana and methamphetamine to the United States. Central American officials have identified gangs, drug trafficking, and trafficking of arms as the most pressing security concerns in that region" (Johnson, 2009, np). According to a 2009 report given in Washington, DC, the main thrust of this initiative should lie in Mexico for a variety of reasons.

> President Calderon has taken decisive action against transnational criminal organizations by conducting counternarcotics operations throughout the country, and initiating large scale police and rule of law reform. As the result of government pressure against the drug trafficking organizations, and conflicts among these organizations over access to prime trafficking routes to the United States, drug-related assassinations and kidnappings have reached unprecedented levels. By some estimates, there were as many as 6,200 drug-related murders last year, including the deaths of 522 military and law enforcement officials, more than double the level in 2007. Narcotics manufacturing in Mexico produced around 18 metric tons of heroin in 2007 and nearly 16,000 metric tons of marijuana. Profits from the drug trade, including the trafficking of cocaine and methamphetamine, generate an estimated $13–$25 billion in earnings per year for the drug cartels. Some 150,000 people are estimated to be directly involved in the narcotics business and another 300,000 are involved in marijuana and opium cultivation and processing. Mexican efforts against the drug gangs coincide with a trend of dramatic reduction in the purity of cocaine and methamphetamines in the United States, as well as an increase in street prices. In recent years, Mexico's drug trafficking organizations have acquired increasingly sophisticated and powerful weaponry—largely from purchases made in the United States. The massive drug profits flowing from the United States are used to finance operations and suborn officials. Arms purchased or otherwise acquired here and smuggled into Mexico equip the cartels with mines, anti-tank weapons, heavy machine guns, military hand grenades, and high powered sniper rifles and high-tech equipment. Smuggling also equips the cartels with night-vision goggles, electronic intercept capabilities, encrypted communications and helicopters. In addition, some of the groups, such as the "Los Zetas" (former military who have become the enforcement arm of the Gulf Cartel), have received specialized training in weapons and tactics. Municipal and state police, and even the military, are woefully ill equipped to confront such well armed and trained forces (Johnson, 2009, np).

The U.S. Congress has allocated $465 million for the Merida Initiative. In order to avoid simply transferring this problem south to Central American countries or the Caribbean, this initiative provides a portion of the funds to these countries.

Some scholars argue that the U.S. war on drugs, both domestically and globally, has largely targeted the poor and lower-level participants in the drug trade. For example, efforts abroad have focused more on poor farmers who grow marijuana and other drug products to support their families instead of focusing on breaking up larger-scale trafficking enterprises; this trend is paralleled in the United States (Sterling, 2001). Milton Friedman argues vehemently that there is no justice in the war on drugs for anyone:

> Our drug policy has led to thousands of deaths and enormous loss of wealth in countries like Colombia, Peru, and Mexico, and has undermined the stability of their governments. All because we cannot enforce our laws at home. If we did, there would

> be no Cali cartel. The foreign countries would not have to suffer the loss of sovereignty involved in letting our "advisors" and troops operate on their soil, search their vessels, and encourage local militaries to shoot down their planes. They could run their own affairs, and we, in turn, could avoid the diversion of military forces from their proper function. Can any policy, however high-minded, be moral if it leads to widespread corruption, imprisons so many, has so racist an effect, destroys our inner cities, wreaks havoc on misguided and vulnerable individuals, and brings death and destruction to foreign countries (Friedman, 2005, pp. 79–80)?

Additionally, though it has become somewhat fashionable to criticize the government's position on the drug war, research shows that supply reduction initiatives like those elaborated above do not work to reduce drug use in the United States. Policies are often politically motivated and therefore not rooted in reducing the impacts of drugs on individuals and societies. Perhaps it is time to explore alternatives.

LEGALIZATION

> "Now what I contend is that my body is my own,
> at least I have always so regarded it.
> If I do harm through my experimenting with it,
> it is I who suffers, not the state."
>
> —MARK TWAIN (1901; AS CITED IN HUGGINS, 2005, P. 245)

"America's highly punitive version of prohibition is intrusive, divisive, and expensive and leaves the United States with a drug problem that is worse than that of any other wealthy nation. Notwithstanding a very substantial investment of resources and of public authority and rhethoric in drug control, there is little sign of major remission in America's drug problems" (MacCoun & Reuter, 2001, p. 1). The current situation in the United States is also counterintuitive: a system wherein we are permitted to use some drugs (prescription drugs, alcohol, tobacco), but not others—decisions based on historical politics and law-making, not on harm of the substance in question. This hypocrisy is noted by former Police Chief Joe McNamara:

> Relatively few of America's estimated 90 million illegal drug users go on to commit non-drug crimes. In fact, the majority of police I hired during my 18 years as police chief in two of the largest cities in America admitted prior use of illegal drugs. They did not commit other crimes and grew out of their early drug use. As one candidate put it to me, "Of course, I smoked pot. I was in the Army. I went to college." And I can remember, some forty years ago, as a young policeman in Harlem, gathering with my colleagues in a tavern after work, listening to them complain vigorously about the junkies who made our work so difficult. During our discussions, we drank prodigious amounts of beer without the slightest awareness that we were consuming a drug that could be as lethal as heroin. Indeed, far more of my fellow police died in driving accidents after these drinking sessions than were slain in the line of duty (McNamara, 2005, pp. 103–104).

At the other end of the continuum of the current U.S. policy of drug prohibition, is a policy of drug **legalization.** This approach to drug policy would call for the creation, distribution, sale, and use of drugs to become legal under a system of governmental regulation, in a way similar to how alcohol is legal in the United States. Throughout history, the campaigns against illicit drugs have been waged so effectively and have convinced Americans so successfully as to the harms that drugs cause, that 75 percent of adults oppose marijuana legalization and between 90 and 95 percent of adults oppose the legalization of other illegal drugs (Goode, 2008). Due to this opposition (not to mention politics), legalization is a proposition unlikely to occur anytime in the near future; it is a position with little political power, but one that is intellectually powerful.

Historically, only controversial figures such as Timothy Leary (advocate of psychedelics), Aldous Huxley (author), Milton Friedman (economist), Thomas Szasz (psychiatrist), or Bob Marley (musician) advocated legalization of illicit substances. In 1988 and 1989, a lot of media attention was given to the debate over proposed legalization of street drugs, such as cocaine, heroin, and marijuana. Kurt Schmoke, a former mayor of Baltimore, started this debate in 1988 at the U.S. Conference of Mayors. Since that time, the legalization position has become more mainstream, with advocates including Ann Landers (advice columnist), George Soros (Wall Street expert), Hugh Downs (talk show host), Joseph McNamara (former Police Chief of San Jose), an increasing number of judges at both the state and federal level, academics, as well as editorial board members of prominent magazines (MacCoun & Reuter, 2001). Supporters of legalization propose that the social and monetary costs of prohibiting the use of illicit drugs are too high (citing that the war on drugs has been ineffective and has cost billions of dollars). Those who support legalization argue that to continue with the model the United States has presently would mean that drug-related crime rates would remain high, civil liberties would remain threatened, high spending on enforcement of drug laws would continue, as would high rates of diseases contracted from the use of dirty needles used by intravenous drug users (Gray, 2001; MacCoun & Reuter, 2001).

Though there have been debates over legalization, there have never been any formal concrete proposals for a workable policy put forward. Numerous questions would have to be answered in such a proposal. The following issues are just a few that would have to be addressed:

- What drugs in particular should be made legal and in what quantities/potencies?
- To whom should these substances be sold (i.e., should there be age limits, or should sales be restricted to those who are already dependent)?
- Where should drugs be sold?
- Should advertising be permitted?
- What restrictions should be placed on use, and what government agency would enforce these restrictions?
- Where should the United States obtain the materials for the drugs? How might this impact our international relationships with chosen countries and with countries not chosen for participation?

This debate poses many questions of interest, some of which can be considered further by an elaboration of the potential advantages and disadvantages of legalization.

Advantages

TAX REVENUE Prohibition of drugs (substances that many people want regardless of illegality) has resulted in highly inflated drug prices for substances that cost little to make. The price of these substances is artificially inflated by the risks of trafficking. If drugs were legalized, they could be controlled and taxed by the government, creating revenue that could be then used for public good (i.e., funding drug treatment and prevention programs). Further, if illicit drugs are legalized, all of the monies spent presently on drug enforcement would be freed up for better use as well. Tax payers would save billions of dollars, as enforcement of drug policy would no longer be necessary (Lyman & Potter, 2007). Instead, users could be taxed when buying drugs (as customers who buy cigarettes are taxed), and those funds could support social programs.

THE PRISON POPULATION Supporters of legalization have argued that drug laws have not been effective in reducing the demand for drugs, and that drug laws have actually bred more harm than drug use itself, specifically in that it has increased street violence, organized crime, and corruption. The argument for legalization is rooted in the concept that "it is impractical to make illegal that which a significant segment of the population in any society is committed to doing" (Inciardi, 2002, p. 278). To do so necessitates punishing a significant number of people, which results unnecessarily in overcrowded courts and prisons. In 2001, there were 1,586,902 drug-related arrests in the United States (Gouvis Roman, Ahn-Redding, & Simon, 2005). Some studies suggest that even with all these drug arrests, enforcement efforts still reach less than 1 percent of all drug users (Lyman & Potter, 2007)! A policy of legalization would result in a significant decrease in the number of individuals in prison, thus translating to a large fiscal saving for the nation.

FOREIGN POLICY CONCERNS If drugs were legalized, it is believed that international cartel activity and organized crime would decrease. These international organizations fund global terrorism and increase the occurrence of violence in the United States. As well, international relations with many countries may improve, as there would be no treaties or mandates on other countries to comply with the U.S. war on drugs. Further, the United States would be less likely to take military action against other countries deemed a drug-trafficking threat if such substances were legal in this country (Inciardi, 2008; Lyman & Potter, 2007).

PERSONAL FREEDOMS Some in the movement to legalize drugs advocate personal freedoms because they are against "moral entrepreneurs" telling individuals what they can and cannot do, and therefore infringing upon personal freedoms. Psychiatrist Thomas Szasz is one of these individuals:

> The plain historical facts are that before 1914 there was no "drug problem" in the United States; nor did we have a name for it. Today there is an immense drug problem in the United States, and we have lots of names for it. Which came first: "the problem of drug abuse" or its name? It is the same as asking which came first: the chicken or the egg? All we can be sure of now is that the more chickens, the more eggs, and vice versa; and similarly, the more problems, the more names for them, and vice versa. My point is simply that our drug abuse experts, legislators, psychiatrists, and other professional guardians of other medical morals have been operating chicken hatcheries: they continue—partly by means of certain characteristic tactical abuses of our language—to manufacture and maintain the "drug problem" they ostensibly try to solve (Szasz, 1976, pp. 11–12).

Other advocates of the legalization position are more concerned with the civil liberties infringements that accompany the current war on drugs. Law enforcement is harsh and often prejudiced in enforcing current drug laws, and these laws typically target minorities in urban areas. If illicit drugs are legalized, many basic civil rights for these individuals would be restored. Some advocates point out that body and property searches would be minimized, random traffic stops would decline, and it would restore the freedom of owning one's body and the right to the "pursuit of happiness" (Cussen & Block, 2000, p. 526). This policy would also decrease the opportunity for police corruption and brutality, due process abuses and denial of constitutional protections, and wrongful arrests.

THE CRIME RATE If drugs were legalized, the prices of drugs would decrease because they would no longer be as difficult to obtain, and dealers and traffickers would not have to combat the risks of being targeted by law enforcement. With drugs priced at a lower, governmentally controlled cost, users would no longer have to participate in secondary crime (such as theft and prostitution) to finance their drug habit. It has been suggested that as a result, the crime rate would drop. Further, if illicit drugs were legalized, their production, distribution, and sale would be regulated by the government and would no longer be controlled by organized-crime families and drug cartels. This would significantly lower the occurrence of drug-related violent crimes, both internationally and domestically (Inciardi, 2008; Lyman & Potter, 2007). With crime related to drug use and possession lowered, law enforcement would be free to focus their attention on other social issues.

PUBLIC HEALTH Supporters make the argument that legalization would not have a significant impact on the level of drug use; considering there is decent access to illicit drugs presently, it is suggested that levels of use pretty much mirror the demand for such substances. Therefore, in following the logic of this argument, there would be no additional public health concerns associated with legalization because levels of drug use would not notably increase. Additionally, legal drug production would be governmentally controlled and users would be guaranteed to receive pure drugs (whereas now many are likely to receive impure substances that are mixed with dangerous additives). Currently, there are no controls on the black market for illegal drugs—there is no guarantee that substances bought on the street are pure, and the level of potency is indeterminable. Legislative control may have the subsequent effect of lowering the incidence of overdose (Inciardi, 2008; Lyman & Potter, 2007). Clean needles would also always be available, thus lowering the incidence of HIV transmission and the transmission of other intravenous diseases (though there are needle exchange facilities that exist presently, many communities are still reluctant to open such establishments).

Disadvantages

PUBLIC HEALTH CONCERNS Opponents of legalization suggest that there are "numerous legitimate arguments against the legalization of drugs [which] have considerable empirical, historical, pharmacological, and/or clinical support" (Inciardi, 2002, p. 281). As such, these opponents have serious concerns about the health implications of legalizing drugs in addition to alcohol and tobacco. The consequences and health impacts (disadvantages) of drug use (by specific drug) have been documented in previous chapters of this book, which point to a number of health concerns:

- Medical issues such as cancer, respiratory problems, seizures, sleep disturbance, overdose, and death;
- Psychological problems such as psychoses, depression, and auditory/visual hallucinations; as well as
- Behavioral problems wherein rather than dealing with personal and interpersonal problems, users tend to turn to drugs to "escape" their issues and frequently experience social problems such as relationship problems and job problems, among other issues.

Therefore, opponents suggest that legalizing such substances could have a tremendous adverse impact on public health. The legal drugs (alcohol and tobacco) are extremely harmful to society in terms of health, why would we want to add other drugs to this list? "The toll of alcohol consumption is well documented in terms of broken homes, violence, ruined careers, accidents, and lost productivity on the job and in the schools. The question is whether legalized alcohol and other drugs would create a worse situation than has been realized by legalized alcohol alone" (Lyman & Potter, 2007, p. 402). To be clear, the public health costs of all illicit drug abuse combined is less than the health costs associated with alcohol abuse (Inciardi, 2008).

THE CRIME RATE Though advocates of legalization suggest that the crime rate would be lowered, opponents take the alternate position and argue that the crime rate would remain high. It is suggested that the street market for drugs would remain for those unable to afford a drug purchase at a licensed facility, for minors, and for drugs that are not legalized (because most advocates of legalization suggest that there are drugs too harmful to legalize, such as PCP or crack). Therefore crime and organized drug-trading activity would revolve around this black market (Lyman & Potter, 2007). Should legalization occur, age limits would most likely be enforced for purchasing drugs. Street dealers/gangs would undoubtedly begin to focus on selling drugs to minors to compensate for their loss of money to governmentally controlled sales of drugs to adults. As well, drug smuggling over state lines would most likely occur after legalization in an effort to escape high state taxes, as taxes on drugs would probably vary by state. Some states are far more conservative than others; if legalization is passed on the federal level, some states may not pass controlled legalization laws, which would also result in smuggling. Admittedly however, this black market would be a fraction of what it is now, should some drugs be legalized. Additionally, drug abusers faced with addiction would have serious difficulty maintaining employment; therefore, though their drug of choice may be legal, they may still commit secondary crimes in order to pay for it due to their lack of employment or lack of stable employment (Lyman & Potter, 2007).

NEW MARKETS AND NEW REVENUES A key assumption of a legalization position is that most individuals who are going to use drugs, already do use drugs, regardless of the fact that it is illegal. "Such an assumption appears to ignore one of the most powerful aspects of U.S. tradition: the ability of an entrepreneurial market system to create, expand, and maintain high levels of demand" (Inciardi, 2008, p. 297). Advertising and marketing tools have been masterful in creating new markets for alcohol and tobacco, and if other substances were legal, why should we not assume this would be the case for these substances as well?

> The successes of tobacco and alcohol advertising programs are eminently conspicuous. The linking of smoking with women's rights has been masterful. The linking of alcohol with the pursuit of happiness after work, in recreational activities, and in romantic liaisons has been so effective that people in the United States spend tens of billions of dollars each year on beer, wine, and distilled spirits. In a United States where drugs are legal, how far would advertisers go? Would they show students, executives, and truck drivers—overworked and faced with tight schedules and deadlines—reaching for a line of cocaine instead of a cup of coffee? Would cocaine be touted as the mark of success in an achievement-oriented society? Would heroin be portrayed as the real way to relax after a harried day? Would the new Marlboro Man be smoking marijuana or crack instead of tobacco (Inciardi, 2008, p. 297)?

Considering that the goal of advertising is to create and sustain demand, these are legitimate questions that, given the successes of past advertising, lead many to believe that new users would indeed be created by a policy of legalization.

COST OF LEGALIZATION Some researchers feel that the inflated cost of illegal drugs keeps levels of use lower than rates would be if illegal drugs were cheaper. If drugs are legalized, the price of drugs would be driven down, which could quite possibly result in more use and addiction: under the theory that addicts would use more if they could afford more, and new users would be more inclined to experiment once the legal sanctions were lifted—therefore, use is correlated with availability. This could increase the amount of health care dollars spent on addicts for emergency room visits, overdose or trauma related to intoxication, and for treatment programs. Using the legal drug of alcohol as an example, the government bears the cost of health care due to addiction, reduced job productivity, lost earnings, crime, and other social welfare concerns, such as inadequate parenting (Lyman & Potter, 2007). This is a significant fiscal toll on society. In addition, law enforcement still needs to provide regulation, as there would presumably be guidelines to legalization of drugs as there are with legalization of alcohol and tobacco. So law enforcement would be responsible for regulating establishments that sell and distribute drugs, ensuring that drugs are not being used by minors, and of course ensuring that "drugging and driving" infractions are not occurring (for which a new roadside test or some other measure to test for intoxication would need to be created). Since the late 1980s, the debate for a strict legalization approach (aside from use of marijuana for medicinal purposes) in the United States has lost momentum as many have moved to support harm reduction or decriminalization instead.

DECRIMINALIZATION

Decriminalization refers to the removal or reduction of legal penalties associated with possession and/or use of illicit drugs. In other words, drugs and drug use would remain illegal, but those caught with small amounts for personal use by law enforcement officials would receive some type of administrative sanction (i.e., a ticket) rather than have criminal charges brought against them. In 1972, the Shafer Commission (known formally as the National Commission on Marijuana and Drug Abuse) created a report that recommended the federal decriminalization of marijuana. One rationale for decriminalization was the nationwide prevalence of marijuana use. A Miami lawyer was quoted in the 1970s as saying:

> *Everybody smokes dope!* This profound statement should not be taken to mean that every person in the country smokes marijuana. It merely means: Policemen smoke dope. Probation officers smoke dope. Narcotic agents smoke dope (and sell it). Judges smoke dope. Prosecutors smoke dope. Plumbers, schoolteachers, principals, deans, carpenters, disabled war veterans, Republicans, doctors, perverts, and librarians smoke dope. Legislators smoke dope. Even writers of articles on drug abuse smoke dope. *Everybody smokes dope* (as cited in Inciardi, 2008, p. 51)!

The movement toward decriminalization was significant in the 1970s in states like Oregon, Colorado, Alaska, Ohio, California, Mississippi, North Carolina, New York, and Nebraska. This was not a national movement however, and Congress would not move to decriminalize marijuana under federal statute. By the 1980s, the decriminalization movement had lost steam, and was an issue left to the individual states.

Currently, twelve states have decriminalized marijuana possession, including Alaska, Colorado, California, Minnesota, Maine, Nevada, Mississippi, New York, North Carolina, Ohio, Nebraska, and Oregon. Individuals found in possession of small amounts of marijuana in these states do not face arrest or imprisonment. Rather, users are required to pay a fine instead, similar to a traffic ticket, ranging from $100 to about $600. It is important to note that in the states where marijuana is decriminalized, policy can vary considerably. What is similar, however, is at the state level a decision has been made to give the enforcement of cannabis possession offenses a very low priority in the war on drugs.

Decriminalization has been described as a **libertarian** policy initiative, meaning that those who support this model feel that the government should not control individual behavior, regardless of whether or not an individual's behavior is self-destructive. One country that has taken this approach is Portugal. In 2001, Portugal decriminalized a variety of drugs (marijuana, cocaine, and heroin) in response to a need for new policy to address a rising drug problem. Under this law, the use and possession of small quantities of marijuana for personal use are no longer considered a criminal offense. Police now ticket drug users but do not arrest them, and then the citation is forwarded to an administrative committee in that district for resolution. The committee determines if the individual is trafficking in drugs, and if so, the case is referred to criminal court. If not, the committee considers whatever evidence is available, and then determines what action is appropriate on a case by case basis. Punishments include fines, revocation of a professional license if applicable, revocation of the right to have a firearm, a ban on certain places/establishments or association with certain individuals, a ban on travel, termination of public financial assistance, and/or confiscation of personal belongings. Committees cannot, however, require that addicts attend treatment (Van Het Loo, Van Beusekom, & Kahan, 2002). Other countries that have adopted a decriminalization approach are Amsterdam and Canada.

Case Study:

Amsterdam

In the early 1600s, the Netherlands traded in opium and coca leaves, the nation earning about 10 percent of its income until 1915 from the opium trade (MacCoun & Reuter, 2001). There was international pressure to pass the Opium Act banning the opium trade, and the Netherlands did so in 1919. Their maximum proscribed penalty for an offense however was only 3 months, increasing to 12 months as of 1928. There were no laws against cannabis in the country until 1953. Several years later, the Netherlands signed the United Nations Single Convention of New York in 1961 which pledged their agreement to limit "the production, manufacture, export, import, distribution of, trade in, use and possession of drugs" (MacCoun & Reuter, 2001, p. 244).

The Dutch perspective on illicit drugs varies from the general views in the United States. Drug use is viewed as an inevitable deviance in an otherwise good society. Rather than try to put an end to the deviance entirely (which is viewed as having the potential to cause social damage), the Dutch instead have decriminalized individual use of what they consider to be "soft drugs" and focus their drug control and enforcement efforts on larger-scale enterprises and the use of hard drugs. In the late 1960s, the Dutch government established several working groups to conduct research regarding drug policy. The Hulsman Committee, established in 1969, made policy recommendations based on the concept that individuals should not be punished for actions that are harmful only to themselves (and the committee sited cigarette smoking as an example—that surely the use of cigarettes would not be outlawed, therefore why should marijuana?). Marijuana use was deemed by the Hulsman Committee to fit into a younger lifestyle that should not be punitively judged by the "majority" of society. They recommended that criminalization be avoided and they warned against harsh law enforcement measures. The revised Opium Act of 1976, which was put forth by the Dutch parliament, decriminalized individual possession and use of "soft drugs" (marijuana and hashish), as these are viewed as less harmful. The act "includes two schedules. Schedule 1 lists a number of substances (opiates, cocaine, amphetamines, LSD) under the heading 'drugs presenting unacceptable risks.' Schedule 2 mentions cannabis only, without mention of unacceptable risks. Penalties for forbidden actions pertaining to schedule 2 are considerably lower than those for schedule 1" (Leuw, 1991, p. 231). In 1976, individuals were permitted to possess up to 30 grams of cannabis without penalty, which was enough for approximately sixty marijuana joints. Succumbing to international pressure, this amount was lowered to 5 grams (enough for about ten joints) in 1995 (Gray, 2001).

> Being realists, the Dutch understood that a ban on marijuana was futile, and since people were going to use it anyway, it was better to have the transactions out in the open rather than in the shadows, and to govern behavior instead. In an attempt to steer a middle course between the futility of Drug Prohibition and the unknown perils of drug legalization, Holland thus began its program of *gedogen* (tolerance) and "decriminalization" of drugs. Under this program, the possession, use, and sale of street drugs are still illegal. But as long as people stay within certain well-known guidelines, and do not otherwise commit any crimes, the police will "look the other way" and not enforce the drug laws. Coffee houses have been established in Dutch cities where patrons can get coffee, tea, and sandwiches, as well as marijuana and hashish. Alcohol and harder drugs are not sold; there is no advertising; sales to minors under seventeen are prohibited; and the sellers at the coffee houses are not allowed to make a nuisance of themselves by hawking passersby on the streets. If those rules are followed, the sellers and the patrons are left alone (Gray, 2001, p. 218).

Today, marijuana possession and use actually remain a criminal offense on the books in the Netherlands; however, legislation has removed the penalty for possession and/or sale of up to 5 grams of marijuana. Additionally, legislation has been passed that allows certain coffee shops to sell less than 30 grams as long as certain legal guidelines are met. In the Netherlands, there are about 1,500 shops that sell cannabis products, with about 450 of them in Amsterdam (MacCoun & Reuter, 2001). These coffee shops sell marijuana and hash from various places across the globe and at various levels of potency. Typically different types or "flavors" are offered, as well as beverages such as coffee or tea, and baked goods that can be purchased with or without marijuana or hashish as an ingredient (MacCoun & Reuter, 2001). What follows is a description of a "typical" coffee shop:

> The setting is considerably less lurid than one might imagine. Sales are low key; customers are more than welcome to simply sip coffee and eat a sandwich. Chess, backgammon, newspapers, and laptops occupy most customers' attention. Music

(*Continued*)

> varies in style (and volume) from bebop to blues to punk to reggae—the latter is especially popular—and many shops are readily identifiable by the Rastafarian imagery in their windows. They are also by the language on their signs; a coffeeshop is often the only establishment on the block with an English name, showing how important tourism is for their sales. The customers are mostly adults; surprisingly many of them in the 30 to 50 age range. Many are aging hippies; others belong to the burgher class, complete with suits and briefcases. For a visitor who prefers to remain "unaltered," the clientele is certainly less menacing than that at the many open-air pubs where tourist youth imbibe large quantities of beer on summer evenings. (MacCoun & Reuter, 2001, p. 242).

Use of "hard drugs" (i.e., heroin, cocaine, etc.) is seen as a public health problem. Dutch government policies focus on harm reduction (treatment and assistance programs, rehabilitation, needle exchange, etc.). Law enforcement comes after social assistance programs; law enforcement, even for the possession of hard drugs, is likely to be more lenient in the Netherlands than in other countries.

The question asked by many critics is: Do such policies lead to increased drug consumption? The answer of most studies is yes: Decriminalization of marijuana in coffee shops, and therefore easier physical access to marijuana, has led to increased marijuana use among Dutch youth. Similarly, research on alcohol and tobacco in the United States found that when such substances are made easily available to youths, use among that age group will increase (Leuw, 1991). That being said, as of the mid-1980s, 17 percent of 18-year-old individuals in the Netherlands reported using cannabis at least once, whereas 57 percent of Americans in the same age group reported using cannabis at least once (Leuw, 1991). So despite decriminalization of marijuana in the Netherlands, the level of drug consumption is still significantly lower than in the United States where marijuana is criminalized.

Drug violence (including violence that surrounds hard drugs) happens at a considerably lower rate in the Netherlands than in the United States. What is pursued aggressively by the Dutch government are harm reduction programs, including drug treatment, needle exchange programs (NEPs), educational programs, any type of program that will reduce the harm associated with drug abuse but is an alternative to a criminal justice response. Supporters of this policy use as one example the lack of availability of crack in the Netherlands:

> even though powder cocaine is available in Holland for people who want it, there is not crack cocaine particularly to be found. Why? Not because it is difficult to manufacture. In fact, any user knows that powder cocaine can be turned into crack by adding baking soda and water and cooking it in a microwave oven. But crack cocaine is much riskier than powder, and users know that, too. So as long as they can afford to purchase powder cocaine, they have no interest in crack. This strongly supports the conclusion that the United States brought the "crack epidemic" on itself as a result of its prohibitionist policy on powder cocaine. In other words, this was not really a "drug" problem, it was a "drug prohibition" problem (Gray, 2001, pp. 220–221).

There are some negative consequences to this approach. One consequence is that because drugs are not legal, those who sell the substances must get them through the black market, which results in drug-related crime and corruption. This is especially problematic for neighboring countries because it increases drug trafficking across their borders. Additionally, the Netherlands is a relatively small country and statistics reveal that of all individuals who use drugs, about one-third are tourists who have come to partake in what is criminalized in their home nation (Gray, 2001). Both of these problems would be reduced (and eventually disappear) as more countries embrace a decriminalization approach. To deal with the issue of trafficking, the Netherlands has taken a crime control approach wherein they focus their efforts on larger-scale trafficking enterprises of hard drugs.

Case Study:

Canada

Canada's Controlled Drugs and Substances Act was passed in 1996 and, similar to U.S. federal legislation, established schedules for controlled substances and the punishments associated with various drug offenses. In Canada, most law enforcement efforts have focused on large-scale drug trafficking, specifically as the nation's "open border policy" with the United States has resulted in the international smuggling of drugs over the Canadian border into the United States. However, despite the fact that drug possession and use are illegal, Canadian courts were typically lenient with small-scale producers and users. Usually, such individuals would be fined instead of receiving prison sentences, and those arrested and brought before the court for drug use were often acquitted because their arrest violated their privacy rights. As such, Canada practiced unwritten decriminalization of illicit substances when the drugs were in an individual's possession for personal use (Gouvis Roman, Ahn-Redding, & Simon, 2005).

In 2001, Canada became the first country to legalize marijuana for medical uses. Patients have the right to grow marijuana themselves or have one other person grow marijuana on their behalf. Patients are, however, prohibited from obtaining marijuana from street dealers. This law allows doctors to make recommendations specific to each individual's case. The law does not limit the quantity of marijuana an individual can be prescribed for medical purposes, but permits each individual to have only a month's supply in his or her possession based on the physician's prescribed recommendation. Canada had been squarely within a harm reduction model historically. Beginning in the 1980s, every Canadian citizen has had access to drug treatment programs through the universal health care system. By way of comparison, in the United States federal funding for treatment basically ceased during the Reagan administration. The tide, however, has begun to turn in Canada, with the government moving away from a harm reduction model toward a crime control model as practiced in the United States. In 2009, Bill C-15 was passed, which essentially authorized the start of a Canadian war on drugs. Both liberals and conservatives joined together to pass this controversial piece of legislation, which will give mandatory minimum sentences to those convicted of drug dealing. Under the amended Controlled Drugs and Substances Act, the following sentences will be mandatory:

(*Continued*)

> A minimum prison term of one year for selling marijuana as part of an organized criminal gang or when a weapon is involved; A minimum of two years in jail for selling hard drugs such as cocaine, heroin or methamphetamine to young people; A minimum of six months behind bars for growing five to 200 marijuana plants without a licen[s]e and two years for cultivating at least 500 plants . . . The bill does give judges some latitude to divert non-violent offenders with substance abuse problems to one of six national drug treatment courts. But most drug dealers will simply be locked up ("Ottawa Embarking on Its Own War on Drugs," 2009).

The tide in Canada turned based on political motives and politicians not wanting to look "soft on crime," not because there is evidence to support mandatory minimum sentences. The bill was approved:

> without any empirical evidence that harsh sentencing laws reduce drug crime. They endorsed the policy without any estimate of how much it will cost to jail thousands of marijuana growers and street pushers. They changed the law without any plan to contain the spread of AIDS, hepatitis C and other drug-related diseases in the prison system ("Ottawa Embarking on its Own War on Drugs," 2009).

And it is not that the empirical studies are not out there, because they are:

> In fact, most studies—including two by the federal justice department in the last seven years—have concluded that mandatory minimum sentences don't work. Most experts, including 13 of the 16 who appeared before the committee, recommended that the government scrap the policy. New York state, which pioneered mandatory sentencing for drug crimes in 1973, has decided to repeal its tough penalties. Michigan, Connecticut, Iowa, Kansas, Louisiana, New Jersey and North Carolina are rethinking their mandatory minimum drug sentences. Yet [Canada] is embarking on its own war on drugs ("Ottawa Embarking on its Own War on Drugs," 2009).

Despite years of research in the United States, which shows that harsh laws do not result in lowered rates of crime and violence but only in overcrowded prisons, Canada has decided to embark on this path in the hopes of appearing "tough on drugs" and subsequently "tough on crime."

Advantages

LAW ENFORCEMENT AND THE CRIME RATE As mentioned earlier, enforcement of harsh drug laws is futile and can create a hostile social environment because drug use in any society is inevitable and will occur to some extent regardless of prohibition legislation. The current U.S. drug laws have not been effective in reducing the demand for drugs. Prohibition has actually resulted in more harm than drug use itself, specifically in that it has increased street violence and organized crime. Current prohibition requires that billions of dollars are spent on law enforcement, imprisonment, probation, parole, and court services, some of which could be transferred to other areas of crime control at the local, state, and federal level if drugs were decriminalized. A policy of decriminalization would remove criminal charges from small drug offenses and therefore free up law enforcement agents to focus on other social issues (rather than processing small-scale drug-related arrests), and would subsequently decrease overcrowding in courts and prisons. Many economists favor abandonment of the present war on drugs because it has resulted in very high spending but has been largely ineffective in deterring street violence and drug abuse/addiction. Instead, many favor legalization and taxation, or at least decriminalization, to decrease the profit organized-crime networks make on illegal drugs (many cite the end of alcohol prohibition and the subsequent breakup of bootleg gangs as an example for this line of thought) (Lyman & Potter, 2007).

PERSONAL FREEDOMS As with legalization, decriminalization would give individuals the opportunity and personal freedom to use any substance they choose (in moderated amounts) without the risk of arrest or significant criminal charges. Civil liberties would be protected by decriminalization, in that the occurrence of search and seizure and wrongful arrests, as well as other violations of civil rights associated with the war on drugs would significantly decrease (Cussen & Block, 2000). Also decreased would be the opportunity for police corruption and brutality, due process abuses and denial of constitutional protections.

PUBLIC HEALTH CONCERNS Supporters make the argument that decriminalization would not have a significant impact on the level of drug use; considering there is reasonable access to illicit drugs presently, it is suggested that levels of use pretty much mirror the demand for such substances. Therefore, it is suggested that there would be no additional public health concerns associated with decriminalization (Inciardi, 2008; Lyman & Potter, 2007).

Disadvantages

INCREASES IN ENFORCEMENT While advocates of decriminalization suggest that there will be decreases in enforcement, opponents suggest that increased enforcement will be required. Rather than punishment via the criminal courts, decriminalization frequently involves police ticketing or providing a summons to those found using or possessing decriminalized drugs. This, opponents suggest, would require increased funding for law enforcement. This is not likely the case however, for two reasons: (1) Decriminalization typically does not involve targeting enforcement but normally permits users to "do their own thing" provided they are not in possession of large quantities of drugs; and (2) If a user is ticketed, he or she would be required to pay a fine, which would offset any increased enforcement costs.

PUBLIC HEALTH CONCERNS Opponents of decriminalization have concerns about the health implications of permitting the use of drugs in addition to alcohol and tobacco. While the consequences and health impacts (disadvantages) of drug use (by specific drug) were documented in previous chapters, health concerns are numerous and include medical issues, psychological problems, and behavioral problems. Therefore, opponents indicate that decriminalization of illicit substances would adversely impact public health, as does consumption of alcohol and tobacco.

THE CRIME RATE Though advocates of decriminalization suggest that the crime rate would be lowered, opponents argue that the crime rate would remain high because a street market for decriminalized drugs would remain. Therefore, crime and organized drug-trading activity would revolve around this black market, as it does currently in a prohibitionist climate. Additionally, it is argued that addicts would have difficulty maintaining employment, which would contribute to secondary crimes in order to pay for their habit (Lyman & Potter, 2007).

COST OF DECRIMINALIZATION Because critics of decriminalization suggest that a greater number of individuals would use drugs, this could increase the amount of health care dollars spent on addicts for emergency room visits, overdose or trauma related to intoxication, and for treatment programs. As such, the government would be forced to bear the cost of health care due to addiction, reduced job productivity, lost earnings, crime, and other social welfare concerns, as the government does currently with alcohol addiction (Lyman & Potter, 2007). This is a significant fiscal toll on society.

In many countries, the tide is starting to turn from a prohibitionist approach, to one that advocates decriminalization and harm reduction. In August 2009, the Supreme Court in a unanimous ruling in Argentina deemed it was unconstitutional for an adult to be punished for private consumption of marijuana, provided it does not harm anyone else ("Argentina Court Ruling Would Allow Personal Use of Pot," 2009). This comes on the heels of a similar ruling in Brazil in early 2009, and a "growing momentum in Latin America toward decriminalization of possessing small amounts of certain drugs" ("Argentina Court Ruling Would Allow Personal Use of Pot," 2009). In addition, Mexico passed a law in August of 2009 that decriminalizes possession of small amounts of a variety of drugs, including not only marijuana, but heroin, cocaine, and LSD as well ("Mexico's New Drug Law May Set An Example," 2009). Additionally, decriminalization for minor drug use is the policy of Belgium, Finland, Greece, Luxembourg, Portugal, Switzerland, the United Kingdom, Ireland, Austria, France, and Italy. This marks a shift toward a harm reduction approach, wherein there is less concern with interdiction and enforcement, and more focus on how to minimize harm to individuals who choose to use drugs, and to society at large from drug's collateral consequences. The underlying assumption is that drug use is not a crime, but an illness, and therefore something that a prison sentence will not solve.

HARM REDUCTION

In a message to Congress on August 2, 1977, President Jimmy Carter was quoted as saying, "Penalties against possession of a drug should not be more damaging to an individual than the use of the drug itself" (as quoted in Huggins, 2005, p. xi). This quote is characteristic of the **harm reduction** model, which focuses on practicality. Rather than attempting to stop or prevent drug use, the harm reduction (or harm minimization) approach seeks to manage drug abuse by minimizing the social harms and consequences of drug abuse to users and nonusers. Those who favor the harm reduction model feel treatment is more effective than imprisonment for addicts, and though harm reduction strategies extend past marijuana, the harm associated with a criminal justice response to marijuana is a good illustration:

> Marijuana prohibition is unique among American criminal laws. No other law is both enforced so widely and harshly and yet deemed unnecessary by such a substantial portion of the populace. Police make about 700,000 arrests per year for marijuana offenses. That's almost the same number as are arrested each year for cocaine, heroin, methamphetamine, Ecstasy, and all other illicit drugs combined. Roughly 600,000 or 87 percent, of marijuana arrests are for nothing more than possession of small amounts. Millions of Americans have never been arrested or convicted of any criminal offense except this. Enforcing marijuana laws costs an estimated $10 to $15 billion in direct costs alone . . . Alabama currently locks up people convicted three times of marijuana *possession* for 15 years to life . . . A parent's marijuana use can be the basis for taking away her children and putting them in foster care. Foreign-born

> residents of the United States can be deported for a marijuana offense no matter how long they have lived in this country, no matter if their children are U.S. citizens, and no matter how long they have been legally employed. More than half the states revoke or suspend driver's licenses of people arrested for marijuana possession even though they were not driving at the time of arrest. The federal High Education Act prohibits student loans to young people convicted of any drug offense; all other criminal offenders remain eligible (Nadelmann, 2005, pp. 221–222).

These types of penalties are perhaps what President Jimmy Carter had in mind when he was speaking of "penalties being more damaging to the individual than the use of the drug itself."

The harm reduction model is guided by five principles:

- Historically, throughout various societies, people have used substances that have the mind-altering effects of illicit drugs for various reasons, such as healing, ritualistic, or religious purposes. Drug use has always existed, despite numerous efforts at prohibition, which can subsequently result in violence and other collateral impacts. Harm reduction seeks to ensure public health and safety without attempting to eradicate drug use.
- Those who abuse drugs should be ensured basic civil rights and should be treated with respect.
- Focus should rest on addressing the social harms of drug abuse rather than focusing primarily on trying to stop drug abuse.
- Drug abusers should be provided with treatment in which they collaborate with professionals to determine their own treatment goals.
- It should be acknowledged that treatment of abusers and harm reduction in communities must be custom-tailored to each individual or community, recognizing gender and culture as components in both policy and treatment (Brocato & Wagner, 2003).

Examples of harm reduction programs include NEPs and methadone maintenance therapy for heroin users. These programs do not necessarily promote or encourage heroin use, but they reduce the harms caused by intravenous drug use by eliminating the opportunity for the spread of HIV. Methadone maintenance therapy also reduces the likelihood of drug-related crime because those on methadone do not feel cravings and are less likely to steal to finance their drug habits. Another more recent harm reduction strategy is the appearance of medical care tents at raves in which water (to prevent dehydration) and any needed medical attention are provided to rave-goers consuming psychedelic drugs.

Seven years after President Jimmy Carter's message to Congress, on September 14, 1986, then-President Ronald Reagan in a White House speech was quoted as saying, "Let us not forget who we are. Drug abuse is a repudiation of everything America is" (as quoted in Huggins, 2005, p. xi). His sentiment indicated the dramatic move away from harm reduction approaches. Recently, however, segments of American society have returned to this approach, seeing the wisdom of programs beyond those singularly advocated by the criminal justice system. California's Proposition 36, which was overwhelmingly approved in 2000, is an interesting example of harm reduction. Under this proposition, many individuals arrested for use of illicit substances are required to undergo treatment. If an individual refuses to undergo treatment, or does not complete treatment successfully, he or she could be sent to jail for the underlying drug offense. This is becoming a more commonplace alternative: treating drug offenders and then imprisoning them only if they fail to comply. Studies estimate that between 1 million and 1.5 million drug and alcohol users enter treatment each year under such propositions (Husak & de Marneffe, 2005). Such proposals are advocated both for their fiscal savings and for the humane treatment of the individual user involved.

Advantages/Disadvantages

Resistance to incorporate the harm reduction model into U.S. policy rests on two arguments: (1) Some argue that if the harms associated with drug use are reduced, drug use will subsequently increase and cause greater public health concerns than those that already exist (i.e., increased crime rate, increased medical costs, increased violence, etc.); and (2) Many also feel that harm reduction policy sends the message that drug use is acceptable. Critics suggest that condoning drug use may result in overall increased use. For example, a user who obtains needles from an NEP may feel safer using the drug, which may lead to increased use, decrease in motivation to stop using, or increase in likelihood to start using. In essence, critics suggest that "micro-level harm reduction among individuals ironically increases macro-level harm for society as a whole" (Jung, 2001, p. 516). Many conservative U.S. policymakers are also hesitant to pursue harm reduction strategies because they fear it is the first step down the road toward legalization. Many who disagree with harm reduction argue that the policy would result in more drug use and addiction among individuals, despite the fact that specific measures may curb violence and the spread of disease—so then it becomes a question of which harm is more socially important and deserves addressing. What critics ignore is that harm reduction approaches prove empirically to be both cost effective (compared to imprisonment of drug users) and a significant improvement in the humane treatment of the individual user involved.

Medical Marijuana

A controversial type of harm reduction is the medical use of marijuana. **Medicalization** of drugs seeks to hand responsibility to physicians for treating drug abusers (including whether or not to have the individual remain on the drug as part of treatment). Historically, marijuana has been used for medicinal purposes for thousands of years. In 1937, however, The Marijuana Tax Act prohibited the recreational use of marijuana in the United States but did not explicitly criminalize medicinal use of marijuana. However, this legislation made marijuana so difficult to obtain that many pharmaceutical companies stopped production. Then in 1970, the Controlled Substances Act classified marijuana as a Schedule I drug, which federally established that marijuana has no medical use, despite much research stating the contrary. Since that time, marijuana has not been legally available as far as the federal government is concerned (aside from a few limited exceptions). Starting in the early 1970s, many states conducted research, with permission from the federal government, on the effects of marijuana use on cancer patients. The THC (delta-9-tetrahydrocannabinol) in marijuana was found to be effective in treating nausea in chemotherapy patients. Subsequently, the federal government approved oral marijuana, but ignored findings that smoked marijuana is more effective. For some patients, oral THC has been found to be far less effective in symptom management; while smoked marijuana is more effective because THC reaches the blood quicker and attains the necessary level at a faster rate. In 1976, the federal government created the Individual Treatment Investigational New Drug Program (also known as Compassionate IND), which allowed the prescription of marijuana to patients whose doctors applied for such a right (in an application process that was extremely long and burdensome). Fewer than forty patients received marijuana through the program before it was ended in 1992 (Grinspoon, 2000).

In recent years, heated debate has surrounded the controversial topic of whether or not marijuana should be legalized, and some moderates argue that it should be legalized for medicinal purposes. Marijuana has been supported by many for the following therapeutic uses:

- Treating cancer patients. The THC in marijuana may help stop nausea and vomiting, which in some patients is so severe that other anti-nausea medications have been unsuccessful in treating the symptom. Marijuana has also been found to relieve anxiety, which could help cancer patients who become nervous prior to chemotherapy sessions. Marijuana could also stimulate appetite and decrease weight loss.

- Treating AIDS wasting syndrome. Marijuana increases appetite and may help to maintain muscle mass in AIDS patients who are losing weight. It may also be helpful in relieving the nausea associated with AZT therapy.
- Treating patients with multiple sclerosis. Marijuana helps treat pain, muscle spasms, and tremors associated with the disease.
- Treating epilepsy patients. In some cases, marijuana may prevent seizures in epilepsy patients.
- Treating glaucoma patients. Marijuana releases pressure on the optic nerve and reduces blood flow to the eye, which may help to prevent vision loss.
- Treating osteoarthritis patients. Marijuana may help treat pain in osteoarthritis patients and may be a much safer alternative to over-the-counter pain relief regimens such as Tylenol, Advil, or aspirin, many of which can cause gastrointestinal bleeding.
- Treating pain. Marijuana can be used as a pain reliever for a number of different ailments, including migraines, back pain, pain associated with various types of physical trauma and/or surgery, etc.
- Treating asthma patients. Marijuana can also be used to relieve asthma symptoms (Ksir, Hart, & Ray, 2008; Liska, 2004).

In the 22-year period between 1978 and 2000, a total of thirty-five states passed legislation acknowledging that marijuana has medicinal or therapeutic value. Not everyone agreed however that this therapeutic value outweighed the potential risks.

The Institute of Medicine reported in 1999, after 2 years of research, that marijuana smoke contained a number of harmful substances (i.e., carcinogens) and alternate treatments should be considered until a cannabinoid drug could be developed that did not require smoking to reap its therapeutic benefits. Additionally, marijuana may restrain the immune system, can cause accidents because of its intoxicating nature, and may cause central nervous system damage. For each medically advocated use of marijuana "there are other modern drugs with greater bioavailability, specificity, and effectiveness . . . Reproducible absorption, consistent and predictable pharmacological effects may not be achieved . . . It appears that it will not become a useful therapeutic agent" (as cited in Ksir, Hart, & Ray, 2008, p. 381). One of the strongest arguments against the legalization of medical marijuana is that it would send the message that marijuana use is acceptable, and therefore promote more recreational use. These are some of the reasons why the federal government is reluctant to legalize medical marijuana. Supporters of the legalization of marijuana state that the negative side effects of smoking marijuana are much less significant than the side effects associated with other approved medical drugs used to treat diseases for which medicinal marijuana would be prescribed, and therefore the benefits of medical marijuana use outweigh the risks.

By 2009, ten states had passed legislation allowing individuals to use marijuana for medical reasons as long as they had permission from their physicians (Alaska, California, Colorado, Hawaii, Maine, Montana, Nevada, Oregon, Vermont, and Washington). Additionally, Arizona has passed a similar law, although they do not have a program in place to administer medicinal marijuana. Medical use of marijuana is supported by two-thirds of the American public (Lyman & Potter 2007). The first states to pass such laws were California and Arizona in 1996. California's law permits an individual to cultivate, possess, and use marijuana in order to relieve symptoms associated with cancer, AIDS, or other illnesses, provided they have been given oral or written permission from a doctor. This law received 56 percent of the vote (MacCoun & Reuter, 2001). Arizona's law permits the prescription of controlled substances including marijuana to seriously or terminally ill individuals, provided the decision is supported by a second physician and backed by medical research. This law received 65 percent of the vote, but was repealed by the legislature and passed for the second and final time in 1998 (MacCoun & Reuter, 2001).

Presently, in states that have legalized medical marijuana, if an individual has a "recommendation" from a doctor to possess marijuana, he or she will not be prosecuted on the local or state level for using marijuana. However, there is no legal way to obtain marijuana, and the drug is not legalized for medical use on the federal level. If a federal official caught a patient using prescribed medical marijuana in a state where medical marijuana was legal, the federal agent still has the authority to arrest the patient for using the substance. This was confirmed in 2005. In *Gonzales v. Raich*, the U.S. Supreme Court upheld that the federal drug laws can be applied to the prosecution of individuals in possession of marijuana, even if they are in a state that permits marijuana for medical purposes, and even if they have a prescription/recommendation from a physician ("Supreme Court Allows Prosecution of Medical Marijuana," 2005). In 2001, the court clarified the precarious position of physicians in prescribing marijuana. In *U.S. v. Oakland Cannabis Buyers*, the Supreme Court upheld that marijuana has no medicinal benefits and the federal government does not recognize the prescription/recommendation for medical marijuana use in cases where patients claim it is the only substance that helps them manage their symptoms. This case enables the federal government to reserve the right to prosecute physicians who recommend/prescribe marijuana, even in states where medical marijuana is legal. So in addition to the patient using marijuana, physicians can be prosecuted on the federal level for prescribing marijuana because it is a controlled substance under the 1970 Controlled Substances Act. (This is why, when drafting legislation on the state level, many states—such as California—allow for the *recommendation* for marijuana use by doctors, rather than the *prescription* of marijuana.) Regardless of wording, this is still a risky business for doctors. Federal prosecution could result in the loss of their medical license and the end of their career.

Needle Exchange

Needle exchange/syringe distribution was a harm reduction initiative that began in Europe in the 1980s in an effort to decrease among intravenous drug users the spread of HIV/AIDS, Hepatitis B and C, as well as more than twenty other blood-borne infections carried in a hypodermic needle ("Point for Point: Canada's Needle Exchange Programs," 2004). Most programs allow users to drop off dirty needles in exchange for clean needles, not only preventing infection in that specific user, but also taking the dirty needles off the street so other users avoid infection as well. Some NEPs additionally distribute bleach kits for the sterilization of needles, provide HIV tests and tests for other sexually transmitted diseases, and provide counseling for other needs as they arise ("Point for Point: Canada's Needle Exchange Programs," 2004).

NEPs are widely used in a variety of European nations such as Spain, Italy, and France because intravenous drug use in these countries is the principal risk factor for the transmission of HIV. As such, HIV is deemed a greater threat to individual and public health than the consequences associated with drug use (MacCoun & Reuter, 2001). It is estimated that an intravenous drug user injects approximately 1,000 times per year, posing a great danger of disease transmission. To deal with this threat, Canada also implemented NEPs beginning in 1989, and currently has more than one hundred facilities nationwide ("Point for Point: Canada's Needle Exchange Programs," 2004).

The United States, however, has not been as receptive to this harm reduction strategy. As of 2003, there were 167 needle exchange clinics in existence in the United States (Brocato & Wagner, 2003). However, NEPs remain at the center of heated debate in this country. From a public health/health care perspective, needle exchange/syringe distribution programs are cost effective because providing clean syringes to users costs far less in the long run than it would be to treat those same users if they were to acquire HIV.

> A study published in the *Canadian Medical Association Journal* in August 1997 concluded that providing sterile needles is an inexpensive means of preventing greater health-care costs. Researchers at McMaster University examined the needle exchange program in Hamilton [Ontario], which provided more than 14,200 clean syringes to 275 drug users in 1995. The authors of the study estimated the program prevented 24 new HIV infections over five years. The study said the cost of treating HIV and AIDS over a person's lifetime could total $1.3 million in direct costs to the health system ("Point for Point: Canada's Needle Exchange Programs," 2004).

So from a fiscal standpoint, NEPs are positive. Do they condone and encourage intravenous drug use, as critics suggest? To test this hypothesis, the Centre for Addiction and Mental Health examined several studies addressing NEPs. The results indicated that such programs result in the effective reduction of disease transmission in drug users and do not increase the number of intravenous drug users or the amount of drugs they inject ("Point for Point: Canada's Needle Exchange Programs," 2004). As well, there has been international support for the research of these programs. "In Southern Australia, 55 [NEPs] serving about 1.2 million drug users resulted in no new HIV infections for three consecutive years" ("Point for Point: Canada's Needle Exchange Programs," 2004). Even U.S. research supports NEPs: "In the U.S., a 1997 National Institute of Health survey demonstrated such programs resulted in a 30 percent reduction in HIV transmission" ("Point for Point: Canada's Needle Exchange Programs," 2004). Despite the positive research findings that such programs work and are fiscally more responsible than imprisonment, it is still not a politically acceptable position to advocate in the midst of a war on drugs.

A NOTE ABOUT ALTERNATIVES

There are many differences between the United States and Europe, so to make a direct comparison that a certain policy works there and so it would or would not work in the United States is a difficult guessing game at best. "The benefits of Europe's drug policy innovations are by no means decisively demonstrated, not for Europe and surely not for the United States. But the results thus far show the plausibility of a wide range of variations—both inside and at the edges of a prohibition framework—that merit more serious consideration in this country" (MacCoun & Reuter, 2005, p. 269). The belief is spreading throughout the world that the war on drugs has cost billions of dollars but has not been a success. In response, countries are rethinking their approaches—even if this means they will be blacklisted by the United States.

> Laws and other policy initiatives must be judged by their consequences, not their intentions. By that measure, the war on drugs over the past three decades has been a colossal failure. The international drug traffickers have been barely inconvenienced while societies in drug-producing and drug-transiting countries have experienced a massive upsurge in corruption and violence. In at least one drug-source country (Colombia), the entire social and political system is in peril. On the domestic front, the sole achievement has been a decline in recreational use of illegal drugs by casual, occasional users. Even assuming that the decline is the result of the prohibitionist strategy and not the effect of educational campaigns about the health consequences of drug abuse, the benefit has been achieved at an enormous cost. We have filled our prisons with drug offenders, diverted criminal justice resources and personnel away from serious crimes to wage the drug war, and badly damaged the Fourth Amendment and other portions of the Bill of Rights (Carpenter, 2005, p. 280).

The United States needs to refocus its efforts and learn from strategies that have been successful in other nations. Americans lose their lives from alcohol abuse, abuse of prescription drugs, and use of illicit drugs every year, so doing nothing is not an option, but proceeding with the same crime control policies and expecting a different result is unlikely to result in change either. American society should focus on the deglamorization of drugs in the media as it is extremely difficult for education and public service campaigns to counter this significant factor, especially when education and prevention programs are underfunded (Lyman & Potter, 2007). Funds also need to be devoted to educational programs, and the development of educational programs that will successfully reach youth. Many of the programs in existence today are not very effective, so it is time to create new strategies and programs geared toward the youth of today. In addition, enforcement efforts should be targeted higher up the trafficking chain. "Experts in organized crime have long argued that criminal organization cannot be controlled by either a 'headhunting' strategy (arresting as many illicit entrepreneurs as possible) or by attacking consumers" (Lyman & Potter, 2007, p. 414). Enforcement efforts need to break up the trafficking businesses by targeting the business-community allies that permit activities such as the laundering of drug money and political corruption. Taking aim at these partners would logistically make drug trafficking much more difficult. A related deterrent would be maintenance of strict forfeiture laws, or even increased forfeiture penalties for individuals convicted of drug trafficking offenses (Lyman & Potter, 2007). What seems clear from an examination of other nations is that to assist the user and his or her family there needs to be a focus on harm reduction and a realignment of our view of drug use as a crime to drug use as an illness or a disease. Greater funding should be devoted to drug treatment programs, treatment should be used as an alternative to prison for drug users, and the focus should be on counseling and rehabilitation. These individuals will be released into the community and American society wants them to be able to reintegrate successfully. With the ease at which prisoners have access to drugs, sending a low-level drug offender to prison seems entirely counter-intuitive if the goal is to one day have him or her be a productive, non-drug-using member of society. The choices in how the "war" on drugs is fought have significant impacts on individuals, families, and communities, so selecting options that are most likely to succeed are paramount. In order to do this, we need to move beyond moral panic and rationally evaluate potential alternatives and lessons we can learn from around the globe.

Summary

- The prohibitionist attitude of the United States toward drugs does not stop at the border, and therefore has had an enormous impact on other countries as the U.S. government lays blame at their doorsteps for America's drug problems. The Foreign Assistance Act of 1971 allowed for monetary aid to other countries for the purpose of controlling the creation and trafficking of drugs. It also called for the halting of foreign monetary assistance and/or military assistance to countries that were not actively taking steps to control the creation and distribution of illicit drugs.
- The war on drugs in America became the initiative and justification for the United States to take military action against several countries. During Operation Just Cause in 1989, the United States invaded Panama for a number of reasons, including the fact that Panama had become a site for trafficking drugs into the United States. Plan Colombia, initiated in 2000, was a $1.3 billion aid package for the purpose of eliminating coca farms and combating illegal drug traders in Colombia, which is also a site for heavy trafficking of illegal drugs.
- The U.S. war on drugs, both domestically and globally, has largely targeted the poor and lower-level participants in the drug trade. Research shows that supply reduction initiatives do not work to reduce drug use in the United States. Polities are often politically motivated, and therefore not rooted in reducing the impacts of drugs on individuals and societies.
- At the other end of the continuum of the current U.S. policy of drug prohibition is a policy of drug legalization. This approach to drug policy would call for the creation, distribution, sale, and use of drugs to become legal under a system of governmental regulation, in a way similar to how alcohol is legal in the United States.
- In the United States, 75 percent of adults oppose marijuana legalization and between 90 and 95 percent of adults oppose the legalization of other illegal drugs.
- Supporters of legalization propose that the social and monetary costs of prohibiting the use of illicit drugs are too high. Those who support legalization argue that to continue with the model the United States has presently would mean that drug-related crime rates would remain high, civil liberties would remain threatened, high spending on enforcement of drug laws would continue, as would high rates of diseases contracted from the use of dirty needles used by intravenous drug users.
- Advantages of legalization would include greater tax revenue, a lowered prison population and lowered crime rate, a decrease in international cartel activity and organized crime, and a reinstatement of civil liberties lost through prohibition. Additionally, drugs would be purer, resulting in fewer public health concerns, and clean needles would be available, thus reducing the likelihood of HIV transmission.
- Disadvantages to legalization would include increased public health costs due to medical, psychological, and behavioral problems resulting from drug use, addicts may still engage in secondary crimes as they are unable to maintain steady employment, and there may be an increase in users as advertisers seek to increase the market and expand revenues.
- Decriminalization refers to the removal or reduction of legal penalties associated with possession and/or use of illicit drugs. In other words, drugs and drug use would remain illegal, but those caught with small amounts for personal use by law enforcement officials would receive some type of administrative sanction (i.e., a ticket) rather than have criminal charges brought against them.

- Currently, twelve states have decriminalized marijuana possession. Individuals found in possession of small amounts of marijuana in these states do not face arrest or imprisonment. Rather, users are required to pay a fine instead. It is important to note that in the states where marijuana is decriminalized, policy can vary considerably. What is similar, however, is that at the state level a decision has been made to give the enforcement of cannabis possession offenses a very low priority in the war on drugs.
- The Dutch view drug use as an inevitable deviance in an otherwise good society. Rather than try to put an end to the deviance entirely, they instead have decriminalized individual use of what they consider to be "soft drugs" and focus their drug control and enforcement efforts on larger-scale enterprises and the use of hard drugs.
- In the Netherlands, there are about 1,500 shops that sell cannabis products, with about 450 of them in Amsterdam. These coffee shops sell marijuana and hash from various places across the globe and at various levels of potency. Typically different types or "flavors" of marijuana are offered, as well as beverages such as coffee or tea, and baked goods that can be purchased with or without marijuana or hashish as an ingredient.
- In Canada, most law enforcement efforts have focused on large-scale drug trafficking, specifically as the nation's "open border policy" with the United States has resulted in the international smuggling of drugs over the Canadian border into the United States. However, despite the fact that drug possession and use are illegal, Canadian courts were typically lenient with small-scale producers and users. As such, Canada practiced unwritten decriminalization of illicit substances when the drugs were in an individual's possession for personal use.
- In 2001, Canada became the first country to legalize marijuana for medical uses. Patients have the right to grow marijuana themselves or have one other person grow marijuana on their behalf. Patients are, however, prohibited from obtaining marijuana from street dealers. This law allows doctors to make recommendations specific to each individual's case and does not limit the quantity of marijuana an individual can have for medical purposes, but permits only a month's supply, based on the physician's prescribed recommendation, to be in a patient's possession.
- In 2009, Bill C-15 was passed, which essentially authorized the start of a Canadian war on drugs. Both liberals and conservatives joined together to pass this controversial piece of legislation, which will give mandatory minimum sentences to those convicted of drug dealing.
- Advantages of decriminalization include lowering of the crime rate, lower levels of required law enforcement, increased civil liberties, and no additional public health concerns.
- Disadvantages of decriminalization include the costs of medical, psychological, and behavioral problems associated with drug use, and no decrease in the crime rate.
- The harm reduction approach focuses on practicality. Rather than attempting to stop or prevent drug use, the harm reduction (or harm minimization) approach seeks to manage drug abuse by minimizing the social harms and consequences of drug abuse to users and nonusers. Those who favor the harm reduction model feel treatment is more effective than imprisonment for addicts.
- Examples of harm reduction programs include NEPs and methadone maintenance therapy for heroin users. These programs do not necessarily promote or encourage heroin use, but they reduce the harms caused by intravenous drug use by eliminating the opportunity for the spread of HIV. Methadone maintenance therapy also

reduces the likelihood of drug-related crime because those on methadone do not feel cravings, and are less likely to steal to finance their drug habits. Another more recent harm reduction strategy is the appearance of medical care tents at raves in which water (to prevent dehydration) and any needed medical attention are provided to rave-goers consuming psychedelic drugs.

- Resistance to incorporate the harm reduction model into U.S. policy rests on two arguments: (1) Some argue that if the harms associated with drug use are reduced, drug use will subsequently increase and cause greater public health concerns than those that already exist (i.e., increased crime rate, increased medical costs, increased violence, etc.); and (2) Many also feel that harm reduction policy sends the message that drug use is acceptable. Critics suggest that condoning drug use may result in overall increased use.
- What critics ignore is that harm reduction approaches prove empirically to be both cost effective (compared to imprisonment of drug users) and a significant improvement in the humane treatment of the individual user involved.
- Medicalization of drugs seeks to hand responsibility to physicians for treating drug abusers (including whether or not to have the individual remain on the drug as part of treatment). Historically, marijuana has been used for medicinal purposes for thousands of years. In 1937, however, The Marijuana Tax Act prohibited the recreational use of marijuana in the United States but did not explicitly criminalize medicinal use of marijuana. However, this legislation made marijuana so difficult to obtain that many pharmaceutical companies stopped production.
- Then in 1970, The Controlled Substances Act classified marijuana as a Schedule I drug, which federally established that marijuana has no medical use, despite much research stating the contrary. In recent years, heated debate has surrounded the controversial topic of whether or not marijuana should be legalized, and some moderates argue that it should be legalized for medicinal purposes. In the 22-year period between 1978 and 2000, a total of thirty-five states passed legislation acknowledging that marijuana has medicinal or therapeutic value.
- By 2009, ten states had passed legislation allowing individuals to use marijuana for medical reasons as long as they had permission from their physicians. This is a position supported by two-thirds of the American public. Presently, in states that have legalized medical marijuana, if an individual has a "recommendation" from a doctor to possess marijuana, he or she will not be prosecuted on the local or state level for using marijuana. However, there is no legal way to obtain marijuana, and the drug is not legalized for medical use on the federal level.
- Needle exchange/syringe distribution was a harm reduction initiative that began in Europe in the 1980s in an effort to decrease among intravenous drug users the spread of HIV/AIDS and Hepatitis B and C, as well as more than twenty other blood borne infections carried in a hypodermic needle. Most programs allow users to drop off dirty needles in exchange for clean needles, not only preventing infection in that specific user but also taking the dirty needle off the street so other users avoid infection as well.
- The United States needs to refocus its efforts and learn from strategies that have been successful in other nations. Americans lose their lives from alcohol abuse, abuse of prescription drugs, and use of illicit drugs every year, so doing nothing is not an option, but proceeding with the same crime control policies and expecting a different result is unlikely to result in change either.

Important Terms

Balloon effect
Decriminalization
Harm reduction
Legalization
Libertarian
Medicalization
Needle exchange

Critical Thinking Questions

1. Do you believe it is appropriate for the United States to take such an active role in the drug policies of other nations? What do you believe is the appropriate level of intervention of the United States regarding the drug policies of other countries?
2. Do you believe a legalization position would work for all illicit substances? Why or why not?

Research Topics

1. Canada has recently made some conservative shifts in drug policy. Research two or three Canadian media sources to determine how the Canadian public feels about these shifts in policies. What do you believe was behind this change in legislation?
2. Write a research paper advocating either a legalization or decriminalization position.

Suggested Readings

Gouvis Roman, C., Ahn-Redding, H., & Simon, R. J. (2005). *Illicit drug policies, trafficking, and use the world over.* Lanham, MD: Lexington Books.

MacCoun, Robert J., and Reuter, Peter. (2001). *Drug war heresies: Learning from other vices, times, and places.* Cambridge, MA: Cambridge University Press.

GLOSSARY

Addictive personality a personality characterized by low self-esteem, insecurity, and anxiety, which is more prone to addiction

Administrative forfeiture when law enforcement seizes possessions that can be moved, but are not illegal, and are believed to be somehow associated with drugs; the owner is then given a specified period of time in which to contest the seizure

Adult Children of Alcoholics (ACOAs) Adult Children of Alcoholics are individuals who, during childhood, experienced a home environment in which one or more parent or caregiver consumed alcohol. Adult Children of Alcoholics can experience significant psychopathology

Affective Model a model of drug education suggesting that youth with high levels of self-esteem will avoid the use of drugs; therefore the goals are to improve communication, self-image, decision making, problem-solving abilities, and abilities to interact within a group of young individuals in order to keep them away from involvement with drugs

Aid Elimination Penalty in 1998 the Higher Education Act was amended to restrict the eligibility of those convicted of certain drug charges for federal financial study aid

Alcohol a potentially dangerous recreational drug; there are three types of alcohol, including rubbing alcohol (isopropyl alcohol), wood alcohol (methyl alcohol), and alcoholic beverages (ethanol); there are three major types of alcoholic beverages: beer, wine, and hard liquor (distilled spirits)

Amotivational syndrome has been observed in individuals who use marijuana, which is characteristic of changes in lifestyle and personality, including decreases in motivation and ambition; individuals become unlikely to accomplish conventional goals, including educational accomplishment

Amphetamines a drug that stimulates metabolism and results in increased energy; they are used to suppress appetite and bring about the release of norepinephrine and serotonin

Anomie results when there is a disjuncture between culturally emphasized goals and prescribed legitimate mean to attain these goals

Anonymous self-help treatment the two most famous anonymous self-help programs are Narcotics Anonymous (NA) and Alcoholics Anonymous (AA) in which the treatment goal is total abstinence through the following of a 12-step program

Anti-Drug Abuse Act passed in 1986 and had a significant impact primarily on the mass incarceration of minority group members for drug possession offenses; expanded in 1988

Arrestee Drug Abuse Monitoring Program (ADAM) a project that involves interviews and urinalysis on recently arrested individuals to assess their involvement with drugs

Asset forfeiture the seizure of personal assets by the government in an attempt to disrupt or dismantle criminal organizations

Attention Deficit Hyperactivity Disorder (ADHD) a syndrome associated with inattention, poor school performance, distractibility, misbehavior, peer conflict, and conflict with authority

Balloon effect the relocation of drug production to another area if pushed out of the original production center

Battered Child Syndrome the collection of injuries sustained by a child as a result of repeated mistreatment or beating

Binge drinking five drinks for men and four drinks for women in less than 2 hours

Biological theories examine the physiological influences that contribute to an individual's progression from drug use to addiction

Birth control a medication that prevents pregnancy and is nearly 100 percent effective

Breathalyzer analyzes one's breath for the presence of alcohol

Bureau of Drug Abuse Control created in the 1960s to focus on the diversion of drugs from legal channels to illegal enterprise

Bureau of Narcotics and Dangerous Drugs the organization under the control of the Department of Justice that was the result of the merger of the Federal Bureau of Narcotics and the Bureau of Drug Abuse Control

Business model of drug distribution retail-level sales are organized hierarchically and drugs are "fronted"

rather than being paid for immediately; at the center is a crew boss who obtains drugs from a wholesaler and then divides the supply among a variety of street-level dealers called "runners"

Caffeine the most widely used psychoactive drug in the world; found in tea and coffee, soft drinks, chocolate, over-the-counter cough and cold medications, herbal remedies, and weight-loss pills; a central nervous system stimulant; considered a recreational drug

Caffeinism psychological dependence on caffeine characteristic of heavy use and preoccupation with caffeinated products; generally involves agitation, anxiety, and heart palpitations

California Civil Addict Program started in 1961; involuntarily committed (mostly) narcotics addicts in order for them to receive treatment; administered by the Department of Corrections and was essentially a diversion method as individuals were provided with this treatment as an alternate to imprisonment

Certification a process by which the United States evaluates the level to which foreign countries cooperate with the "anti-drug" position of the United States; countries are either "certified" or "decertified" and decertified countries are penalized through the withholding of all U.S. aid

Civil asset forfeiture has no relationship to a criminal charge and indeed often proceeds without any criminal charge to follow; property is seized and forfeited irrespective of the guilt or innocence of the property owner; there are three types of civil asset forfeitures: summary forfeiture; administrative forfeiture; and a civil judicial proceeding

Civil Asset Forfeiture Reform Act passed in 2000, this act requires the government to have much stronger evidence of wrongdoing before a person's property can be seized; the burden of proof has been raised from "probable cause" to "a preponderance of the evidence" that the property is linked to a crime; shifts the burden of proof to the federal government

Civil judicial proceeding when a civil proceeding is brought against a defendant prior to the seizure of his or her property; if the defendant loses the proceeding or fails to contest the proposed forfeiture, the property is then seized by law enforcement, which keeps its profits

Claimsmaking is a stage of the social problem creation process in which individuals or groups, often activists, recognize a condition as troublesome and suggest that something should be done to remedy this problem

Classification schemes organize drugs by their common characteristics, allowing the public to grasp their similar generic qualities while isolating and delineating their more specific qualities

Cocaine an illicit stimulant drug derived from a natural substance (the coca leaf); available as "street cocaine," which is white powder that can be snorted or injected intravenously; freebasing is also popular, which is a method in which cocaine is heated and the fumes are inhaled

Codependency a reciprocal relationship between a substance abuser and a non–substance abuser in which the non–substance abuser unintentionally supports and even encourages the substance abuse

Combat Methamphetamine Epidemic Act of 2005 (CMEA) passed as part of the Patriot Improvement and Reauthorization Act of 2005 and requires a variety of actions by merchants involved in the sale of ephedrine, pseudoephedrine, and phenylpropanolamine, in order to decrease the production of methamphetamine

Comprehensive Crime Control Act passed in 1984; permitted the DEA to dictate a substance as illegal for a period of 12 months without review by the current government; increased bail and sentences; increased federal authority to asset forfeiture for individuals convicted of felony drug offenses

Comprehensive Drug Abuse Prevention and Control Act (Controlled Substances Act) passed in 1970 and sought to revise and give uniformity to drug control policy

Compulsory treatment based on the notion that most drug addicts are not intrinsically motivated to seek treatment, or to stay in treatment once admitted, and therefore must be forced to do so

Conflict theory asserts that the powerful in society are able to assert coercive force against the poor and powerless through the illegality of specific drugs and the disproportionate application of these laws

Conformity according to Robert Merton, an individual who internalizes conventional goals and means for attaining success

Controlled buy a monitored undercover informant purchases drugs and the seller is then arrested either immediately or after a period of surveillance

Controlled substance substances (excluding distilled spirits, wine, malt beverages, or tobacco) subject to federal control and punishment under the Controlled Substances Act of 1970 and its amendments

Controlled Substances Act (Comprehensive Drug Abuse Prevention and Control Act) passed in 1970 and used to revise and give uniformity to drug control policy

Crack another form of cocaine made by dissolving base cocaine in alkaline solution (i.e., baking soda); method of ingestion is by smoking

Crimes associated with drug use include crimes that may have occurred while an individual was under the influence of an illegal substance, but the crime was not a direct result of drug use

Criminal asset forfeiture occurs simultaneously with a criminal charge; if the defendant is found guilty, the property in question is forfeited; in a plea agreement, forfeiture of property can often be used to decrease the criminal punishment of a defendant

Critical frame of reference takes a dialectic approach by looking at how the interactions between the objective and subjective approaches for defining, classifying, and labeling drugs translate into meanings that become shared, traditional, and institutionalized by society

Cultural deviance theory asserts that deviance is the result of a combination of social disorganization in an environment and personal strain

Decriminalization the removal or reduction of legal penalties associated with possession and/or use of illicit drugs; drugs and drug use would remain illegal, but those caught with small amounts for personal use by law enforcement officials would receive some type of administrative sanction (i.e., a ticket) rather than face criminal charges

Department of Defense Authorization Act permitted the involvement of military forces in drug interdiction efforts

Direct-to-consumer advertising (DTC) when pharmaceutical companies are permitted to advertise products to consumers directly; allowed only in New Zealand and the United States

Distribution laws prohibit the sale, transportation, or storage of illegal substances

Doping the slang term used most commonly to describe the use of performance-enhancing drugs

Drug abuse (substance abuse) terminology to distinguish acceptable drug use from unacceptable drug use, short of compulsive or addictive behavior

Drug Abuse Resistance Education (DARE) a program developed in 1983 by the Los Angeles Police Department; advocated the well-known "Just Say No" to drugs motto; encouraged self-esteem, taught drug education, stress management techniques, and how to resist peer pressure

Drug Abuse Warning Network (DAWN) a project that gathers data regarding substance use and data from medical examiners and coroners regarding drug-related deaths from hospital emergency room visits

Drug addiction physiological dependence on drugs

Drug court designed to be a judicially supervised program to aid in the treatment of drug abuse for individuals who had committed a drug-related offense; treat an individual's drug offense as not just a concern for the criminal justice system, but also as a public health issue

Drug-defined crimes include the sale and/or possession of an illegal substance

Drug Enforcement Administration (DEA) formed in 1973 to collect and disseminate information related to drug intelligence and to investigate drug-related events

Drug-Free Federal Workforce mandated drug testing for federal agencies; both state and federal governments offered financial incentives for corporations to join the war on drugs and drug test potential and/or current employees

Drug-related crimes include violent behaviors induced by the properties of a drug or illegal activity that occurs to further a drug habit

Drug Resistance Education Model a drug education model (also called the social influence model) suggesting that youth are extremely susceptible to peer pressure and must be taught the skills to make rational decisions to avoid using drugs; as such, once youth are armed with rational decision making skills, they can resist the temptations, both internal and external, and not succumb to drug use (e.g., DARE)

Drug use any consumption of a substance defined or labeled as a drug

Dry county a jurisdictional area prohibiting the distribution of alcohol

Economic–compulsive explanations suggest that drug users engage in various types of crime (which may result in violence) in order to financially support their drug habit

Ecstasy methylededioxyamphetamine (MDMA) is one of 200 drugs from the methylenedioxyamphetamine (MDA) group and the street name "ecstasy" is typically used to refer to all drugs belonging to this family; MDMA is a designer synthetic drug available on the street as either a white powder, or in the form of brightly colored tablets sometimes featuring small pictures or symbols; it is typically administered orally, though occasionally it is crushed and snorted

Eradication policies aimed at minimizing the cultivation and production of drugs on foreign soil

Federal Bureau of Investigation (FBI) in 1982 this agency was given concurrent jurisdiction for drug-law enforcement, with its primary responsibility focused on organized crime as related to the drug trade

Female sexual dysfunction symptoms include decreased sexual desire and arousal, inability to orgasm and pain during sexual intercourse; experienced by 43 percent of women

Fetal Alcohol Syndrome (FAS) a disorder caused by exposure of the fetus to alcohol that results in a variety of both physical and psychological issues; characterized by growth and central nervous system problems, permanent birth defects, and heart and limb defects, as well as behavioral problems and learning disorders later in life

Food and Drug Administration (FDA) in the United States is responsible for approving what products can legally be prescribed or sold as medicine and for regulating the safety of such products

Frames of reference ways of looking at phenomena that can guide our perceptions about drugs

Freelance model of drug distribution dealers who work independent of any large-scale drug organization sell as part of a "cash only" business

Genetic predisposition theory the genetic structure of an individual contributes to his or her susceptibility to addiction

Hague Convention the international effort at narcotics control that was agreed upon in 1912

Hallucinogen persisting perception disorder flashbacks to hallucinogenic trips that occurred possibly years ago; experienced by between 30 and 60 percent of heavy LSD users

Hallucinogens (also known as psychedelics) a complex group of drugs consisting of over ninety naturally occurring plants and even more synthetic substances that produce a variety of consciousness-altering effects and sensory disturbances

Harmful use a pattern of psychoactive substance use that is causing damage to health that may be physical or mental

Harm reduction there is less concern with interdiction and enforcement, and more focus on how to minimize harm to individuals who choose to use drugs, and to society at large from drug's collateral consequences; the underlying assumption is that drug use is not a crime, but an illness, and therefore something that a prison sentence will not solve

Harrison Narcotics Act passed in 1914 to regulate and tax drugs in an attempt to limit drug use

Hazardous use a pattern of substance use that increases the risk of harmful consequences for the user

Herbal supplements include naturally occurring substances, such as plant leaves or nuts, that have (or are thought to have) various health benefits, and that may have psychoactive effects

Herbicide eradication involves spraying herbicides from a small plane onto the illicit crops below

Heroin a semi-synthetic drug made by combining vinegar with morphine; available as a powder or tar, which is injected, snorted, or smoked

Hormone replacement therapy (HRT) used to treat the symptoms of menopause which include irregular menstruation, fatigue, depression, mood changes, decreased libido, anxiety, insomnia, hot flashes, and night sweats; HRT provides the body with hormones once the body's creation of these hormones has naturally slowed

Huffing occurs when chemicals are inhaled through just the mouth, or the mouth and nose

Illegal instrumental use the use of illegal drugs for socially approved purposes

Illegal recreational use the use of illegal drugs for recreational or pleasurable purposes

Incidence the frequency of drug use

Information Model a model of drug education suggesting that when you inform youth of the potential hazards of using drugs, they will use that information to avoid harm because it is believed that information leads to negative attitudes regarding drugs, which results in avoidance of drug use

Inhalants chemicals, including volatile solvents, fuels, propellants/aerosols, anesthetics, or nitrates, that individuals self-administer in order to produce psychoactive effects

Innovation according to Robert Merton, an individual who adopts illegitimate means to attain culturally approved goals

Instrumental drug use the use of drugs, not for the purpose of intoxication, but to engage in drug use to help achieve a goal

Interdiction the attempt to stop drugs from entering the United States, via air, land, or water

INTERPOL the largest international police organization in the world with 187 member countries; works within existing laws by attempting to prevent international crime, including global drug crime

Knock and talk strategy in which law enforcement will arrive at the home of a suspected drug offender and use the element of surprise; they request permission to enter the home after identifying themselves and begin asking questions and asserting allegations about drug offenses, often the offense the officers allege is much more severe than the offense they actually suspect is occurring, and in an effort to "prove their innocence," the homeowners consent to a search of the home

Labeling results in an individual being stigmatized by conventional society, which results in a negative reaction, which frequently fuels the individual's return to the behavior in question

Legal instrumental use the use of either OTC drugs or prescription drugs for socially approved purposes

Legalization this approach to drug policy calls for the creation, distribution, sale, and use of drugs to become legal under a system of governmental regulation (in a way similar to how alcohol is legal in the United States)

Legal recreational use the consumption of legal drugs for recreational or pleasurable purposes

Libertarian a policy initiative suggesting that the government should not control individual behavior regardless of whether or not an individual's behavior is self-destructive

LSD mimics natural serotonin, thereby activating serotonin receptors within the brain; possibly the most potent psychoactive drug known

Macro-sociological theory a theory that focuses on structural issues that shape the whole of society such as strain theory, cultural deviance theory, and conflict theory

Manual crop eradication involves removing the plants from the ground and destroying them, usually by burning

Manufacturing laws prohibit the production of illegal substances

Marihuana Tax Act passed in 1937, the act required a special tax for all marijuana transactions and was modeled after the Harrison Narcotics Act

Marijuana the most commonly used illicit drug in the United States; the largest cash crop in the nation; a preparation of leafs from the cannabis plant that is most typically smoked; it can be consumed in the form of a marijuana cigarette (joint) or rolled in cigar paper (blunt)

Media a wide-ranging group of enterprises that include television, magazines, movies, documentaries, books, newspapers, advertising, information provided by the government, as well as information provided on the Internet

Medicalization seeks to hand responsibility to physicians for treating drug abusers (including whether or not to have the individual remain on the drug as part of treatment)

Metabolic theory suggests that the use of a particular drug for some people results in metabolic change and that this change leads to an almost visceral, chronic, and residual need for the drug

Methadone maintenance a type of pharmacological treatment; involves the use of methadone to treat opiate addiction; a user is "maintained" on methadone so they will not engage in heroin (or other opium) use

Methadone treatment users are stabilized at the same dose over an extended period of time, and some users can eventually be entirely weaned off the drug; those who begin methadone treatment with the goal of being drug-free are usually weaned within 3 weeks; if the treatment extends past that point, it is considered methadone maintenance

Methamphetamine a synthetic drug that can be created using legal substances; stimulants are thought to affect monoamine neurotransmitters within the brain, blocking the reuptake of dopamine, norepinephrine, and serotonin, while also largely increasing the release of dopamine

Micro-sociological theory a theory that focuses on social interaction patterns in specific situations such as social reaction theory, social learning theory, and social control theory

Misuse consumption of a substance not consistent with legal or medical guidelines, as in nonmedical use of prescription medications

Mixed model describes an agriculturally grown substance that is then synthesized into a chemical for consumption (example: heroin)

Monitoring the Future (MTF) a survey conducted on a national sample of high school students to assess their use of illicit substances, as well as their views on drug availability, risks of use, and approval or disapproval of substance use

Moral panic is when a person or group of persons becomes defined as a threat, usually through stereotypical representation by the media, to society at large. This frequently results in legislative changes targeting this group of individuals

Mule a courier of drugs, very often a female

Narcoterrorism a type of terrorism in which terrorist groups are involved directly in the cultivation, manufacture, transportation, and/or distribution of illicit substances

National Survey on Drug Use and Health (NSDUH) a project that involves face-to-face interviews with approximately 70,000 individuals ages 12 and older across the United States on a yearly basis to ask participants about their involvement with illicit drugs

Needle exchange a harm reduction initiative that began in Europe in the 1980s in an effort to decrease among intravenous drug users the spread of HIV/AIDS, Hepatitis B and C, as well as more than twenty other blood-borne infections carried in a hypodermic needle; most programs allow users to drop off dirty needles in exchange for clean needles

Negative reinforcement occurs when a behavior is followed by the removal of an aversive stimuli and the behavior also increases

Neurochemical theory suggests that the use of a particular drug for some people results in neurochemical change and that this change leads to an almost visceral, chronic, and residual need for the drug

Nicotine a mood-altering drug; a volatile alkaloid found in tobacco leafs; known to occur naturally only in tobacco, and is partly destroyed when cigarettes are burned

Objective frame of reference seeks to distinguish drugs by their physical or chemical properties and/or actions through the use of a classification scheme

Office of National Drug Control Policy (ONDCP) created with the Anti-Drug Abuse of 1988 to establish priorities and objectives for the nation's drug control program

Opiates naturally occurring from the opium poppy plant and are used in manufacturing the depressants morphine, codeine, and heroin

Opioids synthetic drugs with the characteristics of opiates

Outpatient treatment the less intense outpatient programs are more educationally focused and can be beneficial to individuals who may not have a life-crippling addiction, but still struggle with substance abuse; the more intense programs are heavily focused on educating the addict, but they also strive to provide patients with a supportive environment and guidance in recommending additional supportive resources to assist in treatment

Partnership for a Drug-Free America (PFDFA) a nonprofit organization which has been integral in the prevention and treatment of drug use among youth in the United States through the use of public service announcements

PCP a dissociative anesthetic which acts on a receptor in the brain that affects glutamate (a neurotransmitter) to produce effects similar to surgical anesthetics, yet the user remains semiconscious

Peyote a cactus growing in northern Mexico and Texas; the entire cactus is psychoactive, however the most powerful psychoactive ingredient is called mescaline and is found in the top of the plant

Pharmacological definition of drugs articles intended for use in the diagnosis, cure, mitigation, treatment, or prevention of diseases, and articles intended to affect the structure or function of the body of man or other animals

Pharmacological treatment uses drugs to counteract the symptoms of withdrawal from narcotics as a form of therapy usually (but not always) in combination with a particular form of behavioral therapy rehabilitation

Physiological dependence symptoms resulting from habitual and prolonged use of particular drugs

Placebo effect many people experience drug actions and effects subjectively; in other words, they experience the effects they expect or believe will occur

Positive reinforcement occurs when a behavior is followed by pleasant stimuli and the behavior then increases

Possession laws prohibit individuals, without a valid prescription, from possessing illegal substances in their home, car, or on their person

Prevalence the number of individuals who engage in drug use

Primary prevention programs drug education programs that are built on the foundation that individuals are less likely to engage in drug use and abuse if the positive aspects of their life are enhanced and risk factors for drug use are diminished

Prison-based treatment could be any type of substance abuse treatment but takes place within a prison setting and is mandated, not voluntary

Project FAST a qualitative study of female drug users in Atlanta to identify the impacts of drug use on women and to explore how social surroundings influence habits of use

Prom Promise a pledge that some students around the United States have taken to not consume alcohol or drugs on their prom night

Psilocybin a serotonergic hallucinogen which mimics natural serotonin, and thereby activates serotonin receptors within the brain; more commonly referred to as "magic mushrooms" or "shrooms"; there are about one hundred mushroom species containing psilocybin

Psychedelics (also known as hallucinogens) a complex group of drugs consisting of over ninety naturally occurring plants and even more synthetic substances that produce a variety of consciousness-altering effects and sensory disturbances

Psychoactive (psychotropic) drugs substances that act upon the nervous system, specifically the central nervous system (CNS) or cerebrospinal axis to affect the mind, moods, and/or behavior

Psychoanalytical approach an approach that suggests that traumatic experiences such as physical and sexual abuse, neglect, and even mild family dysfunction can lead to attempts to medicate the resulting emotional problems

Psychological theories examines the psychodynamic processes and explains drug use and addiction in terms of individual characteristics and experiences

Psychopharmacological explanations provide explanations for drug-related crimes, suggesting that drugs have psychological and physical reactions that increase the likelihood of users getting involved in crime

Public service announcements television or radio spots, print or billboard advertisements, or the like, that advocate anti-drug attitudes and behaviors, typically using an integrated approach to work toward the prevention and reduction of illicit drug use among youth, and seek to support parents in their efforts to keep youth drug free

Pure agricultural model a drug produced using this type of model involves minimal manufacturing and no synthetic production; the drug is harvested and consumed in nearly its natural state (example: marijuana)

Pure chemical model a drug produced using this type of model is created synthetically from start to finish, and does not have an agricultural product as its origin (example: LSD)

Pure Food and Drug Act initially enacted in 1906 to regulate how substances, whether food or drug, were packaged and distributed in order to enhance their safety and to prevent fraudulent marketing

Quackery the business that promotes useless remedies as "cures" for medical ailments

Qualitative participant observation research a type of research method that seeks to capture social life as participants experience it, rather than in categories predetermined by the researcher, and usually involves some participation by the researcher with the group of individuals under study

Racial profiling the use of race or ethnic guidelines, as opposed to behavioral indicators, in the creation of a profiling system for the war on drugs

Rates illustrate the number of individuals using drugs per a certain unit of the population

Rebellion according to Robert Merton, an individual who substitutes alternative goals and means for conventional ones

Recreational drug use the consumption of substances for the purposes of intoxication or getting high

Reinforcement theories based on classical behavioral theories of conditioning and are concerned with the transition from drug use to drug addiction, with a special interest in explaining long-term addiction to street drugs

Residential treatment often referred to as the therapeutic community; the goal of residential treatment programs focuses on the resocialization of people into a life without drugs

Retreatist according to Robert Merton, an individual who is repeatedly unable to attain the culturally approved goals through legitimate means and who does not possess the capability to adopt illegitimate methods

Reverse sting an undercover officer acts as a drug dealer and drug users are arrested after they make a purchase

Ritualism according to Robert Merton, an individual who participates in the socially prescribed means without accepting the goals of society

Rockefeller Drug Laws put forth by Governor Nelson Rockefeller (NY) in 1973 and created mandatory minimum sentencing laws that were intended to crack down on high-level drug offenders, with no consideration given to the offender's circumstances or role in the drug industry during sentencing

Routes of administration the particular method in which a drug is ingested into the body

Secondary prevention programs once an individual begins using drugs, the focus of drug education must become early identification of use and intervention before use of drugs turns into abuse and addiction

Shanghai Opium Commission a group of thirteen nations that met in 1909 to devise a plan for the international control of narcotics

Single Convention on Narcotic Drugs an international treaty among signatory nations to limit to medical and scientific purposes by legal authority more than one hundred drugs and to standardize national drug control laws

Sniffing occurs when chemicals are inhaled through the nose

Social control theory suggests that human behavior is controlled through close associations with institutions and individuals

Social Influence Model a drug education model (also called the drug resistance education model) suggesting that youth are extremely susceptible to peer pressure and must be taught the skills to make rational decisions to avoid the use of drugs; as such, once youth are armed with rational decision-making skills, they can resist the temptations, both internal and external, and not succumb to drug use (e.g., DARE)

Social learning theory asserts that criminal behavior and deviance is learned through human interaction

Social reaction theory also called labeling theory; asserts that some people are labeled negatively by the larger society or those in the criminal justice system, and this negative labeling process results in the individual being shunned and treated differently by conventional society

Sociological theories approaches the use of drugs as a phenomenon embedded in the structural elements of society and believes that social and cultural factors influence our attitudes toward all elements of the drug issue

Strain theory asserts that sharp divisions between the classes creates an atmosphere of envy and mistrust that may lead to deviant behavior

Students Against Destructive Decisions (SADD) formerly known as Students Against Drunk Driving is a nationwide peer organization which seeks to prepare young adults to make responsible decisions for the prevention of underage alcohol and drug use and drunk or impaired driving

Students Against Drunk Driving now called Students Against Destructive Decisions (SADD); it is a nationwide peer organization which seeks to prepare young adults to make responsible decisions for the prevention of underage alcohol and drug use and drunk or impaired driving

Subjective frame of reference challenges us to think about the particular meanings we attach to drugs

Substance abuse (drug abuse) terminology to distinguish acceptable drug use from unacceptable drug use, short of compulsive or addictive drug use

Substance Abuse and Mental Health Services Administration (SAHMSA) uses action-oriented methods to strive toward prevention and early intervention programs in local communities

Summary forfeiture when illegal property is seized by law enforcement on the grounds that one cannot "own" something that is illegal

Systemic explanations suggest that the illegal nature of substances and the underground economy surrounding drug trafficking and selling results in crime as dealers must "settle scores" on their own without legal protection

Systems perspective an interdisciplinary theory that can be applied to the functioning of a family (the family systems perspective is frequently utilized in family therapy); the systems perspective views the family as one functioning unit made up of various parts that affect each other and work together to maintain a certain balance or equilibrium

Temporal disintegration the short-term memory disruption associated with the use of cannabis in which the ability to remember and coordinate information is lost

Tertiary prevention programs treatment programs directed at those individuals already addicted to drugs; focused on rehabilitative efforts and the road to sobriety

Tolerance the need for increasing amounts of a drug to achieve the same intoxicating effects

Treatment Alternatives to Street Crime (TASC) linked treatment and the criminal justice process and was the beginning of the movement toward the creation of drug courts

Undercover buy an undercover officer seeks to purchase drugs and the seller is arrested either immediately or after a period of monitoring by law enforcement

Withdrawal when a person uses large amounts of certain drugs for an extended period of time and then experiences a set of physical symptoms when use is reduced dramatically or stopped abruptly

Zero tolerance policies on school grounds, these policies result in the suspension or expulsion of students for use, possession, or distribution of drugs while on school property

REFERENCES

Abadinsky, H. (2008). *Drug use and abuse: A comprehensive introduction* (6th ed.). Belmont, CA: Thomson Wadsworth.

Abramson, J. (2005). *Overdosed America: The broken promise of American medicine.* New York, NY: Harper Perennial Press.

Ackerman, A. (Director). (1996, February 15). *Seinfeld: The showerhead* [Sitcom: Season 7, Episode 126]. Available from Motion Picture Ventures.

Ackerman, D. L. (1995). Drug testing. In R. H. Coombs & D. Ziedonis (Eds.), *Handbook on drug abuse prevention: A comprehensive strategy to prevent the abuse of alcohol and other drugs* (pp. 473–489). Boston, MA: Allyn & Bacon.

Adrian, M. (2003). How can sociological theory help our understanding of addictions? *Substance Use and Misuse, 38*(10), 1385–1423.

Ads Spur Urge For Drugs. (2008, February 6). *Los Angeles Times.* Retrieved February 18, 2009, from http://articles.latimes.com/2008/feb/06/business/fi-lazarus6

Akers, R., & Lee, G. (1996). A longitudinal test of social learning theory: Adolescent smoking. *Journal of Drug Issues, 26*, 317–343.

American Psychological Association. (1952). *Diagnostic and statistical manual of mental disorders: DSM-I.* Washington, DC: Author.

American Psychological Association. (1962). *Diagnostic and statistical manual of mental disorders: DSM-II* (2nd ed.). Washington, DC: Author.

American Psychological Association. (1986). *Diagnostic and statistical manual of mental disorders: DSM-III-R* (3rd ed.). Washington, DC: Author.

American Psychological Association. (1994). *Diagnostic and statistical manual of mental disorders: DSM-IV* (4th ed.). Washington, DC: Author.

Anderson, E. (1999). *Code of the street: Decency, violence, and the moral life of the inner city.* New York, NY: W. W. Norton & Company.

Anglin, M. D., & Hser, Y.-I. (1990). Treatment of drug abuse. In M. Tonry & J. Q. Wilson (Eds.), *Drugs and crime* (pp. 393–460). Chicago, IL: University of Chicago Press.

Anglin, M. D., & McGlothlin, W. (1985). Methadone maintenance in California: A decade's experience. In L. Brill & C. Winick (Eds.), *The yearbook of substance use and abuse* (pp. 219–280). New York, NY: Human Services Press.

Anglin, M. D., & Westland, C. A. (1989). Drug monitoring in the workplace: Results from the California commercial laboratory drug testing project. In S. W. Gust & J. M. Walsh (Eds.), *Drugs in the workplace: Research and evaluation data* (pp. 81–96). Rockville, MD: National Institute on Drug Abuse.

Argentina Court Ruling Would Allow Personal Use of Pot. (2009, August 25). *CNN.* Retrieved September 1, 2009, from http://www.cnn.com/2009/WORLD/americas/08/25/argentina.drug.decriminalization/index.html

Armor, D. J., Polich, J. M., & Stambul, H. B. (1978). *Alcohol and treatment.* New York, NY: Wiley.

Arrestee Drug Abuse Monitoring. (2003). *2000 arrestee drug abuse monitoring: Annual report* (NCJ 193013). Washington, DC: US Department of Justice.

Asper, K. (2006). Characteristics of adult children of alcoholics. *Center for Substance Abuse Prevention Eye on Prevention Newsletter, 4.* Retrieved August 23, 2009, from http://captus.samhsa.gov/central/documents/4AdultChildrenofAlcoholics.pdf

Baggins, D. S., (1998). *Drug hate and the corruption of American justice.* Westport, CT: Praeger Press.

Ball, J. C., Rosen, L., Flueck, J. A., & Nurco, D. N. (1981). The criminality of heroin addicts: When addicted and when off opiates. In J. A. Inciardi (Ed.), *The drugs-crime connection* (pp. 39–65). Beverly Hills, CA: Sage Publications.

Barak, G., Leighton, P., & Flavin, J. (2007). *Class, race, gender, and crime* (2nd ed.). Lanham, MD: Rowman & Littlefield.

Bard, M., & Zacker, J. (1974). Assaultiveness and alcohol use in family disputes: Police perceptions. *Criminology, 12*, 281–292.

Bateman, N. I., & Peterson, D. M. (1971). Variables related to outcome of treatment for hospitalized alcoholics. *International Journal of Addictions, 6*, 215–224.

Baum, D. (1996). *Smoke and mirrors: The war on drugs and the politics of failure.* Boston, MA: Little Brown.

Becker, H. S. (1953). Becoming a marihuana user. *American Journal of Sociology, 59*, 235–242.

Becker, H. S. (1963). *The outsiders: Studies in the sociology of deviance.* New York, NY: The Free Press.

Best, J. (2001). *Damned lies and statistics: Untangling numbers from the media, politicians, and activists.* Berkeley, CA: University of California Press.

Best, J. (2004). *More damned lies and statistics: How numbers confuse public issues.* Berkeley, CA: University of California Press.

Best, J. (2008). *Social problems.* New York, NY: W.W. Norton & Company.

Bien, T. H., & Burge, R. (1990). Smoking and drinking: A review of the literature. *International Journal of the Addictions, 25*, 1429–1454.

Birth-Control Pill Lands Fairfax Girl 2-Week Suspension. (2009, April 5). *The Washington Post.* Retrieved June 24, 2009, from http://www.washingtonpost.com/wp-dyn/content/article/2009/04/04/AR2009040402591.html

Black Markets for ADD Drugs Exist on College Campuses. (2006, February 27). *Youth Radio.* Retrieved August 3, 2009, from http://www.pbs.org/newshour/extra/speakout/mystory/add_2-24.html

Blumer, H., Sutter, A., Ahmed, S., & Smith, R. (1967). *Add center project final report: The world of youthful drug use.* Berkeley, CA: University of California Press.

Bonds Exposed. (2006, March 7). *Sports Illustrated.* Retrieved July 27, 2009, from http://sportsillustrated.cnn.com/2006/baseball/mlb/03/06/news.excerpt/index.html

Bourgois, P. (1995). *In search of respect: Selling crack in El Barrio.* New York, NY: Cambridge University Press.

Bradshaw, J. (1988). *Bradshaw on the family.* Deerfield Beach, FL: Health Communications, Inc.

Briddel, D. W., Rimm, D. C., Caddy, G. R., Dorawitz, G., Sholis, D., & Wunderlin, R. J. (1978). Effects of alcohol and cognitive set on sexual arousal to deviant stimuli. *Journal of Abnormal Psychology, 87*, 418–430.

Brocato, J., & Wagner, E. F. (2003). Harm reduction: A social work practice model and social justice agenda. *Health & Social Work, 28*(2), 117–125.

Bureau of Justice Statistics. (1992). *Drugs, crime, and the justice system* (NCJ 133652). Washington, DC: U.S. Department of Justice.

Bureau of Justice Statistics. (1998). *Alcohol and crime* (NCJ 168362). Washington, DC: U.S. Department of Justice.

Bureau of Justice Statistics. (1999). *Women offenders* (NCJ 175688). Washington, DC: U.S. Department of Justice.

Bureau of Justice Statistics. (2006). *Intimate partner violence in the U.S.* Retrieved August 9, 2009, from http://www.ojp.usdoj.gov/bjs/intimate/ipv.htm

Bureau of Justice Statistics. (2007). *Drugs and crime facts* (NCJ 165148). Washington, DC: U.S. Department of Justice.

Burns, T. F. (1980). Getting rowdy with the boys. *Journal of Drug Issues, 10*, 273–286.

Caetano, R., Vaeth, P. A. C., & Ramisetty-Milder, S. (2008). Intimate partner violence victim and perpetrator characteristics among couples in the United States. *Journal of Family Violence, 23*, 507–518.

Califano, J. A., Jr. (1999). Least among us: Children of substance-abusing parents. *America, 180*(14), 10–12.

Califano, J. A., Jr., & Sheehan, M. J. (2002, February 11). Religion, science and substance abuse: Why priests and psychiatrists should get their acts together. *America, 186*(4), 8–11.

Campbell, N. D. (2000). *Using women: Gender, drug policy, and social justice.* New York, NY: Routledge.

Canseco, J. (2006). *Juiced: Wild times, rampant 'roids, smash hits, and how baseball got big.* New York, NY: IT Books.

Carpenter, T. G. (2005). A blueprint for peace: Ending the war on drugs. In L. E. Huggins (Ed.), *Drug war deadlock: The policy battle continues* (pp. 273–285). Stanford, CA: Hoover Institution Press.

Caulkins, J. P., Pacula, R. L., Paddock, S., & Chiesna, J. (2004). What we can—and cannot—expect from school-based drug prevention. *Drug and Alcohol Review, 23*, 79–87.

Centers for Disease Control and Prevention. (2002a). Annual smoking-attributable mortality, years of potential life lost, and economic costs—United States, 1995–1999. *Morbidity and Mortality Weekly Report, 51*(14), 300–303.

Centers for Disease Control and Prevention. (2002b, February). Methadone maintenance treatment. *IDU-HIV Prevention.* Retrieved March 29, 2010, from http://www.cdc.gov/IDU/facts/MethadoneFin.pdf

Centers for Disease Control and Prevention. (2004). Use of contraception and use of family planning services in the United States: 1982–2002. *Advanced Data from Vital Health and Statistics, 350.* Retrieved March 29, 2010, from http://www.cdc.gov/nchs/data/ad/ad350.pdf

Centers for Disease Control and Prevention. (2007). *Quick stats: General information on alcohol use and health.* Retrieved August 29, 2009, from http://www.cdc.gov/Alcohol/quickstats/general_info.htm

Centers for Disease Control and Prevention. (2008). Screening high school students for eating disorders: Results of a national initiative. *Preventing Chronic Disease, 5*(4). Retrieved March 29, 2010, from http://www.cdc.gov/pcd/issues/2008/

Centers for Disease Control and Prevention. (2009a). Alcohol use among pregnant and nonpregnant women of childbearing age: United States, 1991–2005. *Morbidity and Mortality Weekly Report, 58*(19), 529–532.

Centers for Disease Control and Prevention. (2009b). *Fetal alcohol spectrum disorders.* Retrieved August 29, 2009, from http://www.cdc.gov/ncbddd/fas

Chadwick, M. J., Gregory, D. L., & Wendling, G. (1990). A double-blind amino acids, l-tryptophan and l-tyrosine, and placebo study with cocaine-dependent subjects in an inpatient chemical dependency treatment center. *American Journal of Drug and Alcohol Abuse, 16*(3/4), 275–286.

Clay, R. A. (2004). Peer-to-peer program promotes recovery. *SAMHSA News, 12*, 1–4.

Clinard, M., & Meier, R. (1998). *Sociology of deviant behavior.* New York, NY: Harcourt Brace.

Cloninger, C. R., Bohman, M., & Sigvardsson, S. (1981). Inheritance of alcohol abuse: Cross-fostering analysis of adopted men. *Archives of General Psychiatry, 38*, 861–868.

Cohen, J. (1996). Drug education: Politics, propaganda and censorship. *The International Journal of Drug Policy, 7*(3). Retrieved from March 29, 2010, http://www.drugtext.org/library/articles/96733.htm

Cohen, S. (1972). *Folk devils and moral panics: The creation of the mods and rockers.* London: MacGibbon and Kee.

Cole, S. G., & James, L. R. (1975). A revised treatment typology based on DARP. *American Journal of Drug and Alcohol Abuse, 2*, 37–49.

Collins, R. L., Ellickson, P. L., & Klein, D. J. (2007). The role of substance use in young adult divorce. *Addiction, 102*, 786–794.

Committee on Armed Services. (1988). *The role of the military in drug interdiction.* Washington, DC: U.S. Government Printing Office.

Court Says Strip Search of Child Illegal. (2009, June 25). *USA Today.* Retrieved June 25, 2009, from http://www.usatoday.com/news/washington/judicial/2009-06-25-scotus-strip-search_N.htm

Curb Aids and HIV by Decriminalising Drugs, Say Experts. (2009). *Guardian: The Observer.* Retrieved July 12, 2009, from http://www.guardian.co.uk/world/2009/apr/19/drugs-decriminalisation-aids

Currie, E. (1993). *Reckoning: Drugs, the cities, and the American future.* New York, NY: Farrar, Straus, and Giroux.

Curtis, R. (1999). The ethnographic approach to studying drug crime. In *Looking at crime from the street level: Plenary papers of the 1999 conference on criminal justice research and evaluation—Enhancing policy and practice through research* (NCJ 178260). Washington, DC: U.S. Department of Justice.

Cussen, M., & Block, W. (2000). Legalize drugs now! An analysis of the benefits of legalized drugs. *American Journal of Economics and Sociology, 59*(3), 525–536.

Date Rape Drugs Explained and De-mystified. (n.d.). *About.com.* Retrieved July 23, 2009, from http://teenadvice.about.com/library/weekly/aa062502a.htm

Death Highlights Drug's Lethal Allure to Doctors. (1995, November 11). *New York Times.* Retrieved June 22, 2009, from http://www.nytimes.com/1995/11/11/nyregion/death-highlights-drug-s-lethalal-lure-to-doctors.html

Decker, S. H., & Chapman, M. T. (2008). *Drug smugglers on drug smuggling: Lessons from the inside.* Philadelphia, PA: Temple University Press.

Delbanco, A., & Delbanco, T. (1995, March 20). A. A. at the crossroads. *New Yorker,* 50–63.

De Leon, G. (1986). Program-based evaluation research in therapeutic communities. In F. M. Tims & J. P. Ludford (Eds.), *Drug abuse treatment evaluations: Strategies, progress, and prospects* (pp. 69–87). Rockville, MD: National Institute on Drug Abuse.

Dole, V. P. (1994). Methadone maintenance: Optimizing dosage by estimating plasma level. *Journal of Addictive Diseases, 13*(1), 1–4.

Domestic Council Task Force on Drug Abuse. (1975). *White paper on drug abuse: A report to the President from the Domestic Council Task Force on Drug Abuse.* Washington, DC: U.S. Government Printing Office.

Donohue, J., Cevasco, M., & Rosenthal, M. B. (2007). A decade of direct-to-consumer advertising of prescription drugs. *The New England Journal of Medicine, 357*(7), 673–681.

Drug Abuse Warning Network. (2002). *Development of a new design: Methodology report* (SMA 02-3754). Rockville, MD: Substance Abuse and Mental Health Services Administration, Office of Applied Studies.

Drug Abuse Warning Network. (2003). *Emergency department trends from the Drug Abuse Warning Network, final estimates 1995–2002* (SMA 03-3780). Rockville, MD: Substance Abuse and Mental Health Services Administration, Office of Applied Studies.

Drug Abuse Warning Network. (2005). *Area profiles of drug-related mortality, 2003* (SMA 05-4023). Rockville, MD: Substance Abuse and Mental Health Services Administration, Office of Applied Studies.

Drug Abuse Warning Network. (2006). *National estimates of drug-related emergency department visits, 2004* (SMA 06-4143). Rockville, MD: Substance Abuse and Mental Health Services Administration, Office of Applied Studies.

Drug Enforcement Administration (DEA). (2005). *Drugs of abuse.* Washington, DC: Department of Justice. Retrieved February 25, 2010, from http://www.justice.gov/dea/pubs/abuse/doa-p.pdf

Drug Enforcement Administration. (2006). *Guidelines for law enforcement for the cleanup for clandestine drug laboratories.* Washington, DC: Department of Justice. Retrieved August 1, 2009, from http://www.usdoj.gov/dea/resources/redbook.pdf

Drug Free Federal Workplace. (1986, September 15). *The National Archives.* Retrieved June 23, 2009, from http://www.archives.gov/federal-register/codification/executive-order/12564.html

Drug Law Denies Aid to Thousands. (2005, September 28). *Inside Higher Ed.* Retrieved June 19, 2009, from http://www.insidehighered.com/news/2005/09/28/drug

Drug Policy Alliance Network. (2009). *Drugs police and the law: Police corruption.* Retrieved August 30, 2009, from http://www.drugpolicy.org/law/police/

Drugs, Y. & the Internet. (2002). *Heroin/Opiates* (#2002-R0430-002). Washington, DC: U.S. Department of Justice.

Dukes, R. L., Stein, J. A., & Ullman, J. B. (1997). Long-term impacts of Drug Abuse Resistance Education (D.A.R.E.). *Evaluation Review, 21*(4), 483–500.

Ellickson, P. L. (1995). Schools. In Robert H. Coombs & D. Ziedonis (Eds.), *Handbook on Drug Prevention* (pp. 93–120). Boston, MA: Allyn & Bacon.

Erlen, J., & Spillane, J. F. (Eds.). (2004). *Federal drug control: The evolution of policy and practice.* New York, NY: Haworth Press.

Eyrich-Garg, K. M., Cacciola, J. S., Carise, D., Lynch, K. G., & McLellan, A. T. (2008). Individual characteristics of the literally homeless, marginally housed, and impoverished in a U.S. substance abuse treatment-seeking sample. *Social Psychiatry and Psychiatric Epidemiology, 43*(10), 831–842.

Fagan, J. (1989). The social organization of drug use and drug dealing among urban gangs. *Criminology, 27,* 633–669.

Fagan, J. (1990). Intoxication and aggression. In M. Tonry & J. Q. Wilson (Eds.), *Drugs and crime* (pp. 241–320). Chicago, IL: University of Chicago Press.

Fagan, J. (1994). Women and drugs revisited: Female participation in the cocaine economy. *Journal of Drug Issues, 24,* 179–225.

Fals-Stewart, W., & Clinton-Sherrod, M. (2009). Treating intimate partner violence among substance-abusing dyads: The effect of couples therapy. *Professional Psychology, 40*(3), 257–263.

Fan, D. (1996). News media framing sets public opinion that drugs is the country's most important problem. *Substance Use and Misuse, 31,* 1413–1421.

Farrell, G. (1998). A global empirical review of drug crop eradication and United Nations crop substitution and alternative development strategies. *Journal of Drug Issues, 28,* 395–437.

Faupel, C. E., Horowitz, A. M., & Weaver, G. S. (2004). *The sociology of American drug use.* New York, NY: McGraw-Hill.

Federal Bureau of Investigation. (2006). *Crime in the United States: Uniform Crime Report 2000.* Retrieved September 4, 2009, from http://www.fbi.gov/ucr/cius_00/contents.pdf

Federal Drug and Cosmetics Act. (1938). Pub L. No. 717, 52 Stat. 1040. Retrieved February 27, 2010, from http://www.fda.gov/RegulatoryInformation/Legislation/FederalFoodDrugandCosmeticAct FDCAct/ucm086299.htm

Fenner, A., & Moore, T. (2006, December 3). The meth menace: Easy and addictive drug is creeping up social ladder. *Daily News.* Retrieved February 27, 2010, from http://www.nydailynews.com/archives/news/2006/12/03/2006-12-03_the_meth_menace__easy___addi.html

Fields, Richard. (2010). *Drugs in perspective: Causes, assessment, family, prevention, intervention, and treatment* (7th ed.). New York, NY: McGraw-Hill.

Finally: New York Repeals Rockefeller Drug Laws. (2009, March 31). *New York Times.* Retrieved August 26, 2009, from http://www.observer.com/2009/finally-new-york-repeals-rockefeller-drug-laws#

Finestone, H. (1967). Narcotics and criminality. *Law and Contemporary Problems, 22,* 60–85.

Finigan, M., Carey, S. M., & Cox, A. (2007). *The impact of a mature drug court over 10 years of operation: Recidivism and costs.* Portland, OR: NPC Research, Inc.

Finn, R. (2004). Alcohol dependence: No magic treatment bullets: Add psychosocial therapy. *Family Practice News, 34,* 22.

Fishbein, M., Hall-Jamieson, K., Zimmer, E., von Haeften, I., & Nabi, R. (2002). Avoiding the boomerang: Testing the relative effectiveness of antidrug public service announcements before a national campaign. *American Journal of Public Health, 92,* 238–245.

Food and Drug Administration. (2009). *FDA 101: Health fraud awareness.* Retrieved February 1, 2009, from http://www.fda.gov/downloads/ForConsumers/ProtectYourself/HealthFraud/UCM167504.pdf

Friedman, M. (2005). There's no justice in the war on drugs. In L. E. Huggins (Ed.), *Drug war deadlock: The policy battle continues* (pp. 77–80). Stanford, CA: Hoover Institution Press.

Gagnon, M. A., & Lexchin, J. (2008). The cost of pushing pills: A new estimate of pharmaceutical promotion expenditures in the United States. *PloS Medicine.* Retrieved July 27, 2009, from http://www.plosmedicine.org/article/info:doi/10.1371/journal.pmed.0050001

Gahlinger, P. M. (2001). *Illegal drugs: A complete guide to their history, chemistry, use and abuse.* Salt Lake City, UT: Sagebrush Press.

Gaines, L. K., & Kraska, P. B. (Eds.). (2003). *Drugs, crime, and justice: Contemporary perspectives* (2nd ed.). Prospect Heights, IL: Waveland Press.

Ganguly, K. (2004). Opium use in Rajasthan, India: A socio-cultural perspective. In R. Coomber & N. South (Eds.), *Drug use and cultural contexts: Beyond the West* (pp. 83–100). London: Free Association Press.

Garrett, J., Stanton, M. D., Landau, J., Hbaciewica, G., Brinkman-Sull, D., & Shea, R. (1999). The 'concerned other' call: Using family links and networks to overcome resistance to addiction treatment. *Substance Use and Misuse, 34,* 363–382.

Gawin, F. H. (1991). Cocaine addiction: Psychology and neurophysiology. *Science, 251,* 1580–1586.

Gieringer, D. (1992). Urinalysis or uromancy? The untold costs of drug testing abuse. In A. S. Trebach,

K. B. Zeese, & K. E. Wring (Eds.), *Strategies for change: New directions in drug policy* (pp. 121–139). Washington, DC: Drug Policy Foundation.

Gilliom, J. (1994). *Surveillance, privacy, and the law.* Ann Arbor, MI: University of Michigan Press.

Glassner, B. (1999). *The culture of fear: Why Americans are afraid of the wrong things: Crime, drugs, minorities, teen moms, killer kids, mutant microbes, plane crashes, road rage, and so much more.* New York, NY: Basic Books.

Goldberg, R. (2006). *Drugs across the spectrum* (5th ed.). Belmont, CA: Thomson Wadsworth.

Goldberg, R. (Ed.). (2008). *Taking sides: Clashing views in drugs and society* (8th ed.). Boston, MA: McGraw-Hill.

Goldstein, P. (1985). The drug/violence nexus: A tripartite conceptual framework. *Journal of Drug Issues, 14,* 493–506.

Goldstein, P., Brownstein, H. H., & Ryan, P. J. (1992). Drug-related homicide in New York: 1984 and 1988. *Crime and Delinquency, 38,* 459–476.

Golub, A., Johnson, B. D., & Dunlap, E. (2007). The race/ethnicity disparity in misdemeanor marijuana arrests in New York City. *Criminology and Public Policy, 6*(1), 131–164.

Goode, E. (1999). *Drugs in American Society* (5th ed.). New York, NY: McGraw Hill.

Goode, E. (2008). *Drugs in American society* (7th ed.). New York, NY: McGraw Hill.

Goode, E., & Ben-Yehuda, N. (1994). *Moral panics: The social construction of deviance.* Malden, MA: Blackwell Publishing.

Goodwin, D. W., Schulsinger, F., Hermansten, L., Guze, S. B., & Winokur, G. (1973). Alcohol problems in adoptees raised apart from alcoholic biological parents. *Archives of General Psychiatry, 28,* 238–243.

Gordon, J. R., & Barrett, K. (1993). The codependency movement: Issues of context and differentiation. In J. S. Baer, G. A. Marlatt, & R. J. McMahon (Eds.), *Addictive behaviors across the life span* (pp. 307–339). Newbury Park, CA: Sage Publications.

Gorman, D. M. (2003). The failure of drug education. In L. K. Gaines & P. B. Kraska (Eds.), *Drugs, crime, & justice: Contemporary perspectives* (2nd ed., pp. 310–317). Prospect Heights, IL: Waveland Press.

Government Accountability Office. (2002). *Prescription drugs: FDA oversight of direct-to-consumer advertising has limitations.* Washington, DC: GAO-03-177.

Government Accountability Office. (2006). *Prescription drugs: Improvements needed in FDA's oversight of direct-to-consumer.* Washington, DC: GAO-07-54.

Gray, J. P. (2001). *Why our drug laws have failed and what we can do about it.* Philadelphia, PA: Temple University Press.

Grilly, D. M. (2006). *Drugs and human behavior* (5th ed.). Boston: Pearson Allyn & Bacon.

Grinspoon, L. (2000). Marijuana should be legalized for medical purposes. In S. Barbour (Ed.), *Drug legalization* (pp. 142–149). San Diego, CA: Greenhaven Press.

Gusfield, J. (1963). *Symbolic crusade.* Urbana, IL: University of Illinois Press.

Hamid, A. (1998). *Drugs in America: Sociology, economics, and politics.* Gaithersburg, MD: Aspen Publishers.

Hanson, B., Beschner, G., Walters, J. M., & Bovelle, E. (1985). *Life with heroin.* Lexington, MA: Lexington Books.

Hanson, G. R., Venturelli, P. J., & Fleckenstein, A. E. (2006). *Drugs and society* (9th ed.). Sudbury, MA: Jones and Bartlett Publishers.

Hanson, M. (1993). Overview on drug and alcohol testing in the workplace. *Bulletin on Narcotics, 2,* 3–44.

Harper, R. L., Harper, G. C., & Stockdale, J. E. (2002). The role and sentencing of women in drug trafficking crime. *Legal and Criminological Psychology, 7*(1), 101–114.

Harrison, P. A., & Sidebottom, A. C. (2009). Alcohol and drug use before and during pregnancy: An examination of use patterns and predictors of cessation. *Journal of Maternal and Child Health, 13,* 386–394.

Hartjen, C. A., Mitchell, S. M., & Washburne, N. F. (1981). Sentencing to therapy: Some legal, ethical and practical issues. *Journal of Offender Counseling, Services and Rehabilitation, 6,* 21–39.

Hartwell, T. D., Steele, P. D., French, M. T., & Rodman, N. F. (1996). Prevalence of drug testing in the workplace. *Monthly Labor Review, 119*, 35–42.

Harwood, H. J., & Myers, T. G. (Eds.). (2004). *New treatments for addiction: Behavioral, ethical, legal, and social questions.* Washington, DC: National Academics Press.

Hawkins, J. D., Lishner, D. J., & Catalano, R. F. (1987). Childhood predictors and the prevention of adolescent substance abuse. In C. L. Jones & R. J. Battjes (Eds.), *Etiology of drug abuse* (pp. 75–126). Rockville, MD: National Institute on Drug Abuse.

Heath, A. C. (1995). Genetic influences on alcoholism risk: A review of adoption and twin studies. *Alcohol Health & Research World, 19*(3), 166–171.

Heath, A. C., & Martin, N. G. (1993). Genetic influences on alcohol consumption patterns and problem drinking: Results from the Australian NH and MRC twin panel follow-up survey. *Annals of New York Academy of Science, 708*, 72–85.

Helfer, M. E., Kempe, R. S., & Krugman, R. D. (1997). *The battered child* (5th ed.). Chicago, IL: The University of Chicago Press.

Hirsch, M. L., Conforti, R. W., & Graney, C. J. (1990). The use of marijuana for pleasure: A replication of Howard S. Becker's study of marijuana use. In J. W. Neuliep (Ed.), *Handbook of replication research in the behavioral and social sciences* (pp. 27–35). New York, NY: Select Press.

Hirschi, T. (1969). *Causes of delinquency.* Berkeley, CA: University of California Press.

Hodgins, E. F. (1981). *A life in our times.* Boston, MA: Houghton Mifflin Company.

Horney, K. (1964). *The neurotic personality of our time.* New York: W. W. Norton & Co.

Hornik, R., Maklan, D., Cadell, D., Prado, A., Barmada, C., Jacobsohn, L., et al. (2002). *Evaluation of the national youth anti-drug media campaign, fourth semi-annual report of findings.* Rockville, MD: Westat.

Huggins, L. E. (Ed.). (2005). *Drug war deadlock: The policy battle continues.* Stanford, CA: Hoover Institution Press.

Huh, J., & Langteau, R. (2007). Presumed influence of DTC prescription drug advertising: Do experts and novices think differently? *Communication Research, 34*(1), 25–52.

Human Rights Watch. (2000). *Racially disproportionate drug arrests.* Retrieved June 1, 2006, from http://www.hrw.org/reports/2000/usa/Rcedrg00-05.htm

Hunt, G. P., & Laidler, K. Joe. (2001). Alcohol and violence in the lives of gang members. *Alcohol, Research, and Health, 25*(1), 66–71.

Husak, D., & de Marneffe, P. (2005). *The legalization of drugs: For & against.* New York, NY: Cambridge University Press.

Hyde, H. (1995). *Forfeiting our property rights: Is your property safe from seizure?* Washington, DC: Cato Institute.

Hyman, S. E., & Malenka, R. C. (2001). Addiction and the brain: The neurobiology of compulsion and its persistence. *National Review Neuroscience, 2*(10), 695–703.

Inciardi, J. A. (1990). The crack-violence connection within a population of hard-core adolescent offenders. In M. DeLaRosa, E. Y. Lambert, & B. Gropper (Eds.), *Drugs and violence: Causes, correlates, and consequences* (pp. 92–111). Rockville, MD: National Institute on Drug Abuse.

Inciardi, J. A. (Ed.). (1993). *Drug treatment and criminal justice.* Newbury Park, CA: Sage Publications.

Inciardi, J. A. (2002). *The war on drugs III: The continuing saga of the mysteries and miseries of intoxication, addiction, crime, and public policy* (3rd ed.). Boston, MA: Allyn & Bacon.

Inciardi, J. A. (2008). *The war on drugs IV: The continuing saga of the mysteries and miseries of intoxication, addiction, crime, and public policy* (4th ed.). Boston, MA: Allyn & Bacon.

Inciardi, J. A., & Chambers, C. D. (1972). Unreported criminal involvement of narcotic addicts. *Journal of Drug Issues, 2*, 57–64.

Inciardi, J. A., Martin, S. S., Butzin, C. A., Hooper, R. J., & Harrison, L. D. (1997). An effective model of prison-based treatment for drug-involved offenders. *Journal of Drug Issues, 27*, 261–278.

Inciardi, J. A., & McElrath, K. (2004). *The American drug scene: An anthology* (4th ed.). Los Angeles, CA: Roxbury Publishing Company.

Inciardi, J. A., & McElrath, K. (2008). *The American drug scene: An anthology* (5th ed.). New York, NY: Oxford University Press.

International Narcotics Control Board. (2005). *Psychotropic substances statistics for 2004: Assessment of medical and scientific requirements.* New York, NY: United Nations.

Jacob, T., Windle, M., Seilhamer, R. A., & Bost, J. (1999). Adult children of alcoholics: Drinking, psychiatric, and social status. *Psychology of Addictive Behaviors, 13*(1), 3–21.

Jaffe, J., H. (1975). Drug addiction and drug abuse. In L. S. Goodman & A. Gilman (Eds.), *The pharmacological basis of therapeutics* (5th ed., pp. 284–324). New York, NY: MacMillan.

Jenkins, P. (1998). The ice age: The social construction of a drug panic. In G. W. Potter & V. E. Kappeler (Eds.), *Constructing crime: Perspectives on making news and social problems* (pp. 137–160). Prospect Heights, IL: Waveland Press.

Jenkins, P. (1999). *Synthetic panics: The symbolic politics of designer drugs.* New York, NY: New York University Press.

Jenkins, P. (2003). The next panic. In L. K. Gaines & P. B. Kraska (Eds.), *Drugs, crime, and justice: Contemporary perspectives* (2nd ed., pp. 87–98). Prospect Heights, IL: Waveland Press.

Johnson, D. T. (2009). The Merida Initiative. *Bureau of International Narcotics and Law Enforcement Affairs.* Retrieved September 1, 2009, from http://www.state.gov/p/inl/rls/rm/120225.htm

Johnson, V. E. (1986). *Intervention: How to help someone who doesn't want help.* Minneapolis, MN: Johnson Institute Books.

Johnston, L. D., O'Malley, P. M., Bachman, J. G., & Schulenberg, J. E. (2006). *Monitoring the future national results on adolescent drug use: Overview of key findings, 2005* (NIH 06-5882). Bethesda, MD: National Institute on Drug Abuse.

Jung, J. (2001). *Psychology of alcohol and other drugs: A research perspective.* Thousand Oaks, CA: Sage Publications.

The Junkie in the O.R. (2006, November). *Men's Health.* Retrieved June 22, 2009, from http://www.menshealth.com/cda/article.do?site=MensHealth&channel=health&category=doctors.hospitals&conitem=d7a4dfaa4d41e010VgnVCM20000012281eac____

Kantor, G. K., & Straus, M. A. (2003). The "drunken bum" theory of wife beating. In J. D. Orcutt & D. R. Rudy (Eds.), *Drugs, alcohol, and social problems* (pp. 219–238). Lanham, MD: Rowman & Littlefield Publishers.

Kappeler, V. E., & Potter, G. W. (2005). *The mythology of crime and criminal justice* (4th ed.). Long Grove, IL: Waveland Press.

Kendler, K. S., Heath, A. C., Neale, M. C., Kessler, R. C., & Eaves, L. J. (1992). Population-based twin study of alcoholism in women. *Journal of American Medicine, 268,* 1877–1882.

King, R. S. & Mauer, M. (2002). *Distorted priorities: Drug offenders in state prisons.* Retrieved April 3, 2008, from http://www.sentencingproject.org/doc/publications/dp_distortedpriorities.pdf

King, R. S. & Mauer, M. (2005). *The sentencing project ~ The war on marijuana: The transformation of the war on drugs in the 1990s.* Retrieved July 1, 2008, from http://www.umsl.edu/~keelr/180/waronmarijuana.pdf

Kraska, P. B. (2003). The military as drug police: Exercising the ideology of war. In L. K. Gaines & P. B. Kraska (Eds.), *Drugs, crime, & justice: Contemporary perspectives* (2nd ed., pp. 288–308). Prospect Heights, IL: Waveland Press.

Ksir, C., Hart, C. L., & Ray, O. (2008). *Drugs, society, and human behavior* (12th ed.). Boston, MA: McGraw Hill.

Lange, W. R., Cabanilla, B. R., Moler, G., Frankenfield, K. L., & Fudala, P. J. (1994). Preemployment drug screening at The Johns Hopkins Hospital, 1989 and 1991. *American Journal of Drug and Alcohol Abuse, 20,* 35–46.

Latimer, D., & Goldberg, J. (1981). *Flowers in the blood: The story of opium.* New York, NY: Franklin Watts.

Lattimore, P. K., Trudeau, J., Riley, K. J., Leiter, J., & Edwards, S. (1997). *Homicide in eight U.S. cities: Trends, context, and policy implications* (NCJ 167262). Washington, DC: Department of Justice.

Lauman, E., Paik, A., & Rosen, R. (1999). Sexual dysfunction in the United States: Prevalence and predictors. *Journal of the American Medical Association, 281*, 537–544.

Lawson, G., Peterson, J. S., & Lawson, A. (1983). *Alcoholism and the family: A guide to treatment and prevention.* Rockville, MD: Aspen Publishers.

Lender, M. E., & Martin, J. K. (1987). *Drinking in America: A history (Revised and Expanded Version).* New York, NY: The Free Press.

LeRoy, M. H. (1991). Discriminating characteristics of union members' attitudes toward drug testing in the workplace. *Journal of Labor Research, 12*, 453–466.

Lesly's Three Year Smoke Free Milestone. (2009, May 25). *About.com.* Retrieved July 15, 2009, from http://quitsmoking.about.com/od/longtermcessation/a/lesly3years.htm

Leuw, E. (1991). Drugs and drug policy in the Netherlands. *Crime and Justice, 14*, 229–276.

Levinthal, C. F. (2008). *Drugs, society, and criminal justice* (2nd ed.). Boston, MA: Allyn & Bacon.

Lieb, J. J., & Sterk-Elifson, C. (1995). Crack in the cradle: Social policy and reproductive rights among crack-using females. *Contemporary Drug Problems, 22* (Winter), 687–705.

Lindesmith, A. R. (1938). A sociological theory of drug addiction. *American Journal of Sociology, 43*, 593–613.

Liska, K. (2004). *Drugs and the human body with implications for society.* (7th ed.). Upper Saddle River, NJ: Prentice Hall.

Livingston, G. (2004). *Inside Colombia: Drugs, democracy and war.* New Brunswick, NJ: Rutgers University Press.

Loe, M. (2004). *The rise of Viagra: How the little blue pill changed sex in America.* New York, NY: New York University Press.

Logan, E. (2003). The wrong race, committing crime, doing drugs, and maladjusted for motherhood: The nation's fury over "crack babies." In L. K. Gaines & P. B. Kraska (Eds.), *Drugs, crime, & justice: Contemporary perspectives* (2nd ed., pp. 368–382). Prospect Heights, IL: Waveland Press.

Lusane, C. (1991). *Pipe dream blues: Racism and the war on drugs.* Boston, MA: South End Press.

Lynam, D. R., Milich, R., Zimmerman, R., Novak, S. P., Logan, T. K., Martin, C., et al. (1999). Project DARE: No effects at 10-year follow-up. *Journal of Consulting and Clinical Psychology, 67*, 590–593.

Lyman, M. D., & Potter, G. W. (2003). *Drugs in society: Causes, concepts and control* (4th ed.). Cincinnati, OH: Anderson Publishing.

Lyman, M. D., & Potter, G. W. (2007). *Drugs in society: Causes, concepts and control* (5th ed.). Cincinnati, OH: Anderson Publishing.

Lynskey, M. T., Heath, A. C., Bucholz, K. K., Slutske, W. S., Madden, P. A. F., Nelson, E. C., et al. (2003). Escalation of drug use in early-onset cannabis users vs co-twin controls. *Journal of the American Medical Association, 289*, 427–433.

MacCoun, R. J., & Reuter, P. (1997). Interpreting Dutch cannabis policy: Reasoning by analogy in the legalization debate. *Science, 278*, 47–52.

MacCoun, R. J., & Reuter, P. (2001). *Drug war heresies: Learning from other vices, times, and places.* Cambridge, MA: Cambridge University Press.

MacCoun, R. J., & Reuter, P. (2005). Does Europe do it better? In L. E. Huggins (Ed.), *Drug war deadlock: The policy battle continues* (pp. 262–269). Stanford, CA: Hoover Institution Press.

Maher, L., & Daly, K. (2006). Women in the street-level drug economy: Continuity or change? In M. S. Kelley (Ed.), *Readings on drugs and society: The criminal connection* (pp. 110–124). Boston, MA: Allyn & Bacon.

Maisto, S. A., Galizio, M., & Connors, G. J. (2008). *Drug use and abuse* (5th ed.). Boston, MA: Thomson Wadsworth.

Martinez, R., Jr., Rosenfeld, R., & Mares, D. (2008). Social disorganization, drug market activity, and neighborhood violent crime. *Urban Affairs Review, 43*(6), 846–874.

Marx, K., & Engels, F. (1964). *The communist manifesto* (P. M. Sweezy, Trans.). New York, NY: Monthly Review Press. (Original work published 1848).

Max, W. (2001). The financial impact of smoking on health-related costs: A review of the literature. *American Journal of Health Promotion, 15*, 321–331.

McAuliffe, W. E. (1982). A test of Wikler's theory of relapse: The frequency of relapse due to conditioned withdrawal sickness. *International Journal of Addictions, 17*, 19–33.

McAuliffe, W. E., & Gordon, R. A. (1974). A test of Lindesmith's theory of addiction: The frequency of euphoria among long-term addicts. *American Journal of Sociology, 79*, 795–830.

McBride, D. C., & McCoy, C. B. (2003). The drugs-crime relationship: An analytical framework. In L. K. Gaines & P. B. Kraska (Eds.), *Drugs, crime }and justice: Contemporary perspectives* (2nd ed., pp. 100–119). Prospect Heights, IL: Waveland Press.

McGwire is Testing a Loyal Baseball Town. (2010, February 1). *New York Times.* Retrieved February 26, 2010, from http://www.nytimes.com/2010/02/02/sports/baseball/02mcgwire.html?scp=4&sq=steroids&st=cse

McKim, W. A. (2007). *Drugs and behavior: An introduction to behavioral pharmacology* (6th ed.). Upper Saddle River, NJ: Pearson Prentice Hall.

McNamara, J. D. (2005). The drug war: The American junkie. In L. E. Huggins (Ed.), *Drug war deadlock: The policy battle continues* (pp. 103–111). Stanford, CA: Hoover Institution Press.

McNaughton, C. C. (2008). Transitions through homelessness, substance use, and the effect of material marginalization and psychological trauma. *Drugs: Education, Prevention and Policy, 15*(2), 177–188.

Meara, E. (2006). Welfare reform, employment, and drug and alcohol use among low-income women. *Harvard Review of Psychiatry, 14*(4), 223–232.

Mental Health America. (2009). *Factsheet: Co-dependency.* Retrieved August 22, 2009, from http://www.nmha.org/gov/codependency

Medical Papers by Ghostwriters Pushed Therapy. (2009, August 4). *New York Times.* Retrieved August 5, 2009, from http://www.nytimes.com/2009/08/05/health/research/05ghost.html?scp=3&sq=hormone%20replacement&st=cse

Merton, R. K. (1938). Social structure and anomie. *American Sociological Review, 3*, 672–682.

Merton, R. K. (1968). *Social theory and social structure.* New York, NY: Free Press.

Messner, S. F., & Rosenfeld, R. (2001). *Crime and the American dream.* Belmont, CA: Wadsworth.

Meth Ads Talk to Teens in Spanish. (2009, June 5). *CNN.* Retrieved June 19, 2009, from http://www.cnn.com/2009/HEALTH/06/05/meth.ads.spanish/index.html

Meth Epidemic Just Media Hype. (2006, June 25). *Arizona Republic.* Retrieved June 1, 2009, from http://www.november.org/stayinfo/breaking06/MediaHype.html

Metzl, J. M. (2007). If direct-to-consumer advertisements come to Europe: Lessons from the USA. *Lancet, 369*(9562), 704–706.

Mexico's New Drug Law May Set an Example. (2009, August 26). *Time.* Retrieved September 2, 2009, from http://www.time.com/time/world/article/0,8599,1918725,00.html?artId=1918725?contType=article?chn=world

Miller, W. R., & Hester, R. K. (1995). Treating alcohol problems: Toward an informed eclecticism. In R. K. Hester & W. R. Miller (Eds.), *Handbook of alcoholism treatment approaches* (2nd ed., pp. 1–12). New York, NY: Allyn & Bacon.

Moilanen, R. (2004, January). Just say no again: The old failures of new and improved anti-drug education. *Reasononline.* Retrieved May 22, 2009, from http://www.reason.com/0401/fe.rm.just.shtml

Moore, M. H., & Kleiman, M. A. R. (2003). The police and drugs. In L. K. Gaines & P. B. Kraska (Eds.), *Drugs, crime, & justice: Contemporary perspectives* (2nd ed., pp. 248–267). Prospect Heights, IL: Waveland Press.

Morgan, J. P., & Kagan, D. V. (1980). The dusting of America: The image of phencyclidine (PCP) in the popular media. *Journal of Psychoactive Drugs, 12*, 195–204.

Morgan, J. P., & Zimmer, L. (1995). The myth of marijuana's gateway effect. *National Organization for the Reform of Marijuana Laws (NORML).* Washington, DC: NORML.

Morris, A. W., Jr., Gadson, S. L., & Burroughs, V. (2007). For the good of the patient: Survey of the physicians of the National Medical Association regarding perceptions of DTC advertising. *Journal of the National Medical Association, 99*(3), 287–293.

Mosher, C. J., & Akins, S. (2007). *Drugs and drug policy: The control of consciousness alteration.* Thousand Oaks, CA: Sage.

Murdoch, D., Pihl, R. O., & Ross, D. (1990). Alcohol and crimes of violence: Present issues. *International Journal of the Addictions, 25*(9), 1065–1081.

Musto, D. F. (1999). *The American disease: Origins of narcotic control* (3rd ed.). New York, NY: Oxford University Press.

Nadelmann, E. A. (2005). An end to marijuana prohibition: The drive to legalize picks up. In L. E. Huggins (Ed.), *Drug war deadlock: The policy battle continues* (pp. 219–235). Stanford, CA: Hoover Institution Press.

Narcotics Anonymous. (5th ed.). (1988). Chatsworth, CA: Narcotics Anonymous World Services, Inc.

National Center for Education Statistics. (2009). *Indicators of school crime and safety: 2008* (NCES 2009-022). Washington, DC: U.S. Department of Education.

National Drug Intelligence Center. (2006). *The impact of drugs on society.* Retrieved August 30, 2009, from http://www.usdoj.gov/ndic//pubs11/18862/impact.htm

National Institute of Alcohol Abuse and Alcoholism. (2000). *Tenth special report to the U.S. Congress on alcohol and health.* Retrieved September 1, 2009, from http://pubs.niaaa.nih.gov/publications/10report/intro.pdf

National Institute of Allergy and Infectious Diseases. (2007, November). *Treatment of HIV infection.* Retrieved January 24, 2008, from http://www.niaid.nih.gov/factsheets/treat-hiv.htm

National Institute on Drug Abuse. (1999). *Principles of drug addiction treatment: A research-based guide* (No. 99-4180). Bethesda, MD: National Institute of Health Publication.

National Institute on Drug Abuse. (2004). *INDA infofacts: Nationwide trends.* Retrieved July 28, 2006, from http://www.drugabuse.gov/infofacts/nationtrends.html

National Institute on Drug Abuse. (2008). *Principles of drug addiction treatment: A research-based guide* (2nd ed., No. 09-4180). Bethesda, MD: National Institute of Health Publication. Retrieved September 4, 2009, from http://www.drugabuse.gov/PDF/PODAT/PODAT.pdf

National Institute of Justice. (2003). *Toward a drugs and crime research agenda for the 21st century* (No. 194616). Washington, DC: National Institute of Justice.

National Poison Data System. (2008). *2007 Annual report of the American Association of Poison Control Centers' National Poison Data System (NPDS): 25th annual report.* Alexandria, VA: American Association of Poison Control Centers.

Newcomb, M. D. (1994). Drug use and intimate relationships among women and men: Separating specific from general effects in prospective data using structural equation models. *Journal of Consulting and Clinical Psychology, 62*(3), 463–476.

Newcomb, M. D., Galaif, E. R., & Carmona, J. V. (2001). The drug-crime nexus in a community sample of adults. *Psychology of Addictive Behaviors, 15*(3), 185–193.

Nielsen, A. L., & Scarpitti, F. R. (1997). Changing the behavior of substance abusers: Factors influencing the effectiveness of therapeutic communities. *Journal of Drug Issues, 27*, 279–298.

Nolan, J. L., Jr. (2001). *Reinventing justice: The American drug court movement.* Princeton, NJ: Princeton University Press.

Normand, J., Lempert, R. O., & O'Brien, C. P. (1994). Impact of drug testing programs on productivity. In J. Normand, R. O. Lempert, & C. P. O'Brien (Eds.), *Under the influence? Drugs and the American work force* (pp. 215–240). Washington, DC: National Academy Press.

Norris, M., Conrad, C., & Resner, V. (1998). *Shattered lives: Portraits from America's drug war.* El Cerrito, CA: Creative Xpressions.

Office of Justice Programs. (1997). *Defining drug courts: The key components.* Washington, DC: National Association of Drug Court Professionals. Retrieved September 1, 2008, from http://www.ojp.usdoj.gov/BJA/grant/DrugCourts/DefiningDC.pdf

Office of Justice Programs. (1999). *Looking at a decade of drug courts.* Washington, DC: Drug Court Clearinghouse and Technical Assistance Project.

Office of Justice Programs. (2000). *OJP drug court clearinghouse and technical assistance project: Summary of drug court activity by state and county.* Washington, DC: U.S. Government Printing, Office.

Office of Justice Programs. (2006). *Drug courts: The second decade.* Washington, DC: U.S. Government Printing, Office. Retrieved August 1, 2008, from http://www.ncjrs.gov/pdffiles1/nij/211081.pdf

Office of Justice Programs. (2008). *Painting the current picture: A national report card on drug courts and other problem-solving court programs in the United States.* Washington, DC: U.S. Government Printing, Office. Retrieved September 2, 2009, from http://www.ndci.org/sites/default/files/ndci/PCPII1_web%5B1%5D.pdf

Office of Juvenile Justice and Delinquency Prevention. (2002). *Battered child syndrome: Investigating physical abuse and homicide.* Washington, DC: U.S. Department of Justice.

Office of National Drug Control Policy. (2001). *The economic costs of drug abuse in the United States, 1992–1998* (NCJ 190636). Washington, DC: Office of National Drug Control Policy, Executive Office of the President.

Office of National Drug Control Policy. (2006). *Girls and drugs: Recent trends, risk factors, and consequences.* Washington, DC: Office of National Drug Control Policy, Executive Office of the President.

Ottawa Embarking on Its Own War on Drugs. (2009, June 12). *The Star.* Retrieved July 14, 2009, from http://www.thestar.com/comment/columnists/article/649475

Palacios, W. R., & Fenwick, M. E. (2006). 'E' is for ecstasy: A participant observation study of ecstasy use. In Paul Cromwell (Ed.), *In their own words: Criminals on crime* (4th ed., pp. 274–280). New York, NY: Oxford University Press.

Pavlov, I. (1927). *Conditioned reflexes.* London: Oxford University Press.

The Payoff. (2007, August 6). *Los Angeles Times.* Retrieved June 24, 2009, from http://articles.latimes.com/2007/aug/06/health/he-effectiveness6

Peele, S. (1995). *Diseasing of America.* San Francisco, CA: Jossey-Bass.

Peled, E., & Sacks, I. (2008). The self-perception of women who live with an alcoholic partner: Dialoging with deviance, strength, and self-fulfillment. *Family Relations, 57,* 390–403.

Peterson, M. (2001, November 21). Increased spending on drugs is linked to more advertising. *New York Times.* Retrieved August 21, 2009, from http://www.nytimes.com/2001/11/21/business/21DRUG.html

PhRMA. (2005). *PhRMA guiding principles: Direct to consumer advertisements about prescription medicines.* Retrieved July 12, 2008, from http://www.phrma.org/files/DTCGuidingprinciples.pdf

Physicians' desk reference. (58th ed.). (2004). Montvale, NJ: Thomson PDR.

Physicians' desk reference for herbal medicines (3rd ed.). (2004). Stamford, CT: Thompson Healthcare.

Physicians' desk reference for nonprescription drugs. (24th ed.). (2003). Montvale, NJ: Thomson PDR.

Pickens, R. W., Svikis, D. S., McGue, M., & LaBuda, M. C. (1995). Common genetic mechanisms in alcohol, drug, and mental disorder comorbidity. *Drug and Alcohol Dependence, 39,* 129–138.

Point for Point: Canada's Needle Exchange Programs. (2004, October 27). *CBC News.* Retrieved September 2, 2009, from http://www.cbc.ca/news/background/drugs/needleexchange.html

Pope, H. G., Jr., Phillips, K. A., & Olivardia, R. (2000). *The Adonis Complex: The secret crisis of male body obsession.* New York, NY: The Free Press.

Pot No Longer Focus of Anti-Drug Campaigns. (2009, July 15). *CBS News.* Retrieved August 26, 2009, from http://www.cbsnews.com/stories/2009/07/15/national/main5161388.shtml

Potter, G. W., & Kappeler, V. E. (Eds.). (1998). *Constructing crime: Perspectives on making news and social problems.* Prospect Heights, IL: Waveland Press.

Preble, E., & Casey, J. J. (1969). Taking care of business: The heroin addict's life on the street. *The International Journal of the Addictions, 4,* 1–24.

President's Commission on Model State Drug Laws. (1993). *Volume 1: Economic remedies.* Washington, DC: The White House.

PR Newswire. (2006, December 21). *Teen drug use declines 23 percent in five years: Marijuana, meth use drop sharply.* PR Newswire Association US.

Public Broadcasting Services. (2008). *Rampart scandal timeline.* Retrieved August 30, 2009, from http://

www.pbs.org/wgbh/pages/frontline/shows/lapd/scandal/cron.html

Radford, B. (2003). *Media mythmakers: How journalists, activists, and advertisers mislead us.* Amherst, NY: Prometheus Books.

Rados, C. (2004). Truth in advertising: Rx drug ads come of age. *FDA Consumer, 38*(4), 20–27.

Reding, N. (2009). *Methland: The death and life of an American small town.* New York, NY: Bloomsbury.

Reefer Madness: Treatment Works. (2009, March 6). *The Austin Chronicle.* Retrieved March 31, 2009, from http://www.austinchronicle.com/gyrobase/Issue/Story?oid=oid:751800

Reinarman, C. (2008). The social impact of drugs and the war on drugs: The social construction of drug scares. In J. A. Inciardi & K. McElrath (Eds.), *The American drug scene: An anthology* (5th ed., pp. 54–62). New York, NY: Oxford University Press.

Reinarman, C., & Duskin, C. (1998). Dominant ideology and drugs in the media. In G. W. Potter & V. E. Kappeler (Eds.), *Constructing crime: Perspectives on making news and social problems* (pp. 317–331). Prospect Heights, IL: Waveland Press.

Reiss, A., & Roth, J. (1993). *Understanding and preventing violence.* Washington, DC: National Academy Press.

Report of Ritalin Risks Prompts a Federal Study. (2005, July 1). *New York Times.* Retrieved August 3, 2009, from http://www.nytimes.com/2005/07/01/health/01ritalin.html?_r=1

Robertson, N. (1988, February 21). The changing world of Alcoholics Anonymous. *New York Times Magazine,* pp. 40–44, 47, 57, 92.

Robinson, A., Hohmann, K., Rifkin, J., Topp, D., Gilroy, C., Pickard, J., et al. (2004). Direct-to-consumer pharmaceutical advertising: Physician and public opinion and potential effects on the physician-patient relationship. *Archives of Internal Medicine, 164*(4), 427–432.

Robinson, T. E., & Berridge, K. C. (2000). The psychology and neurobiology of addiction: An incentive-sensitization view. *Addiction, 95*(2), S91–S117.

Roman, C. G., Ahn-Redding, H., & Simon, R. J. (2005). *Illicit drug policies, trafficking, and use the world over.* Lanham, MD: Lexington Books.

Rose, D. (2002, February 1). Two countries took the drug test: Who passed? *Observer.* Retrieved February 2, 2002, from http://www.observer.co.uk

Rosenbaum, M. (1999). *Safety first! A reality-based approach to teens, drugs, and drug education.* San Francisco, CA: The Lindesmith Center.

Rosenbaum, M. (2001). A focus on safety strikes a universal chord. *Reconsider Quarterly.* Retrieved May 25, 2009, from http://www.reconsider.org/quarterly/2002_Winter/pdf/ReconsiDer_Quarterly_2002_Winter.pdf

Rosenbaum, M. (2004). No silver bullet. *Drug Policy Alliance.* Retrieved June 24, 2009 from http://www.mapinc.org/tlcnews/v04/n182/a06.htm?155

Rosenbaum, M. (2007). *Safety first: A reality-based approach to teens, drugs, and drug education.* San Francisco, CA: Drug Policy Alliance. Retrieved May 23, 2009, from http://www.drugpolicy.org/docUploads/safetyfirst.pdf

Rosenbaum, M., & Hanson, G. (1998). Assessing the effects of school-based drug education: A six-year multilevel analysis of project DARE. *Journal of Research in Crime and Delinquency, 35,* 381–412.

Ryan, K. (1998). Clinging to failure: The rise and continued life of U.S. drug policy. *Law and Society Review, 32,* 221–242.

Sadock, B. J., & Sadock, V. A. (2003). *Kaplan & Sadock's synopsis of psychiatry: Behavioral sciences/clinical psychiatry* (9th ed.). New York, NY: Lippincott Williams & Wilkins.

Sanchez, R. (2000). *My bloody life: The making of a Latin King.* Chicago, IL: Chicago Review Press.

Schempf, A. H., & Strobino, D. M. (2008). Illicit drug use and adverse birth outcomes: Is it drugs or context? *Journal of Urban Health: Bulletin of the New York Academy of Medicine, 85*(6), 858–873.

Schmidt, L., Zabkiewicz, D., Jacobs, L., & Wiley, J. (2007). Substance abuse and employment among welfare mothers: From welfare to work and back again? *Substance Use & Misuse, 42,* 1069–1087.

Schuckit, M. (1985). Genetics and the risk of alcoholism. *Journal of the American Medical Association, 254*(18), 2614–2617.

Senate Backs Sweeping Tobacco Regulation. (2009, June 12). *Democracy Now.* Retrieved February 25, 2010, from http://www.democracynow.org/2009/6/12/headlines#5

Shaw, C., & McKay, H. (1972). *Juvenile delinquency and urban areas* (Rev. ed.). Chicago, IL: University of Chicago Press.

Shepard, E. (2001). *The economic costs of DARE* (Research Paper No. 22). Syracuse, NY: LeMoyne College Institute of Industrial Relations.

Shepard, E., & Clifton, T. (1998). *Drug testing and labor productivity: Estimates applying a production function model* (Research Paper No. 18). Syracuse, NY: LeMoyne College Institute of Industrial Relations.

Shin, H. S. (2001). A review of school-based drug prevention program evaluations in the 1990s. *American Journal of Health Education, 32*, 139–147.

Sinclair, U. (1906). *The jungle.* New York, NY: Penguin Books.

Skager, R. (2001). On reinventing drug education, especially for adolescents. *The Reconsider Quarterly, 1*, 14–18.

Skiba, R., & Peterson, R. (1999). The dark side of zero tolerance: Can punishment lead to safe schools? *Phi Delta Kappan, 80*, 372–378.

Skinner, B. F. (1938). *The behavior of organisms.* New York, NY: Appleton-Century-Crofts.

Soyka, M., & Schmidt, P. (2009). Outpatient alcoholism treatment: 24-month outcome and predictors of outcome. *Substance Abuse Treatment, Prevention, and Policy, 4.* Retrieved, September 7, 2009, from http://www.substanceabusepolicy.com/content/4/1/15

Spitz, H. I. (1987). Cocaine abuse: Therapeutic group approaches. In H. I. Spitz & J. S. Rosecan (Eds.), *Cocaine abuse: New directions in treatment and research* (pp. 156–201). New York, NY: Brunner/Mazel.

Spunt, B., Goldstein, P., Brownstein, H., Fendrich, J., & Langley, S. (1994). Alcohol and homicide: Interviews with prison inmates. *Journal of Drug Issues, 24*, 143–163.

Sterk-Elifson, C. (2005). Determining drug use patterns among women. In W. R. Palacios (Ed.), *Cocktails and dreams: Perspectives on drug and alcohol use* (pp. 43–55). Upper Saddle River, NJ: Prentice Hall.

Sterling, E. (2001). Drug policy: Failure at home. *Foreign policy in focus: A think tank without walls, 6*(16). Retrieved May 2, 2008, from http://www.fpif.org

Stevens, J. W., & Capitman, J. A. (2005). Disaster and loss: Drug research in an urban community. *Families in Society, 86*(2), 279–286.

Strong Views, Pro and Con, on Ads Linking Drug Use to Terrorism. (2002, April 2). *New York Times.* Retrieved June 22, 2009, from http://www.nytimes.com/2002/04/02/business/media-business-advertising-strong-views-pro-con-ads-linking-drug-use-terrorism.html

Students Against Destructive Decisions. (2001). In *Encyclopedia of drugs, alcohol, and addictive behavior.* Retrieved August 16, 2009, from http://www.encyclopedia.com/doc/1G2-3403100433.html

Students for Sensible Drug Policy. (2006). *Harmful drug law hits home: How many college students in each state lost financial aid due to drug convictions?* Washington, DC: Students for Sensible Drug Policy.

Study Say Marijuana No Gateway Drug. (2006, December 4). *ScienceBlog.* Retrieved July 9, 2009, from http://www.scienceblog.com/cms/study-say-marijuana-no-gateway-drug-12116.html

Subby, R., & Friel, J. (1984). Co-dependency: A paradoxical dependency. In R. Subby (Ed.), *Codependency: An emerging issue* (pp. 31–44). Pompano Beach, FL: The U.S. Journal of Drug and Alcohol Dependency and Health Communications.

Subcommittee on Crime. (1985). *Military cooperation with civilian law enforcement.* Washington, DC: U.S. Government Printing Office.

Substance Abuse and Mental Health Services Administration. (1997). *An analysis of worker drug use and workplace policies and programs* (SMA 97-3142). Rockville, MD: Substance Abuse and Mental Health Services Administration, Office of Applied Studies.

Substance Abuse and Mental Health Services Administration. (2004). *Results from the 2003 national survey on drug use and health: National findings.* Rockville, MD: Substance Abuse and

Mental Health Services Administration, Office of Applied Studies.

Substance Abuse and Mental Health Services Administration. (2006). *Results from the 2005 national survey on drug use and health: National findings* (SMA 06-4194). Rockville, MD: Substance Abuse and Mental Health Services Administration, Office of Applied Studies.

Substance Abuse and Mental Health Services Administration. (2009). *The national survey on drug use and health report: Children living with substance-dependent or substance-abusing parents 2002 to 2007.* Washington, DC: U.S. Department of Health and Human Services.

Supreme Court Allows Prosecution of Medical Marijuana. (2005, June 7). *CNN.* Retrieved June 1, 2009, from http://www.cnn.com/2005/LAW/06/06/scotus.medical.marijuana/

Supreme Court Clears $79.5M Award for Smoker's Widow. (2009, March 31). *New York Times.* Retrieved February 25, 2010, from http://www.usatoday.com/news/washington/judicial/supremecourtopinions/2009-03-31-scotus-cigarette-appeal_N.htm

Sutherland, E. H. (1939). *Principles of criminology* (3rd ed.). Philadelphia, PA: Lippincott.

Swena, D. D., & Gaines W., Jr. (1999). Effect of random drug screening on fatal commercial truck accident rates. *International Journal of Drug Testing.* Retrieved June 22, 2009, from http://www.criminology.fsu.edu/journal/drugscreen.pdf

Szasz, T. S. (1976). *Ceremonial chemistry: The ritual persecution of drugs, addicts, and pushers.* Holmes Beach, FL: Learning Publications.

Taking the Side of the Coca Farmer. (2002, August 5). *Time.* Retrieved August 1, 2009, from http://www.time.com/time/magazine/article/0,9171,332053,00.html

Teens and SADD: Organization Helps Kids Make Positive Choices. (2008, April 11). *Suite101.com.* Retrieved July 29, 2009, from http://youthdevelopment.suite101.com/article.cfm/teens_and_sadd

Tonry, M., & Wilson, J. Q. (Eds.). (1990). *Drugs and crime.* Chicago, IL: University of Chicago Press.

Trendy Drug Goes Club-Hopping . . . and Officials are Worried. (1996, August 11). *CNN.* Retrieved July 23, 2009, from http://www.cnn.com/US/9608/10/rave.drug/

Tunnell, K. D. (2004). *Pissing on demand: Workplace drug testing and the rise of the detox industry.* New York, NY: New York University Press.

United Nations Office for Drug Central and Crime Prevention (UNODCCP). (2000). *Demand reduction: A glossary of terms.* New York, NY: United Nations Publications.

United Nations Office on Drugs and Crime (UNODC). (2006). *World drug report* (ISBN 92-1-148214-3). Sweden: United Nations Publication.

United Nations Office on Drugs and Crime (UNODC). (2007). *World drug report* (ISBN 978-92-1-148222-5). Sweden: United Nations Publication.

United States pharmacopeia-national formulary (29th ed.). (2006). Rockville, MD: United States Pharmacopeia.

U.S. Department of Health and Human Services, Children's Bureau, Administration on Children, Youth and Families. (2009). *Parental drug use as child abuse: Summary of state laws.* Retrieved August 16, 2009, from http://www.childwelfare.gov/systemwide/laws_policies/statutes/drugexposedall.pdf

U.S. Department of Health and Human Services, Office for Substance Abuse Prevention. (1989). *Prevention plus II: Tools for creating and sustaining drug-free communities* (DHHS-ADM-89-1649). Rockville, MD: National Clearinghouse for Alcohol and Drug Information.

U.S. Department of Labor. (2009). *General workplace impact: Substance use and abuse in America in 2007.* Retrieved August 30, 2009, from http://www.dol.gov/asp/programs/drugs/workingpartners/stats/wi.asp

U.S. General Accounting Office. (1998). *Law enforcement: Information on drug-related police corruption.* Washington, DC: U.S. Government Accountability Office.

U.S. General Accounting Office. (2003, January 15). *Youth illicit drug use prevention: DARE long-term evaluations and federal efforts to identify effective programs.* Retrieved January 1, 2009, from http://www.gao.gov/new.items/d03172r.pdf

U.S. Sentencing Commission. (1997). *Special report to the Congress: Cocaine and federal sentencing policy.* Washington, DC: USGPO.

U.S. Sentencing Commission. (2007). *Cocaine and federal sentencing policy.* Washington, DC: USGPO.

Valentine, G. (2002). MDMA and ecstasy. *Psychiatric Time, XIX*(2). Retrieved March 29, 2010, from http://www.psychiatrictimes.com/display/article/10168/47391?pageNumber=2#

Vance, D. A. (2007). Premarin: The intriguing history of a controversial drug. *International Journal of Pharmaceutical Compounding, 11*(4). Retrieved March 29, 2010, from http://www.solaltech.com/doctors/3/HOT%20OFF%20THE%20PRESS%20Premarin-The_Intriguing_History_of_a_Controversial_Drug.pdf

Van Het Loo, M., Van Beusekom, I., & Kahan, J. P. (2002). Decriminalization of drug use in Portugal: The development of a policy. *Annals of the American Academy of Political and Social Science, 582*, 49–63.

Vannostrand, L.-M., & Tewksbury, R. (2006). The motives and mechanics of operating an illegal drug enterprise. In M. S. Kelley (Ed.), *Readings on drugs and society: The criminal connection* (pp. 315–328). Boston, MA: Allyn & Bacon.

Vargas, Ricardo. (2002). The anti-drug policy, aerial spraying of illicit crops and their social, environmental and political impacts on Columbia. *Journal of Drug Issues, 32*, 11–61.

Wald, P. M., & Hutt, P. B. (1972). The drug abuse survey project: Summary of findings, conclusions, and recommendations. In The Drug Abuse Survey Project (Ed.), *Dealing with drug abuse: A report to the Ford Foundation* (pp. 3–61). New York, NY: Praeger Press.

Walker, S. (2006). *Sense and non-sense about crime and drugs: A policy guide* (6th ed.). Belmont, CA: Thomson Wadsworth.

Wallace, A. E., & Weeks, W. B. (2004). Substance abuse intensive outpatient treatment: Does program graduation matter? *Journal of Substance Abuse Treatment, 27*, 27–30. Retrieved June 5, 2008, from http://www.dartmouth.edu/~dcare/pdfs/fp/WallaceAmy-SubstanceAbuseIntensiveOutpatientTreatment.pdf

Weil, A. (1972). *The natural mind: A new way of looking at drugs and higher consciousness.* Boston, MA: Houghton Mifflin Company.

Wesson, D. R., & Smith, D. E. (1985). Cocaine: Treatment perspectives. In N. J. Kozel & E. H. Adams (Eds.), *Cocaine use in America: Epidemiologic and clinical perspectives* (pp. 35–49). Rockville, MD: National Institute on Drug Abuse.

Weil, A., & Rosen, W. (1998). *From chocolate to morphine.* Boston, MA: Houghton Mifflin.

Wexler, H. K., & Williams, R. (1985). The Stay'n Out therapeutic community: Prison treatment for substance abuses. *Journal of Psychoactive Drugs, 18*, 221–230.

What Kind of Drug Use Does School-Based Prevention Prevent. (2002, June). *Drug Policy Research Newsletter.* Retrieved June 22, 2009, from http://www.rand.org/multi/dprc/pubs/CP201.02.pdf

What's Behind an F.D.A. Stamp? (2008, September 29). *New York Times.* Retrieved June 15, 2009, from http://www.nytimes.com/2008/09/30/health/policy/30fda.html

White, H. R., & Gorman, D. M. (2000). Dynamics of the drug-crime relationship. In *Criminal justice 2000: Vol. 1: The nature of crime: Continuity and change* (NCJ 182408). Washington, DC: Department of Justice.

Wiebe, R. H. (1967). *The search for order, 1877–1920.* New York, NY: Hill and Wang.

Williams, T. (1992). *Crackhouse: Notes from the end of the line.* New York, NY: Penguin Books.

Wisotsky, S. (1987). *Breaking the impasse in the war on drugs.* Westport, CT: Greenwood Press.

With Anti-Addiction Pill, No Urge No Craving. (2009, April 15). *CNN.* Retrieved August 23, 2009, from http://www.cnn.com/2009/HEALTH/04/15/addiction.cold.turkey.pill/index.html

Wolfgang, M. E. (1958). *Patterns in criminal homicide.* Philadelphia, PA: University of Pennsylvania Press.

Wood, D., Valdez, R. B., Hayashi, T., & Shen, A. (1990). Homeless and housed families in Los Angeles: A study comparing demographic, economic, and family function characteristics. *American Journal of Public Health, 80*(9), 1049–1052.

World Health Organization. (1992). *The ICD-10 classification of mental and behavioural disorders: Clinical descriptions and diagnostic guidelines.* Geneva, Switzerland: Author.

World Health Organization. (2004). *Neuroscience of psychoactive substance use and dependence.* Geneva, Switzerland: Author.

Worrall, J. (2003). Civil asset forfeiture: Past, present, and future. In L. K. Gaines & P. B. Kraska (Eds.), *Drugs, crime, & justice: Contemporary perspectives* (2nd ed., pp. 268–287). Prospect Heights, IL: Waveland Press.

Wright, K. (2001, March 15). DARE rethinks drug prevention. *Seattle Post-Intelligencer.* Retrieved March 15, 2001, from http://www.seattlepi.com.nwsource

Wysong, E., Aniskiewicz, R., & Wright, D. (1994). Truth and DARE: Tracking drug education to graduation and as symbolic politics. *Social Problems, 41*, 448–472.

Wysong, E., Aniskiewicz, R., & Wright, D. (2003). Truth and DARE. In J. Orcutt & D. Rudy (Eds.), *Drugs, alcohol, and social problems* (pp. 93–119). New York, NY: Roman and Littlefield.

Yamaguchi, R., Johnston, L., & O'Malley, P. (2003). Relationship between student illicit rug use and school drug-testing policies. *Journal of School Health, 73*, 159–164.

Young, D. (2002). Impact of perceived legal pressure on retention in drug treatment. *Criminal Justice and Behavior, 29*, 27–55.

Zeese, K. B. (1997). *Drug testing legal manual and practice aids* (2nd ed., Vols. 1–2). St. Paul, MN: West Group.

Zero Tolerance Policies in Schools Need to End. (2009, May 31). *The Providence Journal.* Retrieved June 24, 2009, from http://www.projo.com/opinion/columnists/content/edwatch_0531_05-31-09_HOEGMRG_v7.29f5eaa.html

Zero Tolerance Policies in Schools Under Attack. (2001). *Drug War Chronicle.* Retrieved June 24, 2009, from http://stopthedrugwar.org/chronicle-old/188/zerotolerance.shtml

Zero Tolerance Policy Lacks Flexibility. (1999, April 13). *USA Today.* Retrieved June 24, 2009, from http://www.usatoday.com/educate/ednews3.htm

Zimmer, L., & Jacobs, J. B. (1992). The business of drug testing: Technological innovation and social control. *Contemporary Drug Problems, 19*, 1–26.

Zwerling, C., Ryan, J., & Orav, E. J. (1990). The efficacy of preemployment drug screening for marijuana and cocaine in predicting employment outcome. *Journal of the American Medical Association, 264*(20), 2639–2643.

Zwerling, C., Ryan, J., & Orav, E. J. (1992). Costs and benefits of preemployment drug screening. *Journal of the American Medical Association, 267*(1), 91–93.

INDEX

Note: Page numbers followed by f or t refer to Figures or Tables